AIR COMMANDERS

AIR COMMANDERS

EDITED BY JOHN ANDREAS OLSEN

Potomac Books
An imprint of the University of Nebraska Press

Library of Congress Cataloging-in-Publication Data
Olsen, John Andreas, 1968–
  Air commanders / edited by John Andreas Olsen. — 1st ed.
    p. cm.
  Includes bibliographical references and index.
  ISBN 978-1-61234-576-5 (hardcover : alk. paper)
  ISBN 978-1-61234-577-2 (paperback: alk. paper)
  ISBN 978-1-61234-578-9 (electronic)
1. United States. Air Force—Officers—Biography. 2. Air warfare—United States—History—20th century. 3. Air power—United States—History—20th century. I. Title.
  UG626.O47 2012
  358.40092'273--dc23

                                                                2012031571

Printed in the United States of America on acid-free paper that meets the American National Standards Institute Z39-48 Standard.

First Edition

CONTENTS

ACKNOWLEDGMENTS

This book is the third in a series, sponsored by the Swedish National Defence College and published by Potomac Books, focused on various aspects of air power. The first book, *A History of Air Warfare* (2010), offers a comprehensive analysis of the role that air power has played in military conflicts of the past century, from the First World War to the second Lebanon war, campaign by campaign. The second, *Global Air Power* (2011), provides insight into the evolution of air power theory and practice by examining the experience of six of the world's largest air forces—those of the United Kingdom, the United States, Israel, Russia, India, and China—and of representative smaller air forces in Pacific Asia, Latin America, and continental Europe. By contrast, this third book, *Air Commanders* (2012), centers on individuals and their command and leadership in air warfare. By combining short military biographies and operational analyses, this study explores the careers of twelve senior American airmen and the characteristics of the air campaigns they shaped and led. From "Tooey" Spaatz in World War II to the contemporary "Buzz" Moseley, the case studies highlight the essential qualities of these airmen and how they dealt with the disparate challenges they confronted. *Air Commanders* should be of interest to both general readers and students of military history, particularly those seeking a deeper understanding of the use and development of air power as a national instrument of force.

I would like to thank the authors, all of them prominent experts with practical and scholarly experience in the field of air power. They accepted overall guidance but were given full freedom to develop their narratives and conclusions as they saw fit. I sincerely appreciate the independence of their research and their professionalism. I am once again grateful to Margaret S. MacDonald, who has worked with me on six books since 2007; her crucial advice, encouragement, and excellent editorial skills provide invaluable assistance. Finally, I wish to thank the Swedish National Defence College for financial support of this project, the Air Force Historical Studies Office for providing the majority of the photos, and Potomac Books for once again collaborating with me from idea to implementation.

ABBREVIATIONS

AAA	antiaircraft artillery
AAF	Army Air Forces
ACC	Air Combat Command
ACCE	Air Control Coordination Element
ACM	Air Chief Marshal
ACSC	Air Command and Staff College
ACTS	Air Corps Tactical School
AEAF	Allied Expeditionary Air Forces
AEF	Air Expeditionary Force
AF	air force
AFB	air force base
AFMC	Air Force Materiel Command
AGE	aerospace ground equipment
AIRSOUTH	Allied Air Forces Southern Europe
AMRAAM	advanced medium-range air-to-air missile
AO	area of operations
ARVN	Army of the Republic of Vietnam
ASC	Air Support Command
ASF	U.S. Army Service Forces
ASOC	Air Support Operations Center
ATAF	Allied Tactical Air Forces
ATC	Air Training Command
ATO	air tasking order

AWACS	airborne warning and control system
AWC	Air War College
BDA	bomb damage assessment
BiH	Bosnia and Herzegovina
BSA	Bosnian Serb Army
CAOC	Combined Air Operations Center
CAS	close air support
CASF	Composite Air Strike Force
CBI	China-Burma-India
CBU	cluster munition bomb
CBW	chemical and biological weapons
CENTAF	Central Command Air Forces
CENTCOM	Central Command
CFACC	Combined Forces Air Component Commander
CFLCC	Combined Force Land Component Commander
CFSOCC	Coalition Forces Special Operations Component Commander
CGSS	Command and General Staff School
CINCCENT	commander in chief of CENTCOM
CINCPAC	commander in chief of PACOM
CJCS	chairman of the Joint Chiefs of Staff
CJTF	Combined Joint Task Force
COMO	combat-oriented maintenance organization
COMUSCENTAF	Commander of U.S. Central Command Air Forces
COMUSMACV	Commander of U.S. Military Assistance Command, Vietnam
CONOPS	concept of operations
COSO	combat-oriented supply organization
COSSAC	chief of staff to the Supreme Allied Commander
CSAF	air force chief of staff
CSAR	combat search and rescue
DFC	Distinguished Flying Cross
DMPI	desired mean point of impact
DMZ	demilitarized zone
ETO	European theater of operations

EWO	electronic warfare officer
FAC	forward air controller
FEAF	Far East Air Forces
FECOM	Far East Command
FFI	French Forces of the Interior
FM	field manual
GCI	ground-controlled interception
GHQ	General Headquarters
GPS	Global Positioning System
HVT	high-value target
IADS	integrated air defense system
IPB	intelligence preparation of the battle space
ISR	intelligence, surveillance, and reconnaissance
JCS	Joint Chiefs of Staff
JDAM	joint direct attack munition
JFACC	joint force air component commander
JFC	joint force commander
JSOTF-N	Joint Special Operations Task Force–North
JSTARS	Joint Surveillance Target Attack Radar System
LGB	laser-guided bomb
LORAN	long-range area navigation
MACV	Military Assistance Command, Vietnam
MAF	marine amphibious force
MATS	Military Air Transport Service
MEF	marine expeditionary force
MEW	microwave early warning
MIT	Massachusetts Institute of Technology
MoU	memorandum of understanding
NAC	North Atlantic Council
NASM	National Air and Space Museum
NATO	North Atlantic Treaty Organization
NSC	National Security Council
NVA	North Vietnamese Army
OEF	Operation Enduring Freedom
OIF	Operation Iraqi Freedom

ORI	Operational Readiness Inspection
PACAF	Pacific Air Forces
PACOM	Pacific Command
PGM	precision-guided munition
PME	professional military education
POL	petroleum, oils, and lubricants
POW	prisoner of war
PSAB	Prince Sultan Air Base
R&D	research and development
RAF	Royal Air Force
RoE	rules of engagement
ROTC	Reserve Officers' Training Corps
RRF	rapid reaction force
RVNAF	Republic of Vietnam Armed Forces
SAASS	School of Advanced Air and Space Studies
SAC	Strategic Air Command
SACEUR	supreme allied commander Europe
SAIS	School of Advanced International Studies
SAM	surface-to-air missile
SEAD	suppression of enemy air defenses
SF	Special Forces
SHAEF	Supreme Headquarters Allied Expeditionary Force
SLAM	standoff land-attack missile
SOLE	special operations liaison element
SOS	Squadron Officer School
SPINS	special instructions
STANEVAL	standardization/evaluation
SWPA	Southwest Pacific Area
TAC	Tactical Air Command
TACC	Tactical Air Control Center
TACP	tactical air control party
TAF	tactical air force
TF	task force
TFW	tactical fighter wing
TLAM	Tomahawk land-attack missile

TST	time-sensitive targeting
TTP	tactics, techniques, and procedures
UK	United Kingdom
UN	United Nations
UNPF	UN Peace Force
UNPROFOR	UN Protection Force
UPT	undergraduate pilot training
USAAF	U.S. Army Air Forces
USAF	U.S. Air Force
USAFE	U.S. Air Forces in Europe
USMA	U.S. Military Academy
USSAG	U.S. Support and Assistance Group
USSTAF	U.S. Strategic Air Forces
WAC	Women's Army Corps
WDFM	War Department field manual
WSAG	Washington Special Actions Group
ZOA	zone of action

INTRODUCTION

Some academics and consultants decided to solve the mystery of leader-ship. They had time on their hands—they were on safari. By way of a warm-up exercise they decided to design the perfect predator. Each took responsibility for one element of the predator. The result was a beast with the legs of a cheetah, the jaws of a crocodile, the hide of a rhino, the neck of a giraffe, the ears of an elephant, the tail of a scorpion, and the attitude of a hippo. The beast promptly collapsed under the weight of its own improbability.

Undeterred, they turned their attention to designing the perfect leader. Their perfect leader looked like this: creative and disciplined; visionary and detailed; motivational and commanding; directing and empowering; ambitious and humble; reliable and risk taking; intuitive and logical; intellectual and emotional; coaching and controlling. This leader also collapsed under the weight of overwhelming improbability. The good news is that we do not have to be perfect to be a leader. We have to fit the situation.

—From Jo Owens, *How to Lead*[1]

THE FULL SPECTRUM OF AIR POWER

To many the evolution of air power is a story of "higher, faster, and farther," with a constant drive to improve technology and tactics for getting "bombs on target." To others it represents a quest for concepts and theory to give air warfare a larger meaning and purpose. In essence, technology is an enabler for what we *can do* and *how*, while concepts inform us what we *should do* and *why*. Execution, however—the coming together of what is technologically possible and conceptually feasible—depends on *military leadership*. Achieving strategic effects and optimizing the utility of air power in given politico-military circumstances constitute the art and science of air command and air leadership. In other words, understanding "the whole house of air power," to paraphrase Lawrence of Arabia, requires insight into concepts (ideas), technology (machines), and leadership (people). This book sheds light on the interaction among these three components in various air campaigns, with an emphasis on the latter. The operational narratives focus on personalities, experiences, and styles of leadership and on how those factors translated into battle-space outcomes.

Studies of air warfare and air campaigns in general far outnumber studies of air commanders. Many of these analyses are of admirable quality, but surveys of air power literature lead to the undeniable conclusion that many studies misrepresent the contribution of air power to the resolution of any particular conflict, giving it either too little credit or too much. The obvious reason for this shortcoming is that air power's effectiveness and efficiency are difficult to grasp. Strategic effects are cumulative, cascading, nonlinear, and often secondary and tertiary in nature, not lending themselves to traditional definitions of success and failure. Furthermore, subject matter expertise tends to focus either on details of tactics and technology or on the political setting and overall strategy. Both types of studies underestimate, or even leave out, the operational level, which is the essential link between strategy and tactics.

Airmen often blame the misrepresentation of air power's contribution to modern warfare on ground-centric officers and scholars, but the inescapable conclusion after a hundred years of flight is that airmen have not succeeded in telling their own story convincingly. In their quest to "sell their product" to the public and to politicians, airmen unfortunately often deliver uncritical hymns of praise to air power rather than sound and logical explanations based on their own experience. According to Professor Colin S. Gray:

> The airpower story has been and remains strategically superior to the tale that many of its more devoted advocates have managed to tell. As a result of promising too much, airpower spokespeople actually have promised too little for what they have delivered. Airpower has been undersold in good part be-

cause some among its more dedicated promoters have exaggerated what did not require exaggeration, and—most damaging of all—because they chose to advertise their product in a way that ignored or short-changed much of what it was, did, and could do.[2]

The more zealous among air power advocates have traditionally overstated the strength of the "bolt from the blue" and understated its limitations. Greater knowledge about the history of air power—not only about campaigns but also about the individuals who led these campaigns—might help airmen explain the purpose and effects of air power in a logical, systematic, and coherent fashion. They could do so not through wishful thinking or twisting of the truth but by presenting the use and development of air power factually, analytically, and passionately; the first two characteristics do not preclude the third. This effort should not be taken lightly, as a thorough understanding of air power offers substantial political and military benefits to nations.

Biography—an important but often neglected element of the historiography of air power—has partly failed to give insight into the individual qualities that enable effective leadership in air campaigns. Relatively few air power experts have devoted extensive and serious effort to portraying the lives and achievements of prominent air leaders. Some great books have appeared,[3] but good, solid biographies of great air leaders have lagged behind those of ground commanders, and biographies of senior airmen in command of air forces have left much to be desired. In acknowledging the small but respectable body of biographies of air power commanders, one must also admit that many less serious works available are hagiographical, seek to endow their subjects with prophetic power and greatness, and lack the critical research necessary for accuracy, accountability, and perspective. Others are sketchy biographical notes offering little more than a series of anecdotes, speeches, and testimonies short of contextual basis. Yet others are sensational, speculative, unforgiving, and even spiteful without acknowledging that leaders make decisions under very special circumstances and based only on the information available at the time. "If I knew then what I know now, I would have acted differently" applies to everyone, including military leaders. Unfortunately, relatively few senior airmen have written extensive autobiographies. Our understanding of events would increase if we knew more about what influenced and motivated decisions that played a major role in shaping military history.

THE IMPORTANCE OF GREAT CAPTAINS

This shortage of high-quality biographies and autobiographies in the air power literature is regrettable, because the centrality of warfare to the human experience, and of the individual to history, makes studies of "great captains" a worthy and profitable endeavor. After all, military leaders, or the sword bearers of their nations—entrusted with authority to employ lethal force to achieve national objectives—have primary responsibility for planning and executing the battles and campaigns that, cumulatively, spell victory or defeat. What are the common characteristics of successful generals in modern warfare and of those who have failed the test of leadership? Is there a prototypical archetype that is marked for generalship, or a "general template" applicable to the evaluation, career progression, and selection of junior officers for higher command? These and many other questions call for inquiry and have provoked much scholarship and analysis,[4] but case studies of air commanders are few and far between.

According to Carl von Clausewitz, "the greatest student of strategy who ever lived,"[5] two qualities of leadership are indispensable: "First, an intellect that, even in the darkest hour, retains some glimmerings of the inner light which leads to truth; and second, the courage to follow this faint light wherever it may lead. The first of these qualities is described by the French term *coup d'oeil:* the second is determination."[6] Both of these qualities of leadership are rooted in character more than anything else, and for Napoleon Bonaparte, "perhaps the most competent person who ever lived,"[7] great generalship reflected the realm of genius. At St. Helena "the God of War" summed up his view on the centrality of great captains to warfare:

> The personality (présence) of the general is indispensable, he is the head, he is the all of the army. The Gauls were not conquered by the Roman legions, but by Caesar. It was not before the Carthaginian soldiers that Rome was made to tremble, but before Hannibal. It was not the Macedonian phalanx which penetrated to India, but Alexander. It was not the French army which reached the Weser and the Inn, it was Turenne. Prussia was not defended for seven years against the three most formidable European powers by the Prussian soldiers, but by Fredrick the Great.[8]

In the words of Brig. Sir John Smyth, "No one becomes a general unless he has shown outstanding qualities of knowledge and leadership. . . . The interesting thing is how different generals then stand up to different conditions—which rise to the big occasion and which fail to do so." While acknowledging that "all the time the imponderable actor of luck plays its very important part," he concluded that "leadership is of course the most important quality which every successful battle general must have."[9]

More than a decade earlier, in 1961, Smyth's fellow countryman Field Marshal Bernard Law Montgomery—himself a highly polarizing commander whose record reflects both the most and the least admirable qualities of generalship—enumerated what he perceived as the essential qualities of military leadership required by a successful commander. He noted:

> The man who aspires to rise to high command has got to make an intense study of the military art, and equip his mind professionally with all he needs—so that he will be ready when the moment arises, when the opportunity comes his way. He must be a man of decision and action; calmness in the crisis and decision in action must be his watchwords. . . . He must be a good judge of men, a good picker of subordinates. . . . Then he must be tough, and ruthless in dealing with inefficiency in battle—when men's lives are at stake. The good general is not merely one who wins battles; they must be won with a minimum loss of life. And he must be prepared to take a chance when the situation favours boldness. He will lose part of the fruits of victory if he is never prepared to soar from the known to seize the unknown. . . . He must be absolutely straight and speak the military truth to his political masters, hoping that they will be straight with him.[10]

In essence, great generalship is the art of war.[11]

COMMANDING AIR POWER

With such a perspective as background, this book focuses on personality traits and leadership styles of twelve senior airmen, from "Tooey" Spaatz in the Second World War to "Buzz" Moseley in Afghanistan and Iraq more than a half-century later, who commanded air forces in combat. It does so not to endorse the actions of these men, pay tribute to them, or defend their reputations, but to better comprehend their challenges. In addition to providing insight into their personality traits and leadership styles, the book offers added value by placing these important commanders within a political, operational, organizational, and doctrinal context, which in turn should lead to greater understanding of command in air warfare. As Phillip S. Meilinger notes, the importance of proper balance and proportion cannot be overstated:

> Although biography has its limitations—a tendency to exaggerate the significance of individuals and to forget that institutions, groups, and simple fate can also determine history—the insights into character, culture, behavior, and emotion far outweigh any potential drawbacks. We have much to learn from our past leaders. The challenges they faced are not so different from those we confront today and will meet in the future. Thorough, critical, dispassionate, and honest biographies and autobiographies are essential in assisting future airmen to meet their challenges.[12]

In essence, this book uses short biographies of outstanding airmen who commanded air campaigns in times of war to illustrate how their individual characters and life experiences shaped some of the central air campaigns in history. Each chapter uses a specific campaign as a starting point, but the discussion centers on the life and times of the air commander who gave those campaigns their unique character. The chapters may help to answer such questions as: What does it take to command an air campaign? What qualities do commanders require in terms of personality, leadership, and expertise? What kind of training, education, and real-life experience did these air commanders have before they were put to the test? How did these factors influence their concepts of operations? And, finally, what can we learn from their command experiences?

Ultimately, this volume presents a selection of case studies that will help readers better understand command in air warfare, the very interface between man and machine, and how air leaders in times of conflict linked the theory and practice of air power.

SELECTION CRITERIA

The most difficult task in designing this book was selecting the subjects. Many great airmen throughout the world have shown determination, courage, and wisdom in times of war, with the Second World War offering especially notable examples. Many European commanders—British, French, and German—merit closer examination, or reexamination, as do a range of airmen from Australia, India, and

Japan. This volume nevertheless stays with American airmen and, in particular, those of the U.S. Air Force (USAF) and its lineal predecessors. The book focuses on command in major military conflicts, and often it was a strong American contribution, even in a coalition effort, that proved decisive. Currently the USAF is to many a model of a powerful modern air force and is undeniably the world's supreme air power. This circumscribed focus allows for consistency and coherence among the chapters and sheds light on the institution's organizational, doctrinal, and intellectual development over time, but those advantages admittedly come at the expense of other nationalities and services.

I also decided to focus on the higher military level of air combat command. Wing and squadron commanders are integral parts of any command group, and their strengths and weaknesses in terms of combat and leadership have significant, and interesting, effects on the outcomes of individual battles. No less interesting are air-minded civilian political leaders, such as the first secretary of the air force, Stuart Symington, who fought so hard to form a proper institution in the tumultuous postwar years, and the seventeenth secretary, Donald B. Rice, who sponsored a powerful and insightful white paper titled *Global Reach—Global Power* that has shaped USAF doctrine to the present day. A series of USAF chiefs of staff also held significant command responsibility worthy of scholarly research, as did commanders of the Strategic Air Command (SAC), Tactical Air Command (TAC), and several numbered commands, but I decided to focus the discussion on airmen of general rank who commanded relatively large air forces in combat. To provide the required depth, breadth, and context, with emphasis on modern air warfare, the number of case studies had to be reduced to four for each of three crucial time periods: World War II, the Cold War era, and finally the conflicts of the late twentieth and early twenty-first centuries.

Command of air power in World War I is interesting, and much can be learned from Mason M. Patrick ("the first real head of American aviation"), William "Billy" Mitchell ("the most famous and controversial figure in the history of American airpower"),[13] and others. But at that time air power was still in its early stages as an instrument of force, and most of the command and leadership lessons from that conflict can be captured in sharper relief from experiences during World War II, when it had become far more mature and influential.

Here, too, choices were necessary, because World War II is also the period most often discussed in the air power literature. Many readers will find it surprising and possibly disappointing that Henry H. Arnold, Claire L. Chennault, James H. Doolittle, Ira C. Eaker, Haywood S. Hansell Jr., Elwood R. Quesada, Hoyt S. Vandenberg, Nathan F. Twining, Lauris Norstad, and several other prominent air leaders from World War II are not focal points of this book.[14] They are all worthy candidates, but deeming it paramount to select representatives of strategic, operational, and tactical use of air power, the choice fell on Carl A. Spaatz, George C. Kenney, and Otto P. Weyland respectively. These three also had interesting relationships with well-known superiors, Dwight D. Eisenhower, Douglas MacArthur, and George S. Patton Jr., respectively. The fourth study for the World War II period is Curtis E. LeMay, a man whose determination, critical positions in the military hierarchy, and longevity of service made him tremendously influential. He is perhaps the air commander best known outside air power circles, having become even an icon of sorts, but his contributions are often misunderstood, in no small part because of stories that focus on style rather than substance.

The chapters on these four airmen cover command responsibilities in both the European and the Pacific theaters of operations without the overlap and redundancy that would result from describing the same campaign time and again. Furthermore, all these airmen appreciated the diversity of air power and therefore present a broad spectrum of experiences. While their experiences in World War I strongly influenced Spaatz and Kenney, the younger Weyland and LeMay were more heavily conditioned by events early in World War II. All were "generalists," in the proper sense of the word, as well as generals, with great appreciation of both the strengths and the weaknesses of air power in its multiple roles and missions. Moreover, the length and range of their service and their vast experience across the full spectrum of air power at a time when it was transforming rapidly make them particularly relevant—in the case of Spaatz and Kenney from the western front to the jet age, and in the case of Weyland and LeMay from the late biplane era to the era of supersonic fighters, nuclear-armed bombers, and ballistic missiles. While they had vastly different personalities, they were contemporaries who, to some extent, influenced each other; they also experienced many of the same challenges that remain, in principle, relevant today. Although some might not consider these men the top four air commanders during World War II, they represent the broadest characteristics of air command of that period. Furthermore, they all performed superbly and by any account should be acknowledged as great captains.[15]

Candidates for the Cold War era were fewer, especially given the focus on major operations in which the United States took the lead—the Berlin Airlift, Korea, and Vietnam. William H. Tunner is included for two reasons: airlift is an often overlooked and underestimated function that is essential to operational success, and he played a leading role in developing and implementing the unprecedented airlift into Berlin during one of the first major international crises of the Cold War. George E. Stratemeyer held command under Douglas MacArthur in the first and most crucial year of the Korean War—during the initial response to North Korea's invasion of South Korea on June 25, 1950. Exceptionally knowledgeable about tactical air power, William W. Momyer served as the air commander in Vietnam from July 1966 to August 1968 during the infamous Rolling Thunder campaign. Finally, John W. Vogt Jr., directly appointed by President Richard Nixon and National Security Adviser Henry Kissinger, held command of U.S. air forces during the more successful Linebacker campaigns. Momyer's and Vogt's experiences present an interesting contrast of strategies in the same conflict.

Again, others could have been chosen, such as Earle E. Partridge and Emmett "Rosie" O'Donnell, both distinguished air commanders under Stratemeyer in the Korean War, or any of the three men who commanded the Seventh Air Force in Vietnam in the periods between Momyer and Vogt:[16] George S. Brown, who later became air force chief of staff and chairman of the Joint Chiefs of Staff; Lucius D. "Lou" Clay Jr., later appointed commander in chief of North American Air Defense Command; or John D. Lavelle, who was relieved of command under allegations of having directed unauthorized bombing missions into North Vietnam.[17] Still, Stratemeyer, Momyer, and Vogt held command during the most intensive air operations in Korea and Vietnam and have so far received relatively little attention in the historiography of air power.[18]

Selecting commanders for major air campaigns in the post–Cold War era was easiest of all. Charles A. Horner was the air component commander of Operation Desert Storm (1991), Michael E. Ryan was in charge of air operations during Operation Deliberate Force in Bosnia and Herzegovina (1995), Michael C. Short commanded the air campaign of Allied Force (1999), and finally T. Michael Moseley served as the air component commander of both Operation Enduring Freedom (2001) and Operation Iraqi Freedom (2003). It will become apparent to the readers that these campaigns were fought under different geographical and political circumstances.

THE AIR COMMANDERS: OVERVIEW

These twelve case studies of senior USAF airmen commanding air forces, in short, offer possible lessons for future air leaders or anyone interested in the command, leadership, and history of air warfare. Some readers may disagree with the choices. I hope that future historians will supplement this book with further analyses that give the outstanding leaders covered, and those not covered here, the careful consideration they deserve.

Gen. Carl A. Spaatz

In the first chapter, Richard G. Davis focuses on Gen. Carl A. Spaatz, the man who led the largest strategic air campaign in the history of air warfare—the aerial bombardment of Germany in 1944 and 1945. "Tooey" Spaatz was the premier American air commander in the European theater of war and, according to General Eisenhower, "the best operational airman in the world." Spaatz was the only airman whom Hap Arnold fully trusted; and when the war in Europe ended, Arnold selected Spaatz to lead the strategic air campaign in the Pacific, including the nuclear attacks. After Japan's surrender, Arnold appointed Spaatz to lead the fight for an independent air service, which resulted in the creation of the U.S. Air Force. Spaatz reorganized the air force by establishing two important commands that would define the USAF for more than forty years—SAC to conduct atomic and conventional bombing and TAC to provide aerial and close air support to the army.

Ironically, and perhaps comforting to some, the man who accomplished these tasks hated paperwork, was sometimes labeled an "anti-staff officer," was a poor public speaker, and disliked professional military education. When he graduated from West Point he was viewed as low on motivation with less-than-average prospects for a military career. Later on, his rater at the Command and General Staff School did not recommend this private and modest airman for further staff training. Obviously, outstanding grades in school are not a precondition for great leadership.

Davis paints a picture of an officer who had an extremely broad and deep range of practical experience before he took command of the U.S. Strategic Air Forces (USSTAF) in Europe in January 1944. Spaatz had proved himself time and again as a doer and a problem solver—first as an outstanding pilot and second as a great organizer and excellent commander. Davis attributes Spaatz's high performance to five essential ingredients: luck, management skills, killer instinct, perseverance, and trustworthiness (with superiors and subordinates alike). These qualities manifested themselves when Spaatz led the first American heavy bombers to Britain, ordered the first B-17 raid on a European target, and served in the Mediterranean, where he earned Eisenhower's friendship and learned the ins and outs of coalition warfare. In January 1944 he stepped up to command both the U.S. Eighth and Fifteenth Strategic Air Forces. Benefitting from massive resources, he altered tactics fundamentally by ordering loose escort instead of close escort, a change that led to a crushing victory over the Axis powers. His insistence on bombing German oil plants (rather than transportation lines) resulted in a classic strategic campaign against a target system of decisive importance. He combined this effort with low-level attacks and air attacks on German cities, including the bombing of Berlin with incendiary bombs, convinced that this strategy would help to end the war and thus ultimately save lives. After serving as the first USAF chief of staff, "the Bomber Baron" retired in 1948, but he remained an active supporter of land-based air power for the rest of his life.

Gen. George C. Kenney

In chapter 2 Alan Stephens examines the command and leadership of Gen. George C. Kenney, the most powerful and influential airman in the Southwest Pacific during World War II. Highly skilled in the full spectrum of air power, Kenney became the prototype—or archetype—of the modern concept of "air component commander" under General MacArthur and a master practitioner of what we would later term "operational art." While in tune with the grand strategic and military strategic setting and objectives, and an expert on tactical aviation, engineering, and logistics, Kenney exhibited exceptional skill when it came to orchestrating an air campaign operationally and organizationally. To earn the trust, full confidence, and high regard of the difficult and demanding MacArthur was an achievement in and of itself. Furthermore, the way Kenney set up from scratch, trained, and then led air forces to a spectacular victory in the Battle of the Bismarck Sea was a masterpiece in air warfare. MacArthur himself described it as "the decisive aerial engagement" of the war in the Southwest Pacific. In a matter of months, Kenney reshaped his command's strength, organization, and fighting spirit to such an extent that the Allies enjoyed near-supremacy in the skies over the theater of operations. He did so with limited resources, as the war in Europe had higher priority. That supremacy in turn underwrote MacArthur's famous island-hopping strategy, through which the Allies advanced northward toward the Japanese home islands. By the end of the war Kenney commanded all Allied and American Army Air Forces in the Pacific.

Stephens argues that Kenney's professional mastery—defined by his ability to create certainty, his acute understanding of the strategic environment, his loyalty, his unsentimental (but qualified) observance of realpolitik, and his profound knowledge of every element of air power—was, quite simply, unique. His grasp of the full spectrum of air power—including the integration of intelligence and logistics—as well as his intellect, personal energy, and focus on the morale and well-being of his men (rated and nonrated) set him aside from most leaders. He was, quintessentially, a commander in full and "a kind of renaissance airman." It may therefore be surprising that the most accomplished air commander in the Pacific theater of war was fired from command of SAC three years after the war. Unfortunately, as Stephens concludes, Kenney lost sight of his priorities: he involved himself in interservice rivalry, flirted with national politics, and preferred traveling constantly to give dramatic speeches that promoted air power to attending to the bureaucratic demands of managing SAC. His absence from SAC resulted in a remote management style that stood in strong contrast to the tireless energy and personal dedication that had defined his leadership and command during the war. Having been replaced by Curtis LeMay, Kenney ended his career as commander of Air University, retiring from that position in 1951. He then provided a useful written account of his experiences in World War II, *General Kenney Reports: A Personal History of the Pacific War*.

GEN. OTTO P. WEYLAND

While Spaatz was a champion of strategic air power and Kenney excelled at the operational level of war, no leader was more effective and competent than Gen. Otto P. Weyland when it came to tactical air operations. In the third chapter Richard R. Muller examines the air leadership of "Opie" Weyland, commander of XIX TAC, which fought alongside Patton's Third Army without pause for more than nine months, from August 1944 to the Third Reich's defeat in May 1945. The XIX TAC and Third Army functioned as an effective air-ground team from the day they first went into battle, with Weyland's fighter-bombers essentially providing an aerial flank and protecting the swift advance of Patton's army through

France and its final drive into Germany. These campaigns have often been used since as case studies and models for air-ground cooperation and coordination. Weyland was so successful that Patton, seventeen years older, battle-hardened, and with unparalleled wartime experience, assessed him as "the best damn general in the Air Corps."

Such praise from the flamboyant, eccentric, and demanding Patton is even more impressive when one realizes that Weyland arrived in theater in March 1944 without combat experience and that the operations they fought varied significantly in character. Muller identifies several professional and personal attributes that contributed to Weyland's being "one of the most accomplished practitioners of tactical air support in all of military history." Undeniably, having spent so much time prior to the war in tactical aviation and specializing in observation served him exceptionally well. His grasp of the fundamentals of land warfare was second to none; in his own words he could speak "Army language." Although he was not an operational innovator (others developed most of the techniques of close air support), Weyland did excel in integrating aerial reconnaissance and signals intelligence into his operations. Like Spaatz and Kenney he was no slave to published doctrine; he knew when to adhere to established procedures and when to be flexible. Simply put, he knew his profession. His tactical air power expertise, however, might have availed little had his leadership style not earned him the trust of ground commanders. Weyland was quiet and firm, both confident and self-critical, and loyal to his superiors, peers, and subordinates alike. He demonstrated concern for the well-being of his men and treated captured Germans with professional respect. He did not shy away from challenges and delivered on his promises. Weyland also had a flair for public relations, ensuring that the accomplishments of XIX TAC were widely disseminated. After the war he would again witness combat as both vice commander and then commander of Far East Air Forces in the Korean War. When he ended his career as commander of TAC (1954–1959), he had cemented his reputation as the quintessential tactical airman.

GEN. CURTIS E. LeMAY

In the fourth chapter Williamson Murray examines the most controversial airman in USAF history, Gen. Curtis E. LeMay, who still stands out as a seminal larger-than-life-figure. An outstanding pilot and navigator, with great tactical and mechanical insight, he excelled as an air commander during World War II and then emerged as the ultimate Cold Warrior. Where Kenney failed as commander of SAC, LeMay formed and shaped the command according to his own views, to the extent that he became Mr. Atom Bomb personified, and ended his career as the air force's vice chief of staff (1957–1961) and then chief of staff (1961–1965). LeMay is remembered not only as a great commander of SAC, the leader who built it into an effective and efficient deterrent and war-fighting arm, but also as a rather unsuccessful chief. He never became comfortable working the inner circles of either side of the Potomac River and had uneasy relationships with both the Lyndon Johnson administration (especially Secretary of Defense Robert McNamara) and the chairman of the Joint Chiefs, Gen. Maxwell Taylor.

In this chapter, however, Murray focuses primarily on LeMay's service in World War II, when he clearly displayed his personality as a leader who ruthlessly demanded the best from his air crews, but at the same time never required that they do anything that he had not accomplished himself—sometimes at the risk of his life. Always impatient and lacking in social grace and tact, LeMay drove himself without regard to his health. Murray identifies critical qualities that made for this "airman extraordinary": a blend of intellect, innovation, and courage within the framework of relentless training, plain hard work, and an insistence on leading by example. LeMay began as a group commander in the Eighth Air Force, where he created a combat bomber group out of raw recruits and then led it in some of the first combat missions that the U.S. Army Air Force flew against the Luftwaffe. During his first year in Britain, he tightened up the combat formations to fly straight and level through German flak, and then flew in the first mission. In August 1943, he led his bomb division on the Schweinfurt-Regensburg raid. His performance as a combat leader in Europe led to promotions that took him from lieutenant colonel to major general in eighteen months.

Hap Arnold was so impressed by LeMay's leadership that he put him in command of the Pacific Theater's XXI Bomber Command, which was equipped with prestigious B-29s. Flying from bases in the Marianas, LeMay took the bold and unprecedented decision to abandon the U.S. doctrine of high-altitude, daylight precision bombing. He instead stripped the B-29s of guns, loaded them with incendiaries and high explosives, and sent them against Japanese cities at night and at low level. His crews devastated the country through a series of firebombing raids, of which the March 9–10 attacks on Tokyo are the most infamous. LeMay's incendiary campaign destroyed more than two million houses and left 30 percent of the Japanese population homeless. To the end of his life LeMay believed that the firebombing was morally justified because it brought the Japanese to the brink of surrender without conducting a land invasion, which would have caused more casualties and destruction for combatants and civilians alike. In fact, recent research has revealed that Japan was unwilling to surrender prior to the atomic bomb attacks of August 1945, despite having been defeated militarily through air power.

LT. GEN. WILLIAM H. TUNNER

Moving into the second part of the book—focusing on the commanders of the Cold War era—in chapter 5 James S. Corum examines the career of Gen. William H. Tunner, an airman who showed an unusual talent for developing organizations and concepts for air transportation systems. A mediocre pilot at best and a hopeless flight instructor, Tunner's skills lay first and foremost in organization and management. His personal dedication and drive to improve airlift capacity added a new dimension to timely and efficient methods for transportation of personnel, equipment, and other supplies in times of war, crisis, and peace. He was instrumental in developing the Ferrying Command (where he set up procedures, standardized training programs, and regular inspections), but his breakthrough came in 1944 when he led and directed the Hump airlift over the Himalayas. His fame was ensured when he used those experiences as the de facto air commander of the Berlin Airlift from June 1948 to May 1949. Failure to supply the Western Allied sectors of Berlin would have meant a catastrophic defeat in the early stages of the Cold War. The Berlin Airlift became the West's first real victory in the Cold War and demonstrated American and Western resolve in the face of Soviet aggression.

The formula for Tunner's success over the Hump, in Berlin, and in later contributions during the Korean War, was hard work and dedication combined with an insistence on strict procedures. Standardized flight schedules and flight plans were carefully worked out, firm regulations were established for air control, crew rest and safety regulations were formalized and enforced, and both timely weather briefings and statistical analysis became essential parts of the operational planning and analysis. Tunner also paid close attention to maintenance procedures because, in an airlift, operations and logistics became closely intertwined. With these guidelines in force, tonnage rates improved significantly and accident rates decreased. Efficiency and safety were prime principles for Tunner. In the 1950s, as the Military Air Transport Service commander, "the father of airlift" developed new organizational concepts for a joint airlift system that would make possible the rapid deployment and supply of large American ground forces anywhere in the world. Although Tunner retired in 1960, the American air transport system today retains many of the concepts that he initiated and developed.

In terms of command and leadership, Tunner's strength was his "managerial approach"; he was an excellent organizer and administrator who was dedicated to the mission at hand. At times creative and even visionary, he spoke his mind and never took no for an answer, to the extent that he would work around the chain of command if he deemed it necessary. He gained the highest respect from General Norstad, who saw him as a problem solver who always got the job done, while others found him unpleasant and arrogant. "Willie the Whip" had a mixed reputation among his subordinates. His cold personality, short temper, impatience, and insistence on discipline and internal inspections made him many enemies, and General Twining, who replaced Vandenberg as air force chief of staff, considered Tunner's "irascible personality a source of bad leadership." Regardless, LeMay, at first not too pleased with Tunner's showing up for the Berlin Airlift, concluded that Tunner was "the transportation expert to end transportation experts."

Lt. Gen. George E. Stratemeyer

In chapter 6, Thomas A. Keaney examines the leadership of Lt. Gen. George E. Stratemeyer, who commanded Far East Air Forces during the first year of the Korean War. "Strat" had substantial and relevant experience before assuming that post, having served as the executive officer and later chief of staff for Hap Arnold, air deputy to Gen. Joseph Stilwell in the China-Burma-India theater, commander of the Air Defense Command, and, after the merger of Air Defense Command with TAC, commander of the resulting Continental Air Command.

When he arrived in Korea Stratemeyer had dealt extensively with operational, diplomatic, and interservice matters, but little had prepared him for what proved to be a very different kind of war. The first year encompassed turbulent periods with unready forces waging a desperate defense against the North Korean attack, followed by United Nations forces launching the air-ground-amphibious counteroffensive to reverse the course of the war, and then fighting another grim defense when Chinese forces entered the war, all while avoiding an escalation of the war into a U.S.-Soviet confrontation. Stratemeyer found himself in command of air operations with a force that was drastically downsized from World War II, was in the process of transitioning to jet aircraft, and was lacking doctrinal and organizational frameworks. Outstanding air commanders were pulled out in the middle of the war to serve on the Air Staff back in Washington, indicating the low priority of the war. Stratemeyer chafed against the political restrictions placed on air operations, particularly the prohibition against extending air attacks into Manchuria, and throughout the rest of his life he decried the political interference in the war's conduct.

Just as the Korean War is often labeled the "forgotten war," Stratemeyer, who was less charismatic and spectacular than many of his contemporaries, is a forgotten air commander. Previous accounts have tended to underestimate the complexities of the geopolitical considerations that governed the Korean War, and his organization of air power may well have exemplified the art of the possible given the circumstances he faced. Here Keaney draws the picture of a competent air commander who had considerable insight into both the political and operational aspects of the war and who had a great talent for orchestrating and managing the air campaign through others. While his headquarters remained in Tokyo, he exercised control through three outstanding subordinate commanders: Maj. Gen. Earle Partridge for tactical operations, Maj. Gen. Emmett O'Donnell for B-29 operations, and Maj. Gen. William Tunner for airlift operations. It is interesting to note that O'Donnell's provisional bomber command served under Stratemeyer. This chain of command served as a clear indication of LeMay's trust, since in every other case the command of those SAC bombers deployed during the Cold War remained with SAC.

There are several noteworthy elements to Stratemeyer's command. First, in strong contrast to LeMay and Tunner, for example, he clearly had a talent for interpersonal relations, which was demonstrated by the excellent relationship he enjoyed with Gen. Douglas MacArthur, his superior in the theater who dominated all aspects of the war. Second, Stratemeyer was ahead of his time in recognizing the importance of media relations. Seeing the war as a test of air force capabilities, Stratemeyer attempted to influence news reporting on air force operations, gave many press interviews, and monitored reports coming from the theater for signs of bias, often instigated, he suspected, by members of the army, navy, or marines. Finally, his willingness to delegate tasks to key subordinates sets him apart from several other air commanders scrutinized in this book, particularly the next two men who held command in Vietnam.

Gen. William W. Momyer

Chapter 7 focuses on Gen. William W. Momyer, the theater commander during the discredited Rolling Thunder air campaign in Vietnam. Momyer presents historians with an apparent contradiction. On one hand, he was exceptionally knowledgeable about air power, especially tactical air power, and in this was on par with Generals Kenney and LeMay. He was an outstanding pilot who had commanded one of the U.S. Army Air Forces' finest P-40 fighter groups through combat operations from North Africa to Italy. Momyer returned to the United States to serve on the U.S. Army Air Force Board, an organization that applied the lessons of World War II to equipment testing, tactics, and doctrine. He served on the TAC staff during its earliest days and returned to that staff later in his career, when he would find himself responsible for forging doctrine and planning joint exercises. During the Korean War he served on the Air War College faculty and led the production of the first complete set of air force doctrine manuals. Following the National War College, he commanded fighter wings and divisions during TAC's resource-scarce times. Momyer's tour on the air staff as director of operational requirements put him at the center of planning for the means that would serve the ends of war in the future. His whole career could be seen as preparing him for Vietnam, where as Seventh Air Force Commander from July 1966 to July 1968 he had operational control over hundreds of aircraft and thousands of sorties during the USAF's heaviest participation in the Vietnam War. On the other hand, most historians consider Rolling Thunder an example of the misuse of air power—or of how not to conduct an air campaign. Ironically, this expert pilot and planner was in charge of one of the most condemned air campaigns in history.

The answer to this apparent contradiction is that commanders must fight a war as they find it and not as they wish it were. Although all senior military leaders must take their share of responsibility for the conduct of the war, Case Cunningham explains the difficult command arrangements that Momyer faced, the various agendas at play, and Washington's unprecedented micromanagement of the air campaign. Momyer was not allowed to design and execute the campaign as he saw fit; instead, he was forced to remain within a series of politically dictated constraints and restraints.

In terms of command style he was the opposite of Stratemeyer: stubborn and stern, Momyer did not easily delegate or seek advice, and as a true workaholic who never rested, he saw no need for deputies. Still, he was able to impress most of his superiors, including Robert McNamara. It also reflects well on Momyer that he was selected to command TAC upon his return from Vietnam and held that position from 1968 to 1973. Momyer no doubt understood the full spectrum of air power, but in many ways he has come to symbolize the legacy of tactical air power acumen, extending the legacy of Generals Quesada and Weyland.

After retirement, Momyer led a team that analyzed, reviewed, and wrote about the lessons of the Vietnam War. He emerges as an airman who spent his entire career in the pursuit of the most effective application of air power as a means to end wars. His career culminated in his book, *Airpower in Three Wars*, in which he captured the ideas that underlay his actions.

Gen. John W. Vogt

Moving from Rolling Thunder to the Linebacker campaigns, in the eighth chapter Stephen P. Randolph portrays Gen. John William Vogt Jr., who commanded the Seventh Air Force during the most prolonged combat period of the Vietnam War, at the outset of the Easter Offensive in April 1972. Personally chosen by Nixon and Kissinger, Vogt arrived in Saigon without having held command at any level since World War II and without having served in a flying unit since his combat tour in P-47s ended in 1944. Vogt's selection reflected Nixon's mistrust of the overall theater commander, Gen. Creighton Abrams, whom the president regarded as incapable of summoning the creativity and energy that he sought at that moment of crisis. Throughout his period of command, Vogt sustained his trusted relationship with the Nixon White House and most especially with Adm. Tom Moorer, the chairman of the Joint Chiefs. By contrast, Vogt's relationship with senior air force leaders—such as Chief of Staff Gen. Jack Ryan and Pacific Air Forces commander (and previous Seventh Air Force commander) Gen. Lou Clay—was distant at best and hostile at worst. Having defied the tradition of taking operational assignments and instead spending most of his later years serving in Joint Staff positions and working the military-political interface, Vogt lacked allies or friends among the air force leadership. That he had nominated himself for the position in Vietnam, and had criticized fellow officers for their conduct of operations there, was considered neither collegial nor good generalship. He did not make it easier for himself when, on his first day in theater, he overconfidently abandoned the long-held practice of having command briefings, and his demand for full control of his organization prevented others from demonstrating their own capabilities.

In addition, Vogt faced particularly trying circumstances. The U.S. command structure in Vietnam was convoluted, forcing him to report to four different superiors, and he arrived at a time when a three-pronged North Vietnamese offensive threatened to overwhelm the South Vietnamese defenders. Vogt successfully marshaled air force and navy support for the South Vietnamese and smothered the attacking forces under unremitting air attacks. When Nixon finally reopened the air war over North Vietnam with the Linebacker air offensive, Vogt shaped that air campaign through his insistence on using precision weapons, as American air forces engaged in an intense, though ultimately stalemated, action-reaction cycle with the North Vietnamese. Eight years of warfare had brought a wide range of new technologies to the tactical air forces, and Vogt actively promoted their use in combat. The choice of laser weaponry at the forefront of the campaign, his insistence on building an intelligence fusion center, and the use of acoustic sensors to find artillery and of long-range area navigation to permit flight in poor weather conditions—all demonstrated Vogt's focus on technology. As negotiations stagnated in December 1972, Vogt's forces provided critical support for the Linebacker II campaign, which finally brought the war to an end, and Vogt himself played a constructive role in informing the media about the air war. In retrospect, he secured his place in air power history through his aggressive application of advanced technology. In doing so, he planted the seeds of strategies that later became standard in air operations throughout the 1990s. As was the case of the air commanders before him, he made the most out of the situation in which he found himself.

Gen. Charles A. Horner

In the post–Cold War period, Gen. Charles A. Horner, America's first wartime Joint Force Air Component commander, oversaw the Desert Storm air campaign, the most successful such operation in military aviation history and the antithesis to the restrained approach used during the Vietnam War. Having combined a strategic campaign with tactical operations, Desert Storm set new standards for what the public, politicians, and officers of all services expected from air power. Horner exemplifies the American tradition of the citizen-soldier or, in his case, the citizen-airman. Having come into the service as a reservist eager to fly, he found that he was not only a superlative airman but also ideally suited for greater responsibilities and higher command, eventually retiring as a four-star general and commander of America's space forces. Horner's career spanned much of the post–World War II era of the air force, from the advent of supersonic tactical fighters to the emergence of stealth attack aircraft and space-based capabilities.

Richard P. Hallion examines how several key incidents and experiences strongly shaped Horner's personal and professional outlook. Horner grew up in what has been termed America's "Golden Age of Aviation," and his lifelong interest in flight began because of exposure to aviation and building models as a youth. Early in his air force career he experienced a near-accident that transformed his view of life. Then, while in Vietnam, he witnessed firsthand the dangers of incoherent strategy, of political micromanagement, of "top-down" direction by detached and distant authorities, of an unclear chain of command, and of senior leaders who failed to support their airmen. This experience would shape his approach to planning, command, and combat leadership. Exposure to two senior commanders in particular—Generals William Momyer and Wilbur Creech—greatly influenced his leadership and command style and imparted a vital perspective on the value of decentralizing execution and empowering subordinates to make critical decisions. Just as Kenney and Stratemeyer enjoyed excellent relationships with MacArthur, and Weyland did with Patton, Horner developed exceptionally good relations with his superior in theater, Gen. H. Norman Schwarzkopf. Horner earned Schwarzkopf's trust, remained loyal to his boss (Schwarzkopf), and time and again succeeded in sorting out issues before they became problems. Horner was also mindful of the Coalition's relationships, especially those with Arab partners. His subsequent experience in Desert Storm reaffirmed the lessons he had drawn from earlier in his career. Any officer aspiring to higher command could benefit from studying this supremely successful airman's career.

GEN. MICHAEL E. RYAN

Four years after the stunning success of Desert Storm, the U.S. Air Force became involved in a fundamentally different type of conflict. By 1995, the three warring parties in Bosnia and Herzegovina (BiH)—Serb, Croat, and Bosniak—were poised to seek a final settlement of their differences by fighting it out on the battlefield. The United Nations (UN) was reluctant to support the enforcement measures of the North Atlantic Treaty Organization (NATO) because the warring parties could easily retaliate against the UN peacekeepers. Any authorization to use NATO air power was subject to a dual-key arrangement, whereby the UN and NATO had to cooperate and figuratively turn their separate keys to authorize air strikes; but the UN remained unwilling to turn its key. Thus, despite air power's many positive attributes, it appeared to be the wrong tool to apply in war-torn BiH, where physical and political constraints offered huge challenges. Nevertheless, from the end of August through mid-September 1995, a NATO air campaign seemed to change the entire situation. The civil war ended, and within weeks a lasting political settlement to the war was hammered out in Dayton, Ohio. Mark A. Bucknam tells the story of the two-week air campaign—Operation Deliberate Force—and the man who commanded it, Gen. Michael E. "Mike" Ryan.

The son of a World War II hero, General Ryan was a fighter pilot who led the air campaign in BiH and eventually would go on to earn his fourth star and fill the position his father once held as chief of staff of the U.S. Air Force. His personal and professional background and the factors that shaped his life help explain why he succeeded as an air commander. Bucknam argues that several aspects of Ryan's command of Deliberate Force warrant the attention of students of air power and leadership, and resemble lessons that can be learned from most of the other air commanders discussed in this book. A tactical expert, Ryan was always aware of the significance of proper intelligence as an integral part of operations. He recognized the importance of vision, initiative, planning, and the need to remain within the context of what civilian policymakers found conceptually sound and politically feasible. In essence, this latter point meant that planners must take public relations, as well as simple efficacy, into account and remain sensitive to both friendly and enemy casualties. In addition, Ryan radiated a sense of responsibility toward superiors, peers, subordinates, and those under attack. He worked effectively with a range of players, including Coalition partners, and defied preset organizational lines. Ryan also understood operational art and air power doctrine, and when given the opportunity he used air power as decisively as possible. But when all is said and done, the qualities that defined him, as well as the subjects of the other case studies in this book, were integrity and strength of character—two classic qualities that will never become unfashionable.

Lt. Gen. Michael C. Short

Between March 24 and June 9, 1999, while under American leadership, NATO conducted an air campaign against President Slobodan Milošević's regime in an effort to halt the continuing atrocities and human rights abuses that were being committed against the citizens of Kosovo. Operation Allied Force lasted for seventy-eight days and became the third campaign during the 1990s, after Desert Storm and Deliberate Force, in which air power proved essential in determining a regional conflict's outcome. In this penultimate chapter Rebecca L. Grant focuses on the leadership of the man in charge of the air campaign, Lt. Gen. Michael C. Short. With his extensive experience from Vietnam, several senior command positions, and close involvement in the lead-up to the campaign, which included meetings with President Milošević himself, Short was as prepared as any airman could have been.

But a complex NATO command structure, a complicated target approval procedure, and substantial disagreement with his joint force commander, Gen. Wesley Clark, on what constituted centers of gravity for the Serb regime resulted in challenges no one could have fully foreseen. Short never established the trust and working relations with General Clark that Spaatz, Kenney, Weyland, Stratemeyer, and Horner had with their respective superiors. He was up against a commander who held strong views about how to apply air power, including an insistence on low-level combat flight and the introduction of Apache helicopters—conclusions that Short believed would undermine the very effectiveness of air power and unnecessarily increase the risk to his pilots' lives. Short was not risk averse, but he saw no potential gain in these strategies. At the core of strategic planning and operational art, Clark wanted to go after the Third Army in Kosovo, while Short wanted to go after the Serb leadership in downtown Belgrade on the opening night and ensure that the regime was turned deaf, blind, and mute—or rendered strategically incapacitated—in a model of shock and awe that had proved successful in 1991 against Saddam Hussein. Moreover, Short argued he could be even more successful since he had more precision bombs available and better aircraft, especially B-2 and joint direct attack munitions that could hit targets regardless of how bad the weather was. Grant revisits this debate, based on new and extensive interviews with General Short, and ends the chapter with highlights of this airman's lessons on command relations in particular and Coalition (allied) warfare in general.

GEN. T. MICHAEL MOSELEY

Few senior leaders in USAF history have generated as much controversy as Gen. T. Michael Moseley. Perhaps more than any other air general, "Buzz" Moseley embodies the qualities of the so-called fighter generals who have dominated the senior leadership positions in the USAF since 1982. This book's final chapter focuses on the generalship of an officer who found himself in charge of portions of Operation Enduring Freedom, particularly of the much-discussed Operation Anaconda, and the preparation and conduct of the air portion of Operation Iraqi Freedom, the campaign that sought to topple Saddam Hussein and his regime. James D. Kiras concludes that Moseley exhibited qualities that both inspired his staff and fostered a solid relationship with his commander, Gen. Tommy Franks, who increasingly delegated responsibility to him. In turn, Moseley did the same for his staff, from his deputy and chief of strategy on down. Moseley set high standards of technical and leadership competency for himself, and he expected the same from others. And as senior officers had trusted him throughout his career, he also rewarded others, including field grade officers, with both trust and great responsibilities, particularly in devising solutions to battlefield problems. According to Kiras, Moseley further inspired and fostered trust within the air forces by accepting the risk and responsibility for certain decisions, and by defending risks others had taken on individual initiative, provided they were not irresponsible. Above all else, he held those whom he trusted accountable for their actions, as the opening air-strike of Operation Iraqi Freedom suggests.

For those under his command, Moseley's blunt conviction that technologically advanced systems would deliver powerful solutions was a source of inspiring leadership, while others serving with him had their doubts. During his time of generalship between Operation Anaconda and the end of Operation Iraqi Freedom, Moseley was a strong advocate for the value of air power and the need to integrate air assets within the joint force. He observed the problems that occurred during Operation Anaconda in Afghanistan and sought to correct them. Moseley fought hard to have all air and space assets for the subsequent operations placed under his command to ensure unified control and to provide the joint force commander with the right air power solution for the job. He repaid Franks's trust by remaining flexible and responsive to pressing, unfolding requirements. Throughout Operation Iraqi Freedom he would continue to balance the strategic effects that air power could generate with the operational and tactical needs of the joint force team. His later promotion to chief of staff of the U.S. Air Force is proof positive that both senior political and military leaders recognized his command of air power in the war on terrorism.

CONCLUSION: A QUESTION OF RESPONSIBILITY

The case studies presented in this book focus explicitly on how these twelve air commanders dealt with an array of leadership challenges—all with the goal of assessing the mission at hand and, within it, the utility and effectiveness of air power as it was applied in unique organizational and operational settings. Different airmen faced various levels and combinations of issues related to command and control; personal relationships with superiors and subordinates; the dynamics of the four levels of war (political, military strategic, operational, and tactical); the interactions between political guidance and operations proper, including constraints and restraints; technological innovations and the human aspects of fog and friction; and media relations.

Every contributor to this book has examined the record as conscientiously as possible and has rendered judgment on the performance of air leaders who, at the time they made their decisions, could not know the ultimate outcome. They were obliged to provide such judgment; otherwise, as Robert Dallek has reminded us, "we are no more than chroniclers telling a story without meaning."[19] The authors make clear that commanding air power is different from traditional command, but qualities such as intellect, courage, determination, and character are at the heart of all types of leadership, be it leadership with or without genius.[20]

The case studies are not prescriptive, because there is no magic formula for the development of outstanding air generalship and because each conflict brings its own unique conditions and constraints. Perfection may be sought, but we all fall short of it. This book shows both the diversity of character among successful air leaders and the interplay between personality traits and the circumstances under which leaders exercise command. Being an outstanding student or an excellent pilot does not define leadership; neither does popularity. Some air leaders easily delegated tasks to subordinates; others held power so closely that they crossed into micromanagement. Yet all these airmen have certain traits in common: they fought for a single point of contact for air management against opposition, and they were all experts in the application of air power, combining the finest technology available to them with concepts and leadership skills as best they could, given the goals and conditions they faced. They were not slaves of doctrine but adapted to situations as they saw necessary to save lives and improve effectiveness. And, of profound importance, they all cared about their officers and men.

Notably, successful air commanders considered operations and logistics as two sides of the same coin in which the very currency of that coin was intelligence: from Ultra in World War II and Teaball in Vietnam to the latest operations in Afghanistan and Iraq, intelligence was, is, and will remain alpha and omega. As General Horner and others have noted, air campaigns start and end with intelligence. Consequently, this field must be fully integrated into the planning and execution of air campaigns, large and small.

The chapters in this book reinforce the truth of General LeMay's observation that leaders are not born; they are educated, trained, and made, as in every other profession. This truly sums up the attitudes of the twelve airmen who constitute the subjects of this book.

PART I

1

CARL A. SPAATZ: BOMBER BARON

Richard G. Davis

The candidate should be naturally athletic and have a reputation for reliability, punctuality and honesty. He should have a cool head in emergencies, good eye for distance, keen ear for familiar sounds, steady hand and sound body with plenty of reserve; he should be quick-witted, highly intelligent and tractable. Immature, high strung, overconfident, impatient candidates are not desired.

—From Frank Freidel, *Over There: The Story of America's First Great Overseas Crusade*[1]

It is appropriate that Carl Andrew Spaatz, the man who commanded the largest force of combat aircraft in the history of air power, should lead off this volume. At the height of his command he had direct control of eighty-five heavy bomber and fighter groups, a force whose first-line strength of more than seventy-five hundred combat aircraft exceeded that of the Luftwaffe, the Imperial Japanese Naval Air Forces, and the Imperial Japanese Army Air Forces combined.[2] He also had indirect control of two tactical air forces, with an additional thirty-six hundred combat aircraft,[3] and one of which, the Ninth Air Force, was probably the largest tactical air force ever assembled. In the six months before the Anglo-American invasion of Normandy—the key operation on the western front in World War II and one whose failure would have prolonged the war for years—Spaatz wielded his forces to ensure air supremacy over the beachhead, to begin the strategic air attack on the German oil industry, and to greatly assist in the destruction of the rail and road network between the German border and the invasion beaches. In the eleven months after the invasion, in coordination with British Royal Air Force (RAF) Bomber Command, Spaatz directed a strategic air campaign that suppressed the German fighter force, continuously reduced enemy oil production to a small fraction of Germany's basic requirements, and brought the German railways and war economy to a standstill by February 1945.

At the same time, as a senior member of the Anglo-American military coalition, Spaatz established productive and usually cordial relations with senior British airmen. Likewise, as the most senior American airman in Europe, he closely and successfully cooperated with U.S. Army ground generals to provide strategic bombers for tactical air support to land operations. On February 1, 1945, the supreme commander, Allied Expeditionary Force (SCAEF) Europe, Gen. Dwight D. Eisenhower, rated Spaatz and the senior American ground general, Omar N. Bradley, equally as the two officers under his command who rendered the most valuable service against the Germans. Of Spaatz he said, "Experienced and able air leader: loyal and cooperative; modest and selfless; always reliable."[4]

What personal experiences and background and what circumstances of time and place allowed Spaatz to earn such high praise? How did these factors influence his leadership and success as an air commander? These are the questions that this chapter will attempt to answer.

EARLY CAREER: FROM WEST POINT TO WORLD WAR I

Carl Andrew Spatz was born in Boyerstown, Pennsylvania, on June 28, 1891.[5] He was an indifferent student and preferred the outdoor life to academics. Still, even as a teenager he demonstrated his ability to concentrate on the main task when he had to run the family's newspaper business while his father recovered from severe burns. Spaatz set type, oversaw the small staff, wrote stories, marketed the paper, and delivered it until he could return it to his father's hands. His knowledge of the newspaper business from the ground up would serve him well throughout his life. It enabled him to establish easy working arrangements with the press, ranging from beat reporters to Hollywood script writers, such as Beirne Lay Jr. and Sy Bartlett (the authors of *Twelve O'Clock High!*); photojournalists, such as Margaret Bourke-White; and publishers, such as Arthur Hays Sulzberger of the *New York Times*. The intensely private Spaatz used his ability to charm the press in order to direct it away from himself and toward others.

At the age of nineteen, after a year at the Army-Navy Preparatory School to improve his academics, Spaatz entered the U.S. Military Academy (USMA) at West Point. His four years there produced a permanent distaste for professional military education. For the rest of his career Spaatz attended service schools only when it was unavoidable or as a last resort. He attempted to resign after three weeks—probably for the usual reasons of homesickness and the traditional hazing inflicted on entering cadets—but was dissuaded. His record of demerits at West Point revealed a particular antipathy for what he considered unnecessary spit and polish. He never earned cadet rank and remained a "cleansleeve."[6] He coasted through the academy on wit rather than scholarship, finishing 57th out of 107 class members in academics and 95th in conduct. He excelled in the activities that mattered to him: bridge, poker, and the guitar. *Howitzer*, the West Point yearbook of 1914, caricatured him with his guitar in hand, and the editors commented on his silent demeanor, his ability to recite with confidence on subjects he had not read about, and his "independent attitude generally."[7] By the time of his graduation, his independence, taciturnity, and impatience with stultifying routine had become fixed.

The editors' comment on his "silent demeanor" may have referred to a problem that would plague Spaatz throughout his career: he did not perform well in scripted settings such as public speeches and important briefings. He did not freeze, but he tended to speak woodenly and failed to engage his audience. At such events his fund of dry wit and one-liners, which endeared him to friends and close associates, dried up. Perhaps this reaction reflected a painful, and apparently permanent, case of stage fright—one he could only control at the expense of his normally more open style of speech. While somewhat debilitating, this flaw seldom caused him serious harm.

Spaatz also left the USMA with three items that stuck to him for the rest of his life: a nickname, a desire to fly, and a reputation for honesty. First, Spaatz had the kind of pale, freckled complexion typical of redheads, and it so happened that he shared this trait with a certain upperclassman, Francis J. Toohey. In short order his classmates stopped calling him "Carl," and he became "Tooey" Spaatz permanently. Second, on May 29, 1910, early aviator Glenn Curtiss flew over West Point on a trip from New York City to Albany. Spaatz watched him fly past and then and there decided that he too would learn to fly. And he did.

As for honesty, Spaatz demonstrated it at the academy in a typically damn-the-consequences way. When Spaatz returned to the post after an evening out and a gate guard asked if he had come from an off-limits drinking establishment, Spaatz promptly replied yes. No one else had seen him there, so after some head scratching, the honor committee, which could have expelled him, refused to punish him. The committee ruled that he had simply told the truth; therefore, the academy's Code of Honor could not be used against him.

West Point did not simply anneal many of Spaatz's personality and character traits. As an institution it played an important role in his and other graduates' subsequent careers. It provided the initial—and one of the most significant—common bonding experiences to the men who would serve as the future leaders of the U.S. Army. It also allowed them to share this experience not only with their peers but also with superior officers, subordinates, and all the other men who had served in a long line of officers extending back to 1802. The esprit de corps and cohesiveness of USMA graduates persisted throughout their careers, as did the friendships (or enmities) and personal judgments formed during their stay. Spaatz may not have appreciated every aspect of West Point, but he certainly recognized and appreciated the higher values of the institution. More than thirty years later, both as chief of staff of the U.S. Air Force and in retirement, he worked tirelessly and effectively to establish a U.S. Air Force Academy that would impart similar values and internal cohesion to its graduates and their new service.

The army allowed new graduates from the academy to express a preference for their branch of service. The top graduates had their wishes met first. In 1914, as in earlier years, they pointed either to the Corps of Engineers or, if not mathematically inclined, to the prestigious and seemingly romantic cavalry as first choice. When the cavalry billets filled, cadets went to the branches of their second or lower choices. As a new second lieutenant who had graduated in the lower half of his class, Spaatz found himself assigned to the all-black Twenty-Fifth Infantry Regiment stationed in Hawaii. It made little difference to him, as he knew he would not be there long. In that infant era of air power and aircraft, the army had assigned all its aircraft to the Signal Corps, and regulations required that an officer serve for at least one year of service in a regular branch of the army before transferring to one of the technical branches.

In his later years Spaatz claimed he had "enjoyed that year of service with that outfit as much as any year in the service." He thought his men "made fine soldiers easily disciplined by white officers and easily kept in control." But in 1945, as the second-highest-ranking officer in his service, he told the Gillem Board for Utilization of Negro Manpower (three army generals appointed by Assistant Secretary of War John J. McCloy and known as the Gillem Board after its head, Lt. Gen. Alvan C. Gillem), which was investigating the role of black servicemen in the post–World War II era, that blacks should not serve in integrated units and that they would be more effective in support and service units than in combat units.[8] Throughout his career Spaatz continued to evince the paternalistic attitude shared by men of his rank and station toward blacks. He never seemed to question their low status within the military.

Spaatz may have made no lasting mark on the Twenty-Fifth Infantry, but he did succeed in making an indelible impression on Ruth Harrison, the eighteen-year-old daughter of cavalry colonel Ralph Harrison. Even her father's objection that there was "obviously no future" in aviation failed to sidetrack the relationship.[9]

When his tour in the infantry ended, Spaatz reported to North Field, San Diego, California, on November 25, 1915, to begin flight training. This preparation consisted of five hours of dual flight instruction with additional training in how to inspect an aircraft for safety and how to assemble and disassemble its motor. On his first solo flight his engine quit, but he managed to glide to a safe landing. In May 1916, he joined the First Aero Squadron, based at Fort Sam Houston, San Antonio, Texas, for a tour of duty with Brig. Gen. John J. Pershing's punitive expedition in Mexico. His squadron commander, Capt. Benjamin D. Foulois, would become a senior airman under Pershing in World War I and chief of the U.S. Army Air Corps in the early 1930s. Spaatz was promoted to first lieutenant on July 1, 1916. As one of the army's sixty-five flying officers, he was promoted to captain on May 15, 1917, six weeks after the United States declared war against Germany.

On July 26, 1917, two weeks before Spaatz was scheduled to depart for Europe, he and Ruth Harrison gave her parents twelve hours' notice and married. The marriage lasted fifty-seven years, until Spaatz's death in 1974. They had three daughters.

It should be noted that while Spaatz remained a man of his times in racial affairs, in gender matters he took the lead. While in no way a flirt or a ladies' man, he knew how to listen to women and respected their viewpoints. He allowed his wife and daughters great independence. He even went so far as to let Ruth act in a national touring troupe in the early 1920s while he stayed at home with his daughters, a state of affairs almost unheard of in the sexist army of his time.

Twenty years later Spaatz enthusiastically supported the assignment of Women's Army Corps (WAC) personnel to U.S. Army Air Force (AAF) units and headquarters under his command. So determinedly did Spaatz press the commander of the AAF, Gen. Henry "Hap" H. Arnold, to provide WACs that in February 1944 Arnold succeeded in obtaining an AAF allocation of WACs separate from that of the European theater of operations (ETO). The AAF in Europe had a quota of 4,448 WACs as opposed to a quota of only 1,727 for the ETO. By June 6, 1944, the AAF had female personnel assigned throughout its bomber, fighter, and troop carrier commands and its bombardment divisions, even down to individual combat wings. Spaatz's own executive officer, Capt. Sally Bagby, ran his unique personal/military headquarters. Spaatz was the highest-ranking officer in the theater to assign a woman to such a position.[10]

WORLD WAR I AND THE INTERWAR YEARS

Under orders from the War Department, Captain Spaatz quickly organized the Thirty-First Aero Squadron and shipped out for France. He arrived there on September 19, 1917, where his unit was immediately broken up for replacements to other American air units.

After three weeks in Paris in charge of enlisted men's mechanical training, followed by a month-long assignment to the air supply section of Pershing's American Expeditionary Force Headquarters, Spaatz became commander of the Third Aviation Instruction Training Center at Issoudun, France, approximately 130 miles south of Paris. He would have preferred, of course, a combat assignment, but as a regular officer and a trained pilot he was one of the few men with any qualifications to fill the job, even though he had never flown a modern fighter and had no formal instruction in aviation training.

Upon assuming command of the center Spaatz immediately found himself battling a situation that even the air service's postwar report termed "to say the least disheartening." Barracks and shops were of the crudest construction or uncompleted, and the rainy season had started before roads were in place, making the center a sea of mud. On the flying field, mud churned up by landing wheels broke propeller blades as fast as they could be replaced, and the center had no machine shops or matériel to build them.[11] By the time Spaatz left, in September 1918, Issoudun had become the largest training field in the world and the army air service's chief facility for training pursuit or fighter pilots, with eighty-four hangars, fourteen airfields, and numerous warehouses, shops, and barracks.[12] In all, the center graduated 766 pilots.[13] Sadly, during Spaatz's tenure the base also suffered fifty-six training fatalities. This rate was actually lower than the air service's overall death rate for pursuit training.[14] During the war, American pursuit pilot students, who trained on the hottest and most technologically advanced aircraft available, suffered a staggering one death for every 9.2 graduates.[15]

This assignment gave Spaatz valuable experience as a trainer and administrator of a rapidly expanding but woefully inexperienced air force. His work also earned him promotion to major in June 1918.

Brig. Gen. William L. "Billy" Mitchell, the chief of the air service in Europe, valued this hard-won knowledge and ordered Spaatz to return to the States to upgrade training. Spaatz objected and managed to obtain permission for two weeks at the front. He found an empty space in the Thirteenth Aero Squadron, Second Pursuit Group. Spaatz immediately won over the outfit's pilots, mostly first and second lieutenants who had entered combat five weeks before his arrival, by removing his major's insignia of rank and becoming one of them.[16] When his first two weeks were up, he ignored his orders and stayed two more weeks. On September 16, 1918, despite the repeated jamming of his machine guns, he shot down his first German plane. Ten days later he earned a Distinguished Flying Cross in a stunt that made the *New York Times*: "Flying Officer shoots down three planes— two German and his own."[17] Spaatz had concentrated so hard on his dogfighting that he neglected to check his fuel gauge, causing the loss of his own SPAD aircraft. Fortunately when he crash-landed in no-man's land between the trenches the French *poilus* (infantrymen), rather than German grenadiers, won the race to his plane. Mitchell, of course, soon learned of Spaatz's latest adventure, which added proof of bravery and determination to Spaatz's evident skills in training and organization. He promptly ordered Spaatz back to the United States to serve as a troubleshooter for pursuit training, telling him, "I will be glad to have you command a group at any time under my command."[18]

Spaatz arrived in New York City on October 13, 1918, and traveled to Washington, D.C., where he was appointed to the U.S. Air Services' Training Department as the inspector of pursuit training. He quickly embarked on an inspection tour of U.S. pursuit training facilities. The end of the war on November 11, 1918, found him in El Paso, Texas. He emerged from the war as a recognized expert on air training and pursuit aviation.

He also was convinced that the army's air arm deserved more autonomy within the service. Much later he recalled, "My own feeling was all in favor of getting it out of the Signal Corps. . . . I wanted an air force on the same level as the infantry."[19] Within a few years Spaatz and many other air officers would want not simple autonomy in the army; instead, they wanted independence from it.

In December 1918 Spaatz returned to Rockwell Field, California, to begin the task of demobilizing the air service. Spaatz began the typical treadmill existence of an American officer between the world wars: repeated changes of post, lack of public regard, low pay, and agonizingly slow promotion. Although from 1918 to 1920 he changed posts twenty times, he had two advantages over most of his fellow officers—flight pay (a cause of much jealousy among nonflying officers) and seniority as a major for all but three months of the next seventeen years, when he was temporarily reduced to the rank of captain. By contrast, many of his contemporaries permanently lost their wartime ranks and toiled for years as captains or even lieutenants.

At Rockwell Field, he formed a close professional and personal friendship with Maj. Hap Arnold, West Point class of 1907. At one point in the demobilization Spaatz outranked Arnold but refused to take advantage of the situation. Sure enough, a few days later the War Department reversed itself and Arnold was again the senior of the two. Thanks to the strict workings of the U.S. Army's seniority promotion system, Arnold stayed a step ahead of Spaatz for the rest of their careers, but he remembered the consideration Spaatz had shown and their friendship became firm. Arnold was not Spaatz's mentor; instead, he was a close and equal confidant and confederate. They became a team, with Arnold serving as the good long-range planner and Spaatz as the solid operations specialist. Both firmly shared the belief that air power was the future of warfare, and having met Mitchell early in their careers, they had become believers in his doctrine of air autonomy.

To his friends, Arnold demonstrated a charm, openness, and exuberance that earned him the sobriquet "Happy" or plain "Hap." To opponents he was "a real SOB." Once Spaatz had earned his trust, Arnold willingly supported him throughout his career. Late in life, Spaatz said of Arnold, "I know he had confidence in me, because of the relationship we had before. With me, he might sound impatient, but when I responded and gave him the reason for what I was doing, that would end it."[20]

This duo soon found another partner in Lt. Ira Eaker, who was serving at Rockwell Field at the same time. For the next twenty-four years the three worked closely to advance the cause of ground-based air power.

During the early 1920s Spaatz commanded the First Pursuit Group, the army's only active fighter group, and arranged numerous inspections and visits from his old boss Mitchell. He also served in key positions in the Office of the Chief of the Air Corps. Throughout this period he actively participated in critiquing and writing manuals on fighter tactics, close air support, and autonomy of the air arm. He was recognized as an expert in tactics in his own right. He had long conversations with Mitchell and corresponded with him frequently. Spaatz certainly favored more independence for the air service,[21] and he had no qualms about expressing his opinions about the flaws in the War Department's treatment of its fliers. In July 1925 he gave public testimony before the Lampert Committee of the U.S. House of Representatives, which was investigating the air service. He stated that the next war would start in the air, and if it did so in the near future "this country is absolutely defenseless."[22]

Naturally, he also chose to speak out at the famous court-martial of Mitchell, which ran from late October to November 1925. Eaker served as assistant defense counsel. Arnold and Spaatz, in part because of their relative seniority in the air service and in part because of the official positions they then held, readily volunteered to become chief and expert witnesses for the defense. Spaatz, then serving as the assistant for training and operations in the Office of the Chief of the Air Service, forthrightly told the highest-ranking court-martial board in U.S. history that the air service had only fifty-nine modern airplanes and that "by dragging all administrative officers from their desks" the service might field fifteen pursuit aircraft. When asked the key question of whether the War Department was slowing the development of air power, he quickly answered yes, beating the prosecutor's objection. Spaatz was warned that his testimony might damage his career, but he refused to trim to the prevailing wind. He noted, perhaps naively, "They can't do anything to you when you're under oath and tell them the answers to their questions."

In late 1928, the army air corps needed publicity to demonstrate the potential of air-to-air refueling. First Lt. Elwood "Pete" Quesada had the first germ of such an idea when, working with a U.S. Marine pilot, he designed a Marine air-to-air refueling mission to beat the Belgians, who currently held the air endurance record. When he heard of the scheme, Spaatz's friend Capt. Ira Eaker appropriated it entirely for the Air Corps alone—with the permission of Eaker's boss, Assistant Secretary of War F. Trubee Davison. Davison agreed only upon being convinced that air-to-air refueling had military applications. Spaatz got the job of leading the project.[23] Spaatz's friend Eaker came up with the idea of carrying out a world record endurance flight and chose Spaatz as one of the aircrew. During January 1–7, 1929, Spaatz, Eaker, Quesada, Lt. Harry A. Halverson, and Staff Sgt. Roy W. Hooe kept their modified Atlantic-Fokker C-2A airplane, *Question Mark*, aloft over Southern California for eleven thousand miles and a then–world record 150 hours, 40 minutes, and 15 seconds. In doing so, the crew also consumed 33,950 pounds of aviation gasoline and earned Distinguished Flying Crosses.[24]

Early in the mission, an accident caused Spaatz to be drenched in high-octane aviation gasoline. The crew quickly took off his clothes and rubbed him down with zinc oxide to prevent serious burns. He instructed them, "If I'm burned and have to bail out, you keep this plane in the air." On the next refueling, Spaatz manned his post wearing only skin cream, goggles, a parachute, and a grin.

Spaatz became a lieutenant colonel in 1935. With the promotion came orders to attend the U.S. Army Command and General Staff School at Fort Leavenworth, Kansas, which Spaatz gratefully observed had recently shortened its course from two years to one. He went to the school only to get away from Washington and made little attempt to conceal his dislike for a curriculum that lacked an appreciation of modern air power. He graduated 94th out of 121 students, with an unfavorable recommendation for further staff training.

Spaatz went from Leavenworth to Langley Field, Virginia, home of the Second Wing. He stayed until November 1938, when then–Major General Arnold called him to Washington to help plan the air portion of the rearmament program President Franklin D. Roosevelt had instituted in recognition of the war looming in Europe and the Far East. As head of the air corps's plans section, Spaatz helped to implement an ever-growing program. Pilot training alone increased a hundredfold.

From late May to early September 1940, Spaatz served in Great Britain as an official air corps observer. During the dark days of the fall of France and the Battle of Britain, he remained confident the RAF would win out over the Luftwaffe. He shared that view with William J. Donovan, Roosevelt's special envoy. Donovan, in turn, convinced the president to continue supplying aid. Spaatz left England, having made many friends within the RAF and still certain the air corps was correct in backing the development of strategic bombardment. In June 1941, when Gen. George C. Marshall, army chief of staff, authorized the creation of the U.S. Army Air Force (AAF), Chief of the AAF Hap Arnold named Spaatz as the first chief of the Air Staff.

THE EIGHTH AIR FORCE AND THE MEDITERRANEAN

After the attack on Pearl Harbor brought the United States into World War II, Arnold assigned Spaatz to command the Eighth Air Force, which was to spearhead the American strategic bombing campaign against Germany from bases in England. Spaatz possessed the personal qualities that fitted him for his assignment. Unlike many managers, Spaatz believed in delegating authority as well as responsibility. Once he assigned a task he gave his subordinates wide latitude to fulfill it. Spaatz loathed staff work; consequently, he ran his headquarters more as a household than as a general staff. He and the immediate members of his staff roomed, messed, and played together. Gen. Curtis LeMay, who served under Spaatz in both the Pacific and European theaters of World War II and later became air force chief of staff, recalled many years after the war that he "never got any direct orders from General Spaatz on anything," but after a few hours of playing evening poker and sitting at the same table he had a good idea of exactly what Spaatz wanted him to do. As noted earlier, Spaatz, who possibly suffered from stage fright, was very shy in public and spoke woodenly at staff meetings, never straying from the prepared text he brought with him. His shyness in public contributed to his reputation for taciturnity, as did his dry and sardonic wit.

From his arrival in June 1942 until November, Spaatz assembled units and completed their training. Getting this hastily fielded force across the Atlantic to newly built stations took time. Spaatz, now a major general, could not launch his first heavy bomber raid until August 17, 1942. He had to withstand pressure both from Washington to begin operations immediately and from London to defend British airspace and switch to nighttime bombing operations. By October 1942 the Eighth had dispatched a thousand bomber sorties. Then grand strategy intervened.

On November 8, 1942, the Anglo-American Allies began their invasion of French North Africa. Gen. Dwight D. Eisenhower, the invasion commander, soon realized that he needed closer coordination between his air and ground units. Spaatz was awarded the job of providing this coordination and eventually received a third star. First as an adviser, next as a coordinator, and last as Ike's overall air commander, he smoothed tangled air-ground relations, integrated the AAF and RAF operations, and conducted a devastating anti-air and interdiction campaign against the Axis powers in Tunisia. The Ultra code-breaking intelligence operation (discussed later) played a large part in Spaatz's success, for it gave him the exact time schedules and routing of all Axis shipping and air ferrying from Sicily to Tunisia.

The combat experience that the AAF gained under Spaatz's command in North Africa, and in particular his excellent relationship with U.S. ground generals such as Eisenhower and George S. Patton, resulted in the modification of the U.S. Army's ground-air doctrine. The War Department's Field Manual 100-20 (FM 100-20) Command and Employment of Air Power, of July 21, 1943, became the AAF's declaration of independence from the army ground forces. Its first sentence, all in capital letters, made clear the new relationship between air and ground forces: "LAND POWER AND AIR POWER ARE CO-EQUAL AND INTER-DEPENDENT FORCES: NEITHER IS AN AUXILIARY OF THE OTHER." This manual served as the basis for future air support of army operations and would provide key ammunition for the eventual postwar fight over the AAF's independence.

After the Axis powers in Africa surrendered in May 1943, Spaatz's Northwest African Air Forces paved the way for the Allied invasions on Sicily and Italy. The American bombing of Rome on July 19, 1943, may have been the final straw in causing the fall of dictator Benito Mussolini on July 24 and his replacement by an Italian government anxious for peace.

Later in the summer and fall of 1943 Spaatz made a further, and key, contribution to the American strategic bombing campaign by convincing the Combined Chiefs of Staff of the need to establish a second U.S. strategic air force in Europe. The Fifteenth Air Force, a new cog in the offensive machine directed at Adolf Hitler, was created in November 1943 and based in Italy. It opened a new air front, forcing Germany to spread its defenses and giving the Allies the capability to attack a new range of targets, especially the Romanian oil fields, which supplied much of the Nazis' fuel.

PRE–D-DAY OPERATIONS

The recipe for being a successful general, admiral, or air marshal is as infinitely varied as the men who have achieved that distinction. In this author's opinion, however, there are five essential ingredients, with each differing in measure according to the man. First is a sprinkling of luck—not the luck of Napoleon Bonaparte, who supposedly said, "Give me a lucky general over a good one," but that of American football warrior Vince Lombardi, who said, "Luck is the residue of hard work and skill." Second is the ability to participate in and manage modern combined, joint, and national command structures—a skill that French marshal Ferdinand Foch demonstrated and Douglas MacArthur lacked. Third is a helping of the killer instinct of Gen. Robert E. Lee—not simply the desire to destroy one's enemy, which is something any soldier must have, but also the ability to send men one admires and respects to their death. Too little produces a George B. McClellan, whose squeamishness at Antietam cost the republic two and a half more years of war and 200,000 more dead. Too much yields a Sir Douglas Haig, who wasted hundreds of thousands of his men by refusing to discontinue failed attacks. Fourth is a pinch of the perseverance of Robert the Bruce or George Washington, two leaders who refused to give up even though their military fortunes seemed to hit hopeless rock bottom against vastly superior English foes. Last comes a healthy portion of George C. Marshall's ability to inspire the trust of peers, subordinates, and superiors. Carl Spaatz had all these qualities.

LUCK

Luck often boils down to uncontrollable variables resolving in one's favor. The manner in which a general exploits this gift determines his fate. The shortcomings of his enemies gave Spaatz opportunity. The systematic Anglo-American breaking of German operational-level and lower message traffic codes, a program known as Ultra, vouchsafed all Allied commanders an unparalleled knowledge of their enemies' intentions and situation. Perhaps more than any other leader and command, Spaatz and the U.S. Strategic Air Forces (USSTAF) in Europe used and relied upon these intercepts. He was aided by two fortunate circumstances. First, the Luftwaffe had the worst signal security of any of the German armed forces, which made its Ultra codes much easier to break. This gave Spaatz reliable access to the actual conditions and status of his opponent. In some cases, Spaatz read Luftwaffe reports before they landed on Göring's, or his subordinates' desks. Second, two of the allied air forces' major target systems, synthetic oil and railroad marshaling yards, had their own Ultra machines, also decrypted by allied intelligence. The rail and oil reports of damage to their Headquarters gave the allies accurate and speedy bomb damage assessments upon which to base follow-up raids. Intercepts of Luftwaffe traffic also validated the effectiveness of new American air tactics.[25]

The very nature of the Nazi state and ideology played into the Allied air leaders' hands. Hitler's personal isolation, coupled with his propensity to divide responsibility for the war economy into competing fiefdoms, all dependent upon himself, resulted in staggering mismanagement. With the notable exception of Albert Speer, the Nazi minister of armaments production, the highest Nazi leadership had little conception of the interrelationships among resources, research, design, labor, tooling, organization, and other factors in the industrial process.

The experience of the Henschel aircraft firm provides but one example. The company undertook to build the Junkers Ju 88 bomber/night fighter with a new assembly system called the "hole system," which replaced jigs with prefabricated holes in the airframe components. As long as the design remained stable the system could turn out airframes at a remarkable pace. However, when Henschel had finished the design and tooling of 80–90 percent of the assembly process, the firm was ordered to switch production to a newer and significantly different model, the Ju 188. This shift required a complete redesign of the firm's assembly system. As a result it wasted two to four million man-hours and produced not a single aircraft. The Allies had similar tales, but not as many, and they could absorb the loss of resources far more easily than the Germans could.

Almost all major German war production decisions and priorities rested not on economic efficiency but on the self-interest of the entities involved. The refusal of Hermann Göring, commander in chief of the Luftwaffe and number two man in the Nazi regime, to relinquish a single iota of his authority and his lack of understanding of technical matters gravely hampered aircraft production. Not until February 1944 did much of the aircraft industry come under Speer's Armaments Ministry, which in any case did not control manpower allocations. Likewise, Speer did not gain authority over both civilian and military production until September 1943. Only in August 1944, far too late in the conflict, did Hitler finally allow complete mobilization of the German economy for the war effort.[26]

While Germany frittered away much of its industrial strength, the Nazis' ideology and individual outlook further sapped their efforts. Having gained power using tactics of terror and intimidation, Hitler and others preferred retaliation and counterterror operations to seemingly passive defensive measures. The resources expended on the V weapons produced little beyond technical triumphs, which came at the direct expense of aircraft production. Likewise, the fighter aircraft lost over Normandy and the Bulge stripped German industry of its strongest defenses. Had the Germans decided to focus on fighter production and to concentrate that production in defense of industry in 1942 instead of 1944, they would have made Spaatz's task far more formidable. Even weakened and misdirected as they were, the German air defenses had halted American deep penetration raids and increased the RAF Bomber Command's losses to almost prohibitive levels by as late as November 1943.[27]

Not only did Spaatz have opponents who actively contributed to their own defeat, but he also possessed resources far greater than his predecessor had. For Lt. Gen. Ira Eaker, commander of the Eighth Air Force from January 1942 to December 1943, increases in force had come slowly and behind schedule. By contrast, the logistics and aircraft supply pipeline overflowed for Spaatz. It took the Eighth seventeen months to establish twenty and a half heavy bomb groups. Its first long-range P-38 fighter escorts did not become operational until the day after the second Schweinfurt raid, on October 14, 1943. As for the Fifteenth Air Force, it began life on November 1, 1943, with six heavy bomb groups that had been in the Mediterranean since May 1943. By May 1944 the Eighth had grown to forty-one heavy groups and the Fifteenth to twenty-one. During that same period the number of U.S. fighter groups in the Eighth and Ninth Air Forces in England available to fly long-range escort missions in support of the bombers going deep into Germany grew from twelve to thirty-three. Many of them were equipped with the extremely long-range P-51 fighter, and all were capable of using range-extending drop tanks, whose production bottlenecks had been solved.[28] A massive air training program supplied the strategic air forces with enough trained airmen to provide each aircraft with almost two crews.

Finally, the introduction, in the fall of 1943, of airborne radar bombing devices, initially borrowed from the RAF, allowed for bombing through clouds, albeit only with extreme inaccuracy. When bombing through completely overcast skies, only one bomb in seventy landed within a half mile of the aiming point.[29] In comparison, bombing of a target one mile in diameter in good visual conditions was fifty times more accurate.[30] While Eaker had only a few radar sets, Spaatz received enough to outfit all of his groups, enabling him to put a much higher percentage of his bombers into the air a much higher percentage of the time.

With radar bombing came city bombing. Its first raid with radar, conducted against Emden on September 27, 1943, was also the Eighth's first mission ordered to target the center of the city rather than to hit industrial or transportation targets.[31]

Spaatz and his subordinate air force commanders, Lt. Gen. James H. Doolittle (Eighth Air Force) and Lt. Gen. Nathan F. Twining (Fifteenth Air Force), capitalized on German inefficiency, American prodigality, and airborne radar by greatly increasing their rates of operation. The combination of higher operations rates and more aircraft gave Spaatz a far bigger hammer than Eaker had possessed. Spaatz wielded that hammer to smash his opponent.

Spaatz and his best-known subordinate, Doolittle, made one key change in the doctrine Eaker had followed. Perhaps because of the relatively few escort fighters he possessed, and their short range, Eaker had ordered his fighters to fly "close escort" for bombers, meaning that the fighters would stay near the heavy bombers and attempt to break up German fighter attacks. With Spaatz's complete support, Doolittle reversed this tactic, which he felt deprived the American fighters of a fighter aircraft's natural and very great offensive capabilities. Instead, Doolittle ordered his fighters to fly "loose escort," which meant that the American fighters were to hurl themselves at German fighters as soon as they spotted them. This tactic (greatly aided by the hundreds of fighters that Eaker never had) revolutionized daylight air warfare over Germany. American P-51s, P-38s, and P-47s pursued and destroyed the Luftwaffe's day fighter force from the tops of the clouds to the tops of the trees and even as they landed and took off. This tactical advantage served as a catalyst that enabled all the American advantages discussed in this section to work against the enemy.[32]

Management Skill

A secret and not often recognized ingredient of generalship, especially modern generalship, is an ability to conduct effective bureaucratic warfare. This trait has become even more important as modern warfare has forced high-level commanders to deal with ever more complicated situations of combined command with allies, joint command with other same-nation service components, and close supervision and contact with their nation's highest command authorities, such as their joint chiefs of staff, ministers of defense, and chief executives. Spaatz, who appeared to many as the "anti-staff officer" and who ran a loose and casual staff, would prove surprisingly adept in exercising this skill.

Shortly after his arrival in the United Kingdom on January 1, 1944, Spaatz established a new headquarters, the USSTAF Headquarters in Europe. There he instituted a system in which operations and administration received equal attention. This double deputy arrangement stemmed from his dual responsibilities as both the commander of USSTAF, having operational control of the Eighth and Fifteenth Air Forces, and the head of the AAF in Britain, in charge of administration for the Eighth and Ninth Air Forces. The Ninth, a tactical air force, made up the U.S. contingent of Air Chief Marshal (ACM) Sir Trafford Leigh-Mallory's Allied Expeditionary Air Force (AEAF). Spaatz appointed Brig. Gen. Hugh J. Knerr as his deputy for administration, with directorates subordinate to him for personnel, supply, maintenance, and administration. Maj. Gen. Frederick L. Anderson became Spaatz's deputy for operations, with directorates for operations and intelligence under him. The postwar U.S. Air Force official history commented that this arrangement "integrated operations and logistics in one headquarters to a degree never before attained and represented a triumph for the concept that logistics was of equal importance with operations."[33] By elevating logistics to the same command level as operations, Spaatz increased the status and morale of his logistics organizations. The move also emphasized his administrative control over the Ninth Air Force by placing that control at the same level as his control over the Fifteenth Air Force. By tying the Eighth and Ninth together administratively, Spaatz made it harder for the Ninth to separate itself completely from Spaatz's headquarters.

His new system also underscored that the AAF was independent from both the RAF and the U.S. ground forces. A few months later Spaatz commented, "The Maintenance and Supply functions of our Air Forces cannot be integrated into the British Maintenance and Supply system for obvious reasons. Therein we have a firm foundation upon which to build our effort to regain and retain complete control of all U.S. air units in all theaters."

Not only did the new organization help to maintain independence from the British, but it also helped to maintain institutional independence from the U.S. Army Service Forces (ASF). In the same letter Spaatz added, "We must always be alert that the A.S.F. does not extend its control of ground services to the Air Forces through lack of an organization of our own capable of rendering all manner of base services to air units in the combat zone."[34] Finally, in keeping with Spaatz's desire to avoid as much administrative detail as possible, the reorganization reduced the number of people reporting directly to him to three: the two deputies and his chief of staff.

Spaatz overcame the worries of ACM Sir Charles "Peter" Portal, the RAF chief of staff, and General Marshall that his headquarters would graft a new and large layer of bureaucratic staff onto the already awkward air command arrangements in England. His new headquarters simply moved in on Eighth Air Force Headquarters, abolished it, absorbed most of it, and sent the rump to the headquarters of VIII Bomber Command. In turn, the latter became Doolittle's new headquarters, redesignated Headquarters, Eighth Air Force.

Maj. Gen. Walter Bedell Smith, Eisenhower's chief of staff, participated in the discussions about the new organization. On January 1 he assured Eisenhower, who had returned to the United States for a short visit, that "the above planned Organization represents NO repeat NO increase in personnel and NO repeat NO increase in the number of Headquarters."[35] The same day, Spaatz and Smith agreed to locate Eisenhower's Supreme Headquarters at the same place as USSTAF: Bushy Park, code-named WIDEWINGS.[36] Spaatz believed that this arrangement overcame one of the basic flaws of the Mediterranean organization, which had allowed the different service commanders to locate their headquarters in areas widely separated from the theater commanders and each other.

The decision to colocate USSTAF and the Supreme Headquarters Allied Expeditionary Force (SHAEF) gave Spaatz an advantage over the other air leaders, as his geographical proximity to Eisenhower provided greater access to the supreme commander's ear. Smith's and Spaatz's agreement ruined the plans of Leigh-Mallory, who had intended to move Eisenhower into Bushy Heath, a group of buildings adjacent to Leigh-Mallory's own complex at Stanmore, the headquarters of No. 11 Group. With perhaps the finest communications network in Britain, much of the Battle of Britain had been directed from Stanmore, and its facilities had expanded since then. Before Leigh-Mallory and Lt. Gen. Sir Frederick Morgan, the principal planner for Operation Overlord and designated chief of staff to the supreme Allied commander (COSSAC), could explain the situation to Smith, however, several battalions of U.S. engineers had descended on Bushy Park and erected Eisenhower's headquarters there. When Smith learned that Morgan and Leigh-Mallory had meant to place the SHAEF at Stanmore, he remarked, "My

God, I've married the wrong woman."[37] From the beginning of the campaign, Spaatz thus gained an advantage in the fight over the air command arrangements that would plague the Allies until April 1944.

KILLER INSTINCT

A general is, by definition, a killer of men—the enemy's and his own. Spaatz was no exception. In the winter and spring of 1944 he began a campaign of straight-forward attrition against the Luftwaffe's day fighter force with the purpose of extinguishing its capacity to interfere with the American bomber operations and the upcoming cross-Channel invasion. It would also adversely affect the Luftwaffe's night fighter force, the majority of which took part in daylight interceptions. By the time he had returned to the United Kingdom in December 1943, Spaatz knew from Ultra that fuel shortages and deficiencies in pilot training had already begun to impair the Luftwaffe's readiness. The same source informed him that the Germans had reduced their number of routine reconnaissance flights and had reassigned test and ferry pilots to daylight fighter formations. In January 1944 he learned that the Luftwaffe had cut back meteorological operations and shortened the recuperation period for wounded pilots. On February 6 he found out that the Luftwaffe had launched a systematic comb-out of its noncombatants to provide more pilots.[38] The knowledge of his enemy's increasing weakness and vulnerability to sustained losses added to Spaatz's determination to increase pressure on the foe.

This air campaign would not only demolish German aircraft, but it would also eviscerate the Luftwaffe's air leadership cadres, forcing it into a descending spiral of inexperience and increasing losses from operations and accidents. Within a few weeks of his arrival in London, Spaatz authorized Doolittle to implement the fighter escort tactics the two men had already used during their previous tour in the Mediterranean. Doolittle ordered his fighters to fly loose escort, giving them the initiative to take the offensive and to attack and pursue German fighters, instead of maintaining close escort, which had forced the American fighters to absorb the first blow.[39] The commander of the Eighth Fighter Command, tough ex-marine Maj. Gen. William E. Kepner, supposedly wept with joy at the change, but the bomber commanders winced, because the new tactics moved their status from protected cows to bait.

Spaatz and Doolittle risked their bombers in order to expose the enemy. As the aerial combat raged and as the escort fighters flew to and from their rendezvous with the bomber stream, individual fighter pilots, with a greater sense of mayhem than self-preservation, found themselves at low altitudes and proceeded to strafe targets of opportunity. When Ultra intercepts alerted the American air leaders that this practice caused havoc, especially to German aircraft taking off from and landing at their airfields, Spaatz encouraged the practice by allowing pilots credit for destroying ground aircraft as well as for those in the air. In April 1944 Spaatz informed Arnold that his pilots had been instructed "to shoot up any moving target within Germany."[40] The enemy responded by setting up flak traps at likely strafing targets. These traps killed, wounded, or resulted in the capture of more American fighter pilots than any other single tactic.[41] Soon the Luftwaffe could no longer conduct any operations, including training and air transport, without fear of interference. Spaatz did not discontinue low-level attacks until April 1945.

In order to force the Luftwaffe to accept battle, Spaatz ordered a continuing series of deep penetration missions into the Reich. Starting on January 11, 1944, the Americans attacked the German air industry. Both sides suffered heavy losses. When cloud cover prevented precision bombing of air plants or other specific targets, Spaatz ordered area raids on German cities, particularly Frankfurt. Forty percent of all city area raids that the Eighth Air Force ordered or authorized took place between February and May 1944.[42] The Germans sent their fighters up to oppose most of these raids but—at a cost to civilian morale and production—they sometimes allowed the city attacks to go uncontested.

In mid-February, under orders from Arnold, Spaatz and Doolittle extended the bomber crews' combat tour from twenty-five to thirty-five missions over the protests of the group commanders. At the end of the month the Americans conducted Operation Argument, or "Big Week," which dealt a body blow to the enemy air industry. Spaatz was determined to initiate and continue the operation, even though it cost two hundred bombers on the first day.[43] Although not as decisive as American air leaders then believed, Big Week prompted the Germans' decision to disperse their air industry. This move placed an additional load on the rail system, which had to schedule, load, transport, and unload aircraft subassemblies and engines at widely separated assembly plants. It also sacrificed all economies of scale in production, making the aircraft greatly more expensive in terms of resources. Big Week also delayed German fighter production for approximately sixty days. This delay pushed the bulk of new German fighter construction into the beginning of May 1944, a period of training restrictions and grave fuel shortages, which virtually nullified the benefits of the increased numbers of operational aircraft produced.

After Big Week, Spaatz wished to switch target priorities to the German synthetic oil industry, a system whose sovereign importance to the entire German war machine would require the Luftwaffe to defend it or die trying. This series of missions, however, was delayed until May. Thus, at the beginning of March, Spaatz ordered a series of area attacks on Berlin instead. The attacks went straight over the top, making no attempt to deceive the defenders about their intentions and target. The importance of the city as an industrial, transportation, and administrative center guaranteed a fierce response. In its first major attack on the German capital on March 6, the Eighth lost sixty-nine heavy bombers—the highest number of American bombers ever lost in a single mission. On March 8, the Americans lost another thirty-seven bombers over the "Big B," but the next mission encountered no aerial opposition. By June 6, the Americans had achieved daylight air superiority over Europe at the cost of more than twenty-seven hundred bombers, almost a thousand fighters, and more than eighteen thousand casualties. These losses were 50 percent more than they had suffered in all of 1942 and 1943 combined.[44]

PERSEVERANCE

Spaatz certainly had the ability to persevere with the courage of his convictions. In the months preceding the cross-Channel invasion two fundamental questions directly affected Spaatz: in what manner could the strategic bombers best aid the invasion, and who would control the bombers? Spaatz had always assumed that at some point before the invasion his command would come under Eisenhower's direction. However, he objected strenuously to being subordinate to Eisenhower's air component commander, ACM Leigh-Mallory, who as a former commander of RAF Fighter Command had no experience commanding strategic bombers or conducting ground support operations. Spaatz personally disliked Leigh-Mallory and flatly refused to serve under him, as did, eventually, ACM Sir Arthur "Bomber" Harris, commander of Bomber Command, the RAF strategic air command.[45] Both Spaatz and Harris, the so-called Bomber Barons, insisted that they be allowed to continue raids deep into Germany and feared they would not be able to do so if they were too tightly tethered to direct support of the invasion. Eisenhower, however, demanded complete control of the strategic forces and threatened to resign. Finally, the Allies reached a compromise. They assigned control (indirectly through

Eisenhower) of the strategic bombers to Eisenhower's deputy supreme commander, ACM Sir Arthur Tedder, who was one of the finest air leaders of the war. They then left the tactical battle to Leigh-Mallory. Although they did not always see eye to eye, Spaatz had an easy working rapport with Tedder. Most important, the new arrangement worked.

The question of how the strategic air forces could best aid the invasion was, of course, a matter of greater significance. Leigh-Mallory and Tedder advocated the transportation plan, which called for the attritional bombing of the French and Belgian rail systems to render them incapable of allowing speedy reinforcement or easy logistical support of the German forces opposing the invasion. In the beginning of March, Spaatz's headquarters originated a competing oil plan, which called for the destruction of Ploesti, the Axis' principal source of natural oil, and then the destruction of the Germans' synthetic oil industry. The oil plan was the quintessential strategic bombing plan. Losing the oil fields would fatally hamper any German response both to the invasion and to the Soviet summer offensive. Spaatz estimated that it would take only twenty-one days of visual bombing of the synthetic oil plants to destroy this compact and absolutely crucial target system, and thus the strategic air force would make an important, relatively inexpensive, and noticeable contribution to the end of the war.

For Spaatz the oil plan had two additional advantages. First, it would allow the Americans to continue the attrition of the Luftwaffe and to fly precision missions into Germany, which justified AAF strategic doctrine, not to mention the national investment in the AAF's bombardment theories. Second, it would leave Harris and Leigh-Mallory to conduct most of the transportation bombing missions. Spaatz, naturally, realized that weather conditions would often limit the Eighth to striking French rail yards because it could not fly into the Reich. After bitter bureaucratic infighting among the Allied ground and air staffs, Eisenhower chose the transportation plan on March 25 because it offered measurable results, while the effects of the oil plan, while logical, could not be verified with existing Allied intelligence.

In practically every major decision—be it military, corporate, or political—there is one faction or man who will not accept that decision as final. In April 1944 Spaatz was that man. Throughout March, ACM Portal, the RAF chief of staff and the officer charged with direction of the combined bomber offensive by the Combined Chiefs of Staff, had refused to allow Spaatz to order the Fifteenth Air Force to attack the Ploesti oil complex, which produced 25 percent of Germany's oil. In part Portal did not want to draw the Fifteenth away from its duties to Operation Pointblank, the joint bombing offensive against the German aircraft industry, and its assistance to the Allied ground forces, and in part Portal regarded the bombing of Balkan rail yards as more militarily effective than bombing oil fields would be. An attack on the Romanian oil fields would also strengthen Spaatz's hand in the oil versus transportation dispute. Spaatz realized that successful oil strikes on Ploesti would increase German reliance on their synthetic oil plants, which, in turn, might give the oil plan advocates a trump card to play against the transportation plan.

On April 5, Spaatz resorted to subterfuge. Under the guise of attacking Ploesti's main rail yard (each oil refinery had its own such yard), the Fifteenth made its first raid on Romanian oil. As the U.S. official history noted, with some satisfaction, "Most of the 588 tons of bombs, with more than coincidental accuracy, struck and badly damaged the Astra group of refineries."[46] On April 15 and 26 the Fifteenth returned. Again they somehow missed the main rail yard and "unfortunately" damaged more Axis refineries. As a result of this "transportation" bombing German imports of finished petroleum products fell from 186,000 tons in March to 104,000 tons in April. In May, when Portal finally granted permission to bomb Romanian oil fields, German imports of finished petroleum products dropped to 81,000 tons and dropped further, to 40,000 tons, in June.[47]

In the meantime from the United Kingdom, the Eighth continued its duel with the Luftwaffe day fighters. On April 18 and 19, however, the Germans offered little resistance to large, clear-weather missions near Berlin and Kassel. Rather than elating Spaatz, this circumstance seemed to confirm one of his worst fears: the Germans had begun a policy of conservation in anticipation of the invasion. Also on April 19 the British invoked the emergency clause in their agreements with the Americans. Tedder phoned Spaatz's headquarters to inform the Americans that the potential threat of the Germans' V-1 pilotless jet-propelled bombers had caused the War Cabinet to declare the security of the British Isles at risk. Tedder thereupon moved Operation Crossbow, the bombing of the V-weapon sites, to a top priority and ahead of countering the Luftwaffe.[48] The British move, a shortsighted and certainly uneconomical diversion of force undertaken for domestic political considerations, threatened to gut the AAF's entire bombing effort at precisely the time when, in Spaatz's estimation, he needed to offer the Luftwaffe even more provocation to fight. The Luftwaffe, of course, had never bothered to resist Crossbow bombing of the French coast.

Spaatz went to Eisenhower that evening and found that the supreme commander was upset with the AAF for his own reasons. In spite of the March 25 decision in favor of attacking transportation rather than oil fields, the Eighth had yet to bomb a single transportation target, and the invasion was only seven weeks distant. Second, on the previous evening one of Spaatz's generals, Maj. Gen. Henry Miller, had become drunk at a large night club in London and had proceeded loudly and openly to take bets that the invasion would occur before June 15.

Spaatz responded promptly to the matter of discipline. He picked up Eisenhower's personal phone, called Ninth Air Force Headquarters, and placed Miller under house arrest. Eisenhower followed up by demoting Miller to colonel and returning him to the States (where he eventually retired as a brigadier general).[49] The discussion of policy matters took longer and generated more heat. Spaatz may even have threatened to resign. At last Eisenhower agreed to allow the Eighth to use two visual bombing days before the invasion to strike oil targets and test the Luftwaffe's reaction. For his part, Spaatz appears to have agreed to devote more energy to transportation bombing.

The next morning Spaatz visited Tedder.[50] They agreed that on the next suitable day the Eighth would raid Crossbow targets and then on the next two suitable days the Americans would hit oil. Later that day Doolittle sent almost nine hundred heavy bombers against Crossbow targets, encountering no aerial opposition. On April 21 foul weather forced cancellation of the first oil mission, and on the next day Spaatz began to fulfill his other pledge: 638 bombers attacked Hamm, the largest rail yard in Europe. Not until May 12 did the weather allow a strike against oil targets.

The first oil strike vindicated Spaatz's judgment. The 800 attacking bombers hit six synthetic oil plants and lost 46 bombers (a single group that missed its escort lost 12 out of 16 aircraft). The Germans reacted strongly, and the American escort of 735 fighters claimed 61 destroyed in the air and 5 on the ground. Luftwaffe records confirmed 28 pilots dead, 26 wounded, and 65 fighters lost.[51] In a bit of serendipitous good fortune, the attack on Merseburg-Leuna also destroyed a laboratory engaged in heavy water research for the German atomic bomb program.

Ultra revealed the Germans' immediate and alarmed response. On May 13 the Luftwaffe Operations Staff ordered the transfer of antiaircraft guns from fighter production plants and the eastern front to synthetic oil facilities. A week later Oberkommando der Wehrmacht (Supreme Command of the Armed Forces) ordered increased conversion of motor vehicles to highly inefficient wood generators.[52] When Tedder heard of the intercepts he remarked, "It looks like we'll have to give the customer what he wants."[53]

To Speer the mission signaled that the end had come. In his postwar memoirs he stated, "I shall never forget the day May 12 . . . on that date the technological war was decided. Until then we had managed approximately as many weapons as the armed forces needed, in spite of considerable losses. But with the attack of . . . the Eighth Air Force upon several fuel plants in central and eastern Germany, a new era in the air war began. It meant the end of German armaments production."[54]

A week after the raid Speer reported to Hitler, "The enemy has struck us at one of our weakest points. If [he persists] at this time, we will soon no longer have any fuel production worth mentioning. Our one hope is that the other side has an air force General Staff as scatterbrained as our own."[55] In that desire he was disappointed. Two further raids, on May 28 and 29, lost 66 bombers and 19 fighters, while claiming 121 German aircraft destroyed in the air and on the ground. Once the invasion was established ashore, the Allies moved raids on oil production to the highest priority and kept it there until the end of the war.

In April the Luftwaffe had consumed 156,000 tons of the 175,000 tons of aviation fuel produced, an average daily production of 5,850 tons a day. After May 12 daily production fell to 4,820 tons a day (an 18 percent drop). It had recovered to 5,500 tons daily until the raids at the end of the month reduced production to 2,775 tons daily.[56] Total production was 14,000 tons short of essential planned consumption. On June 7 Ultra deciphered the following message, dated June 5: "As a result of renewed encroachment into the production of a/c [aircraft] fuel by enemy action, the most essential requirements for training and carrying out production plans can scarcely be met with the quantities of a/c fuel available. In order to ensure the defense of the Reich and to prevent the readiness of the G.A.F. [German Air Forces] in the east from gradually collapsing, it has been necessary to break into the strategic reserve."[57]

TRUSTWORTHINESS

Spaatz possessed a good measure of the fifth necessary ingredient of a successful general, that is the ability to inspire trust in both superiors and subordinates. In an oral history interview with then-Maj. Ronald R. Fogleman, Spaatz's principal subordinate commander, Jimmy Doolittle, stated: "I suppose if it were possible for one man to love another man, I love General Spaatz. I guess it's . . . better . . . [to say] that I idolize General Spaatz. He is perhaps the only man that I have ever been closely associated with whom I have never known to make a bad decision."[58] This praise, coming from a man of Doolittle's enormous physical and moral courage and high intellect, speaks for itself. Meanwhile, Spaatz was probably unknown to most of the rank and file of his command, in large part because of his shyness, his inarticulateness in front of crowds and even during briefings, and his avoidance of the limelight. Interestingly enough, he visited his bases far more often than did his RAF counterpart, Harris, and showed genuine concern for his troops' well-being and morale.

In the much smaller circle of his superiors Spaatz inspired great trust. He was Arnold's personal friend, confidant, and favorite. Unlike others, such as Eaker and Haywood Hansell, Spaatz retained the AAF commanding general's faith through-out the war. In fact, Arnold purposely placed Spaatz in positions that would in-crease Spaatz's importance and influence, not so much because Spaatz's actions would reflect favorably on Arnold but because he knew that Spaatz's first loyalty was to the service. In February 1944 Arnold told him:

> Another and perhaps equally important motive behind the formation of the United States Strategic Air Forces in Europe was my desire to build an American Air Commander to a high position prior to the defeat of Germany. It is that prospect in particular that has impelled me in my so far successful fight to keep your command parallel to Harris' command and, therefore, parallel to Ike's. If you do not remain in a position parallel with Harris the air war will certainly be won by the RAF, if anybody. Already the spectacular effectiveness of their devastation of cities has placed their contribution in the popular mind at a high plane that I am having the greatest difficulty in keeping your achievement (far less spectacular to the public) in its proper role not only in publications, but unfortunately in military and naval circles and, in fact, with the President himself. Therefore, considering only the aspect of a proper American share of credit for success of the air war, I feel we must have a high air commander some place in Europe. Today you can be that commander.[59]

Arnold's abiding trust and confidence meant that Spaatz always had support in the highest areas of decision making.

Spaatz also earned Eisenhower's esteem. From June 1942 through May 1945 the two worked hand in hand, becoming close friends—even to the unlikely extent of Spaatz accompanying the supreme commander's singing on the guitar when the two relaxed at parties. However, the friendship did not affect Eisenhower's judgment. In June 1943 he wrote of Spaatz:

> I have an impression he is not tough and hard enough personally to meet the full requirements of his high position. He is constantly urging more promotions for his subordinates and seeking special favors for his forces [such as a regular liquor ration]. My belief in this regard is further strengthened by the type of staff officer he has accumulated around him. He has apparently picked officers for personal qualifications of comradeship and friendliness than for their abilities as businesslike, tough operators.[60]

Although Spaatz did have his share of World War I "retreads" on his staff, he also had other excellent officers, such as Hoyt Vandenberg, Lauris Norstad, and Fred Anderson. By January 1945 Ike had changed his opinion. In urging Spaatz's promotion to a fourth star he stated: "That no one could tell him that Spaatz was not the best operational air man in the world, [although] he was not a paper man, couldn't write what he wanted, and couldn't conduct himself at a conference, but he had the utmost respect from everybody, ground and air, in the theater." As for Spaatz's decisions, Eisenhower commented that they were "sound and he knew exactly what he was doing."[61] In 1948 Eisenhower wrote to Spaatz, "No man can justly claim a greater share than you in the attainment of victory in Europe."[62]

The AAF's pre–D-Day operations, directed by Spaatz, cost the air forces dearly in blood and matériel. From January 1 through May 31, the Eighth and Fifteenth Air Forces lost 2,351 heavy bombers (and their respective ten-man crews) on combat missions. They wrote off another 254 from accidents and irreparable battle damage. The Eighth and Ninth Air Forces lost 983 fighters and suffered 18,403 casualties (5,427 killed in action, 11,033 missing in action or interned, and 1,943 wounded). Ninety percent of those men, most of whom were missing in action or prisoners of war, would not fight against Germany again. The Fifteenth and Twelfth Air Forces lost 595 fighters and sustained 7,285 casualties (2,780 killed in action, 3,452 missing in action, and 1,053 wounded). The Fifteenth probably suffered 80 percent of the AAF's personnel losses in the Mediterranean. This expenditure of manpower and matériel, however, gained the Allies air supremacy over Europe. With air supremacy came the freedom both to bomb at will any target in Germany and to conduct the invasion of France without Luftwaffe interference.

The achievement of air supremacy over France, especially over the invasion area, and of air superiority over Germany before D-Day was the decisive contribution of Spaatz and USSTAF to Operation Overlord. Being forced to battle for control of the skies on the day of the invasion might have ruined the Allies' ability to achieve their objectives. By forcing the Luftwaffe to concentrate its chief defensive effort over Germany, Spaatz left the Luftwaffe unable or unwilling to oppose the Allied interdiction air campaign in northern France.

The Eighth's contribution to the transportation bombing plan, although not niggardly, amounted to less than one-third of Bomber Command's: 13,000 tons to 46,000 tons.[63] During the first three months of 1944, 70 percent of the Eighth's bombs hit German soil.[64] In April the Eighth Air Force dropped 62.5 percent of its bombs on Germany; in May the figure was 57 percent.[65] Given the increase in bombers available to Doolittle in April and May, actual tonnage dropped on the Reich went up in both months. Thus the preinvasion plan to bomb transportation, although a diversion, did not greatly cut into the combined bomber offensive. For the first five months of 1944, Crossbow targets received more bomb tonnage—16,082 tons—than did the transportation plan's targets.[66] This result represented a dead loss to the Eighth's war effort, because Crossbow neither involved Luftwaffe fighter opposition nor substantially delayed the Germans' deployment of the V-1s. Transportation plan bombing at least aided the invasion.

D-DAY TO VE-DAY

Spaatz had performed well in the first and crucial phase of his air campaign, but he was now faced with carrying the campaign through to its conclusion. This effort would require a different formulation of the factors of luck, management skill, killer instinct, perseverance, and trustworthiness.

Although his actions had contributed greatly to the success of the invasion, Spaatz had been, at best, a less than wholehearted participant in combined and joint operations. In the circumstances of most U.S. air operations since 1991, where the daily air tasking order transparently reveals every combat sortie of the day and its target, Spaatz's failure to support the joint campaign plan completely might even have been cause for removal. However, after the successful Anglo-American lodgment on the continent, he willingly provided direct support for ground operations. In July and August he committed the Eighth to three attacks: two in support of the British and one in support of the Americans. On July 18, in cooperation with RAF Bomber Command, Spaatz sent U.S. heavy bombers to support Operation Goodwood, an attack designed to break the British out of the Normandy beachhead. This attack was ineffective, as was the attack on August 8. On July 24–25, missions in support of the American Operation Cobra, although marred by highly controversial short bombings that killed 141 U.S. soldiers and wounded more than 500, pulverized the German defenses and aided in Cobra's decisive breakout from the beachhead.[67] In both operations ground commanders had asked for the heavy bombers' firepower because the beachhead's limited logistics (the Allies had not yet captured and repaired a major port) could not provide the heavy guns and prodigious advance stockage of shells that usually preceded a major ground offensive. In the case of Cobra, air firepower provided a key piece of the formula for destroying entrenched defenders—a massive, concentrated, and quickly delivered initial bombardment. The Americans' immediate follow-up ground attack with overwhelming numbers broke through the German defenses. Allied tactical air power prevented the Germans from shifting their limited reserves to seal the front, and the Allied ground forces broke into the clear, beginning the drive that would sweep the Germans out of much of France.

During the Allies' logistics crisis in late August 1944 Spaatz offered the ground forces a different kind of support. He ordered more than two hundred of his bombers to transport gasoline from dumps in England to airfields in France and Belgium for the advancing Allied armies' use. Two later ground support attacks by heavy bombers, however, reverted to the ineffective norm of such missions. On November 9, more than twelve hundred heavy bombers carrying 2,000- and 1,000-pound bombs hit concrete fortifications near Metz to support Lt. Gen. George S. Patton's Third Army.[68] Operation Queen on November 16 supported Lt. Gen. Courtney H. Hodges's First Army in Rur by striking the German front line with 1,191 bombers and 3,846 tons of fragmentation bombs.

Spaatz also ordered the Eighth to fly several ground missions to support troops during the December 1944–January 1945 Battle of the Bulge. This effort included the Eighth's largest mission of the war, when its leaders ordered "everything that could fly" into the air on Christmas Eve and dispatched 2,046 bombers.[69] Later,

Spaatz made the entire Second Air Division—more than five hundred B-24s—available for the entire month of January 1945 to attack targets supporting the German counteroffensive.

While Spaatz accommodated the ground forces' needs, naturally he focused on his principal mission, the strategic bombardment of Germany. He was aided in his ability to target as he wished first by Eisenhower's loose reins and second by the Combined Chiefs of Staff's decision on September 13, 1944, to remove both Harris and Spaatz from Eisenhower's direct control and place them under their respective service's chief of staff.[70] Harris proceeded to virtually ignore his RAF boss, ACM Portal, while General Arnold, head of the AAF, gave Spaatz carte blanche to determine his targets and priorities. From June 1944 through April 1945 Spaatz kept his sights (and those of his bombardiers) on the German oil industry as a first priority. The plants' relatively small size made them difficult for radar (at least the primitive air-to-ground radar available in 1944–1945) to locate through clouds. Even so, his consistent and heavy bombing of this vital target system, which consumed most of the discouragingly few days of daylight bombing, left Spaatz with considerable bomb lift for other targets. By the end of October 1944 he had agreed with Tedder to make the German railroad transportation system his second priority. Every town in Germany had a rail marshaling yard and the labor force to repair it quickly. The German rail system could absorb, for a while, the excess bomb lift of the Allied strategic air forces. The bombers' radar could also identify, to some degree, the marshaling yards. Better still, unlike France (where more than half of the rail capacity supported the French civilian economy and whose loss inflicted hardship on the Allies), all losses of transport capacity in Germany affected the enemy's war economy and populace.

Bombing the rail system had a dark side. Rail marshaling yards were located in or adjacent to cities. Given the abysmal accuracy of radar bombing, a well-hit rail yard meant dozens of 500-pound bombs smashed into the surrounding urban area and thus caused the death or injury of dozens or more men, women, and children in each raid, every time.

Inevitably Spaatz, as the man who ordered so many of these raids, was drawn into the wartime and postwar debate concerning the bombing of civilians or, to use the military euphemism, "collateral damage." Like any man of fundamental decency, he was troubled by the difference between what he ought to do and what he had to do, especially on a scale such as this war demanded. Unlike Harris, who was under specific orders from his government to bomb German cities,[71] Spaatz and the AAF had no such directives, and they had developed their precision bombing doctrine to maximize efficiency, not terror. From January 1942 through April 1945 RAF Bomber Command targeted 56 percent of its sorties and 500,000 tons of bombs on city areas, whereas the Eighth only devoted 21.5 percent of its heavy bomber sorties to area or area-like bombing during the same period.[72]

What was Spaatz's role in this strategy? When he arrived in England in January 1944 the Eighth Air Force had already begun to fly radar-directed city raids. Spaatz encouraged and expanded this practice, not to kill civilians, but to kill the Luftwaffe fighter force. He continued to order city raids until late July 1944, which marked the high point of American-ordered area bombing. At that time his operations deputy issued a directive to the Eighth and Fifteenth Air Forces that categorically denied any intention to conduct area bombings, but he noted, "We will continue to conduct bombing attacks through the overcast where it is impossible to get precision targets. Such attacks will include German marshalling yards whether or not they are located in German cities."[73] This memo stilled the American reporting of area bombing missions but not the practice. Spaatz himself would have been highly offended if anyone had accused him of supporting an area bombing policy. Yet a month later, on August 27,[74] Spaatz informed Arnold that he had rejected a British proposal to associate the AAF with a British plan to inflict 137,500 dead in a combined raid on Berlin. Spaatz stated: "There is no doubt in my mind that the RAF very much wants the U.S. Air Forces tarred with the moral bombing aftermath, which we feel will be terrific."

In this author's opinion, Spaatz never believed he had conducted an area bombing campaign. Instead, he would have argued that the greatest evil he could have committed would have been to allow the vast daily killing of World War II to continue without using every means at his disposal to end it. Not even his position as the ranking officer in the operational chain of command that ordered the A-bomb drops on Hiroshima and Nagasaki would have changed his reasoning.

Once committed to attacking the German transportation system Spaatz pursued this goal with typical ruthlessness. Again Ultra eased the way with accurate bomb damage assessments that kept the Allies well informed of the injury inflicted and when the system had healed enough to warrant another blow. Attack followed attack; repairs followed repairs (aided by 250,000 slave laborers specifically assigned to the task). But each repair consumed limited, irreplaceable supplies of spares and returned the yard to a lower capacity than before. The overall capacity of the system rapidly declined, disrupting the flow of matériel, industrial resources, and the supply of railroad engines and rolling stock. In February 1945 Germany banned the shipment of industrial subassemblies, which finished it as an industrial power. By March 1945 coal, the lifeblood of German industry and electrical power, had ceased to flow from the pits to the consumers, and marshaling yard superintendents began to push rolling stock off the tracks to clear the way for the higher priority troop and ammunition trains. Even as the Allied ground forces kicked open the last doors of Hitler's empire, the strategic bombers were collapsing it from above. From August 17, 1942, through May 2, 1945, American heavy bombers dropped a million tons of bombs on Europe, 75 percent of them after September 1944. Spaatz had directed the bulk of this effort. By mid-April 1945 his heavy bombers could no longer find targets within the detritus of the Nazi state. Spaatz therefore called off the strategic offensive and offered his forces to assist the ground armies. On May 8, 1945, he was present when the Germans surrendered to the Anglo-American forces at Reims, France. The next day, appointed by Eisenhower as the American representative, he attended the surrender of the Germans to the Soviets in Berlin. After the ceremony he toured the city he had done his best to wreck from end to end.

FROM VJ-DAY TO CHIEF OF STAFF OF THE U.S. AIR FORCE

Spaatz had not completed his wartime service. At the end of May 1945 Arnold plucked Spaatz from his upcoming assignment as commander of the Continental Air Force (the U.S. home air force) and thrust him into the complicated U.S. command and control situation in the war against Japan. There Spaatz would have to take on such icons as Fleet Adm. Chester Nimitz and General of the Army Douglas MacArthur, as well as the die-hard servants of the emperor of Japan. Arnold wrote to Spaatz, "I can see nobody else who has the chance to save for [the AAF] a proper representation in the air war in the Pacific and who can assure that we will have bases from which we can launch and express a proper level of air effort against the Japs."[75]

Fortunately for Spaatz, Arnold and the other Joint Chiefs of Staff had done most of the spadework in reconciling the conflicting army- and navy-led campaigns of MacArthur and Nimitz, respectively, for the initial invasion of the Japanese home island of Kyushu (Operation Olympic). While MacArthur had primary responsibility for the landing itself, Spaatz was directed to cooperate with Nimitz, who had the responsibility for planning the landing's amphibious phase. The Twentieth Air Force, the AAF's B-29 bomber-equipped strategic air force in the Pacific, would cooperate in the execution of Olympic and might be placed under the direction of Nimitz or MacArthur to support either's operations. MacArthur would also have direct control of Gen. George C. Kenney's Far East Air Forces, comprising the AAF's tactical Fifth, Seventh, and Thirteenth Air Forces.[76]

By mid-July 1945 Arnold succeeded in inserting Spaatz into this structure. The heretofore independent Twentieth Air Force, the Eighth Air Force (redeploying from Europe to Okinawa), and their supporting units would be placed under Spaatz in a new headquarters, U.S. Army Strategic Air Forces in the Pacific. The headquarters was subject to the directives already imposed on the Twentieth Air Force, and both MacArthur and Nimitz were to keep it supplied. This move increased the status of strategic air by giving it a four-star commander and ensured that the strategic bombardment of Japan would not be subsumed into tactical operations.

On July 29, 1945, after a short rest with his family, Spaatz arrived on Guam. His first duty was to inform Nimitz and MacArthur of the existence of the A-bomb. Neither man saw any reason to modify his planning. Even as Spaatz performed this task the 509th Composite Group, the AAF's one atomic-capable bomb group, worked feverishly to complete preparations for an early August bomb drop. Upon receiving authorization from President Harry S. Truman and Army chief of staff Marshall, Spaatz gave the order for the atomic bombing of Hiroshima and Nagasaki.

On the sixth of August the first atomic bomb exploded over Hiroshima. Three days later a second atomic bomb struck Nagasaki. But the Japanese still hesitated. On August 14 Spaatz sent the entire Twentieth Air Force, or 828 heavy bombers carrying more than eight thousand tons of bombs, against precision targets in Japan.[77] Because the Eighth Air Force could double this total in a few weeks, Spaatz clearly had the power to crush any target in Japan. The next day (motivated more by the atomic weapons than by conventional tonnage), the Japanese surrendered. Spaatz had spent exactly seventeen days in combat in the Pacific. On September 2, 1945, standing on the USS *Missouri*'s deck, Spaatz witnessed the final Axis surrender and became the only American general to attend the three major ceremonies ending the war.

The shooting had stopped, but Spaatz immediately found himself in the midst of the most bruising bureaucratic fight in American history as the armed services unified under a single Department of Defense. Arnold had made it possible by gaining Marshall's agreement to a separate air force, but Arnold's bad heart forced him from active duty by November 1945. Someone else would have to do the hard work of fighting it out with the navy, creating a new service, and presiding over the destruction of the largest aerial armada ever created. As the second and last commanding general of the AAF, Spaatz was assigned the job. Fortunately for the air service, Spaatz had an excellent and tested working relationship with the army's new chief of staff, Eisenhower. They formed an effective, although not uniformly successful, tag team against the navy.

Even as the great struggle for unification of the services (and relative autonomy for the U.S. Air Force within that structure) began, Arnold sent Spaatz charging over the top by calling on him to clarify the air service's role in the atomic era. The bid for unification could not be allowed to founder because the AAF could not state a new goal and the route to it. In October 1945 Arnold appointed what came to be known as the Spaatz Board, consisting of Spaatz and two of his protégés—Lieutenant General Vandenberg, the wartime commander of the U.S. Ninth Air Force, the world's largest tactical air force, and Major General Norstad, an experienced operations and staff officer. The three men attacked their task with determination. By the end of October they issued the first section of the "Spaatz Report," which they apparently intended for fairly wide distribution. In November they released the second part, possibly aimed at only the few high-ranking officers in the service with top security clearances.[78]

The report reflected Spaatz's practical outlook. It offered no out-of-the-box thinking.[79] Part 1 contained a review of strategic bombing as conducted in World War II. It also assumed that any opponent would have the secret of the A-bomb, since it would be suicidal to attack the United States without one's own nuclear weapons. This line of reasoning led the report to confirm some of the time-tested tenets of the prewar Air Corps Tactical School (ACTS), which, in spite of its name, had been the intellectual hotbed of the AAF's strategic bombardment doctrine. In particular, the report accepted two ACTS premises: "Future wars will begin by air action. Thus we must have an adequate standing air force to ensure our defense and to begin immediate offensive operations. We must place ourselves in a position to begin bombardment of the enemy as soon as possible. . . . The current limited range of our aircraft requires the acquisition of allies to provide forward bases in order to begin action as soon as possible."[80]

Consequently, and since an enemy's atomic attack could decide a war before mobilization could even occur, the United States should maintain an air service capable of stopping an enemy air offensive dead in its tracks and of launching a crushing attack of its own. This force must always be ready to fly at any moment. This philosophy meant that the AAF must be, to the extent possible, forward based and always fully on alert. Unlike the other services, which would require time to mobilize, the AAF could not adopt a status of tiered readiness. The service supported this position for the next fifty-three years, until it was forced to adopt the aerospace expeditionary force scheme. Finally, the first report called for an air force of 400,000 personnel and seventy combat groups (about ten thousand aircraft) of coequal status with the nation's ground and naval forces.[81]

The second portion of the Spaatz Report, which was declassified in the 1980s, took a close look at the role of nuclear weapons in modern warfare. It reiterated the call for a standing nuclear strike force with overseas basing. It also stressed the need for an effective continental air defense force (which never became a reality because of budget restrictions), the requirement for a greatly expanded intelligence network (Spaatz and Vandenberg realized that they could not allow a future force to be as strongly dependent on a single source of information as they had been on Ultra during the war), and the necessity for an immediate improvement of the AAF's research and development establishment (the AAF had begun the war with severe deficiencies in radar and engine research).[82] The service now had a blueprint for unification.

In March 1946, in the midst of the struggle, Spaatz began to implement this blueprint by reorganizing the AAF's basic structure. He created three major commands based on function: the Air Defense Command, which would protect the homeland; the Strategic Air Command, which contained all the AAF's nuclear-capable and other heavy bombers and would clearly serve as the nuclear force; and the Tactical Air Command. The formation of a tactical command reassured the army that the air force would meet its airlift and close air support needs. It also dampened the army's separate campaigning for its own air arm. These commands would form the combat backbone of the U.S. Air Force for more than forty years.

In June 1946, Spaatz strengthened the ability of the United States to respond to Soviet aggression when he concluded a "handshake" agreement with the RAF chief of staff, his old comrade in arms Sir Arthur Tedder. The two agreed, without the formal consent of their governments, that the British would immediately build two airfields capable of handling American B-29 bombers carrying atomic bombs.[83] This understanding was followed by many more formal agreements granting the United States forward basing rights and leading to facilities that would eventually ring the Soviet Union.

With the creation of the U.S. Air Force in September 1947, Spaatz made two further contributions to his service. First, he established the Air Staff. As befitted a man who loathed paperwork, the organization chart for his initial staff was the simplest in the institution's history. Spaatz's Air Staff reflected his wartime experience with the deputy system. It granted responsibility and authority to four deputy chiefs of staff: (1) operations, (2) matériel, (3) personnel, and (4) administration, as well as an air comptroller. It reduced the number of officers reporting directly to him from thirteen to seven. Perhaps the subsequent expansion of the U.S. Air Force's Air Staff has reflected the growing complexity of the modern military; perhaps not.

Second, in March 1948, he met with the other service chiefs and Secretary of Defense James Forrestal in Key West, Florida, where, after a good deal of head butting, they reached an agreement defining the roles and missions of each service. This accord confirmed the air force's primary role in performing continental air defense, providing tactical support to the army, and conducting strategic air warfare.

A few days later, worn out by almost nine years of unremitting labor, Spaatz retired from active duty to enjoy time with his family and grandchildren. His official retirement date was June 30, 1948. Later that year he joined *Newsweek*, a nationally distributed magazine, as its military editor. For the next thirteen years he used this platform to advocate interservice cooperation and support for air power (without navy supercarriers) and to recommend continued backing for the North Atlantic alliance as a strategic priority. He wrote many articles on the Korean War, where he served for a while as a war correspondent. Demonstrating that he was not infallible, he argued for bombing China and committing the Taiwanese armed forces of Chiang Kai-shek.

In 1950–1951, Spaatz once more gave proof of his commitment to advancing the case of land-based air power by serving one term as chairman of the board of the Air Force Association, the U.S. Air Force's leading public and political advocacy group. Later, his support was instrumental in founding the Air Force Histori-cal Association, whose meetings he often attended.[84] In the mid-1950s he served on the committee that established the USAF Academy and selected its site at Colorado Springs. Thanks in part to Spaatz's suggestions the new school adopted more of a liberal arts curriculum than its more technically oriented fellow acad-emies had. Spaatz died from the complications of a stroke on July 14, 1974, and is buried at the Air Force Academy.

Spaatz stands in the front rank of air power leaders. He was a man who, when he spoke at all, told the unvarnished truth, often to superiors. He hated paperwork and disliked professional military education. He simply got things done.

2

GEORGE C. KENNEY: "A KIND OF RENAISSANCE AIRMAN"

ALAN STEPHENS

George Churchill Kenney was arguably World War II's outstanding operational-level air commander. Highly skilled across a remarkably wide range of military disciplines—piloting, engineering, logistics, strategy, operations, tactics, administration, research and development, doctrine, campaign planning, weapons application, organizational politics, and leadership—Kenney was "a kind of renaissance airman."[1]

When he became the Southwest Pacific Area's (SWPA's) senior airman in August 1942 the Allied air forces were in disarray. They had not merely been defeated by the stunning Japanese strikes against Malaya, the Philippines, and Pearl Harbor in early December 1941, they had been humiliated. The theater's supreme commander, the imperious Gen. Douglas MacArthur, had become distrustful of air power and had sacked Kenney's predecessor, Lt. Gen. George H. Brett. Kenney's main assets—the U.S. Army Air Forces (USAAF) and the Royal Australian Air Force (RAAF)—were ill prepared, poorly equipped, and suffering from indifferent leadership.

Yet only seven months later Kenney led those same forces to a spectacular victory in the Battle of the Bismarck Sea, an action General MacArthur later described as "the decisive aerial engagement" of the war in the SWPA. Never again were the Japanese in a position to take the strategic offensive; instead, they were forced into a defensive posture from which victory was unlikely. Bismarck Sea was a master class in air warfare.

By early 1944, within eighteen months of taking over, Kenney had reshaped his command's strength, organization, and fighting spirit to such an extent that the

Allies enjoyed near supremacy in the skies over the SWPA. That supremacy in turn underwrote MacArthur's so-called island-hopping strategy, through which the Allies advanced northward toward the Japanese home islands. MacArthur's distrust had been transformed into absolute confidence in his senior airman's leadership and judgment and in his ability to deliver control of the air, to strike, to maneuver (airlift), and to conduct reconnaissance and a host of other capabilities as and when required.

It might seem extraordinary, therefore, that only three years after the war Kenney was sacked as commander of the U.S. Air Force's Strategic Air Command (SAC).

All of the elements of command and leadership in war are evident in the contrasting experiences that in sum constituted Kenney's military career. Some of those experiences were within his province to control or at least to manage; others were not. In short, as is the case for all of us, George Kenney's professional life offered opportunity and choice, sometimes favorable, sometimes disagreeable; and it was the way in which he prepared himself for and dealt with those events that determined his performance as a wartime commander.

COMMANDING AIR POWER

Before examining General Kenney's approach to command and leadership, a template against which he (or any other commander) can be assessed must be established. That template has three components: professional mastery, personal qualities, and an unsentimental appreciation of Realpolitik, or of dealing with the world as it is rather than how we might like it to be.

Samuel Huntington's classic study *The Soldier and the State* contends that professional mastery is based on the notions of "expertise" and "responsibility."[2] Expertise is derived from a high degree of competence within specialized military skills (pilot, infantryman, engineer, and so on) and from a broad liberal education, including military history and its associated disciplines. Responsibility, Huntington argues, exists in the social compact an individual has with the state to perform his duties as and when required. That compact rests essentially on a moral base and may be defined as much by unwritten norms as by any binding legal document.

Also central to any analysis of an individual's ability to command and to lead is the concept of the "management of violence." Formalized by Harold Lasswell, the concept argues that the special skill of a military officer is the "direction, operation and control of a human organization" in which the prime purpose is the application of violence.[3] It is important to understand that the concept's definition specifically excludes committing an act of violence. In other words, dropping a bomb does not qualify, but directing the operations of a flight of bombers does.

Another perspective of the command template has been provided by John Keegan, who has noted that analyses of commanders tend to focus on one or both of two sets of personal qualities.[4] The first is individual characteristics, which are usually defined in terms of intellect, energy, decisiveness, self-confidence, and professional expertise. The second is behavior, which is perhaps most usefully described as the capacity to get things done; that is, it is the way in which a commander chooses to direct subordinates and fighting forces using one or a combination of encouragement, dissuasion, coercion, inspiration, and so on.[5] Keegan's "characteristics" and "behavior" might be regarded as analogous to Carl von Clausewitz's *coup d'oeil* and resolution.[6]

Also worth mentioning is Martin van Creveld's shrewd analysis of military command, which turns on an individual's skill in the search for certainty—"certainty about the intentions of the enemy, the environment of battle, and the character of one's own forces."[7] This search is both competitive and continuous. One of its key effects is the creation of confidence up and down the chain of command, with superiors and subordinates alike. The ability to create certainty is shaped partly by training, socialization and experience, and partly by innate qualities.

Few organizations rival advanced defense forces in providing whole-of-career access to training, education, and personal development courses. Thus, the extent to which an individual cultivates the range of skills needed to command and to lead is to a fair degree within his or her control. Plainly some people are smarter or more physically capable or more courageous, and so on, than others are, but in general it is reasonable to suggest that motivated individuals are masters of their professional destinies.

At the same time, it is important to acknowledge the reality of the objective circumstances under which a commander operates—that is, those forces beyond his control, such as the era, the political context, the geography, the industrial base, and so on, which obtain at the time he occupies center stage. There are two points here. First, because of those objective circumstances, what works for one (in a particular setting) will not necessarily work for all. And second, successful commanders understand that they must deal with the world as it is and shape their behavior accordingly.

For example, in 1863, Ulysses S. Grant was the right commander in the right place at the right time. Prior to that, Grant had often been the wrong man in the wrong place at the wrong time. An undistinguished West Point graduate who had dropped out of the army mid-career and who had been a failure as a businessman, Grant knew what had to be done to win the American Civil War. President Abraham Lincoln had become increasingly frustrated by the reluctance of a succession of his generals to fight. Like Lincoln, Grant appreciated that the North had an overwhelming material advantage over the South. As long as the Union's armies kept engaging those of the Confederacy and were competently led, they would eventually win. Grant was not afraid of fighting—of risking lives and matériel—as he relentlessly closed with Robert E. Lee's forces, finally driving his opponent to an almost inevitable surrender. (That description is something of an oversimplification, neglecting as it does Grant's brilliant logistics planning, especially his use of rivers for transportation, and his astute understanding of people, but it is essentially accurate.)[8]

One hundred and twenty-six years later, in the 1991 Gulf War, public opinion would never have allowed Gen. H. Norman Schwarzkopf to have contemplated the model of attrition warfare that was logical for Grant. Schwarzkopf's command considerations had to include possible enemy, as well as friendly, casualties; and he had to make allowance for the fact that his every action would be watched by a world audience of hundreds of millions. He did all of those things brilliantly. In short, like Grant, he operated within the objective circumstances as he found them.

The final observation in this section concerns a feature of command and leadership that is distinctive to air forces. As John Olsen has noted, airmen are "a different breed of cat."[9] Air forces have a small warrior caste, mostly limited to aircrew in general and pilots in particular. Pilots comprise only 15 percent of an air force's officer corps, yet since 1914 the mystique of the pilot has loomed large in shaping air forces' ideas and command styles. It is noteworthy that, unlike their army and navy counterparts, air force pilots do not lead their troops into battle. Moreover, a substantial number of biographies, memoirs, and critiques indicate that many senior air force officers have defined their professional status more through their skill as pilots than through the command qualities identified by Huntington, Lasswell, Keegan, and van Creveld.[10] That is not to say this has necessarily been good or bad, but it is to say it has been different.

Precisely how General Kenney fits the template for commanding air power is the subject of the rest of this chapter.

EARLY CAREER

George Kenney was born in Canada in 1889 and grew up in Massachusetts.[11] Important influences on his early development included three years studying civil engineering at the prestigious Massachusetts Institute of Technology (MIT), having to support his family when his father deserted them while Kenney was still at MIT, and attending an "air meet" in Boston in 1910. The need to earn a living prevented Kenney from graduating from MIT, but the management and engineering experience he gained was to be a great asset throughout his career. That career was never in doubt following the air meet. "From then on," he stated, "I knew that was what I was going to do."[12]

Family responsibilities meant that it would be another seven years before Kenney could take flying lessons. In the meantime, he accumulated an impressive range of technical and managerial experience, working as a civil engineer for companies that built office blocks, homes, railroads, bridges, and roads. He was also involved in complex engineering projects that required innovative solutions, such as erecting buildings and seawalls near swamps and other wetlands. By his mid-twenties he had become president of an engineering firm and had started his own business. In doing so, Kenney had incidentally demonstrated many of the qualities needed to succeed at the highest levels of the profession of arms.

By the time the United States entered World War I in 1917 Kenney's family circumstances had eased, and he was finally able to pursue his ambition to become a pilot. In June he enlisted as a flight cadet in the aviation section of the army's Signal Corps. Flight school presented few problems. Aged twenty-seven and already a successful engineer and businessman, Kenney was mature and confident. The most noteworthy incident from his flight training offers a revealing insight into his personality. Ignoring the syllabus, Kenney made his first three solo landings without engine power. Forced landings were common at the time, but to practice them so soon was strictly against the rules. Kenney's attitude was indicative of someone who was in a hurry and who was constantly challenging himself. As he told his instructor, Bert Acosta (subsequently to achieve a degree of fame himself as the world flight endurance record holder), "Any damn fool can land if the motor is running. I just wanted to see what would happen in case [it] quit."[13]

Lieutenant Kenney arrived at the Western Front in France early in 1918 classified as a pursuit (fighter) pilot. In reality, while he was competent in basic flying sequences, he was inadequately prepared for combat operations and advanced aircraft types. The environment was dangerous and demanding: life expectancy for new pilots was about one month. It was typical of Kenney that he simply got on with the job, learning from his senior colleagues and trying to stay out of trouble while he gained experience.

By the end of the war Kenney had flown seventy-five combat sorties. His mission experience included reconnaissance, sometimes deep into enemy-held territory; ground attack; army liaison; communications; and furious dogfights that could involve scores of aircraft, and in the course of which he shot down two German aircraft and was shot down once himself. Respected for his courage and his ability quickly to assess a situation, he had risen to the rank of captain and had been decorated with the Silver Star and the Distinguished Service Cross—the latter presented personally by the senior U.S. airman on the Western Front, Brig. Gen. William "Billy" Mitchell.

Those were fine achievements. However, within the context of commanding air power, Kenney's rapid development as a military thinker was far more significant. Unlike most of his colleagues, he took a keen interest in how the missions he flew at the tactical level of war related to the broader operational and strategic situations; that is, his attention was turning to Lasswell's "management of violence" as opposed to its mere application. Notwithstanding his junior rank, he quickly became one of the charismatic Mitchell's closest confidants.

Kenney's combat experience left him with two enduring doctrinal convictions. The first was that control of the air was the prime air campaign—the essential precursor to every other war-fighting action, whether on the surface or in the sky. This was a seminal conclusion, because during the 1920s and 1930s the relative importance of control of the air (fighters) and strategic strike (bombers) would become the most hotly contested debate within the air corps. His second conviction was that men and morale, not machines, win wars. First-rate weapons systems are highly desirable but in themselves are useless if the human element is weak. Kenney was not one of those officers who paid mere lip service to the fundamental importance of people in combat: he was utterly committed to the principle.

CONSOLIDATING PROFESSIONAL MASTERY

The period between the world wars was a time of both frustration and excitement for the U.S. Army Air Corps (USAAC). Frustration came in the form of the constant battle for recognition from the broader army, whose land-centric generals continued to regard air power as an enabling capability, notwithstanding clear evidence to the contrary from World War I. Consequently, for many members of the air corps, the interwar period was defined by limited resources, restricted opportunities, exasperating doctrinal battles, overt hostility from the army's senior echelons, and bleak promotion prospects. The other side of the coin, however, was the undercurrent of excitement associated with the true believers' conviction that, from now on, air forces were not just going to be equal with armies and navies, but would become the dominant form of military power. Securing independence from the army in order to pursue that belief became an over-riding air corps ambition.

Kenney experienced his share of setbacks and unreasonable treatment. But despite having to wait seventeen years for promotion from captain to major, he refused to let peremptory behavior undermine his convictions or inhibit his energy. His exceptional qualities were recognized within the air corps, most notably by Generals Mitchell, Benjamin Foulois, Frank Andrews, and Henry "Hap" Arnold, all of whom were influential at different times. And while circumstances might have prevented the corps hierarchy from promoting Kenney, the appointments for which he was chosen tacitly acknowledged his unique skill set. Among other things, Kenney served as a squadron commander, engineer, logistician, staff officer, and instructor. He was also a key member of various air corps "brain trusts," both formal and informal.

Following his return from France, Captain Kenney flew security patrols along the U.S.-Mexican border, after which he completed a demanding engineering course. He was then appointed chief of the factory section at the army's Air Service Engineering School at Wright Field, Ohio. Kenney was unimpressed by much of the school's official research, but his position gave him the opportunity to broaden his technical knowledge and to conduct his own experiments.

Two of his innovations were especially significant. Disregarding strident engineering objections, in 1922 he had machine guns successfully fitted to the wings of a de Havilland DH-4 fighter (previously guns had been mounted on engine cowlings), an initiative that increased the number of guns and, therefore, the aircraft's firepower.[14] Wing-mounted guns became standard on fighters around the world for the next three decades. He followed this some years later by designing the "parafrag" bomb. Kenney wanted to develop a fragmentation weapon that would be effective against soft-skinned targets such as parked aircraft, fuel dumps, and personnel, and could be dropped from very low levels (thus maximizing accuracy) without exposing crews to blast and shrapnel damage. The drag of the parachute increased the bomb's drop time, which allowed the crew to egress before the warhead detonated; it also facilitated a high degree of accuracy because the weapon was released almost directly above the target. At the time, high-explosive bombs usually weighed between 40 and 250 pounds, but after a series of trials Kenney opted for a 24-pound weapon so that more bombs could be carried to saturate a target area. Years later, Kenney was to employ the parafrag to considerable effect during the war in the Pacific.

Technical innovation was complemented by robust doctrinal dialogue. Throughout the 1920s and 1930s, Kenney was a leader in the air power debate as he and like-minded colleagues fought to establish an independent air force. In 1925 he was posted to undertake the intellectually stimulating, even radical, course at the Air Corps Tactical School (ACTS) at Langley Field, Virginia. This was a time when the classical air power theorists Giulio Douhet, Hugh Trenchard, and Billy Mitchell were arguing that air strike would dominate future warfare. The ACTS was a vibrant environment in which the prevailing army- and navy-centric warfighting orthodoxies were vigorously challenged. Also argued with passion by staff and students were the evolving and sometimes competing elements of air power doctrine: fighter versus bomber, precision attack versus area attack, organizational independence versus integration, escorted versus unescorted bomber fleets, and so on. Many of the men who were to lead the USAAF during World War II were involved in the discussions at the ACTS (which in 1931 relocated to Maxwell Field in Montgomery, Alabama).[15] Kenney participated energetically and wrote a textbook on air attack.

Notwithstanding his conviction that air forces had become the decisive expression of military power, Kenney was not intellectually dogmatic and remained open to new concepts. In the opinion of one respected commentator, "He showed the least tendency to get hung up on tactical method and dogma, [and would] seek for success by alternatives within the general framework of air power."[16]

The ACTS brought Kenney into contact with fellow creative thinker Capt. Hugh Knerr, who believed that aerial warfare's intensely technological nature meant that its single most important component was not operations (control of the air, strike, etc.) but logistics.[17] Knerr was overstating the case: as the experiences of Italy in World War II, Egypt in the Six-Day War, and Iraq in the first Gulf War have shown, an air force that is well equipped but operationally inept is likely to fail. Nevertheless, it is noteworthy that Kenney's mastery of logistics was to be a distinctive feature of his command in the SWPA.

The professional growth Kenney enjoyed at Langley and later Maxwell was enhanced by courses at the army's Command and General Staff School and then the War College, and by a posting back to the ACTS as an instructor. One of his colleagues on his return to the ACTS was Maj. Frank Andrews, subsequently a towering figure in U.S. military aviation. Andrews recognized in Kenney someone whose mind "crackled with ideas and opinions, most of them strongly held."[18] Andrews's assessment was shared by the then-chief of the air corps Maj. Gen. Benjamin Foulois, who in 1933 directed Kenney and his friend and mentor Hap Arnold to have a summary of Douhet's theories on air warfare translated into English and distributed to "influential contacts."[19] Although only a junior officer, Captain Kenney had established himself as one of his service's foremost air power thinkers.

Kenney's intellect and staff skills were acknowledged by his assignment to the Plans Division of the chief of the air corps in the mid-1930s. Among the important policy papers he helped to prepare was the framework for establishing the General Headquarters Air Force (GHQ AF), a vital organizational step in the corps's progress toward independence. When the GHQ was formed in March 1935 to take command of all army air combat units, Kenney was among the handful of "energetic, dedicated, determined, individualists" chosen to provide the command's intellectual horsepower.[20]

His conceptual policy work was complemented by a wide range of more practical tasks, such as determining the force structure an independent service would need, auditing the corps's flying practices, and boosting its public image. Thus, Kenney strongly supported the Boeing Company's project B-299, a four-engine bomber that promised to revolutionize the air corps's strategic potential, and which eventually entered service as the iconic B-17 Flying Fortress. As far as flying practices were concerned, five years before the Battle of Britain, Kenney devised an "ingenious" early warning fighter alert system that more often than not enabled defensive forces to scramble in time to intercept attacking (exercise) bombers.[21] His extraordinarily eclectic approach to professional mastery was further demonstrated through his role in convincing the air corps to pay more attention to instrument flying and night flying—emerging skills that were to become crucial in World War II.

Turning to publicity, Kenney knew that spectacular achievements would promote the air corps's fight for identity; in particular, any flight that set a world record was likely to capture public attention. He was the driving force behind a number of highly publicized events. Perhaps the most successful was the nonstop, overwater flight from Puerto Rico to the U.S. northeast coast made in June 1936 by Frank Andrews, by then a major general and chief of GHQ AF. Andrews's twin-engine Douglas YOA-5 amphibian, nicknamed *The Big Duck*, was supposed to reach Newark, New Jersey, but strong headwinds forced a diversion to Langley Field. Nevertheless, the eleven-hour flight almost doubled the existing record and attracted favorable publicity.

Kenney might have enjoyed the respect of influential air corps officers, but the fact remained that he was a junior officer and an airman in the army, an organization that discouraged challenges to intellectual orthodoxy. On occasion the senior soldiers liked to exert their authority, and Kenney was among those fliers whose careers sometimes went into a nosedive because of arbitrary postings to remote or trivial jobs. In May 1936 he was transferred from Andrews's staff at GHQ AF to be an instructor at the army's Infantry School, despite strong protests from his air corps mentors. The message was not subtle. Kenney was being banished from the center of the air power movement and reminded of the army's one true faith.

But by the late 1930s the manifest threats of Germany in Europe and Japan in the Asia-Pacific had made that kind of petty behavior unacceptable. War seemed inevitable, and the best people were needed in the most important jobs. Kenney's rise to the top began in earnest once General Arnold became chief of the air corps in 1938. In addition to being a close personal friend, Arnold—perhaps the greatest air commander in U.S. history—regarded Kenney as his top "trouble shooter."[22] He rotated Kenney through a variety of postings intended to rapidly expand his understanding of military affairs, especially the political dimension. At the start of World War II and before the United States had joined the struggle, Arnold sent Kenney and another of his most trusted lieutenants, Col. Carl "Tooey" Spaatz, to serve as observers with the Royal Air Force (RAF), a deployment that included the Battle of Britain. Spaatz and Kenney provided Arnold with "many accurate reports," including their assessment that the USAAC lagged far behind the Luftwaffe in equipment and operational proficiency.[23] Air corps war plans were amended accordingly. Kenney also gained experience with the U.S. Navy on sea maneuvers, as an assistant air attaché in Paris, and as head of the air corps's Experimental Division.

Intensive exposure to strategic activities was accompanied by swift promotion. In contrast to the dismal progress over the past two decades, Kenney advanced four ranks in only four years, from major to major general. By 1942 he was commanding the Fourth Air Force in California, where his performance was widely regarded as "brilliant."[24] When serious problems arose with the conduct of the air war in the Southwest Pacific, it was natural for Arnold to turn to one of his best and brightest.

THE POLITICS OF COMMAND

Late in March 1942 the Allied Combined Chiefs of Staff designated the Pacific region as an American sphere of strategic responsibility and created two theaters— the SWPA and the Pacific Ocean Area. Gen. Douglas MacArthur was appointed commander in chief of the former, Adm. Chester Nimitz of the latter.

MacArthur had regrouped in Australia following his flight from the Philippines and had wasted little time in sacking his air commander, Lt. Gen. George H. Brett. His treatment of Brett was probably unfair, but by the same token the USAAF had scarcely distinguished itself during the brief Philippines campaign. Major General Kenney arrived as the new air commander in August.

Although his air forces were in poor shape, Kenney knew that his first and most critical task was political, not military. Before doing anything else he had to gain MacArthur's confidence and then sort things out with the Australians, with whom Brett had established a politically unacceptable organizational structure.

The egotistical MacArthur was the top priority; without his trust and respect it would not matter how good an air commander Kenney might be. The sensitivity of the situation was tacitly acknowledged in Washington, where General Arnold and the chairman of the Combined Chiefs of Staff, Gen. George C. Marshall, had issued Kenney the most uninformative command brief imaginable: "Simply report to General MacArthur."[25] Arnold's faith in his favorite was tempered somewhat by his concern that Kenney's straight talking might offend MacArthur. Kenney, however, was far too astute for that.

Brett had failed with MacArthur on several counts. The fiasco in the Philippines was one: humiliated by his defeat and looking for scapegoats, MacArthur had (unreasonably) placed much of the blame on his fliers, whom he described as "incompetent, bungling nincompoop airmen." Another issue was Brett's inability to deal with MacArthur's aggressive and overprotective chief of staff Maj. Gen. Richard K. Sutherland. Brett lacked the gravitas and confidence to stand up to Sutherland and consequently found it difficult to gain access to MacArthur, let alone influence him. Exploiting Brett's lack of authority, Sutherland increasingly took it upon himself to draft air operations orders, despite his ignorance of the subject.

Kenney immediately gauged the situation and dealt with it in characteristic fashion. In a scene often fondly recalled by airmen, he confronted Sutherland in his office. Placing a blank sheet of paper in front of the infantry officer, he marked a solitary dot with a pencil and said, "That dot represents what you know about air operations, the entire rest of the paper what I know."[26] He then suggested to Sutherland that they should see MacArthur at once to find out who was running the air war. Sutherland backed down, and from then on he and Kenney enjoyed a productive working relationship.

During his first meeting with MacArthur, Kenney spoke frankly about the difficulties that had affected air operations and of the USAAF's shortcomings in the theater. He outlined his plans for fixing things and for ensuring that in future the theater commander would receive the best possible support from his air forces. He assured MacArthur that he "knew how to run an air force as well or as better than anyone else and, while there were undoubtedly a lot of things wrong with [the] show, [he] intended to correct them and do a real job."[27] He would, he continued, work tirelessly to ensure that MacArthur "owned" the air in the SWPA. In conclusion, he promised MacArthur his absolute loyalty. By the time Kenney had finished speaking, MacArthur's previously hostile mood had evaporated. The foundations had been laid for an air-land command relationship that was to be the equal of any in the war.

Kenney moved swiftly to show MacArthur that he was more than just talk—that he could deliver on his promises. At the time of their meeting, the Australian Army in New Guinea was under intense pressure from Japanese forces that had advanced along the Kokoda Trail to within twenty-five miles of the vital Allied base at Port Moresby on the south coast. MacArthur was deeply worried, and reinforcements were urgently needed. Kenney proposed an audacious solution. He convinced a somewhat hesitant MacArthur to let him airlift an infantry company from Australia to Port Moresby instead of relying on the much slower alternative of sea transport. It was a characteristically bold idea, not least because the Allied air forces' airlift assets were modest and poorly organized. Kenney was undeterred, seizing the situation by the scruff of the neck. Through sheer force of character and intellect, he pulled together an air transport system almost overnight. An ad hoc fleet of Douglas C-47s and Lockheed 12s was assembled, load plans drafted, and flight schedules prepared. MacArthur was delighted when his soldiers arrived in New Guinea without a hitch, days earlier than would otherwise have been the case.

Encouraged by his success and taking advantage of MacArthur's newfound confidence, Kenney convinced the commander in chief to expand the airlift program. Yet again he thought laterally, this time by enlisting the assistance of the Australian minister for air to borrow twelve DC-3s from local airlines to supplement his fleet. He also requisitioned USAAF bomber aircraft that were not equipped for their primary mission but that could still transport people, and he commandeered civilian crews and aircraft that had been ferrying supplies to Australia from the United States.[28] An airlift schedule that could shift six hundred troops a day from Australia to New Guinea was established. It was a masterful demonstration of command and leadership at both the political and the operational levels. In a remarkably short period, Kenney had created an environment of certainty for MacArthur. Shortly afterward he was promoted to lieutenant general.

Incidentally, the measures Kenney was prepared to take to foster his relationship with MacArthur are worth mentioning. MacArthur had a monumental ego and a passion for favorable publicity. Kenney was happy to cater to his chief's campaign of self-promotion, even to the extent of issuing false media reports. For example, some months later, a series of air raids against the major Japanese base at Rabaul was the subject of a special public relations communiqué which claimed that 177 aircraft had been destroyed and the enemy had "sustained a disastrous defeat."[29] In distant Washington, General Arnold responded to Kenney's hyperbole by describing the action as a "Pearl Harbor in reverse." In fact, the attacks were nowhere near as destructive as claimed. Only fifty-five Japanese aircraft had been lost, and a post-raid assessment had concluded that Rabaul remained "immensely strong." An official U.S. war historian later concluded that "never . . . have such exorbitant claims been made with so little basis in fact."[30] In the meantime, however, the air-land command relationship in the SWPA flourished.

Returning to Kenney's early weeks in the SWPA, once he had established himself with MacArthur, he turned his attention to his other crucial political concern, namely, the command arrangements between the USAAF and the RAAF.

Prior to Kenney's arrival, Brett and his RAAF counterpart, Air Chief Marshal Sir Charles Burnett, had agreed that Allied air power in the SWPA should be integrated. But the U.S. Joint Chiefs of Staff in Washington disliked the proposal, which could have placed American forces under foreign (Australian) command, something they had traditionally rejected.[31] Their dissatisfaction was shared by MacArthur, an unabashed believer in American exceptionalism. Kenney acted promptly to ensure that the air war would be conducted strictly along national lines, and that all important decisions would be made by the United States.

The Australian government had previously placed the RAAF's operational units under the authority of the commander of the Allied Air Forces, SWPA (formerly Brett, now Kenney), on the understanding that, as per the Brett-Burnett agreement, the higher organization would be fully integrated. But while in theory Headquarters Allied Air Forces (AAF) was to draw its staff from both the USAAF and the RAAF, in practice all of the key positions were filled by American officers.

Kenney formalized that de facto segregation by forming two new war-fighting organizations, one American and the other Australian, which were subordinate to Headquarters AAF and which to all intents and purposes operated independently from each other. The American organization was known as the Fifth Air Force and was nominally headed by Kenney himself, but was run on a day-to-day basis by his right-hand man, Maj. Gen. Ennis C. Whitehead. Concurrently, Kenney grouped his Australian units into an organization named RAAF Command, headed by Air Vice Marshal Bill Bostock. It was the start of a process through which the RAAF was purposely consigned to a secondary role.

This is not a criticism of Kenney; on the contrary, the difficulties inherent in combined air operations have been apparent since World War II and continue today, with recent examples including Operations Deliberate Force in 1995, Allied Force in 1999, and Unified Protector in 2011.[32] Notwithstanding seemingly close ties of culture and tradition, nations historically have struggled to integrate their armed forces and to function comfortably under foreign command. In this instance, Kenney and MacArthur wanted to do things their way, and that would be easier if their air forces were not integrated with those of another nation. Kenney's approach might have upset the Australians, but that was their problem. Command in war and its associated politics is a tough business, and Kenney understood the rules.

At the same time, he demonstrated clear-headed pragmatism by not hesitating to draw on the RAAF's operational expertise while his unproven USAAF crews gained experience. Unlike their American counterparts, Kenney's Australian airmen had been fighting the Nazis since September 1939 and had accumulated a great deal of combat experience. Given the maritime nature of the SWPA, pilots and planners familiar with contemporary fighter, strike, and anti-shipping operations were especially valuable.

Boosted by the return of veterans from Europe and North Africa, Australian forces had regrouped speedily following their early defeats in Southeast Asia and on the Australian mainland. In the months preceding Kenney's arrival, RAAF squadrons had played a vital role in the war against Japan in the successful battles to defend Port Moresby from air attack (April/May 1942) and from amphibious invasion (August/September). By contrast, USAAF units were suffering from serious skill shortfalls, particularly in instrument flying, navigation, and bomb-aiming.[33] Kenney found it necessary to withdraw entire USAAF groups from combat for intensive remedial training; simultaneously, he seconded experienced Australian pilots and navigators to USAAF units, and used RAAF Catalina and Hudson crews to lead American bomber formations on raids. He also acknowledged that "the Australian planning was much better [than the USAAF's]."[34]

Kenney was, however, simply biding his time. As the USAAF gathered strength, he increasingly relegated the RAAF to supporting roles, such as garrisoning bypassed territory and protecting the flanks of MacArthur's main air and land forces as they pushed northward toward the Philippines and Japan. He was assisted in his approach by a damaging rivalry between the RAAF's two most senior officers in the SWPA—Air Vice Marshals George Jones and Bill Bostock. The tension between Jones and Bostock was never satisfactorily resolved and complicated the RAAF's command arrangements throughout the war. Kenney played the politics of the situation deftly, noting that while the feud "sometimes was a nuisance" he "liked the situation as it was."[35] He regarded Bostock and Jones as capable within their respective appointments and believed that their infighting did not diminish the RAAF's performance in the field. As far as he was concerned the situation made it easier for him to support MacArthur's preference to preserve the prestige and honor of the ultimate victory against Japan for his own forces.

It is noteworthy, incidentally, that the Australians were not the only "outsiders" Kenney deliberately pushed into the background. Adm. William F. Halsey Jr., commander of the Pacific area, felt compelled to intercede with MacArthur on behalf of the First Marine Air Group, which he claimed was either being deliberately ignored by Kenney or assigned tasks "far below its capacity."[36]

Kenney continued to play alliance politics hard. Because the SWPA was designated as an American sphere of strategic responsibility, Kenney (as MacArthur's delegate for air operations) was responsible via General Arnold for all new aircraft allocations in the theater. Early in the campaign the RAAF and the Australian government had lobbied Kenney strongly for heavy bombers, believing that they offered the best means of taking the fight to the enemy. Kenney, however, had resisted, wanting to build up the USAAF and use the RAAF as a supporting force.

In April 1943 Kenney had dismissed yet another RAAF request for heavy bombers.[37] Six months later, however, he suddenly changed his position. Claiming to have become aware that the United States now had a "surplus of B-24s pouring out" of its factories, Kenney asked General Arnold to start allocating heavy bombers to Australia immediately, with the intention of forming RAAF squadrons to replace USAAF squadrons stationed at Darwin in mainland Australia.[38] This apparent change of heart was entirely politically motivated. Once the RAAF was armed with B-24s, the American squadrons would be released to take part in the push against the enemy's homeland, leaving the newly formed Australian squadrons behind to look after mopping-up operations. In order to hasten the process Kenney even lent the RAAF six of his own B-24s, to which Arnold added another dozen, along with the promise of regular supplies.

From the Australian perspective these long-awaited bombers seemed the ideal weapon with which to hit back at a brutal and despised enemy. In fact, the Liberators were being provided by Arnold and Kenney with precisely the opposite intention in mind—their objective was to deny the RAAF a role in any strikes against the Japanese homeland. As late as March 1945 the Australian government was still earnestly expressing its (unrealized) hope that the RAAF might yet be allowed to "offer a substantial force in the final bombing of Japan."[39] The contrast with Kenney's tough and, it must be emphasized, valid application of command Realpolitik could scarcely have been more pronounced.

STRATEGIC PLANNING

Kenney was right to make the politics of command his priority. His success in that aspect of his personal challenge was, however, only the first step along the path of contributing to victory by conducting effective air operations. Other critical early steps included ascertaining the nature of the theater and getting hold of the best available men and machines to execute his campaign plan.

General Marshall believed that if the strategic character of a conflict were correctly defined, then even a lieutenant—in other words, almost anyone—could write the campaign plan. Understanding the nature of the theater is the essential starting point for that process. Military history is replete with instances of commanders who came to grief because they did not fully comprehend the conditions in which their forces were fighting. In that context, geography was a powerful factor in the SWPA.

Only two days after arriving in Australia, Kenney flew to New Guinea to see the place and the people for himself, and to talk to the men in charge on the scene. It was a practice he was to continue for the next three years. Even before, he knew that the SWPA was different. Thousands of islands, impenetrable jungles, towering mountain ranges, vast oceans, volatile weather, primitive facilities, and sparse populations—many of whom were little advanced from the Stone Age—made it unlike anywhere else. "I'd studied all the books," he told *Time* magazine in 1943, "and [New Guinea] was not in any of them."[40] Topographical information was "meagre to non-existent."

Few if any more incisive strategic analyses were made during World War II than Kenney's assessment of the nature of the war in the Pacific. It was Kenney who defined the method that came to be known as MacArthur's "island-hopping" strategy. In a letter he wrote to General Arnold soon after arriving in the SWPA, Kenney noted that the conflict in the Pacific was above all else a war of frequent, large-scale movement.[41] Moreover, unlike the campaigns in Europe, North Africa, Central Asia, and North Asia, that movement could not take place over land. Instead, the SWPA consisted of "a number of islands," and those islands in turn were "nothing more or less than aerodromes" from which operations could be launched. Sometimes they were "true" islands, like Wake and Midway, and sometimes they were isolated areas, like Port Moresby, Lae, and Buna, that shared a common land mass (New Guinea) but that realistically could be linked only by air.

In this theater, he told Arnold, tanks and heavy artillery had no place; instead, "the artillery flies." Other, lighter weapons, such as mortars, machine guns, rifles, tommy guns, and grenades, were carried by men "who fly to war, jump in parachutes, are carried in gliders and who land from air transports on ground which air engineers have prepared. These engineers have landed also by parachute and glider with airborne bulldozers, jeeps, and light engineer tools." Furthermore, the whole operation was "preceded and accompanied by bombers and fighters."

"Each time one of these islands is taken," Kenney continued in a telling judgment, "the rear is better secured and the emplacements for the flying artillery [strike aircraft] are advanced closer and closer to Japan itself." In effect, Kenney was presenting the case for a "rolling" front line of fighter and bomber bases that would mount offensive air operations to neutralize (or bypass) enemy strongholds and to capture the next airfield. It was a concept which implicitly challenged the army dogma of taking and holding ground as an end in itself, and that promised both to expedite MacArthur's push towards the Philippines and Japan and to reduce casualties. As the official U.S. history later acknowledged, it was a "daring estimate of the future role of [Kenney's] air forces."[42]

Kenney's masterful analysis led to four planning imperatives. The first concerned the ineluctable force of geography. Perhaps more than anywhere else, the sheer overwater distances involved meant that the danger of strategic overreach was constantly present. Airlift thus became fundamental to the planning and conduct of land operations. Second, and again because of distance and remoteness, gaining command of the sea would depend on air power to find and to strike convoys—that is, to interdict sea lines of communication. Third, no operation of any magnitude was likely to succeed if control of the air had not first been established. As Kenney explained to Arnold, "If we take out his fighters, his bombers won't go. If his fighters don't go, his troops and boats don't go either."[43] And finally, as MacArthur's army progressed northwards, only air power had the range and speed of response to protect its constantly expanding western and eastern flanks. In short, campaigning in the SWPA was even more dependent on air power than were the campaigns in Europe, where armies had a far greater capacity to maneuver independently.

Kenney acted boldly to translate his analysis into practice. During his initial reconnaissance of New Guinea he had noted the potential of the Wanigela Mission area, north of the looming Owen Stanley Mountains, as a forward base. At the time the Allied Air Forces were stationed south of the Owen Stanleys, but most enemy formations were to the north. The daily requirement for aircraft to climb over terrain that often was shrouded in dense clouds was exacting a heavy cost in reduced flying distances and excessive engine wear (high engine power settings were needed to clear the mountains), lighter weapons loads, and an unacceptable accident rate. Establishing a major base north of the mountains would with one stroke alter the air power calculus in the theater. After some hesitation on MacArthur's part, Wanigela was occupied by Allied air and ground forces in early October 1942 and was quickly built up as an important facility.

Because of the urgency of securing Wanigela, a maximum-effort airlift was organized to complement the movement of men and equipment by land and water. Once again Kenney demonstrated his flair for improvisation, drafting B-25 Mitchell attack aircraft into service to paradrop supplies, with considerable success. When it was discovered that some trucks would not fit into C-47 airlifters, Kenney had the chassis frames cut into halves with acetylene torches, stuffed into the aircraft, and welded together again after delivery. The most significant feature of the operation, though, was that Wanigela became a prototype for other advanced bases as Kenney pushed his air forces forward and on to the offensive. It is noteworthy, incidentally, that those bases relied on the Allied Air Forces for resupply for almost a year. Kenney had made maneuver via airlift an integral component of warfare in the SWPA.

The capture of Wanigela established an operational model. For any major action, Kenney's first objective was to achieve control of the air and also, therefore, its corollary in the SWPA, control of the sea. Once that was done, air (and, if applicable, naval) strikes would soften-up the target area, which almost invariably was one of Kenney's "isolated areas" or "true islands." Simultaneously, the enemy's supply lines, more often than not maritime, would be interdicted in order to isolate his garrison. Finally, during the amphibious/land assault phase, Kenney's air power would provide close attack, reconnaissance, resupply, and so on. The captured ground would then become the next airfield and the process would start again, as the Allies gradually moved northwards toward the Japanese home islands.

Sometimes geography and/or the relative lack of major targets led to variations in Kenney's model: for example, the softening-up bombardment phase might not be necessary. Or, better still, an entire enemy garrison might be bypassed. Because AAF fighters and strike aircraft dominated the theater's lines of communications, many enemy garrisons could not be resupplied, reinforced, or relieved, and Mac-Arthur saw little point in expending lives and resources by attacking strongholds that had become isolated. Consequently, huge numbers of Japanese forces in New Guinea, New Britain, New Ireland, and the Solomons were simply bypassed.[44] (This approach, incidentally, remains an intriguing doctrinal case study, and receives insufficient attention from contemporary army strategists.)

By pushing his forces forward and going on the offensive, Kenney had challenged the control of the air and sea that was the key to the Imperial Japanese Army's ability to maneuver and, therefore, to dominate the theater. By the end of 1942, captured Japanese documents despondently noted that the Allies were able to "fly above our position as if they own the sky"—a dramatic turnaround from the situation only a year before in the Philippines, Malaya, the Netherlands East Indies, and New Guinea.[45] Kenney was pleased but circumspect, welcoming 1943 with the observation that he and his command had learned a great deal in the preceding six months, and promising that the coming year would "be better."[46] In the event, it was to be much more than that.

CREATING CERTAINTY

The most brilliant strategic analysis is likely to fail if a commander does not have the right people to implement his plans, and if those people do not trust his leadership. Kenney was equally as assiduous in choosing his senior lieutenants and looking after his personnel as he was in attending to the politics of command and to strategy. The essence of his personnel management style was to create confidence and, therefore, certainty, for the thousands of men and women who relied on him.

Just as MacArthur had been unimpressed with Brett, so too was Kenney unimpressed with a number of his predecessor's senior staff. As he flew around the SWPA inspecting his new command he was constantly observing individuals and forming impressions: one officer might be assessed as "miscast" in his job; another as "not an operator"; another still as "active, intelligent, knows the theater, and has ideas about how to fight the Japs," and so on.[47] He dismissed five of his senior subordinates and left the others in no doubt that a new order was in place and that dramatic improvement was required.

His single most important personnel decision was to place his full trust in Brigadier General Whitehead. Kenney knew and respected Whitehead from previous associations at the ACTS and GHQ AF. Tough and uncompromising, the no-frills Whitehead thrived under Kenney's certain leadership and became an invaluable right-hand man as the campaign in the SWPA unfolded. "He had brains, leadership, loyalty, and likes to work," Kenney later wrote in a passage revealing of his command style. Other astute appointments included Brig. Gen. Kenneth N. Walker, an expert in bomber operations, and Brig. Gen. Donald Wilson, who became Kenney's chief of staff. Both Walker and Wilson, like Kenney and Whitehead, had served at the ACTS.

Initially Kenney worked closely with his senior staff on the detail of rebuilding the AAF and then deploying them aggressively against the enemy. As those efforts began to yield results, the span of operations broadened and command responsibilities changed. Kenney became increasingly concerned with strategic-level issues, which meant that Whitehead often assumed the responsibilities of the commander of a numbered air force, even of a theater air commander. It was an arrangement that suited the changing dynamics of the campaign, and that could not have prospered without the two-way confidence that Kenney's leadership style inspired.

That style had several non-negotiable components. Kenney demanded professional expertise, total dedication to the job at hand, and loyalty to the USAAF in general and to himself in particular. His emphasis on "loyalty," with its sense of constancy and fidelity, can be seen as an expression of Huntington's "responsibility" and of the implicit compact all service members have to perform their duties to the best of their ability. Details such as rank, reputation, past performance (including, on occasion, transgressions against the established order), and unconventional attitudes did not matter if Kenney believed an individual would perform his duties to the very best of his ability and was utterly committed to winning the war. An airman who demonstrated those qualities knew he would have his commander's full support.

Kenney's inclination to chance his arm on mavericks deserves comment, because it was a feature of his leadership. His "gadgeteer par excellence," for example, was an idiosyncratic former civilian pilot-come-engineer, Major Paul I. "Pappy" Gunn. It was Gunn who, with his "why not?" attitude, translated a number of Kenney's technical concepts into operational form. The same kind of trust was extended to the RAAF's Group Capt. W. H. "Bull" Garing, something of an eccentric who had a mixed reputation in his own service. Garing, however, had spent two years fighting the Germans in Europe with the RAF's Coastal Command and impressed Kenney with his intelligence, aggression, and "ideas about how to fight the Japs."[48] Garing had flown the length and breadth of New Guinea; indeed, he had drawn Kenney's attention to the potential of the Wanigela region as a forward base. Ignoring RAAF criticisms of Garing, Kenney "decided to keep my eye on him for future reference." Subsequent events were to prove it a shrewd assessment.

Intuition had also shaped Kenney's decision when, as commander of the Fourth Air Force in California in July 1942, he had decided not to court-martial a young fighter pilot, Lt. Richard I. Bong, for flying loops around San Francisco's Golden Gate Bridge. The reprieved Bong went on to become the leading USAAF ace in the SWPA with forty kills and a recipient of the Congressional Medal of Honor.

Attending to the welfare of the thousands of people for whom he was responsible was the other main ingredient of Kenney's approach to personnel management. The SWPA was a debilitating environment, with its isolation, primitive facilities, jungles, mountains, heat, humidity, and tropical disease. Dysentery and malaria were rife, and it was common for men to lose twenty pounds during a tour. Easing those conditions was one of Kenney's priorities. He built extra main-base hospitals, formed mobile hospitals, and improved the standard of living quarters. He also insisted on regular medical checks and the implementation of health education programs. Because personnel numbers were insufficient, he introduced frequent short-leave stays in Australia, where the men were encouraged to rest and eat healthily; simultaneously, he lobbied General Arnold for reinforcements.[49]

On one hand Kenney's self-confidence and his ability rapidly to assess personalities were usually major strengths. On the other hand, the same qualities could sometimes lead him into impetuous judgments. One such incident was extremely harmful to a prominent Australian commander.

When Kenney arrived in the SWPA in August 1942, Australian reserve force soldiers were fighting a desperate rear-guard action to save the city of Port Moresby, which was the key to holding New Guinea. If Port Moresby fell, Australia itself might be vulnerable to invasion. The fight seemed to be going badly. The Australians had been pushed back over most of the Owen Stanley ranges and the Japanese were only twenty-five miles from the city. Kenney was quick to question the Australians' fighting ability, reporting to MacArthur that he "had no faith in the Australians holding Kokoda Gap" (the vital pass across the Owen Stanleys).[50] He was especially critical of the Australian land force commander, Brig. Sydney

Rowell, whom he described as "defeatist." Yet unlike Kenney (or indeed any American officer), Rowell had already been fighting for two years (in Greece and Libya) and was highly regarded by his British contemporaries. Moreover, the situation in New Guinea was more complex than Kenney realized.

Rowell was well aware of the limitations of his reservists and had skillfully managed their fighting withdrawal along the Kokoda Trail, a maneuver that had gradually extended the enemy's supply lines to dangerous proportions. Rowell also knew that experienced Australian soldiers from North Africa were being rushed to New Guinea as reinforcements. Events were soon to prove Rowell right and Kenney wrong. The Japanese were stopped, they began to retreat back over the Owen Stanleys to the north coast of New Guinea, and the Australians' eventual victory became a turning point in the war in the Southwest Pacific. To add to Kenney's embarrassment, shortly afterward he learned that soldiers from the U.S. Army's Thirty-Second Division had been "avoiding action and [were] scared to death" of Japanese snipers and had abandoned their weapons as they "ran away in panic."[51]

All of this information was cold comfort for Rowell, however, who in the meantime had been relieved of his command, largely because of Kenney's peremptory appraisal. As the Australian official historian Douglas Gillison later wrote, "Perhaps it was typical of the ebullient, egocentric Kenney that he should make a snap judgment on a land-force situation for which he had no direct responsibility. Yet his ignorance of the nature of the battle . . . was lamentable in the commander responsible for air support." Kenney's criticism of Rowell was, Gillison concluded, "unjustified and ill-timed."[52]

Gillison's censure has been cited here not to denigrate Kenney but rather to remind us that even the great commanders do not get it right all the time. The very same qualities that enabled Kenney to assess events and people astutely could also, on occasions, draw him into injudicious judgments.

LOGISTICS AS AIR POWER

As noted previously, Kenney's colleague from the ACTS, Capt. Hugh Knerr, believed that logistics was the key to air power. Knerr's view may have been extreme, but he had a point. Kenney's firsthand involvement in all aspects of maintenance, engineering, resupply, and weapons performance was so important to his success as a commander in the SWPA that it warrants elaboration. In addition to his premilitary experience managing a variety of civil engineering projects, Kenney had been the army's liaison officer with the Curtiss aero-engineering company and chief of the Materiel Division's production engineering section. His knowledge of logistics was exceptional by any standards, let alone those of a senior pilot.

The logistics system Kenney inherited in the SWPA was, he observed, "appalling." Coordination was poor, the disposition of spares illogical, and the administration tortuous. It was common for weeks to elapse from the time a part was ordered from a depot in one location until it arrived at an operational base in another. More often than not, parts were never received; instead, requisitions were returned with the annotation "not available" or "form improperly filled out."[53]

Kenney intervened at both the macro and micro levels of management. At the macro level, he ordered all service units to move forward from their comfortable but remote rear-echelon locations. Some were sent to New Guinea, and others to Townsville in northern Australia, where No. 4 Aircraft Depot became one of the largest supply and maintenance centers in the Pacific theater.[54] For a time, while order was being restored, the depot was directed to work twenty-four hours a day, seven days a week. Low-performing officers were replaced; and a former vice president of the Douglas Aircraft Corporation, Lt. Col. Victor E. Bertrandias, was brought in as the depot's commander. The combination of Bertrandias's expertise and Kenney's understanding and flair generated a dramatic improvement in aircraft availability and quality.

At the micro level, Kenney instructed logistics officers to forget paperwork and to get the supply chain moving. Every task was to be treated as time-critical. He forbade engineers to raid damaged or unserviceable aircraft for spare parts; every bomber had to be rebuilt. He stopped all heavy bomber operations for a week while as many aircraft as possible were restored to full serviceability. At one stage, small bullet holes were patched with flattened tin cans. Specialist groups were formed to tackle complex one-off tasks: for example, on one occasion, a hand-picked technical crew was sent forward to Nadzab in New Guinea to expedite the modification of P-38 fighters for extra-long-range operations, a job that was completed "in record time."[55]

Aircraft allocation was another critical dimension of logistics management. General Arnold had informed Kenney that, although he had his full support, the Pacific campaign was secondary to the fighting in Europe, a strategic reality that would affect resources. Rather than wasting time and energy pestering Arnold for equipment he was unlikely to receive, Kenney made the best of the hand he had been dealt by identifying aircraft types that had not proven especially popular in Europe but that he believed would suit the Pacific.

Vast distances, the maritime nature of the theater, and a less-technologically advanced enemy were the keys. Thus, Kenney asked for, and was satisfied to receive, B-24 Liberator bombers, which, with their supercritical wing, had an exceptional range and endurance; and P-38 Lightning fighters, which also had an excellent range and which, unlike the P-40 Kittyhawks they replaced, were competitive in air-to-air combat against the previously all-conquering Zero. The same logic informed Kenney's willingness to take as many B-25 Mitchell and A-20 Havoc[56] light bombers as Arnold would give him—while both types might have been marginal in the land-attack role in Europe, Kenney was confident they would be effective in the anti-shipping role in the Pacific. The case of the A-20 was particularly instructive. Early production models were tricky to fly and technically unreliable, earning the aircraft the nickname "Widow Maker." Senior members of Kenney's staff wanted it scrapped. Kenney, however, believed the A-20 had potential and intervened to keep it in service.[57] Technical modifications were made, flight training programs were customized, and the Havoc became a very good light attack/bomber in the SWPA.

That kind of firsthand intervention into logistical problems was a distinctive feature of Kenney's command style. Three other noteworthy examples involved parafrag bombs, skip bombing, and "commerce destroyer" aircraft.

As noted previously, Kenney had developed the parafrag bomb in the 1920s when he was chief of the factory section at the Air Service Engineering School. If he had been hoping to deploy the weapon operationally, he could not have found a more suitable setting than the Pacific. Until the USAAF's strategic bombing offensive against Japan's cities began in late 1944, targets in the Pacific tended to be small and of relatively low value, such as fuel storage depots, cargo ships, parked aircraft, wharf facilities, and personnel. All were vulnerable to fragmentation weapons. The first batches of parafrags dropped operationally by Kenney's airmen were fitted with small warheads, consistent with the trials their commander had conducted at the engineering school years ago, but bomb damage assessment revealed that they were not causing enough damage. Kenney consequently ordered the manufacture of 300- and 500-pound parafrags, which were wrapped with heavy steel wire and fitted with an instantaneous fuse on the end of a six-inch pipe extension. When a bomb detonated just above the surface, the wire shattered into hundreds of pieces from six inches to two feet long, "cutting the limbs off trees [and, it was left unsaid, humans] a hundred feet away."[58] It was a terrifying and effective weapon.

Skip bombing also combined technical and tactical innovation and proved well suited to the maritime environment of the SWPA. Prewar air corps doctrine had envisaged antishipping strikes being conducted by formations of about nine aircraft that would attack from different altitudes. Kenney knew that the SWPA's unpredictable weather and frequent heavy cloud buildups made that a dubious proposition; furthermore, bombing accuracy from medium and high altitudes was poor. Accordingly he advocated very low-level strikes, down to mast-top height if necessary, even for multiengine bombers such as the B-17. The introduction of skip bombing was a result of this tactic.

Kenney's objective was to devise an antishipping flight profile that would mitigate the effects of weather, minimize his crews' exposure to anti-aircraft fire, and maximize accuracy. Pilots on a skip-bombing run would approach their target at high speed and very low level. About one hundred yards from the ship they would release a stick of two to four large bombs fitted with delay fuses. The bombs would skip across the water before (ideally) exploding against the ship's hull at the waterline, or sinking and detonating under the hull. Bombs that missed might still ricochet and explode above the deck. Whether or not the technique was original is moot; the point is that Kenney introduced it into the SWPA to considerable effect.[59]

Kenney was also the driving force behind the development of antishipping "commerce destroyers": heavily armed B-25 attack aircraft that complemented skip bombing. Modified by "Pappy" Gunn to carry eight .50-caliber machine guns, the commerce destroyers would sweep in low and fast, laying down withering fire that suppressed ships' anti-aircraft defenses, destroyed their superstructure, and killed their crews.

All AAF aircraft were subjected to Kenney's continual demand for greater range, regardless of their role, size, or type. Throughout the campaign in the SWPA he constantly urged his engineers and supporting industrial bases in Australia and the United States to develop bigger and better fuel drop tanks. Thus, the 110-gallon tank originally built for his P-39 and P-40 fighters was modified for use on the P-47 Thunderbolt when it eventually arrived in-theater; and a 200-gallon tank developed in Brisbane became standard equipment for a variety of aircraft types throughout the Pacific.[60]

In short, Kenney's approach to logistics management was characterized by personal expertise, firsthand involvement, a sensible acceptance of what was and was not possible, adroit personnel selection, innovation, and dynamic leadership. It was an approach that transformed logistics into a war-winning capability.

MASTER CLASSES: BISMARCK SEA AND LAE

Allied air power had been in disarray when General Kenney assumed command in the SWPA in August 1942. The mismanagement of USAAF heavy bomber operations typified the situation. Targets in New Guinea were selected by staff in Brisbane, who had little knowledge of the theater and were further handicapped by sketchy intelligence and poor communications. Raid details, such as they were, were sent to the bomb group, some 250 miles away but still on the Australian mainland. The group commander assembled however many crews and aircraft he could muster and sent them off to Port Moresby, another 750 miles away, for a final briefing. Mission plans rarely nominated a formation leader or applied the principle of concentration. On average only 30 percent of crews reached their targets. If they encountered enemy fighters they jettisoned their bombs and auxiliary fuel and abandoned the mission. Poststrike analysis was to all intents and purposes useless. The whole setup was, Kenney recorded, "chaotic."[61]

Yet only seven months later, in the Battle of the Bismarck Sea, Kenney led those same forces to one of the most comprehensive victories of World War II. Perhaps because the fighting in the Pacific was regarded as secondary to the war in Europe, and perhaps because (with some notable exceptions) air battles receive less scholarly and popular attention than land battles, the combat in the Bismarck Sea is not well known. That is regrettable, because it was not only decisive, but also a tour de force of leadership, planning, and execution. The battle and the subsequent assault on the vital enemy garrison at Lae are recounted in detail here to epitomize the hundreds of actions George Kenney commanded in the SWPA and to illustrate his war-fighting mastery.

The triumph of American naval air power at Coral Sea and Midway in May and June 1942 and Australian successes on land at Milne Bay and along the Kokoda Trail in August and September had halted Japan's march through New Guinea. Further Allied progress on the northeast coast at Buna-Gona and Sanananda between November 1942 and January 1943 had left the Japanese position significantly weakened. Intercepted radio messages indicated that an enemy convoy would sail from Rabaul in late February with reinforcements for Lae. This was likely to be Japan's last throw of the dice in New Guinea.

General Kenney immediately began preparing for a major assault on the convoy. He would rely on reconnaissance aircraft to detect the fleet, which initially would be attacked by long-range USAAF bombers operating from the Australian mainland and Port Moresby. Once the convoy was within range of the Allies' potent anti-shipping aircraft—USAAF B-25 Mitchells and Havocs, and RAAF Beaufighters—based in New Guinea, an all-out attack would be mounted from medium, low, and very low altitudes. In consultation with his senior commanders, Kenney envisaged large numbers of aircraft striking the convoy from different directions and altitudes, with precise timing. Knowing that inexperienced crews would find the task challenging, Kenney took the unusual measure of ordering a full-scale dress rehearsal.

Because Kenney expected the battle to take place in the Huon Gulf he selected Cape Ward Hunt, ninety miles to the southeast, as the strike force's rendezvous point. Each formation would have to overfly Cape Ward Hunt at precisely the right time if the desired degree of concentration and coordination above the enemy convoy were to be achieved. For the dress rehearsal, crews were briefed to rendezvous at Cape Rodney, ninety miles southeast of Port Moresby, and to carry out a simulated strike against a wrecked ship in Port Moresby harbor. Kenney and his senior commanders, the USAAF's General Whitehead and the RAAF's Group Captain Garing, observed the exercise from a nearby hill.

The dress rehearsal proved invaluable, as potentially disastrous mistakes were made—some aircraft arrived over the wreck twenty minutes late. Thorough debriefings were held and problems were resolved. During the waiting period, crews honed their bombing and gunnery skills.

Some sixty-four hundred Japanese troops embarked at Rabaul between February 23 and 27, 1943, and the convoy of eight merchant ships and eight destroyers sailed before midnight on the twenty-eighth, planning to arrive at Lae on March 3. Air cover was provided by about one hundred fighters flying out of Japanese bases in New Ireland, New Britain, and New Guinea.

Initially the enemy convoy was favored by poor weather, which hampered Allied reconnaissance. It was not until mid-morning on March 2 that USAAF

B-24 Liberators sighted the ships. General Kenney immediately launched eight B-17s, followed shortly afterward by twenty more. The B-17s attacked from an altitude of six thousand feet with 1,000-pound demolition (blast effect) bombs. Later in the day another strike was made by eleven B-17s whose crews claimed large numbers of hits and reported that vessels were "burning and exploding . . . smoking and burning amidships" and "left sinking." Up to three merchant ships may have been sunk.

By nightfall the enemy had reached the Vitiaz Strait, which meant that in the morning it would be in the Huon Gulf and within range of the entire AAF strike force. If the coordinated attack were to succeed, the precise location of the convoy had to be known at daybreak; consequently, throughout the night the convoy was tracked by an RAAF Catalina, which occasionally dropped bombs to keep the Japanese troops in a state of anxiety.

The moment General Kenney's crews had been waiting for came on the morning of March 3, 1943, when the Japanese convoy rounded the Huon Peninsula. For much of the time adverse weather had helped the enemy to avoid detection, but now clear conditions favored the Allies. More than ninety aircraft took off from Port Moresby and set heading for Cape Ward Hunt. By 9:30 a.m. the AAF formations had assembled, and by 10 a.m. the Battle of the Bismarck Sea had started.

The Allies attacked in three waves and from three levels, only seconds apart. First, thirteen USAAF Flying Fortresses bombed from medium altitude. In addition to the obvious objective of sinking ships, those attacks were intended to disperse the convoy by forcing vessels to break station to avoid being hit.

Second, thirteen RAAF Beaufighters struck the enemy from very low level, lining up on their targets as the bombs from the Flying Fortresses were exploding. With four cannons in its nose and six machine guns in its wings, the Beaufighter was the most heavily armed fighter in the world. The pilots' job was twofold—to suppress antiaircraft fire and to kill ships' captains and officers on their bridges.

The Beaufighters initially approached at five hundred feet in line astern formation. The pilots then dived to mast-level height, set full power on their engines, changed into line abreast formation, and approached their targets at 270 knots. It seems that some of the Japanese captains thought the Beaufighters were going to make a torpedo attack because they altered course to meet the Australians head-on, to present a smaller profile. Instead, they made themselves better targets for strafing. With a slight alteration of heading, the Beaufighters were now in a position to rake the ships from bow to stern, which they did, subjecting the enemy to a withering storm of cannon and machine gun fire. According to the subsequent official release, "Enemy crews were slain beside their guns, deck cargo burst into flame, superstructures toppled and burned."

With the convoy now dispersed and in disarray the third wave of attackers was able to concentrate on sinking ships. Thirteen USAAF B-25 Mitchells made a medium-level bombing strike while, simultaneously, a mast-level attack was made by twelve specially modified USAAF B-25C1 "commerce destroyers." The commerce destroyers were devastating, claiming seventeen direct hits. Close behind the Mitchells, Havocs added more firepower.

Following the coordinated onslaught, Beaufighters, Mitchells, and Havocs intermingled as they swept back and forth over the convoy, strafing and bombing. Within minutes of the opening shots, the battle had turned into a rout. At the end of the action, "ships were listing and sinking, their superstructure smashed and blazing, and great clouds of dense black smoke [rose] into a sky where aircraft circled and dived over the confusion they had wrought among what, less than an hour earlier, had been an impressively orderly convoy."[62]

Above the surface battle, twenty-eight USAAF P-38 Lightning fighters provided air defense for the strike force. In their combat with the Zeros, which were attempting to protect the convoy, three of the Lightnings were shot down, but in turn the American pilots claimed twenty kills. Apart from those three P-38s the only other AAF aircraft lost was a single B-17, shot down by a Zero.

With their armament expended the AAF aircraft returned to Port Moresby, but there was to be no respite for the enemy. Throughout the afternoon the attacks continued. Again, USAAF B-17s struck from medium level, this time in cooperation with USAAF Mitchells and RAAF Havocs flying at very low level. At least twenty direct hits were claimed against the by-now devastated convoy.

That was the last of the coordinated attacks. The battle had been won. For the loss of a handful of aircraft the Allied Air Forces had sunk twelve ships—all eight of the troop transports and four of the eight destroyers—and killed three thousand enemy soldiers. The brilliantly conceived and executed operation had smashed Japanese hopes of regaining the initiative in New Guinea and had eliminated any possibility Australia might be invaded. In Douglas MacArthur's words, the Battle of the Bismarck Sea was "the decisive aerial engagement" of the war in the Southwest Pacific.

But there was a "terrible yet essential finale" still to come. For several days after the battle, General Kenney sent his crews back to the Huon Gulf to strafe barges and rafts crowded with survivors. It was grim and bloody work, but as one pilot said, every enemy they prevented from getting ashore was one less for their army colleagues to face. And after fifteen months of Japanese brutality, the great immorality, it seemed, would have been to have ignored the rights of their soldiers. Japanese media never mentioned the battle, but in a macabre footnote, two weeks later, Tokyo announced that in future all Japanese soldiers were to be taught to swim.

The AAF's victory in the Bismarck Sea had isolated Japanese bases along New Guinea's northern coast, but the threat they posed still had to be neutralized before MacArthur's campaign could continue northward. The garrison at Lae was the key: if it were taken, the maritime passages to the north would be open. MacArthur decided to occupy Nadzab, twenty miles west of Lae, as a staging base for the assault. Nadzab's position astride the Markham Valley led directly to Lae, and would allow an occupying force to dominate land movement in the region. As part of the air-land assault, General Kenney mounted another textbook operation, only this time emphasizing aerial delivery.[63]

The paradrop into Nadzab was set for September 5, 1943. In the preceding week, Kenney's air forces conducted a series of strikes intended to destroy fuel supplies, interdict surface transport, negate the enemy's air and sea power, and weaken the garrison at Lae. Immediately before the paradrop, enemy airfields in the region were bombed and strafed by B-25s, A-20s, B-17s, and B-24s. Other aircraft laid a smokescreen to cover the paradrop. Ninety-six C-47s carrying seventeen hundred paratroops with their artillery and supplies then completed a near-perfect drop. The C-47s flew in three columns, each of which carried a battalion and had its own drop zone. Close-cover fighters flew 1,000 feet above the C-47s, more flew at 7,000 feet, and more still were staggered between 15,000 and 20,000 feet. Only 2 of the AAF's 302 aircraft were lost.

Once the paratroops were safely on the ground, five B-17s converted for supply dropping began orbiting Nadzab, on call to release their loads as required. They remained overhead for most of the day. General MacArthur observed the operation from another B-17 with barely contained excitement. Lae fell to the Allies eleven days later.

The Battle of the Bismarck Sea and the assault on Nadzab-Lae were exemplary applications of the principles of war. All of the tenets that should guide military operations were evident, from selection and maintenance of the aim through to concentration of force, surprise, offensive action, flexibility, maneuver (airlift), unity of command, and high morale. General Kenney had provided a masterful demonstration of air command in war.

POSTSCRIPT

By mid-1943, just a year after taking command, General Kenney had established an operational model that to all intents and purposes remained intact for the rest of the war. As MacArthur pushed northwards toward the Philippines and Japan, the pattern of reconnaissance, control of the air, strike, interdiction, close attack, and maneuver was repeated through such places as Hollandia, Aitape, Biak, and Morotai. Ever-increasing Allied air dominance was complemented by larger allocations of more capable aircraft, which in turn facilitated more effective operations. Of particular note were the massive (for the theater) B-24 strikes against the oil refineries at Balikpapan in Borneo, one of the few genuinely strategic targets in the theater.

In mid-1944, Kenney was appointed commander of the U.S. Far East Air Forces (FEAF), which essentially comprised the USAAF's Fifth and Thirteenth Air Forces. Kenney remained head of the AAF, through which he commanded operational RAAF units and other allocated Allied air forces (primarily from the Netherlands East Indies and New Zealand). The new arrangement had two notable features. First, by formally separating the USAAF and the Allied Air Forces, MacArthur (and Kenney) had made it organizationally easier to take American units forward on the drive north, and to leave the Allies behind. And second, in an attempt to encourage his senior FEAF commanders to fully exploit the innate flexibility of air power, Kenney relaxed conventional organizational boundaries. Although all air units were still allocated to specific geographic areas, in practice they were authorized to cross nominal boundaries at their commander's discretion and with the concurrence of the relevant area commander. Kenney urged his senior leaders to take full advantage of the concept, and showed his trust in their judgment by simply requiring them to keep him informed of their decisions, and to talk regularly amongst themselves.[64]

MacArthur honored his celebrated pledge to return to the Philippines during the Battle of Leyte, from October to December 1944. A noteworthy aspect of the fighting there, incidentally, was the extensive use by the Japanese of kamikaze air attacks, a sign of an air force that had, in effect, given up (an organization that accepts suicide as a routine mission is not only depraved but also cannot regenerate itself). By then the nature of the air war in the Pacific and Kenney's role in it had changed. Because the Allies had captured islands (and airfields) within range of Japan, the focus of the air campaign shifted away from Kenney's "airfield hopping" strategy and its associated operational model and toward strategic bombing, B-29 Superfortresses, and their commander, Gen. Curtis E. LeMay.

Following victory in Europe in May 1945, the Allies turned their full attention to the war in the Pacific. Kenney's magnificent performance had been recognized by his promotion to full (four-star) general in March. Simultaneously, the U.S. Joint Chiefs appointed him commander of all USAAF in the Pacific, with the exception of the B-29s of the Strategic Air Forces, which they continued to control themselves. In the event, the strategic bombing campaign that culminated in the atomic attacks against Hiroshima and Nagasaki on August 6 and 9 meant that Kenney had little opportunity to do anything of note before Japan announced its surrender on August 15. Kenney's mission in the SWPA was finished.

World War II may have been won, but the USAAF still faced the challenge of gaining its independence from the army. The hero of the liberation of Europe and chief of staff of the army, Gen. Dwight D. Eisenhower, supported air force autonomy, but only if the new organization included a strong tactical air command, which would exist primarily to cooperate with land-force operations, and which consequently would emphasize close attack and airlift missions.[65] The USAAF's senior commanders, led by "Hap" Arnold, accepted Eisenhower's condition. Their private agenda, though, was to promote the primacy of strategic bombing, which they believed would be the decisive factor in future warfare and which they regarded as their doctrinal raison d'être.

American air power gained its independence with the formation of the U.S. Air Force in 1947, and George Kenney was acknowledged as one of the new service's outstanding commanders when he was appointed to lead Strategic Air Command (SAC). As the world's only nuclear-armed force, SAC was the ultimate deterrent and symbolized four decades of air power doctrine. It should have been an ideal post for Kenney.

For perhaps the first time in his career, however, Kenney lost sight of his priorities. Given the circumstances under which the USAF had been formed and SAC's symbolism, Kenney's sole objective should have been to ensure that his command became as strong and effective as possible, as soon as possible. Instead, he remained deeply involved in inter-service politics, constantly traveling to give speeches on the allegedly decisive capabilities of strategic air power.[66] To make things worse, some of his public statements were unnecessarily inflammatory: for example, his assertion that aircraft carriers were obsolete was inconsistent with the experience of World War II.[67] It was also politically careless and personally damaging. His attention was further diverted by a brief appointment as military adviser to the newly formed United Nations Organization.

Kenney's frequent absences from SAC led to a remote management style that contrasted starkly with the intense personal engagement that had defined his leadership in the SWPA. Too many important decisions were left to deputies who lacked Kenney's understanding of air power, and SAC's efficiency, energy, and morale rapidly declined.[68] The USAF's first chief of staff, General Spaatz, tried to refocus his friend's attention, but Kenney continued to devote himself to other matters at the expense of his command.

Spaatz's successor, Gen. Hoyt S. Vandenberg, was approached by a number of senior officers who had become concerned by SAC's parlous state. Vandenberg appointed the legendary aviator Charles Lindbergh to inspect the command, and when Lindbergh presented a damning report, Vandenberg had no option other than to replace Kenney. The unrivaled airman of World War II had committed one of the cardinal sins of command by confusing his priorities. It must be stressed that in no way did this reversal of fortune diminish Kenney's achievements in the SWPA, nor should it diminish his status as a great captain. It does, however, serve to emphasize the importance of politics in command, and of understanding priorities.

Kenney was reassigned as commander of the Air University at Maxwell Air Force Base, an appointment with a certain amount of prestige, but one far removed from the centers of power and often regarded as a sinecure for senior officers who have run their race. Kenney used his time at Maxwell constructively, among other things writing his memoir of the war in the Southwest Pacific, a book that is one of the very best histories of the campaign, and one of the very best wartime accounts ever written by a senior officer. After retiring in 1951 he continued writing (including biographies of "Pappy" Gunn and Dick Bong) and contributing to military affairs.

George Kenney died in Florida in 1977 and is buried at the Arlington National Cemetery. Douglas MacArthur had already provided a fitting valedictory: "Of all the air commanders in the war, none surpassed him in those three great essentials of successful combat leadership: aggressive vision, mastery over air tactics and strategy, and the ability to exact the maximum in fighting qualities from both men and equipment."[69]

CONCLUSION

A number of great air commanders emerged during World War II but few, if any, matched George Kenney's remarkably eclectic range of skills, and none dominated his theater of operations to the same extent. Kenney's professional mastery—defined by his ability to create certainty, an acute understanding of the strategic environment, loyalty, an unsentimental (but proper) observance of Realpolitik, and a profound knowledge of every element of air power—was, quite simply, unique. Gen. George Kenney was more than just a practitioner of air power: he was an air commander in the full sense of the term.

3

OTTO P. WEYLAND: "BEST DAMN GENERAL IN THE AIR CORPS"

RICHARD R. MULLER

In 1949, an ailing Gen. Henry H. "Hap" Arnold, who had commanded the United States Army Air Forces (USAAF) throughout World War II, published a memoir titled *Global Mission*. In it, he liberally distributed honors to the victors in the recent war. He singled out Maj. Gen. Otto P. "Opie" Weyland of XIX Tactical Air Command (TAC), which supported Gen. George S. Patton's Third Army from August 1944 to May 1945, as the exemplar for all successful USAAF tactical air operations: "To General Weyland [Patton] turned over the task of taking care of his south flank, completely and entirely—certain proof of the confidence Patton had in his air support."[1] Arnold might well have selected Lt. Gen. Elwood "Pete" Quesada, the innovative commander of IX TAC, or Lt. Gen. John K. "Joe" Cannon, who did yeoman service with Twelfth Air Force in the Mediterranean and southern France—both worthy candidates. What was it about Weyland that made Arnold hold him up as the ideal? What led the exacting Patton to proclaim him the "best damn General in the Air Corps"?[2]

THE MAKING OF AN AIRMAN

Otto Paul Weyland was born a child of immigrants in Riverside, California, on January 27, 1903.[3] His father was a German musician who was the bandmaster on an ocean liner. Fearing conscription, the elder Weyland jumped ship when it was docked in New York. He traveled the country and ended up in California, where he met and married Opie's mother, a woman of English extraction. The family moved to Texas in 1909, where Weyland's father abandoned music for farming.

Otto attended Texas A&M University, graduating in 1923 with a degree in mechanical engineering.

That same year, Weyland began his flying career. By his own account, he had a strong desire to fly but was ambivalent about a military career, which in his view brought with it "too much red tape." As a newly minted engineer, Weyland thought he could get the best of both worlds. He could pursue a day job with Western Electric in Chicago while playing "the flying game" as a reservist. After a four-month flying course at Brooks Field, Texas, he earned his wings. Back in Chicago, he continued to indulge his aviation passion on weekends at Chanute Field. By then it had dawned on him that industry had as much red tape as the military, if not more. He left Western Electric and passed his examination for a regular commission in the U.S. Army Air Service in June 1924. Further training opportunities followed at Brooks, Kelly Field (where one of his classmates was Charles Lindbergh), and Fort Sam Houston. Weyland briefly considered attending the air service's engineering school at McCook Field, Ohio, but his tactical work with the army at Fort Sam Houston captured his interest. He noted decades later that this choice was fortuitous: most McCook graduates of that era remained in the Materiel Command and were denied the chance to serve in the combat zones.[4]

The U.S. Army's Second Division was stationed at "Fort Sam," and Weyland was assigned to the attached Twelfth Observation Squadron, flying de Havilland DH-4s. He found that his fellow pilots (mostly World War I veterans senior to him) were more interested in flying than in observation and were willing to let Weyland shoulder the army cooperation work. He seized the opportunity to hone his craft, attending ground force planning sessions and debriefings, mastering map reading, becoming informed about logistics and supply problems, and experimenting with air-to-ground radio communications. As he put it, he "learned a hell of a lot about the ground forces. . . . I got to know the ground forces backwards and forwards. I learned to determine how long a division would be, or what an artillery battery looked like on the road, or when they were allegedly concealed and in firing position. I would adjust the artillery for them from the air."[5] Weyland's strong identification with aerial reconnaissance endured to the end of his career. Even as a general officer, he continued to fly occasional wartime reconnaissance missions until his high security clearance required that he be grounded.[6] This early exposure to the army was the beginning of a lifetime in tactical aviation.

Following a four-year stint at Kelly Field as an instructor, Weyland commanded the Fourth Observation Squadron at Luke Field, Hawaii, flying Thomas-Morse O-19 biplanes. The presence of an army division, coast artillery batteries, and pursuit and bombardment squadrons enabled Weyland to continue gaining experience working with air and ground units. While in Hawaii, he met and married Kathryn McFarland, known as "Tinker." His Hawaiian sojourn was followed by a return to Kelly Field, selection as chief of the observation section, and promotion to captain in November 1935.

From 1937 to 1938, Weyland attended the Air Corps Tactical School (ACTS) at Maxwell Field, Alabama. Originally created simply as a branch school for aviators seeking to attend Command and General Staff School (CGSS) at Fort Leavenworth, Kansas, ACTS earned the reputation as the crucible of strategic bombing theory in the air corps. By the time Captain Weyland entered its doors, the climate of intense air power evangelism had abated somewhat. With the basic principles of high-altitude precision daylight bombing well established at the school, research efforts and seminar discussions focused on fleshing out the mature theory with tactical "map problem" exercises and detailed target set analysis.[7]

Weyland certainly came into contact with key members of the school's "bomber mafia." Haywood Hansell, Lawrence Kuter, and Harold George were leading members of the faculty at the time, as was Weyland's future boss Hoyt S. Vandenberg, who headed the pursuit section.[8] Weyland respected the intellectual firepower of the bomber mafia (he noted "there were some pretty damn smart boys over there"), but he did not fully imbibe the strategic bombing theory. He accepted the basic principles of air power as a powerful contributor to victory in war but was not overly enamored of doctrinal prescriptions. This stance did not prevent him from graduating at the top of his ACTS class. He attributed his success to two factors. On air power issues, he always provided the faculty with the approved "school solution," while noting parenthetically that he would not necessarily do things that way. And his detailed knowledge of army ground forces enabled him to excel at the more land-centric portions of the program, including the attack and observation aviation courses.

Weyland's ACTS student paper, completed in May 1938, had the innocuous title "Training Program for Observation Aviation."[9] In it, he examined the training programs involving aerial reconnaissance that the various army branch schools offered and found them wanting. He attributed this outcome to "a general tending [*sic*] in the Air Corps to ignore ground troops and observation aviation." He applauded the recent redesignation of observation units as "reconnaissance," because the former term, with its passive connotations, had become a stigma. Weyland called for more extensive and realistic theoretical and practical training throughout the army and air corps. Though some of Weyland's recommendations did not stand the test of time (for example, he asserted that tethered observation balloons still had a major role to play in future war), it is hard to argue with his overall conclusion: the objective of all such training was to inculcate "mutual understanding and respect," which in turn would "result in the greatest tactical efficiency in the minimum amount of time."[10]

From his successful year at ACTS, Weyland went straight on to CGSS at Fort Leavenworth. Again, his mastery of the principles of ground warfare stood him in good stead. In fact, he noticed that Maxwell and Leavenworth used many of the same exercises. He knew the school was supposed to be tough, "but it held no terror" for him. "No one in my class committed suicide," he wryly noted.[11] After graduation in June 1939 he reported to the National Guard Bureau in Washington, D.C., as assistant chief of the Aviation Division. He recalled his time at the Guard Bureau as not terribly demanding and with plenty of opportunities to fly out of nearby Bolling Field. The war in Europe began shortly after he arrived at the bureau. Though he spent nearly two and a half years in the nation's capital, he knew the United States would eventually be drawn into the war, and "smart, young Weyland didn't want to be in Washington if a war started."[12] He worked a transfer to the Panama Canal Zone as commander of the Sixteenth Pursuit Group and chief of staff of Sixth Air Force. There, Weyland assisted with the development of an integrated air defense plan for the canal zone and oversaw the group's conversion from P-36s to P-40s; this transition was almost complete at the time of Pearl Harbor. In the wake of the Japanese attack, Weyland drew the ire of the security-conscious military district commander as he kept the lights burning in his hangars so his crews could work around the clock to ready the new planes for combat.

After the likelihood of an Axis attack on the canal zone receded, Weyland returned to Washington and an assignment to the newly reorganized Air Staff for the Operational Commitments and Requirements Branch. The massive buildup of the U.S. Army Air Forces was in full swing, and Weyland—by then a colonel—threw himself into what he termed the "numbers racket." He became "one of Arnold's favorite whipping boys," as the impatient USAAF chief was constantly buzzing him with questions about the location and allocation of newly manufactured aircraft. This assignment afforded Weyland the opportunity to observe—albeit at a distance—the activities of one of Arnold's rising stars, George C. Kenney of the Fifth Air Force in the southwest Pacific. Kenney was constantly demanding more assets for his operations in support of Gen. Douglas MacArthur. In particular, Kenney attempted to divert P-47s already earmarked for Europe to his own command. Weyland admired his ingenuity but concluded Kenney was "not living within his means."[13] Arnold was impressed by Weyland, even though their relationship was turbulent at times; Weyland reported that Arnold was once so displeased with him that he threw an inkwell at him. In September 1943, Weyland pinned on his brigadier general's stars, and two months later he finally departed for the European theater of operations (ETO) as commander of the Eighty-Fourth Fighter Wing. His star was about to ascend.

PREPARATION FOR COMBAT

When Weyland arrived in the ETO, years of combat experience and successful completion of a steep learning curve within both the Royal Air Force (RAF) and the USAAF had significantly redressed earlier shortcomings in Allied tactical aviation. At the war's outset, both Allied air arms had emphasized strategic bombardment to the detriment of developing workable procedures to support ground forces, particularly armored or mechanized forces operating in a fluid environment. British air and ground commanders in the Western Desert from 1941 on developed new practices and techniques, including colocating army and air force headquarters and establishing mutually acceptable liaison procedures between air and ground units. By November 1942, when the USAAF arrived in strength in the Mediterranean theater, corresponding doctrinal developments were already under way. These doctrinal improvements, coupled with the swift assimilation of lessons gleaned from the RAF, enabled the USAAF to institute more effective practices fairly rapidly. An update of Field Manual (FM) 31-35, *Aviation in Support of Ground Forces*, in April 1942 had at least partially addressed a yawning gap in USAAF theory and practice. The manual codified the need to centralize all aviation forces (with the exception of organic light aviation) under an air commander while also recognizing the need to lay out procedures for effective air-ground cooperation in the battle area.[14]

To be sure, the USAAF suffered in its early efforts to gain air superiority and provide tactical support during the battles for Tunisia in 1942–1943. This failure was more a function of inadequate training and lack of experience than of any inherent shortcomings in FM 31-35. Still, perceived dissatisfaction with the manual was part of the impetus for the War Department's drafting of FM 100-20, *Command and Employment of Air Power*, which appeared in July 1943. As well as boldly asserting the "co-equal and interdependent" nature of air and ground forces, FM 100-20 noted that the necessary concentration of an "air striking force" was only possible through centralized command and control.[15] The manual stated that air forces consisted of separate strategic and tactical components. The tactical air forces were to conduct three missions in a rigid priority order: achieve air superiority, isolate the battlefield (interdiction), and carry out direct support missions in the zone of contact (close air support). Direct support missions were "the most difficult to control, are most expensive, and are, in general, least effective."

Despite some hope in the USAAF that FM 100-20 might supersede FM 31-35, both manuals remained in force throughout the war, as FM 100-20 lacked the specific procedures contained in the earlier publication. Doctrinal debates aside, the formal guidance clearly proved practical and flexible enough in the hands of such commanders as Weyland to bring about success on the battlefield.

Weyland would inherit a system that was battle tested and join an organization poised to put earlier hard-won lessons into practice. The Ninth Air Force transferred from the Mediterranean to England on October 16, 1943. Its purpose was simple: "to serve as the American Tactical Air Force which would cooperate with the ground forces in the Allied invasion of Europe."[16] The Ninth was under the command of Lt. Gen. Lewis H. Brereton; Lieutenant General Vandenberg replaced him in August 1944, at about the same time XIX TAC went into battle. On June 1, 1944, Ninth Air Force flying units consisted of IX Troop Carrier Command, IX Bomber Command (operating mainly medium bombers), and IX Fighter Command. Under IX Fighter Command were two TACs: IX TAC and XIX TAC. These groups had originally been designated "Air Support Commands" but were renamed "TACs" to avoid the subordinate connotations of "support." The IX TAC would provide tactical air power to the First Army under Lt. Gen. Omar Bradley, while XIX TAC would operate alongside Patton's Third Army when it became operational in August 1944.

The Ninth also had a full complement of engineering and support units. One of Brereton's operating principles was "Keep mobile."[17] Weyland would benefit from the work of IX Engineer Command, especially in the realm of airfield selection and construction. Theirs was not an easy lot. Often the engineers would barely have gotten a base up and running, with pierced steel planking in place, before Patton's rapid advance would outrun the useful range of fighter-bombers operating from the newly constructed airfield. Yet as the XIX TAC war diarist noted at the end of the campaign, "The success of Engineering construction may be summed up with this statement: Over a period of 9 months no more than 20 planes were lost because of runway or taxiway difficulties and very few missions were cancelled owing to temporary failure of runways."[18]

The Ninth Air Force and its attached TACs functioned as streamlined organizations while providing air support to the Allied lodgment, but they were part of a larger air organization that bore the marks of inter-Allied and interservice rivalry. All Allied forces in Europe were under the command of Supreme Headquarters Allied Expeditionary Force (SHAEF), which was headed by Gen. Dwight D. Eisenhower. Eisenhower's deputy was Air Chief Marshal Sir Arthur Tedder, a brilliant tactical airman in his own right. Allied tactical air forces—the U.S. Ninth and the British Second Tactical Air Force (2 TAF)—were beneath another layer of command, Air Chief Marshal Sir Trafford Leigh-Mallory's Allied Expeditionary Air Forces (AEAF). RAF Bomber Command, led by Air Chief Marshal Arthur Harris, and the United States Strategic Air Forces in Europe, commanded by Gen. Carl A. Spaatz, reported directly to Eisenhower. Both strategic forces were sometimes reluctant partners in the pre-Overlord preparations, as both preferred to attack strategic targets deep inside Germany. To complicate matters further, Spaatz also exercised administrative control of the Ninth. In practice, however, the convoluted command arrangements at the top seem to have had little impact on Ninth Air Force operations. Weyland's boss was undeniably Vandenberg, but his close (coordinating) relationship with Third Army led many to assume (erroneously) that he worked for Patton. That this arrangement rubbed along free of strife was a tribute to all concerned.

The air war in Europe took a decisive turn in the spring of 1944. The USAAF strategic air forces had achieved air superiority over the continent after a bruising, years-long battle of air attrition over the Reich. A punishing campaign against German synthetic oil production by both the USAAF and RAF Bomber Command that began in May 1944 crippled both the Luftwaffe's remaining front line and its ability to train new pilots. Both strategic and tactical air forces conducted wide-ranging interdiction campaigns, softening up the continent for the cross-Channel assault.

The Ninth Air Force played its part in this effort. In the months prior to D-Day, the fighter groups assigned to XIX TAC learned their craft, participating in bomber escort missions, air superiority combat, armed reconnaissance, interdiction strikes, and strafing runs from their bases in England. Weyland took over IX Fighter Command from Quesada when the latter went to France after D-Day. His job was to move the fighter groups to the continent as soon as bases were ready to house them. The IX Fighter Command, never much more than a thin layer of administration between the Ninth Air Force and the TACs, was essentially deactivated when Weyland himself relocated to France in late July.

PATTON AND WEYLAND: A BEAUTIFUL FRIENDSHIP

Shortly after being named commander of XIX TAC, Weyland met Patton for the first time. Without a doubt Patton was the most storied and controversial character on the Allied side in the ETO. In the fullness of time a consensus has emerged: Patton was the outstanding American battlefield commander of the war. Part of Patton's genius was his ability to get the most out of his assets, and XIX TAC would loom large as one of those key assets. He possessed extensive war experience, which Weyland lacked. Some thought Patton would simply steamroller his airman.[19] Weyland certainly knew it would not be an easy assignment; he recalled, "Nobody was just real anxious to do it."[20]

The forging of the Patton-Weyland partnership invites contrast to that between Douglas MacArthur and his supporting airman, George Kenney. On the surface, there were certain similarities. In both cases, a flamboyant and controversial ground commander who felt ill served by tactical aviation earlier in the war was suddenly paired with a junior air commander who was confident in his own credentials as a tactical airman. The stage was set for confrontation, yet from all accounts the Patton-Weyland teamwork functioned smoothly and without drama from the beginning. Patton, though his experiences with Air Marshal Arthur "Maori" Coningham in Tunisia still rankled, appreciated the value of tactical air power from his time in the Mediterranean and was an enthusiastic amateur pilot.[21] And Weyland was no pugnacious Kenney. Seventeen years younger than Patton, the airman was deferential and did not respond to Patton's bluster.[22] He built up confidence by touring Third Army units with a presentation on the value of tactical air support, summarizing the experience in North Africa and Italy, and reassuring the ground forces that the Ninth Air Force had a well-established air support system in place.

The closest thing to a confrontation between the two men came during one of Patton's visits to a fighter-bomber group. At the end of the mission briefing the pilots "hacked" (synchronized) their watches. Patton suspected that all of this emphasis on precise timing indicated a snow job and confronted Weyland after the briefing. Weyland set him straight, quietly but firmly explaining the difference between a 30-mile-per-hour road march and a 400-mile-per-hour air mission— "and there are no maps to read." Patton silently watched the fighters start up, take off, assemble over the field, and set out on their mission, timed to the second. Finally he spoke, "Well, I'll be goddamned."[23] Patton never challenged Weyland again. Early in the campaign, the two men cemented their friendship over a bottle of bourbon.[24]

Weyland was justifiably confident in the capabilities of XIX TAC on the eve of battle. At any one time, his force contained anywhere from three to nine fighter-bomber groups. The paper strength of the command was misleading, for groups were transferred between it and IX TAC with regularity as the tactical situation demanded. At the end of the war in Europe, for example, XIX TAC contained one P-51 group (the 354th, the "Pioneer Mustangs") and six P-47 groups (the 48th, 362nd, 367th, 368th, 371st, and 405th) for a total of 476 fighter-bombers.[25] Other flying units included the 10th Reconnaissance Group and 425th Night Fighter Squadron. XIX TAC had a robust signals organization (including aircraft warning and tactical air control units), an intelligence branch, and a liaison branch with the service commands of the Ninth Air Force. Weyland noted almost from the outset that the number of air liaison officers was inadequate and increased them accordingly; such modifications and improvements would continue throughout the campaign.

The heart of XIX TAC's striking power was its Republic P-47 Thunderbolt fighter-bomber. This powerful and rugged radial-engine fighter could carry a ton of bombs, although two 500-pound bombs was the normal load for supporting armored advances in open country. It was augmented by the P-51 Mustang, a better air superiority fighter but with a more vulnerable liquid-cooled engine.

In addition to carrying bombs and .50-caliber machine guns, XIX TAC fighter-bombers often dropped napalm.* Weyland once noted with satisfaction that "20,000 gal[lons] German gas to be returned to Germans in form of Napalm."[26] Some of the P-47s were equipped with unguided rockets as well. In October 1944, the first P-61 Black Widow night fighters were assigned to XIX TAC, eventually equipping a single squadron.[27] These aircraft found little employment in their intended role—engaging German night harassment aircraft—and were instead used for armed reconnaissance and night intruder operations.[28]

A vitally important, if unsung, component of Weyland's air force was the reconnaissance arm, usually abbreviated "recce." The North American F-6, which was the recce version of the P-51, and the F-5, which was a modified P-38 Lightning with camera equipment replacing the nose guns, carried out daylight tactical reconnaissance. A version of the A-20 Havoc medium bomber was the primary nighttime photoreconnaissance platform.

Weyland arrived on the continent in late July and established his prospective headquarters near Patton's Third Army command post. When the Third Army was activated on August 1, XIX TAC formally came to life as well. By that time the D-Day landings in Normandy had succeeded, the bridgehead had been consolidated and expanded, and the lengthy and frustrating fight in the bocage country was almost at an end. Operation Cobra at St. Lô, preceded by a mass carpet bombing of the German lines, had succeeded brilliantly and the long-awaited breakout was about to begin. The Third Army took up its positions and was poised to launch one of the most remarkable mobile campaigns in modern military history.

"TWELVE THOUSAND FIGHTER-BOMBER SORTIES": XIX TAC IS UNLEASHED

Weyland and XIX TAC fought alongside Patton's Third Army without a pause for nine months and eight days, from August 1944 to the final collapse of the Third Reich in May 1945. During those months the operations were remarkably diverse, with periods of breakneck armored advances followed by frustrating positional warfare. Weather, terrain, fortifications, logistical difficulties, and enemy countermoves all shaped the campaign. Such operations demanded maximum flexibility

---

* A jellied mix of gasoline and naphthenic and palmitic acids; hence, it was often described in contemporary documents as NaPalm.

and resourcefulness from soldiers and airmen alike. The following account tracks the organization as put forth in various XIX TAC internal histories, operational narratives, and after-action reports (some of which were written within weeks of the events described). These histories divide the operations of XIX TAC and the Third Army in France, ending in Lorraine; then the Ardennes; and the final drive into Germany into nine distinct phases: the first phase, the "end run across France" in August and September 1944, was in many ways the most dramatic.[29] The XIX TAC and Third Army fought in three directions—west, south, and east. The XIX TAC's own reports spoke of "operations on fronts 350 miles apart . . . which proved entirely practical because of the flexibility and range of air power."[30] In mid-August units of the Third Army and XIX TAC were operating simultaneously at Brest far to the west, in central France north of the Loire, and in the battle of the Falaise pocket. In the confident words of the XIX TAC operations summary,

> The Third Army-XIX TAC team burst out of Normandy [at Avranches] and into Brittany, conquered all of that peninsula except three stubborn ports, and swept 140 miles past liberated Paris to within 60 miles of the German border. During most of September, General Patton's spearheads continued prodding the Nazi remnants toward the Fatherland at a pace which was literally a run in many cases, because of the immense quantities of motor transport and rolling stock knocked out by the air.[31]

This campaign was the defining moment for XIX TAC and earned the command its most enduring laurels for the almost unprecedented use of air power to cover Patton's open flank to the south and for its role in compelling the surrender of 20,000 German troops. At the same time, its efforts to reduce the fortress of Brest revealed the limits of tactical air power in 1944.

On August 1, XIX TAC kicked off its war by sending three P-47 groups into action. Two P-51 groups joined them the following day, and the groups flew armored column cover and armed recce for Patton's advancing spearheads. In what Weyland's war diarists termed "Blitz warfare—US Style," the command flew 1,088 sorties in its first five days.[32] The XIX TAC history noted, "XIX TAC would find its targets in the field, would plan as it flew."[33]

Even while the drive into Brittany was unfolding, part of the Third Army was driving east and south toward the Loire. Patton's right flank was thinly held, and he turned the security of that flank entirely over to XIX TAC.[34] "Never in military history had a ground commander entrusted the defense of his flank to tactical aircraft," observed the XIX TAC scribe.[35] It was a daring move but not a rash one. Patton needed only a few days of combat to come to trust Weyland implicitly, and his Ultra intelligence officer was able to assure him that the German forces on the flank, though numerically large, were in poor condition and posed little real danger.[36]

To support its expanding roster of duties, on August 7 XIX TAC's strength was increased to nine fighter-bomber groups: 36th, 358th, 362nd, 371st, 373rd, 405th, 406th (P-47s), 354th, and 363rd (P-51s). These fighter-bombers flew armored column cover, "long route" and area reconnaissance over the Loire flank, and close air support. During the August–September advance, Weyland's headquarters could not keep up with Patton's forces. The solution was to create a small advanced XIX TAC echelon, and Weyland flew up every other day in a spotter plane for personal conferences with Patton and his staff.[37]

Even as the Third Army besieged the Brittany ports and drove eastward, the German army, on Hitler's personal order, launched a desperate counterattack designed to cut through the Allied breakthrough area at its narrowest point. Ultra betrayed Hitler's direct order to Field Marshal Günther von Kluge, the commander in chief in the west, on August 6. The objective was to reach the sea at Avranches.[38] Informed of the plan at the Third Army's Ultra intelligence briefing, Weyland contacted his counterpart Quesada at IX TAC to the north. In his diary, he noted, "German counterattack. XIX TAC can divert fighter-bombers to threatened area anytime—will coordinate between two TACs."[39] The XIX TAC engaged the Luftwaffe over the battle area and flew extensive fighter-bomber missions (August 9 was the most active day for the command thus far, with 780 sorties). Much of the effort was over the Mortain-Falaise-Argentan battlefield as the German offensive was first stopped in its tracks, then encircled. Though many German forces ultimately escaped that poorly executed encirclement, the Ninth Air Force and 2 TAF still wrought bloody execution in the Falaise pocket.

At times, XIX TAC received requests for emergency support from the First Army to the north. In these missions, XIX TAC racked up a substantial toll of German motor vehicles, rolling stock, and even horse-drawn transport and individual cyclists. Desperate Germans who had been listening in on U.S. tactical communications attempted to radio misleading messages to the fighter-bombers.

In one instance a pilot, detecting a slight Teutonic accent, demanded that the speaker sing "Mairzy Doats." "The Heinie could not make the grade," TAC's history reports.[40] On August 18 a XIX TAC recce mission spotted two massive concentrations of more than 1,000 German vehicles "bumper to bumper" in the areas of Argentan-Trun and Falaise. To their frustration, XIX TAC "missed the big jackpot," as most of this lucrative target was in the area assigned to 2 TAF.[41]

With the Falaise battle winding down, XIX TAC shifted its attention to the Seine River crossings in an effort to interdict barge and ferry traffic as the remnants of the German Seventh Army streamed eastward. The command also focused on what was left of the German air force in France. In August 1944 the Luftwaffe in the west was hard pressed. The Luftwaffe command had planned to meet the invasion in France with the combat units of Luftflotte (Air Fleet) 3—bomber, ground attack, and fighter units. In the days following a landing the Luftwaffe planned to send massive reinforcements by staging fighter units assigned to the Reich defense organization into the front lines. The Luftwaffe command succeeded in getting a large number of fighter aircraft into the invasion zone in the days following the landing and would continue to reinforce them in the following weeks.

Yet this force could accomplish little in the face of crushing Allied air superiority. German fighter pilots were hastily trained in ground attack procedures and bomb racks were added to the fighters, but the poorly trained pilots were unable to operate them effectively. As XIX TAC was demonstrating, ground attack is a skill that must be consistently honed, and it had long vanished from the syllabus at German training establishments. The German pilots who did get into action faced, in the words of a tactical assessment by the Luftwaffe high command, a "continuous air umbrella" over the battle zone.[42] Close cooperation between Allied fighters, fighter-bombers, and medium bombers was evident, and the Germans made special note of the thoroughness of Allied air reconnaissance over the battlefield. The ubiquitous *Jabos*, or *Jagdbomber* (fighter-bombers), were everywhere, restricting most major movements to the hours of darkness when possible. Many Luftwaffe reports simply referred to the French battle zone as a *Jabo-Rennstrecke* (fighter-bomber racetrack).

German army units did become adept at using camouflage and concealment and light antiaircraft artillery; XIX TAC reports pay tribute to the efficacy of German camouflage procedures and to the lethality of their flak defenses. Still, by late August, the Allies had all but eliminated the Luftwaffe as a threat on the western battlefields. Both IX and XIX TAC on August 25 launched a series of fighter sweeps and strafing attacks on overcrowded German airfields, which had been precisely located thanks to Ultra.[43] These strikes destroyed or damaged some 171 German planes for a loss of 27 American aircraft and "broke the back of the German fighter force in France."[44] To be sure, XIX TAC never had to face an unbroken Luftwaffe. The strategic bombing campaign of 1943–1944 had all but assured that outcome.

Tributes flowed in to Weyland during the August end run. In a letter to Hap Arnold on the seventeenth, Patton spoke of

> the swell job which your Air Force, particularly . . . the fighter-bombers of the XIX Tactical Air Command under General Weyland is doing. After we got the enemy on the move, the tanks pushed him so hard he could not deploy but had to stick to the roads, and the fighter-bombers would then come down and get him. For about 250 miles I have seen the calling cards of the fighter-bombers which are bullet marks in the pavement and burned tanks and trucks in the ditches.[45]

Patton told Weyland personally at the latter's Bronze Star award ceremony that "the superior efficiency and cooperation afforded this Army by the forces under your command is the best example of the combined use of air and ground troops I have ever witnessed."[46]

Yet amid this tremendous success were reminders that air power was not omnipotent. The heavily fortified Breton port of Brest, its fanatical German defenders led by veteran paratrooper Generalleutnant Hermann-Bernhard Ramcke, held out for weeks against a furious Allied assault. The XIX TAC's fighter-bombers were heavily committed to the attack, even at the expense of interdiction missions that might have helped cut off the retreat of many German troops to the south and east.[47] Its after-action report concluded, "Strong fixed fortifications are improper targets for fighter-bomber attack. . . . Far greater destruction and loss can be inflicted upon the enemy by employing these aircraft against proper fighter-bomber targets. . . . The fruits of the program of interdiction would have been considerably larger had it not been interrupted by concentration at Brest."[48] In the last stages of the assault, "fighter-bombers were directed to attack individual houses which were obstructing progress of the ground attack—in effect, street fighting with P-47s."[49]

The town finally fell (in ruins—Ramcke had completely demolished the port) on September 19.

Some weeks after the siege of Brest ended, Weyland made a poignant notation in his diary. Maj. Gen. Donald A. Stroh, commander of the Eighth Infantry Division, sent Weyland a letter on October 14, thanking him for XIX TAC's tireless efforts during the assault on Brest. Stroh's son, Capt. Harry R. Stroh, a P-47 pilot in Weyland's command, had been killed in action supporting his father's division on August 27, 1944.[50]

One event in XIX TAC's end run through France that loomed large was its role in one of the first mass surrenders of German troops during the campaign. By mid-August the remaining German forces in southwestern France were in a precarious position. The German high command issued orders for the troops to withdraw in three march groups. The first group, containing most of the vehicles and combat formations, managed to escape the American trap. The last group, a foot column under the command of Generalmajor Botho Elster, was not so lucky. Harried by XIX TAC and attacks by the French Forces of the Interior (FFI), Elster's column stood little chance of making it across the Loire. French resistance fighters informed Maj. Gen. Robert C. Macon, the commander of the Eighty-Third Infantry Division (part of the Ninth Army operating north of the river), that the Germans might be in a mood to surrender.[51] With XIX TAC Thunderbolts orbiting above, Elster received a delegation from the Eighty-Third led by its commander. Elster told him, "Keep the Jabos off my men and they will march north to the Beaugency bridge [southwest of Orleans] and surrender." Years later Weyland more colorfully recalled Elster's surrender: "Christ, I'd like to turn in my suit and surrender if you'll just call off that goddamn air power." Elster's command, permitted to keep its weapons to fend off the ever-present FFI, marched north to the surrender site in good order.

Weyland was invited to be present at the ceremony on September 16 "because XIX TAC was instrumental in the surrender."[52] He also witnessed an embarrassing breach of protocol. The Ninth Army was running the surrender ceremony, despite having only recently taken over the sector from the Third Army. When it came time for Elster to surrender his sidearm to Macon, the German snubbed the division commander.[53] "He turned over his pistol to me, not to the Army general," Weyland proudly noted.[54] Elster wanted it made clear that he was surrendering to the Third Army and XIX TAC.

Despite what some accounts imply, "Gruppe Elster" was not a battle group; it was a somewhat ragtag collection of rear-echelon personnel armed with many obsolete weapons. But by any measure, a surrender of nearly twenty thousand enemy troops is impressive. While Weyland managed to be magnanimous, noting that the prisoners were to be treated in accordance with the Geneva Conventions, a XIX TAC publication titled "Fly, Seek, Destroy" gloated, "Gen Elster disliked XIX TAC."[55] Always thinking of his men, Weyland requested a number of Lugers as presents for his key staff. When they were duly delivered courtesy of General Macon a few days later, Weyland set one aside for Vandenberg.[56] Eight days after the surrender, Weyland noted with satisfaction that Arnold and Vandenberg were delighted by his air power coup.[57]

The epic dash across France finally came to a halt some 350 miles from its starting point at Avranches. The advance was stopped not by the German defenders but by logistical shortfalls and fuel starvation, exacerbated by the Allies' shift in resources necessary to support Field Marshal Bernard Montgomery's Market Garden operation in mid-September. By any measure, XIX TAC's shakedown campaign had been a tremendous success, and the units assigned to it performed the whole range of tactical operations with skill and flexibility. To be sure, supporting maneuver warfare on widely separated fronts strained the command's capabilities and sometimes surpassed them.[58] The days of breakneck advances were, for the time being, over. "One of the greatest offensives in history," the XIX TAC diary sadly noted, "had lost its momentum at last."

The second phase of the Third Army–XIX TAC campaign, the buildup along the Moselle River in late September–early November 1944, was a different kind of war. In Weyland's words it "presented wholly different problems" than those encountered during the dash across France.[59] For nearly two months, the Third Army's front remained largely static. The XIX TAC took advantage of this operational pause, bringing up much-needed supplies, recovering its scattered groups (one fighter-bomber group involved in the Brest siege finally rejoined the main body of XIX TAC from its Cherbourg base some four hundred miles behind the front), readying new airfields, and generally "tidying up the battlefield." The Fighter Control Center also benefited from the lull and was at last able to bring up its microwave early warning radar and forward director posts.[60] Direct air support to the Third Army all but ceased, and the fighter-bomber groups turned to interdiction operations as the U.S. Army prepared for the attack on the fortified city of Metz.

Air attacks on the forts protecting Metz in large measure underscored the lessons of Brest. Using 1,000-pound bombs and napalm, P-47s conducted largely futile attacks against pillboxes and armored turrets. Weyland concluded that these were "not a proper target" for his fighter-bombers.[61] One of the few bright spots was P-47s dropping 1,000-pound bombs and busting the Dieuze Dam to prevent the Germans from blowing it themselves at an inopportune time. Yet, all told, this phase was frustrating, although XIX TAC did assist the Third Army in securing jumping-off positions for the forthcoming major assault on Metz.

The third distinct phase in the campaign was the carefully planned attack on Metz. It began with massed fighter-bomber attacks on November 8 (weather forced cancellation of the planned accompanying medium and heavy bomber strikes, which were delayed until the next day). In some respects this entire phase was dominated by adverse weather, which affected both air and ground action. The XIX TAC aided the Third Army's slow, methodical advance. Both attackers and defenders were largely confined to the roads, and every village seemed to be a strong point. Histories from XIX TAC tell of grim attacks on villages with high explosives, fragmentation bombs, and napalm while taking casualties from massed German light flak batteries. The XIX TAC did make further progress in its air-ground cooperation procedures by establishing a Combined Operations Office down to combat command level. It physically colocated the G-3 (operations officer, air), the tactical air liaison officer, and appropriate communications equipment, ensuring maximum cooperation among air, artillery, and ground forces. Patton's advance eventually bypassed Metz and drove on toward the Siegfried Line.

Operations from December 1 through December 19 that aimed at piercing the once-formidable Westwall, known to the Allies as the Siegfried Line, comprised the fourth phase. The offensive began with a sharp reverse, a hard lesson learned, and later success, all to be derailed by an unexpected enemy counteroffensive. The Allies' first order of business was to seize a bridgehead across the rain-swollen Saar River. The first attempt at Merzig featured a smaller-scale attempt to replay Operation Cobra, with an intense carpet bombing of the German defenses. The air attack went off as scheduled, but a delay in launching the follow-up ground assault allowed the resilient Germans the opportunity to rebound. As a result, "the air effort proved absolutely wasted."[62] The TAC's after-action report noted that an immediate follow-up is essential for carpet bombing to prove successful. This lesson was immediately put into practice, and the next offensive, at Saarlautern, succeeded in establishing a bridgehead.

All attention now turned to the massed assault on the Siegfried Line itself. Weyland took an almost proprietary interest in planning the massive combined arms attack, even to the extent of christening it Operation Tink, after his wife.[63] On December 6, Weyland met with Spaatz, Vandenberg, Patton, and Lt. Gen. James Doolittle to plan the attack in the vicinity of Zweibrücken.[64] The launch date was set for December 19, and Weyland predicted that with three thousand bombers it would be "the biggest operation of its kind in history."[65] But Operation Tink was not to be. On December 16, 1944, Hitler threw his last remaining Panzer armies into a desperate bid to split the Allied front and take Antwerp.

The fifth phase, the Ardennes counteroffensive that is commonly known as the Battle of the Bulge, lasted from December 16, 1944, to January 28, 1945. The Bulge would be XIX TAC's second "finest hour," yet Weyland was uncharacteristically slow to realize the implications of the offensive. His diary reveals that he spent the first three days of the German offensive desperately lobbying to keep Operation Tink alive. Only on December 19 did Weyland finally admit that "Tink was scrubbed." He noted on December 20, "Per SHAEF decision yesterday TUSA [Third U.S. Army] pulls 1st Army chestnuts out of the fire by taking over the VIII Corps & shifting weight to north to counter German thrust to Liege."[66]

For nearly a week, terrible weather largely grounded the Allied air forces, and the German offensive made good progress. Yet once the weather cleared XIX TAC found the narrow Ardennes roads choked with German armor and motor transport. This situation presented a delicate problem, as many German columns had a fair proportion of captured American vehicles among the Panzers, and this led to several friendly fire incidents. The XIX TAC's strike aircraft returned again and again to the fray as fast as they could be turned around on their airfields, attacking German columns with high explosives, fragmentation bombs, and napalm. Weyland's command also assisted in the support and relief of Bastogne. In particular, its Tenth Photo Group supplied the cut-off garrison with up-to-the-hour photographs of German positions surrounding the town. Vandenberg hailed their work at Bastogne as "the outstanding performance of night photography done anywhere at any time."[67]

On the morning of January 1, 1945, the Luftwaffe demonstrated that it still had some fight left when it launched Operation Bodenplatte, a dawn attack against sixteen Allied airfields in the Netherlands, Belgium, and France. Nine hundred German fighters organized into thirty-four groups—an unheard-of armada at this late stage of the war—were committed to this last effort. Ten groups never found their targets, nine others made ineffectual attacks, and others targeted vacant airfields or other worthless targets.[68] But eleven groups made successful strikes on viable targets, including the Metz-Frescaty airfield, home of XIX TAC's 365th Fighter Group, the "Hell Hawks."[69] Fifty Messerschmitts struck the airfield in a low-level attack with machine guns and cannon. In minutes, they had destroyed twenty-two P-47s and damaged eleven. One of the Bf-109s belly-landed near the field; during the pilot's interrogation, he pointed at the smoldering Thunderbolt wrecks and asked, "What do you think of that?" One of Weyland's squadron commanders had to excuse himself from the interrogation lest he punch the arrogant German in the nose. The XIX TAC's verdict on the attack was "quite effective, although costly for the attackers." This observation was an understatement: Bodenplatte cost the Luftwaffe 300 planes and 214 pilots, including 19 formation leaders. The strike on Metz-Frescaty alone resulted in 20 German fighters destroyed and 7 damaged out of 50, or a greater than 50 percent casualty rate.[70] German fighter inspector Generalleutnant Adolf Galland recalled, "We sacrificed our last reserves."[71]

During the reduction of the Bulge, XIX TAC's intelligence branch collected many prisoner of war testimonials about the effectiveness of tactical aviation in the battle. Alongside the reports of carnage along the roads, some prisoners reported that no food had reached them for days owing to USAAF interdiction efforts; hunger had led to their decision to surrender. Captured artillerymen also said that ammunition was as scarce as the rations. Other prisoners stated that entire units had been captured because they were unaware of the Third Army's rapid advance, so disrupted were their communications.

A break in the weather on January 22 ushered in what Weyland called the "Biggest Day in TAC history of destruction."[72] An enormous column of more than fourteen hundred German vehicles, fleeing the collapsing Bulge, was spotted opposite XX Corps. Tactical reconnaissance planes led the fighter-bombers as well as Ninth Air Force medium bombers to the target. The carnage was judged to be "worse than the Falaise pocket." On January 28, 1945, Weyland noted that the Bulge had been officially eliminated. The XIX TAC and Third Army would resume their drive to break through the Siegfried Line and reach the Rhine.

Phase 6 of the Third Army–XIX TAC advance would fulfill the objectives of the canceled Operation Tink, now rendered unnecessary after the Germans' defeat in the Bulge. From January 28 to March 13, Patton's forces would battle their way through the Siegfried Line, then make a quick drive to the Rhine. During the first stage of the operation XIX TAC rendered close air support. Throughout the campaign, Weyland's forces made time for "nontraditional" missions. In one instance, XIX TAC dropped blood plasma in drop tanks to pinned-down troops;[73] and another cut-off infantry unit also received drop tank largesse from XIX TAC—this time containing emergency rations.[74] On February 10, Weyland was promoted to major general. The Third Army pulled out all the stops with an honor guard and a band for the occasion.

The XIX TAC also carried out interdiction operations along the Third Army's right flank, attacking bridges over the Moselle. One bridge at Bullay had resisted attacks by the IX Bombardment Division's medium bombers, but on February 10 one of Weyland's P-47 squadrons managed to drop the span. The resulting exchange of letters between Weyland and the bomber commander, Maj. Gen. Samuel E. Anderson, reveals the spirit of friendly but edgy competition between the two men: "Dear Sam: Here's the newest picture of that Bullay Bridge you were interested in for some time. Any time you find some little job that's too tough for your mediums, just call on us for a few of our P-47 heavy bombers. Insultingly yours, 'Opie.'" Not to be outdone, Anderson replied, "Dear Opie: Congratulations on the Bullay Bridge job! In view of the fact that it had been severely weakened by medium bomber attacks (photographs enclosed) I am not surprised that your pea-shooters were able to collapse a span. Also, in view of the fact that O.R.S. [Operational Research Section] tells me that your claims as to bridges destroyed and railroad cuts made are about 70% greater than actual damage, I can appreciate your elation over having one picture to prove one claim. Insultingly yours, Sam."[75]

On February 22, XIX TAC played its part in Operation Clarion, a controversial mass aerial assault on German transportation targets, even those located in towns too small to have warranted air attack earlier. The raids are sometimes seen as a promiscuous "piling on" at a late stage of the war, but the results of Clarion enabled XIX TAC to reap a rich harvest of bottled-up rail traffic.

The final drive to the Rhine was reminiscent of the heady days of the drive across France the previous August. Once again, the XIX TAC diarists noted, "the right flank of the Army was protected only by a river and by the air."[76]

The Third Army was poised, in conjunction with the Seventh Army to the south, to proceed to phase seven, which involved "springing the Saar-Moselle-Rhine trap." From March 13 through March 23, 1945, the enemy forces were put to flight, and the result was "a fighter-bomber's paradise." By this stage of the war, almost no German tanks remained operational. As a result heavier weapons like rockets were not needed, so the fighter-bombers used machine guns almost exclusively.[77] They suspended using even standard high-explosive bombs, knowing cratered roads would only impede Patton's advance. A XIX TAC diarist recorded the observations of a staffer from Third Army headquarters who traversed a road after Weyland's fighter-bombers had visited it: "The passerby first notices a few scattered vehicles and dead horses; then it seems to grow in crescendo until finally he is in the midst of such a twisted mass of death and destruction that single items can no longer stand out. . . . It is a scene that should be photographed for the Master Race. Let them see the 'Road to Glory,' by courtesy of the Air Corps."[78] On March 19, Thunderbolts struck Field Marshal Gerd von Rundstedt's headquarters at Ziegenburg. Despite Weyland's high hopes for the mission—he believed that Hitler and Reichsführer Heinrich Himmler might have been visiting at the time—the attack missed any high-ranking targets.

Phase eight, known as "crossing the Rhine and disemboweling southern Germany," which took place from March 22 to April 22, 1945, and culminated in cutting the Third Reich in two, was almost anticlimactic. The actual Rhine crossing, aided by an extensive program of fifty-seven railway cuts to ensure no German reinforcements could move into the area, was compared to a "Ft Belvoir maneuver." The dying German air force, crowded into poorly defended second-line airfields, was shot out of the sky or strafed on the ground by Eighth and Ninth Air Force fighters. On April 12, the Third Army made a grim discovery at the newly liberated Ohrdruf concentration camp. One of Weyland's officers stated that the appalling sights made it very clear what the war was all about.[79]

All that remained of the war in Europe was the endgame. The ninth and final phase of the Third Army's and XIX TAC's air-land battle for Europe took place from April 22 to May 9, 1945. The Third Army drove to the southeast, with XIX TAC again covering its flank and dealing with the last remnants of the Luftwaffe. German forces were disintegrating in its path as the final acts in the drama played out. On April 28, four Mustangs of 354th Fighter Group, the Pioneer

Mustangs, did slow rolls over Moosburg prisoner of war (POW) camp. The Allies liberated the camp the next day and freed 110,000 Allied POWs, including a number of XIX TAC pilots.[80] The skies were uncharacteristically filled with German warplanes, but instead of attacking, they were coming in to surrender. Seventy Luftwaffe aircraft landed at XIX TAC bases on May 8, 1945, alone. "The Germans came prepared to stay. Some brought wives or mistresses (or even both) and personal luggage include everything imaginable, with baby carriages topping the list of unpredictable equipment!"[81] On May 9, 1945, Weyland issued his final general order. He predictably spoke of "the effectiveness of the XIX Tactical Air Command–Third Army team, which has carried air-ground cooperation to new heights of combat efficiency."[82]

For Weyland, VE-Day marked the end of his war. He took over the Ninth Air Force from Vandenberg. The force began a move to the Pacific, but VJ-Day intervened. In the wake of what Weyland admitted was a "tearful" parting, he sent his last official message to Patton, revealing the depth of his feelings. On November 26, 1945, not quite two weeks before Patton's fatal road accident, Weyland wrote, "I feel that the Third Army has died. To me, the Third Army meant Patton. When you left it, it ceased to be a thing alive. In a way I'm glad—a fighting Army and a peacetime Army are two different things."[83] Weyland's final verdict on Patton, and one that many modern historians have come to share, was that "he was a great man to work with, in my view he was probably the greatest field general the world's ever known."[84] Note Weyland's careful choice of words: the airman worked *with* Patton, not *for* him.

WEYLAND'S FORMULA FOR SUCCESS

The impressive record of XIX TAC speaks for itself. Without a doubt, Weyland was one of the most accomplished practitioners of tactical air support in military history. During and after the campaign, plaudits rained down on him from on high: Patton, Arnold, Spaatz, and Vandenberg. One of Patton's no-nonsense corps commanders, Lt. Gen. Walton Walker, probably spoke for most ground-pounders when he told Weyland, "Without your efficient and well planned operations we would have suffered far greater casualties and taken a much longer time to reach our objectives." From a ground commander to a tactical airman there can be no higher praise.[85] Yet what personal and professional attributes did Weyland possess that account for this success?

LEADERSHIP AND COMMAND

Weyland's success originated in his approach to leadership and service. His loyalty to his superiors and peers was unquestioned, and that loyalty extended to subordinates as well. Although his oral history reveals a tendency toward salty language, Weyland was the furthest thing from a loudmouth. In his dealings with Patton, his quiet, deferential, yet confident demeanor went a long way toward cementing the partnership. Most of Patton's biographers credit Weyland with eliminating Patton's lingering mistrust of the air force. Weyland summed up, "We thought we were a pretty goddamned good pair."[86]

In return, Patton never failed to support his airman. Historian David Spires, the most thorough chronicler of XIX TAC's war, notes only two occasions when Third Army staff attempted to strong-arm Weyland; in both cases, when Patton learned of it he interceded on Weyland's behalf.[87] One of these incidents involved Maj. Gen. John S. Wood, the Fourth Armored Division commander, who refused to return a communications officer borrowed from XIX TAC. When Wood's division later ran into trouble during the assault on Metz, Weyland, who was not above indulging in a bit of Schadenfreude, commented, "Wood yelled for help."[88]

The records show no sign of friction between Weyland and any of his USAAF superiors. He got along especially well with Vandenberg, whom he knew not only from ACTS but also from his early flight school days.[89] There are indications he felt some competitiveness with his counterpart Quesada at IX TAC, who possibly resented sharing the stage with XIX TAC on the continent.[90] Weyland's mostly good-natured rivalry with Anderson at IX Bombardment Division has already been noted.

His dealings with subordinates indicate a sure touch. When confronted with evidence that one of his reconnaissance pilots had violated standing orders and engaged and shot down several German aircraft in the course of a mission, Weyland displayed both firmness and flexibility. The pilot's lame explanation—"Gee, I'm kind of sorry about that, but he was just right there in front of me and I just shot him"—did not satisfy Weyland, but he had to acknowledge that his pilot not only displayed superior airmanship but also brought back superb photographs. "So I gave him a DSC [Distinguished Service Cross] and chewed the hell out of him."[91]

His observation background gave him an easy familiarity with army troops. "Ground soldiers sensed that I was simpatico with them . . . when I had to get a little hard-nosed about the proper employment of air power, they would take it from me."[92] Weyland also worked hard to smooth over any friction between air and ground forces. When his aircraft inadvertently attacked friendly ground forces during the Battle of the Bulge, he moved swiftly to avoid any repetition. When army gunners shot down a P-47 and killed its pilot, Weyland ensured that Patton's regrets were passed on directly to the squadron involved. "Do not want bad feeling," he noted.[93]

In sharp contrast to Patton, who believed that shell shock was no more than a euphemism for cowardice, Weyland was sensitive to such human factors as psychological stress and combat fatigue. This awareness is especially remarkable as—unlike Patton—Weyland had never seen combat up close until he arrived in the ETO. Early in the campaign, he made it his business to ensure that rest facilities (similar to the "flak houses" for Eighth Air Force personnel) were available on the continent. He recognized that the stress of constant low-level air action in the flak-filled skies of France would often try the nerves of even the bravest men.[94]

This empathy also extended to foreign nationals. His normally matter-of-fact diary betrayed his shock and horror at the sights he saw after the liberation of Ohrdruf concentration camp on April 12, 1945. He wrote of the stacked corpses and of survivors "too weak and emaciated to be evacuated!"[95] This experience must still have been weighing on his mind when, in his VE-Day message to his command, he referred to the "German enemy's career of crime."

Yet at the same time—and in stark contrast to Eisenhower, who refused to meet with captured German generals (or even shake their hands)—Weyland treated captured enemy commanders with professional respect. This magnanimity was evident both during the war (witness his sympathetic treatment of Elster at his surrender) and afterward. In July 1945, Weyland arranged and conducted a collegial interview with captured German field marshal Rundstedt. The two discussed various topics, such as the nature of Luftwaffe-army cooperation, the effectiveness of Allied tactical air (tacair) power on the western front, the value of reconnaissance, and the March 19, 1945, XIX TAC raid on Rundstedt's headquarters.[96] He was even tolerant of captured Stuka ace Hans-Ulrich Rudel when the German colonel proposed that Luftwaffe units join with Weyland's XIX TAC against the Soviets.[97]

Weyland undeniably possessed an ability to engage in critical self-assessment. The after-action reports and summaries issued with his signature bear this observation out: they are replete with observations about shortcomings, areas for improvement, and candid assessments of the limits of tactical air power. When necessary, he acted swiftly to make corrections. Notably, on the very afternoon of January 1, with Thunderbolt wrecks still smoldering after the surprise Luftwaffe attack, a thorough overhaul of airfield defense procedures was under way throughout his command.

Yet this soft-spoken, down-to-business character occasionally displayed the slightest hints of vanity. Weeks after the capitulation of Elster's column, Weyland was still searching for evidence and documentation that his fighter-bombers were the key factor in the Germans' surrender. And sometimes his diary betrays a craving for approval. He scrupulously recorded bits of praise from Arnold, Spaatz, and Vandenberg, and once even noted, "Gen Ike paid high tribute to XIX TAC-3rd Army action and relations—said nice things about W."[98] Yet such observations do nothing to diminish Weyland's stature. They simply make him more human.

TACAIR AND DOCTRINE

Unlike Quesada or Air Marshal Coningham, who actually developed the tactical air operations principles and procedures that came to fruition in northwestern Europe in 1944–1945, Weyland was not an innovator. The tactics he employed from August 1944 onward—including the use of air support parties, the employment of armored column cover, and armed reconnaissance—had been well developed by others by the time he took the field.[99] He certainly refined the existing procedures and synthesized them to great effect, but only in the area of integration of his reconnaissance activities (as discussed later) could he claim to have made an original contribution to tactical aviation.

Nor did he ever claim otherwise. In his earliest briefings to XIX TAC and Third Army personnel after he assumed command, he specifically mentioned that the tacair he would deliver was first developed in North Africa, was refined in Sicily and Italy, and had been honed by Quesada at IX TAC. In a postwar interview he summed up his lessons-learned approach: "We tried to improve on what they had learned and their tactics and tried to start out a little bit fresher with a somewhat fresher approach, but not by any means discarding the lessons that they had learned."[100]

Weyland was not overly concerned with formal doctrine. The after-action assessments from XIX TAC issued with Weyland's signature all assert that war experience fully validated the principles of FM 100-20. "In nine months of intensive air operations . . . the experience of XIX Tactical Air Command proved the concepts of FM 100-20 . . . basically sound. Tactical missions were planned and executed in order of priority laid down in that document: (1) Attainment and maintenance of air superiority. (2) Isolation of the battlefield. (3) Close air cooperation with ground units in combat."[101] In fact a review of XIX TAC's actual activities shows only a loose correlation with the spirit, and not the letter, of FM 100-20. In particular, the weight of effort placed on the three air missions is revealing: XIX TAC devoted 18 percent of its missions to air superiority, 40 percent to interdiction, and 42 percent to close air support.[102]

Undoubtedly by the end of the war XIX TAC had raised the level of direct air support to new heights. A remarkable incident from February 24, 1945, partly captures the level of cooperation Weyland's command had achieved:

> An OP [observation post] of the 10th Armd Div [Armored Division] reported, at 1630, a column of vehicles, of which he could see only six, moving into the town of OBEREMMEL. The information was immediately communicated by the G-2 [intelligence officer] of the division to the G-2 of XX Corps, who in turn informed XX Corps G-2 Air and requested that the movement be investigated as soon as possible by a Tac/R plane. The G-2 stepped across the room to convey the information to the Tactical Air Liaison Officer [TALO]. The TALO replied by handing him the headphones. 'Hear 'em burning?' he asked. Fighter bombers, already vectored to the spot by the Division TALO, had just finished destroying the vehicles, fifteen in all. The trucks had been spotted, reported, and destroyed in just under five minutes, an outstanding example of ground-air cooperation.[103]

INTEGRATION OF AERIAL RECONNAISSANCE AND OPERATIONS

If there was one single attribute that set Weyland apart from even his most successful contemporaries, it was the amount of attention he paid to the activities of his reconnaissance units and the integration of those activities into his larger combat actions. Weyland never forgot that he learned the business of operating effectively with the army during his early days with the Twelfth Observation Squadron at Fort Sam in the 1920s. Successful commanders are not supposed to favor any of their subordinate units over others, yet Weyland made no secret of his affinity for his recce units. He used to joke that "a recce pilot is a real smart fighter pilot—just a little smarter than the others." He took particular interest in the activities of the

Tenth Photo Reconnaissance Group and its commander, Col. Russell A. Berg. The group's motto was "We make pictures that even generals can interpret."[104] That said, Weyland came to value the reports of his fighter-bombers performing armed reconnaissance (termed "tactical recce" or "TACR") via radio messages even above those coming from photoreconnaissance, because the former could be acted upon much more quickly. It is difficult to see how XIX TAC could have guarded Patton's right flank on the Loire so effectively—to say nothing of its ability to execute far-flung simultaneous operations—without the seamless integration of day and night, or of photo and visual reconnaissance activity with that of his fighter-bombers.

When Patton's intelligence officer suggested gaining operational control over XIX TAC's reconnaissance activities, Weyland demurred. Much to his satisfaction, "Gen Patton backed us up very thoroughly. He said, 'That is the way . . . My G-2 had the mistaken idea that he ought to be running reconnaissance, and Weyland can run it a hell of a lot better than he. Besides, his reconnaissance had a hell of a lot more to do than just take pictures for the Third Army. Vandenberg is right as hell—centralize control of all of the air.' Old Patton was a believer."[105] The XIX TAC's after-action reports amplified this conclusion: "Without such [centralized] control it would be impossible to achieve the swift and close air-ground cooperation which means success in battle." In practice, XIX TAC's staff reconnaissance officer and the Third Army G-2 air had the closest possible cooperation.[106]

Weyland always spoke of "this teamwork of reconnaissance and combat aviation" when accounting for XIX TAC's accomplishments.[107] It is not too great a stretch to see the antecedents of later concepts, such as the reconnaissance-strike complex and time-sensitive targeting, in Weyland's pioneering work with XIX TAC.

SIGNALS INTELLIGENCE

Closely related to Weyland's effective use of air reconnaissance is the powerful contribution of signals intelligence, above all the intelligence gleaned from intercepts and decrypts of high-level German message traffic using the Enigma machine. David Spires is correct in stating that the direct impact of such information, classified as "Ultra," on air operations is somewhat questionable.[108] Certainly the Ultra decrypts did not yield the hour-by-hour information on fleeting targets that aerial observation could provide. Yet recent scholarship suggests an important triangular relationship between Ultra information, Patton's scheme of maneuver, and the activities of XIX TAC.[109] In particular, a remarkable partnership existed between Lt. Col. Melvin C. Helfers, Third Army's Ultra officer, and Maj. Harry M. Grove, his counterpart at XIX TAC.[110] From August 1944 on, Patton was an eager consumer of Ultra information, and there is little doubt that Ultra intelligence informed many of the major operational decisions that shaped Third Army's drive across Europe. In particular, the involvement of XIX TAC in the Mortain operation on August 6–13 and the attacks on Luftwaffe airfields at the end of the month were conducted on the basis of Ultra information.[111] Weyland, of course, never revealed the existence of Ultra in any of his wartime writings, but he did write guardedly of "cloak and dagger sources" or "special intelligence" at times.[112]

PUBLIC RELATIONS

In 1944–1945, the USAAF was an extraordinarily media-savvy organization. In September 1944, Arnold insisted to Spaatz that "our press releases [must] more nearly picture in proper balance the relative contribution of ground, sea, and air forces in our approach towards complete victory over our enemies. . . . I will scour the country to provide you with the men most capable of putting into words the achievements of the Army Air Forces."[113] Weyland needed no urging. He seems to have had a natural flair for public relations, both to motivate his own troops and to gain the confidence of his superiors, as well as to assist in the drive for a postwar independent air force. His command excelled in turning out eye-catching and hard-hitting publications for internal and external consumption. He even took time during the first tense day of the Battle of the Bulge to note in his diary Arnold's congratulations on the report "Twelve Thousand Fighter Bomber Sorties," which had recently arrived stateside.[114] In this effort he was certainly assisted by Patton, who constantly told war correspondents, "Now I would appreciate it if you all could integrate in your stories the Third Army and the XIX Tactical Air Command, because the XIX TAC has done a great job with us."[115]

In February 1945, Weyland jumped at an opportunity offered by Lt. Gen. Barney Giles, deputy USAAF commander and chief of Air Staff. Giles arranged for a visit by Capt. Maitland A. Edey of the USAAF Publications Section, who was a former editor at *Life* magazine. Edey was collecting information on USAAF tactical operations for possible inclusion in a future issue of *Impact*, the USAAF's confidential journal, which in fact enjoyed wide distribution among policymakers.

Giles asked Weyland to extend Edey "the fullest cooperation of the members of your Command with whom he must work."[116]

Weyland's response exceeded Giles's expectations. The XIX TAC rolled out the red carpet for Edey, who later wrote effusively to Weyland, "I can't tell you how the cooperation given me by you and your staff helped me in my job." The special issue of *Impact*, featuring a striking red cover with the title "U.S. TACTICAL AIR POWER IN EUROPE" in huge white letters, was so successful that the publisher was preparing an unclassified version for Congress.[117] Unsurprisingly, XIX TAC material (especially photographs and charts willingly provided by Weyland's staff) figured prominently in the issue.[118] As in so many other matters, Weyland was ahead of his time in what are now known as strategic communications.

All of these elements contributed to Weyland's formula for success. Truly, Weyland embodied a three-dimensional form of Gen. Ulysses S. Grant's observation on the art of war: "Find out where your enemy is. Get at him as soon as you can. Strike at him as hard as you can and as often as you can, and keep moving on."[119] Weyland might have added, "And be sure to tell everyone about it."

AFTERWORD AND SIGNIFICANCE

Weyland went on to even greater achievements in the postwar years. On his return from Europe in the autumn of 1945 he served as vice commandant of the CGSS at Fort Leavenworth. After two headquarters tours with the USAAF and the newly independent United States Air Force (USAF), he spent two years as deputy commandant of the National War College. He took command of TAC briefly in 1950, but the North Korean invasion of the south in June 1950 brought Weyland to Tokyo the following month as Gen. George E. Stratemeyer's vice commander for operations of Far East Air Forces (FEAF). Weyland returned briefly to TAC the next year, only to be called back to take over FEAF after Stratemeyer suffered a heart attack in May 1951.

As the senior American airman in the theater, Weyland steered the USAF through its first war as an independent service. In some respects, he reprised his World War II role as a tactical air commander while painting on a larger canvas. The almost complete lack of strategic targets and the need to avoid a direct confrontation with the Soviet Union combined to keep the war limited. Weyland recognized that the air war on the Korean Peninsula would therefore be primarily an interdiction effort, although close air support for imperiled United Nations forces would also be necessary. He credited the interdiction and air pressure campaigns with setting the conditions for the eventual 1953 armistice.

Weyland also grappled with several vexing interservice disputes, most notably the command and control of close air support. His army counterparts were, in his view, more difficult to deal with than Patton had been. Weyland fended off successive attempts by army commanders Matthew B. Ridgway and Mark Clark to place tactical aviation under the army's control.[120] Weyland's management of the air war in Korea was entirely consistent with his World War II modus operandi: he firmly adhered to the principle that an airman should have centralized control of air operations and should take a flexible approach to applying air power on the battlefield. A recent history of the air war in Korea flatly declares, "No one would influence the course of the air war over Korea more than he."[121]

After the armistice and a period spent helping to build up the Japanese Air Self Defense Forces, Weyland returned to take over TAC in May 1954. His part in the nuclearization (some would say SAC-umcizing) of TAC is undeniable. Weyland recognized that the service needed a nuclear strike capability if it was to survive during the years of President Eisenhower's New Look national security policy. He was also the author of the "Concept for Employment of Tactical Air Worldwide," a rationale for creating the Composite Air Strike Force, a forerunner of today's air expeditionary force concept.[122]

Weyland retired in July 1959 and died on September 2, 1979. He unfortunately did not write a memoir, but he did sit for an engaging and candid oral history and kept a regular diary during the 1944–1945 campaign in Western Europe.

Clearly his later success owed much to his World War II experience. In a major article in *Air University Quarterly Review*, summarizing the lessons of the Korean War, Weyland made an observation that could have applied equally to the battle zone of Northwest Europe in 1944–1945. He wrote:

> One thing that should be clear to everyone by now is that airpower is indivisible. . . . Attempts to classify it by types of aircraft, types of operations, or types of targets, have led to confusion and misunderstanding. For this reason I have tried to think of it in terms of objectives, threats, and opportunities. The results desired, balanced against threats and opportunities, determine

the weight, timing, and phasing of air attacks. Successful integration of these considerations into a pattern of employment is a complex business. Successful resolution of these problems is the primary aim and responsibility of the airmen.[123]

Today's airmen still grapple with these concepts.

Otto P. Weyland ranks among the greatest tactical airmen of World War II. He certainly stands beside Maori Coningham, George Kenney, Arthur Tedder, Wolfram von Richthofen, Pete Quesada, and A. A. Novikov. If his postwar accomplishments are factored in, he eclipses most of these great airmen (with the exception of Tedder, who served magnificently as deputy supreme commander of the Allied Expeditionary Force) in terms of influence and impact. Yet Weyland himself would probably have rejected being labeled a "tactical airman." He was simply an airman.

4

CURTIS E. LEMAY: AIRMAN EXTRAORDINARY

WILLIAMSON MURRAY

Curtis Emerson LeMay is an American legend and still to this day the most controversial senior leader in the history of the United States Air Force (USAF). Pictured on the cover of *Time* magazine on August 13, 1945, less than a week after the first nuclear bombs were dropped on Nagasaki and Hiroshima, he was the very symbol of a war hero: "LeMay of the B-29s" had brought the war with the Japanese to an end. Five years later he was again featured on the cover of *Time*, now with the caption "Strategic Air Commander LeMay," as the man who had built and shaped the Strategic Air Command (SAC) into an effective and efficient deterrent and war-fighting arm.

Having served as the SAC commander for ten years, vice chief of staff of the USAF for four years, and finally chief of staff for another four years, LeMay remains the longest serving general in modern American history. Though widely recognized as a great commander of war and peace during the administrations of both Harry S. Truman and Dwight D. Eisenhower, he had a troubled tenure as chief of staff under John F. Kennedy and Lyndon B. Johnson. Being portrayed as the mad general in Stanley Kubrick's *Dr. Strangelove* did not improve his public reputation; neither did his unsuccessful stint at a political career as George C. Wallace's running mate in the 1968 presidential campaign.

This operational biography seeks to revisit the man and his career. To give the bottom line up front, LeMay was intelligent, innovative, and courageous—three qualities essential for successful military leadership—but the real reason for the success of this "airman extraordinary" was his insistence on seeing any job through to its completion. Determination, expressed through relentless training, hard work, and always leading by example, provided the foundation for his achievements.

FORMATIVE YEARS

The eldest of seven children, Curtis LeMay was born in Columbus, Ohio, on November 15, 1906, to working-class parents. His mother, Arizona Carpenter, a woman of English stock, was the role model of the family, instilling in her children a strong sense of honesty, moral integrity, ambition, and drive—characteristics that would remain with Curtis throughout his life. His father, Erving LeMay, of French extraction, could never hold a job and used to beat his son; from him Curtis inherited a belief in strict discipline and a rather dark and forbidding personality.

From early childhood on, Curtis LeMay felt obligated to earn money for the family. He learned that hard work was a basic part of life and developed a deep sense of responsibility for himself and those who were close to him. He grew up during an era in which virtually all young Americans were fascinated by cars and airplanes, both of which remained LeMay's passion throughout his life. He saw his first airplane when he was barely five years old, and it was love at first sight.

For those who were willing to devote self-discipline and diligence to the business of getting ahead in the 1920s, America was the land of opportunity. At the time, high school marked the highest level of educational attainment for most Americans, not only because most teenagers had to work in order to help support their families, but also because the standards in American high schools were such that few college graduates in the United States today could meet them. LeMay did not merely graduate from high school, but he had worked at so many part-time jobs—full time in the summer—that he could pay the initial fees at The Ohio State University in Columbus. Thereafter, he continued to pay his way through college by working full time in a steel foundry while taking a complete course load and joining the Reserve Officers' Training Corps (ROTC). His major was engineering, then as now one of the most demanding disciplines in the academic world.

LeMay's enlistment in ROTC clearly represented an effort to open the door to a flying career in the army after graduation. In October 1928, one year before the Wall Street crash, he received his commission as a reserve officer in the army's artillery branch, but he failed to graduate on time and earn his degree—an omission he rectified while serving as a flying officer on detached duty in the Columbus area in the mid-1930s. At that time, he fulfilled his military duties while earning the academic credits and completing the thesis he needed to earn his bachelor of engineering degree.

To get into U.S. Army Air Corps flying school, LeMay had to resign his reserve commission, enlist in the National Guard, complete the trying syllabus the army inflicted on its aviation cadets, and then resign his National Guard position to accept a regular commission in the air corps. Although nothing came easily to LeMay, he never complained about the hard road he followed, and he was struck with pure luck and good fortune in one aspect of life. He may have been shy and somewhat ill at ease around women, never putting much effort into socializing and dating, but with Helen Maitland, as with the airplane, it was love at first sight. They met when he was twenty-five years old, and from that time on she would stand by his side in good and bad days, for better or worse—his most positive and important personal relationship.

On the professional side, LeMay's service until the mid-1930s was as a "crew dog," learning the ins and outs of flying and serving in a military organization. The air corps was starved for money and given tasks for which the officers had little preparation, such as flying the air mail when Franklin Roosevelt briefly canceled the government's contracts with the airlines and supporting the Civilian Conservation Corps. This situation created an atmosphere in which one either adapted or found oneself looking for a new job in the midst of the Great Depression, when there were no jobs to be had. LeMay thrived, but promotions were few and far between. Throughout the decade before the war, Congress refused to fund the air corps at anything but the most minimum level. In early 1940, ten years after he had graduated from flight school, LeMay found himself still a first lieutenant.

But by the late 1930s LeMay had established a reputation as a leader of men in an operational environment and as an officer who could get things done in the practical world of a service dominated by technology. In particular, he played a major role in the development of navigational and blind flying techniques. Recognizing that the men flying long-range aircraft, such as the B-17s that began arriving in the air corps inventory in the late 1930s, would require more sophisticated methods of navigation, LeMay pioneered the development of navigation technologies and the creation of schools to train navigators. In 1938, in one of the propaganda coups executed by the air corps's leadership, he navigated a flight of B-17s to intercept the Italian liner SS *Rex* 610 miles out in the Atlantic Ocean—an effort to prove that aircraft could play as important a role in America's defense as the navy did. That year LeMay also served as the navigator for pioneer flights to South America with B-17s—an effort that demonstrated air power's increasing range.

Some of the characteristics that were to define LeMay became visible early in his career: hardworking and independent, he was self-driven, self-sustained, self-reliant, and essentially self-made. He was certainly reserved in social settings, lacking polished manners, natural charm, and charisma. He also had a no-nonsense personality and was brutally honest and forthright; in fact, he was tactless to the point of rudeness. He developed an argumentative speaking style, relying heavily on logic and experience rather than on persuasion. Some appreciated these qualities, others did not, but something about his style, dedication, and technological insight made officers and men trust him. Subordinates and superiors simply came to respect his views and have confidence in him when it came to war.

THE ARMY AIR CORPS DAYS

During the 1930s the theorists in the army air corps developed a complex doctrine aimed at achieving that organization's independence from the army. Their theories resembled those of Giulio Douhet in Italy and Hugh Trenchard in the Royal Air Force (RAF). Inspired by Billy Mitchell, they argued that in future wars large bomber formations, protected by their defensive armament, would be able to fly deep into enemy territory at high altitude, bomb specific targets in an enemy country, and return, while suffering only "acceptable damage." In other words, these self-defending formations could attack and destroy key nodes of an enemy nation's industrial web, such as ball bearing factories, oil refineries, or transportation centers, and this devastation would result in second- and third-order effects that would spread throughout an enemy's war economy.[1]

Above all, the theorists of air power explicitly rejected the lessons of military history, including the experiences of World War I, which suggested that air power made its greatest contribution when it executed a broad array of missions. Those lessons had also indicated that without air superiority, bombing efforts invariably resulted in unacceptable losses among attacking aircraft. Moreover, they underlined that finding and then hitting targets represented problems of great difficulty, especially in the appalling weather conditions that generally characterize northern Europe. The most dangerous error was a doctrinal belief, bordering on dogma, that not only was a long-range fighter technologically impossible, but also unnecessary. As the British prime minister Stanley Baldwin had claimed in 1934, the bomber would always get through. Moreover, fighters were only for defensive purposes, and the fewer the better—a belief that the leaders of the army air corps and the RAF, with the exception of Hugh Dowding of Fighter Command, happily endorsed.

Interestingly, the Germans, who devoted considerable effort to examining the lessons of the last war realistically, developed a more broadly based air power doctrine that took into account the other missions that had made air power a key contributor to combat throughout World War I. The unfortunate result was that, with the exception of the Battle of Britain, the Germans utilized air power more effectively in the opening years of the war than did their opponents.[2] It was not until the 1942–1943 period that the Anglo-American air forces caught up to the Germans. At that point the overwhelming productive abilities of the Allied economies allowed the Americans and the British to swamp the Luftwaffe.

While intelligent and very capable of matching conceptual acumen with technological insight, LeMay was a practitioner, not a theorist. He had virtually nothing to do with these intellectual exercises, which he would have equated to attempting to determine how many angels could dance on the head of a pin. In the early 1980s, at Maxwell Air Force Base (AFB), this author overheard LeMay commenting to Maj. Gen. Haywood "Possum" Hansell, "I had no interest in that doctrine stuff, Possum. I was only interested in trying to figure out how to fly more intelligently and safely." LeMay's interests centered on the practical application of technology and tactics to flying, as well as the use of air power, as would become apparent during the biggest test of all, the war of national survival.

WORLD WAR II: PREPARING THE FORCE

While LeMay's first decade in service had been one of preparation and minimal promotions, the outbreak of World War II radically altered the framework within which airmen operated. It was a period that saw the transformation of the minuscule army air corps into the massive army air forces of 1945. That transformation created unheard-of opportunities for men with drive, imagination, and ruthlessness to rise quickly to ranks that previously had taken decades in military service to reach. In January 1940 LeMay was a first lieutenant; four years and two months later he was a major general, commanding a vast number of B-29s in the Pacific. It was a hard road, but it was a road for which LeMay had been preparing himself throughout his whole life.

Between 1940 and 1942, LeMay found himself engaged not only in the desperate task of attempting to ready units for future deployment either to Europe or the Pacific but also in a number of specialized tasks, such as using the B-24 to establish an air bridge between the United States and the United Kingdom. While executing that task he met future air vice marshal D. C. Bennett, who was engaged in the same task for the RAF and who would eventually create and lead Bomber Command's Pathfinder force. LeMay would have fully agreed with the sentiments Bennett later expressed when asked about the disastrous Battle of Berlin, which almost wrecked Bomber Command in the winter of 1943–1944: "If I were ever to lead a similar effort, I would make every air vice marshal who commanded a group [equivalent to an American bomber division] fly on active operations, and for every one I killed, I would save 200 crew lives."[3]

LeMay's admiration for Bennett underlined his penchant for connecting with others who were willing to follow the same hard path that he followed. Few individuals received unalloyed praise from him in his memoirs. Bennett was one; interestingly, Mao Zedong was another. In spite of his rabid anticommunism, LeMay noted with considerable admiration that the Communists not only built the airfields he needed in China for his B-29s far more expeditiously than did the Nationalists but also that Mao himself was out one day a week doing manual labor to set an example for the workforce of peasants and soldiers whom the Communists had dragooned into leveling the landscape and preparing an adequate field.

The real challenge LeMay confronted, as did so many other veterans of the air corps from the 1930s, was creating deployable units that could fight and survive in the ferocious combat environments of Europe and the Pacific. American commanders faced the frustrating situation that they had to create such units from scratch. Then they had to watch as higher headquarters stripped them of skilled pilots, navigators, and other officers to create new units, as what was soon to be called the army air forces expanded at a dizzying rate.

Moreover, unit commanders found themselves responsible for creating bases where quite literally nothing existed but the empty landscape. Runways, taxiways, roads, command posts, hangars, barracks, and mess halls all had to be thrown together, while at the same time the officers were molding aircrews and ground crews out of the ill-disciplined civilians of American society. It represented a herculean task, but LeMay understood it was essential to welding the disparate backgrounds of air and ground crew into fighting outfits.

The task of building a combat unit out of nothing was one at which LeMay excelled. Admittedly he was a workaholic, but he also was technically gifted in all aspects of the profession of airman. He proceeded to demand the very best from everyone who worked for him—and he got it, because those who served under him not only feared his ferocious demeanor but also knew that he was not asking them to do anything that he was not willing to do himself and in most cases could do better than they could. He certainly did not win any popularity contests, nor was he to win any in the course of his air force career. Nevertheless, he earned the respect of his men, who eventually tagged him with the nickname "Old Iron Ass"—one that he richly deserved—and his unrelenting insistence on training would save many of their lives in the air battles over Germany.

In May 1942 LeMay received orders to command the 305th Bomb Group located near the barren salt flats around Salt Lake City, Utah. The outfit had been activated two months earlier and consisted of virtually nothing except its name on pieces of paper that assigned individuals, supplies, and aircraft to it. A few Flying Fortresses arrived from the factory to serve as the training vehicles for the air and ground crews. LeMay had his newly arriving crews fly the aircraft into the ground, sometimes quite literally. In late May, he was ordered to take his few aircraft and crews north to Spokane, Washington, where he then commanded a composite group of B-17s and B-24s that would address the emergency occasioned by the Japanese move against Midway. When that crisis died down, he went back to Salt Lake City to continue working up crews. The group he led at times had at most seven or eight aircraft assigned to it, and at other times as few as three B-17s, but would routinely lose half of its bombers to another group that was beginning the business of working up.

In September 1942, the 305th had reached a state of readiness and received the warning orders for movement to the European theater of operations. As the ground crews departed for England by boat, LeMay's aircrews deployed to Syracuse, New York, to await the balance of their new B-17s, coming straight from the factory. Despite their newness, all the aircraft required extensive checkouts and modification. That done, LeMay and his almost totally inexperienced aircrew set off for Gander, Newfoundland, and the great hop across the Atlantic to Prestwick, Scotland. The sound of the propellers whirring through the wretched fall weather of the North Atlantic seemed to stir up lyrics in LeMay's mind as he struggled with the thought of leading these men and their aircraft into combat:

Rmmmmm. Crews are not coordinated. . . . Pilots come straight from basic trainers to B-17s. . . . Rmmmmm . . . Navigators . . . we got a lot of 'em just two weeks before we started overseas. . . . Most of the gunners haven't fired. No range. No gunnery school. . . . Bombadiers haven't had much practice. . . . Rmmmmm . . . And no formation flying. We've never had enough airplanes to fly formations. We'll have to fly our first formation in England.[4]

Conditions were no better in England. He found airfields only in the first stages of completion, bad food, unheated buildings, seas of mud everywhere, and, from the aircrews' point of view, the hideous practice of drinking warm beer. Nevertheless, LeMay got along well with the British in getting the work done that American air bases required. Throughout his period of service in Britain, however, LeMay had little connection with the RAF and with the Allies generally because his tasks involved the day-to-day business of operating combat units, that is, ensuring that they dropped their bombs accurately on targets that others selected.

Creating the conditions that would maximize aircrew capabilities and allow for successful maintenance of B-17s tried LeMay's patience. Almost immediately, he recognized that the then-current bombing practices, which called for the bombers to jink when they came under German antiaircraft fire from high-velocity 88mm and 105mm guns, were fundamentally flawed. LeMay suspected that such maneuvering would produce miserable performance in finding and bombing targets. He checked post-mission photographs, which more than confirmed his worst fears.

LeMay calculated that it would take the Germans 372 rounds of flak to hit a single B-17 during a ten-second run in on its target. In fact, he was crediting the Germans with a greater degree of accuracy than they possessed. That year the Luftwaffe had estimated that the number of 88mm shells required to bring a bomber down was so high that antiaircraft defense was not cost effective, and it recommended that the Reich's air defenses shift from the emphasis on antiaircraft guns to night and day fighters.[5] However, Hitler and the civilian air defense authorities refused to authorize such a change, because they believed the firing of antiaircraft guns helped improve civilian morale. This decision illustrates that Nazi scientists and technologists, despite the superiority of German technology in general, never possessed the imagination to develop proximity fuses, which the U.S. Navy was already in the process of creating at this point in the war.[6]

As he always did when he believed he was right, LeMay went against conventional wisdom. In the few training missions he could arrange to work on the 305th's formation flying, Iron Ass ensured his crews would fly in a disciplined formation, which eventually became the model that all the bombing formations of Eighth Air Force followed, and thus in their practice bomb runs the group would fly on a straight and level course. On November 23, 1942, LeMay demonstrated the effectiveness of this new bombing approach. Unlike the other bomber formations of the tiny Eighth, the 305th took its final run into the target straight and narrow, despite anguished protests from the aircrews. But as was to become a habit throughout the war, LeMay led from the front and the rest followed. As he told the men: "If we're going to St. Nazaire we're going to drop some arms on that target, by God. And this is the only way I can see to do it."[7]

Not only did LeMay's bombers achieve remarkable bombing accuracy compared to that of the other bomb groups, he also did not lose a single aircraft to flak, although his attacking formation did lose two B-17s to Luftwaffe fighters. Therein lay the rub, because, as the Americans soon discovered, the German fighter, not antiaircraft fire, posed the greatest danger to their daylight bombing offensives. In late 1942 few American bombers were available in England, since Operation Torch (Novemver 1942) had siphoned off many to the Mediterranean. Thus the only daylight bombing attacks were into occupied France, most of which was within the range of Allied fighters, and U.S. losses therefore remained at acceptable levels unless the bombers reached beyond fighter support. When they did, however, losses on each raid began to approach the 10 percent mark, which was totally unacceptable for the maintenance of a sustained aerial offensive.

Slowly but steadily, over the winter of 1942–1943, American bomber strength in England climbed, as production of aircraft and crews in the United States ratcheted upward. By late April 1943 Ira Eaker, commander of the Eighth Air Force, was able to begin sending bomber formations against the fringes of the Luftwaffe's daylight air defense system. Nevertheless, he was unwilling to attack targets too deep into Germany until the Eighth Air Force could mount raids with upward of 250 to 300 aircraft. Still, even on the fringes of the Reich, American losses mounted alarmingly. From April through August 1943 the Eighth Air Force was losing on average 30 percent of the crews on active duty at the beginning of the month and an even larger percentage of its bombers.[8] What saved the American bombing offensive was the swelling tide of aircraft and crews that stateside factories and training bases in the United States produced and sent to England every month. Thus, in spite of extraordinary losses, the Eighth Air Force's strength continued to increase.[9]

In addition to his constant insistence on leading from the front, LeMay emphasized that navigators and bombardiers should be trained to new standards of competence. By early summer Eaker and a number of other leaders in Washington had recognized the outstanding job that LeMay was doing. In May, they promoted him to command of the Provisional Combat Wing, which in September became the Third Air Division. To his new assignment LeMay brought the same ruthless emphasis on constant, grinding training when the crews were not flying combat missions over Nazi-held territory.

The results manifested themselves in the great Schweinfurt-Regensburg mission of August 17, 1943—one of the darker episodes that marked Eighth Air Force's efforts in 1943. It certainly underlined the weaknesses in American doctrine and understanding of the Luftwaffe's capabilities. The assumption that underlay Eaker's planning of the mission was that the daylight air defense of Germany was a brittle affair. Supposedly, once a large formation had punched through the Germans' hard outer layer of defenses, the remainder of the mission would prove relatively easy. But not until mid-August did Eaker believe that he possessed sufficient numbers of bombers for the Eighth Air Force to fight its way through the outer shell of the Luftwaffe's air defenses.

The plans for the mission itself involved two distinct parts. LeMay's Provisional Combat Wing (already known by most as the Third Air Division) would lead the way through the German air defenses. The target was the aircraft factories in Regensburg, where the Messerschmitt Company produced a substantial number of Bf-109s. Afterward, instead of returning to their bases in England, LeMay's aircraft would continue on to land at bases in North Africa. Meanwhile, the German fighters, waiting to ambush the B-17s on their return, would see nothing but empty sky. The waiting German fighters would expend much of their fuel in attacking LeMay's bombers and eventually would have to land to rearm and refuel. Approximately half an hour after LeMay's mission had pushed on to Africa, a second great wave of B-17s would arrive in German airspace to find the Luftwaffe fighters on the deck and the way cleared to bomb the factories in Schweinfurt that produced nearly 60 percent of Germany's ball bearings.

On August 17, the Third Air Division launched 146 bombers from its bases in England, and First Air Division launched 183 bombers. But as happens so often in war, Clausewitz's frictions intervened. That morning found the airfields in England socked in with the kind of fog known as a "pea souper." LeMay had trained his aircrews to take off and form up in such conditions, but the First Air Division's commander had not, and his aircraft could not take off in the fog. Thus, the third Air Division, with LeMay leading in the first B-17 in the Ninety-Sixth Bomb Group, formed up and departed for Regensburg, because it had to arrive in North Africa while there was still enough daylight for the crews to find and land at unfamiliar airfields.

The Germans took a terrible toll on LeMay's bombers, shooting down twenty-four B-17s; a number of other aircraft were written off in North Africa because of battle or crash damage. The First Air Division, however, could not get airborne until the fog had cleared. By the time it arrived over Schweinfurt, the Bf-109s and the FW 190s had rearmed and refueled, and they savaged the second great American bombing attack. Altogether the Americans lost another thirty-six B-17s, which were shot down over German-held territory. The total loss was nearly 20 percent for the combined mission, a rate no military force could sustain. The message was clear: daylight air operations over the Reich desperately needed the cover of long-range escort fighters. However, Eaker would not recognize that reality until October.

One should not assume that the Combined Bomber Offensive was failing to have a significant impact on the Third Reich's ability to support the war. Recent research has underlined that Bomber Command's attacks on the Ruhr in spring 1943 had brought the expansion of the German war economy to a screeching halt.[10] The American attack on Regensburg significantly lowered the Germans' production totals for new fighter aircraft, while the threat of daylight attacks forced the Luftwaffe to terminate most of its air operations over France, the Mediterranean, and the Eastern Front so that it could concentrate its fighter strength on defending the homeland. For the remainder of the war, German ground forces would have to conduct their battles without protection from the increasing numbers of Allied tactical aircraft.

For LeMay, the other front-line commanders, and the crews, air combat over Germany had turned into a terrible battle of attrition that was to last for more than a year. In September the Eighth Air Force launched a massive raid of 407 bombers to attack targets in the Stuttgart area. A ferocious air battle quickly developed, and that day the Americans lost forty-five bombers, or more than 10 percent of the attacking force. In his memoir LeMay noted that on the following day 177 Eighth Air Force bombers attacked targets in Belgium and France, all within range of escort fighter support, and lost not a single aircraft.

Nevertheless, Eaker made one more major attempt to fly huge, unescorted formations of B-17s through the German air defenses. In the week of October 8–14, he came close to destroying Eighth Air Force by mounting a series of major attacks deep into the Reich's airspace. The worst day came on "Black Thursday," October 14, when Eighth Air Force returned to Schweinfurt. The mission was a disaster. Out of 229 bombers that crossed into enemy airspace, the Americans lost 60, with more than 20 others written off for battle damage after their return. Nearly every bomber that survived the mission suffered some sort of battle damage. The 305th, LeMay's old outfit, lost 13 out of the 15 aircraft that it put up that day.

There are some indications that at this point a general crew revolt took place, making it clear to the Eighth's commanders that deep penetration raids without long-range fighter escorts were no longer acceptable. Eaker finally absorbed the harsh reality, and, not surprising, long-range escort fighters suddenly appeared at the top of his list of priorities. But in December 1943, Gen. Henry "Hap" Arnold, the chief of the army air forces, saw fit to move Eaker to the Mediterranean, while Jimmy Doolittle and Carl "Tooey" Spaatz took over the business of running the daylight campaign against Germany.

It was not until February 1944 that the Americans were able to resume their daylight air offensive against targets deep in Germany. This time they were accompanied on the last leg by the magnificent P-51, an aircraft which neither the British nor the Americans had wanted but which turned out to be not only the best single-engine piston fighter of the war but also a long-range fighter capable of accompanying the bombers all the way to Berlin. Arnold gave explicit orders to Doolittle, now in charge of Eighth Air Force, that the immediate target was to be the production base of the Luftwaffe, and the American bombers succeeded in substantially damaging the overall production ability of the German aircraft industry.

The real impact of the American air assault on German factories that produced aircraft and their engines lay in the second-order effects. With its production base under terrible threat, the Luftwaffe sent its fighters up to attack the B-17s, with the B-24s serving as the bait. From mid-February through April a ferocious battle of attrition took place in the skies over Germany. From January through May 1944, the Luftwaffe's average fighter pilot strength on active duty was 2,283 pilots.[11] In that five-month period, the Germans lost 2,262 fighter pilots, killed, injured, or missing. In May the German fighter force cracked, never to recover for the remainder of the war.[12]

In March, Doolittle made the crucial decision to release the escort fighters from close-escort support of bomber formations. LeMay and other bomber commanders complained vociferously, but Doolittle refused to listen. He would not make the mistake that Reich Marshal Hermann Göring had made during the Battle of Britain by restricting fighters from fulfilling their mission of seeking out and destroying the enemy's fighters. That decision still upset LeMay well after the war, and it was understandable given that his bomber formations were losing more than 30 percent of their aircraft and crews every month from February through April. Not until May did the appalling losses abate, in a direct indication that the Luftwaffe had finally broken and that the American air offensive had won air superiority over all of Europe. LeMay at least saw the result of that contribution when he visited the Normandy battlefield in June 1944. But he was not to remain long in the European theater. Hap Arnold and the masterminds in Washington had a new assignment for him.

WORLD WAR II: ENDING THE WAR WITH B-29S

When France fell in 1940, army air corps leaders had decided that if Britain were also to fall they might have to wage an air campaign against the Third Reich from North America. The program they created aimed to push the technology as far as it could possibly go. Similar to the German Heinkel He 177, the B-29 was inordinately expensive in terms of the resources it gobbled up and was also a killer of those brave enough to fly the first test prototypes. The engines were a nightmare; again like those of the He 177, they had a tendency to explode in flight, more often than not with lethal effects on the test crews. Possum Hansell had less-than-fond memories of the B-29's engines, even after the aircraft had deployed to the field: "The engines of the B-29 had developed a very mean tendency to swallow valves and catch fire. The magnesium crank cases burned with a fury that defied all efforts to put them out."[13] But Hap Arnold was betting that the army air forces would ride on the back of that aircraft into the future as the United States Air Force.

The first deployed unit of B-29s, the XX Bomber Command, went to eastern India. There the crews were to hone their skills by bombing the Japanese in Southeast Asia and prepare for a move to bases in China, from which they would bomb

Japan's industry. LeMay received the assignment to command that group, and after a month transitioning into the B-29 in Nebraska, he found himself in the China-Burma-India Theater. It was a difficult assignment, because Arnold was simply not going to tolerate failure.

In fact, from the military perspective the whole idea of bombing Japan from China represented the worst sort of insanity. The Chinese had to use coolie labor to carve out the great runways and taxiways the B-29s needed. For a government that had nothing but contempt for its people, mobilizing peasants who lived on a starvation diet represented no great problem. But the logistical requirements of a great air campaign required an immense tonnage of fuel, bombs, supplies, and spare parts, all of which transports had to fly across the Himalayas. And then there were the Japanese, who had a vote in the matter. As soon as they recognized that the Americans would launch bombing raids from China, their army set off to capture the bases, which it soon did. Meanwhile, LeMay wasted his immense energy and organizational abilities on attempting to execute a strategic bombing campaign from India against Japanese targets in China and Southeast Asia. Occasionally, his logistical staff managed to acquire sufficient fuel and bombs in China for a few B-29s to strike at the Japanese home islands from bases in China before the Imperial Japanese Army arrived.

Eventually Washington realized that the army air forces were wasting LeMay's talents in India and China. At the beginning of 1945, LeMay found himself ordered to Guam to relieve Hansell as the commander of the XXI Bomber Command. In spring 1944 the U.S. Navy had won a great naval battle over the Imperial Japanese Navy in the Battle of the Philippine Sea, while marines and soldiers had seized Tinian, Kwajalein, Guam, and almost all of the Marianas. Almost at once engineers had begun creating great air bases from which B-29s could attack Japanese industrial sites. Hansell led that effort in fall 1944 with the explicit aim of destroying key targets in the Japanese industrial web, as American doctrine had called for at the beginning of the war.

But Hansell's campaign immediately ran into the inevitable frictions of war. As American airmen had discovered in Europe, the weather in much of the rest of the world rarely resembles that of the training areas of the Arizona desert in the summertime. Adding to the problems posed by uncooperative weather was that the ferocious jet streams at the altitude at which the B-29s had been designed to fly made accurate bomb aiming impossible. Blown about by the high-altitude winds,

U.S. bombers dropped their loads all over the Japanese landscape. Moreover, Japan's economic structure was entirely different from those of the European powers or the United States. It was largely decentralized, with few major nodes whose destruction would result in second- and third-order effects on other portions of war production. Spread out among Japanese cities, Japanese war production offered no clear targets for the B-29 offensive.

Confronted with the problems of bombing Japan as well as the continued teething problems in the B-29, Hansell failed to meet Arnold's expectations. Thus, Arnold sent Hansell home to command training establishments for the remainder of his career. There would be no further promotions for him. Maj. Gen. Lauris Norstad, Arnold's representative, greeted LeMay with a clear warning: "You go ahead and get results with the B-29. If you don't get results, you'll be fired."[14] Implicit in his warning was that the failure of the B-29 offensive would force the American high command to launch an amphibious landing on the Japanese home islands, leading to hundreds of thousands of Allied casualties.

LeMay immediately drew on his intuition regarding the operational aspects of air power and grasped that the American approach in Europe—which accorded with the prewar doctrine—was simply not applicable to the new set of circumstances in the Pacific. What Hansell and the B-29s had attempted over the past several months had not worked. In retrospect, Hansell's approach exemplified that of a commander taking into war his prewar assumptions regarding future conflicts and then attempting to fit reality to those assumptions rather than adapting to face reality. But that was not how LeMay operated. Ever the pragmatist and realist, he took the facts as they were and adapted his operational approach to them.

Moreover, LeMay had absorbed the experiences of the RAF's Bomber Command in executing the nighttime offensive against Germany's cities. And were not Japan's major cities even more flammable than Germany's, since they consisted almost entirely of wood and paper? LeMay decided to discard the XXI Bomber Command's approach to bombing Japan. The B-29s would bomb at night rather than during the day. Ground crews would strip the bombers of their defensive armament. The bombers would go in at low altitude, rather than the high altitudes where the jet stream had so disturbed their flight patterns. Instead of high-explosive bombs aimed at specific military targets, the B-29s would carry napalm and magnesium incendiaries. In other words, the American approach would be similar to Bomber Command's area bombing campaign and would aim as much at destroying the willingness of the Japanese people to continue the war as at demolishing the enemy's war-fighting capabilities. Simply put, LeMay was ditching the entire American doctrine of precision bombing in favor of straight-out attacks on enemy population centers.

Aircrews, of course, vehemently protested. Many feared attacks at low levels would expose them to a greater density of antiaircraft fire, others objected that their training had not prepared them for extensive nighttime flying in combat conditions, while still others suggested that Japanese night fighters would have a field day against the American bombers. Officers at the staff and command levels muttered that they had not done it this way in Europe. None of these objections bothered LeMay. His head and American lives were on the line, and he did not intend to follow a path that had dismally failed in the raids on Japanese industrial sites. Moreover, he doubted that the Japanese possessed many low-level antiaircraft guns.

Thus, in the early evening hours of March 9, LeMay dispatched 325 B-29s loaded with incendiaries to attack Tokyo. Instead of bombing at 20,000 feet, the bombers attacked at altitudes between 5,000 and 9,000 feet. Over the night of March 9–10 they dropped 1,665 tons of ordnance on Tokyo. The resulting firestorm burned the heart out of the city, killed more than 100,000 civilians, and destroyed some 250,000 buildings. Out of the attacking force XXI Bomber Command lost only fourteen bombers. Attacks against smaller targets followed over the next few days. Two days after the destruction of Tokyo, XXI Bomber Command wrecked Nagoya, the center of Japan's aircraft industry. Osaka became the next victim, on the night of March 13–14. It was Kobe's turn on the night of March 16–17, and three days later the B-29s returned to Nagoya. The B-29s left a trail of devastation at every target they bombed. Some crews toward the tail end of raids could smell the burning human flesh that the fires below had already reached.

At least in its images, the bombing of the Japanese cities represented total war at its worst. A few of the victims of the attacks died a relatively painless death from carbon monoxide poisoning, but most suffered excruciating deaths from the fires that engulfed whole cities. The Japanese fire departments proved wholly inadequate to dealing with the fires that spread from one house to another with almost lightning speed, while fleeing civilians made fighting the fires almost impossible. And, not surprisingly, Japan's medical services completely broke down in the face of the tens of thousands of burn victims who required attention. Desperate city dwellers attempted to flee the fires only to run into swelling fires in their path. In every respect the raids underlined the hopelessness of Japan's position, yet the swath of destruction seems to have made little impression on Japan's rulers. Shortly after the devastating first raid on Tokyo, the emperor visited the burned-out areas, but thereafter he made no attempt to persuade his military leaders that the time had come to deal with the Allies.

While the bulk of his B-29 force savaged Japanese cities, LeMay and his bombers cooperated in two other major operations against the Japanese. The first was extensive raids against the air bases in southern Japan, from which the kamikazes were savaging the American carriers and other fleet units that were supporting the marines and soldiers in the amphibious operation to seize Okinawa. Between April 6, when the landings began, and June 22, 1945, approximately 1,900 kamikazes flew missions against U.S. and U.K. naval forces. Fighters on combat air patrol and antiaircraft fire shot down most of the Japanese, but the few that penetrated the Allies' multilayered defenses did terrible damage. The attackers sank a number of ships and severely damaged several fleet carriers. The U.S. Navy suffered 4,907 killed and 4,874 wounded in these attacks. Adm. Chester Nimitz, overall theater commander, ordered LeMay to attack Japanese airfields throughout Kyushu to suppress the attacks. LeMay did not like the mission and complained to Arnold, but LeMay lost the argument. In retrospect, he was probably right about the effectiveness of attacking the airfields, but given the losses the kamikazes were inflicting on the navy, he had no other choice but to obey.

The B-29s executed other missions in their support for the navy's campaign. They not only cut off Japan's sea-lanes of communication with Korea, China, and Southeast Asia but also strangled the seaborne trade among the home islands. American submarines had already sunk most of Japan's merchant fleet. The B-29s now carried out extensive mining operations around every major port in Japan and all the main costal routes between the islands. By July the movement of goods and military forces on the coastal waterways had virtually ceased, yet their situation, hopeless in Western terms, seems to have made little impression on a Japanese high command determined to fight to the end and take Japan's entire population along with them to utter destruction.

To the end of his life LeMay believed that the firebombing of Japan's cities had brought the Japanese to the brink of surrender. Appearing in the brilliant historical documentary *The World at War*, he argued that by the time the atomic bomb exploded over Hiroshima, XXI Bomber Command had almost finished destroying all of Japan's major cities, and once it had struck all of its targets, Japan would have surrendered. In this assertion, however, he was wrong. Recent research, much of it based on the declassification of the Magic intercepts of high-level communications among Japan's military leaders, reveals the Japanese had no intention of surrendering.[15] The carnage that the raids occasioned among the civilian population of Japan's cities moved the Japanese military leaders not at all. In fact, the generals intended to conduct a desperate, suicidal defense of the home islands, even though the consequences for the Japanese people would have been horrendous. The weight of historical evidence now indicates that only the dropping of the atomic bombs forced the emperor to order his military commanders to surrender.

The timing of that surrender proved providential, particularly for the Japanese people. With virtually all of Japan's cities wrecked, XXI Bomber Command was about to move on to a new target set, namely, Japan's transportation network, which was both vulnerable and primitive in comparison to those of Europe and the United States. Here Allied experience during the attacks on the French (1944) and German (1944–1945) transportation networks played a role in future planning. Had the B-29s carried out the planned raids, they would have destroyed that network in short order; however, American occupation authorities would then have had no means to transport the food supplies that prevented mass starvation of the Japanese people over the winter of 1945–1946.

For most of the airmen the dropping of the bombs meant the end of the war, and a chance to return home to their civilian lives. For LeMay, nuclear weapons would open a whole new chapter in his military career.

THE BERLIN AIRLIFT

LeMay returned to the United States as one of the three premier American combat airmen of the war, the other two being Jimmy Doolittle and George Kenney. Doolittle almost immediately returned to civilian life, while Kenney was to fail as the first commander of SAC and almost immediately retire. LeMay, meanwhile, remained on active duty for the next twenty years and put an indelible mark on the culture of the USAF, which had emerged from the war as an independent service.

LeMay's first appointment in the postwar period was as leader of the new service's research and development (R&D) effort. During those two years he tried to salvage as much funding as possible while Congress drastically cut the defense budget, which had swollen to gigantic proportions during the war. However low the funding levels were in the immediate postwar years, a significant number of crucial R&D ventures began under LeMay's oversight, including the initial expansion of the rocket work the Germans had begun with their V-2 ballistic missile program.

But in 1947, as relations with the Soviet Union steadily worsened, LeMay was shipped to Wiesbaden, Germany, to command USAF units deployed to support the American occupation forces in Germany and Italy. Promoted to lieutenant general in January 1948, at the age of forty-one he was the youngest USAF officer at that level. If LeMay had any vision of a restful tour in the palatial quarters of a general charged with occupation duties in a defeated nation, the Soviets soon shattered such illusions. In spring 1948 Joseph Stalin imposed a total road and rail blockade of the American, British, and French zones in occupied Berlin. Together with Maj. Gen. William H. Tunner, who arrived on July 28, 1948, LeMay played an essential role in organizing the aerial bridge of U.S. and Allied aircraft that supplied the German capital with food, coal, and the other necessities required to maintain the portions of the city not under Soviet control.

In every respect the Berlin Airlift represented a triumph not only of LeMay's skills as an airman but also of his immense organizational strengths and his ability to cut through red tape. For example, by having his crews fill out their flight plans while in the cockpits of their aircraft as the Germans unloaded the cargo, he was able to save fifteen minutes per flight. While seemingly inconsequential by itself, the time saved was cumulatively a significant enabler, considering the hundreds of aircraft sorties each day. By the time Stalin finally admitted defeat in 1949, the Berlin Airlift had carried 2,223,000 tons of fuel (mostly coal), food, and other necessities into the city's airports.[16] In every respect the airlift served as a wonderful representation of the flexibility that air power conferred on those with sufficient numbers of aircraft.

FATHER OF THE STRATEGIC AIR COMMAND

Almost immediately after returning from Germany, LeMay found himself confronting the enormous job of turning SAC into a deterrent force that could prevent war between the United States and the Soviet Union. The chief of staff of the newly established USAF, Gen. Hoyt Vandenberg, named him to replace Lt. Gen. George Kenney, who had proven himself to be one of the most innovative

American airmen during the fighting in the Pacific theater. Kenney had faced the difficult task of creating a new command in the midst of huge dislocations as the U.S. Army Air Forces demobilized. Moreover, the new service had minimal resources and had no control over the few nuclear weapons that the United States possessed during the first years after World War II.

Vandenberg picked LeMay precisely because of his extraordinary record in leading air units in combat. Despite a considerable lack of resources and serious handicaps, he had proven in the 1940–1945 period that he had the ability to create effective combat forces that could complete their missions. The secret of LeMay's success lay not in his dour demeanor, one exacerbated by the fact that he had suffered from an attack of Bell's palsy, but in the fact that LeMay's air and ground crews knew that he could and would perform their tasks better than they could. They knew he had led the great Regensburg mission in the lead aircraft— the most dangerous position. His aircrews respected rather than loved their commander, but respect in military organizations is far more important than love.

In building SAC as a formidable military force, LeMay demanded the impossible and in doing so created a command that from top to bottom did its job in a most effective fashion. Because its mission encompassed nuclear deterrence, it was also a highly centralized organization that in the Linebacker II campaign at the end of the Vietnam War proved to lack the flexibility needed to adapt to new circumstances. But SAC's mission of deterrence demanded close control from the top, because its forces possessed a huge and growing arsenal of nuclear weapons. LeMay's success stemmed from his establishing a command that both posed a terrible threat to the Soviet Union's existence and proved sufficient to keep the peace.

Given the problems in the immediate postwar period, the fact that LeMay found the command in general collapse is not surprising. He quickly learned that SAC was not prepared for war. Its aircraft could not reach, much less find, their targets; civilians had control over the few atomic bombs the United States possessed; maintenance rates were appallingly low, while accident rates remained as high as they had been throughout World War II; and SAC's bases were a ramshackle collection of airfields that had been hurriedly constructed during World War II in the rush to train aircrews for service in Europe and the Pacific. However, LeMay was fortunate in taking over SAC at a time when the Cold War was reaching a fever pitch. The period of demobilization had ended, resources again had begun to flow into the military system, and, most important of all, SAC had become the focus of the initial buildup of the U.S. military, since nuclear weapons appeared to be the only deterrent to the vast conventional forces that the Soviets had amassed in Central Europe. Thus, it is no surprise that LeMay succeeded where Kenney had seemingly failed.[17]

In 1948, SAC had only forty-five thousand airmen and fourteen bomber wings, which were equipped almost entirely with B-29s and B-50s, which were nothing more than glorified B-29s. The first six-engine B-36s were arriving in the command, but that aircraft had experienced almost as many difficulties during its development as the B-29 had. The accident rate for the command was an appalling sixty-five major accidents for every 100,000 hours flown. The command's first major exercise—simulated night-bombing runs at altitude—was a disaster, with hardly any of the aircraft reaching and making simulated attacks on its target of Dayton, Ohio.

LeMay set about to fix what he viewed as inexcusable shortcomings. Crews would reach higher standards or they would leave the command. With SAC's acquisition of nuclear weapons, LeMay drastically tightened security procedures. The increasingly intense Cold War gradually solved the problem of adequate resources, and the Korean War and the massive American rearmament following that conflict turned on a steady stream of support. In October 1951, in recognition of his contribution to national defense, LeMay was promoted to full general in the USAF. Moreover, Eisenhower's New Look national security policy and defense budget of 1953 emphasized air power as the primary deterrent force to prevent the outbreak of World War III. Accordingly, the air force received the lion's share of defense budgets.

SAC's capabilities and front-line strength steadily increased in tandem with the defense budget. In 1955 LeMay's SAC had reached nearly 200,000 airmen, who supported twenty-three wings of the new jet-powered B-47s (1,200 total), six wings of B-36s, and the first wing of B-52s, the production run having begun that year.[18]

LeMay's emphasis on more thorough training of flight crews and maintenance crews also had a great impact on the command's safety record. By 1957 SAC experienced only three major accidents per 100,000 flying hours, an enormous change from World War II, when in 1943 alone the army air forces suffered 20,389 major accidents that killed 2,264 pilots and 3,339 other aircrew members while training in the continental United States.[19] LeMay's ruthless punishment of aircrews who made mistakes did not always sit well with those who remembered that LeMay had crashed an aircraft in the 1930s—a picture of which is included in his autobiography. But LeMay proved himself a very successful commander, again through determination, intellect, and plain hard work. He would identify a problem, fix it, and move on to the next, always more concerned with substance than with form.

SAC quickly became synonymous with the B-52 and LeMay, who essentially transformed the command into an extremely effective military unit. All in all, LeMay's force represented a terrifying capability to destroy that served to deter the worst instincts of the Soviet leadership. By the early 1960s SAC had a new supersonic bomber, the B-58, which set the speed record for a flight between Los Angeles and New York.[20] The last bomber to begin development under LeMay, the XB-70, never saw production beyond the first two prototypes, because a new secretary of defense, Robert McNamara, calculated that the ballistic missile would provide a more effective deterrent than the bomber.

CHIEF OF STAFF OF THE AIR FORCE

In 1957 LeMay was promoted to vice chief of staff of the USAF. Four years later, President Kennedy would swear him in as the chief of staff of the air force. LeMay enjoyed neither job. During the last years of the Eisenhower administration, the air force and SAC continued to enjoy the administration's enthusiastic support. Matters changed, however, when Kennedy became president, and the American military came under the scrutiny of Robert McNamara and his cadre of systems analysts known as the "Whiz Kids." Kennedy had won the 1960 election partly on the spurious claim that there was a missile gap between the Soviet Union and the United States. From LeMay's point of view it really did not matter whether or not such a gap existed, because he believed that SAC had more than enough bombers on airborne alert as well as on ground alert to blow the Soviet Union to smithereens should its leaders attempt to launch a first strike at American bases throughout the world.

But LeMay could not tolerate the efforts of McNamara and his band of intellectuals to tinker with American nuclear strategy. From his standpoint the Eisenhower administration's approach of mutually assured destruction was more than sufficient. As LeMay saw it, the use of atomic bombs in 1945 hardly differed from other bombing attacks; after all, the first incendiary raid on Tokyo killed more people than either atomic bomb did. McNamara wanted the air force to focus on missiles, which he argued were more cost effective, while LeMay believed in a new generation of supersonic bombers, the B-70, which would be able to replace the B-52s in time. The Bay of Pigs operation in 1961 violated every military principle that LeMay could think of, and he considered the final negotiated settlement with the Soviet Union over Cuba an appeasement on a par with the 1938 Munich Agreement. That civilians had devised the new strategic approach of flexible response in Vietnam was not only deeply annoying, but it also intruded on what he regarded as the military's preserve. It did not help that the secretary of defense had been one of the analysts of strategic bombing during World War II but had never been exposed to enemy fire. To put it mildly, McNamara and LeMay had an uneasy relationship. In retrospect, LeMay had a better sense of the North Vietnamese than did McNamara and the Whiz Kids, who modeled the war with their new computers and calculated the "proper" signals to send to the North Vietnamese by a carefully calibrated bombing campaign of the north.

Relatively speaking, the Eisenhower years had been ones of relative restraint in the contest between the Soviets and the United States. However, the Kennedy administration faced what appeared to be a far more dangerous world in which the Soviets were willing to challenge the Americans on a number of fronts: Europe and the Berlin Wall crisis of 1961, the Cuban missile crisis of 1962, and the increasingly serious threat of growing Communist insurgencies in both South Vietnam and Laos.

SAC and LeMay's huge air force represented a deterrent of such magnitude that, with the exception of the Cuban missile crisis, the Soviet Union never really dared to push the United States too far and too hard. Did LeMay ever urge his superiors to attack the Soviet Union in a preventive war? The record suggests he did not, although undoubtedly, as Buck Turgidson boasted in Stanley Kubrick's movie *Dr. Strangelove*, LeMay did inform them that the United States could wreck the Soviet Union from one end to the other should a war start. To paraphrase LeMay, "What is the purpose of deterrence if you cannot tell anybody?"

But challenging American interests in the third world was another matter. Here the Soviets had real proxies—China, to supply arms and act as a threat, and, of course, the North Vietnamese themselves, who managed to combine Vietnamese nationalism and dislike of foreigners with the enthusiasm of Maximilien Robespierre's French Revolution. Adding to the difficulties that LeMay and American military leaders confronted in terms of the insurgency in South Vietnam were the proponents of the bizarre theory of graduated response and their apparent willingness to fight an insurgency as if the past did not matter. In fact, through a series of war games called Sigma, planners clearly demonstrated that the path of graduated response that McNamara and his Whiz Kids had designed for Lyndon Johnson had little chance of working, particularly given Ho Chi Minh's ferocious brand of nationalism. To LeMay that outcome was obvious from the beginning. However, while his solution—a massive air campaign to wreck North Vietnam from one end to the other—might have worked, it would certainly have given the rest of the world a negative perception of the United States.

While constantly quarreling with McNamara about whether the XB-70 prototype should go into production, LeMay had troubles on other fronts. Chairman of the joint chiefs of staff (JCS) Gen. Maxwell Taylor, whom some consider to have been the most dishonest officer to hold that position,[21] certainly annoyed LeMay, who also disagreed with virtually all of the chairman's policies. To retaliate against Taylor, who was a nonsmoker, LeMay did not simply smoke cigars in the "Tank" where the JCS met but at times even blew some of the smoke in Taylor's direction.

Fundamentally, however, LeMay's air force was not prepared to fight a conventional war, much less a war against insurgents. It consistently confused numbers and graphs with reality and displayed little interest in the realities of the war against Viet Cong insurgents. USAF fighter-bombers could not hit targets accurately, because virtually all of their practice drops were simulated nuclear deliveries. As a result, Tactical Air Command (TAC) failed to destroy the major railroad bridges outside Hanoi during the entire Rolling Thunder campaign, which lasted from summer 1965 to summer 1968. Its tactical fighters achieved the worst exchange ratio in air-to-air dogfights with enemy fighters in the history of American air power. Graduated response, in terms of both air and ground power, proved as dismal a failure as the Sigma war games had predicted.

Nineteen years after the firebombing of Japan's cities, LeMay noticed a newspaper item that indicated American bombers had been dropping chemicals to help extinguish a massive fire in Japan's main oil refinery. He did not miss the irony. He retired as the air force chief of staff in 1965, a time when Johnson and McNamara were ramping up a war that the United States could not win.

It is fair to argue that LeMay's combative and argumentative nature and his black-and-white view of right and wrong did not serve him particularly well in a politically charged environment. During his time as vice chief and chief, he had certainly been forceful in meetings with the administration and other service chiefs, the president, the secretary of defense, and the chairman of the JCS, but LeMay never exceeded his authority. He was undoubtedly loyal to his political masters (otherwise they would not have extended his term as air force chief of staff), but he was never afraid of offering opposing ideas, believing that the last thing the president needed was a yes-man.

When LeMay's tenure came up for renewal in 1964 President Johnson suggested the possibility of an ambassadorship instead. LeMay answered bluntly and in his typical commonsense style: "It didn't make much sense to stop doing something I knew something about to take on something I knew nothing about."[22] His tenure was renewed for another year, but McNamara and Taylor consulted him less frequently and even ignored him. Both Johnson and McNamara dreaded meetings with LeMay because he made them uncomfortable.

VENTURE INTO POLITICS

LeMay's retirement might have brought some personal happiness to a man who had done so much to mold the culture of the USAF; instead, he felt a great deal of bitterness as he watched politicians and "pointy-headed intellectuals" fight the Vietnam War in a way that he considered so blatantly incompetent. It was probably his frustration with the Kennedy-Johnson policy in Vietnam and the Cold War that drove LeMay into a brief attempt at a political career in 1968. He seems to have believed that by running for vice president with George C. Wallace Jr., the racist former governor of Alabama, the American Independent Party would take votes away from Hubert Humphrey and strengthen Richard Nixon's chances to win the election. LeMay's decision to run with Wallace also reflected his profound contempt toward the counterculture and the attitude young Americans were displaying toward his values. LeMay believed he could use the opportunity of running for vice president to argue that the Johnson administration had engaged in a prolonged and unwinnable war in Vietnam. In retrospect he was right about the appalling mismanagement of the war, but his solution, including the potential use of nuclear weapons, was equally flawed in terms of American grand strategy to win the Cold War.

Spaatz, Eaker, and LeMay's family urged him to stay out of politics. After all, he did not like people who talked a great deal, he did not like speaking to reporters, he did not even like giving speeches—and, equally important, he was not particularly good at it. LeMay had a national standing, represented politically conservative views, and could give a great deal of advice based on his experience, but being an adviser is far different from being a political leader. He first declined the offer to become Wallace's running mate, but when approached again he changed his mind. The experiment failed. LeMay was a poor match for Wallace, he spoke his mind rather than follow the party platform, and his gruff exterior did not appeal to the media. Wallace and LeMay ultimately earned 13 percent of the vote and won five states, but the association with Wallace would taint LeMay for the rest of his life. The younger generation simply remembered the airman for being a failed politician, for being the running mate of a segregationist candidate, and for including the following quotation in his 1965 autobiography: "My solution to the problem would be to tell them frankly that they've got to draw in their horns and stop their aggression, or we're going to bomb them back into the Stone Age. And we would shove them back into the Stone Age with Air power or Naval power—not with ground forces."[23]

LeMay did little to dispel this negative image; he told friends and colleagues that he did not care much what other people said and thought about him. He retired from public life after the election, enjoying a relaxed existence in Bel Air, California. He did some consulting work for National Geographic, spent time with his family, and relished repairing cars and engines, fishing, and hunting—hobbies for which he had had little time during his active duty service. At the age of eighty-five, he died at home from a heart attack on October 1, 1990, and is buried at the Air Force Academy Cemetery in Colorado Springs. Fittingly, Gen. John Chain Jr., the SAC commander, offered the eulogy.

CONCLUSION

Curtis LeMay was a man of his times. He emerged from the school of hard knocks that had produced most of the men who succeeded in the Depression, and he had little patience with people who had followed a softer road. LeMay consistently set an example for his men. In the terrible trials of World War II he led from the front. He never asked his crews to do anything he had not already attempted. When he demanded that they fly straight and level on their bombing runs, he was in the lead aircraft. Moreover, LeMay's persistent interest in technology and the wider aspects of using air power allowed him to see what others consistently missed.

That capacity to analyze and shed new light on complex issues stood him in good stead when he confronted the difficult and ambiguous dilemmas that the conduct of an air campaign would bring.

LeMay was a child of a harder, leaner America. That country was one in which a diligent, intelligent, imaginative, and tough man could get to the top, but it was also a country in which most could never even aspire to succeed. The effort that LeMay expended to become the best of the best represented a level that few, if any, human beings could even consider. In retrospect, LeMay succeeded not by trampling on others but by the sheer unremitting toil that he was willing to expend in the pursuit of excellence. Moreover, he engaged in that quest not merely to promote himself above others but also to preserve the lives of the crews who served under him. In the end, he recognized that while SAC possessed awesome combat capabilities, its greater mission—as found in its motto, "Peace is our profession"—was to preserve the peace. The motto, of course, is also featured prominently on a sign in a fighting scene in *Dr. Strangelove*.

In the decades that have followed the end of the Cold War it is easy to see that the organizational perfection pursued at SAC and eventually in the whole USAF in the 1960s was a target no human organization could reach. Yet, despite all the difficulties the air force confronted in adapting to the complexities of the Vietnam War, it is well to remember that the mission of LeMay's air force, as well as of SAC during his tenure, was to ensure, first, that the Soviet Union was deterred from aggression and, second, that no nuclear accident occurred that would do irreparable harm to the nation. In the early 1990s, USAF chief of staff Gen. Merrill McPeak merged SAC with TAC into the organization that is today called Air Combat Command. The decision represented the triumph of the "fighter jocks" over the supposedly mindless bureaucratic mumbo jumbo of the "bomber mafia." In 2007, however, the careless procedures of that new command allowed several of its bombers to depart their home base fully loaded with nuclear weapons, and no one in the command apparently recognized the situation until the aircraft had landed at another American base. Such a sloppy approach to the duties with which the government of the United States charged the officers responsible for the security of these weapons would never have occurred on LeMay's watch.

PART II

5

WILLIAM H. TUNNER: MASTER OF AIRLIFT

James S. Corum

More than fifty years after his retirement, the effects of Lt. Gen. William H. Tunner's ideas, policies, and leadership style can still be clearly seen in the U.S. Air Force's (USAF's) organization, doctrine, and culture. That is the kind of impact that few military leaders ever achieve. Even airmen who have never heard of Tunner operate according to the procedures that he set up and work with organizations that he brought into being. In short, Tunner was a creative and transformational leader whose forte was in building effective processes and structures. The organization that he largely fashioned—a centrally controlled and directed military air transport system—is today considered one of the great strengths of American military power.

Although the primary mission of armed forces is winning wars, they can also win victories in support of national objectives by means other than combat. The Berlin Airlift is a prime example. As an air leader, William H. Tunner was a special kind of visionary: a man who could articulate the vision and make it realizable in practical terms. Although air power theorists and practitioners had occasionally spoken about the potential of air transport during the first forty years of air power, the military application of air transport was still the most neglected form of air power until World War II. Tunner, who was not particularly distinguished for special talents or rapid advancement before the war, being only a major when the war broke out, showed a unique ability to analyze complex problems and develop highly effective solutions to major strategic challenges. What seem today to be commonsense solutions were then revolutionary conceptual advances in a military culture that had not seriously considered the possibility of large-scale transport of personnel and cargo by air.

Rising from the rank of major to general in four years, Tunner was acknowledged as America's premier air transport specialist by the end of World War II. The subsequent Cold War conflicts and crises would require Tunner's involvement as an air leader for the next fifteen years. By the time of his retirement, the American air transport system that he had largely created was acknowledged as a key element of American grand strategy.[1]

This chapter examines the career of William H. Tunner with the intent of distilling the key traits and methodologies that made Tunner such an effective and innovative leader. Although he is known primarily for his magnificent performance in organizing and directing the Berlin Airlift, Tunner also successfully carried out several other missions of equal importance during his thirty-two-year career. Indeed, Tunner was no "one-trick pony," only proficient in his chosen field of airlift. For example, one of his major accomplishments was his innovative strategic leadership in the 1950s as commander of the U.S. Air Forces in Europe (USAFE). At that time the German rearmament program, a central part of the defense strategy for the North Atlantic Treaty Organization (NATO), had encountered great difficulties. The main problem was poor planning and management on the German side. In helping to build the new German Luftwaffe, Tunner stepped into the breach, identified the problems, immediately applied the necessary resources, and developed the solutions to get the German program back on track. After his highly successful tour in Europe, Tunner returned to the United States to lead the Military Air Transport Service (MATS). He ended his career by a dramatic confrontation with the Pentagon leadership over the future of the airlift system. Defeated in his attempts to establish a properly unified transport service equipped with modern jet aircraft, he retired in 1960. Yet, within a few years of his retirement, he would see his key ideas adopted in full by the Kennedy administration, which funded the C-141 jet transport and finally consolidated the military air transport forces into one Military Airlift Command (MAC).

EARLY CAREER

Born on July 14, 1906, Tunner came from a middle-class family of five in New Jersey and went to West Point in 1924 largely because it offered a first-rate free education. While at West Point, cadets received an orientation to all the different branches of the army before they had to request their branch assignments in their senior year. The air corps orientation that Tunner received included visiting army airfields and taking several orientation flights in two-seater aircraft. Tunner was enthralled and liked everything he saw about aviation and the air corps. When he graduated from West Point in 1928 he was one of the seventy-seven men in his class who opted for the air corps.[2]

His first year in the air corps consisted of basic and advanced pilot training. He was sent to the air corps's premier training bases in Texas, where he underwent the standard flight course at Brooks Field and advanced training at Kelly Field and became qualified to fly both fighters and bombers. His flight instruction was tough, and Claire Chennault was his instructor for fighter planes. In training and in later assignments Tunner compiled only an average record as a pilot. In fact, he failed a few check rides and had to retake his tests.

From pilot training he began the usual career path of an air corps officer in the late 1920s. In those days officer pilots were generalists and could be expected to spend time in fighters, bombers, and reconnaissance craft, as well as serving in various squadron- and group-level staff jobs. Right out of flight school in 1929, his first assignment was to a bomber squadron at Rockwell Field near San Diego. One day he was directed to fly a detachment of a dozen soldiers in a Fokker tri-motor transport to Sacramento. His first experience in piloting a transport illustrates the air corps's attitude toward flying in general, and air transport in particular. Tunner had never flown a transport, and no pilot was available to give him a check ride or orientation. Finally a mechanic showed him the aircraft instrument layout and gave him some pointers on the plane's flight characteristics, but no one gave him a weather briefing or a flight plan. Issued a California road map by the operations officer, Tunner set out for Sacramento with his soldier passengers. Luckily, the weather was clear, he could easily follow the landmarks on the ground, and he reached his destination without mishap. After this brief transport adventure, Tunner returned to the usual round of duties.[3] The experience led him to become a systematic, well-organized, and somewhat careful pilot, always concerned with safety. He remembered, "Though I thought nothing of my first transport flight then, I have certainly recalled it many times over the years since . . . to make sure that no other pilot or crew member . . . under my command would be checked out with such casualness."[4]

At that time the army air corps had only a few transport aircraft available and no specialized units for air transport until the late 1930s. Transports were used as squadron utility planes to run errands and to ferry ground personnel and supplies to advanced airfields when a fighter or bomber squadron deployed on maneuvers. Because officers routinely flew both bombers and fighters, a transport was simply another craft to fly. At a time when instrument flying was being introduced—Lt. James "Jimmy" Doolittle made the first all-instrument flight in 1929—the air corps's procedures for long-distance flying were relatively haphazard. In an interesting contrast to the current situation, in the 1920s and 1930s the army and navy lagged behind the private sector in many aspects of aviation. The civilian airlines in America were growing rapidly and already using all-metal monoplane transports. Unlike military pilots, civilian transport pilots could safely and efficiently fly scheduled routes at night by following light beacons. Soon they would be navigating by radio direction finding.

After his tour with the bomber squadron Tunner was assigned to flight instructor duty, an area where he did not shine at all. He was evaluated as only an average instructor and pilot at best, and efficiency reports also referred to him as temperamental. However, in his next assignment, as a group operations officer and chief of antiaircraft intelligence for the air corps in Panama, he began to stand out as an officer with a high degree of drive and a talent for innovation and management. He enthusiastically organized a series of exercises and training to test and improve the air defenses of the Panama Canal. As operations officer he demonstrated an aptitude for staff work and for developing solutions that made military routines more efficient and effective. Scheduling and maintenance—not especially glamorous aspects of aviation—greatly interested him. If a more efficient maintenance program could be worked out and if aircraft could be efficiently scheduled, then the air corps could maximize the number of aircraft and pilots available for active operations. In analyzing operational methods and creating new systems and standard procedures, Tunner significantly improved both air operations and aircraft availability for the air corps in Panama.

By the mid-1930s he was beginning to earn a reputation in the air corps as a problem solver. His approach was especially valued in the air corps culture when Henry "Hap" Arnold became the corps's chief in 1939.

Tunner was transferred from Panama to Fort Benning, Georgia, where he served from 1937 to 1939 as operations officer for the air corps unit that supported the training at the Infantry School, then the army's premier post for innovative thinking and tactical experimentation. This assignment provided a useful education regarding the support needs of the ground forces. As usual, he excelled at a job that required management and planning skills and won exceptional efficiency reports from his superiors. But his assignments in the 1930s also put him outside the mainstream of the air corps, which was centered in the Air Staff in Washington and at the Air Corps Tactical School at Maxwell Field in Alabama. There the core group of World War II leaders—men committed to the heavy bomber and strategic bombing as a war-winning strategy—was emerging. Tunner spent little time at Maxwell, only passing though for the short version of the captain's course. He was always more interested in the practical application of air power than in theory and doctrine.

Some of Tunner's basic character traits became evident early in his career. He showed enthusiasm for whatever job he was assigned. An exceptional staff officer, he was attentive to detail and had a ready grasp of such key issues as maintenance and logistics. Whenever he was given a task he had the unusual ability to look at a mission with fresh eyes and see if it could be made simpler, safer, or more efficient. He lived up to his personal motto, which was famously captured in his irritable rejoinder to a young officer who expressed dissatisfaction at being assigned to a staff job: "When you get a job to do, do it."

Outside of his family Tunner had only a few close friends.[5] In many respects he had a cold personality. He was never known as being especially sociable. He drank moderately, carried out his basic social obligations, and focused on his career, but that was as far as it went. He had what many described as a short temper, and he did not suffer fools gladly. While he would blow up at a subordinate who made a mistake, he would then immediately move on and discuss with the officer how the mistake could be fixed. With superiors he was honest and blunt to the point of brusqueness. He was ready to challenge their thinking, a trait that some liked and many disliked and that caused him considerable friction in his later career.

One of the key experiences that helped Tunner in his later career occurred in 1939 when, as a captain, he was assigned to command the small air corps detachment in Memphis, Tennessee. In addition to managing its depot at Memphis he was responsible for recruiting civilian pilots in Mississippi, Tennessee, Arkansas, and Louisiana to join the army reserve. At the time the United States was slowly, but steadily, building up the armed forces, and the air corps was looking for civilian pilots who could be given reserve commissions and be available in time of war. Tunner's mission was to make contact with civilian professional pilots—airline pilots, crop dusters, and private pilots—and recruit them for the air corps's reserve program. Tunner proved surprisingly successful in this task. First of all, he got along well with civilian aviators and civilians connected with the aviation industry. In fact, he often related better to civilians than to soldiers. He dealt with civilians as one professional to another, and he paid less attention to a person's rank than to that person's competence.

As noted earlier, the U.S. air transport industry was rapidly becoming a successful business model for the world, and Tunner's job required him to become familiar with commercial airlines, pilots, and ground crews. Working in a mostly civilian environment, he came to understand industry's way of managing aviation, and he found it often more effective than the air corps's methods and "seat of the pants" approach to flying.[6] While the air corps was beginning to form its first transport squadrons, Tunner was working closely with people for whom air transport was a profession, and he demonstrated an openness to civilian approaches. Whenever a civilian procedure, technology, or training program proved effective, Tunner was quick to advocate its adoption by the air corps.

It proved important that Tunner was educating himself about civilian air transport methods at this time, because in July 1940, in response to the crisis in Europe, Congress voted a major rearmament program for the United States. As part of the program the air corps would be quickly built up into a force of thousands of planes. In addition to the fifty-four combat groups, the air corps was to establish six air transport groups, units for which the air corps had little doctrine or organizational understanding.[7] Tunner's limited knowledge of civilian aviation put him far ahead of most air corps officers. Even more important, Tunner was ready and willing to learn about air transport.

CREATION AND EVOLUTION OF FERRYING COMMAND

In early 1941, Tunner's reputation for competence as a staff officer led to his assignment to air corps headquarters. There he served on the staff of Col. Robert Olds and set up a brand new command, known as Ferrying Command, responsible for delivering aircraft to Great Britain under the newly passed Lend-Lease Act. Supplying Britain with war matériel in 1941 was a top priority for the United States, and a whole system for delivering the thousands of aircraft then beginning to pour off the assembly lines had to be worked out from scratch.[8]

The air corps was singularly unprepared to organize a major air transport effort in 1941. Although the corps had given some thought to the use of air transport, it had done little of practical value. In 1924 the Air Corps Tactical School had stated that the combat air force would require air transport in wartime, but it had not proposed an organizational model. The air corps assumed that civilian air transport would be readily available in case of war, so the army bought only a few transports, which were scattered among the combat units.[9]

Although in 1933 the air corps proposed planning for wartime air task forces that included long-distance air transports, the airmail fiasco of 1934 demonstrated how weak the air corps was in even the practical application of air transport and long-distance flying. After taking over airmail operations in February 1934 the air corps suffered fifty-seven accidents and twelve deaths in a few weeks. Because the pilots had not mastered the fundamental skills of navigation and instrument flying, air corps units were finally ordered to fly mail routes only in good weather conditions.[10] By May the civilian companies had reclaimed the airmail mission and resumed flying at night and in poor weather with few problems. The disaster had shown how poorly trained the air corps was in the skills necessary for flying at night and over long distances.[11] It took some time for the air corps to recover.

By the late 1930s the air corps's leadership thought of air transport only as a tactical means to move vital air corps personnel and supplies to forward bases and never considered the concept of using air transport to support large army or navy forces at the front.[12] Even if someone had made such a proposal, the leadership would have quickly suppressed it, being focused single-mindedly on using the corps's limited resources to build up the heavy bomber force.

In 1941 Tunner, then a major, proved exactly the right man to develop the new organization and system needed to move thousands of aircraft efficiently from factories in the United States to the war in Europe. The corps had to check and test the aircraft, supply them with pilots, and then schedule the aircraft to be flown first to Canada and then over the Atlantic to Britain. Moreover, Ferrying Command had to recruit pilots, many of them reservists and civilians; train them; and then organize regular routes to enable rapid movement of aircraft with minimal friction. As mobilization of the U.S. war capability shifted into high gear, Ferrying Command assumed responsibility for transferring aircraft from factories to centers for modifications and weapons installation and then to U.S.-based units ready to deploy overseas. Within weeks Ferrying Command was moving large numbers of aircraft both inside and outside the United States.

When the United States entered the war in December 1941 the situation became more urgent as the regular and reserve air corps pilots assigned to Ferrying Command were transferred to army flying units. To carry out its ongoing mission Ferrying Command recruited more than thirty-five hundred civilian pilots. Further, Tunner shocked the corps culture by strongly advocating the use of women pilots. General Arnold, chief of the Army Air Forces (AAF), initially resisted this approach, but wartime requirements finally pushed the AAF leaders to hire women pilots and create an auxiliary branch of the AAF, which became the Women's Auxiliary Ferry Squadron. Ferrying Command recruited several hundred women pilots who provided outstanding service while transporting all types of aircraft, from fighters to heavy bombers, and doing so with a better safety record than their male counterparts.[13]

From 1941 to 1943 Tunner headed all of Ferrying Command's domestic operations, which transferred more than ten thousand aircraft a month to U.S. and overseas destinations in a safe and efficient manner.[14] The success of Ferrying Command was largely owing to Tunner's ability to solve organizational problems by adapting the best civilian management practices to carry out the command's mission. To ensure efficiency, Ferrying Command classified pilots into six categories according to the types of aircraft in which they were qualified and their instrument rating. The command set up additional training to ensure pilots were checked out in the aircraft they were to ferry. Standardized flight and safety procedures brought down the accident rate while increasing the number of aircraft and hours flown.[15] Tunner's attention to procedure and standardized training paid off, and by the end of 1943 more than fifteen thousand pilots had gone through the well-designed Ferrying Command training program that Tunner had created.

In 1942 Ferrying Command took a big step forward when the name was changed to Air Transport Command and placed under the command of Brig. Gen. Harold George. Tunner was soon promoted to full colonel. With the command's new name came a new concept: its mission was no longer simply to ferry aircraft but also to direct what was quickly evolving into a worldwide air transport system, with regularly scheduled flights to Europe, Africa, and throughout the Pacific region.[16] In June 1943 Tunner was promoted to brigadier general. By that time Air Transport Command had evolved into a major system and had created several overseas routes to support the combat theaters.

During his service at Ferrying Command and Air Transport Command one of Tunner's most significant innovations was his adoption of a civilian safety culture. In essence, Tunner eagerly applied the famous Taylor model of American business management to the air corps's ferry and transport operations.[17] He noted that American insurance companies found it good business practice to have teams of safety experts inspect the factories and large facilities they insured to reduce the risk of fire and accidents. Fewer accidents translated into greater efficiency and greater profits. Tunner adopted this model and established a safety office and safety officers in all the units under his command. In addition to emphasizing the culture of safety, he tasked his staff officers to collect statistics on all aspects of operations so that the command would have benchmarks to measure the effectiveness of standard procedures, maintenance, and scheduling. They carefully measured the effects of training, routing, and aircraft performance and availability as a means of identifying problems, solutions, and best practices.

Although described by many as somewhat cold, rather arrogant, and not a "people person" in any sense, Tunner possessed common sense about commanding airmen. He knew the value of having ground crews and aircrews that were rested, well trained, and working with good morale. Therefore, Tunner was never shy about going to his superiors to demand adequate funds to pay and house his largely civilian workforce and to ensure that when each flight was completed the pilots would be out-briefed, given good food, and provided with comfortable quarters while waiting for their next flight.

The development of large-scale ferrying routes for domestic and overseas operations led to new missions for the Air Transport Command. Air transport for personnel had been rare before 1942, but by 1943 air transport of personnel along regular routes was becoming routine. Aircraft returning from overseas were used to evacuate badly wounded personnel to better medical care in the United States. Indeed, medical evacuation (medevac) transport, a program that saved thousands of American and Allied lives, grew from a sideline into a major operation. By May 1945 more than eighteen thousand wounded military personnel had been transported to the United States for medical care.[18]

In his two years as a top commander in Ferrying Command, Tunner had gained an in-depth education in managing and directing large organizations and creating systems. He learned that to fulfill its mission a unit had to cover every aspect of operations, from recruiting pilots to training, maintenance, scheduling, weather reporting, and planning. The air corps had never done such work before, so he had no military model to follow. He therefore adopted and adapted civilian corporate models that provided exactly the right solutions in terms of fulfilling the air corps's mission.

FLYING THE HUMP: INNOVATION IN THE CHINA-BURMA-INDIA THEATER

In the spring of 1942 the Japanese defeated the British and Chinese armies in Burma and overran the entire country, thus severing the only land route from the Western nations to China, which was then facing the onslaught of the Japanese war machine. The China-Burma-India (CBI) theater thus depended upon air transport. The transport units in the CBI theater were placed under the command of the U.S. Tenth Air Force even though Air Transport Command already had demonstrated its ability to handle large-scale air movement. In the CBI theater the Tenth Air Force had a dual mission—to fly supplies into China to support the Chinese Army and the U.S. Fourteenth Air Force, and to support the Chinese and Allied ground forces fighting in northern Burma in their effort to reopen land communications with China.

The CBI theater had too much territory, too many missions, too little infrastructure, and too few planes. To keep the Chinese in the war, Chiang Kai-shek demanded in 1942 that five thousand tons of weapons and supplies be flown from India to southern China every month. Allied strategists, eager to keep China in the war and thereby tie down huge numbers of Japanese troops, accepted his incredible requirement.

Maintaining the Chinese forces and the USAAF units flying in support of the Chinese would demand a major transport effort, larger than any sustained air transport effort conducted to date. While sometimes facing Japanese fighters, pilots would have to fly hundreds of miles over largely uncharted jungle country and the eastern part of the Himalayas known as "the Hump." In 1942 Lt. Gen. Joseph Stilwell, the commander of the U.S. forces in the CBI theater, estimated that flying five thousand tons over the Hump would call for 304 transport planes, 275 men in flight crews, and 3,400 men on the ground as well as five airfields at both ends of the route, each able to handle fifty aircraft.[19]

Yet what was seen as impossible in 1942 was slowly realized. In 1943 the U.S. War Department agreed to support an air transport effort that would deliver seven thousand tons a month to China by July of that year and ten thousand tons a month by September.[20] Given the incredibly difficult terrain, the lack of a developed infrastructure in either India or China, the bad weather, and the poor working and living conditions for the air and ground crews, supplying China by air became one of the most difficult major logistics operations of World War II.

In 1943 Air Transport Command, an organization that by then had developed some maturity and experience, took over the management of the CBI airlift. However, it still operated under the general direction of the Tenth Air Force and could have its aircraft diverted to other missions as the theater commanders dictated. In addition to supporting China, the Air Transport Command units in the theater had to support the ground operations of the British Fourteenth Army and Stilwell's Chinese army in the battle to retake Burma in 1943 and 1944.[21] Furthermore, Maj. Gen. Claire Chennault, commander of the U.S. Fourteenth Air Force based in China, insisted in the summer of 1944 that his forces needed ten thousand additional tons of airlifted supplies for their operations.[22]

Meanwhile, in the spring of 1944 Tunner was told that he would take command of the air transport effort in the CBI theater as of August. Unlike Ferrying Command, he would not be starting from scratch. By that time, Air Transport Command, flying with inadequate C-46 and C-47 transports, overworked crews, and inadequate maintenance, was meeting the transport goals that the Allied commanders had established the previous year. But the Allied counteroffensive in the theater, as well as the decision to base B-29s in China, would require greater amounts of supplies to keep the Chinese Army and Chennault's Fourteenth Air Force in the battle.

As an acknowledged expert on air transport, Tunner was sent on an inspection tour to the CBI theater in June 1944. Once in India he insisted on boarding a C-46 and flying over the Himalayas to China so he could get a "feel" for what his men had to do. As commander he would later fly the Hump as a transport pilot on many occasions.

As he had done with the Ferrying Command, Tunner sent his staff to all the Air Transport Command units in the theater with a questionnaire and collected detailed data on every aspect of the operation, including maintenance, crew rest, rations, fuel management, and so on. Armed with comprehensive data, Tunner set out to remake the airlift system as efficiently as possible.

Tunner analyzed every aspect of the system and implemented standardized maintenance and cargo-handling procedures that improved the speed of loading and made turnaround rates for aircraft faster. Most important, he lobbied AAF headquarters in Washington to send him new C-54 four-engine transports, and some began arriving in the fall of 1944. The C-54 revolutionized airlift operations. Whereas the C-46 could carry four tons of cargo and the venerable C-47 could carry three tons, the new C-54 could easily carry ten tons, making each plane more than three times more capable than the C-47s that had been bearing most of the burden in the theater.

The CBI theater possessed the worst flying conditions of any World War II combat theater. Owing to horrendous weather over the Himalayas and the lack of navigational aids, the CBI theater also had the highest accident rate of any theater of the war. China was being supplied, but only at a high cost in men and airplanes: in January 1944 Air Transport Command in the theater suffered two accidents for every 1,000 flying hours.[23] When Tunner arrived he set up a safety office modeled on the one he had created at Air Transport Command and mandated standardized flight and maintenance procedures. The accident and loss rate dropped dramatically, to 0.301 accidents per 1,000 flying hours by January 1945.[24] Yet, despite the lower accident rate, aircraft still went down over the mountains and jungles, so Tunner set up a jungle orientation and survival course to improve the aircrews' likelihood of survival if they crashed, and he established a search and rescue organization to extricate them.

Considerable credit for the improved conditions in the theater during Tunner's command also goes to the battlefield success of the British and Chinese armies in Northern Burma. The Allied offensive in the summer of 1944 finally cleared the Japanese out of much of northern Burma. The forced retreat of Japanese fighter planes allowed U.S. air transport pilots to fly a more direct and southerly route into China and avoid the worst of the mountains.[25] The easier route, combined with Tunner's reforms, brought about a significant improvement in the air transport system. In June 1944 deliveries to China had amounted to 18,000 tons. In July the figure was 25,000 tons, in August almost 30,000 tons, in October 35,000, and in November 39,000.[26] Even when land travel reopened in January 1945, the air route still delivered more tonnage to China than the land route did, and considerably more efficiently. In July 1945, the busiest month of the war for Tunner's airlifters, Air Transport Command delivered 71,042 tons of supplies to China with an accident rate of only 0.239 per 1,000 flying hours.[27] At the end of the war, Tunner managed the huge job of shifting Chinese and American troops throughout the theater by airlift, which was the only practical form of transport in China.

Tunner demonstrated a unique leadership style in his first combat area command. On the one hand, to counter the low morale among the airmen in the theater he fought to obtain better food, housing, and recreation facilities for them. He argued that men could not work hard for sustained periods without good living conditions. On the other hand, he was ruthless in punishing disciplinary infractions and was especially hard on men who demonstrated a sloppy approach to their duties. Tunner strictly enforced personal appearance and uniform standards and mandated regular parades. He was sometimes viewed as inflexible and overly concerned with discipline. He showed little patience with officers and men who complained. The nickname "Willie the Whip" did not bother him at all because he wanted results. If that outcome came at the expense of popularity, so be it. Tough on his subordinates, he was also impatient with his superiors when they made impossible demands or pushed him to support only their command to the exclusion of the requirements of the entire theater.

This type of confrontation was characteristic of Tunner throughout his career. In the Ferrying Command, in the CBI, and later in Korea, Tunner always viewed the mission in terms of the "big picture." It was, and is, an unusual trait in military leaders. Most air and ground commanders tend to look at strategy and operations only in the context of their slice of the mission. In the CBI theater Tunner tried to institute organizational and procedural reforms that met the needs of the whole theater while facing constant criticism from superior officers who fought his concepts. General Chennault, who always demanded top priority for his Fourteenth Air Force, was a particular headache for Tunner during 1944 and 1945. But although Tunner was never popular with either subordinates or superiors in the CBI theater, he earned the respect of all for his unwavering dedication to professional excellence. Everyone could tolerate a tough and cold commander who obviously knew what he was doing.[28]

The CBI airlift operations were regarded as a triumph for Allied ingenuity, and they made a lasting impression on U.S. air doctrine. According to historian

Charles Miller, the great lesson of the CBI airlift "was that a properly supported and managed airlift could achieve results never dreamed of before World War II."[29]

THE WEST'S FIRST VICTORY OF THE COLD WAR:
THE BERLIN AIRLIFT

In late 1945 Tunner was transferred to the United States, where he was made the air inspector of the Air Transport Command. In July 1946 he was promoted to major general. When the U.S. Army Air Forces became the U.S. Air Force (USAF) in September 1947, the MATS was born from the consolidation of the Air Transport Command and the Naval Air Transport Service. Tunner was made the MATS deputy commander for operations. He had barely settled in to his new job when a crisis in Europe erupted that would make him famous well beyond the ranks of the air force.

The ongoing confrontation between the Soviets and the Western powers over the status of Germany and Berlin had escalated steadily since May 1945. By 1948 it was clear that the Soviets were determined to build a puppet state in their part of Germany. The British and Americans responded by combining their zones of Germany into one economic unit, allowing free elections, and nurturing a West German government under liberal and pro-Western reformers to build a democratic state in the West. The Soviets perceived the introduction of a new currency in West Germany in the spring of 1948 as a threat to their grand plans, as indeed it was. They decided upon a power play to push the Allies out of Berlin.

On June 21, 1948, the Soviets closed all the land routes of transport to the Western sector, which was occupied by the British, Americans, and French. The Soviet action was intended to force the West Berliners to register in East Berlin and accept Soviet authority in order to get ration cards. As West Berlin only had a thirty-day food reserve it was a sound assumption on the Soviets' part, yet the Soviets did not count on the will of the West Berliners to resist such blatant aggression. Few West Berliners accepted Soviet ration cards, and on June 24 more than eighty thousand West Berliners rallied to support Mayor Ernst Reuter and the democratic reforms introduced under the Western powers. The dramatic demonstration of the West Berliners' resolve to support democracy made it vitally important for the Allied powers to win this test of wills.

Rather than revoke their reforms in West Germany, the Allies responded to the Soviet land blockade by enacting an airlift of food and coal through the three air corridors allowed into West Berlin by the occupation agreement. It was an almost foolhardy move. When the airlift began only 102 C-47s (three-ton cargo capacity) and only two C-54s (ten-ton cargo capacity) were available in theater. Planners estimated that West Berlin would need a minimum of four thousand tons of food and coal per day to survive. This requirement was far beyond the capacity of the air transport forces in the area.[30]

The Berlin Airlift is the first example in history of an air campaign conducted outside the context of a shooting war. It came down to a matter of strategic options. The military position of the Western Allies in Europe was very weak. France had focused on reestablishing its armed forces and fighting insurgents in Indochina. Britain was overcommitted to solving Commonwealth problems. The U.S. Army had only one division stationed in Europe. Thus, the Western Allies could draw on only a minuscule conventional force to face off the Soviets. However, caving in to the Soviets' demands would soon lead to the neutralization of Germany, with the Soviets in the dominant role in Central Europe's largest and potentially richest nation. No stable and democratic Europe was possible under those conditions. To avoid the direct risk of open war left only an airlift as a response that could meet the Soviet challenge.

In 1948 Lt. Gen. Curtis LeMay was serving as the commander of the U.S. Air Force in Europe (USAFE). LeMay had emerged from World War II as a famous senior combat commander who had led the strategic bomber offensive against Japan and dropped the atomic bombs that ended the war. At key moments, LeMay had been at the center of the air war in the Pacific. Tunner, meanwhile, was well known only to a few airmen and to the few senior officers who had served in the CBI theater. Although the performance of the Hump airlift to China was impressive, the operation was carried out in a little-known and low-priority theater of war. However impressive the organizational success of Tunner's command had been, no one could claim that CBI was a decisive theater or that the successful airlift had even a fraction of the effect on the outcome of the war that LeMay's air raids on Japan did. In short, airlift still had to prove that it could play a decisive role.

With his characteristic drive and energy LeMay had implemented the Berlin Airlift, known as "Operation Vittles," as soon as possible. The commander of the airlift itself, Brig. Gen. Joseph Smith, was another USAF combat veteran, but he lacked airlift experience. LeMay was out of his depth when it came to managing such an operation, but he believed that Smith was the right man for the job.

When the Berlin Airlift began it quickly ran into trouble. The USAFE had no experience in organizing a major airlift. With their small load capacity the C-47s available for the initial effort were inefficient cargo carriers. Weather and air control problems soon became evident even as additional transport units were committed. Tunner recalled:

> To any of us familiar with the airlift business, some of the features of Operation Vittles which were most enthusiastically reported by the press were contradictions of efficient administration. Pilots were flying twice as many hours per week as they should, for example: newspaper stories told of the way they continued on, though exhausted. I read how desk officers took off whenever they got a chance and ran to the flight line to find planes sitting there waiting for them. This was all very exciting, and loads of fun, but successful operations are not built on such methods.[31]

Having served for much of the war in Washington, Tunner knew his way around the Pentagon and the military bureaucracy. When the airlift began Tunner began lobbying the USAF chief of staff, Gen. Hoyt Vandenberg, for command of the operation. At first Vandenberg favored Smith for the job but was convinced otherwise when he realized that an airlift of this magnitude required special expertise and experience.[32] At a meeting of the National Security Council in late June, Vandenberg put forward Tunner's name as the logical man to run an airlift. The other services supported the idea of sending Tunner. Lt. Gen. Albert C. Wedemeyer, chief of operations on the Army Staff, had seen Tunner in action in China and proposed him for the airlift command as well. He stated that "Ton-Mile" had performed "unbelievable feats" during the war and was ideal for the task.[33] It is a remarkable testimony to Tunner's reputation among the U.S. military's top leaders that, when an airlifter was needed, Tunner was the choice.[34]

When Tunner was told that he would be taking over the airlift, as he had expected, it was with the authority of the Joint Chiefs of Staff behind him. He was ready with a list of twenty key officers, most of them with CBI experience, whom he wanted attached to his staff immediately. To the consternation of General LeMay and General Smith, when Tunner arrived as airlift commander he brought his own complete staff with him. Tunner found a rather chilly atmosphere upon arrival: "We went to Germany and reported in to LeMay. He wasn't very pleasant, he was very cold. He said, 'Well, you'd better get started.' So I said, 'Tell Smith I'm here and taking over.' He said 'Goodbye.' I said, 'Goodbye,' and that is about all the conversation we ever had."[35]

Tunner arrived in Wiesbaden in late July 1948 and assumed command of the task force that had been recently organized to manage the airlift effort. He found an exhausted, disorganized, and demoralized command. After flying some missions into Berlin to see the conditions the pilots faced, Tunner immediately began reorganizing the entire effort.

The problems that the U.S. and British forces confronted in the airlift could be broken down into six key components: the type and number of transport aircraft and their cargo capacity, the capacities of the airfields sending supplies to Berlin, the capacities of the airfields in Berlin to receive supplies, efficient cargo and aircraft ground handling, flight rules and scheduling, and aircraft maintenance. For the airlift to succeed, the Allies would have to overcome problems and maximize efficiency in all six areas.[36] Luckily, the highest military and civilian leaders supported the airlift, and Tunner could count on the USAF to meet his requests for most of its available C-54 transports. Within hours of his arrival, Tunner's experienced staff went to work to collect data and develop a comprehensive plan that addressed all the key issues. Tunner would also walk around at different times of the day and night to check on the staff. "The word got around that the General had been there during the small hours. It was a twenty-four-hour operation everyday, and I wanted everyone in the Airlift to remember that."[37]

One thing that Tunner immediately understood, but LeMay and Smith were slow to grasp, was that the airlift to Berlin, and the Cold War itself, represented a new kind of campaign in which military actions would have to be tied to and supported by the highest political authorities. The old divisions between the military and the civilian leadership had to be mended to enable an effective strategic response. In particular, because the airlift was linked to the German economy and required large amounts of support in the form of West German labor and German funds and resources, success would hinge on the closest cooperation between the German political authority, embodied by the U.S. high commissioner to Germany, Gen. Lucius D. Clay, and the airlift task force. But the U.S. military command structure in Europe cut General Clay out of the loop on airlift issues and required Tunner to coordinate only through General LeMay on all issues related to support from the Germans. This arrangement slowed down the implementation of some key decisions for the airlift.

Keeping the planes flying at maximum efficiency required a large number of mechanics—more than the USAF had readily available. The problem could be easily solved, since many highly trained former Luftwaffe mechanics were available who could do the job; however, to employ them Tunner needed General Clay's approval. Rather than go through the USAF staff process, Tunner arranged to run into General Clay "accidentally" during one of Clay's inspection trips to Berlin. When Clay asked Tunner how the airlift was going, Tunner told him of the urgent need for mechanics. Clay immediately approved Tunner's proposal to hire Germans to support the airlift and provided an ex-Luftwaffe general to help organize the effort.[38]

Bucking the normal command channels in this manner was characteristic of Tunner and caused considerable friction with other senior U.S. officers. Tunner had spent enough time in Washington to know how to circumvent official procedures and to get decisions made quickly. Tunner also had an advantage in that the Joint Chiefs of Staff and USAF chief of staff Vandenberg had sanctioned his mission and were ready to commit most of America's airlift assets to make this one operation succeed.

The airlift also called for a coalition effort that had to be negotiated at the top military levels. In many respects, the airlift was a forerunner of NATO in terms of negotiating basing rights, equipment use, and common procedures and doctrine, and especially in terms of developing a combined command arrangement. The British were key partners in the airlift. Although the Royal Air Force (RAF) had only a limited transport force, its two airfields at Celle and Fassberg in northern Germany allowed for shorter and simpler flights into Berlin than did any air bases in the U.S. sector and could significantly speed up the operation.[39] By using the British bases as the airlift's primary fields, the task force could fly more sorties and at lower altitudes and deliver greater tonnages with the same number of planes.

The only problem was working out an allied command system. The RAF senior commander in Europe, well aware that his force would be the junior partner in the endeavor, offered the RAF's full support if the airlift were managed by an Allied committee that would make the key decisions and would review all decisions and operations. To LeMay and Tunner, this arrangement was unacceptable. They felt the airlift's success would require a unified command under a single commander. After hours of negotiations the RAF gave in and accepted an American task force commander having the final say in all airlift operations.[40] Soon the greater part of the USAF effort was staged out of the British bases. This cooperation proved central in the airlift's success.

Tunner understood that success depended on achieving the greatest possible efficiency from each aircraft. This effort meant putting an airplane in the air for the maximum hours per day, ensuring rapid loading and unloading at each end, establishing a safe and effective air control system, providing smooth and efficient engine and aircraft maintenance, and making certain that pilots and aircrews were rested, available, and trained to do their job. When short on American personnel he used German labor for maintenance, cargo loading, and administrative tasks. As when he hired women pilots in World War II, Tunner's latter idea was met with skepticism at first, but his judgment was proved right. He also emphasized that tonnage should not take priority over safety, another criterion for overall success.

The C-47s, excellent tactical planes for front-line operations, were clearly unsuitable for this kind of airlift. Tunner therefore requested that a large percentage of the American four-engine C-54 transport force be deployed immediately to Germany. As he had learned in China, fewer but larger planes did a much better job of airlifting than smaller planes could.[41] In addition, Tunner's staff reviewed the efficiency of the maintenance system and determined that the operation required a centralized engine repair facility. Again coalition operations came into play. The quickest solution was to reopen a major repair depot in Britain that the AAF had used during the world war.

Solving the problems related to developing practical standardized flight procedures and efficient aircraft ground handling was also central to the success of the airlift. Essentially, Tunner instituted a system that worked brilliantly. All planes flew through the three air corridors to Berlin spaced three minutes apart and followed a set instrument flight path. If a plane missed an approach, it turned back rather than "stacking" in a holding pattern. This procedure simplified air control and ground handling. The turnaround time for aircraft in Berlin was thirty minutes, enabling transports to fly several trips per day.[42]

Tunner understood the political requirements of a Cold War air campaign before his colleagues in the U.S. military did and brought with him to Germany a highly talented press officer who would ensure that the airlift efforts received maximum international coverage.[43] Tunner understood that the airlift was much more than a logistics exercise, it also had vital psychological and symbolic significance. The USAFE staff initially wanted the daily airlift cargo data to be classified, but Tunner insisted on publishing the tonnage figures daily and on giving the international press full access to the airlift crews. The airlift would be a major propaganda victory for the West. When one transport crew began using handkerchief parachutes to drop candy to children in West Berlin, Tunner made the program of "candy bombing" a regular part of the airlift routine. A photograph of American airmen who, only three years before had dropped bombs on Berlin, were now "bombing" Berlin children with candy became one of the iconic images of the airlift. He was the "peace warrior."

Tunner's task force was quickly able to meet Berlin's daily requirements for four thousand tons of food and coal. From then on, it became a competition to exceed the minimum, and every day that the task force succeeded was a huge morale victory for the Western nations. Tunner's policy of publishing the daily tonnage figures encouraged a healthy spirit of competition among all the units involved in the airlift. On April 16, 1949, U.S. and British airmen, in an all-out effort, delivered 12,941 tons of coal and food to Berlin. It was a significant humiliation for the Soviets.[44]

Finally, on May 12, 1949, the Soviets ended their blockade of Berlin, after the airlift had delivered more than two million tons of food and coal and after General Tunner had firmly announced, "We can keep pouring it in for 20 years if we have to." It was the West's first real victory of the Cold War. It heartened the Western Allies, who now knew that the Soviet threat could be met and overcome. Berlin gave an impetus to the Western Allies at the start of the NATO alliance, proving that Allied cooperation and effort and American leadership and technical know-how could overcome seemingly insurmountable problems. General Vandenberg summed it up: "Above all the Berlin Airlift has provided the United States Air Force an opportunity to demonstrate to the American people, whose instrument it is, and to the world at large, what it can do and what it will continue to do the best of its ability to make air power a true force for peace."[45]

LeMay, for his part, would later refer to Tunner as "the transportation expert to end transportation experts."[46] A distinguished combat commander and always results oriented, he came to appreciate Tunner for his expertise. He basically allowed Tunner to run the airlift without micromanagement. LeMay's replacement,

Lt. Gen. John K. Cannon, who arrived in October 1948, did not feel the same way about Tunner, and the two developed an uneasy relationship. As USAFE commanding general, Cannon insisted that everything should go through him, an arrangement that Tunner found detrimental to an efficient operation. When Tunner could not convince Cannon he simply bypassed the chain of command.

The two clashed, for instance, on how to deal with the personnel. According to Tunner:

> He [Cannon] always wore a big smile, and he liked to go around listening to the troubles of the GI's. If the story was good enough, he'd send the man home regardless of his duties, or how long he had been in Europe. Word of this got around, and the more members of the Task Force began to think of Uncle Joe Cannon as sympathetic and kind-hearted and fair, the more their commander, I, became by contrast harsh and cold and a miserable guy to work for.[47]

Cannon found that Tunner had an abrasive personality and that his bluntness and tactless behavior did not inspire loyalty. But results speak for themselves: when the airlift ended, 276,926 flights had delivered 2,323,067 tons of supplies to Berlin[48] and the Soviet Union had backed down. Tunner had preferred to be assessed by results than popularity. His primary loyalty and dedication were to the mission, not to his commander.

THE KOREAN WAR

The next crisis came in June 1950, when Soviet-backed North Korea mounted a massive invasion of South Korea with the intent of quickly overrunning that small nation. The United States immediately intervened to oppose the North Korean attack, rapidly followed by allied forces from the United Kingdom, Canada, Australia, France, Greece, the Philippines, Turkey, South Africa, and others. The United States and allied nations under a United Nations (UN) resolution would eventually turn the tide, but in the early days of the Korean War it seemed likely that U.S. support would not arrive in time.

When the Korean conflict began Tunner, now known throughout the world as the man who had run the Berlin Airlift, was dispatched to Korea to organize the air transport effort for the U.S. and UN forces. He arrived in theater on August

26, 1950, to assume command of the Combat Cargo Command.[49] At the start of the conflict the U.S. Far Eastern Air Force had only the 374th Troop Carrier Wing with two squadrons of C-54s and some C-47s assigned to tactical troop carrier units.[50] The undermanned and poorly trained and equipped U.S. Army units in the region had been dispatched to Korea in July 1950, and the North Koreans had soundly beaten them in early battles. Even though a steady stream of U.S. reinforcements was arriving, by August 1950 the North Koreans had steadily pushed U.S. and South Korean forces far south, to a small perimeter around Pusan. In order to merely hold on, the UN forces in Korea needed all the air support, including airlift support, that could be mustered.

When Tunner went to Korea the U.S. airlift position had improved thanks to the addition of the C-119 transport to the airlift fleet. The C-54 needed large and developed airfields, while the C-119 could carry even more cargo and could operate effectively from short, rough airfields. In short order Tunner created a provisional troop carrier group to handle the four C-119 squadrons that had arrived in the theater. Another group with C-46 and C-47 squadrons quickly reinforced it.[51]

To illustrate how much U.S. doctrine had changed since 1944, airlift played a central role in all U.S. military operations in Korea from the beginning of the conflict. The first American units to go into combat to defend South Korea were airlifted from Japan. Vital supplies were flown in and wounded soldiers taken out by medevac flights. A transpacific air operation was soon in place to move personnel to and from Korea and the United States.

In Korea the centralized use of assets was a key part of Tunner's organizational changes. To the navy's dismay, Tunner convinced the theater commander, Gen. Douglas MacArthur, to place the marine air transport units under his command. To ensure that airlift and his limited resources were used properly, Tunner established a single theater agency to manage all airlift requests and empowered his airlift managers to reject any requests that did not meet the requirements of military necessity.[52] Tunner advocated establishing a single transport agency for the theater that would manage all transport assets—air, sea, and land—in a centralized manner. It was a sound proposal and would become the standard U.S. military practice in the 1960s, but such a concept was still too extreme for the services to accept in the early 1950s. The army clung stubbornly to the tactical troop carrier units assigned to tactical army support in the belief—later proven wrong in Vietnam— that ground forces would not receive full support from a centralized transport force under USAF command. Tunner's strong advocacy for a centralized transport command earned him the enmity of some senior army leaders.[53]

By October 1950 Tunner's reorganized and centrally directed air transport effort was able to move hundreds of passengers and more than fourteen hundred tons of cargo throughout the Korean Peninsula on a daily basis. It was recognized as an airlift operation second only to the Berlin Airlift.[54] As the UN forces counterattacked at Inchon in September 1950 and began a rapid advance into North Korea, they soon outran their supply lines using Korea's poor road network. Tunner's airlifters flew fuel and ammunition to forward airfields as soon as they were captured, thus enabling the UN forces to sweep up to the Yalu River and overrun almost all of North Korea by November 1950. General MacArthur was so impressed by Tunner's performance that he personally presented Tunner with the Distinguished Service Medal.

In November 1950 the Red Chinese armies intervened in Korea and isolated and sometimes cut off UN troops. Throughout the retreat of UN forces during November 1950 to January 1951, Tunner's command supplied cut-off units by air, evacuated thousands of casualties, and even ran an airlift in December 1950 to move thousands of South Korean orphans out of the advancing Communist forces' path.[55] Throughout the advance and the crisis of retreat, Tunner's improvised organization did all that was asked and ensured that a setback for the UN forces did not become a catastrophe.

Tunner stayed in Korea until February 1951. The systems that he had put into place in Korea functioned exceptionally well and became a model for an effective theater air transport system. Before Korea, air transport had never been considered a key part of a theater combat plan. Tunner and the airlifters' performance in Korea changed that thinking.

THE BATTLE FOR ORGANIZATIONAL AND TECHNOLOGICAL INNOVATION

As the Korean War wound down, the Eisenhower administration faced the dilemma of meeting numerous international military commitments without breaking the budget. All conventional forces—naval, air, and ground—faced major cuts as the United States moved to a policy of reliance upon nuclear weapons as the primary means of deterrence. Determining the means to maintain the U.S. deterrent power with a smaller U.S. conventional force was a key strategic issue at the end of the Korean War.

When he returned to Washington in 1951 Tunner became deputy director of the Air Force Materiel Command (AFMC).[56] He worked closely with USAF chief of staff Vandenberg and the Air Staff to develop a new doctrine that would meet current requirements for worldwide military obligations. Given the success of airlift in Korea in moving troops into theater, supplying forward units, and delivering key items of equipment, combined with the capabilities of prototype large transport aircraft that could carry far more passengers and cargo than the C-54s and C-119s, General Vandenberg proposed new conventional deterrence concepts to the Joint Chiefs of Staff and Defense Department. Coached by Tunner, Vandenberg argued that instead of maintaining large supply depots in forward areas of likely conflicts, airlift could provide a better and more flexible, not to mention much less expensive, means to support U.S. forces rushed into a combat theater. In essence, an enlarged American airlift force equipped with cutting-edge large transports could replace much of the logistics system.[57]

It was a revolutionary concept and not an impractical one, given the new technology becoming available in the mid-1950s. However, the army was suspicious of placing too much reliance upon the USAF and was reluctant to change its traditional logistics system, which was built on forward basing and depots. The Eisenhower administration considered the USAF proposals but soon rejected them as being too costly.

In Washington Tunner was fully engaged in promoting newer and larger transports to follow the C-124 Globemaster, which had been introduced into service as a strategic airlifter during the Korean War. The Globemaster represented an impressive advance in airlift capability as it could carry twenty-five tons of cargo—even armored vehicles—across long distances. But Tunner was looking to the future development of large jet transports with intercontinental range. In his previous jobs he had developed doctrine, procedures, and plans for a theater force. Now he could do the same for the whole USAF and, indeed, for the entire defense establishment. His job as deputy commander of AFMC put him at the center of developing technology and concepts for the USAF, and he proved to be talented at both. Unfortunately, Tunner was looking to develop and expand the airlift system as a national asset at a time when defense cuts were the order of the day. During his tenure at AFMC from 1951 to 1953 he was able to move only a few of his ideas forward.

USAFE COMMANDER

In 1953 Tunner, now a lieutenant general, was selected to command USAFE and take over from Gen. Lauris Norstad, who had been promoted to NATO commander. While Lt. Gen. Nathan F. Twining, who had succeeded Vandenberg as chief of staff, once noted Tunner's irascible personality and leadership ability had a negative effect on subordinates,[58] General Norstad thought very highly of Tunner and specifically requested Tunner to serve as his air commander.

When Tunner arrived in Europe the buildup of the NATO allies was well under way, and for the next four years he would face a new set of challenges that he would, in characteristic fashion, manage to solve. During the Korean War the U.S. forces in Europe had gone from one to more than five divisions, and USAFE had also increased in size. However, as the U.S. buildup still could not match the Soviet conventional threat, NATO needed the newly created and increasingly prosperous West German state, under the leadership of Chancellor Konrad Adenauer, to join NATO and develop armed forces within the NATO context. Germany was willing to rearm, and its entry into NATO was negotiated with the major Western powers. In 1955 the Federal Republic of Germany formally joined NATO and began to establish the new Bundeswehr (Federal Defense Force), committed to the defense of Western Germany and Western Europe.[59]

Creating a modern air force was an exceptionally difficult task for the Germans. While Germany had fielded a few jet aircraft in the last year of World War II, the country had been without an air force during an intensive period of technological development in aeronautics. By the time Germany began to rearm, the United States and Great Britain had technologically sophisticated forces flying their third and fourth generations of jets. In contrast, a new German air force would have to be developed virtually from scratch. A few officers of the old Luftwaffe could provide leadership, but Germany would have to recruit and train a new corps of pilots, mechanics, and support personnel for the jet age. To meet the goal of standing up a large air force in a few years, the West Germans would have to mount a huge training effort. To speed up the process, they opted to outfit their new air force with American equipment and to follow American procedures. For its part, the USAF would act as trainer and mentor for the new Luftwaffe.[60] Tunner, with his ability to create and adapt organizations and develop training programs, was again the right man in the right job.

Because a strong German Luftwaffe would be an enormous asset to NATO, the NATO commander accorded a high priority to the USAF program to train and develop it. Tunner worked in close partnership with General Norstad, who readily provided him with the resources and personnel to make the training program work.

During 1955 Tunner and the new Luftwaffe staff finalized plans to build a large German air force over a period of five to six years. To establish a basic training program for German pilots and ground personnel the USAF set up a provisional training command under a brigadier general and designated four air bases in Germany to serve as training schools for the Luftwaffe. A training wing of approximately a thousand personnel would staff each base. The initial pilot and ground crew training would be carried out in Germany, and advanced training for pilots would be conducted in the USAF schools in the United States. Eventually, American-trained German personnel would take over the training of the Luftwaffe, and the four bases would be turned over to the new Luftwaffe.[61]

The well-planned system that Tunner set up almost collapsed in 1956 when the German Bundestag (Parliament) failed to allocate the defense funds for the Bundeswehr. It was less a political crisis than sheer incompetence on the part of West Germany's first defense minister, Theodor Blank. The lack of funding was about to shut down all the training programs for the new Luftwaffe in midcourse. However, Norstad and Tunner, who had carefully followed the West German defense ministry's administrative mess, had readied a plan to continue the German training program with funding from various U.S. sources until Adenauer and the Bundestag could resolve the problem.[62] As they predicted, the Germans soon solved their budget predicament, the USAF was reimbursed, and training continued without interruption.

Norstad and Tunner had demonstrated good coalition leadership skills by understanding the problems the NATO Allies faced and anticipating the likely obstacles to mission accomplishment. Thanks to Tunner's planning skills and political sense, what could have been a major crisis for German rearmament and for NATO expansion was averted. When Tunner left Europe the West German Luftwaffe's training program was running smoothly, the bases had been transferred to its control, and its first combat units had been activated.

THE VISION FOR GLOBAL STRATEGIC AIR TRANSPORT

In 1957, after his tour as the USAFE commander, Tunner was transferred to Washington. On July 1, 1958, he was given the post to which he was especially suited: commander of MATS. Succeeding his old rival Joseph Smith, Tunner had authority over most of the U.S. strategic military airlift assets. During the next two years he pushed for the adoption of a new air transport organization and doctrine for the U.S. military.

Through the years of the Eisenhower administration the president and defense secretary had resisted any significant expansion or development of America's conventional capability. Toward the end of the decade, the USAF still had as its main strategic airlifter the C-124 Globemaster, an aircraft that was rapidly wearing out. Moreover, it had no plans for a new generation of strategic airlift planes.[63]

In addition, the air force confronted a doctrinal and organizational debate about centralizing the U.S. airlift fleet or dispersing it among the tactical commands. Despite ample evidence from recent conflicts, many at the top of the defense establishment still failed to recognize the importance of a strong airlift force to enable quick reaction. As Tunner assumed the MATS command in 1958 two crises occurred that illustrated the importance of a modern, centrally commanded strategic airlift force. First, the United States deployed more than twenty thousand American troops to intervene in the civil conflict in Lebanon. Immediately, MATS was able to allot a force of Globemasters to fly high-priority supplies and personnel to Lebanon. On the other side of the world, a confrontation between Red China and Taiwan in the Taiwan Strait required the immediate deployment of F-104 fighters, parts, and aircrews across the Pacific. Again, the C-124 Globemasters carried out this mission quickly and efficiently.[64] Despite this clear evidence of the effectiveness of a centralized air transport system, the Pentagon directed Tunner to shift half of the MATS transport aircraft to the tactical air forces. It seemed that every theater commander wanted his own transport force.

In Tunner's view, the United States was setting itself up for strategic failure in the future. From Berlin to Korea to the recent crises, a centralized system for strategic airlift had proven more efficient and cost effective than dispersed airlift assets. Indeed, since World War II, America's strategic airlift capability had made a huge difference in terms of military capability and power projection. Now, narrow-minded service interests and theater commanders wanted to wreck the system.[65]

To prove how effectively centralized airlift could respond to a crisis Tunner organized a large-scale joint maneuver in which more than twenty thousand army troops and their equipment and logistics were transported from the continental United States to Puerto Rico, and then sustained completely by airlift. Tunner managed the feat through a brilliant piece of planning and scheduling, and he did it without disrupting the normal support that MATS gave to the major commands.[66] It was a real piece of showmanship intended to counter the Defense Department's refusal to support a stronger conventional military capability. However, the grand airlift exercise was aimed less at the Eisenhower administration, which Tunner by this point believed was unteachable, than at the U.S. Congress.

In his last months as MATS commander Tunner openly defied the Eisenhower administration over its strategy of reliance on nuclear weapons and its failure to properly fund the conventional forces. In 1959 and 1960, Tunner argued several times before Congress that a strong, centralized airlift system would enable the United States to respond quickly and effectively to any limited war or major crisis. Tunner told Congress that the U.S. airlift fleet was obsolescent and that current and future threats required an airlift force equipped with an intercontinental jet airlifter capable of carrying forty-plus tons of equipment and supplies to points thousands of miles distant. He insisted that the failure to fund a modern airlift fleet was a strategic mistake that would leave America vulnerable. Tunner furthermore asserted that the troop carrier transport units that still belonged to the tactical air forces and were trained to support army paratroop operations should be placed under the command of MATS. He assured Congress that such a move would not reduce the army's support assets; rather, it would simply offer a far more cost-effective means of organizing the transport system. Finally, Tunner argued that his own agency, MATS, should not operate under the air force's direct command; instead, along with all other strategic transport assets, MATS should be placed under the direction of the Joint Chiefs of Staff as part of a single, centrally directed, strategic transport agency.[67]

Tunner knew full well that advocating such programs in congressional testimony would mean the end of his career, but he firmly believed that establishing a strong airlift system as part of a joint force was worth his losing out on further promotion and a fourth star. In a formal report to Congress in April 1960 Tunner openly advocated a policy that the Eisenhower administration was resisting: one of flexible response supported by airlift. Tunner noted that "the limitations of the majority of the present MATS aircraft seriously limit the size of the United States Forces which can be deployed to distant overseas destinations in acceptable periods of time."[68] Tunner's forthrightness had the expected consequence. After only two years as chief of MATS Lieutenant General Tunner retired from active duty on May 31, 1960, having successfully organized and commanded the three largest airlift operations up to that time.

Tunner was soon able to see that his testimony had borne fruit. By all accounts, he had made a strong case before Congress. The Kennedy administration that came into office in January 1961 was bent on overturning the policy of over-reliance on nuclear weapons and on adopting a strategy of flexible response, which meant developing larger and more capable conventional defense forces. Tunner's airlift vision fit perfectly into the new administration's concepts, and within weeks of Kennedy's assuming office the administration announced that it would fund the new intercontinental strategic airlift plane, the C-141 jet transport, which would serve in the U.S. inventory for more than forty years. The rest of Tunner's vision was realized in 1965 when MATS was converted into the Military Airlift Command, a centralized strategic transportation agency operating under the direction of the Joint Chiefs. Tunner believed that the realization of his airlift vision was worth stoking the Pentagon's ire and taking an early retirement.

During his retirement years Tunner often spoke and wrote about airlift, and in 1964 the air force published his autobiography, *Over the Hump*. He remained a staunch advocate of airlift as a national strategic asset. He died on April 6, 1983, at age seventy-six, in Ware Neck, Virginia, and was buried with high honors at Arlington National Cemetery.

CONCLUSION

William Henry Tunner should be remembered as a leader and manager who met a variety of complex challenges, created organizations, and established new concepts for the practical application of air power. Today's military leaders are expected to be warriors, not managers. Indeed, the managerial approach to leadership is viewed with some disdain in most military circles. But in the case of organizing strategic transport, a managerial approach is certainly more effective than reliance on a warrior ethic. General Tunner was a man and commander who raised the process of transferring civilian management and business approaches to solve problems in a military context to a fine art. From the earliest days of his career

Tunner had learned from his own experience and from that of civilians. More than most military leaders, he was ready to apply models from civil aviation and private industry to the armed forces. Moreover, to the irritation of many, he proved that his solutions worked better than others did.

From Tunner the USAF received not only much of its current airlift doctrine and strategy but also its approach to safety, and operational management. His cost-effectiveness studies were a model for their time. Further, he proved that his centralized system of maintenance and standardized procedures not only made mission success more likely but also saved lives and money. Today General Tunner still serves as the model of a rational commander, one who constantly learns, adapts, focuses on solving the problem at hand, and anticipates future problems and formulates plans to deal with them.

Tunner also is an example of a commander who never hesitated to tell his superiors the unvarnished truth as he saw it. He did not willingly pick fights, but when the mission was at stake he acted without hesitation. Tunner never argued with superiors at an emotional level; instead, he based all of his positions on solid research and fact finding. Because he knew exactly what he was talking about, he usually won his organizational and doctrinal battles. He spoke out many times, and each time it was to the long-term advantage of the USAF. During his final years as a senior commander he showed moral courage in defying his superiors as a matter of principle and accepting retirement as the price of honesty. Today, when one sees many aggressively careerist officers in the top ranks of the U.S. armed forces, one could hope that Tunner's honesty and openness to innovation might again become the accepted model of air leadership.

6

GEORGE E. STRATEMEYER: ORGANIZER OF AIR POWER

Thomas A. Keaney

Less than five years after World War II ended, the U.S. Air Force (USAF) entered the Korean War as an organization with great confidence in its ability and its doctrine for applying air power. Commanded by Lt. Gen. George E. Stratemeyer, USAF units in the western Pacific and East Asia, the Far East Air Forces (FEAF), included personnel well experienced in conducting close air support (CAS), air interdiction, and strategic bombing in the prior war, but both the commander and his command faced great difficulties in adapting to a very different kind of war in Korea. Even without considering the changed conditions of the war, the state of the force itself—newly equipped with jet aircraft, but only a shell of its former self and woefully lacking in training—brought great difficulties for the FEAF. Stratemeyer himself had little firsthand experience in using air power as an operational commander, but through a series of assignments since the 1920s he had gained in-depth familiarity with the broad scope of the air arm's activities. Further, his World War II experience had prepared him well for managing the design and execution of operations by others—the particular role he would again assume in the Korean War.

The title "organizer of air power" describes the essential role Stratemeyer played as a commander in 1950. In no sense meant as a pejorative, the term indicates the nature of the tasks required to convert an ill-prepared organization to effectiveness in combat. Flush with success from its World War II performance but essentially dismantled during the five years since, the air force in 1950, similar to the other services, had not anticipated engaging in another war so soon and least of all a war of the kind experienced in Korea. Employment doctrines abounded, but the essential elements of training and providing for support of air power—maintenance, supply, intelligence, and command and control, among others—had atrophied where they had existed at all.

Stratemeyer's performance during the Korean War has received scant attention, good or bad, but his experiences deserve further examination, both for what they show about the war itself and for the many factors that affect an operational commander in a complex conflict such as that faced in Korea. Stratemeyer—a contemporary of Carl Spaatz, the first USAF chief of staff; George Kenney, the first commanding general of the Strategic Air Command (SAC); and other airmen involved in the early days of military aviation—rose to the rank of lieutenant general in World War II while dealing with the operational, diplomatic, and interservice matters that concern any commander. Still, events in 1950 introduced far different situations. The USAF was less than three years old when the Korean War started and recently had endured not only the stress of coping with drastic downsizing of the force but also that resulting from the bitter interservice disputes, which had emerged in the late 1940s. Moreover, the war itself involved rapid shifts: from the desperate efforts to defend against the North Korean attack after June 25, 1950, to the decisive counteroffensive of United Nations (UN) forces following the Inchon landing that September, and to the just-as-desperate defensive actions to meet the Chinese forces' entry into the war two months later. Furthermore, air operations took place amid concerns about their possible implications for the U.S.-Soviet relationship and the danger that the fighting might escalate to a world war between the two superpowers.

In addition to concerns over intensifying the war, Stratemeyer encountered issues about the use of air power that represented a continuation of disputes originating during World War II: the relative attention that should be given to CAS versus air interdiction, the value of strategic bombing, and the centralized control of air assets. Several new technologies complicated these debates, principally the introduction of the atomic bomb and jet aircraft. The former brought an entirely new dimension to strategic bombing and even to war itself; the latter initiated disputes over the ability of jets to conduct CAS effectively. Meanwhile, many in the army wondered if the air force's embrace of these technologies would further separate the new service from its roots.

Disputes among the services were fodder for political debates in Washington over the wisdom of America's entry into the war and the appropriate military actions for conducting it. Would bombing Chinese forces across the Yalu River in Manchuria further widen the war? Would attacking Soviet aircraft at air bases in Manchuria bring about Soviet military involvement? Did air power's performance in the war invalidate or confirm recent decisions regarding the roles and missions assigned to each of the services? Proponents of each position presented their arguments in the press, in Congress, and in the Pentagon, using selective evidence to support their various cases. The Korean theater was not simply a spectator to these debates; Stratemeyer himself, his staff, and the staffs of the other services forwarded their positions, both formally through channels and informally through contacts with reporters covering the war. Such activity was not new, of course, but the sensitivity of these matters to the conduct of the war and to longer-term decisions on force structure and service roles gave them increased importance.

Although apparently not a charismatic leader, Stratemeyer was recognized as a steady, reliable, and skilled diplomat. Gen. Earle Partridge, his immediate subordinate in Korea, saw him as "a gentleman of the old school, warm, generous, thoughtful, low key." Another former subordinate, Gen. Jacob Smart, called him "sharp intellectually and in appearance" and an "intuitive" commander. They agreed that he was intensely loyal to subordinates, gave them broad latitude in doing their jobs, and acknowledged that his own successes, whatever they might be, had been achieved through the work of others.[1]

No discussion of the Korean War in its first year can be complete without mentioning General of the Army Douglas MacArthur, the UN forces' commander in Korea and commander in chief of U.S. Far East Command (FECOM) before and during the war. MacArthur's name and actions dominated the news of Korea in the war's first year, and his pervasive influence extended to both his subordinates in theater and to the military and civilian leadership in Washington. His two immediate subordinates, Lieutenant General Stratemeyer (FEAF) and Vice Adm. C. Turner Joy (Naval Forces Far East), enjoyed good relations with MacArthur; indeed, they were much better than MacArthur's dealings with the Joint Chiefs of Staff (JCS) and civilian officials, up to and including President Harry Truman. Stratemeyer himself began as and remained an ardent admirer of MacArthur's and continually referred to him in superlative terms. Following the Inchon landing in September, he told MacArthur that "there was a great affection for him and that we in FEAF appreciated his brain power, his leadership and his strategy." In early April 1951, shortly before MacArthur was relieved of command, Stratemeyer wrote, "I have always been greatly impressed with anything and everything that General MacArthur has had to say."[2] For his part, MacArthur maintained a close and cordial relationship with Stratemeyer and in all important matters seemed to trust his judgment.

While relations between these two principals remained amiable, coordination between MacArthur's FECOM and Stratemeyer's FEAF was often tenuous. Difficulties arose because even though MacArthur held both the position of commander in chief, Far East—a unified (i.e., joint service) command—and that of commanding general, U.S. Army Forces, FECOM, he did not maintain a separate unified staff; his Army Staff also served as the unified command staff. Without USAF (or navy) representation on the staff, the only routine contact concerning joint USAF-army issues took place between the principals, MacArthur and Stratemeyer. Needless to say, coordination that first required agreement or meetings between the principals would be, and was, an inadequate substitute for day-to-day coordination at the working level. When the staffs did meet, differences in procedures, in service doctrines, and in priorities among air force, army, and navy forces often led to conflicts that almost automatically called for the senior leaders to step in and act as intermediaries—or peacemakers—between the respective staffs for lack of more established procedures that might govern these disputes. Stratemeyer himself frequently served in this capacity.

BACKGROUND AND EXPERIENCE

Born on November 24, 1890, in Cincinnati, Ohio, Stratemeyer grew up in Peru, Indiana. At age nineteen he was selected for the U.S. Military Academy as a member of the class of 1914, along with his friend Carl Spaatz. Stratemeyer was not a strong student, and because of his poor grades in a philosophy course the academy set him back to the class of 1915. That class became "the class the stars fell on," with 59 of 164 graduates becoming general officers—the most for any West Point class before or since. In that class, Stratemeyer finished 147 out of the 164 students, his highest-rated subject being drill regulations and his lowest being practical military engineering.[3] A year after graduation, he married Annalee Rix; the marriage lasted until his death in 1969. From his graduation until the time he assumed his position as theater air commander in Korea, Stratemeyer pursued a varied career that included extensive administrative, logistics, educational, interservice, and coalition experience, spanning nearly every aspect of early military aviation. By 1950, except for a handful of soon-to-retire generals such as George

Kenney, Stratemeyer brought more to the position than any other officer then available in the air force. That varied experience, however, came at a cost; it kept him from accumulating extended service in the operational force.

Carl Spaatz, George Stratemeyer, and George Kenney were contemporaries in age and time of service when the United States entered World War I in 1917. While Spaatz and Kenney received assignments that sent them to France to fly in fighter squadrons, and thus gained recognition and combat experience, Stratemeyer became a test pilot for a short time and then commander of the Air Service Mechanics School at Kelly Field in Texas, a position he held until 1921.[4] Then, after three years' service in Hawaii, he moved on to a series of education and training assignments, beginning with a five-year tour as a tactics instructor at West Point. That assignment led to his attendance at the Air Corps Tactical School at Langley Field, Virginia (later moved to Maxwell Field, Alabama)—a necessary stop for air corps officers at the time. He then went to the Army Command and Staff College, where he remained for two more years as an instructor, and finally went to the Army War College. Thus, he spent eleven of the sixteen years from 1924 to 1940 as a student or an instructor. His only operational assignment was as commander of the Seventh Bomb Group (B-10 aircraft) at Hamilton Field, California, from 1937 to 1939.[5] The Seventh Group was a part of the First Air Wing, whose commander had been Brig. Gen. Henry "Hap" Arnold. While having only limited operational experience, Lieutenant Colonel Stratemeyer established a reputation for engaging in experimentation and using innovative methods for training his crews—an important trait he would continue to exhibit throughout his career.[6]

Stratemeyer's career path definitely set him apart from the typical air corps officer. Until 1935, for example, few air corps officers attended the U.S. Army Command and General Staff School (CGSS).[7] Their attendance increased only when Gen. George Marshall, army chief of staff, demanded it. Ironically, Stratemeyer had written to his friend Spaatz to ask whether he might be interested in joining him on the CGSS faculty, but it had no appeal whatever to Spaatz. Even when Spaatz had to attend the school because of Marshall's directive, he showed his lack of interest by finishing close to the bottom of his class and receiving negative reviews of his promotion potential.[8] Thus, while Stratemeyer did not become one of the Billy Mitchell–trained airmen involved with the operational development of aircraft and air power, he achieved distinction in other areas of the air corps. When General Arnold became chief of the U.S. Army Air Forces (USAAF) in mid-1941, he selected Stratemeyer to be his executive officer with the rank of brigadier general. Then, following an assignment as commander of Southeast Air Corps Training Center, Stratemeyer received a promotion to major general and returned to Washington in 1942 as chief of the Air Staff.

In his new position, Stratemeyer was at the center of all decisions affecting air operations in every theater of the war, and by all accounts Arnold gave him great latitude as his spokesman in dealing with commanders in the field.[9] But being at the center of USAAF decision making did not equate to being a theater commander. One is left to conclude that while Stratemeyer enjoyed Arnold's complete confidence, he still ranked below those officers, such as Generals Ira Eaker, Spaatz, Kenney, or Jimmy Doolittle, whom the USAAF commander had chosen to run a theater of war—an assessment that Arnold himself implicitly acknowledged later.[10] Stratemeyer's opportunity for a theater command did come, however, and the experience no doubt proved important for his later service in the Korean War.

In 1943, Arnold sent Stratemeyer to command the USAAF in the newly formed India-Burma sector of the China-Burma-India theater of operations. Stratemeyer's organization involved perhaps the most complex command arrangements of the war. Its elements were anything but typical. First, along with commanding USAAF forces, Stratemeyer also led Eastern Air Command, an integrated USAAF–Royal Air Force (RAF) operational force. Second, he was also commanding general of Theater Air Forces, Southeast Asia. Finally, although his command was not part of the China theater, Stratemeyer was responsible for supplying and assisting air forces in China—the famous airlift operations "over the Hump," or the Himalayas—then under the command of Brig. Gen. Claire Chennault, and at times for advising Generalissimo Chiang Kai-shek, the Chinese Nationalist leader. All the while, Stratemeyer answered not only to Arnold but also to the India-Burma sector commander, Lord Louis Mountbatten. Dealing simultaneously with Mountbatten, Chennault, Chiang, and Lt. Gen. Joseph Stilwell, commander of the China theater, was challenge enough. But the initiation in 1944 of Operation Matterhorn, the program to deploy B-29s to China through India for the strategic bombing of Japanese forces—with the B-29s remaining under Arnold's direct command—made coordination between all elements operating in the theater nearly impossible.

Especially valuable in this situation was Stratemeyer's talent for coordinating the actions of others, not for conducting operations under his own control. His diary entries during this period center on his efforts to coordinate operations, on command relationships, and on logistics, and they contain little about the operations themselves. No doubt they were a good indication of the thrust of his activities.[11] He knew his theater had one of the lowest priorities for resources, and by 1944 it was becoming more of a backwater in the war against Japan. He admitted to journalists the mainly administrative nature of his duties, noting that his key responsibility had become supporting the war by assisting forces in China and not by carrying out operations in his own theater.[12]

All indications are that Stratemeyer performed exceptionally well in the circumstances.[13] Unlike most USAAF officers, including General Arnold, he had a good working relationship with Claire Chennault, an old friend from before the war, and their relationship endured even through Chennault's forced retirement in 1945 while Stratemeyer was his supervisor.[14] The diary portrays Stratemeyer as someone who took readily to the multiple functions he had to perform and seldom lost his focus or his control of the situation. His temper and patience were tested only once in a confrontation with his boss Lord Mountbatten, and it involved a communication between Arnold and Stratemeyer about which Mountbatten had been not informed. Since Stratemeyer had at least two direct bosses—Arnold and Mountbatten—such situations were inevitable. In this case, Mountbatten sent a cable to Field Marshal Sir John Dill, the senior British representative to the Combined Chiefs of Staff in Washington. In the cable, the contents of which were leaked to Stratemeyer, Mountbatten compared Stratemeyer's actions to those of Field Marshal Bernard Montgomery, who was well known for working outside the chain of command. In response, Stratemeyer informed Lord Mountbatten that he (Stratemeyer) also reported directly to Arnold and that if Mountbatten did not like it, he "would go to the Southwest Pacific to serve under Kenney as a corporal."[15] That exchange seemed to be the extent of the dispute.

Two other aspects of Stratemeyer's command experience during World War II, both positive, would be reflected in Korea. First, he supported and monitored closely the experimentation with the guided, or "smart," Azon (AZimuth ONly) bombs used against bridges in Burma. Despite the bombs' numerous initial mechanical failures, Stratemeyer persisted in these attempts when he might well have abandoned the effort as nonproductive, and, in the end, the Azon bombs achieved a significant success rate.[16] In Korea he would push for developing a later generation of these bombs. Second, he appeared totally committed to achieving harmony in his India-Burma combined command. In a meeting with his staff, he emphasized the need for total cooperation among and integration of British and U.S. officers, stating that he would relieve officers who could not wholeheartedly support that level of integration.[17]

Though committed to interservice and combined forces cooperation in the India-Burma sector, Stratemeyer also paid close attention to instances when he felt his own service (the USAAF) did not receive proper recognition (examples of such perceived neglect would arise numerous times during the Korean War). In one instance, after reading a news report on an RAF operation, he lodged a complaint with the paper, citing the even greater participation by American forces and pointing out that the article had pictured only the RAF aircraft involved without including a photo of a USAAF B-24.[18] Whether such concerns over publicity in this instance were worth his time is debatable, but they would occupy even more of his attention in Korea, when he saw the stakes as being even higher.

Between World War II and the Korean War, Stratemeyer, now a lieutenant general, headed two major USAAF and air force commands. In 1946, he became commander of Air Defense Command, and in 1948, when Tactical Air Command (TAC) was downgraded and merged with Air Defense Command into Continental Air Command, he became commander of the new organization. At the time, many saw the merger as evidence of the air force's disregard of tactical aviation and aircraft support of the army. The air force not only defended the consolidation as a needed budgetary measure, but it also indicated the relatively lower priority given to tactical air support operations as below that of strategic attack (through SAC) and air defense of the United States. In 1950, as air commander in Korea, Stratemeyer would have to face direct criticism of the USAF lack of emphasis on supporting land forces.

The years after World War II also saw the retirement of many of Stratemeyer's contemporaries—Spaatz, Eaker, Doolittle, and Kenney—and the emergence of a new generation of air force leadership. Taking over the leadership in Washington were Gen. Hoyt Vandenberg as air force chief, Gen. Lauris Norstad, Gen. Nathan Twining, and others, while Curtis LeMay succeeded Kenney as SAC commander. Thus, Stratemeyer remained as one of the few old guard still in active service.

One can view Stratemeyer's assignment as commander of FEAF in 1949 as a natural progression, since his experience in command of U.S. air defenses fit perfectly with FEAF's primary mission of providing the air defense of Japan, Okinawa, the Marianas, and the Philippines (but not Korea). At the time he received his assignment, no one anticipated that U.S. forces in the Far East would engage in combat, so constraints on the military budget meant there would be little support for training or equipment for FEAF missions other than defense. The JCS war plan saw the major threat as coming from a Soviet attack in Europe.[19] Whether the USAF leadership would have selected Stratemeyer for this command if the Far East had been considered the major threat area must remain an open question.

FEAF IN JUNE 1950

When the North Koreans invaded South Korea in June 1950, FEAF had to adapt its mission radically, as did all U.S. and Allied forces that were to join the UN coalition. Basically, FEAF had to shift from its primary mission of air defense to one of stopping a ground attack, and it did so through air interdiction of the attacking Korean People's Army and CAS of the defending force, mainly the U.S. Eighth Army. Air superiority—the strength of FEAF—was rapidly achieved against the negligible North Korean air force, but performing CAS and air interdiction while also providing air transport of troops to Korea and evacuating U.S. officials, civilians, families, and many others proved far more difficult.

The FEAF organization was not prepared to fight a war. Like all other U.S. military units in Japan at the time, FEAF experienced shortages in almost every area, including aircraft, personnel, and funds for training. The command possessed between eleven hundred and twelve hundred aircraft, divided among three air forces: the Fifth Air Force in Japan, the Twentieth Air Force on the island of Okinawa, and the Thirteenth Air Force in the Philippines. As part of FEAF, each had air defense as a primary mission, with the Twentieth Air Force's defense region including the Marianas. Fifth Air Force became the premier USAF combat unit of the war, while the Twentieth and Thirteenth served as force suppliers and augmented the Fifth. In addition, each of these units, even the Fifth Air Force, had to maintain its air defense role throughout the war, a mission that limited the aircraft available for use in Korea to roughly half of the total number in theater. The only unit not tasked with air defense was the B-29-equipped Nineteenth Bombardment Group, which was part of Twentieth Air Force at the beginning of the war. Besides lacking full complements of men and planes, every FEAF unit confronted even more severe shortages in aircraft maintenance and other ground support elements and lacked funds to train aircrews in weapons delivery, to operate with army units, or to deploy to and operate from forward bases.

In 1950 FEAF depended on the F-80C Shooting Star, the most numerous platform in its arsenal, as its leading combat aircraft. This first-generation jet had a primary role as an air interceptor and had a capability for ground attack. Unfortunately, the F-80C had limited range and armaments for use in a ground-attack role. Jets consume large amounts of fuel at low altitude, need longer runways than do propeller aircraft, and are highly vulnerable to engine damage when operating from unimproved airfields.[20] The F-80C armament of .50-caliber machine guns and rockets was well suited for air-to-air fighting, but the plane could carry only two bombs (if they were substituted for rockets on the aircraft's rails). Adding fuel tanks on the wings increased its range but at the expense of its bomb load. As a result, without additional runway construction, F-80s had to operate from bases in Japan, greatly reducing the length of time the aircraft could remain on station in the Korean target area to usually less than twenty minutes. Runway construction on bases in Korea would have helped enormously, but those facilities depended on the availability of USAF engineering units, which were in short supply.

Supplementing the F-80s were a number of piston-engine aircraft: the F-51 Mustang, the premier U.S. fighter-bomber and fighter interceptor during World War II; the F-82 Twin Mustang, which saw little action in Korea; the B-26 light bomber, a redesign of the World War II A-26; and the B-29 medium bomber, designated a heavy bomber in World War II but displaced to medium when a larger aircraft, the B-36, came along. Each of FEAF's air forces also possessed reconnaissance, weather, utility, and cargo aircraft, with the last being a particularly valuable asset in the war. C-54, C-47, and C-46 transport aircraft, all veterans of World War II, assumed an early and vital role owing to the environment in Korea, where few roads existed to accommodate land transportation. Because of their important function, cargo aircraft came to be organized into a separate command within FEAF.

In addition to its primitive road system (no paved roads outside of the main cities), South Korea presented other physical problems hindering military operations. It had only two rail lines, those between Pusan and Seoul, and only one airfield of any size and capability, Kimpo outside of Seoul, which the North Koreans quickly overran.

A major strength of Stratemeyer's command proved to be the experience and capabilities of his subordinate commanders. Maj. Gen. Earle Partridge, the commander of Fifth Air Force, had held the position for nearly two years before the war and had commanded several bomber units in World War II, ending the war as commander of Eighth Air Force. Partridge deployed to Korea early in the conflict and maintained his headquarters alongside the Eighth Amy commander, who was also the commander of ground forces in Korea—Lt. Gen. Walton Walker until his death in December 1950 and his successor, Lt. Gen. Matthew Ridgway. In addition to leading the Fifth Air Force, Partridge was responsible for developing a workable air-ground communications system to enable CAS missions and for developing tactics appropriate to the Korean scenario.

Soon after hostilities began, Stratemeyer established a subordinate command to conduct strategic bombing, a role the air force believed would be essential in the war. While FEAF possessed the Nineteenth Bombardment Group on Guam, Stratemeyer requested, and USAF chief of staff Vandenberg approved, the deployment of two groups of SAC B-29s. These units joined the B-29s already in the theater to form Far East Air Force Bomber Command (Provisional) under the leadership of Maj. Gen. Emmett "Rosie" O'Donnell, who at the time was commander of the Fifteenth Air Force. O'Donnell, in addition to being a key member of SAC's leadership, had commanded a B-29 group in the Marianas that conducted bombing raids on Japan during World War II, so he was familiar with the region and with B-29 operations. Both he and Stratemeyer would see, however, that the political context of the Korean War would affect the role of strategic bombing more than any other aspect of air power would. Of note, O'Donnell's provisional bomber command served under Stratemeyer as the overall commander in the theater; in every other case when SAC strategic bombers deployed during the Cold War—such as during the Vietnam War—command of the bombers remained with SAC.

Because of the critical need for airlift, Stratemeyer established another independent command, the FEAF Combat Cargo Command, to take charge of all airlift of troops and supplies—including paratroopers—within the theater. This command organized all cargo aircraft from the three FEAF air forces, including those arriving from USAF units around the world. To lead this organization, Stratemeyer selected easily the most qualified individual then in the air force, Maj. Gen. William Tunner, who had organized the Hump airlift into China during

World War II and directed the Berlin Airlift in 1948–1949. In this command Tunner controlled all cargo aircraft in the theater, but this feat was not easily achieved, as the army, navy, and marines each sought to retain some of these aircraft for their own use.[21]

Under these three subordinate commanders—Partridge, O'Donnell, and Tunner—Stratemeyer established the command structure with which FEAF would operate during the war's first year. O'Donnell's Bomber Command would be responsible for deep interdiction and strategic attack; Partridge's Fifth Air Force would conduct tactical air operations (i.e., CAS and interdiction near the front lines, later called "battlefield interdiction"); and Tunner, of course, would direct air transport.

To this group of subordinate commanders the air force leadership added one other senior leader, Maj. Gen. Otto Weyland. General Vandenberg had apparently recognized a potential shortcoming in the Far East commanders: neither Stratemeyer nor Partridge had any firsthand experience of conducting tactical air operations, which were sure to be an important factor in the war. Therefore, in the first month of the conflict he sent General Weyland to FEAF as Stratemeyer's vice commander, even though Weyland had recently assumed leadership of TAC. Weyland had established an outstanding record as the air commander for Gen. George Patton's Third Army during World War II and was highly regarded in the army. His reputation, along with his tactical air experience, made him especially valuable in Korea. Stratemeyer had little to say in his diary about this move, other than to acknowledge that the assignment had taken place.[22] Weyland later admitted that he saw his role as being proactive in asserting the USAF position on providing tactical air support and not simply acting as a vice commander. While he did not clash with Stratemeyer, Weyland did view him as too much of a "nice guy" and not willing to be "mean and nasty" when required.[23] As Weyland saw it, dealing with the army-dominated FECOM staff would require some nastiness.

Although FECOM was an army-dominated organization, Stratemeyer enjoyed good relations with his superior, General MacArthur, in large measure because of MacArthur's World War II experience. In his island-hopping campaign in the southwest Pacific, MacArthur had depended on airlift to transport troops and on tactical air to secure the region and make possible the next advance. For these tasks, he had relied on his air deputy, General Kenney, and from all accounts Kenney served brilliantly in this role, earning MacArthur's admiration, which Kenney reciprocated.[24] Because of this experience MacArthur developed a high regard for the use of air power and remained open to the ideas of his new air deputy in Korea. That Stratemeyer also held MacArthur in high regard did not hurt at all. The two worked together successfully, but their harmonious one-on-one relationship did not extend to relations between their staffs.

The final element of Stratemeyer's command relationships concerned those with General Vandenberg and his staff in Washington. Here again, the relationship proved positive and useful. As noted earlier, in assigning General Weyland to FEAF, Vandenberg had not hesitated to insert himself into theater operations. Nonetheless, Stratemeyer considered the USAF chief someone with whom he could communicate openly; only rarely did he question Vandenberg's motives or interference.[25] In fact, Stratemeyer's diary lists his frequent communications with USAF Headquarters, requesting additional aircraft, personnel, and other resources. As the only theater commander then engaged in combat, Stratemeyer received a sympathetic hearing, at least in the early days of the war. If the initial response from Washington was not satisfactory, Stratemeyer persisted. Since he knew the generals involved personally and had at one time outranked all of them, he may have felt increased confidence in conducting these discussions.

With the war taking place entirely on the Korean Peninsula, one might ask if Stratemeyer's headquarters should have moved forward from Tokyo, but several factors made that relocation unwise. First, the command's relationship with General MacArthur made it imperative that the two headquarters remain together. Second, the level and frequency of communications with Washington called for a communications capability not available in Korea. Further, while General Partridge moved his headquarters to Korea to direct tactical air operations more effectively and to link with Eighth Army headquarters, Stratemeyer's other two subordinate commanders, Generals O'Donnell and Tunner, had their headquarters in Japan.

A headquarters in the relatively plush surroundings of Tokyo provided a setting quite unlike that of locations in Korea. Stratemeyer's diary, for instance, records the frequent cocktail parties and dinners he and his wife, Annalee, hosted or attended and the considerable time he spent on the golf course. The other side of that coin, however, was the large number of visitors he had to host. They included active duty and retired (including Spaatz and Kenney) military officials, congressional delegations, inspection teams, and many journalists. Stratemeyer was not required to host reporters, but his concern for how they reported on the air force made this effort one of his special interests. At a "small" (his words) dinner party he hosted in September 1950, for example, those present included the general officers on his staff, Generals Spaatz and Kenney, Al Jolson and his accompanist (on a United Service Organization tour), and journalists from *Newsweek*, United Press International, and *Collier's*.[26]

Throughout the war, Stratemeyer tried his best to influence news reporting on air force operations. Thus, he loudly announced cancellation of his *New York Times* subscription, accusing the paper of being biased against the USAF, and urged acquaintances in the United States to take up this cause. At the same time, he asked his subordinate commanders to give personal attention to discussing the air force's performance in tactical aviation with the news media and with visiting private citizens.[27] For his own part, Stratemeyer gave many press interviews and in each week of his tour sent a letter to a particularly influential American journalist, Gill Robb Wilson (World War I aviator, founder of the Civil Air Patrol, reporter for the *Herald Tribune*, and editor of *Flying Magazine*). The general's diary records the dispatch of the weekly letter, no matter how busy his schedule. Nor was press reporting Stratemeyer's only concern. On more than one occasion, he received queries from the Pentagon, including personal communications from General Vandenberg, asking him to provide positive news on USAF operations to balance the effect of laudatory accounts of other services' operations.

MEETING THE NORTH KOREAN ATTACK, JUNE TO SEPTEMBER 1950

In the desperate early days of the war, June to September 1950, all of FECOM faced perhaps its toughest test as the unprepared and ill-equipped forces attempted to blunt the North Korean attack. The initial attack had shattered the small South Korean forces, captured Seoul on the third day, and continued a rapid march south. The arrival of the first U.S. ground forces on July 4 and of follow-on forces of two U.S. divisions slowed the North Koreans' advance, until a month later U.S. and South Korean troops held at what came to be known as the Pusan Perimeter. After FEAF quickly defeated the North Korean air units, it focused almost entirely on tactical operations supporting the U.S. Army, probably the command's most neglected role until the war began. Air force and army units had essentially no joint training (indeed, FEAF's crews were only partly trained in their own operations) and little written doctrine to guide them. Moreover, neither service had the air-ground communications equipment necessary for effective joint operations. Air-ground operations had to cope with and solve three major issues, all of them contentious and all of them related to one another: How should the air-ground system work? Who would pick the targets? And, more generally, who would control the aircraft?

The first weeks saw air force and army units struggle to slow the North Koreans' advance while at the same time hastily developing a system to deliver air support to the rapidly retreating South Korean troops. An air-ground communications procedure existed on paper, but the army was not able to supply the required personnel to man its half of the system, the air force had insufficient radio equipment for the task, and the equipment available was frequently damaged during transport on the Korean Peninsula's poor to nonexistent road system. Problems with target selection also impeded the provision of CAS. The air force had discontinued the airborne forward air controller (FAC) system used in World War II, and that decision—an error that the air force would repeat in Vietnam—left a critical deficiency. The army-dominated FECOM headquarters, dissatisfied with FEAF's performance in target selection, assumed that role itself but used inadequate maps. As a result, of the 220 targets initially identified from data on the maps, 20 percent no longer existed.[28] Target area operations also proved difficult. As noted previously, a lack of suitable bases in Korea itself meant that F-80s had to fly from Japan, drastically reducing their time on station. Because the command's F-51s, in the process of being retired, could fly from dirt airstrips in Korea, they suddenly assumed a critical role, carrying the burden of air strikes in the early days of the war. Rather than retire these aircraft, Stratemeyer directed that they be refurbished and also requested that all F-51s available in the United States be sent to the theater. Some F-51 squadrons had transitioned to F-80s, and FEAF had them change back to F-51s.[29] Finally, adding to the complexity of command arrangements, arriving on the scene were strike aircraft from the navy (in July) and marines (in August) that had to be integrated into the air-ground system. Since their aircraft radios proved incompatible with the USAF systems, the addition of these aircraft increased the difficulties that FEAF encountered. In short, sorting out U.S. military operations became almost as difficult a task as fighting the enemy was.

Stratemeyer left solving the problems associated with CAS to Partridge, who, as previously noted, had set up his headquarters next to the army ground commander,

General Walker. Aided by officers who had arrived with Weyland, Partridge worked hard to make the air-ground system operate effectively. He established a joint operations center, though initially manned only by air force personnel, and oversaw the reinstitution of airborne FACs. The FACs flew a USAF training aircraft, the T-6 (redesignated the AT-6), which Partridge often flew himself while accompanied by Walker.[30] In addition to the AT-6s, Partridge employed F-51s, F-80s, B-26s, and, at times, B-29s to support the army. The air force might have expected to have the F-51s and F-80s undertake CAS, with the B-26s concentrating on air interdiction and B-29s on attacking strategic targets, but in the early days of the war such role assignments did not hold.

B-29s required special handling, since their use in the war diverged greatly from air force doctrine. O'Donnell had deployed as commander of FEAF Bomber Command with the intent of reinstituting the same kinds of raids conducted against Japan in 1945. After meeting with Generals MacArthur and Stratemeyer, however, O'Donnell was informed by Stratemeyer that the tactical emergency required his missions to focus on interdicting supply routes and at times supplying CAS. It became clear immediately that B-29s were ill suited for CAS, but Stratemeyer, knowing MacArthur had directed this assignment, continued using them in this role. In mid-July, General Vandenberg visited the theater and attempted to impress on MacArthur the proper use of B-29s—strategic bombing—but with no effect. Prior to a subsequent meeting between Vandenberg and Partridge, Stratemeyer, having promised to use B-29s as MacArthur had directed, told Partridge not to discuss the subject of B-29 employment. In his briefing to the arriving B-29 crews, Stratemeyer stressed that they "would have to throw the book away and get in and pitch and destroy the targets that would be assigned to them."[31]

During the campaign, the B-29s saw action not only in CAS but also in nighttime missions targeting North Korean supply routes. The latter required the bombers to find their own targets, a capability these aircraft and crews did not possess. These night missions achieved little, and in late September, they were canceled for B-29s and left to B-26s. Recognizing the limits of the crews' low-level navigation capability, Stratemeyer backed off and, to O'Donnell's evident relief, promised that the B-29s would receive their targets prior to takeoff.[32] Stratemeyer kept up the pressure on O'Donnell, however, and even suggested to General LeMay that SAC begin to train its crews on low-altitude visual bombing.[33] LeMay's response is not recorded, but SAC, on its way to becoming a force whose only mission was delivery of nuclear weapons, would have had no interest in such training. It was not the last time that Stratemeyer would clash with the wishes of his bomber command.

Partridge's efforts established the CAS system that would operate during the war, and in so doing he gained the confidence of General Walker, one of the few army generals to have a positive impression of USAF support operations. Stratemeyer faced a greater obstacle in dealing with the army-dominated FECOM staff and with opinions in Washington. He feared both their misunderstanding of the air force's capabilities and deliberate undermining of its status as an independent force. To address both of these difficulties, Stratemeyer used his access to MacArthur to bring about changes not possible through lower-level interaction with the Army Staff. First, Stratemeyer convinced MacArthur to sign an order putting into effect the air-ground support arrangement that Partridge and Walker had developed. Then, taking advantage of the initiative of Weyland, who was trying to establish a joint system of air interdiction targeting to replace the army-only committee, Stratemeyer also succeeded in convincing MacArthur to set up an ad hoc committee that included Weyland as well as army and navy representatives to select air interdiction targets.[34]

In dealing with the FECOM staff, Stratemeyer and others found MacArthur's chief of staff and friend, Maj. Gen. Edward "Ned" Almond, opposed to the air force's concept for conducting air operations. Almond, who had attended the Air Corps Tactical School prior to World War II and had experience during that war as a division commander in Italy, had definite ideas about using and managing air power. In Almond's view, and contrary to the joint army–air force decision on service roles and missions made in 1947–1948, the army should have taken over the CAS mission and have operated like the Marine Corps in this regard, with the ground units owning the support aircraft. In Korea, Almond had fought the decision on control of targeting and become a constant critic of how the air force operated. He had an ally in Gen. Mark Clark, who in 1950 was the chief of army field forces and advocated that USAF tactical air operate under the command of the ground commander.[35] While Stratemeyer could deal with Almond by operating through MacArthur, Clark continued to have strong influence in Washington.

Perhaps the most significant disagreements among Stratemeyer, Almond, and others concerned the control of the aircraft in theater. What had been an army–air force issue at the beginning of the war became more complicated when navy and marine air forces joined the fight. The navy and marines had developed their own doctrines and control procedures concerning aircraft—procedures that were often incompatible with USAF doctrine and equipment. Air force doctrine and Army Field Manual 31-35 *Air-Ground Operations* specified that the theater air commander (Stratemeyer in this case) had authority over all tactical air forces. The air-ground system between the army and the USAAF in Europe in World War II had of course grown up without the presence of navy or marine aviation.[36] Though neither the air force nor the army agreed with all elements of FM 31-35—and many members of the army units in Korea had never read it—no other guidance existed, so Stratemeyer petitioned MacArthur to send out a directive authorizing its use. Specifically, Stratemeyer sought operational control of navy (and later marine) aircraft except for those units engaged in aerial mining or antisubmarine warfare. The petition, moreover, came as aircraft carriers had entered the theater.

MacArthur decided the matter but not in a way that provided any real guidance. Instead of giving Stratemeyer *operational* control, he authorized *coordination* control, leaving undefined what the latter term meant.[37] Essentially, it meant nothing. Coordination implies communication between groups but says nothing about one group's having any control over another's actions. In fact, communication was all that happened. For all practical purposes, the air force, navy, and marines retained considerable autonomy in operations. Those arrangements came to mean physical separation of these forces and the assignment of separate operating areas, similar to the air force's and navy's later "route packages" of the Vietnam War.

Almond's preference for having Marine Corps aircraft conduct CAS drew Stratemeyer's particular ire. The status of Marine Corps air as being solidly linked to the ground commander, its large complement relative to the size of the ground force, and its ability to have aircraft on station all appealed to Almond's view of what air support should entail. The air force's response, maintaining that it lacked the number of aircraft required to provide the army with similar support, did not satisfy Almond and his supporters; instead of an aircraft shortage, they perceived the air force as lacking an interest in the CAS mission. Some evidence supported the army's argument—the air force had downgraded TAC two years before and had neglected CAS training while the marines had given it special emphasis.

Stratemeyer's reaction to these claims led him in several directions. First, he pointed out that marine air could be as effective as it was only because the air force had achieved air supremacy, a claim that, while true, was somewhat off the subject. Second, he pointed out to all who would listen the far greater number of CAS sorties that the USAF aircraft conducted compared to the number carried out by the navy and marines. He might well have also pointed out that USAF B-26s, B-29s, and other aircraft flying operations to interdict supplies to the North Korean army may have been as important as CAS sorties in stopping the North Korean advance. Finally, he expressed privately to members of his staff his irritation that army and marine forces had come to rely so heavily on CAS as simply heavy artillery: "It is my opinion that the American ground forces are not taking the initiative and fighting. It is further my opinion that they are not aggressive unless they have total, all-out air support. . . . I wonder what would happen within our lines if there was enemy air and it had killed 1,200 of our people in a division front as we did yesterday in front of the 3d South Korean Division."[38]

Beyond Almond's complaints, Stratemeyer took special notice of and offense at navy and marine fliers who denigrated USAF capabilities in comments to the press. Stratemeyer viewed these reports as more than simply casual talk among pilots. Instead, behind the sniping about air force tactical air he saw navy public affairs officers as deliberately attempting to embarrass the air force in retaliation for its role during the controversy surrounding the B-36, which ultimately had resulted in cancellation of the carrier *United States* in April 1949. He stated this view in a letter to his air force commanders and staff, and in the same letter he noted that Clark, the army field forces commander, was running an undercover campaign aimed at securing tactical air as part of the army.[39]

AFTER INCHON, SEPTEMBER TO NOVEMBER 1950

The Inchon landing on September 15, 1950, saw the recently formed X Corps (consisting of U.S. Army, Marine Corps, and South Korean ground forces) under the command of General Almond (moved up from his position as MacArthur's chief of staff) achieve rapid success, and it did so with the support of only navy and marine aircraft, no doubt an arrangement specified by Almond himself. Stratemeyer's diary rather remarkably makes no mention of the Inchon landing or of the air support arrangements other than to point out the important role of air force cargo aircraft in resupplying the ground forces; the shallow harbor at Inchon greatly limited the ability of ships to provide that support. During the Inchon operation, the Fifth Air Force concentrated on aiding the breakout of Walker's Eighth Army from the Pusan Perimeter, with next to no coordination between the two forces except for the timing of the assaults.

The success at Inchon began a new phase of the war and, in the minds of many, the start of preparations for ending the conflict. Arguments over CAS roles became a moot point; instead, air operations focused on destroying the fleeing North Korean forces. By late October, believing the targets and tasks did not justify their use, Stratemeyer cleared two B-29 bomb groups to return to the United States and began taking steps to dismantle O'Donnell's provisional bomber command—actions that Stratemeyer would soon reconsider.[40] On the assumption that the war would soon end, Stratemeyer also prepared what he thought at the time was his final report, specifically writing an introductory section and guidance for the individual reports by the Fifth Air Force, Cargo Command, and Bomber Command on their operations. Stratemeyer's report, which was never published in final form, shows great understanding of the various elements of air power and how they should be integrated. This observation does not mean his judgments were necessarily correct, but they clearly reflected Stratemeyer's personal views as recorded in his diary.

In the report, Stratemeyer focused on lessons *not* learned, given the lack of an air opponent. His thesis was that the presence of hostile (jet) aircraft would have completely changed the ability of cargo aircraft to operate in support of the ground forces; indeed, it was fallacious to think that American fighters could escort bomber and cargo aircraft, since those fighters would be needed to gain air superiority. As a result, army personnel in rear areas and truck convoys could not have operated freely, calling into question the army's ability to sustain front-line operations from Pusan. Further, the navy's carriers would have been sitting ducks for a hostile bomber force, and U.S. Air Force and Army bases in Japan, including the U.S. military headquarters—the centers of command and sources of the logistical strength of forces in Korea—would have been drastically affected.

Stratemeyer also paid special attention to the command of air forces, then a subject of intense debate in Washington as well as in the theater. In his view, coordinating the multiple actions of bomber escorts, air-to-air fighting, and air defense required a single air commander. In this respect, he singled out Marine Corps air-ground units, citing their value for amphibious landings but maintaining that such a force structure would establish an invalid precedent for army operations. In the first place, he stated, the government could not afford to equip ground divisions with their own tactical air packages, but, even if that arrangement were possible, it would result in the loss of air power's flexibility.

Finally, Stratemeyer addressed a tactical matter concerning the F-80s, then the subject of a controversy regarding the relative value of F-80 jets versus F-51 propeller aircraft. He used the report to restate the judgment that F-80s could carry the same payload and suffer only one-fourth the combat losses as the F-51s, losses in the main stemming from ground fire.[41] However, he did not mention the F-80's liability in having far less time on station. In a way, he opened a debate that would continue well into the future regarding the relative merits for CAS missions of high-performance jets versus slower but better-defended, more time-on-station aircraft. Stratemeyer later recorded in his diary two lessons that should be taken from the war—the need to develop better equipment and tactics for attacking ground-based air defenses and the necessity for good night photography—as both handicaps had persisted throughout the war.[42]

After the Inchon landing, a flurry of awards to general officers reflected poorly on those involved, including Stratemeyer. In October 1950, MacArthur awarded the Distinguished Service Cross to the operation's key commanders: Generals Walker, Almond, Partridge, and Stratemeyer, among others. The medal, second only to the Medal of Honor, is awarded for exhibiting extreme gallantry and risking one's life in combat. Three days after Stratemeyer received his award, he submitted MacArthur's name for the Distinguished Flying Cross, based on the several flights MacArthur made (with Stratemeyer) as he toured the front lines and defensive positions before, during, and after Inchon. Less than a week later he used a similar justification in recommending MacArthur for the Medal of Honor. Stratemeyer pushed for this award based both on his high regard for MacArthur and on his belief that MacArthur's view of air power's value could assist the air force. He admitted as much in a letter to Vandenberg in which he asked for support on the recommendation, pointing out that "[MacArthur] believes in air power, he knows how to use it, and he has backed me one hundred percent in my position as Commanding General, Far East Air Forces." Curiously, during the same period, Stratemeyer met with Partridge to discuss the command's generous award practices, but the diary does not record Partridge's position on that subject.[43]

Stratemeyer's attitude, though not unprecedented, reflects a view of awards not in keeping with their intent. He seemed to view decorations, such as those for MacArthur and members of his own staff, as rewards for service, not for bravery or gallantry. When Vandenberg challenged Stratemeyer's recommendation that Silver Stars be awarded to several of his commanders and staff members, Stratemeyer justified the awards on the basis that the officers he had recommended, although not required to fly missions, had done so voluntarily. In other words, he based his recommendation not on what they had done but on their voluntary status.[44] By that logic, all crew members on similar flights would routinely have received Silver Stars, but of course that was not what Stratemeyer had in mind.

By mid-October, the sense of how the war might end began to change. UN forces had moved across the thirty-eighth parallel, with the anticipation both that the reeling North Korean forces would surrender and that, following an armistice, a brief occupation would ensue with free elections taking place throughout the country. Those assumptions held during the October 15 meeting between General MacArthur and President Harry Truman on Wake Island, but even then events in Korea had begun to undermine that scenario. Though persistent reports indicated Chinese "volunteers" were entering Korea across the Yalu River, the possibility that regular Chinese or even Soviet forces might have entered the war were dismissed. At the same time, the North Korean leadership had refused all requests for an armistice or even further discussions through third parties. In these circumstances, the strategy of how to win the war became contentious between the theater commanders, U.S. political leadership, and UN coalition allies.[45]

Meanwhile, a major external factor began to affect decisions on Korea: the United States began shifting its focus toward building up the military strength of the North Atlantic Treaty Organization (NATO) to counter a possible Soviet invasion of Western Europe. This turn made events in Korea somewhat of a sideshow or, worse, possibly a trigger for an outbreak of war in Europe. Great Britain, the other major power with significant forces in the UN coalition, particularly feared such a scenario.

In these circumstances, a gap developed between the stated political objectives and the military objectives pursued by FECOM, leaving its military strategy relatively unconstrained. UN resolutions and U.S. policy diverged somewhat regarding the form of any postwar settlement. No one wanted a long occupation that might distract from the focus on Europe, but the conditions that might lead to stability in Korea were unclear. Meanwhile, MacArthur's strategy sought the destruction of the North Korean army and was not influenced by the ultimate effects that strategy would have on cities—whether the environment would be conducive to holding free elections—or on events outside the theater. In that atmosphere, communications between the theater and Washington became more frequent and often more acrimonious, as theater military operations increasingly affected the tense political situation in Asia. Two particular controversies concerned Stratemeyer and his air operations—the political effects of air strikes near the Chinese and Soviet borders with Korea and incursions by U.S. aircraft across those borders.

Navigation errors had resulted in U.S. aircraft straying across the Korean-Manchurian border, beginning in August with an F-51 strafing workers on an airstrip in Antung, Manchuria, a city five miles from the Yalu River. A month later a B-29 flight attacked marshaling yards at Antung. In each case the United States accepted blame and promised restitution, and in each case Vandenberg sent strong messages to Stratemeyer, directing him to institute further precautions to avoid such incidents. In spite of the warnings, two weeks after the B-29 incident, two F-80s apparently became disoriented in the weather, broke out of the clouds, and, seeing what they thought was their target, strafed a Soviet air base near Sukhaya Rechka, which was south of Vladivostok and more than sixty miles into Soviet territory. Again, the incident involved a navigation error and perhaps overeager pilots, and Stratemeyer sent an extended report to Generals MacArthur and Vandenberg. Though Stratemeyer disclosed that he had relieved the fighter group commander concerned and court-martialed the two pilots, these actions did not seem to have their logical consequences. Both pilots went on to long and distinguished careers in the air force. In fact, one of the pilots was next assigned as aide-de-camp to the air force general in charge of Japan's air defense—an unprecedented posting for a recently court-martialed officer.[46] From all indications, the aircraft incursions were in fact accidental, and Stratemeyer treated them as errors and not as deliberate acts.

By contrast, in 1952 and 1953 U.S. pilots commonly flew into Manchuria either in pursuit or in search of Soviet-made, swept-wing MiG-15s. No one acknowledged these incursions at the time, but they were frequently discussed by the pilots and must have been known to and ignored by the USAF leadership.[47] Though neither the Soviets nor the Chinese did more than make diplomatic protests for the incursions, the Pentagon reacted by becoming wary of sending any flights even close to the Korean border—a factor that would become important when Stratemeyer sought to conduct those kinds of flights in November. His diary only referrred indirectly to the deliberate reconnaissance overflights of Soviet and Chinese territory that U.S. RB-45 aircraft conducted, but Stratemeyer's command did not conduct these operations.

MacArthur had voiced little concern over the possibility of Chinese intervention in the war, but as reports of Chinese troops crossing the Yalu River and entering Korea became more frequent, halting such movements became vital even if China did not officially enter the conflict. For this task, air power was MacArthur's only weapon, and he took an active role in directing its use. Planned air operations involving bombing up to and including the Yalu River crossing were sensitive undertakings, since even the slightest error would mean attacks on Manchuria or possibly Soviet territory. In addition, sending bombers to the Yalu River took a dangerous turn at the beginning of November 1950, when MiG-15 fighters began flying over the northwest corner of North Korea, a region that came to be known as "MiG Alley," and attacking USAF and navy aircraft operating there. The MiG-15 could outperform any of the air force or navy fighters then in Korea. The air force had planned to use its only aircraft in the same class, the swept-wing F-86, for homeland air defense, but Vandenberg agreed to rush two squadrons to Korea so the U.S. forces could meet the emerging threat to air superiority in the region. The F-86s, however, would not arrive and enter service until December.[48]

In spite of the difficulty of bombing targets that bordered China-Manchuria and lay in a region patrolled by MiG-15s, in early November MacArthur directed an all-out bombing effort against the Yalu River bridges even though the flights were bound to be politically sensitive. The JCS initially denied permission for any strikes within five miles of the border but relented a short time later when MacArthur announced to the JCS that his command would be in danger without them.[49]

MacArthur and Stratemeyer were of one mind regarding the use of air power in this manner; indeed, Stratemeyer may have been the more aggressive of the two. During operations earlier in the war Stratemeyer had used leaflet drops to warn civilians in North Korea of air attacks and had restricted bombing to purely military targets, but he now planned to use the B-29s as O'Donnell had advocated soon after his arrival in the theater and firebomb cities. In October Stratemeyer proposed to MacArthur that they bomb the city of Sinuiju on the southern banks of the Yalu River, which was a major transportation hub for Chinese troops and supplies. He presented MacArthur with four options for carrying out the attacks, with the most severe being attacks "over the widest areas of the city without warning, by burning and high explosives," and with the least severe being attacks against "military targets in the city, with high explosives, with warning." Stratemeyer recommended the most severe option, but MacArthur withheld approval of any of the four alternatives because of restrictions Washington had imposed.[50] Those restrictions concerned bombing close to the Manchurian border, but they did not prevent the use of incendiaries or mandate attacking only military targets. Even so, both missions were soon undertaken. Flight operations close to the border remained a concern, but the use of incendiaries against North Korean cities continued throughout the war.

Stratemeyer followed an aggressive course in combating the MiG-15s, but in November he not only lacked aircraft capable of matching the MiGs' performance but also could not carry out tactics on equal terms. The MiGs flew from a base in Antung, located right across the border in Manchuria, and in sight of U.S. aircraft patrolling only a few miles away. The MiGs' tactic was to dart across the border, attack the U.S. aircraft—often B-29s with little capability to maneuver—and then quickly return to Chinese airspace. Both Generals Partridge and Stratemeyer petitioned Washington to allow "hot pursuit" of the MiGs into China, and no doubt to attack the base at Antung as well, but at a time when air strikes that approached the border required special permission, Washington denied their requests. Nor did it grant approval at any time during the war.[51] As noted earlier, however, later in the war the practice of hot pursuit became common, even without official approval.

Reaching back to his experience in World War II, Stratemeyer promoted the use of precision weapons to take out the Yalu River bridges. The use of Razon (range and azimuth-directed) bombs—upgraded radio-controlled Azon bombs of World War II—by B-29s promised to be effective against the well-constructed bridges. Though initially faced with control problems—one-third of the bombs did not respond to the guidance—their effectiveness improved dramatically, and Razon bombs were credited with destroying fifteen of the bridges. By December 1950, the use of precision weapons expanded to include Tarzon bombs, which had a similar guidance system but were mated with a 12,000-pound explosive instead of the 1,000-pound Razon payload. Though the larger payload promised a greater impact, the Tarzon had many more misses than hits, in large part owing to the crews' inexperience with the ordnance. Additionally, a flaw in the release system caused the bombs to detonate even when they were jettisoned without being armed, and one such occurrence killed the group commander of the Tarzon unit in March 1951.[52] The Tarzon program soon ended, and the air force would not use precision weapons for another twenty years, this time against targets in North Vietnam. Although the bombs achieved only limited effectiveness for both operational and technical reasons, Stratemeyer's championing of precision weapon development showed considerable foresight. The military might have developed the program further, but the subsequent dominance of nuclear weapons made radio-controlled bomb releases irrelevant.

THE UNITED STATES ON THE DEFENSIVE

The Chinese ground offensive that began on November 25, 1950, routed the UN forces from their positions near the Yalu River and at the same time prompted a review of U.S. objectives in Korea, as well as Korea's place in national strategy. Reports were not long in coming. Perceiving the attack as a feint to distract the United States from a Soviet attack in Europe, on December 15, 1950, President Truman declared a national emergency, called for new appropriations to enlarge the U.S. military, and announced that troops would be sent to Europe as soon as possible.[53] Defending Europe and Japan had become the priority, with a focus on a developing Cold War in preference to the hot war in Korea. The war in Korea, in fact, had now become at most a distraction, if not an incitement to a general war with the Soviets. All military actions in Korea came to be seen within that context. On December 29, 1950, President Truman informed MacArthur of the new U.S. policy: "We believe Korea is not the place to fight a major war. Further, we believe that we should not commit forces in Korea in face of the increased threat of general war. . . . Since developments may force our withdrawal from Korea, it is important, particularly in view of the continued threat to Japan, to determine in advance, our last reasonable opportunity for an orderly evacuation."[54]

Meanwhile, meetings of the JCS considered how to address the military crisis in Korea while refocusing on Europe and strengthening NATO for an anticipated attack there. The results of that review put military operations in Korea under additional restrictions. First, no further reinforcement of U.S. forces would go to Korea; whatever new forces became available would be committed to NATO.

Next, not only would there be no relaxation of restrictions on cross-border hot pursuit or bombing close to the border, but any actions thought likely to threaten an expansion of the war were also forbidden. In short, instead of seeking to win the war or even confine it to the Korean Peninsula, the Americans' new policy, heavily influenced by its allies (particularly the British), was to end UN involvement in the war as quickly as possible and even to evacuate the peninsula without an armistice if necessary.

As the president and JCS made clear, they would disregard MacArthur's request and send FECOM no reinforcements from the United States, its allies, or Nationalist China. They also denied MacArthur's proposal, fully supported by Stratemeyer, to blockade the Chinese coast and attack targets in Manchuria or elsewhere in China. MacArthur placed a great deal of the blame on British influence in denying him these options. Stratemeyer appears to have adopted the same view of undue political interference in military affairs and would emphasize it in his later pronouncements.[55]

During the dark days of December 1950, the possible use of atomic bombs became a prominent topic of discussion in both political and military circles, but the subject arose and played out in Washington, not in the theater. Neither MacArthur nor Stratemeyer ever advocated their use. They did respond when the JCS queried them on the most appropriate targets for such weapons and made preparations in case their use were authorized, but both officers rightly saw that with principal attention focused on Europe, atomic bombs would only be used in Asia in retaliation for their use against U.S. forces.

Within the narrow constraints of U.S. policy, Stratemeyer conducted perhaps his most effective leadership in the war. He had two immediate tasks, both of which required extensive coordination and frequent adaptation—evacuating air and ground forces and their equipment before they could be overrun by the Chinese–North Korean offensive and conducting an all-out interdiction effort against those enemy forces. His diary contains the minutes of frequent meetings with his commanders and messages to those commanders, to General Vandenberg, and to the Air Staff on requirements, logistics capabilities, and limitations of his forces; tactical details on confronting the MiG-15s; and the destruction of forward-based airfields and construction of fallback positions in both South Korea and in Japan. In the minutes of these meetings, Stratemeyer portrays himself as taking a proactive role—questioning, directing actions, and coordinating among his command elements. He had experienced commanders in Partridge, Tunner, and O'Donnell, but records of discussions at the meetings demonstrate that Stratemeyer was not a passive supervisor.[56]

In one important instance, Stratemeyer's advice might have had a significant impact on how the war would later unfold. Stratemeyer met with MacArthur and the visiting army chief of staff, Lt. Gen. J. Lawton Collins, on December 4, 1950. In that meeting, MacArthur stated that, as a last resort, he intended to retreat and hold two beachheads—one at the Inchon-Seoul area for the Eighth Army and the other at Hungnam on the northeast Korean coast for X Corps. That strategy meant abandoning the rest of the peninsula to the Chinese and North Korean forces. A day later, Stratemeyer hand-delivered a personal message to MacArthur opposing this plan. His arguments centered on the use of air power, highlighting the resulting loss of their air bases in Korea, the difficulty in conducting CAS from bases in Japan, and, even more vitally, the almost certain loss of South Korea. Stratemeyer instead advocated a fighting retreat back to the Pusan area, if necessary, and holding there. Moving in that direction would cause the Chinese forces to extend their supply lines and make them more vulnerable to air attack. In another meeting two days later, MacArthur gave his support to Stratemeyer's plan.[57] It unfolded as anticipated, and air interdiction of the extended Chinese–North Korean supply lines had the intended effect even sooner than had been expected (the offensive essentially ended south of Seoul by January 15). One is left to wonder, however, what the status of Korea would be today if MacArthur's original plan had gone into effect in early December.

Meeting the Chinese–North Korean offensive presented USAF units with severe challenges, but their missions were no different from those undertaken since June 1950. The offensive particularly stressed airlift and air interdiction efforts and, in contrast to prior operations, created serious difficulties in maintaining the air superiority that UN forces had up to then achieved as a matter of course. The offensive brought two factors into play that would threaten the use of air power. First, as noted previously, the introduction of the MiG-15 immediately trumped the capabilities of all UN aircraft except the F-86, which did not become operational in Korea until mid-December 1950. Unfortunately, that time coincided almost exactly with the loss, or impending loss, of the Korean air bases from which the F-86s could operate. Having to retreat to bases in Japan meant that, because of their range limitations, F-86s could not reach MiG Alley or other areas in North Korea that the MiGs now patrolled. That condition lasted until mid-March 1951, when South Korean bases could be put back into commission. Second, the Chinese army brought to the peninsula a far superior ground-based air defense system to what had existed before November. Antiaircraft guns, rockets, machine guns, and searchlights began to affect bombing effectiveness significantly. Aircraft had to fly higher, decreasing bombing accuracy by a factor of three from earlier results, and aircraft loss rates increased accordingly. Moreover, the relatively slow piston-engine aircraft suffered disproportionately. Navy F4U Corsairs and USAF F-51 Mustangs saw several times the loss rate of their jet counterparts: the navy F9F Panthers and USAF F-80 Shooting Stars and F-84 Thunderjets.[58]

An even more serious air threat emerged for the B-29s, which until late 1950 had enjoyed a relatively permissive bombing environment. By the spring of 1951, B-29 missions close to the Manchurian border required a high level of fighter escort, and the B-29s had to revert to night operations. On April 12, 1951, during a bombing mission near the Yalu River, MiGs shot down three B-29s and damaged seven others. Within a thirty-day period a total of eight B-29s were lost.[59] By the fall of 1951, all B-29s had to revert to night-only operations for the remainder of the war. In SAC, Eighth Air Force veterans of World War II must have recalled that even in the dark days of the strategic air campaign against Germany in 1942–1943 the USAAF had resisted attempts to make them revert to night-only operations, but Korea was a different war with different conditions.

With these new conditions now evident, Stratemeyer raised with the Air Staff a growing problem with crew morale and the need for a crew rotation policy and limits on the number of missions flown, similar to policies that had been in effect in World War II. He suggested a set number of missions for each aircraft: a hundred missions for fighters, seventy-five for light bombers (B-26s), and sixty for medium bombers (B-29s). Eventually, the air force accepted those standards with some modifications and with crews exceeding those limits when the situation dictated, but meeting these restrictions called for a steady flow of replacement crews.

Here again, the relatively low priority of the Korean War in USAF planning became evident. Because of the air force's state of readiness when the war began in 1950, World War II veterans were the only immediate source of crew members. Recalled to active duty, they deployed to Korea and continued to carry the load during the first year of the war and beyond. In fact, in the early days of the war, 80 percent of the personnel in FEAF had been recalled from the National Guard or the U.S. Air Force Reserve. Even by April 1951, 72 percent of the officers in FEAF were reservists; in other words, they were officers who, for the most part, had not expected to continue flying in the air force after they had completed their service obligations.[60] Since a rapid expansion of the air force and other services had taxed the training organizations, as new units formed they sought officers and airmen who would grow with the organization and not leave the service at the first opportunity. As a result, those Stateside units had first call on new inductees, with the needs of FEAF having to compete with those of an expanding SAC and of air force units deploying to Europe. Most personnel assigned to Korea continued to be recalled reservists.

Inevitably, the toll on the crew members was high, particularly with the increasing lethality of low-level flying. The command saw a significant increase in "fear of flying" cases involving aircrew members, nearly all of them reservists recalled to active duty, and crews flying on ground attack missions in F-51s, F-80s, F-84s, and B-26s. In one instance, Stratemeyer had to deal with a situation in a B-26 group in which three or four navigators had refused to fly after completing fifty missions. In this case, Stratemeyer relieved the wing commander, a one-star general, for deficient leadership.[61]

In addition to a shortage of crews and aircraft, Stratemeyer also had to compensate for the reassignment of his major subordinate commanders. The first to go in January 1951 was O'Donnell, who was replaced by a series of brigadier generals on four-month rotations from SAC. Next, in February 1951, the air force reassigned Tunner to Air Materiel Command as its deputy commander. In April, Stratemeyer lost Weyland to TAC, although Weyland was to return to FEAF in June as its commander. And, finally, though discussions of his replacement had taken place earlier, in June 1951 General Partridge left to become commander of the Air Research and Development Command. None of these officers was reassigned for lack of ability; in fact, all went on to higher levels of command. Instead, the moves illustrated the air force's focus on creating its postwar organization even while the war continued. They provided the most capable future leadership for the air force, but one would be hard pressed to find another example of so many wartime commanders transferred to a peacetime environment while a war continued to be fought.

THE POLITICAL BATTLES, JANUARY TO MAY 1951

A final major distraction to the conduct of the Korean War concerned the possibility of a Soviet attack on the United States and how it would involve FEAF. That fear became explicit at the time of the Chinese offensive in November 1950 and continued thereafter. What in December and January had been a fear of another Dunkirk-style evacuation for UN forces by February 1951 had become a fear of a Pearl Harbor–type of attack on U.S. forces as part of a general war begun by the Soviet Union. Since Stratemeyer's command had responsibility for both air operations in Korea and the air defense of Japan, he now had to reconsider his allocation of aircraft and crews to these two missions while facing shortages in both. Frequent communications with General Vandenberg and others on the Air Staff concerned these allocations. Decision makers in Washington and in the theater recognized the almost impossible situation that simply not enough crews or aircraft were available for the task. Vandenberg and Stratemeyer discussed the need for dispersing air units so as not to present too inviting a target—a measure that would exacerbate the strain on logistics—and whether to assign the higher-performance F-80s to Japan while leaving the more vulnerable F-51s in Korea. Stratemeyer opted to leave the F-80s in Korea.[62] In hindsight, one might view the fear of a Soviet air attack as exaggerated, but at the time, and given the long-term importance of Japan over that of Korea, American concerns about such an attack took on increased significance. No one wanted to preside over another Pearl Harbor. In Stratemeyer's first meeting with General Ridgway after the latter succeeded MacArthur, the main subjects under discussion were the buildup of Soviet aircraft in Siberia and Manchuria and plans for countering an attack.[63] In this discussion, no option appeared promising.

Stratemeyer's command of FEAF ended in the spring of 1951 with two unexpected events—MacArthur's removal from command on April 11 and Stratemeyer's heart attack on May 20. Five days before being relieved of command, MacArthur had briefed three congressmen on the general situation in the Far East (Stratemeyer recorded that he had "never spent a more inspiring 55 minutes.")[64] On April 9, MacArthur recommended Stratemeyer for promotion to four-star rank (along with General Ridgway and Admiral Joy), an action that would be overtaken by subsequent events. Hearing the news of MacArthur's dismissal, Stratemeyer appeared devastated both personally and professionally. For the first time in his diary he expressed political views: "To me, it means capitulation of our government and all that it has stood for to our 'Pinkish' State Department, the British government, and Moscow. Every Red, regardless of his place in the world, was gleeful at this drastic order."[65] After his retirement, Stratemeyer would expand on these views.

Stratemeyer's diary for the following weeks never again referred to MacArthur's removal from command. He quickly began to develop a working relationship with General Ridgway, and all of his correspondence concerned his daily work as FEAF commander: support for B-29 operations, reports on the continuing buildup of Soviet air forces in the region and planned actions in case of a Soviet air offensive, provision of hospitals and flight surgeons, assignments of key staff members, and discussions and reviews of news stories that appeared in the United States. The only comment of a more general nature appeared in a message to the USAF deputy chief of staff for operations, Lt. Gen. Idwal Edwards. It ended: "I urgently request that you exercise your good office in the Headquarters of the United States Air Force and in the joint bodies on which you sit to start a change in thinking that this is a minor skirmish and that this it is not having any lasting effect. All the services need all-out assistance in Korea as long as this is the only place where actual war exists."[66]

LATER CAREER

Following a severe heart attack on May 20, 1951, Stratemeyer quickly left the scene. He remained hospitalized in Japan for months before returning to the United States. MacArthur's recommendation for four-star rank never took effect, and Stratemeyer retired immediately thereafter. For the remainder of the Korean War, Stratemeyer refrained from any public comments, but beginning in 1954 he took an active political role in attacking administration policies. He appeared before congressional committees to castigate the State Department for its actions during the Korean War and asserted that "we were not allowed to win it." He continued to praise MacArthur's role and began to associate more and more with partisan politics. Among other actions, he led an unsuccessful movement to stop the censure of Wisconsin senator Joseph McCarthy that the latter's Senate colleagues sought for his accusations against the army.

During the remainder of the 1950s Stratemeyer essentially cut his ties with the air force and became associated with various causes supporting both anticommunist, pro–Nationalist China positions and the avoidance of any involvement in a Korean War–type military action, but he quickly lost his platform and faded from sight. General Smart, one of his former subordinates, visited him in retirement at his home in Florida and saw him as "a man possessed with exaggerated if not irrational perceptions of reality." Stratemeyer died in the summer of 1969, during the depths of the nation's involvement in the Vietnam War and a particularly divisive time in U.S. politics.[67]

No doubt Stratemeyer's controversial involvement in politics after his retirement and his close association and continued support of MacArthur affected others' judgments of his leadership of FEAF and resulted in little, if any, extended assessment of his service there.[68] Part of the explanation may lie in the difficulty of separating his actions from MacArthur's dominant presence during the first year of the war. A triumphant MacArthur would have had a positive impact on Stratemeyer's legacy; a fired commander had the opposite effect. Another part of the explanation may stem from the way that the air force and others set aside the experience of the Korean War and its lessons, including assessments of its leaders (notably excepting MacArthur). With regard to Stratemeyer, it is also difficult to judge his contributions apart from those of his major subordinate commanders who executed the operational and tactical aspects of the war and from the role of the leadership in the Pentagon. Since Stratemeyer's role had been to prompt, support, and encourage the work of his subordinates and not to pursue independent actions himself, his more often behind-the-scenes influence remains hard to assess. Other general officers of the time presented accounts of their own service in the war but left few comments, good or bad, about the theater air commander.

An examination of Stratemeyer's personal records, however, shows him to have been an extremely knowledgeable and involved commander who was well attuned, if perhaps overly sensitive, to public perceptions of his command's operations and of the air force in general. In a way Stratemeyer was seemingly denigrated when others described him in such terms as "affable," "genial," or "low key"; these descriptions confuse style with substance. Stratemeyer perceived as well as anyone the type of leadership required of him in the war, and, fortunately for the air force, his background prepared him to carry out that role as well as anyone could have done. It was his unenviable task to lead FEAF during the most vital and turbulent period of the war, a period in which the war itself took no better than second place to other U.S. military responsibilities. Denied the air force's preference for conducting a World War II–type strategic bombing campaign during the

Korean War's first year, Stratemeyer led his command in adjusting to alternative uses for its bombers. He remained open to innovative uses of air power and its technologies, most notably to using precision weapons and instituting air refueling of aircraft in his theater (although it was never actually used during the war).

The Korean War presented Stratemeyer with a situation in which doctrine existed for air control and targeting, but no system was in place to translate doctrine into action. Only the adjustments and compromises of his command, made on the fly, achieved that objective. He also had to deal with the reality that command of the air did not prevent the appearance of a ground-based air defense system using World War II–type weapons that were lethal to his low-level operations. Stratemeyer steadfastly faced these issues in Korea, but they came to the fore again in a different context, bedeviling Generals William Momyer, John Vogt Jr., and others in Vietnam.

7

WILLIAM W. MOMYER:
AN AIR POWER MIND

CASE CUNNINGHAM

On November 10, 1942, Lt. Col. William Wallace Momyer started the engine of his P-40 Warhawk on the deck of the U.S. Navy escort carrier USS *Chenango*. The recently promoted commander of the Thirty-Third Fighter Group prepared to launch with seventy-seven P-40s for the Port Lyautey airfield in French Morocco as a part of the Western Task Force of Operation Torch.[1]

Less than twenty-four years later, Lieutenant General Momyer would stand on the ramp at Tan Son Nhut Air Base, Saigon, South Vietnam, and assume responsibilities as the Seventh Air Force commander and deputy commander for air operations of Military Assistance Command, Vietnam (MACV). When he arrived in South Vietnam in 1966, he would have operational command of more than eight hundred aircraft. By the time he left in 1968 that number would have more than doubled to more than eighteen hundred aircraft with twenty-three squadrons of fighter, bomber, or attack aircraft.[2]

Between those two moments, William "Spike" Momyer would see combat through North Africa and Italy, fight doctrinal battles at the U.S. Air Force's Tactical Air Command (TAC) and Air University, and dedicate endless hours of thought to a concept of the application of air power. This chapter tells the story of the development of an air power mind.

EARLY YEARS AND COMMAND IN WAR

A native of Muskogee, Oklahoma, the son of an attorney and a schoolteacher, Momyer first got the aviation itch crawling around the cockpits of World War I–era De Havilland aircraft at Hatbox Field, east of town. A few years before Momyer entered high school, his father passed away, and his mother moved the family to Seattle, Washington. Although he thought of following in his father's footsteps and attending law school after graduating from the University of Washington in 1937, the call of the air spoke louder than family tradition. He joined the U.S. Army and traveled to Randolph Field in San Antonio, Texas, for flight school.[3]

At Randolph Field, Momyer quickly realized that he wanted to be a pursuit pilot. In February 1939 he accomplished his goal when he graduated from flying school. Days later, he arrived at Langley Field, Virginia, and reported to the Thirty-Fifth Pursuit Squadron. In June 1940, the squadrons of the Eighth Pursuit Group became the first to fly the Curtis P-40 Warhawk. During this transition, Momyer spent time at Wright Field, Ohio, conducting the first service tests for the aircraft. After completing the tests and nearly another year of flight duty, Momyer prepared to travel across the Atlantic to Africa.[4]

On March 23, 1941, Lieutenant Momyer departed Washington, D.C., for Cairo, Egypt.[5] Although Momyer's primary duty in the Western Desert was aiding the British with the P-40s and passing lessons to Washington, D.C., he also found time to fly in combat with the Royal Air Force (RAF). Momyer took part in enough combat operations with the RAF to see "what it was like to be shot at and to shoot."[6]

Upon his return to the States, First Lieutenant Momyer became the second in command of the Sixtieth Pursuit Squadron of the Thirty-Third Pursuit Group at Bolling Field, Washington, D.C. Charles Duncan, a pilot in the Sixtieth Pursuit Squadron, recalled that Momyer "would not permit pilots of the 60th [to] do but two things while in operations when they had free time. One was to read technical orders and the other was play checkers."[7] Momyer left Bolling Field for Norfolk, Virginia, in March 1942 and assumed command of the Fifty-Eighth Pursuit Squadron on March 23.[8] Shortly thereafter, now-Major Momyer replaced Col. Elwood Quesada as the Thirty-Third Fighter Group commander.[9]

As Momyer took command of the Thirty-Third, Brig. Gen. Jimmy Doolittle, the leader of Twelfth Air Force, made plans to bring the group on board to support Operation Torch. Under the Twelfth, Doolittle created a suborganization—the XII Air Support Command (XII ASC), commanded by Brig. Gen. John Cannon—to cooperate directly with the Western Task Force's landings in French Morocco.[10] Momyer's Thirty-Third Fighter Group fell under the XII ASC and would make the transit to French Morocco on an auxiliary aircraft carrier.[11] The

Thirty-Third loaded up on the recently converted *Chenango* at Norfolk, Virginia, on October 22, 1942. A few days before the invasion, the captain of the *Chenango* announced that America and its Allies were now taking the offensive in the Mediterranean area and that the task force was headed for West Africa.[12]

As they crossed the Atlantic to join the war, the men of the Thirty-Third could not have felt thoroughly prepared for battle. Momyer later recalled that the experience level of the group's pilots was very low; indeed, most of them had only recently graduated from flight school.[13] A major factor hindering the preparations of the U.S. Army Air Forces (USAAF) was the state of air power doctrine in 1942. No organization or individual in the USAAF had yet established a formal set of tactics for providing close air support or for attaining air superiority. The most recent U.S. Army Field Manual, FM 31-35, *Aviation in Support of Ground Forces* (April 1942), focused more on the organization of air power than on its use. Even in that regard, the manual called for the air support commander to come under immediate control of the ground force commander. Along with the lack of doctrine, the USAAF also suffered from a lack of training in direct support of ground operations. In fact, since the attack on Pearl Harbor in December 1941, the Thirty-Third had spent the majority of its time sitting alert for coastal defense.[14]

On November 8, 1942, after sixteen long days and nights at sea, the task force arrived off the French Moroccan coast. As the battle raged on land, Momyer and the other pilots of the Thirty-Third waited on standby in their aircraft, ready to take off at a moment's notice. Their objective was the airfield at Port Lyautey, the only "all-weather concrete landing strip in northwestern Africa," a perfect first home for the fighter group.[15] Although the beach assaults were supported by carrier-borne naval aviation, capturing Port Lyautey would allow the Thirty-Third and the rest of XII ASC to sustain air support for Torch.[16]

Finally, after the assault force secured the Port Lyautey airfield on the morning of November 10, the Thirty-Third received the call to launch. Momyer took off with the first group of P-40s that left the ship at two-minute intervals. The catapulting was uneventful, but the landing at Port Lyautey was not. The shelling from the navy ships and the navy aircrafts' attacks on the French aircraft on the field had left the airfield in great disrepair, and three large craters pocked the airfield's hard surface runway. Each pilot tried to find his own way around these craters, but a number of the first pilots crashed their P-40s on landing. With the approaching runway looking similar to the moon's surface, Momyer tried to stop before reaching the first crater. Unfortunately, he landed short and caught his landing gear on the edge of the pavement, shearing it from the aircraft.[17]

Luckily unhurt, Momyer climbed out of the wreckage to survey the field. Realizing that the entire landing operation and the fate of his group were in jeopardy, he assessed the situation on foot and under the heat of enemy sniper and artillery fire. As he relayed the field's grim status to the *Chenango* and ordered the second wave of P-40 launches to delay, another pilot crashed and his aircraft flipped upside down. Momyer began to run toward the wreckage. Though realizing that the aircraft could explode into flame at any moment, Momyer calmly removed the pilot from the tangled metal and moved him to safety. His heroism on that day would later earn him the Silver Star, the third-highest combat military decoration that can be awarded to a member of any branch of the armed forces for valor in the face of the enemy.[18]

On the morning of November 11, after a night devoted to runway repair, the Thirty-Third's remaining P-40s began launching from the deck of the *Chenango*. The group's aircraft arrived late in Torch's timeline, and none of them participated in combat in that operation.[19]

As the Thirty-Third settled in French Morocco, the Germans began an invasion of their own through Sicily into Tunisia. To stop the advance, Allied commanders started moving aircraft forward to the Tebessa region of eastern Algeria.[20] The Thirty-Third began to filter into Thelepte, the most forward base in the Tebessa region, early in December 1942. The group's movement coincided with the forward movement of its parent organization, the XII ASC, which Gen. Dwight Eisenhower had attached to the U.S. II Corps.[21]

The forward position of Thelepte made it not only valuable to the Allies but also highly vulnerable to attacks from German aircraft. The Axis powers almost daily attacked the airfield with both fighters and bombers. Initially, the Allies had no early warning radar, and the Thirty-Third depended on French observers in the hills surrounding the airfield. As an added measure, the Thirty-Third kept two aircraft flying combat air patrol at all times during the daylight hours. Dogfights between P-40s and German Messerschmitt Bf-109 fighters often occurred over the field.[22]

The XII ASC set the objectives for Momyer's men at Thelepte. They were to gain air superiority in the II Corps area of operations, support the ground forces with both reconnaissance and attacks on enemy troops, and provide maximum protection for Allied ground units against enemy air attack. Command arrangements gave II Corps operational control of XII ASC aircraft, often limiting the freedom of XII ASC. On more than one occasion, II Corps leadership denied air support to French units under attack less than a hundred miles from the field at Thelepte.[23]

After arriving at Thelepte on January 4, 1943, Momyer scored his first aerial victories. On that day, six German Junkers Ju 88 bombers attacked the field with Bf-109s as escort. When the attack commenced, Momyer ran to his P-40 and scrambled to meet the marauders. Moments after Momyer became airborne, the six .50-caliber machine guns of Momyer's P-40 had found their mark, and a German Ju 88 plummeted to the earth. Four days later Momyer shot down his second and last aircraft for the month, a German Bf-109 fighter in a bombing escort mission, over a German truck park east of the field.[24]

Although the Thirty-Third's first operations supported II Corps on the southern portion of the lines, in late January the Germans began to focus attacks on the French center sector. As January turned to February, the Thirty-Third began to feel the impact of a month of combat operations at the foremost Allied field. Despite the Axis's numerical superiority and vastly greater combat experience, the Thirty-Third traded their aircraft for enemy aircraft on a roughly one-to-one ratio. But both the constant attacks on Thelepte and flight operations under what was, for all practical purposes, Axis air superiority had taken its toll on the Thirty-Third in manpower and matériel. Combat fatigue had begun to set in, and on February 9 the Thirty-Third received orders to withdraw from the front and reorganize.[25]

After only a month away from battle, the context changed drastically for Momyer and the men of the Thirty-Third. By early March it was apparent that the Axis forces were fighting a losing battle in Tunisia, and it was only a matter of time before they would be expelled from North Africa.[26] Toward the end of March, after the Allies had pushed back the Axis lines, the Thirty-Third was once again assigned to the XII ASC and moved to the most forward Allied airfield, Sbeitla, thirty-five miles east of Thelepte. In this phase of the Tunisian campaign, the Thirty-Third began to feel the positive effects of the new air organization created by the Casablanca Conference of January 1943. In orders to his commanders, Air Marshal Arthur Coningham, now Momyer's superior as the commander of recently formed Northwest African Tactical Air Force, stressed the importance of air superiority over the battle area. Specifically, the objective was to "provide maximum support for air operations" with two supporting courses of action: "(1) A continual offensive against the enemy in the air, and (2) Sustained attacks on enemy airfields."[27]

The war diary of the Fifty-Eighth Fighter Squadron records a typical mission for the Thirty-Third Fighter Group during this time.

> This morning, at 0915 hours, the 58th, with other members of the 33rd Group, including Colonel Momyer, escort the American bombers over the Axis landing-strip [north of Djebel Tebaga]. Before reaching the target, an unknown number of German fighters rise up, through their own flak, to intercept the bombers. The P-40s return their fire. Colonel Momyer, while over the target, choosing between two German fighters—one, above, and, one, below—goes for the ship beneath him. Giving one burst, he drops the Me-109.[28]

In a situation not atypical of life on the front lines, the dogfights over the Axis airfields had migrated over the field at Sbeitla, and the entire group witnessed Momyer's victory over the Bf-109—his fourth of the war. One more would bring him the coveted title of ace.

Some of the most intense ground action of this portion of the campaign occurred between the forces of Maj. Gen. George Patton and Field Marshal Erwin Rommel near El Guettar in late March.[29] On the afternoon of March 31, Momyer took off from Sbeitla leading a force of thirty-six P-40s on a bombing and strafing mission against a concentration of enemy troops near El Guettar.[30] The Thirty-Third met a large force of Bf-109s and Stuka dive-bombers over the battle lines. Momyer recalled the aerial battle that ensued years later: "The Germans had come in with this formation of Stukas to hit the tank formation that we had. After I made the identity, I told the wingman that we would slide up the back end of the formation and work our way through. So, with that I started out to shoot the Stukas, and I shot four Stukas down real quick. Bang! Bang!"[31]

While Momyer's personal recollection of the battle reveals his feelings at the moment, it does not fully capture the heroism of his actions. He first led his flight in the attack on twelve Bf-109s. Emerging from this attack with his wingman, Momyer spotted a formation of eighteen Stukas escorted by three more Bf-109s. In the turn to attack, enemy fire hit Momyer's wingman, and he could not continue. Recognizing that the enemy formation had the Allied ground forces in their sights, Momyer attacked the large formation as a formation of one. The account from a friendly aircraft above the fight confirmed that Momyer destroyed four aircraft and damaged seven. He continued the attack on the enemy aircraft until his fuel ran dangerously low, and then he returned to Sbeitla through a barrage of enemy antiaircraft fire. For his actions that day, Momyer not only earned the title of ace but was also awarded the Distinguished Service Cross, second only to the Medal of Honor in the U.S. Army hierarchy of awards for gallantry and risking one's life in combat.[32]

The Thirty-Third closed out operations at Sbeitla in a much healthier condition than when they left Thelepte. The XII ASC now traded approximately one of its aircraft for every two and a half Axis aircraft. In mid-April, the Thirty-Third moved to Ebba Ksour, Tunisia, to follow up the continued advance of Allied troops.[33] In this fourth phase of the campaign, Coningham placed even greater stress on air superiority. With the Axis in retreat, Coningham planned to precede the Allied ground offensive with air operations "directed to the weakening and, if possible, the elimination of this fighter force."[34] In the campaign for air superiority, HQ XII ASC employed Momyer's P-40s almost exclusively as fighter-bombers to attack airfields, vehicle traffic, gun installations, and enemy force concentrations. Now six squadrons of Spitfires were under the XII ASC to support the fighter sweep mission.[35]

As group commander at the Thirty-Third, Momyer would gain a great deal of experience with both the tactical and operational aspects of using air power.[36] In May, the Axis forces began their evacuation from North Africa, and Momyer's men continued to harass them, attacking boats, supplies, and equipment. On May 13, 1943, the Axis commander in North Africa accepted the Eighth Army's surrender terms, officially ending the hostilities in Tunisia. A little more than five months later, and after nearly a full year of command in the Mediterranean theater, Col. William Momyer left the Thirty-Third and departed for the United States. With more than two hundred combat hours and eight confirmed kills, Momyer had experienced more in a year than many would experience in a lifetime of aviation service. After North Africa, Momyer had led the Thirty-Third through the air operations over Pantelleria, the Allied invasion of Sicily, and the amphibious assault on Italy at Salerno. Momyer's leadership was essential in transforming the group from a green bunch of pilots who had recently emerged from pilot training to one of the most respected fighter groups in the USAAF. "Moe's Mob," as the newspapers had tagged the Thirty-Third, had played a major role in the campaigns that helped develop tactical aviation in the U.S. armed services.

A FOCUS ON AIR POWER THOUGHT

On December 17, 1943, Momyer reported for duty on the USAAF Board in Orlando, Florida. Although a world away from combat duty in the Mediterranean, Momyer's time at Orlando would nonetheless keep him well connected to air power thought and practice. The USAAF Board, according to Maj. Gen. Muir S. Fairchild, the Air Staff director of military requirements, would "study the overall picture of Air Force matters with a view to making recommendations to the Commanding General, Army Air Forces, on such matters as Air Force strategy, technique, organization, equipment, training, etc., of all units making up an Air Force and of the Air Forces as a whole."[37]

Brig. Gen. E. L. Eubank, the executive director of the USAAF Board, assigned Momyer to the Tactics Division. Much later, Eubank remembered that Momyer's presence brought the board "more influence because we were bringing back people from overseas who had been in combat and who had some personal knowledge of what it took to do certain things in combat."[38] Although, as Eubank once stated at a morning staff meeting, they were "a helluva long way from the War," Momyer and the other members of the USAAF Board could still contribute to the fight.[39]

In March 1944, Momyer became chief of the USAAF Board's Combined Operations Branch, which had primary responsibility for projects concerning the interdependence of air power with the land and sea components. In July 1944, the board began a study on coordinating the use of air and land power, specifically seeking to determine the "doctrine and tactics for the isolation of a battlefield by employment of air power."[40] Using data on the Allied campaigns in Normandy, southern France, and Italy and the inputs of personnel with recent air and ground experience in combined operations, Momyer led the effort to "evaluate the experience to date of combined air-surface operations, and to derive therefrom certain principles and methods of air attack which can be used as the basis for the planning and execution of such operations." The completed study noted that the "attack on enemy rear area objectives and sea forces for the purpose of isolating the battlefield" was second only to achieving air superiority while accomplishing the phases of a tactical air campaign. The document framed a general plan for conducting future interdiction operations.[41]

Momyer served on the USAAF Board until its dissolution in June 1946. "It was a fine outfit and provided a very needed service to the Air Force," Momyer recalled in 1972. "We don't have anyplace in the Air Force today that ties together new concepts, doctrine, and hardware. The board provided this essential task in a very productive manner."[42]

As the board disbanded, Momyer learned that he would once again work for General Quesada.[43] In May 1946, recognizing the need to be close to those army and navy organizations that would be crucial to the cooperation required in tactical air power, Quesada had moved TAC Headquarters from Tampa, Florida, to Langley Field, Virginia. The headquarters of Army Ground Forces, located at Fort Monroe, and the Atlantic Fleet Headquarters at Norfolk were both a short drive from Langley. To support his mission of "providing and operating that portion of the USAAF which is maintained in the United States . . . for cooperating with land and sea forces in the conduct of land and amphibious operations," Quesada built a headquarters staff on a traditional "A-Staff" structure with sections for personnel, intelligence, operations, and resources. Not until Momyer's arrival at Langley in July 1946, however, did Quesada create an A-5 section for plans, putting Momyer at the helm.[44]

Momyer supervised the staffs that created war plans, doctrine, and exercise plans for TAC. As Quesada stated in an interview many years later, Momyer was the "driving force very often behind joint maneuvers with the Army, and he believed in [joint maneuver] very deeply."[45] Momyer would soon have more opportunity to develop these thoughts as he packed up his effects in August 1949 and departed Langley for Montgomery, Alabama, and a year at the Air War College (AWC).

At the end of the academic year in Montgomery, Momyer submitted his completed thesis to the AWC faculty. Titled "A Concept of Tactical Air Operations," the thesis built directly on his air power experiences to that point. His goal was to provide a concept of tactical air operations "particularly oriented on the new era of atomic weapons." In pursuing this goal, Momyer briefly analyzed "pre-World War II, World War II, and post-war concepts to determine their applicability, if any, to a future concept."[46] In one of the most insightful observations in his thesis, Momyer states simply, "Another basic portion of the proposed concept is the treatment of Air Power as an entity, and not as self-contained component parts unrelated. The arbitrary division of Air Power into Strategic and Tactical has tended to compartment the thinking of air strategists so as to compromise an exploitation of the full potential of Air Power as a whole."[47] Momyer seems to have been at the leading edge of the development of this theory of indivisible air power, since

USAF historian Robert Futrell subsequently credited Gen. Hoyt Vandenberg, the USAF chief of staff, with a similar statement in the summer of 1950.[48]

Momyer was selected to stay as a member of the AWC faculty after his graduation in June 1950. While many of Momyer's peers fought in Asia, he remained at Maxwell, preparing to instruct students in his first AWC class.[49] His time as an instructor helped Momyer to think even more deeply about his experiences thus far. In June 1951 he assumed a position that would further refine his air power mind and became director of the AWC Evaluation Staff.[50]

By mid-1951, Momyer's Evaluation Staff had responsibility for approximately twenty-five projects. Most interesting in the context of air power thought was the project to write twelve doctrine manuals covering the air force's major mission areas. As director, Momyer supervised the completion of these manuals. He also served as the project officer for Air Force Manual (AFM) 1-2, *United States Air Force Basic Doctrine*. Because this manual was to form the foundation of the other doctrine documents, it received the highest priority.[51] AFM 1-2 presented the basic USAF doctrine in seventeen pages. Characteristic of air power thought at the time, it cited the dominant role of air forces in war. More important, AFM 1-2 described formally how the air force would accomplish its missions. This how-to of basic doctrine emerged from what the foreword to the document called "experience gained in war and from analysis of the continuing impact of new weapons on warfare."[52]

In chairing the latter stages of the production of AFM 1-2, Momyer produced the first officially sanctioned basic doctrine document for the independent U.S. Air Force—a monumental achievement. Nearly simultaneously with the publication of AFM 1-2, Momyer's staff forwarded four additional operational doctrine manuals to the Air Staff for approval: the manuals for theater air operations, air defense operations, air transport operations, and strategic air operations. The manual on theater air operations would prove especially relevant to Momyer's experience and his future commands. This document sought to provide "principles for the conduct of air warfare in a theater of operations and for the command and control of air forces" and served as a basic guide for "correlating and coordinating the operations of Air Force forces with other forces in the theater."[53]

Momyer completed his tour at Maxwell in August 1953. In his years of service at Air University he left an indelible mark on the canvas of air power thought. As he arrived in Washington, D.C., for another year of senior service school at the

National War College, the air force distributed approved copies of the doctrine manuals. Momyer entered the halls of the National War College as one of the most knowledgeable USAF officers on the subject of air power doctrine and a firm believer in the flexibility and lethality of air power under the central control of a theater commander.

A SHORT RETURN TO COMMAND

Momyer graduated from the National War College in June 1954, and on August 4 he took command of the Eighth Fighter-Bomber Wing at Suwon Air Base, South Korea. For a brief six months he oversaw the wing's move to Japan.[54] In February 1955 he returned to Korea and took command of the 314th Air Division and operational control of all Fifth Air Force units in the country. He also had operational control over shore-based navy and marine fighters in air defense or offensive roles, operational control over navy and marine antiaircraft artillery units in support of air defense, and supervision of an air defense control center. In this role, Momyer was ultimately responsible for the air power aspects of enforcing the armistice agreement and the air defense of South Korea. Again serving only a short tour, Momyer departed Korea in late August 1955 for command assignments in the high desert of New Mexico.[55]

Upon arriving in New Mexico, Momyer took command of the 312th Fighter-Bomber Wing at Clovis Air Force Base.[56] On December 13, 1955, the air force promoted Momyer to brigadier general.[57] Since he had spent nearly thirteen years as a colonel, the promotion seemed to be a long time coming; however, considering that Momyer's promotion to colonel came four years after he was commissioned and when he was only twenty-six, the significant time lapse appears more reasonable. In an era of Strategic Air Command (SAC) dominance, the promotion of a "tactical Airman" to general officer rank signaled that the air force had selected Momyer as one of the men to carry the torch of tactical air power as he moved on to senior leadership positions. The burden was great, but Momyer was more than up to the task.

As 1956 closed, what is now Cannon Air Force Base expanded to accommodate additional fighters, and TAC located a second fighter-bomber wing there. A new organization, the 832nd Air Division, was established to manage the two wings, each made up of four fighter-bomber squadrons,[58] as well as the air base group. In October 1957, Momyer moved from the 312th and took command of the division.

BACK TO STAFF

Shortly after assuming command of the 832nd Air Division, Momyer once again left the life of the combat forces for the life of a staff officer at TAC. On August 4, 1958, Brig. Gen. William Momyer replaced Maj. Gen. John D. Stevenson as the TAC director of plans on the staff of the deputy commander for operations. In August 1959, Gen. Frank F. Everest took command of TAC. Since Momyer was one of Everest's key deputies, they interacted a great deal. Later, Everest recalled his time with Momyer:

> He was hardheaded, and we had some debates. He was one of the few guys that I allowed to come back in the office to discuss the same subject the second or even third time. He was hard to convince. It always got to the point where I would have to say, "Spike, I have talked with you all I intend to about this subject. You are going to do it my way. Now let's get that thoroughly understood." He always said, "Yes, sir," and he would get up and leave the office . . . you couldn't ask for a more loyal—he was at times hard to convince, but once he was convinced or directed, then he would follow his instructions right to the letter, never any question about that.[59]

Although the strength of Momyer's convictions meant that he fought hard for what he believed was right, he knew when to salute smartly and carry out the orders of the boss.

In October 1961, Momyer replaced Lt. Gen. Bruce K. Holloway as the director of operational requirements on the air staff.[60] As the chief of requirements for the air force, Momyer held a very important job, and the force of his personality and the strength of his ideas made it even more influential. "Christ, I can remember briefing him," Col. William Hovde recalled, "and [Gen. Curtis] LeMay said, 'Colonel Hovde, you go tell General Momyer.' I said, 'Tell him? I'll suggest, sir.' He said, 'I think that is a better word, yes.'"[61]

At the time, Col. (later Maj. Gen.) Richard Catledge was serving in the staff of the deputy chief of staff for operations. "As I looked and listened," Catledge recalled from his first meeting with Momyer in attendance, "I realized this two-star Gen. Spike Momyer ran the Air Staff—very strong-minded individual, very knowledgeable individual, who did his homework on everything. He just knew so much more than anybody else that he just really ran the Air Staff."[62]

Maj. Gen. Gordon H. Austin, who was Momyer's deputy when he first arrived in Washington, later commented: "I think that he is a brilliant man, and he has wide experience. Momyer is a fast reader; he can read an ordinary book in about 20 minutes and get 80 percent of it." He noted, however, that Momyer did not want a deputy; thus, Austin lost the responsibility he had had under Holloway's leadership. "He took it all unto himself," Austin remembered, "and he had the capability to handle it."[63]

Reflecting on his time with Momyer on the Air Staff, Gen. Gabriel Disosway, a future TAC commander, later remarked:

> Spike is so fast and so smart and knows so much that he could do the work of ten people and I'd keep telling him, I'd say, Spike, that's not the idea. I said, you're up here for two purposes; one is to train officers and the other is to get work done, but it doesn't do any good if you do all the work. . . . I said, you've got to train the other fellow to take over some day. But it was much easier for Spike to do it all himself.[64]

In early summer of 1964, Lt. Gen. Robert W. Burns, the commander of Air Training Command (ATC) at Randolph Air Force Base, applied for medical retirement, and Momyer was selected as his replacement. As a major command, ATC required a three-star general to lead it, so Momyer was promoted upon his assumption of command on August 11, 1964. Interestingly enough, in the past, generals who were on their last assignment prior to retirement had filled the ATC commander's position. Momyer's case was different.

Brig. Gen. Kenneth R. Johnson, who was a staff maintenance officer at ATC during Momyer's tenure, recalled that "he's absolutely brilliant. . . . He's tough as nails. He reads about thirteen hundred words a minute and he's got a recall that's like an iron mousetrap." Johnson, who was responsible for briefing Momyer on ATC maintenance issues each day, noted, "That was a real challenge. I used to sit up at nights figuring out how I was going to brief him on some of the tougher things." He soon learned to prepare for the tough briefs. "I'd carry in my board and I'd have a special briefing on the back of it. Whenever he'd hit me on that point, I'd flip my board around and give him that briefing. One day I went in there and we finished the briefing and I didn't even get caught on anything. He said, 'What did I miss?' I said, 'You didn't miss anything,' and he said, 'Turn your board around.'"[65]

Momyer's time at Randolph Field would be short. In May 1966, Momyer received official word that on July 1 he would assume duties as deputy commander of the Military Assistance Command Vietnam (MACV) for air operations and as commander of the Seventh Air Force. Momyer left Randolph on June 26 bound for the Pacific.[66]

VIETNAM

In retrospect, the first twenty-eight years of Momyer's career all seem to have served as preparation for his assignment in Vietnam. Finally, as the Seventh Air Force commander, Momyer would command air power in war.

Although Momyer appeared to have been bred for the Seventh Air Force job, one of his longtime mentors, Lt. Gen. Elwood Quesada, played at least a supporting role in sending Momyer to Vietnam. The recently retired Quesada managed to secure a trip to Vietnam with the help of Senator Stuart Symington. Quesada later recalled that after his visit to Vietnam "I recommended very strongly that . . . you need somebody there who understands the use of air power and doesn't give a goddamn about getting along. I suggested Spike Momyer."[67]

LINES OF COMMAND

Gen. William C. Westmoreland was the commander of the U.S. MACV (COMUSMACV), a sub-unified command under Pacific Command (PACOM), and thus in many ways he was Momyer's new boss. Westmoreland greeted Momyer as he arrived at Seventh Air Force Headquarters at Tan Son Nhut Air Base, Saigon, South Vietnam, on June 30, 1966. The next day, in a ceremony at the base, Momyer succeeded Lt. Gen. Joseph H. Moore as the Seventh Air Force commander and the deputy commander for air operations of MACV.

Although Westmoreland reported directly to PACOM, Momyer's responsibilities were far more complex. For air operations in South Vietnam, Laos, and the southernmost part of North Vietnam, Momyer worked for Westmoreland and commanded air force aircraft based throughout South Vietnam. For air operations in the rest of North Vietnam, Momyer reported to General Hunter Harris, the commander in chief of Pacific Air Forces (CINCPACAF), who in turn reported to Adm. U. S. Grant Sharp, the commander in chief of PACOM (CINCPAC). In this capacity, Momyer had operational control of USAF assets flying from South Vietnam and of aircraft from Thailand—but only when they were airborne. When these aircraft were on the ground, they were the responsibility of the Thirteenth Air Force in the Philippines. In accordance with a geographic division of Vietnam known as the "route package system," these aircraft operated primarily in certain parts of North Vietnam. The navy assets flying into the coastal sections of North Vietnam came under the operational control of the navy's Task Force (TF) 77, which operated in the Gulf of Tonkin with a number of aircraft carriers.

The B-52 sorties in South Vietnam remained under the operational control of SAC. Momyer firmly believed that other services could not be expected to offer control of their air power if the USAF would not even provide the component control of its assets. He wrote later to a colleague:

> We can't have a "cake and eat" attitude, that all Naval air elements operating in a theater should come under the operational control of the theater commander and at the same time withhold SAC forces employed in the furtherance of the theater mission. We agreed that the Seventh Air Force should have operational control not coordinating authority of Naval air units of TF-77 when employed in Southeast Asia, which included Laos, South and North Vietnam. Yet, we turned around and agreed that B-52s, Drones, MSQs, SR-71s and KC-135s shouldn't come under the operational control of the Seventh Air Force.[68]

Although Momyer had operational control of tactical sorties tasked for southern Laos, the U.S. ambassador to Laos had to approve the targets. Marine aircraft operating in the northern part of South Vietnam reported to Westmoreland but operated independently of Momyer.

Although this structure of command relationships could not have been the type that Momyer had hoped to inherit, there was no better person to make a convincing argument for change.[69] Momyer later summed up his opinion of the command arrangements in one sentence: "With so many different people and organizations involved, it was not possible to lay out a single plan of action for employing the air resources across the spectrum of tasks that had to be accomplished." He believed that "PACOM was really limited to the role of dividing the targets between PACAF [Pacific Air Forces] and PACFLT [Pacific Fleet] and establishing the times when the targets would be struck." PACAF and PACFLT were also inefficient in their command arrangements because the lack of communication infrastructure prevented the two commands from keeping abreast of what was occurring in an often rapidly changing environment. Reflecting on the communications limitations, Momyer believed that in a theater of war, "it is imperative that the command directing the war be located in close proximity to the fighting."

Since there was no centralized control of air assets, only coordination authority, the route package system had been developed to deconflict navy and air force operations. Reflecting on these arrangements later in his life, Momyer wrote, "Dividing North Vietnam into route packages compartmentalized our Airpower and reduced its capabilities."[70] Further, "any arrangement arbitrarily assigning air forces to exclusive areas of operation will significantly reduce Airpower's unique ability to quickly concentrate overwhelming firepower wherever it is needed most."[71] When discussing the command and control of the route package system in Vietnam, Momyer later stated that MACV should be responsible for missions into all the route packages since "the entire air campaign against the LOCs [lines of communication] was meant to affect the battle in South Vietnam."[72] He noted the difficulty of cycling forces in carrier operations and the inherent range limitations of naval aviation, but Momyer did not believe a fragmented command structure was the best way to accommodate these issues. As he would do in many later documents, Momyer recommended establishing a Southeast Asia theater of operations as the optimum command arrangement. Mirroring his experience in the Mediterranean, he held that this arrangement, with separate components for land, sea, and air, would provide an environment where command trumped coordination—instead of the opposite.[73]

ROLLING THUNDER

As the Seventh Air Force commander during the majority of Operation Rolling Thunder, Momyer played a key role in what has been called "the longest aerial-bombardment campaign in the history of American air power."[74] While Rolling Thunder had many purposes, Momyer viewed it as an interdiction campaign to lessen the flow of supplies from North Vietnam to South Vietnam. He recognized that Rolling Thunder reflected President Lyndon Johnson's "strategy of steadily increasing pressure"; however, Momyer noted, "senior airmen felt strongly that the initial conception of Rolling Thunder was too restrictive." In later writings, Momyer described the airmen's concept of Rolling Thunder as a "strategic air offensive" and viewed the "vital elements of the system" in relation to the North

Vietnamese logistical network. This view also addressed the reality that "as supplies funneled southward, it became increasingly difficult to destroy them in large quantities because of the absence of open terrain and natural choke points." Momyer wrote, "The dissemination of supplies among hundreds of jungle trails and thousands of porters guaranteed that air attacks in the south would be less efficient than attacks against the Kep Marshalling Yard, the Paul Doumer Bridge, or the ports at Haiphong."[75]

Momyer thought that "Airpower was beginning to have an effect on the enemy's logistical system," but he and other senior airmen did not believe "that our Airpower could be as effective as it had been in World War II unless we were authorized to strike the full range of interdiction targets." While permission to bomb North Vietnam's oil storage facilities in June 1966 brought more pressure on the enemy, "this piecemeal application of Airpower was relatively ineffective because it still avoided many of the targets that were of most value to the North Vietnamese."[76]

Although Momyer had operational control of air force missions in Rolling Thunder, his control of air strategy for air operations in North Vietnam was minimal. If Momyer and his staff wanted to request a particular target in North Vietnam, that request had to be forwarded to the PACAF commander for approval and then on to CINCPAC. Next, CINCPAC would integrate the air force's requests with the navy's requests and forward both specific targets and campaign concepts to the Joint Chiefs of Staff (JCS). These proposals would be integrated with the recommendations of a group on the Joint Staff to produce a targeting "package." The service chiefs would then meet and discuss both the concepts and the individual targets in the proposed package, and either change the concepts and targets or approve them. Next, the chairman of the JCS would discuss the package with the secretary of defense, who would then discuss the package with the secretary of state and send it on to the president for final approval.[77]

The nature of the campaign's target approval process did not contribute to the ability to build a "coherent, coordinated and flexible air campaign." Momyer wrote, "I suppose this dilemma will prevail as long as there are so many agencies in the chain of command between the source directing the overall conduct of a war and the intervening headquarters which interpret and pass down the detailed instructions." In the target approval process Momyer also perceived a dilemma in that "if we lost too many aircraft on a target it was withdrawn and if we didn't hit the target in a given period of time, it was subject to withdrawal."[78]

Because of his position as deputy chief of staff at Seventh Air Force, Maj. Gen. Gordon Blood had a good perspective on how the targeting process played out at Seventh Air Force. He stated that, for operations in South Vietnam, General Momyer "knew the requirements from COMUSMACV for in-country operations, where the pressures were in which Corps, and what type of support we needed for any particular campaigns." Momyer would then allocate his forces in South Vietnam to meet those requirements.[79] Momyer later noted that by 1967 there could not possibly be enough air power to support the hundreds of thousands of ground troops in South Vietnam if air assets were allocated to individual units as they had been in the early days of North Africa. Centralized control of air power for supporting ground troops, Momyer believed, would allow him to concentrate firepower where it was needed. Harking back to lessons from World War II and Korea, Momyer stressed that the best way to support these troops was through preplanned missions. In the 1965–1968 period, Momyer wrote, 65–70 percent of the support missions were preplanned, since the ground forces' large conventional movements often required such planning. The remaining portion of air support was for immediate requests or troops-in-contact situations. These requests were filled by retasking lower-priority preplanned missions or through aircraft on ground alert.[80]

Blood also recalled that for the operations in North Vietnam, Momyer "provided the strategy within the guidelines and constraints and targets that had been approved from Washington or PACOM level." Momyer then "took the targets available and the armed reconnaissance areas available; and he discussed the strategy with us on Saturday for a weekly meeting." The overall strategy would also be discussed at daily planning meetings when the targets for the next day's strikes would be nominated. Once Momyer reviewed those targets, "he would give us some guidance for the next two or three days on how he'd like to apply the force in the Hanoi area." When laying out his guidance, Blood remembered that Momyer liked to prioritize the targets in order to minimize losses while maximizing the destruction and impact on the enemy. From his perspective, Blood felt "sometimes it was an hour-by-hour change in strategy based on what the enemy did in the morning. Sometimes it was day-by-day based on the weather, what targets were available. Sometimes it was a week-by-week based on what JCS targets were released to us and what flexibility we had to do the job."[81]

A 1967 *Time* magazine article described Momyer's "typical" day in South Vietnam. Momyer would arrive at "7 a.m. every day to read the reports on the previous night's raids, then assembles his staff in his war conference room to plot the day's operations." In planning operations, Momyer used "weather and intelligence reports" and checked "reconnaissance slides projected on an 8-ft-by-10-ft screen." If intelligence discovered new targets that were not on the approved target list, "the request goes up the chain of command to CINCPAC in Hawaii or, if it is a particularly sensitive target, to the Joint Chiefs of Staff in the Pentagon, the Secretary of Defense or even the White House." As the missions began to take off, Momyer would move to either the plotting room for Operation Rolling Thunder or a nearby, similar room for strikes ongoing in South Vietnam. In either room, "sitting in a glass 'cab' in the center, he is surrounded by 23 maps and charts that rise seven feet from the floor." If he wanted to see a section of the map and its associated strikes in more detail, he could just press the map and that section would light up. The author of the article wrote that if Momyer wanted to change anything about the ongoing operations, he could "be in touch within 60 seconds with any pilot flying anywhere in Southeast Asia."[82]

In an interview for another magazine, Momyer described some of the challenges of his job. "There is one fundamental aspect of military operations I think we are inclined to lose sight of," he told the reporter, "and that is that military power is applied to accomplish certain desired political objectives in war." Momyer believed that "for any military force to satisfy these objectives, it must be able to perform within the demand of these national goals." This single statement says a great deal about Momyer's understanding of a fundamental aspect of the Vietnam War. This war, unlike World War II, was not about fighting for the unconditional surrender of North Vietnam or of the Communists in South Vietnam. Instead, he had to apply air power within the constraints of the war's political goals and objectives, which in fact were limited in nature. What he also hinted at here, if ever so subtly, was a possible mismatch between the stated objectives and the military's ability to attain them.

Momyer's challenge, he felt, was to employ air power in such a way that it would respond effectively to the dynamic and changing face of the war in Vietnam. When asked why air power was so important in Vietnam, Momyer responded:

There are numerous tasks which could not be performed without tactical air power. It takes aircraft to find and engage the enemy beyond the range of ground penetration. Because there is no other effective means of transportation, it takes airlift to move ground troops into battle or to supply food, weapons, equipment and ammunition in a land of heavy jungle, soggy rice fields, and unusable roads. It takes air-delivered firepower to soften up landing areas and to even the odds against human-wave attacks at remote villages and outposts. We even use air power to provide light to beleaguered villages and outposts that are under attack at night. There is no doubt that air power has struck the biggest, and most telling blows against the Viet Cong and against the North Vietnamese regulars. Air power has interdicted the enemy's men, his supply lines, and sources of supply in the north. In short, air power is an essential element in almost every facet of the complicated and demanding conflict in Southeast Asia.

This explanation reflects Momyer's all-encompassing view of Southeast Asia as a theater of war. He specifically mentioned this point again in a response to a later question: "In my judgment, the air war we are waging in the north is inseparable from the air and ground operations in South Vietnam."[83]

In another part of the interview, Momyer described his conception of an ideal air campaign in Southeast Asia.

I believe we must maintain total pressure against all parts of his military structure. . . . It is the accumulation of a large number of attacks against many diversified targets which limits his ability to fight at the required level of effort. When he cannot fight at the rate necessary to counter our forces, it is inevitable that he will be forced from both the air and ground battlefield. This is what we seek to achieve, and our tactical air force is making a contribution to this goal.

Momyer went on to comment that the future of the war in Vietnam would likely be a "long and hard struggle. I don't see any indications that North Vietnam is ready to stop the fighting." Recognizing this resolve, Momyer stated that "the enemy must be forced to realize the pressure will not be relaxed and that his military forces and structure will be brought under attack wherever they are found." Although he did not say it explicitly, these words make it clear that Momyer believed the air effort was constrained by political considerations that denied a campaign of sustained pressure against all parts of the enemy's military structure.[84]

In July 1967, Secretary of Defense Robert McNamara made a trip to Vietnam to gain a better sense of the air campaign's progress from those who were most familiar with its day-to-day operations. During that visit, Momyer presented a briefing outlining the operations of the Seventh Air Force and his perspectives on the progress of Rolling Thunder. After outlining the progress of operations, Momyer stated that, "as a field commander directing the day to day air effort against North Vietnam in Route Package V and VIA, there is no question in my mind about the very profound effect we are having on the enemy's fighting ability."[85] Momyer summed up his brief by stating that this belief was based on eight major factors.

1. The Seventh Air Force was able to sustain a level of effort not previously possible. Momyer based this assumption on both the number of aircrews available and the improvements in weapon systems that permitted more effective operations.

2. The loss rate of American aircraft had decreased while the number of flights that the Seventh Air Force was able to generate over enemy territory had increased. Momyer attributed this development to tactics that the newer weapons permitted, which put the American aircraft in less danger from enemy fire. Fewer aircraft losses meant more effectiveness per sortie.

3. The enemy's surface-to-air missile firings had dropped significantly in the past year. Momyer believed that this decrease indicated a strain in the enemy's logistic system (their ability to resupply missiles) and thereby indicated success in the interdiction efforts.

4. The volume of antiaircraft artillery (AAA) fire from the enemy was fluctuating even though the American effort remained strong. Momyer believed that since AAA inflicted the most losses on American aircraft, any fluctuation in the amount of fire indicated both a stressed logistical system (the enemy was conserving ammunition or simply did not have enough) and the psychological toll of daily bombing. In his opinion, this variation indicated that the United States should maintain pressure on the enemy and presented an argument against the frequent bombing pauses that took place for diplomatic reasons.

5. The Seventh Air Force had had no engagements with enemy aircraft in two months. Momyer claimed that this lack of contact showed that the enemy's air force had been defeated and would suffer the same fate if it attempted to fly again. He attributed the defeat to the authority to attack the enemy's

airfields. Further, because no enemy aircraft were flying, U.S. pilots had to jettison fewer bombs before reaching their targets,[86] resulting in more efficient air operations.

6. The Seventh Air Force was successful at disrupting the operations of North Vietnam's northeast railroad line. Where North Vietnamese forces encountered breaks in the rail lines, they had to transfer the cargo to trucks, thus decreasing the efficiency of the enemy's operations.

7. The enemy was taking a longer time to repair bridges and marshaling yards. Since these facilities were essential to the transportation of needed matériel, Momyer felt that this prolonged repair time highlighted the stress on the enemy's system.

8. Last, the sheer number of boxcars (a thousand) that air attacks had destroyed during the month of June put a significant strain on the enemy's supply system.[87]

The briefing was truly a work of art in the way Momyer presented his conception of the interdiction campaign. Momyer was an extremely analytical and thoughtful professional, and evidently he paid extra care to deconstruct the operation into its component parts and presented it in a light that enabled McNamara to perceive progress. By doing so, he specifically showed how operations were impacting the enemy system. This approach undoubtedly struck a chord with McNamara, as it put the air war in Vietnam in the context of systems analysis. McNamara, a former USAF officer who had served in the Office of Statistical Control, had instituted this system in public policy. Momyer used McNamara's language.

In fact, Momyer's briefing made a significant impression on all of the attendees. Walt Rostow, President Johnson's special assistant for national security affairs, wrote a note to the president that accompanied the paper copy of the briefing, saying that the briefing "helped convince a number of those in Secretary McNamara's party that we are making headway in the bombing of transport in the northern part of North Vietnam."[88] In an interview with Kenneth Crawford of *Newsweek* shortly after the visit, President Johnson said that McNamara was more impressed with Momyer than with anyone else he had met on his trip.[89]

During this period, President Johnson was using Lt. Gen. Andrew Goodpaster, the commandant of the National War College, as an intermediary with former president Eisenhower for obtaining his military suggestions concerning the

Vietnam War. The president's staff provided Goodpaster with the text of Momyer's briefing to obtain Eisenhower's thoughts on the air war's progress. According to Goodpaster, Eisenhower was extremely interested in the briefing and "especially interested in the mutually reinforcing effects" of the factors outlined in the briefing. Eisenhower "recalled from his own experience the appearance of such mutually reinforcing effects in Europe when the tempo and systems coverage of the bombing campaign were brought to the proper level."[90]

A few days later, Momyer traveled to Washington and appeared before the Preparedness Investigating Subcommittee of the Senate Armed Services Committee with Gen. Earle G. Wheeler, the chairman of the JCS. The hearing's purpose was to gain information on the conduct and effectiveness of the air war against North Vietnam. Although Admiral Sharp was responsible for conducting the air campaign against North Vietnam, General Wheeler provided senior oversight to all operations in Southeast Asia and served as the president's senior military adviser. Momyer appeared with Wheeler, but he spoke relatively infrequently during the hearings. His testimony, as it appears in the *Congressional Record*, reveals some of the challenges he faced in Vietnam.

One of Momyer's most substantive responses during the hearings dealt with the nature of an air interdiction campaign. "The interdiction campaign really begins in the heart of the enemy, where his supplies and equipment are more vulnerable," Momyer said. "And by eliminating those supplies and equipment in their most vulnerable position, we begin a process of denying what residual can get to the battlefield." Momyer saw the second element of an interdiction campaign as "some kind of formalized ground campaign in which there is a line between the two opposing forces, in which you can launch an offensive that forces the enemy to consume logistics faster than he can get them down and replenish them." Momyer continued, "The third element is the interdicting of the flow between the heartland and the enemy field forces."[91]

After describing these three elements, Momyer related them to the difficulty of the situation in Vietnam. First, "most of these war materials [are] coming from external sources." This situation meant that "you have to disrupt and constantly disrupt, because they can be replenished, and there is no way under [the] circumstances that you can constantly cut them out." Momyer stated, "It is not like it was in Germany [in World War II], when the war resources were being fabricated in country." The second difficulty was that "the enemy, due to his elusiveness, sometimes will stand and fight, and sometimes he won't stand and fight; and, as a consequence, you can't put the strain on his logistics that you can in that formalized method." The formalized structure of two opposing forces, Momyer believed, was not present "in South Vietnam as you had in Italy, or in Europe, or even as you had in Korea." Given these limitations of the war-fighting environment, Momyer felt that air interdiction was effective at what it could be expected to do.[92]

When asked what Momyer felt could make it easier for him to bring the war to a conclusion, he replied, "Give me more flexibility for targets of opportunity, the reinforced target list that [Wheeler] has mentioned. . . ; and to give me greater capability to maximize against the lines of communications." Here Momyer was referring to a statement in which Wheeler advocated "more area for the application of our air power" that would then give field commanders such as Momyer authorization to "strike military targets in accordance with the pattern which they determined to be most applicable to the situation."[93]

On December 14, 1967, General Westmoreland and his deputy, Gen. Creighton W. Abrams, pinned the fourth star on Momyer's uniform.[94] "Delighted to see in the morning mail that you had received the fourth star," General Disosway wrote. "Certainly the fine job you are doing over there deserves it." In closing, he said, "Now that you have got four stars, let some of those other people over there do part of the work and save yourself for something in the future."[95] In an earlier letter, Gen. John D. "Jack" Ryan, the air force chief of staff, had also recognized how hard Momyer was working. "I was serious when I told you that I expected you to get out of that place prior to [Maj. Gen. Gordon M.] Graham's departure," Ryan wrote. "I strongly recommend that you take some leave before he goes. No man is made of iron and I think a week to ten days break for you is most appropriate."[96]

It was obvious by late 1967 that the enemy was planning a major attack against South Vietnam. As the year drew to a close, the Communist forces continued to increase the number of offensive operations across South Vietnam but specifically in the areas near the demilitarized zone (DMZ). Marine Corps firebases in this region were taking as many as a thousand rounds of artillery per day. Momyer determined that air power could lessen these attacks and locate and annihilate enemy forces staging for the offensive. The intensified air campaign, code-named "Neutralize," started on September 11, 1967. This operation massed air power in a way that "finally broke the siege of these northern bases, which had been under intensive attack for more than 49 days." Momyer also believed that "it was the constant pounding of airpower that the enemy had not foreseen when planning this offensive." Because the targets were often difficult to find, Momyer set up an intelligence center to interpret photographs from RF-4 reconnaissance sorties flown along the DMZ. These intensive reconnaissance and intelligence efforts were known as SLAM operations: seek, locate, annihilate, and monitor.[97]

The large buildup of enemy forces in the area surrounding Khe Sanh evoked images of the 1954 French battle with the Vietnamese at Dien Bien Phu. President Johnson visited Cam Ranh Bay during Christmas 1967, and when he brought up the question of defending Khe Sanh, Momyer "reassured him that with the massive use of airpower, the base could be defended." In addition to the direct support effort, Momyer believed that the associated interdiction effort of the supply lines surrounding Khe Sanh "would have not only an effect on the battle for Khe Sanh, but also an influence on the strategy of the forthcoming Tet Offensive." Seeing this looming fight as a psychological battle as well as a military one, Momyer believed that "an unequivocal setback was essential to neutralize the political offensive against the South Vietnamese and U.S. home fronts."[98]

As the enemy moved troops and personnel into the area surrounding Khe Sanh, General Westmoreland prepared for battle. On January 6, 1968, he directed General Momyer to "prepare a plan to concentrate all available air resources into the Khe Sanh area."[99] The goal of this operation, Niagara, was to disrupt a major potential offensive that the enemy might launch in the northern portions of South Vietnam.[100]

In light of this situation and pending operations, on January 18, 1968, General Westmoreland sent a message to Admiral Sharp. Westmoreland stated, "In view of the increased deployment of Army forces into I Corps, impending battles and the need for having more operational flexibility of the air effort available to me, I am contemplating placing operational control of the I Marine Air Wing under my Deputy for Air."[101] While this idea had been developing for some time, this note would fuel the fires of what would come to be known as the "single manager for air controversy."

The marines viewed the operation at Khe Sanh as a fit for their air-ground team cooperation. Momyer, however, did not believe the Marine Corps's system was robust enough to coordinate or control all of the air traffic needed around Khe Sanh to bring the full weight of air power to bear. He thought that "centralized control of the air had become absolutely essential." Further, Momyer wrote, without centralized control "Khe Sanh could well be lost."[102] On January 21, General Westmoreland wrote to Admiral Sharp that "the anticipated enemy attack on Khe Sanh was initiated last evening." With a good dose of military understatement, Westmoreland also wrote that "the next several weeks are destined to be active."[103]

Two battles were fought in parallel in the early months of 1968—one for Khe Sanh and the other for the control of air assets supporting it. On February 20, 1968, Lt. Gen. Robert Cushman Jr., deputy commander of III Marine Amphibious Force, and Momyer met at the former's headquarters to discuss the management of air resources. In a message to Westmoreland after the meeting, Cushman wrote that "although the briefing conducted by General Momyer was well done . . . several points were raised by me or my staff."[104] In his own letter to Westmoreland, Momyer wrote, "The question was not whether there should be one man responsible for all air operations but how best to accomplish this arrangement while preserving the principle of Marine air units supporting Marine ground units whenever the tactical situation permitted."[105] Lt. Gen. Victor Krulak, the commanding general of the Pacific Fleet Marine Force, received General Cushman's daily updates on the battle for control. After reviewing Cushman's inputs on Westmoreland's plan, Krulak wrote, "When you wrestle further with Momyer on this and have the draft document in hand, send it to me at once so that I can go to work on my approach to Sharp."[106]

Although many probably viewed the battle as an air force power play to gain control of marine air, Westmoreland saw the single manager concept as the best way to manage the air assets at play. The scale of operations in previous months had been conducive to the "Marine air for Marines" concept, but Westmoreland believed that the number of aircraft from Seventh Air Force, aircraft carriers, Thailand-based forces, and B-52s involved now required a greater level of integration. On February 24 he wrote to General Wheeler, "The problem is one of coordination and directing all of these diversified air elements so that air support can be put where and when needed in the required quantity. I do not see how this can be accomplished without one airman fitting all air into schedules that do not conflict with one another."[107] To demonstrate the exact level of effort involved, three days later Westmoreland's daily Khe Sanh situation report to the White House listed the total number of sorties flown on February 27 by component: 157 marine sorties, 153 air force sorties, 105 navy sorties, and 33 B-52 sorties.[108]

On February 28, the Seventh Air Force's director of operations, Major General Blood, personally presented the single manager plan to Admiral Sharp and an audience that included his staff and General Krulak. In a memo to Cushman, Krulak described the presentation: "The air control brannigan began with a presentation by MGen Blood of 7th AF Headquarters. He illustrated with charts, and in the most dramatic way he could, the problems that are generated by the creation of the provisional corps, Vietnam with respect to air support." Krulak finished his note to Cushman with dry humor and an estimate of what was to come: "I expected to be telephoning from the jail tonight, but we are still at large. My guess is that Sharp is going to search for some sort of compromise. However, I sense that the Air Force is in concrete, and I doubt if Momyer will give at all."[109]

By the beginning of March, Westmoreland submitted the slightly revised single manager concept to Admiral Sharp. This time Sharp approved it with the caveats that marine emergency calls for air support would not go through Seventh Air Force Headquarters and that the Marine Amphibious Force commander had a right to appeal any tasking. Westmoreland implemented the plan on March 7, but the first missions under this arrangement were not flown until March 22. By that date, Momyer had become responsible for assigning individual missions and operational control for all strike and reconnaissance aircraft throughout South Vietnam. If at all possible, marine aircraft would be tasked to support marine ground units.[110] Interestingly, the press received news of the controversy that arose over the control of air power in and around Khe Sanh. Although many believed that the air force may have leaked the "victory" to the press, General Cushman thought otherwise. "Spike is not that gauche. Stupid, he ain't."[111]

As March drew to a close, the enemy effectively abandoned their pursuit of defeating the American forces at Khe Sanh. American aircraft supported the last sorties in Niagara on March 31. Since January 22, 1968, the opening day of the effort, American pilots had flown 24,400 tactical sorties and 2,500 B-52 sorties.[112] C-130s and C-123s completed 1,120 missions. Over 450 of these missions involved landings at the dangerous field. The airlifters delivered over 12,400 tons of precious supplies.[113] General Momyer not only orchestrated the defense of Khe Sanh in what was called the "greatest sustained concentration of air power in the Vietnam conflict to date,"[114] but he also drew on his World War II experience and his many years of thought on the command and application of air power to play a large role in denying the Vietnamese another Dien Bien Phu–style victory. Earlier in the conflict, Westmoreland had said to Momyer, "Spike, Khe Sanh has become a symbol. It is of no importance to me, but it has become of great psychological importance to the United States. . . . Spike, if I lose Khe Sanh I am going to hold the United States Air Force responsible."[115] Momyer did not disappoint him.

For Momyer, "Khe Sanh was probably the turning point in the enemy's strategy for Tet." He believed that if "Khe Sanh had fallen, the regular NVA [North Vietnamese Army] troops would have moved against the major cities that were initially assaulted by VC [Viet Cong] local forces. The fact that there were no significant actions by regular forces indicated the enemy backed away from a combined military-political offensive."[116] General Westmoreland also believed that "the key to our success at Khe Sanh was . . . principally aerial firepower."[117] Even those outside the inner circles of MACV held this belief. On March 28, Walt Rostow wrote to President Johnson to inform him of Momyer's upcoming visit to Washington, D.C. In recommending that the president meet with Momyer, Rostow wrote simply that Momyer had "managed the defense of Khe Sanh by air power. You'd find him interesting."[118]

Momyer later wrote that, at the conclusion of the Tet Offensive, "the expected effect on the South Vietnamese people didn't materialize . . . and not a single province fell to the enemy." The battle, had by all accounts, resulted in an overwhelming defeat for Communist forces in South Vietnam; however, the offensive had "succeeded in the effect that the North Vietnamese hoped to achieve on the U.S. home front." Momyer believed that the resultant loss of U.S. political will meant that "instead of being able to follow-up the Tet offensive with a major military effort in South Vietnam and an all-out bombing campaign in the north, which would have been consistent with fundamental principles for applying military power, the President was compelled to suspend the bombing and step down as a candidate for reelection."

Momyer recognized the Tet Offensive as a "resounding psychological victory" for the enemy. Despite this setback, Momyer felt that the air effort during the offensive once again pointed to the benefit of centralized control of air power. Because the Tet Offensive occurred simultaneously in a number of cities in South Vietnam, air assets had to be allocated effectively in order to mass effects at the right places and right times. Troops had to be moved in cargo aircraft to meet the threat and reinforce defenses in the cities, and more than 16,000 sorties were flown in support of ground forces.[119]

A 1968 story in the *Air Force and Space Digest* captured how Momyer interacted with those he commanded. In the article, one of Momyer's aides commented,

> The pilots are invariably amazed at his detailed knowledge of the mission they flew. "Let's see," he'd say, "that day you were in White flight and you came in from this altitude on this heading. You had to break left . . ." and he'd go, right through the whole mission. He'll talk with these kids for the longest time, discussing bedrock details, and getting their ideas on tactics. . . . The one time he really relaxed was when pilots were brought in to be cited for some outstanding performance. When he talks with them he goes back twenty years. He leans back in his chair, puts his hands behind his head, and a big smile brightens his face.[120]

In Vietnam, Momyer built this familiarity with operations by participating in the actual missions. He took every opportunity to fly so that he could experience the conditions that the men operating under him experienced every day. He flew in "at least one of each of the 30 types of missions, from reconnaissance to rescue operations that are flown over North Viet Nam." Not only did he fly in every type of mission, but he also flew "in every kind of U.S. aircraft in use in Asia, from little Cessna spotter planes to the fleet F-4 fighter-bomber."[121]

As Momyer's time in Vietnam drew to a close, the American level of effort there began to decrease. At the end of March 1968, President Johnson halted all bombing above the twentieth parallel and effectively eliminated the ability to strike targets in nearly 75 percent of North Vietnam.

LEGACY

In July 1968, Momyer departed Southeast Asia for Langley Air Force Base and command of TAC. Before his departure, Secretary of the Air Force Harold Brown described Momyer in a letter to Secretary of Defense McNamara, noting that Momyer "knows more about the air war in Southeast Asia than any man on earth, and this belief together with a high regard for him is shared by General Wheeler, General [J. P.] McConnell, General Westmoreland and General Abrams."[122]

Momyer would command TAC for a little more than five years before retiring from the air force in September 1973. While at TAC, Momyer remained intimately involved in the conflict in Vietnam, as a large majority of TAC's assets and aircrews continued to operate in Southeast Asia. While providing and training the forces to fight a war in Southeast Asia, Momyer led a command that also prepared to fight a possible future conflict on the plains of Europe. During his time at TAC, Momyer maintained his reputation as the air force's expert on tactical air power. When the most difficult issues arose in Washington, D.C., the director of legislative liaison in the Office of the Secretary of the Air Force often called Momyer to testify for congressional hearings. "It was magnificent," he recalled, largely because Momyer was "the one man who had fought for tactical air from WWII to Vietnam and was an undisputed leader and scholar in this entire discipline."[123]

After retirement, Momyer led an air force team in assessing the lessons learned in Vietnam. This five-year undertaking inspired Momyer to write a book about air power. "If all goes well," Momyer wrote in a letter to a colleague, "there should be a book on the shelf next fall that says what airmen believe about airpower—at least what Momyer thinks they believe."[124] In another letter, Momyer wrote,

> I have set forth many of the doctrinal positions we believe about airpower. I am sure the Army, Navy, and Marines aren't going to be happy with some of the passages, but it is high time for airmen to say what they believe about airpower and quit worrying about what other people think, including the other services. I have tried to set forth these beliefs in a rational but, obviously, in a somewhat biased manner. How else can one recite his beliefs? So the charge of parochialism is inevitable, and I'm prepared to accept it.[125]

The resulting publication of *Airpower in Three Wars* made Momyer one of the only USAF airmen to have both led air forces in combat and written about the philosophy that inspired his actions.

Perhaps the best summation of Momyer's legacy came from the man who served as his vice commander at TAC from 1970 to 1972, Lt. Gen. Jay T. Robbins:

> Momyer was very demanding. . . . I always had a tremendous respect for him. I think he is one of a kind . . . in the Air Force. He has a keen mind on strategy and tactics, and he is a historian. He has read all about military doctrine. . . . I think he was the most knowledgeable man in the Air Force, the Air Force has ever had in terms of tactical airpower. . . . I never really got to be where I felt I was a strategist, maybe a tactician in some respects but

never did I think in the broad, strategic terms of tactical air power. Spike Momyer did. . . . There won't be another one like him come along for awhile neither.[126]

It is hard to imagine an officer better prepared to take on the challenges that Momyer faced in the years he fought in Vietnam. Many may take issue with what he did or how he thought, but few could dispute that he had the courage of convictions forged by experience, study, and thought. He had a vision for the way air power could most effectively be brought to bear.

Without a doubt, Momyer's time in North Africa provided the foundation for all that followed. As the battles raged on land and in the air, Momyer lived the impact of the evolution of air power doctrine. He saw his men die and felt the commander's burden, wondering if he could do more to protect them while searching for the best way to fight the enemy from the air. He later recounted in a letter to a fellow veteran of the North African campaign the impact of those times. "This was the beginning of trying to find out how to fight an air force. I have looked back on those days with a great deal of pleasure. For my part, they were the most trying and demanding times I have been through, but every day something was learned on how to fight airpower. . . . I wouldn't trade anyone for that experience."[127] With that experience in hand, Momyer spent the majority of the time leading up to his assignment in the Seventh Air Force thinking about air power and how best to apply the means to meet desired ends. He worked with the other services to integrate air power into the overall objective through both exercises and an endless quest for common ground on the most efficient and effective use of air power in a campaign.

Through these experiences, Momyer became a deliberate and thoughtful air power philosopher. If asked what they thought of his leadership, most who served with him would not use the word "charismatic" and "Momyer" in the same sentence. In fact, one would be more likely to hear such words as "stubborn" and "stern" from Momyer's detractors. But for those who knew him best and relied on his leadership and scholarship when times were tough, he was steadfast and stable. As an air power leader, Momyer was firm and resolute, with an unwavering commitment to the pursuit of objectives through the efficient, effective, and exact control and application of air power. He stood tall for what he believed. Although these qualities likely never truly endeared Momyer to those who served under him, time and time again it made him the air force's most valuable player when championing the cause of air power.

History does not regard Rolling Thunder as a successful application of air power. Although those operations did not capture all of Momyer's responsibilities in Vietnam, they were certainly the most visible. Had the application of steadily increasing pressure against North Vietnam actually caused Hanoi to cease its aggression in South Vietnam, Momyer's role as the air force's top combat airman in Vietnam would likely have earned him a much higher spot in the pyramid of combat air power leaders. It was not to be. Perhaps as a way of accepting this verdict, Momyer reflected on the topic after he left Vietnam and while he led a command that continued to support combat operations in Southeast Asia. "The political objectives must be consistent with the capabilities of the forces," Momyer wrote in 1970. "If there had been a more valid evaluation of our political objectives in Vietnam, I believe it would have revealed our military forces couldn't produce the conditions dictated by the specifics of the objectives. Thus, there would have been a change in the political objectives or a decision not to commit forces with a consequent loss of the country."[128] He was well aware that an air commander's success is closely tied to the political environment in which he operates.

Popular culture often remembers Momyer as the commander who criticized the efforts of the Tuskegee Airmen who served under his command in 1943. Here, without question, Momyer was wrong. Some might also claim that he brought an inflexible World War II mind-set to a counterinsurgency in Southeast Asia. History would have to be rewritten and relived to accommodate those who believe that other approaches would have prevailed under the same set of political constraints. It would not be inconsistent to accept those criticisms and others yet still acknowledge the contributions of an airman who spent more than thirty-five years in the service of his nation and commanded air power in the pursuit of national objectives. Although he spent much of his career in tactical aviation, Momyer believed in air power as an entity. His comprehensive understanding of all the elements of an air campaign and his masterful ability to articulate strengths and weaknesses at every level set Gen. William Momyer apart from all but a few airmen of his generation and those of generations to follow.

8

JOHN W. VOGT: THE EASTER OFFENSIVE AND NIXON'S WAR IN VIETNAM

Stephen P. Randolph

The dawn of contemporary warfare arrived in the spring and summer of 1972, in a war so unpopular that no one even noticed. President Richard Nixon, determined to defeat a dramatic North Vietnamese invasion of South Vietnam, ordered a massive reinforcement of American air and naval forces in theater, mined the harbors of North Vietnam, and directed a sustained, brutal air campaign code-named "Linebacker." The operation was designed to punish North Vietnam, isolate that nation from its Communist sponsors in the Soviet Union and China, and cut off the flow of matériel to the battlefields in the south. That air offensive would take advantage of technologies developed over nearly a decade of war, as precision weapons, satellite-based imagery and communications, night vision equipment, digital fire control systems, intelligence fusion centers, and computer-based mission planning and tasking would all come together in the battle.

As powerful and advanced as these systems were, they had been developed in isolation and, in many cases, to deal with far different operations than those in which they were now employed. It fell to Gen. John W. Vogt Jr. the commander of the Seventh Air Force, to pull these systems together to support the ambitious, challenging range of missions that Nixon expected the Seventh Air Force to execute over the coming months.

For Vogt, it all began in early April, in a turbulent few weeks that fundamentally changed the direction of his life. By that point, Vogt had served on the Joint Staff for the past three years, first as director of operations, then as director. He had established a strong relationship with the chairman of the Joint Chiefs of Staff (CJCS), Adm. Thomas Moorer, and had worked closely with the White House from the first months of the Nixon administration. Then he had been assigned a sunset tour as the chief of staff at the North Atlantic Treaty Organization headquarters, a comfortable pathway to an obscure retirement.

Then in late March, Seventh Air Force commander Maj. Gen. John "Jack" Lavelle was relieved from command for filing false mission reports to conceal unauthorized air attacks against North Vietnam. (He was cleared of these charges in 2010.) Almost immediately thereafter, on March 30, 1972, the North Vietnamese Army (NVA) launched its go-for-broke spring offensive, shattering South Vietnam's ring of defenses along the demilitarized zone (DMZ) and threatening to annihilate the Republic of Vietnam Armed Forces (RVNAF).

America's combat role in ground fighting had dwindled over the previous years and was essentially at an end by early 1972. The military response to the NVA's offensive would have to be conducted entirely by air power. But the Seventh Air Force—stunned by Lavelle's removal, stymied by bad weather, and hamstrung by the effects of the years-long withdrawal from the war—responded sluggishly to the offensive, immensely angering Nixon and his national security adviser, Henry Kissinger. Both men had a deep-seated mistrust of and frustration with the air force, born of frequent disappointments in earlier air operations; indeed, they had no faith in the U.S. military as a whole. They shared the conviction that, left to their own devices, the military leadership then in theater—especially the commander of the U.S. Military Assistance Command, Vietnam (COMUSMACV), Gen. Creighton Abrams—would never respond with the creativity and energy that the situation demanded. The president had completely lost his confidence in Abrams during Operation Lam Son 719, the South Vietnamese incursion into Laos in February and March 1971. Nixon had kept Abrams in Saigon because he expected no more ground fighting for American forces and wanted to avoid the inevitable political cost in removing his field commander. Nixon also suspected his secretary of defense, Melvin Laird, of concealing the extent and seriousness of North Vietnam's offensive from the White House in order to minimize the American response to the NVA action.

Their feelings still raw from the Lam Son 719 experience, Nixon and Kissinger felt an urgent need to "get ahold of this thing," as Nixon put it.[1] From far away they had the perception that the early response to the NVA offensive was a repeat of the confusion and discord seen in the Laotian incursion. As Kissinger commented, "It's my instinct . . . there's some blight on that operation. . . . I think Laird has drilled into their heads so much to do nothing, that they just don't react."[2]

In that tension-wracked setting, Moorer sent Vogt over to the White House to brief Kissinger on the ongoing air operations. Nixon's chief of staff, H. R. Haldeman, later recorded the result: "Vogt mentioned to Henry that he was terribly distressed with the way the military and particularly the Air Force were handling the Vietnam situation, particularly their failure to carry out the Presidential orders and an even worse failure to come up with any ideas on their own on how things ought to be handled. Vogt made the comment to K that he would like to give up his 4th star and get the thing straightened out."[3]

The seed planted, Kissinger repeated the remark to Nixon. Vogt was someone they knew and trusted, a general they could expect to understand and respond to White House priorities and to inject the urgency and creativity they demanded from the air force in this time of emergency. Kissinger called Moorer, who ran the idea by the air force chief of staff, Gen. Jack Ryan. Ryan agreed, and the deed was done. Vogt would take over the Seventh Air Force.[4]

Given the stakes involved in this offensive and the role that the White House expected Vogt to play, Kissinger suggested to Nixon that it would be helpful for the president to talk with the new Seventh Air Force commander and ensure that the general exactly understood the president's estimate of the situation and his expectations for air operations. Nixon agreed, and on April 6, at 10:04 a.m., Vogt found himself entering Nixon's hideaway office at the Executive Office Building, Kissinger at his side, to meet with the president.

It was a remarkable meeting, even by the standards of the Nixon White House. Nixon came quickly to the point. "The performance of the Air Force," he charged, "has not been, in my view, adequate. The reason it has not been adequate is not because of the bravery of the people . . . but the reason it's not been adequate, it's been routine, it's been by the numbers, there's been no imagination." And the president charged Vogt, "Let's see some imagination and drive. . . . I'm going to watch this every morning and every night . . . you're going out there on a rescue mission." From there the commander in chief went on to outline his view of the theater commander: "a splendid man, a magnificent record in World War II—a fine record in Vietnam—he's been there too long. He's tired, unimaginative. What's going to determine this is not what Abrams decides, because he's not gonna take any risks at this point, but what *you* decide." Nixon had an abiding interest in concentration and shock in military affairs, and he urged Vogt to proceed along those lines: "He who concentrates his forces wins the battle; he who spreads his forces out gets the hell kicked out of him."

In closing, Nixon asked Vogt if he needed anything. Vogt answered that it would be helpful if he could be named deputy commander of Military Assistance Command, Vietnam (MACV), instead of the deputy commander for air. Nixon replied, "Work it out. The reason it should be worked out isn't because of personalities, the reason it should be worked out is that all the goddamned thing is about now, is *air*."[5] This change would seemingly be well within the president's authority, especially since the JCS had already approved the reorganization, which was to be implemented in July. But despite the president's approval, the change would have to await the overall reorganization of MACV that summer.

Though happy with his assignment and this opportunity, Vogt was well aware of the reaction it would trigger from Abrams. He raised the issue with Kissinger, commenting that "I definitely will have a problem at the other end." Kissinger, flush with his authority, responded, "We will make heads roll. You do what is wanted and he's got to get out of the way."[6] On the day of his departure for Saigon, Vogt spoke once more with Kissinger, who again emphasized Vogt's standing and closed with, "You have our backing. Come to us if you have trouble."[7]

So Vogt was going out to Southeast Asia to seize control of the situation, inject energy into the operation, and serve as the White House's man on the spot for operations. He would have credibility in his advisory role far exceeding that of his nominal superior, Abrams. By this point in their administration, Nixon and Kissinger were used to operating in a tightly closed circle, with deception and deceit everywhere around them. Now they had exported that environment into the military chain of command.

BACKGROUND

The career path that brought Vogt to this point was remarkable, although it began conventionally enough. John William Vogt Jr. was born on March 18, 1920, in Elizabeth, New Jersey. He acquired a lifelong love of sailing and the sea from his father, a German immigrant who was, in Vogt's words, "the world's greatest fisherman." Vogt attended Thomas Jefferson High School and then went off to Tusculum College in Tennessee. The Presbyterian college held strongly to its origins, focused on building a Judeo-Christian environment and educating students in moral values and civic service. More than forty years later, Vogt would recall, "I've had three years at Yale, two years at Columbia, and a year at Harvard, and the two most valuable years that I had in college were those two years that I had at this little Presbyterian school in Tennessee."[8]

While there Vogt saw the war clouds gathering over the nation. He was determined to get into the conflict and joined the Aviation Cadet Program of the U.S. Army Air Forces on September 2, 1941. Earning his wings at Ellington Field, Texas, on April 29, 1942, he was assigned to the Sixty-Third Fighter Squadron, Fifty-Sixth Fighter Group—Hub Zemke's Wolfpack—for his first operational assignment.

It was a dream assignment under the legendary Zemke, one of the finest tacticians and leaders in the army air corps. Vogt adapted well to the P-47, known as the "Jug." A massive aircraft for its day, it was not agile, but if well flown it was capable of inflicting and absorbing massive punishment and was a match for any aircraft in the skies. On January 6, 1943, Vogt boarded the RMS *Queen Elizabeth* in New York harbor and five days later disembarked in Scotland, en route to his duty station at Royal Air Force (RAF) Kings Cliffe. The following May, while still a first lieutenant, he was named a flight commander. During that first tour in combat he was credited with five kills, earning ace status among the highest-scoring fighter group in Europe. In February 1944 he was assigned as commander of the 360th Fighter Squadron in the 356th Fighter Group. Only twenty-four years old, he was an ace and a squadron commander. Through the spring he joined the masses of American and Allied forces as they prepared for the return to the European continent.

Major Vogt fought through the drama of D-Day, leading his squadron as they took station at dawn over the invasion fleet, waiting for the German air attacks that never came. He earned a Silver Star on August 4 for leading his squadron in an engagement with thirty Bf-109s and shooting down two Messerschmitts. In the early autumn his unit was assigned the task of interdicting German forces responding to Operation Market Garden, the parachute assault in Arnhem, the Netherlands, to capture the famous "bridge too far." Expecting little resistance, Allied forces instead faced a Panzer division and devastating antiaircraft fire. Vogt's squadron lost half its men in a two-week campaign, leaving him with an abiding respect for the importance of intelligence.[9] He finished his second combat tour in October with eight kills, a coveted ace plaque, and, more important, the status as an ace, which would remain his proudest achievement and place him in an exclusive fraternity.

That status had come with a price, though. At a time when 200 hours of combat time gave a pilot credit for a combat tour, Vogt had amassed 440 combat hours, adding the stress of squadron command to that incurred during combat. Completely overwrought, his nerves shot, Vogt returned to the United States on October 21, 1944, and the next day was placed on inactive status, a victim of what was then known as combat fatigue. He returned to active duty in June 1945 and was sent to Recife, Brazil, to command the air base that served as part of the air bridge supporting the redeployment of U.S. forces from Europe to the Pacific theater.

From that point, Vogt embarked on a career path that was unique among his generation of military leaders. After three months in command, he returned to the United States to resume his education at Yale University. He separated from the army air forces on November 10, 1945, expecting to become a foreign service officer after completing his college education. But after marrying Doris "Kathie" Adams in April 1946, Vogt rejoined the army air forces and graduated with a bachelor's degree in international relations in 1947.[10] After a brief stint as an intelligence officer, Vogt returned to college—this time to Columbia University—and earned a master's degree in international relations in 1951. He then served until August 1955 as the special assistant to the JCS for National Security Council (NSC) affairs. He acquired firsthand experience of the interface between the military and civilian policymakers while working on the first NSC staff under Presidents Harry Truman and Dwight Eisenhower. He also gained his initial exposure to Southeast Asia in that position. Among other activities, he traveled to Paris after France's defeat at Dien Bien Phu to consult with the French about supporting noncommunist elements in Vietnam.

Subsequently, he served in an ascending series of policy planning positions, beginning the sequence with a tour in the Pacific theater—first in Japan as a planner with Headquarters, Far East Air Forces, and then in Hawaii as special assistant to the chief of staff of Pacific Air Forces (PACAF) from 1956 to 1958. At that point, Colonel Vogt undertook his third educational program in the Ivy League. This time he was a fellow at the Harvard Center for International Affairs, where he studied under Henry Kissinger and established a relationship that would have fateful consequences a decade later. From there he returned to the Pentagon, with stops on the Air Staff as a joint planner and as director of Robert McNamara's policy planning staff in the Office of the Secretary of Defense from 1963 to 1965. In August 1965 he moved to Honolulu, serving as the director of operations for PACAF during the three years of the Rolling Thunder campaign.

In June 1968 Vogt left Hawaii for another Pentagon tour, this time a series of three positions over a four-year span: first on the Air Staff, then in August 1969 as director of operations on the Joint Staff, and finally in July 1970 as director of the Joint Staff. From the first days of the Nixon administration Vogt had the opportunity to collaborate with Kissinger, and he built the relationship that eventually led to his selection for command. At every crisis—the Cambodia incursion in 1970, the Laotian operation a year later, and finally the Easter Offensive—Vogt worked closely with the White House, coordinating political-military action as part of the Washington Special Actions Group (WSAG), Kissinger's interagency mechanism for managing crisis action.

This succession of high-level policy positions had given Vogt a broad knowledge of the political and operational framework of the air war. He had developed relationships with senior leaders, both civilian and military, across the government and most recently with the innermost circle of the Nixon administration. But since his experience in World War II, as he rose through the ranks from major to general, Vogt had never held senior command and in fact had not served in a flying unit. An unbridgeable gap in experience, perspective, skill set, and knowledge exists between staff positions and command, and Vogt had not crossed that gap in a quarter of a century and through two wars. Inevitably, too, this background shaped his relationships with the senior military leaders with whom he dealt daily, men who had earned their positions through more conventional means. In gaining this command, Vogt had violated the military tradition of working assignments through the military chain of command; he had freely criticized air force operations and decision making to the highest level of national political authorities; and he had circumvented the air force hierarchy in furthering his ambitions. His path to senior command did not endear him to his peers.

In fact, his entire career trajectory set him aside from his contemporaries. An Ivy Leaguer in a world of West Point graduates, he was a general who had never undertaken the professional military education that was the staple of career progression at the time and who had followed a career path that repeatedly took him into policy positions at the expense of operational experience. This path to his position would have a lasting effect on Vogt's working relationships with his nominal superiors in the chain of command.

Vogt's air force career was driven by a set of values, both positive and negative, that was distinctly his own. He carried into every assignment and every decision a rigid sense of duty and an absolute commitment to the task at hand. His demand for full control of his organization often crossed the line into micromanagement, a tendency strengthened by his complete self-confidence. He felt bound always to reach for greater responsibility and never to turn away from work or risk, and he was delighted to be at the center of a crisis, where military actions met political requirements.

That combination of confidence and his perception of his duty as a military officer propelled him throughout his career and into command of the Seventh Air Force, and it shaped his experience and his results there. In stepping forward at that time of crisis in April 1972, he found himself facing responsibilities for which he was almost entirely unprepared. His self-promotion, which at first glance seemed a manifestation of sheer, naked ambition, could again more accurately be attributed to his sense that a bad situation existed in Indochina and that it was his duty to do something about it.

While Vogt would do anything to live up to his concept of his responsibilities, he would do nothing outside that definition. The politics of his service were of no interest to him. He had no allies or friends among the air force leadership, having spent most of his career in joint assignments. He had no cadre of trusted subordinates and made no effort to extend his professional relationships into a personal or social framework. Thus, he had no network to sustain him in hard times, and aside from CJCS Moorer he had accumulated no reservoir of trust and confidence among his peers as he entered the complex, critical arena of senior command.[11]

His situation would have been complicated in the best of circumstances. The American command structure in the Vietnam War made little sense at any time, with responsibility for the air war in Indochina fragmented across services, commands, and embassies scattered across Indochina and around the globe. In commanding the Seventh Air Force, Vogt worked for four superiors, all with different criteria for success. He was General Abrams's air force component commander, responsible for air support of ground forces in South Vietnam and for attack into the southernmost panhandle region of North Vietnam. He worked for Gen. Lou Clay Jr., the PACAF commander, in executing strikes further north in North Vietnam. Beyond that formal relationship, Clay had commanded the Seventh Air Force earlier in the war and was not shy about offering his recommendations to Vogt on all aspects of operations. General Ryan, as the air force chief of staff, had no formal authority over operations but offered a large measure of informal input and exercised control over personnel and mobilization of the air force resources supporting current operations. All the while, Vogt was keenly aware that his real bosses were half a world away in the White House, where Nixon and Kissinger saw him as their man in theater. They trusted his views, and they had sent him out to the war specifically to ensure that it was run along the lines they wanted.

THE EASTER OFFENSIVE

Vogt's baptism in senior command occurred in the opening days of the bloodiest campaign of the Vietnam War, as North Vietnam made its bid for a decisive victory. The North Vietnamese Politburo, after an extended and contentious internal debate, had ordered planning for a massive offensive nearly a year earlier. Defense Minister Vo Nguyen Giap had cautioned against the campaign, being concerned for his army's logistics in the face of American air interdiction, but the Politburo's majority supported the attack. Their strategic estimates of the situation projected that Nixon's response would be constrained by the impending presidential election and by strategic factors—primarily the still-fragile relationship with Communist China and the Moscow summit planned for late May. They expected Nixon to restrict air attacks to the North Vietnamese panhandle, perhaps with limited strikes farther north. They were confident that the president would not redeploy American ground forces into the theater and that NVA forces could withstand the level of air attacks permitted under the constraints that they expected Nixon to face. They believed that their own offensive would rout the South Vietnamese main forces, triggering local uprisings that would bring down the government of South Vietnamese president Nguyen Van Thieu and lead to a negotiated settlement and a quick transition to a Communist-controlled government. It was an immensely costly and risky strategy, but these risks were well worth taking in view of their strategic objective: to achieve, at last, an end to the thirty-year-long war, first with the French and then with the Americans, for the liberation and unity of their country.[12]

By early April, the outlines of the offensive had become clear. The NVA had first struck in the north, along the DMZ, annihilating the ring of firebases and observation positions that the Army of the Republic of Vietnam (ARVN) manned along the border and opening the way southward along the coast toward the ancient capital city of Hue. Days later, the NVA opened a second front north of Saigon, bursting out of Cambodian base camps toward the provincial capital of

An Loc. In early April a third front had begun to take shape in the central highlands and the coastal lowlands of central South Vietnam. Across the board, on all three fronts, the South Vietnamese defenders had cracked quickly, especially unnerved by the NVA's superiority in artillery and their use of tanks. The long-standing weaknesses of South Vietnam's military leaders, tolerable when the South Vietnamese forces were backed by the full might of America's military, were now exposed, and a lack of decisive leadership and command cohesion hamstrung the ARVN's response to the offensive in every sector.[13]

America's reaction to the NVA invasion was shaped and orchestrated in the White House, without input from the theater commander, the JCS, or the secretary of defense. Nixon and Kissinger had foreseen this climactic offensive a year earlier and had tried to forestall it through a negotiated settlement. Once the attack occurred, though, Nixon resolved to respond with every weapon at his disposal, short of recommitting U.S. ground forces into the theater. He ordered a massive reinforcement of air and naval forces, sent B-52s to Guam and Thailand, re-Americanized the theater air control system, and committed the United States to unlimited logistics support for the ARVN. Meanwhile, he and Kissinger took the diplomatic offensive against the Soviet Union and China, warning the superpower sponsors of North Vietnam that their support for their ally in this peripheral conflict could jeopardize their greater interest in a relationship with the United States. The White House worked to characterize the NVA offensive as an overt invasion of the south and a challenge to America's role in the world—messages designed to allow Nixon freedom of action in his military response.[14]

Finally, immediately upon receiving confirmation that the offensive had opened, Nixon ordered air strikes into North Vietnam. He did so partly to crush the air defenses shielding NVA attacks along the DMZ and equally to send a signal to the Politburo, warning that if the offensive continued America's response would stop at nothing. These actions were all ongoing before Vogt arrived in theater, and in fact the first reports from the attacks on the north had begun arriving as he walked into Nixon's office on April 6. His entry into high-level command would take place in an intense, complicated, and contentious setting.

VOGT ARRIVES IN THEATER

Vogt took command of the Seventh Air Force on April 10, 1972. Like any commander, he saw his first task as getting a grip on the operation. The importance of this requirement was heightened by the complexity of the situation, Vogt's lack of detailed knowledge of the staff procedures and the personalities under his command, and his awareness that he was being injected into an atmosphere of suspicion and resentment, probably inevitable given the means by which he had been appointed to his position. Despite the assurances that Nixon had offered Vogt in their meeting days earlier, Kissinger had done nothing either to have Vogt dual-hatted as the MACV deputy commander or, more broadly, to smooth his path into MACV. General Abrams by that point in the war was deeply resentful of the White House, sullen in his interactions with Moorer, and so difficult to deal with that the CJCS worked as much as possible with others in the chain of command. Moorer was especially cautious about calling Abrams late at night, when, as Moorer put it, COMUSMACV was likely to have been "partying."[15] Abrams viewed Vogt as a political general, or an extension of Kissinger into his command, and he made no effort to establish a basis of trust with his air force component commander. That attitude, of course, leached into the heavily army-centric MACV staff, which was deeply loyal to Abrams.[16]

Given his career path, as noted earlier, Vogt had no stable of talented subordinates to take with him into this environment, but he did have his deeply devoted administrative assistant, executive officer Nancy Collins, who had been with Vogt since his first days as a general. She would maintain iron control of his calendar and all access to him and would serve as his executive secretary, taking the dictation that would fill Vogt's days in the weeks to come. Vogt still needed someone to manage his personal affairs, however, since his wife, Kathie, was living in Bangkok. Immediately on his arrival in Saigon, he asked his personal instructor pilot, Maj. Bill Goodyear, to serve as his aide. Vogt emphasized to Goodyear in their first conversation that "I want to spend all my time and energy running this war and I want you to take care of all other aspects of my life." Goodyear was a B-52 pilot then flying T-39s, and he had neither experience as an aide nor any particular desire to gain that experience. But he agreed to the dual-hatting as instructor pilot and aide and served Vogt loyally until July.

It now remained for Vogt to structure his command's procedures, and he placed his unique stamp on the command in his first day at the Seventh Air Force. That morning he arrived for the daily staff meeting as scheduled, personable and open as always, and sat through the normal presentations: weather, a summary of the previous day's operations, plans for the day, and issues raised by the staff sections. At the scheduled closing time he stood up and announced to the staff, "We could be looking at these slides all morning, and be losing the war and never even know it. This is unsatisfactory." With that, he closed the meeting; he never again held the morning staff meeting that had been a staple of Seventh Air Force procedures since its first days. Instead, he met with his deputies one-on-one in his office. He permitted full access by those directly involved with combat operations: his director of operations, Maj. Gen. Alton Slay; his director of intelligence, Maj. Gen. Jimmy Jumper; and his vice commander, Lt. Gen. Winton "Bones" Marshall, another ace in whom Vogt placed complete confidence. The other members of his staff were required to work through Collins for appointments. Vogt kept track of the war through frequent visits to Blue Chip, the Seventh Air Force command post, and by monitoring the army's FM net via a receiver in his office, paying special attention to the "troops in contact" calls to ensure that tactical air (tacair) was responding effectively.

As with his self-nomination to command, his abolition of the staff meeting was an act of supreme self-confidence: the man without senior command experience dismantled the planning and execution processes that had existed for longer than a decade and did so on his first day in theater. Staff meetings are notoriously boring and inefficient, but they serve an indispensable function in providing a common forum for the commander, in ensuring the staff has a shared perspective on issues and priorities, and in establishing working relationships across the organization. Now all that was gone, and Vogt would be faced with developing another means of synchronizing staff activity in a high-tempo, complex operational setting.

Only a few days into the offensive, Abrams and his commander in chief were already locked in a bitter impasse over the use of air power, with Vogt stuck squarely in the middle. It was a classic and often repeated conflict in the history of air power, and it played out as a repeated series of confrontations from April until Abrams's departure at the end of June. Abrams was intensely focused on the ground battle and keenly aware that air power was the only force he had to forestall a collapse of South Vietnam. For Nixon, though, the war in Southeast Asia was part of a larger fabric of strategic and political concerns. As he had summarized at the outset of the offensive, Nixon was playing "a bigger game—we're playing a Russia game, and a China game, and an election game, and we're not gonna have the ARVN collapse."[17] It was essential to that bigger game that Nixon demonstrate brutality and strength not only to Hanoi but also to Moscow and Beijing.

And so recurrently through April, as the Moscow summit neared, Nixon directed B-52 raids into southern North Vietnam. The raids were militarily insignificant but served as potent signals of his determination to stop at nothing in halting the north's offensive. Each of these raids triggered another transpacific debate with Abrams, who was not as concerned about the B-52s per se as he was about the dozens of fighter sorties that would be absorbed in the support packages. In mid-April, with Kissinger on the verge of a secret visit to Moscow, Nixon ordered airstrikes against Hanoi and Hai Phong that were aimed at sending a message of toughness and resolve to leaders in both Hanoi and the Soviet Union. Abrams raised such a protracted and bitter resistance to the strike, however, that it was nearly aborted in midair.[18]

The contention between Nixon and his theater commander reached a point where Nixon sent his most trusted military adviser, Maj. Gen. Alexander Haig, out to Saigon in mid-April specifically to talk with Abrams about the broader strategic context at play. It was a very long trip that did no good at all. The entire sequence only further strengthened the mistrust of Laird and of Abrams endemic in Nixon's inner circle; now the White House suspected Laird of trying to minimize the use of force and Abrams of posturing and creating a record in case of failure. It was, as Moorer summarized, "a hell of a way to run a war."[19] In that complicated setting, Vogt struggled to balance the competing demands of countering Communist offensives on three fronts in South Vietnam, dealing with ongoing wars in Laos and Cambodia, conducting a gradually escalating air offensive into North Vietnam, and supporting the White House–directed B-52 raids into the north.

He faced challenges on each of those fronts. On the positive side, Nixon had sent a flood of reinforcements into the theater, and the sortie count rose rapidly during Vogt's first weeks in command. In the first week of the offensive, air force and navy fighters flew 1,101 sorties over North Vietnam; the following week that number reached 2,722; and in the third week sorties increased again, to 3,183.[20] Concentrated in the highest-priority battle areas, these sorties began their work of smothering the NVA offensive short of its major objectives.

It was easier to send in aircraft, though, than to ensure their effectiveness. The long years of the drawdown had dislocated the theater air control system and had especially damaged the forward air controller (FAC) force, or the men directly observing and targeting the NVA forces. Only two weeks prior to the NVA offensive, the Seventh Air Force had dissolved the 504th Tactical Air Support Group, which became a victim of the relentless reduction of U.S. forces in South Vietnam. For years that organization had provided central direction of the FAC forces across South Vietnam. Now, only days before the offensive, the FAC units underwent a reorganization that placed them under the command of their host wings, and decisions on FAC deployments came directly from the Seventh Air Force and were largely made by men who were unfamiliar with the capabilities of the different aircraft and units in the FAC force. The wing commander at Korat Royal Thai Air Force Base later summarized the effects: "Unfortunately, vast inefficiencies in the employment of the 'beefed up' strike forces were soon apparent because the command and control system (both ground and air) was too inflexible to be quickly expanded along with the size of the strike forces."[21] As one disgusted squadron commander later noted, at the outset of the offensive a series of ill-informed, hasty decisions on the employment of FAC forces "ended up with night-qualified FACs and aircraft flying in the daytime, day-qualified FACs and aircraft flying at night, both in unfamiliar areas and both working with a vastly inadequate command and control system! There has to be a better way."[22]

Navy tacair added to the confusion, as carriers conducting cyclic operations offshore launched dozens of fighters into constricted airspace, saturating the air control system and overwhelming the ability of the FACs to provide effective control. The navy pilots returned to their carriers to report that about 40 percent of their sorties were essentially dumping their bombs either into the jungle or into the water. Finally, the South Vietnamese Air Force (VNAF), now much larger and more capable than it had been during the earlier phases of America's involvement, was generating attack sorties while operating under its own FACs and thus creating further chaos over the battle area.[23] This confusion reigned over both An Loc and the DMZ front, where further complications arose from ARVN artillery and from naval gunfire support.

Vogt had little time to remedy this situation before facing his first crisis in command: the NVA launched an all-out assault on An Loc on April 13. A combination of B-52 strikes, helicopter and fixed-wing gunship attacks, and air force and navy tacair stymied the three-wave attack, but the response again highlighted the shortcomings in the tactical air control system. As an AC-130 gunship pilot summarized, "Mass confusion reigned supreme most of the time we were in the area. . . . It was interesting because a flight of VNAF A-1s kept flying through our shooting orbit."[24] This trial by fire triggered a rapid upgrade in control procedures—

separating VNAF and U.S. operating areas and establishing a hierarchy of U.S. FACs operating over the town, with a "King FAC" receiving tacair allocations and allocating those assets to two other FACs assigned to An Loc. U.S. and South Vietnamese forces used this system in the NVA's follow-on attack on April 15, and the city held. The NVA, gravely weakened by their losses in these attacks, settled into a siege and awaited the reinforcements they would need to resume their attacks.

Meanwhile, the Seventh Air Force and Task Force 77, the carrier task force executing air operations under the Pacific Fleet, returned to sustained operations over North Vietnam for the first time since 1968. The air offensive that Nixon had ordered, Operation Freedom Train, reintroduced air force and navy pilots to the high-threat environment over the north, though they were restricted to attacks below the twentieth parallel. The operation resembled the incremental, limited, escalatory air strategy of the Lyndon Johnson years, as Kissinger carefully orchestrated military, political, and diplomatic action. The air force conducted 628 tacair and 82 B-52 sorties in these attacks, focusing mainly on airfields and transportation nodes. Over the five weeks of the operation, air force pilots reported 487 surface-to-air missile (SAM) launches, and the Seventh Air Force lost eleven aircraft in the meat grinder near the DMZ and from operations in the north. In light of the massive air offensive shortly to follow, this brief period of gradual escalation provided a welcome transition into higher-intensity operations and a chance to work out tactics that would soon prove invaluable over the NVA heartland. For example, Seventh Air Force fighters laid down chaff corridors for the five B-52 strikes into the north during April. The intricate operation badly needed testing in a relatively benign environment, for it would prove an essential element in the later Linebacker missions.

In late April the ground situation, which had stabilized after the NVA's first assault, deteriorated and threatened to collapse. In the north, along the DMZ, command dysfunctions dislocated the South Vietnamese defenses, enabling the NVA to overrun Quang Tri. The first provincial capital to fall in the war, it appeared to be only a stopping point on the way to a still greater disaster. The ancient capital of Hue was due south, and nothing seemed to be standing in the way of the NVA advance. The North Vietnamese recognized full well what they could achieve by taking Hue; indeed, their campaign plan for that phase of the offensive projected that "if large numbers of enemy forces are annihilated and Hue is lost, this will affect the very nature of the war and will cause the collapse of the Thieu regime."[25] North of Saigon, An Loc was under a protracted siege, reminiscent in fury and human misery, if not in scale or climate, of the Stalingrad siege in World War II. In the Central Highlands the NVA had eradicated a regiment at Dak To and had laid siege to the provincial capital, Kontum, threatening to achieve a long-standing Communist goal of slicing South Vietnam in half.

It was a theater-wide crisis, a moment at which America's stake in Indochina seemed in imminent peril. That nightmare was vivid enough, but to Nixon further specters lurked, all to be wakened if America's war in Vietnam ended in failure. Immediately ahead, capping the triumph of the February visit to Beijing, was the summit in Moscow that would reshape the Cold War. Nixon could not imagine visiting Moscow and exchanging toasts with the Soviet leaders while Soviet-supplied NVA tanks rolled through the streets of Hue. He would cancel the summit rather than meet Leonid Brezhnev under those conditions. This military crisis in what had become a strategically peripheral conflict threatened to unravel Nixon's grand diplomatic construct. Following that May summit loomed the electoral campaign, inexorably driving toward the date that so impelled action both in Hanoi and Washington—November 7, 1972, Election Day. Given the impossibility of recommitting ground forces to the war, Nixon had to rely on air power to stymie the North Vietnamese offensive. Although later historians would focus on the dramatic air offensives against North Vietnam, it was in the south that the war could be lost and where immediate disaster threatened.

It was perhaps Vogt's finest hour, and it arrived only a month into his command. His time working with the White House had left him with no doubt of the importance of Hue, especially as Nixon's summit with the Soviets loomed in the immediate future. So Vogt threw the air force into every role conceivable in support of the ground battle, compensating for the lack of effective ARVN defenders. By this point the aircraft and carriers that Nixon had sent into the theater were fully engaged, and American air forces could generate about nine hundred tacair sorties per day, along with nearly eighty B-52 strikes and thirty gunship sorties.[26] On April 30 and May 1, as the ARVN defenses around Quang Tri crumbled, Vogt worked with Abrams's deputy, Gen. Fred Weyand, to extract the 127 American advisers and controllers from Quang Tri city. They completed the mission on May 1.

That same day Vogt alerted Washington to the SAM sites now under construction in RVN territory and, still worse, to the apparent deployment of a second-echelon NVA division, the 325th, into the offensive against Hue. Vogt reported:

"I have had armed recce [reconnaissance] aircraft working over the routes down which they might travel. Today, a flight of armed recce aircraft discovered about 100 trucks working down Route 137 and heading for the Ban Karai Pass. They attacked, destroying a number of trucks and large amounts of supplies stockpiled along Route 137. . . . I plan to have F-4s with flares working 137 this evening." The next day he sent 421 tacair sorties into the defense of Hue, and another 181 sorties pounded NVA forces in the North Vietnamese panhandle. The day after that, the ARVN forces around Quang Tri largely dissolved, "streaming out on foot," as Vogt described it, and the Seventh Air Force was called on to destroy the tanks and artillery that the ARVN forces had abandoned and at the same time to screen the retreating troops.

The Politburo, far away in Hanoi, was exerting all the pressure in its power to encourage its commanders to press the attack on Hue. The NVA were as subject as the Americans to political interference in combat operations, and the forces operating north of Hue were to pay a terrible price for these urgent attacks.[27] The next day, even before the ARVN had established a fixed defense north of Hue, FACs and armed recce uncovered and destroyed a tank force moving down Route 1 toward the battle area. Vogt reported, "I kept the road covered all night long with Owls, which are flare-equipped F-4s. We employed the same tactics we had the previous night up in the Route 137 area." He also directed twenty-four-hour coverage of the principal ingress routes and river crossings leading toward Hue.

By now this intensive air interdiction effort had given the ARVN forces a respite, and, better still, for the first time in the war they now had a capable corps commander. The crisis in early May forced South Vietnamese president Thieu to replace all three of the corps commanders involved, and he finally chose competence over loyalty in the ARVN high command. In I Corps, defending northern South Vietnam, Gen. Ngo Quang Truong moved decisively into command, demonstrating the energy, urgency, and ruthless determination that had been so sadly lacking to that point in the ARVN defenses. More important, he was a skilled tactician who knew exactly how to take advantage of the exorbitant amounts of firepower and matériel that the Americans placed at his disposal.

Truong's greatest concern was not the NVA infantry or their tanks, which he could deal with; he was most worried about their artillery, specifically their Soviet-supplied 130mm M-46 cannon, now being used for the first time in South Vietnam. The M-46 could outrange any ARVN or U.S. field artillery piece, and the NVA had adopted tactics designed to counter the air threat they faced by dispersing and camouflaging their forces. Vogt set about countering this threat, first looking toward his AC-130 gunships, which had a variety of sensors—infrared sensors, lowlight television, and electronic detection devices—coupled with digital fire control systems and an array of cannon. Over time he would try to locate the M-46 artillery pieces by using acoustic arrays and by blanketing their operating areas with FACs, slowly whittling down their numbers through simple attrition.

Meanwhile, the NVA continued to force its troops southward into the teeth of American air attacks and naval gunfire, and Vogt continued to concentrate his tacair and B-52 sorties against every sign of NVA movement or logistics support. On May 5 he reported attacks on a large crane the NVA was attempting to use in replacing a bridge over the Ben Hai River in Quang Tri; the suicidal move, impelled by Politburo direction, resulted only in the crane's destruction. That same day U.S. Air Force and U.S. Navy fighters worked over a convoy moving south through the battle area. Vogt reported, "We have destroyed every bridge on QL-1 from friendly positions north to the DMZ" and that "following a detailed photo analysis, we believe we have determined the fords being used by the enemy across the Ben Hai River and have effectively damaged them with laser bombs."

The next day the NVA sent more than twenty tanks along the beach southward toward Hue. First the navy pounded them with gunfire, then air force fighters used laser-guided weapons, and finally navy aircraft dropped cluster bombs. Trapped out in the open, subjected to ceaseless air attack, the tank force was annihilated. The next day Vogt reported, "In MR-I I have directed that every bridge, ferry and ford be destroyed or cut. The enemy is making a desperate attempt to repair these much needed arteries in order to bring his heavy tanks southward for the battle for Hue."[28] By that time, the North Vietnamese offensive had reached its culminating point, with its strength sapped by constant devastating air attacks in all three sectors. Though nobody could be certain at that moment, the threat of South Vietnamese military collapse had passed.

In that same message, Vogt reported, "We are scheduling strikes against two targets in the Hanoi area tomorrow. . . . We are also selecting key interdiction points on both the Northeast and the Northwest rail lines for subsequent operations when authorized. We will attempt to keep these lines cut employing primarily smart bombs."[29] It was a quiet beginning to a dramatic and protracted air campaign that would absorb Vogt's attention, and that of the nation's highest authorities, for the remaining months of the war.

LINEBACKER

Back in Washington, as combat in Indochina reached a climax, Nixon and his cohorts sketched the outlines of a crushing air offensive against North Vietnam in a rambling discussion on May 4.[30] Nixon had long contemplated launching a massive attack on the north, directing an intensive planning effort as early as 1969 and repeatedly reconsidering it in the years since. Now the time had come. The NVA had committed open aggression against the south, pouring across the DMZ in a naked, conventional armored offensive. It was using Soviet-supplied weapons and had apparently dropped any pretense of a popular uprising against the government of South Vietnam. Nixon now had the political and strategic cover he needed, and he was determined to take advantage.

The conversation among Nixon, Kissinger, Haig, and John Connally drew the broad outlines of the air strategy that the U.S. military would execute through the following months.[31] The Americans would close the NVA harbors quickly and cleanly through naval mining operations and set a tight cordon on the North Vietnamese coast to prevent lightering operations. Air force and navy air would shut down the rail and road systems along routes to the northeast and northwest that led from the North Vietnamese heartland to the NVA's supply sources in the Soviet Union and China. Finally, a brutally aggressive air offensive would destroy the north's supplies of petroleum, oils, and lubricants (POL) and shut down movement to the southern battlefields. This battering would continue relentlessly, ceaselessly, until North Vietnam agreed to terms.

Conceptually, the operation originated in the early days of the Nixon presidency. In 1969, frustrated by the lack of military and diplomatic progress during the administration's first months and convinced that the American public would never stand for a protracted withdrawal from the war, Kissinger directed an extensive political-military planning effort, exploring the idea of a destructive air campaign conducted in a series of short, spasmodic, violent phases. In time, that concept morphed into a more conventional air campaign almost exactly foreshadowing Linebacker. The campaign was to begin with a mining operation, codenamed "Duck Hook," combined with an intense attack phase to eliminate North Vietnam's air defenses, isolate its heartland, and crush its war-making capacity and its economy. It would emphasize shock, concentration, mass, and surprise to magnify the more purely military effects.

All of the key figures in Linebacker had taken part in that earlier planning effort: Nixon, Kissinger, and Haig from the White House; Moorer as the chief of naval operations and acting CJCS; and Vogt as the Joint Staff's director of operations. It was Vogt's first extended exposure to the Nixon inner circle, and clearly the experience established a greater basis of trust. All of these men worked through the logic and sequence of the campaign. As Linebacker opened, White House expectations were shaped by this previous concept of a cataclysmic, brutal air offensive, annihilating North Vietnam as a society, and bringing its leaders to their knees.

This vision aligned perfectly with air power theory from the first days of military aviation. Now, it would be necessary to build that campaign and prosecute it in the real world of unpredictable weather, limitations on technology and proficiency, and the countermeasures of a committed, resourceful enemy. Vogt, however, would enjoy two major advantages over his predecessors in the Rolling Thunder era. First, he would have the use of precision weapons, predominantly the laser-guided bombs (LGBs) that multiplied strike effectiveness by several orders of magnitude. LGBs would be Linebacker's signature weapon, and Vogt shaped his strike tactics around their use and protection. His second key advantage was the strategic leadership shaping the campaign. He would face neither the incrementalism and micromanagement of the Johnson years nor the hesitant and half-hearted escalatory pathway that air operations had followed in the earlier administration. Instead, his president demanded a rapid and full-scale application of air power, and Nixon vowed that he would "watch this every day" to ensure that Vogt delivered.

On May 8, Nixon took the issue to the NSC, seeking its members' views on the proposed air offensive. Moorer attended the meeting, returned to the Pentagon at about 12:30 p.m., and within forty minutes called Vogt—waking him at 1 a.m. Saigon time—to talk about the initial day's targeting and the interdiction campaign that was to follow. Vogt suggested that the first day's strikes go after the road and rail bridges into Hanoi and bottleneck traffic so that later strikes could take out the rail yards once they were filled. Moorer accepted that recommendation, setting the stage for the most dramatic day of air combat in the entire Vietnam War.

In that one brief conversation Vogt made two other proposals to which Moorer also agreed and that in large part defined the Linebacker air operation—

for better and for worse. Kissinger had urged that the air force open the Line-backer campaign with B-52 strikes on the rail yards in Hanoi and then continue to use the heavy bombers throughout the campaign. Vogt objected, arguing that "actually I can do better with TACAIR using laser guided bombs than they can with the 52s . . . every time you use 52s up there we have to put in [a] tremendous package for them—takes me more TACAIR to get 52s out of there than it does to do the job myself." So rather than use the B-52s that the White House initially favored, air force and navy fighters would execute the opening strikes in this strategic air campaign and would carry the weight of the offensive throughout the following months.

Moments later, Vogt took another initiative in structuring the campaign. He suggested that the upcoming air operation take the form of the earlier Rolling Thunder campaign, separating North Vietnam into geographic areas divided between the navy and the air force. "I would just go back to that," he said. "We wouldn't have any problem."[32] Vogt's comment committed Linebacker to the same system of route packages that had hamstrung Rolling Thunder. Perhaps the choice was inevitable given the limited time available to build an alternative system, but Vogt would later come to regret this decision.

Five hours later Vogt was back on the phone with Moorer, who was now armed with details of the president's decision and the mining plan. Together they worked through the overall strategy—the mining and blockade and interdiction—and Vogt asked for authority to strike the North Vietnamese air defense command center at Bac Mai as the campaign opened. Moorer suggested that the Seventh Air Force simply hit the command center the next time it struck Hanoi without asking for formal clearance, as Kissinger had specified that these strikes would not be dispersed on air defense targets. As Moorer summarized, "I have been working on [Kissinger] for a long time and haven't gotten him educated yet, that you have to take out the defense and then place total attention on the job at hand. He always said that pilots want to attack airfields instead of attacking supplies."[33]

These two conversations put the general structure of the plan in place. Nixon's air offensive would follow the general outline of Rolling Thunder, opting for simplicity at the cost of the ability to mass air force and navy aircraft. The use of precision weaponry would define the campaign, and the interdiction of supplies flowing southward would depend on cutting bridges to interrupt traffic reaching Hanoi from China. The White House essentially prohibited preparatory suppression of air defenses; instead, elaborate strike packages would have to be structured to protect the precision strikers against MiGs and SAMs, attack by attack. This strategy would prove a heavy and constant drain on the air offensive.

Vogt's decision to rely on a few laser guidance pods as the foundation of the air campaign had a series of direct and indirect consequences that he would face daily over the coming months. The laser designators were few and precious. He had only six in theater at the outset of the campaign, with no prospect of replacements. Their protection was imperative if the campaign was to succeed, so Vogt and his staff structured elaborate support packages to suppress the formidable defenses that the strikers would face. These packages would come from units stationed all across Southeast Asia, creating endless coordination and communication problems that had to be addressed mission after mission. These complexities, in turn, placed a premium on aircrew proficiency and experience, effective radios, and timely mission scheduling—none of which could be taken for granted. In fact, the F-4's problems with radios had been thoroughly documented for years, had seriously affected Rolling Thunder operations, and had somehow remained unaddressed despite the huge influx of advanced technologies reaching the air force during this phase of the war. Similarly, a series of assessments through the previous winter had warned that air force pilots reaching the squadrons lacked both experience and sufficient air-to-air training in their upgrade programs. These problems would play out week after week throughout the Linebacker campaign.

Vogt's insistence on the laser weaponry reached back to his days at PACAF during Rolling Thunder. As he summarized the following January:[34]

I appreciated, having been out here as Chief of Operations in PACAF back in the Rolling Thunder days from 1965 to 1968, the difficulty of trying to interdict along the rail lines which involved the destruction of many small bridges using conventional ordnance. It was a tough job and we never did really succeed in interdicting those rail lines in the Rolling Thunder campaign. . . . I knew that we couldn't do the job that was asked of us, namely to fight a major war in-country with a major invasion underway and at the same time take on a major interdiction program in the north, without a quantum jump in our effectiveness. So we forced the development of new tactics for the proper employment, in the high-risk areas, of these laser-guided weapons. . . . I insisted on it because I knew we couldn't do it any other way.

The curtain went up on May 10, as Nixon unleashed his air campaign. The first raid set a pattern that would continue through months of Linebacker air operations. From its bases in Thailand, the air force launched an elaborate and complex strike force consisting primarily of a few F-4s carrying LGBs and electro-optical weapons. Other F-4s deployed a chaff corridor, still others provided SAM suppression, and yet others flew air-to-air sweeps and combat air patrols. Meanwhile, from carriers offshore, the navy launched three waves of strikes, smaller and simpler than those of the air force strike forces, without the vast advantage offered by precision weapons but with far better flight cohesion, training, and tactics.[35]

The North Vietnamese responded in force, launching MiG-17s, -19s, and -21s, and triggering the largest and most dramatic air battles of the war. Engagements rippled across North Vietnam, from near Yen Bai in the west to the coast near Hai Phong. By the end of the day the Paul Doumer Bridge in Hanoi, significant both as a transportation node and a symbol, had been put out of action with a single air strike, immediately demonstrating the value of the new tactical array assembled by Seventh Air Force. That night, in a bunker near Hanoi, Gen. Vo Nguyen Giap reviewed the day's events with his air force leadership and ruled against any further mass engagements with the American strike forces. Giap was not a fighter tactician, but he understood attrition very well and fully recognized what would ensue if his tiny air force continued to challenge the Americans head on. The NVAF shifted to a strategy of small hit-and-run engagements, a tactic designed to draw blood and keep the primitive air force in the battle. It was the first move in a ceaseless action-reaction cycle that would continue for months, until an uneasy peace finally settled over Vietnam.[36]

The first day's attacks provided a dramatic and promising opening to the campaign, and Vogt worked to build on the initial success in the days to come. As he did so, he faced squarely the many forms of friction built into this air operation: bad weather, maintenance issues, enemy defenses and countermeasures, problems with coordination and aircrew proficiency, and conflicting requirements on the southern battlefields. Nonetheless, Seventh Air Force fighters claimed some remarkable early successes—not only dropping two spans of the Paul Doumer Bridge but also putting the Thanh Hoa Bridge out of action and knocking down bridges along the northeast and northwest railroads to China. These first successes led Vogt to claim that these rail lines had been effectively interdicted, but the same report notifying Washington that the Thanh Hoa Bridge had been destroyed brought news that the North Vietnamese had already deployed a pontoon bridge for truck traffic a bit downstream from the Paul Doumer Bridge in Hanoi. Moreover, the NVA were redeploying their SAM battalions from the southern battlefields to defend their national heartland and to cover the northeast railroad. Surprised by Nixon's decision, North Vietnam was now responding to this new situation.[37]

Those first days of Linebacker coincided with the NVA's last push to take An Loc, creating a direct competition for sorties between the strategic campaign over the north and the demands of this key battle. The battle triggered a fundamental shift in the relationship between Vogt and Abrams. Ever since Vogt's arrival, Abrams had maintained his distant and resentful attitude, which was amplified in the MACV staff. In early May, as NVA forces marshaled for their go-for-broke attack on An Loc, III Corps senior adviser Maj. Gen. James Hollingsworth recommended a change in the standard allocation of B-52 sorties, moving away from the basically even allocation across the military regions to concentrate the strikes around An Loc. Hollingsworth was intensely involved in the campaign, orbiting the besieged town daily in his helicopter, and he was convinced that the NVA would attack on May 11. On the recommendation of the MACV staff, however, Abrams rejected the new targeting plan.[38]

Vogt received an information copy of Hollingsworth's message in his office and heard that Abrams had rejected his recommendation. Convinced that Hollingsworth was right, Vogt drove to MACV headquarters and talked with Abrams, arguing that, given the stakes at play, "even if [Hollingsworth] was wrong we wouldn't lose very much, but if he was right and we didn't do it, it would be a colossal loss." The MACV staff again asserted that no evidence supported Hollingsworth's recommendation, and Abrams turned to Vogt and said, "You're overruled. Stick to the old schedule. Meeting dismissed."

Irritated, Vogt returned to his headquarters and called the FACs who had been operating over An Loc to come to his office that afternoon and report on the situation. They supported Hollingsworth's analysis, and Vogt decided to try once again to persuade Abrams to change his decision. By that time it was evening, and Abrams's staff was with him in his quarters, drinks in hand, when Vogt arrived. Once again he made his arguments, this time spelling out the strategic consequences at play: Nixon's position at the Moscow summit would be terribly weakened if An Loc were to fall. Abrams was livid, convinced he was being lectured and reminded once more of Vogt's ties to the White House. Still later that evening, to his eternal credit, Abrams called Vogt at his quarters. After chewing Vogt out for embarrassing him in front of his staff, he abruptly commented, "You're right," and hung up. The next day the B-52s went to Hollingsworth, who placed the strikes precisely on the marshaling NVA forces and crushed the offensive once and for all.

From that day on, with Abrams having gained a new respect for Vogt, their relationship vastly improved. Over a four-day period, U.S. forces carried out 812 fighter attack missions, 31 gunship sorties, and 96 B-52 strikes in direct support of An Loc. This cascade of firepower ended the NVA offensive, leading Abrams to comment that "without the air power we have employed here, South Vietnam would have long since been gone."[39]

Then the weather went bad up north, and Linebacker ground to a temporary halt despite the presidential priority placed on the operation. From May 14 to May 16 the weather shut down operations around Hanoi. The following two days were marginal; the next day conditions were again unworkable. For Nixon, receiving reports in the White House, they seemed to repeat the old story of the air force promising much and delivering little.

It all came to a head on May 19, on the eve of Nixon's departure for Moscow. Vice President Spiro Agnew recently had returned from a largely ceremonial trip to Asia and dropped in on Nixon to give a report. Kissinger was with the president, and the two men listened with commendable patience as Agnew summarized his tour. In an offhand remark, completely unaware of the charged context, Agnew commented that some among the military were frustrated about bombing restrictions. It was as if he had lit a fast-burning fuse. Nixon and Kissinger angrily exploded, each heaping more invective on the air force. Kissinger hurried off to bring in Moorer, who was waiting for Kissinger downstairs, to see the president, and the CJCS walked into "a session like you never heard," as Haig later summarized it. Nixon's diatribe culminated with the president's pounding his fist on the table and shouting, "Ryan is out—out—out—out!" He targeted his anger at the air force chief of staff, who was far removed from campaign planning, rather than at Vogt, who was directly responsible for Linebacker. As with most of Nixon's outbursts, nothing came of it, but the incident provides a glimpse into Nixon's acute and continuing vexation with the air force.[40]

As the weather improved somewhat and as planners and aircrews developed tactics and proficiency, Linebacker settled into a rhythm. Day after day, attack packages targeted the road and rail systems leading to China, destroying bridges with an effectiveness never seen in the Rolling Thunder days. The North Vietnamese quickly countered, moving to road-rail shuttles and bypasses and shifting much of their logistics backbone from rail to road traffic. Vogt was well aware that he could not stop trucks operating north of Hanoi, so he sent raids against the truck storage and repair facilities, against electrical power plants, and against the pontoon and cement factories turning out matériel for road and bridge repairs. These strikes worked, knocking out North Vietnam's tiny industrial infrastructure with little effort. The question remaining was whether this level of destruction would translate into the strategic effect that the president demanded—the isolation of North Vietnam and the suppression of its economy and war effort.

By this point Vogt had also settled into a routine in command and a daily rhythm that enabled him to focus on matters he found important. In the morning he received an essential weather briefing, as the treacherous weather in Indochina shaped the day's activities. Then he would attend to the day's operations, generally in the Blue Chip command post, and monitor communications to stay abreast of the situation. At about 10:30 he and Lieutenant General Marshall would drive to the MACV staff meeting, and General Slay occasionally accompanied them when operational issues were to be addressed.

On most afternoons, Vogt blocked off a two-hour period to give newsmen one-on-one background briefings on air operations. In these carefully prepared sessions, Vogt was armed with photographic evidence of the effects of air operations, or mosaics to provide a comprehensive picture. With his education and his career background, Vogt was the ideal voice for the media, and he took that role seriously. Coherent and articulate, he used no notes and no script, instead relying on memory and his wit to master the situation. It was a role to which he was uniquely suited and one in which he was urgently needed. By that point in the war, Abrams was as deeply mistrustful of the media as he was of the White House, so almost all information flowing out of the command came from Vogt.[41]

Moorer, in fact, asked Vogt to send him detailed assessments of air operations daily, as Abrams's reports in the first days of the NVA offensive provided little insight into the air forces' role in slowing the North Vietnamese attack. The CJCS needed more information to calm the anxieties in the White House. So, late in the afternoon, Vogt would work with Collins to add his personal assessment to the staff's daily summary going to Washington. He would gather his source material on a table in his office and dictate to Collins his summary of the day's events, plans for the near future, and any issues worth raising. Occasionally he advocated for having particular targets cleared for attack. Usually Vogt would call Moorer at 8 p.m. Saigon time, closing his day and sketching the state of affairs in theater for the CJCS as Moorer started his day halfway around the world.

By early June American intelligence had discovered that the North Vietnamese had begun constructing two oil pipelines from the Chinese border to Hanoi, and that these were clearly going to be linked to the pipelines built earlier to send POL to the southern battlefields. These pipelines would replace the seaborne tankers that had previously brought oil into the country and would largely negate the effects of the mining operations against Hai Phong and the other ports. This effort was the most visible and effective measure in North Vietnam's nationwide initiative in support of the transportation system. The North Vietnamese mobilized their workforce, rerouted weapons shipments through China, shifted to nighttime transportation, built out waterways to supplement the road network, and demonstrated their usual persistence and skill in repairing bridges and roadways. Although labor-intensive and inefficient, these countermeasures offered a low-technology response to the overwhelming firepower and technology wielded by the air assault. Instead of delivering the crushing shock promised by air theory and doctrine, Vogt found himself directing a campaign of grinding attrition while fending off constant criticism and suggestions from PACAF on the effectiveness of his interdiction campaign.

Slowly the air campaign fell into the trap of predictability, driven by maintenance cycles, weather, and the complexity of the force packages.[42] Once everyone found a system that worked, inertia took hold. It all played into the hands of the North Vietnamese, who spared no effort to study the patterns of the air attacks, seeking exploitable weaknesses. Other problems developed as well and became the subjects of a series of messages from Vogt's superiors that began within two days of the campaign's opening. Clay, in particular, was deeply concerned about reports of recurrent errors in tactics, radio and flight discipline, aircraft maintenance and scheduling, and aircrew proficiency. From his seat in Hawaii, the PACAF commander perceived the Seventh Air Force was conducting a chaotic and unprofessional campaign over North Vietnam. He saw no sign of improvement, only a failure that pointed straight to the highest level of command.[43]

The campaign hit its low point on June 27. Vogt opened his daily report with the line, "This was one of those days."[44] He went on to recount the full story.

The day had begun with a Linebacker attack on the NVAF air defense command post at Bac Mai, and a Soviet SA-2 SAM destroyed one chaff bomber. A MiG-21 shot down a second F-4 Phantom on egress, with two more fighters falling victim to MiGs while attempting to locate the crew members ejecting from the earlier shootdown. The rest of the day was absorbed in efforts to rescue the six survivors, but these attempts were put on hold when the two helicopters committed to the rescue operation developed engine trouble. The entire sequence reflected the problems that had been evident since the first days of the campaign: communication shortfalls, poor tactical decision making, unreliable missiles, and breakdowns in flight discipline.[45]

The losses in late June crystallized concerns that had been growing among the air force leadership since the first days of the campaign, and suddenly Vogt was getting more help than he ever wanted. In rapid succession, he hosted Maj. Gen. Frederick "Boots" Blesse, the legendary Korean War ace who was now the PACAF director of operations; Maj. Gen. John J. Burns from the Air Staff, conducting an informal inspection at the direction of General Ryan; a study group from the Fighter Weapons Center; and finally, in early July, a visit from Ryan himself, traveling halfway around the world to review operations in a manifestation of his uneasiness with the status of the air offensive. Gen. William W. Momyer, commander of Tactical Air Command, also added his views from Langley. This barrage of technical and tactical assistance could be viewed as giving Vogt the opportunity to draw on the resources of the greatest air force on earth. Vogt, however, took all this attention as unfair carping and backseat driving. He pointed out in some testy exchanges with Clay that Linebacker was inflicting far greater damage, with lower overall loss rates, than Rolling Thunder had ever achieved; that problems with missile maintenance and aircrew proficiency were long standing and not readily fixable; and that he and his command were taking aggressive action to address the problems.

Dissatisfied, Clay and Ryan took direct action. Returning from his visit to Saigon Ryan promptly relieved Slay from his duties as Seventh Air Force director of operations. To remedy the shortcomings, Ryan sent Maj. Gen. Carlos Talbott to Saigon to straighten out the mess Ryan had found in his visit. Talbott was appalled at the changes that Vogt had made in the management of operations and later offered a scathing indictment of the situation he found on his arrival:

That place was a shambles. All the systems that we had established, even in Joe Moore's day [in the early 1960s], had been cast aside. Things were in utter chaos. There were no planning meetings. Sometime in the afternoon the [director of intelligence] would be running wildly down the hall headed for Vogt's office with some pictures. He and Vogt would plan what they were going to do up north tomorrow. The [director of operations] wasn't even consulted. There was no morning meeting to review what transpired yesterday; no evening planning meeting where the whole staff was brought in to discuss these things. The frag order was getting out about 2:00 or 3:00 in the morning, much later than it should have been. . . . I couldn't believe how bad it was.[46]

While Talbott rebuilt the planning and tasking cycles from earlier days, Ryan and Vogt stepped in to push the development of a fusion center, later named Teaball, designed to provide real-time operational use of the warning data scooped up by the various intelligence sensors operating in theater. In his daily report on July 5, Vogt noted that in an engagement costing two Phantoms, ground-controlled interception (GCI) had missed the MiGs making a low-level ingress for their attacks. "I am urgently investigating a way to give our pilots real time [Special Intelligence] information. . . . We must offset the GCI capability available to the MIGs by a dramatic improvement in our own capability if we are to get on top of the MIG problem."[47] The relevant information had long been secured in intelligence channels but kept away from the very pilots who desperately needed the warning and situation awareness that this system would deliver. Teaball was operational by early August, and, though hamstrung by complex and limited communications capabilities that reduced its reliability, it proved an important factor in reducing the air force's loss rate in the air-to-air arena.[48]

Ryan directed a second change to operations that reflected his concern over the Seventh Air Force's slow advance up the learning curve. Ultimately, the deepest cause of concern to Ryan and Clay was the command's failure to correct what they viewed as serious errors in planning, coordination, and execution that were frequently repeated across the elements of the Linebacker strike packages. Ryan therefore ordered the command to hold face-to-face poststrike debriefs, with every wing that contributed to a mission sending representatives. Gathering these men from all over Indochina was a logistics nightmare, and naturally participants were initially reluctant to air their dirty laundry in this open forum. But the benefits of these conferences were so clear that the meetings soon grew to include members of the support packages and controllers as well. The discussions there fed back to the Seventh Air Force planners, leading to subtle but important shifts in mission planning that strengthened Linebacker's effectiveness. Combined with the inevitable growth in aircrew proficiency over time and the attrition that wore down the tiny NVAF, the balance of losses quickly swung in favor of the United States and would stay that way until the end of the war.

Vogt's work in that period was further complicated by having to plan and execute the continuing drawdown of the Seventh Air Force, part of the Americans' withdrawal from South Vietnam that continued even in this time of crisis. The reductions only made sense in light of election-year domestic politics, and they continued regardless of how the loss of personnel might complicate combat operations. The Seventh Air Force staff decreased from twelve hundred men to five hundred and, coincident with General Abrams's departure, officially merged with MACV on July 1.

Vogt finally obtained the MACV deputy commander assignment that he had asked Nixon to bestow months earlier. Equally important, at that same time General Weyand succeeded Abrams as commander of MACV. Vogt had a close and trusted relationship with Weyand, both personally and professionally, and the lingering strains of working with Abrams vanished. Vogt had two offices in the reorganized MACV headquarters—one for his role as deputy COMUSMACV and the other for his role as commander of the Seventh Air Force, where he would do the bulk of his dictation. Vogt later considered his dual role to have been a mixed blessing:[49]

> I had to pick up duties which the Seventh Air Force commander before had not been required to do. For example, to hold tri-partite meetings with the Cambodians and South Vietnamese, which had previously been the function of the Deputy Commander here. . . . I spent a great deal of my time traveling around to the corps areas on matters that were strictly military command business rather than Seventh Air Force business. But I benefited by it too because I got, for the first time, a feel for what was going on with the South Vietnamese forces out in the field with the enemy, and I was able to contribute better in support of those activities since I knew more about them than the previous commanders had had a chance to find out.

So there was an increased effectiveness—there's no doubt about that. What I might say, then, is that in the ten months I've been here I've had one day off—I took one day off to go see my wife—on Christmas day—and I've worked every day, seven days a week, twenty hours a day to stay ahead of this thing.

By this time the air campaign was three months old, and the U.S. attacks and the North Vietnamese countermeasures both had been fully developed. A Central Intelligence Agency (CIA) analysis from early August summarized the balance that had been struck in this action-reaction cycle—essentially, the result was a stalemate, though one that favored the North Vietnamese. The NVA had managed to move their logistics system to the roads and rails extending from China, thus compensating for the loss of their ports. The bombing and mining had cut North Vietnam's imports in half, from about 6,100 tons per day to about 3,000 tons, but this tonnage level still met the north's requirements to feed the war effort and to sustain its already minimal level of economic activity. Moreover, by early August, as an NSC summary noted, "The degree of damage on the North has bottomed out; in fact, the North may be recovering in some ways."[50] The analysis took care to note, "The fact that physical damage levels has bottomed out does *not* mean the pain suffered isn't increasing. In fact the difficulties and discomforts will build over time. But it does indicate that if the North is in fact getting sufficient imports . . . we can't expect our air operations and mining to be crucial in [Politburo] policy decisions." The paper concluded with the ominous question, "Do we really have a strategy for our operations; what targets are they focusing on and why are the operations of the Seventh Air Force, SAC [Strategic Air Command], and the Navy [not] fully integrated?"

By that time, however, the stagnation in the NVA offensive in the south had begun to nudge the North Vietnamese toward genuine negotiations for the first time in the war. Nixon now needed an intense air operation both to serve as a bargaining chip in negotiations and to coerce the North Vietnamese into a settlement. By late July Nixon was concerned that he had "lost control" of the bombing, and he wanted the attacks intensified in the northern route packs. As usual this demand filtered down through Admiral Moorer. Always reluctant to tell his field commanders how to "suck eggs," in his phrase, Moorer broke that pattern with a message to the commander in chief of Pacific Command (CINCPAC) on

August 6, summarizing the White House's concerns and providing specific operational direction to the theater commander:

> You should note that the picture as seen from here is that a disproportionate share of the air effort is programmed in the NVN [North Vietnam] panhandle at the expense of targets in the northern route packages. To illustrate my point, less than 25 percent of the validated targets in RP [route package] V and VI have been struck. . . . While the need for strong interdiction operations in the lower route packages is certainly appreciated, the limited weight of effort against key targets in the northern area of NVN raises questions as to whether we are holding to our priorities.[51]

In response, Vogt and his staff developed a system that enabled two Linebacker missions a day, taking advantage of the reduced tempo now prevailing in the ground fighting in the south. Through August, however, the unworkable weather continued to constrain the air offensive in the northern route packs.

As always in such situations, Vogt looked toward a technological solution, and this time he had the long-range area navigation (LORAN) system developed by the Coast Guard. The LORAN system, which measured signal time differences from three ground stations to determine aircraft position, was now pressed into service for bombing in instrument conditions. Vogt inherited the program that his predecessor in command, General Lavelle, had developed, so he emphasized it, expecting orders to continue the air campaign through the winter. LORAN yielded acceptable results in the south and in Laos, where the transmitting stations were relatively close and the antiaircraft defenses were less formidable than those in the North Vietnamese heartland. An area bombardment system at best, it was highly unreliable in bad weather and with aircraft maneuvers and had a limited range. As it was the only apparent solution, however, Vogt continued to press for its use.[52]

While NVA counters stymied operations in the North Vietnamese heartland, air attacks through North Vietnam's panhandle were far less constrained by weather, fuel limitations, and enemy defenses, and the results favored the American air forces. Through the summer Vogt and the Seventh Air Force poured sorties into the areas immediately north of the key battlefield along the DMZ, devastating the flow of NVA forces and logistics toward the grinding battle around Quang Tri. Once they fully overwhelmed NVA offensives in the other two sectors, Vogt increasingly focused his air effort on supporting the ARVN counteroffensive toward the DMZ. Finally, in mid-September, this effort enabled the South Vietnamese to retake the rubble that was once Quang Tri. That battlefield victory translated into a turn on the diplomatic front that would finally move the war toward a resolution.

TURNING ON BOTH SIDES: LINEBACKER II

As the NVA offensive crested in late June, the Politburo met in Hanoi to review the state of the war and the negotiations. Deciding that the NVA had gained as much as it ever would through its offensive and hoping to take advantage of the American election to gain concessions from Nixon, the Politburo resolved for the first time to move "toward the peace path."[53] From that point, Kissinger and Le Duc Tho gradually converged on a settlement and on October 8, 1972, the North Vietnamese, in a dramatic breakthrough, agreed to an arrangement that would leave Thieu in power. A feverish round of meetings followed, culminating in an agreed text between the North Vietnamese and the Americans on October 17.

It was an astonishingly rapid conclusion to the negotiations after four years of complete stagnation. The question remaining was whether President Nguyen Van Thieu and the South Vietnamese would accept a solution that left the NVA in position in South Vietnam and provided political legitimacy to the Communist front organization in South Vietnam. Kissinger met with Thieu in Saigon from October 20 to 23, hoping to gain his agreement, but the discussions were a nearly complete disaster. Thieu absolutely rejected Kissinger's terms, demanding the NVA forces' complete withdrawal from the south and refusing to accept the settlement's political terms. The only saving grace was that Thieu agreed not to go public with his position. His intransigence left Kissinger with the painful task of reopening negotiations with the North Vietnamese and seeking some middle ground between these two Vietnamese parties divided by decades of war, even though both sides now completely distrusted him.

Kissinger and Le Duc Tho met in November and again in December. No amount of diplomatic legerdemain could overcome the visceral hatred separating North and South Vietnam or bridge their irreconcilable war aims. Nixon and Kissinger found themselves trapped between the Vietnamese parties. While the Americans desperately needed a settlement, they were unable to budge Thieu toward agreement. On November 30, Nixon gathered the JCS for the first time that year with two goals in mind. First, he needed to outline the peace agreement to the chiefs to ensure their acquiescence and support. Second, he needed them to prepare military plans for either a North Vietnamese violation of the peace accords or a breakdown in negotiations. These plans would call for overwhelming force applied to the North Vietnamese heartland in Hanoi and Hai Phong.

Kissinger returned for another round of talks with Tho beginning on December 4. On December 7, as negotiations stalled, Haig drafted the conceptual framework to guide operational planning for a last-roll-of-the-dice air offensive. His remarkable document was also a remarkable basis for military planning. Explicitly rejecting military considerations for operational planning, Haig specified that the campaign would focus on psychological outcomes:[54]

> The strike plan . . . must be so configured as to create the most massive shock effect in a psychological context. There is to be no dissipation of effort through scattered attacks against a number of varied targets, but rather a clear concentration of effort against essential national assets designed to achieve psychological as well as strategic effects. . . . We cannot permit purely military considerations such as long-term interdiction, etc. to dominate the targeting philosophy. Attacks which are launched when the weather permits must be massive and brutal in character. No other criteria [sic] is acceptable and no other conceptual approach will be countenanced.

A week later, on December 14, Nixon, Kissinger, and Haig gathered in the Oval Office to review the situation. Kissinger, having arrived from Paris, reported on the frustrating tactics of the North Vietnamese and the stalemate that now existed. Thieu was still obstinately resisting the settlement despite all the Americans' promises, threats, and blandishments. Moreover, Thieu felt the choices before him were between a rapid defeat for his nation if he rejected the settlement and a slower death if he accepted it.

Only one option remained: as Kissinger phrased it, they had to "turn on both sides," imposing the full weight of American power on both Vietnamese parties to force a settlement. Nixon would send SAC's B-52s in a crushing assault on downtown Hanoi while threatening Saigon with an imminent shutoff of American military, economic, and diplomatic support. For Nixon, it was a desperate gamble that he had fervently hoped to avoid. In the media, he came under attack for conducting "warfare by tantrum," but more accurately it was warfare by lack

Gen. Carl A. Spaatz. *Courtesy Air Force Historical Studies Office*

Gen. Carl A. Spaatz. *Courtesy Air Force Historical Studies Office*

Gen. George C. Kenney. *Courtesy Air Force Historical Studies Office*

Gen. George C. Kenney. *Courtesy Air Force Historical Studies Office*

Gen. Otto P. Weyland. *Courtesy Air Force Historical Studies Office*

Gen. Curtis E. LeMay. *Courtesy Air Force Historical Studies Office*

Gen. Curtis E. LeMay. *Courtesy Air Force Historical Studies Office*

Lt. Gen. William H. Tunner. *Courtesy Air Force Historical Studies Office*

Lt. Gen. William H. Tunner. *Courtesy Air Force Historical Studies Office*

Lt. Gen. George E. Stratemeyer. *Courtesy Air Force Historical Studies Office*

Lt. Gen. George E. Stratemeyer. *Courtesy Air Force Historical Studies Office*

Gen. William W. Momyer (left) with Gen. Bruce K. Holloway.
Courtesy Air Force Historical Studies Office

Gen. William W. Momyer (left) with Gen. John P. McConnell.
Courtesy Air Force Historical Studies Office

Gen. William W. Momyer. *Courtesy Air Force Historical Studies Office*

Gen. John W. Vogt Jr. *Courtesy Air Force Historical Studies Office*

Chuck Horner at Shaw AFB taking to his crew after a mission in his F-16 before the war, 1990. *Courtesy Air Force Historical Studies Office*

Chuck Horner in Riyadh, Saudi Arabia, immediately after the war in March 1991, talking to some crew members about their experiences. *Courtesy Air Force Historical Studies Office*

Chuck Horner, University of West Florida, 2002. *Courtesy Gen. Charles A. Horner*

Chuck Horner with his wife, Mary Jo, London, 2004.
Courtesy Gen. Charles A. Horner

Capt. Mike E. Ryan (right) and his brother, Capt. Jack Ryan (left), with their father, Gen. John D. Ryan, at Udorn Air Base in Thailand in 1968. The brothers were flying combat missions, primarily over North Vietnam. General Ryan was the Commander of the Pacific Air Forces and later the 7th Chief of Staff of the USAF. *Courtesy USAF*

Col. Mike E. Ryan, the 432nd Wing Commander delivering the first F-16 to Misawa Air Base, Japan, in 1985 during the Cold War build-up in the Pacific. *Courtesy USAF*

Gen. Michael E. Ryan, USAF Chief of Staff, October 1997 to September 2001. *Courtesy USAF*

Lt. Gen. Mike E. Ryan, Commander Air South/Sixteenth Air Force at Aviano Air Base, Italy, after an F-16 mission over Bosnia. *Courtesy USAF*

Mike Short in Saudi Arabia the night his wing flew attack missions against Iraq in response to no fly zone violations, January 1993. *Courtesy Gen. Michael C. Short*

Michael Short with his daughter Jennifer when she was a student at navigator school, May 1995. *Courtesy Gen. Michael C. Short*

The Short family at Davis-Monthan AFB, Arizona, July 1996—both General Short and son Chris were undergoing A-10 training—from the right General Short, daughter Jennifer (en route to Survival School after completion of NAV school), General Short's wife, Jini, daughter-in-law Brooke, granddaughter Emily, and son Chris. *Courtesy Gen. Michael C. Short*

Michael Short in the aircraft of the Bulgarian chief of the air force during his visit to Sofia, December 1998. *Courtesy Gen. Michael C. Short*

Michael Short with son Chris preparing to fly A-10s, Spangdahlem Air Base, March 1998. *Courtesy Gen. Michael C. Short*

Capt. T. Michael Moseley, F-15 weapons officer and instructor pilot, Twelfth Tactical Fighter Squadron, Eighteenth Tactical Fighter Wing, Osan Air Base, Republic of Korea, 1982. *Courtesy Gen. T. Michael Moseley*

Lt. Col. T. Michael Moseley, F-15 squadron commander, USAF Fighter Weapons School, Nellis AFB, Nevada, flying F-15 Eagle, 1988. *Courtesy Gen. T. Michael Moseley*

CAOC, Prince Sultan Air Base, Saudi Arabia—receiving President Bush's order to execute Operation Iraqi Freedom on March 19, 2003. From left to right: Group Capt. Geoff Brown (RAAF), Gen. Tommy Franks (commander of U.S. Central Command), Lt. Gen. T. Michael Moseley (Combined Forces Air Component commander) and Air Vice Marshall Glenn Torpy (RAF). *Courtesy Gen. T. Michael Moseley*

Commanders of U.S. Central Command at Saddam Hussein's palace, Baghdad, April 16, 2003, immediately after liberation of the city. From left to right: Vice Adm. Tim Keating (U.S. Navy), Lt. Gen. Buzz Moseley (US Air Force), Gen. Tommy Franks (U.S. Army), Lt. Gen. Earl Hailston (U.S. Marine Corps), Brig. Gen. Gary Harrell (U.S. Army), and Lt. Gen. David McKiernan (U.S. Army). *Courtesy Gen. T. Michael Moseley*

General Moseley, officiating at arrival ceremony for the first F-22 Raptor delivered to Seventh Fighter Squadron, Forty-Ninth Fighter Wing, Holloman AFB, New Mexico, 2008. *Courtesy Gen. T. Michael Moseley*

Gen. T. Michael Moseley, USAF Chief of Staff, September 2005 to July 2008.

of any apparent alternative. He was reluctant to order the bombing, well aware of the domestic political price he would pay, but he believed that the relentless march of events had left him without other options.[55]

That day Moorer called Vogt in Saigon, and the two conducted a conversation uncannily similar to the phone calls in early May on the eve of the Linebacker campaign. Moorer wanted to give Vogt advance notice of the administration's thinking and to exchange ideas about targeting. Confident in the progress that he had seen in the LORAN system, Vogt assured Moorer, "We can hit any tacair target right now regardless of the weather because we have the coordinates all worked out up there. . . . We'll be ready and we'll work out the problem . . . if you decide to send us ahead of time we're ready to go." And, as in May, Vogt proposed targets: "I got some plans for the Power Station right in town and Railroad Station right down town and, from a psychological point of view, it would have the maximum impact . . . lots of supplies and it is a good, legitimate target right down town."

Using the cover story of an intense operation in the NVN panhandle, Vogt directed his staff and the wings to begin planning the operation; however, he and his planners at all levels were stymied by the lack of any data from SAC, where operational planning for the offensive was now under way. The air force planning for the support packages therefore followed the templates established in earlier B-52 raids in the North Vietnamese panhandle.

SAC planners had worked intensively since August on a target list that would take the bombers over Hanoi. But SAC's planning showed little feel for the realities of conventional warfare in Indochina, which was perhaps not surprising in view of SAC's location half a world away from the fight. Given the technical complexities of the attack, SAC focused its attention on the radar returns and offset aim points that the United States would use in its targeting, rather than on the enemy defenses that they would face in this offensive.[56] There was never an attempt to conduct joint planning of the attacks—planning that would synchronize the B-52s, air force and navy support packages, and intelligence packages. Instead, SAC turned out a plan deeply influenced by its nuclear heritage, rigid and inflexible, with little regard for the opponent's likely defensive measures. These factors were compounded by SAC's protracted planning and maintenance cycles, all of which locked the offensive into a stereotyped, predictable attack pattern over the first few days of Linebacker II. The North Vietnamese air defenders, fighting on their home ground, could assess and adjust their operations in a matter of hours.

They were operating well within the Americans' decision cycle, and the results showed as the operation progressed.[57]

That situation was bad enough for the SAC units, but it was murderous for the support packages. The Seventh Air Force played a supporting role in Linebacker II, but it was a complex and vital role nonetheless. Vogt was responsible for the escort packages protecting the B-52s and for the F-111 airfield attacks that would suppress the MiG-21 threat. Moreover, while the command supported operations throughout the night, it also conducted day strike missions designed to keep the pressure on the enemy all day, every day. It was an early form of the "hyperwar" concept that became famous nearly twenty years later in Operation Desert Storm.

The planning problems originating in Omaha played havoc with planning for the escort aircraft. Vogt's crews were receiving their taskings at step time (the time the crews depart the squadron operations facility) for their missions—missions that would take them into the most heavily defended area in the world, at night, in bad weather, and in incomprehensibly complex attack forces. Vogt addressed this problem a few days into the campaign, as losses mounted and pressures rose, and sent a message to the SAC commander, complaining that "often we receive final information on ingress, egress, spacing between cells, etc. after our frag should have been disseminated. This severely constrains us in planning optimum tactics, and the end result is that the Wings have inadequate time to prepare for their missions."[58] Right before Christmas, CINCPAC delegated coordinating authority for the strikes to the Seventh Air Force, giving Vogt the formal authority he needed to ensure effective mission planning.

In a general sense, during Linebacker II the air force again went through the painful and expensive climb up the learning curve that it had undertaken in the first phase of Linebacker II. Many of the problems encountered in May and June—confusion on the tankers, saturated communications, no common call signs, predictable operations, and late frag orders—had also plagued the first attacks in Linebacker.[59] The operation hit its low point during the raids on December 20–21. It was the third night of the attacks and the third night in which the B-52s had followed the same timing, routes, and altitudes in their approach to Hanoi. The NVA air defenders had sharpened their techniques and overcome their fear of the B-52s, and they shot down three bombers in the first wave. The news of these losses, coming after a loss-free night on Day 2, sent shock waves through the American chain of command all the way to Washington. Moorer talked with Gen. John C. Meyer, the SAC chief of staff, in Omaha and then with Vogt in Saigon. Nobody could be sure how the North Vietnamese success rate had escalated so quickly. Were these optical launches enabled by a moonlit night or a new radar tracking technique or a breakdown in the chaff protection? Given this uncertainty, Vogt recommended to Moorer that the strike force abort the entire second wave of attacks—a rare misstep on Vogt's part. Moorer later noted that aborting this strike would have been "disastrous," basically conceding the NVA a victory in this war of perceptions. Meyer made the decision to abort two cells of bombers going into Hanoi, and the other attacks proceeded as planned.

In time the operation righted itself. On December 26, after a one-day stand-down for Christmas, 126 B-52s executed a raid that was elegant in concept, flawless in execution, and brutal in effect. From that point the B-52 loss rate declined, as the North Vietnamese faced missile shortages and the B-52s moved to targets outside the North Vietnamese heartland. Meanwhile, the Seventh Air Force conducted less-noticed daytime strikes, which succeeded despite the weather and the NVA. The Seventh used LORAN for most attacks and took advantage of brief intervals of good weather to send LGB-armed Phantoms against power plants in Hanoi. Postwar assessments concluded that Vogt's confidence in the LORAN system's capability over the Red River Valley was wildly excessive, however; a PACAF history described the LORAN bombing as "totally nonproductive." Despite its limitations, though, the LORAN system provided an essential means of keeping pressure on the enemy in bad weather situations and, perhaps more important, of sustaining the sortie count that the president demanded.[60]

After some diplomatic skirmishing, Kissinger and Le Duc Tho agreed to resume negotiations, and Linebacker II drew to a close on December 28. Operations continued in the North Vietnamese panhandle, as Nixon resolutely refused to repeat Johnson's error of halting the bombing before the North Vietnamese offered reciprocal concessions. Finally, in late January, Thieu collapsed under the weight of American pressure and agreed to the peace settlement although he was fully aware that this arrangement would not bring peace but an extended war.

Through this final phase of the war, while directing Seventh Air Force operations, Vogt was deeply involved in defining the postwar American force structure in Indochina. Well aware of the fragile nature of the peace, Nixon directed the air force to leave substantial forces in Thailand and maintain a visible readiness to resume operations over either North or South Vietnam. An extended skirmish took place in the joint arena over the command and control for the postwar presence, with the army supporting a subunified command headquartered in Thailand and Moorer and Vogt supporting a less visible footprint in theater. In the end, Vogt's views won out, and he took command of the successor to MACV, the U.S. Support and Assistance Group. From there he directed the continuing air operations in Cambodia until Congress mandated an end to American air action in August 1973.[61]

That October Vogt moved to command of PACAF, and in June 1974 he went to Europe to take command of U.S. Air Forces Europe (USAFE), becoming the only man ever to command both PACAF and USAFE. Upon his arrival, he was shocked to find that none of the technological advances he had encouraged in Southeast Asia had been adopted in Europe. There was no fusion center, no computerized mission planning, and not even a single laser-guided weapon in theater.[62] He set about moving the alliance toward implementing these systems, but he ran out of time before he could make major inroads in this huge project.

Given his pivotal role in ending the Vietnam War, Vogt felt he had earned Nixon's support to succeed Moorer as CJCS. In the rotation system then used, the air force would hold the CJCS position next, and, as he viewed it, no one else had better served the White House in its efforts to close out America's involvement in the war. Instead, Kissinger offered Vogt the job as chief of staff of the air force. Vogt was skeptical about Kissinger's making the offer and was completely uninterested in the position, which Vogt considered merely administrative in nature. Meanwhile, Gen. George S. Brown got the nod for CJCS. Vogt then heard talk of his becoming the commander in chief of Pacific Command, taking over a command that had been a navy prerogative since the advent of the unified command system. Vogt had little confidence that this would be possible, given the inter-service politics involved, and so he decided to retire. He filed his papers and returned to the United States without even holding a retirement ceremony. He retired on August 31, 1975.[63]

The next year Vogt participated in the "Team B" analytical effort, joining Paul Nitze, Paul Wolfowitz, and other colleagues from the policy community in assessing the CIA's evaluations of the strategic balance over the preceding years. Later he played a minor role as a policy adviser in Ronald Reagan's presidential campaign in 1980. In that same period, William Shawcross published *Sideshow: Nixon, Kiss-*

inger, and the Destruction of Cambodia, a passionate attack on the spread of the Vietnam War to Cambodia and that country's subsequent descent into genocide.[64] Vogt entered the controversy, defending the American air offensive's targeting, accuracy, and effectiveness against the accounts of civilian casualties and widespread collateral damage. Vogt's last publication, "A Commander's View of the Vietnam War," presented his attempt to shape the historical narrative of the conflict.[65] In his later retirement he lived quietly in Melbourne, Florida, until his death on April 16, 2010.

SUMMARY

John Vogt will stand out in the history of air operations for his role in the technological revolution that dawned under his command. Vogt was enthusiastic about technology and aggressive in its application, though sometimes he was too optimistic in his expectations of what it could accomplish given its limitations at the time. He shaped the Linebacker attack packages around the few laser designation pods available, building complex, layered attack packages to exploit this new capability. Like so many airmen both before and after his time, Vogt was frustrated by the inability to attack in bad weather and worked hard to develop the blind bombing capability of the LORAN system. Success lay beyond the technology of the early 1970s, and the air force had to await the joint direct attack munition guidance kit before it could meet this requirement. Similarly, Vogt tried to lash up acoustic sensors to detect and target the NVA's 130mm guns, which dominated the battlefield along the DMZ. This effort, too, failed. While not nearly as effective as Vogt later claimed, the Teaball intelligence fusion center did play a role in reducing the air force's losses to MiGs in the later months of Linebacker.[66] The seeds planted in Linebacker, and nurtured by Vogt, grew over time to form the technologies that would define attack aviation for the succeeding decades.

Vogt had little to do with shaping the theater strategy or even the air strategy to be pursued. Those plans originated in the White House, as Nixon, Kissinger, and Haig increasingly concentrated decision making in their own hands. It is remarkable, in fact, that each of the air offensives conducted in 1972 reflected the personalities and the philosophies of power of their primary architects. Freedom Train, the initial response to the NVA invasion in April, was all Kissinger: incremental, tightly controlled, centrally orchestrated. Linebacker was Nixon, calling for the relentless application of brute force, month after month, tied to a negotiated settlement. As negotiations stagnated in December 1972, Alexander Haig's unflinching advocacy for the maximum use of force stiffened both Nixon and Kissinger and, in the end, led to the waves of B-52s striking the North Vietnamese heartland, night after night, in Linebacker II.

Linebacker never achieved Nixon's vision of a cataclysmic, overwhelming offensive to shatter North Vietnam and bring his enemy to his knees. Nor did it achieve its more mundane goal of isolating North Vietnam from its sources of supply in China and the Soviet Union. Some dramatic successes have defined the historical memory of the campaign: dropping the Paul Doumer Bridge in Hanoi, taking down the Thanh Hoa Bridge further south, and executing precision strikes on the North Vietnamese power grid. But North Vietnam's counters to these and dozens of similar attacks were sufficient to continue bringing supplies into the country and moving them toward the battle area in the south.

It was on the southern battlefields that Vogt's forces achieved their greatest military effect. Throughout the war, Communist forces had relied on dispersion and deception to nullify the massive firepower and mobility of American air forces. In the Easter Offensive, the NVA was forced to concentrate its forces and to settle into linear or siege warfare on all three fronts. In that setting, American air power exerted a devastating impact. Taking a longer view, this strategy had the damaging effect of reconfirming the South Vietnamese Air Force's reliance on massive air support, which would not be forthcoming after America's withdrawal from the war. But that problem lay in the future. The immediate problem was to stabilize the battlefield, to preserve South Vietnam, and to avoid the terrible strategic and political costs of failure. Air power delivered in that time of crisis.

Another, more experienced commander might have taken control of the Seventh Air Force in the early days of the Linebacker campaign and driven the command more rapidly toward tactical proficiency. Clay, for example, had already commanded the Seventh Air Force, and he could have stepped in quickly and aggressively and possibly addressed the problems in tactical performance that hindered Seventh Air Force operations early in the campaign. But neither Clay nor anyone else could replace the easy relationship that Vogt enjoyed with Moorer, and nobody else in the air force enjoyed the confidence of the White House.

Through this climactic year of the war, Vogt was among only three American military members who worked effectively with Nixon and his inner circle. Haig served effectively as the principal military adviser to the president, as the JCS entirely lost their influence with the National Command Authority. Admiral Moorer served the White House in orchestrating the execution of decisions reached there, and in ensuring that senior operational commanders understood the president's objectives and sense of urgency. Vogt was the White House's man on the scene, trusted to ensure the war effort met the president's demands. He sustained that trust through eight turbulent months, despite the failure of the Linebacker air offensive to meet the White House's expectations. It was a remarkable achievement.

PART III

9

CHARLES A. HORNER:
DESERT STORM MAESTRO

Richard P. Hallion

In February 1991, when the American-led Coalition ejected Saddam Hussein's military forces from Kuwait, taking eighty-seven thousand prisoners and leaving images of shattered buildings, ruptured aircraft shelters, exploded tanks, and broken bridges, it signaled a new stage in the evolution of military operations and capabilities. Afterward President George H. W. Bush, himself a World War II naval aviator, told graduates at the 1991 commencement of the Air Force Academy that "Gulf Lesson One is the value of air power."[1]

The teacher of that lesson was Desert Storm's Joint and Combined Force Air Component commander, then–Lt. Gen. Charles "Chuck" Horner. As the Coalition's air power concertmaster, Horner oversaw the planning and execution of the air campaign. Higher commanders' postwar assessments supported the centrality of his contribution. "Chuck was the man who integrated the thousands of aircraft, U.S. and allied alike, into one integrated theater air campaign [that constituted] the most devastating employment of air power since the introduction of aircraft into warfare," wrote Gen. H. Norman Schwarzkopf. Further, he added, "Lt. Gen. Horner's outstanding leadership and warrior spirit contributed immeasurably to the overall success and superior performance of our air forces during the Gulf War. His commanding presence, detailed planning, and inspirational leadership ensured the near flawless execution of every phase of Operations Desert Shield and Desert Storm. . . . He's the kind of warrior we need leading our Air Forces."[2]

Lt. Gen. Sir Peter de la Billière, commander of the United Kingdom's forces, recalled:

After Schwarzkopf, the American whose ability I admired most was Chuck Horner, the Air Force general. With his slouching posture, his crumpled bloodhound face and his habit of cussing and swearing, he neither looked nor sounded much like a top-class officer; but his professional ability was phenomenal. He knew his aircraft and his pilots inside out, and the plan for the air war which he worked out with his assistant Brigadier General Buster Glosson (another Vietnam veteran) was nothing short of a masterpiece.[3]

THE MAKING OF A CITIZEN-AIRMAN

Desert Storm marked the pinnacle of Horner's progression from combat pilot to combat leader. Charles Horner was born in 1936 into a close-knit Iowa family imbued with strong traditions of faith, work, integrity, and duty. "I'm very confident in myself," he said. "I was a loner and I kind of raised myself."[4] As befit America's "golden age" of aviation, he built model airplanes and followed the exploits of famous aviators. During World War II, a cousin he idolized was killed piloting a bomber over Italy, forever in Horner's mind associating aviation with violent death. Later, a brother-in-law crashed during a post–Korean War training mission. Both tragedies strengthened rather than discouraged his interest in flying.[5]

Horner entered the University of Iowa in 1954, graduating in June four years later with a diploma and a commission as a second lieutenant in the U.S. Air Force (USAF) Reserve. An aggressive, confident airman, he never feared "washing out" of pilot training, just not getting assigned to fighters. In October 1960, he earned his wings and a fighter slot, transitioning into the F-100D Super Sabre and joining the 492nd Tactical Fighter Squadron at Lakenheath, England.[6]

While at Lakenheath, he had two close calls—an emergency night landing in fog and a near-collision caused by another pilot during a deployment to Wheelus Air Base, Libya. Horner was forced to take such violent evasive action that his fighter stalled, snap rolling and "mushing" toward earth in a nose-high attitude. Well outside survivable limits for his ejection seat, he fought to remain aloft, convinced, "I'm going to die out here in the shitty, nowhere desert, splattered like road-kill," leaving a pregnant widow.[7] Then he recalled another pilot had once saved an F-100 under similar circumstances by going into afterburner. The plane sank so low that he saw sand dunes passing on either side before he began climbing away. Already religious, he was convinced his survival signaled his life must revolve around "what God wanted me to do, not what I wanted to do."[8] Now a captain with a regular commission, he returned to the United States at the end of 1963, converting to the F-105 Thunderchief. Afterward he joined the Fourth Tactical Fighter Wing (TFW) at Seymour Johnson Air Force Base (AFB), North Carolina.

ROLLING THUNDER: HOW NOT TO EMPLOY AIR POWER

Affectionately known as the "Thud," the F-105 passed across the history of the air force as though it were a particularly spectacular meteor, which, even if quickly extinguished, nevertheless is remembered for the brilliance of its passage. Its crews flew deep into North Vietnam, braving surface-to-air missiles (SAMs), fighters, and intense antiaircraft fire.[9] "I think to understand the success of Desert Storm, you have to study Vietnam," Horner recalled after the Gulf War. "That's where the lessons were learned—you don't learn from success, you learn from failure, and we had plenty of failure in Vietnam to study, things like gradualism, things like not fighting a war decisively, things like not fully understanding the political goals, and limiting those goals within the military operations to the things the military can achieve."[10]

Horner and his comrades were sacrificial pawns in Rolling Thunder—the Johnson administration's efforts to use air power to send signals rather than achieve decisive effects.[11] Lacking a logical strategy and then shifting policy, President Lyndon Johnson, Defense Secretary Robert S. McNamara, and other senior administration officials crippled efficient target planning.[12] Micromanagement abounded, with the president bragging he oversaw targeting so closely that airmen couldn't "bomb the smallest outhouse . . . without checking with me."[13] A Joint Chiefs of Staff (JCS) history rightly concluded that "lacking an integrated and coherent political-military strategic foundation, the air campaign proceeded by fits and starts, sputtering most of the time."[14] Even in the military, the chain of command was convoluted, with the North divided into service-specific "route packages" that further frustrated any unified effort. Faulty prewar assumptions and institutional failures meant that most aircrews were inadequately trained and equipped, leading to disturbing losses.[15]

Horner went to Korat Royal Thai AFB in June 1965 for a six-month tour with the 388th TFW. His initiation to combat convinced him that "air war planning was being done by people far away from the theater of operations who had no appreciation for the realities" and that "a bunch of amateurs were running things."[16] He was lucky to survive. On July 27, 1965, Horner and twenty-three other pilots flew the first-ever anti-SAM mission, relying on high speed at low level for safety, and they encountered a flak trap. "The mission was just stupid," Horner recalled. "I couldn't believe it. We lost six airplanes that day."[17] He later added, "I concluded at that time that low-level attack was a loser"—a lesson he carried into Desert Storm.[18]

At the end of the year he left Thailand, having completed forty-one missions. By now, the air force had a SAM killer called the "Wild Weasel," a two-seat F-105F fighter with SAM radar- and launch-warning receivers, the radar-homing air-to-ground AGM-45 Shrike missile, and an electronic warfare officer.[19] Horner volunteered for Weasel school, returning to Korat in May 1967. While the counter-culture embarked on a dreamy "Summer of Love" in the United States, Thud fliers embarked on a harrowing Summer of Attrition. Eventually, 334 F-105Ds and Fs, with 353 crewmen, were shot down in Southeast Asia. Many airmen entered— and some perished during—brutal captivity.[20]

In June 1967, in marked contrast to Rolling Thunder, the Israeli Air Force showed what a properly conceived air campaign could achieve. In November, his leadership discredited even within the administration, McNamara announced his resignation, leaving office in February 1968. Rolling Thunder lasted another eight months.[21] By then Horner was back at Nellis AFB, Nevada. He had returned from Thailand in September 1967 and saw "how dysfunctional our operations were, how our leaders failed to work together and allowed agendas to come between the efforts of the various services." He recalled:[22]

> All of us in *Desert Storm* had memories of Vietnam and we were determined not to repeat the mistakes of that war. . . . I would accept information and advice from any source, but I maintained strict control of targeting. Rules of engagement were formulated in a manner so that a captain could remember them when getting shot at, and did not risk our lives needlessly. In Vietnam answers that did not please Washington or even higher headquarters were unacceptable, so we lied. . . . We simply told the headquarters what they wanted to hear. The effect was corrosive. We lost integrity, the only thing that really matters to the military.[23]

MOMYER, CREECH, AND THE MAKING OF AN AIR COMMANDER

In the years after Vietnam, the air force underwent great transformation.[24] In late 1969 Horner joined the planning staff at Langley's Tactical Air Command (TAC), which was then commanded by Lt. Gen. William "Spike" Momyer. Fresh from commanding the Seventh Air Force, Momyer was outspoken about the top-down Pentagon-centric direction that had fatally hobbled Rolling Thunder, and he often drew upon this and other historical examples while mentoring junior officers, such as Horner, who enthusiastically absorbed it all.[25] More influential still was Momyer's successor (once removed), Gen. Wilbur Creech. A formidable personality, similar in stature to Gen. Curtis LeMay, Creech exemplified TAC as LeMay had embodied Strategic Air Command (SAC).[26] After taking charge in 1978, the heart of the "Hollow Force" years, he set out to destroy overcentralization and bureaucratic inefficiency. He emphasized integrity and personal responsibility; inculcated a culture that stressed decentralized control, empowerment, and personal initiative; and mentored gifted subordinates, Horner among them.[27]

Horner got to know Creech after he returned to the Fourth TFW in 1976.[28] Not initially a Creech fan, he soon "became one of his biggest advocates," as he was impressed by the TAC commander's approach to leadership, discipline, training, and operational efficiency.[29] For Creech, integrity was paramount. He had no time for commanders who ruled through intimidation, who distorted unit performance, or who abused their position. Remembering his own origins in the enlisted force, he never forgot his airmen, making certain commanders took care of their people.[30] Like Horner subsequently, he tolerated good-faith error. "He always forgave honest mistakes, as long as you only made them *once*," Horner noted. "Subordinates need to be encouraged to admit their mistakes so all can learn from their experience. . . . In Desert Storm we accepted the fact that we would make mistakes [therefore] aircrews were encouraged to admit mistakes when things had gone wrong, then we got the word out so that we could preclude others from duplicating the errors."[31]

Creech's desire to improve readiness led him to create the Combat-Oriented Maintenance Organization and the Combat-Oriented Supply Organization.[32] He reestablished the authority of crew chiefs, who now effectively "owned" their aircraft and were empowered to make all decisions affecting their planes' maintenance and servicing. He replaced bureaucratic shuffling with commonsense solutions. At the wing and squadron levels, Horner recalled, we practiced, we exercised, and we modified organizations and procedures. Most of all we got better and better and it surprised everyone when our efforts made a very complex difficult operation called Desert Storm look easy [where] in-commission rates were in the high 90% and those who were not ready to fly were being repaired from battle damage or being serviced after landing. All of this was the result of years of practice, organization and planning that Bill Creech brought to the Air Force.[33]

By the time Creech retired from TAC in 1985, Horner had earned the reputation as TAC's "fireman," or someone who was brought in to fix troubled units. When Gen. Robert Russ succeeded Creech as TAC commander, he brought Horner, now a major general, back to Langley as deputy chief of staff for plans.[34] Horner's subsequent experience participating in various joint exercises and planning hardened his belief that air operations should be controlled by a single air commander. While not "an air power *über alles* kind of guy," he believed under the right circumstances it could have decisive effect.[35] He reflected later, "It really bothered me that airmen in the past and during my career had not been able to date get their arms around the management of the air."[36]

In 1987, Lt. Gen. William "Bill" Kirk left his position as the Ninth Air Force and U.S. Central Command Air Forces (CENTAF) commander to take over U.S. Air Forces in Europe (USAFE). Into his place, promoted to lieutenant general, stepped Chuck Horner. Aged fifty-one and still routinely pulling 9Gs while flying various types of air combat sorties against pilots scarcely half his age, he was approaching his moment in history's spotlight.[37]

PREPARING TO CONFRONT THE IRAQI THREAT

In 1979, the shah of Iran had fallen from power, triggering a decade of unrest in the Persian Gulf. In response, the Pentagon formed a rapid deployment force, which evolved into U.S. Central Command (CENTCOM), which was established on January 1, 1983, and headquartered at MacDill AFB, Florida.[38] CENTAF constituted the winged sword of CENTCOM.[39] Horner's predecessor had convinced Gen. George Crist, the then–commander in chief of CENTCOM (CINCCENT), to employ a joint force air component commander (JFACC) as a single air commander.[40] Crist was commendably supportive of joint operations; given his Marine Corps roots, he could easily have rejected the suggestion. Indeed, while he accepted the idea, as a group CENTCOM's Leathernecks did not. Consequently, Horner "had an ongoing fight with the Central Command Marine Corps at every exercise."[41]

After the army's H. Norman Schwarzkopf became CINCCENT, he continued the JFACC practice. Schwarzkopf and Horner crafted a frank, mutually trusting relationship. "He really was a profound individual," said Horner, "very smart, one who appreciated what air could do for everyone."[42]

In November 1989, fresh from a visit to Kuwait, Schwarzkopf called a meeting with Horner.[43] The Warsaw Pact was crumbling, the Berlin Wall was rubble, and the Joint Chiefs were still focused on a possible Soviet threat to Iran. Instead, he was "really concerned" about Saddam Hussein, debt ridden and with a "huge" military. Horner remembers Schwarzkopf saying, "He's sitting right next to the world's largest bank in Kuwait and Saudi Arabia. We're no longer going to fight the Russians, we've got to keep an eye on Iraq." Horner said okay and when he asked who would be the land component commander, Schwarzkopf said he would. To which Horner responded,

Okay. Now I want *you* to understand something: I'm going to talk to you in a way that you're not going to like, because you're going to be ground-centric and you'll want to do things that are stupid, and I'm going to tell you they're stupid. Then you can put on your Unified Commander hat, your Joint Force Commander hat, and after you decide what you're going to do, I'll obey. But when we're in the *planning* or *thinking* stages, I'm going to talk to you as a *ground* commander counterpart.[44]

Horner and his staff immediately set to work.[45] By April 1990 they had fleshed out a three-phased approach. First, they would establish an air defense and power-projection deterrent, using the existing Saudi air defense system architecture and the Saudis' E-3 Airborne Warning and Control System (AWACS) aircraft. Second, if Iraq invaded, they would delay and attrit its mechanized forces. Finally, they would support a counteroffensive. The approach stipulated attacks on airfields, chemical weapons storage facilities, Scud launch sites, refineries and power plants, and transportation choke points.[46]

Horner warned Schwarzkopf that since Hussein had chemical and biological weapons (CBW) and possibly nuclear ones, he wanted to develop a "list of strategic targets" that could deter the dictator's possible recourse to such weapons—words that came back to haunt him only four months later.[47] Remembering a previous war game where Scud-like missiles "were just driving us out of our gourd," Horner conceptualized using the army's Patriot SAMs to counter them, even though the Patriot was regarded primarily as an antiaircraft, not antimissile, system.[48] Working within the existing Saudi air defense architecture offered another benefit, Horner thought; that is, they could retain the unity of the Coalition's air effort. "If the Americans went in and built their own architecture, then the Marines could carve out a piece of it and say 'this is Marine air space.'"[49]

Anticipating both the "very fluid" nature of any likely war and the "inclination of the corps commanders to try and tie up air" in anticipation that the army would need close air support (CAS), Horner came up with a scheme he called "Push CAS. " Inspired by the air campaign against Field Marshal Erwin Rommel's Afrika Korps, Horner reviewed its lessons and was convinced that he had to feed

> airplanes over the battlefield 24 hours a day, as much air as I could generate [with] a command and control network that would allow me to divert it where it needed to go. If there was no divert requirement, no meeting engagement by tanks-on-tanks, then I would just continue that sortie, and it would go on and strike a valid target; go back and land, rearm, and go again. So I always had my air employed: I didn't have the planes holding; I didn't have the planes waiting, tasking, or sitting on the ground idle. [Schwarzkopf] bought that 100 percent.[50]

In less than a year, Push CAS would work to deadly effect in Desert Storm.

In July, a CENTCOM war game called "Internal Look" modeled an Iraqi invasion of Kuwait, followed by an invasion of Saudi Arabia. The results were "bleak."[51] The analytical model used to assess results, TACWAR (tactical warfare), predicted Iraqi armor would inflict heavy casualties. But in retrospect it was TAC-WAR, not the plan, that had problems, underestimating the effects of U.S. weapons and overestimating the resilience of mechanized forces exposed to air attack. Unfortunately, TACWAR led Schwarzkopf to establish a 50 percent attrition goal for Iraqi units, an ultimately meaningless figure driven by an unrealistic combat model.[52] CENTCOM was still digesting the results of Internal Look when Hussein invaded Kuwait on August 2, 1990.

IMMEDIATE CHALLENGES: CREATING A COALITION
AND FRAMING A RESPONSE

Months before, Schwarzkopf had gone to Horner with a problem. Joint doctrine held that as the joint force commander in any conflict he was "supposed to apportion air," but, he confessed, he had "no idea how." Horner replied,

> Nobody knows how to apportion air. You can't do it. The Joint Force Commander needs to tell the JFACC what things have to be done to achieve specific goals. I will then (in cooperation with the other components) put together the best air plan, the Air Tasking Order, to accomplish what you want done. After we fly, we will count the sorties for close air support, for interdiction, for counter-air, and for any other mission categories. *That's* the way to apportion air. It's all *after the fact*. It's all accountants, recordkeeping. Anybody that says "well, we're going to do 30 percent close air support" and so on, is a damn idiot.[53]

Horner always favored ad hoc, pragmatic, "do what works" solutions rooted in an air commander's personal experience and common sense rather than passively accepting top-down-driven strategy and tactics emanating from the White House or the Pentagon. To Horner, air war planning demanded reliance upon basic, fundamental, historically rooted principles, not on doctrinal esoterica. Those principles included: gain control of the air; use air power to achieve decisive effects; do not divide or parcel out the air effort, either by geographic area or by military service; do not be slaves to a plan, and retain the ability to react to changing circumstances; carefully control targeting authority; and place air under a single air commander working for the theater commander.[54] These time-tested truths were fundamental, and to Horner the last factor was most important of all: assign a single air commander, the JFACC.[55]

Although the Bush administration condemned Iraq's invasion, key officials differed on what to do next. While Chairman of the JCS Gen. Colin Powell fretted over policy implications, Secretary of Defense Dick Cheney wanted to know "what carriers could be deployed, what air wings [could be] sent, how soon they could get there," and options and plans. Cheney reminisced afterward that "Powell seemed more comfortable talking about poll numbers than he was recommending military options."[56] Meanwhile, National Security Adviser Brent Scowcroft thought, "Now is the time to get the Saudis everything we have."[57] On August 4, Schwarzkopf and his component commanders flew to Camp David to brief the president.[58] There, in the rustic Laurel Lodge, Schwarzkopf emphasized the size and strength of Hussein's military, stressing that CENTAF's air power constituted "the option most immediately available." Horner promised four hundred aircraft in eleven days, adding that his airmen were "ready to go."[59]

But would Saudi Arabia's King Fahd permit American forces on Saudi soil? Bush feared Fahd might "strike some kind of behind-the-scenes arrangement with Saddam."[60] Saudi ambassador Bandar bin Sultan (a former fighter pilot) urged Cheney to "demonstrate to the king that you are serious," and so Cheney left for Saudi Arabia the next day, accompanied by Schwarzkopf, Horner, and other senior officials.[61] Powell remained in Washington; Cheney feared the chairman's hesitancy might reinforce that of Fahd. After strenuous discussions, Fahd agreed to accept American forces.

Schwarzkopf turned to Horner and said, "Chuck, start them moving."[62] When the question now arose regarding who would act as "CENTCOM Forward," Schwarzkopf selected the airman. "Please God," Horner thought, "keep me from screwing things up."[63]

On August 7, the First TFW at Langley AFB launched F-15Cs, which flew nonstop to Dhahran, air-refueling seven times en route. In addition, two DC-10s left Pope AFB, North Carolina, carrying 520 paratroopers from the Eighty-Second Airborne Division. Two days later, Margaret Thatcher ordered twenty-four Royal Air Force (RAF) Tornadoes and Jaguars to the Gulf.[64] The Coalition was gradually coming together. By the end of the first week, the USAF had deployed ten fighter squadrons to the Gulf, or double the initial estimates of the forces that could be sent in that time. "The squadrons of F-15 and F-16 fighter planes," Schwarzkopf recalled, "flowed to Saudi Arabia wonderfully."[65] In the first eighteen weeks, airlift moved almost three times the payload carried in the Berlin Airlift of 1948–1949.[66] "The challenges associated with the bed-down of the numbers of personnel and equipment were enormous, to say the least," Horner stated afterward.[67] It was a tempting target, and Schwarzkopf feared a surprise Iraqi attack that would cripple CENTCOM's growing air power. He challenged Horner: "Guarantee me that not one airplane is going to get through your air defense net." Horner serenely replied, "Not one airplane will get through. You don't have to worry about that."[68]

As a precaution he inspected air units, ordering at least one of them to disperse its aircraft with a stern, "This is not Red Flag!"[69]

As CENTAF commander, Horner worked "very hard . . . to fit my personality to my Joint Force Commanders, Generals Crist and Schwarzkopf, in order to be able to influence them in a meaningful way." He noted, "[Their] agenda became my agenda, and, as a result, [they] grew to depend on me in my area of expertise, air power." He regarded Crist and Schwarzkopf as "very intelligent leaders who, although they may not have had a lot of air power experience, knew a good thing when they heard or saw it." Horner told air force historians in 1992, "Schwarzkopf is a hero *because he did not want to spend a life unnecessarily of a single soldier*," a legacy of the army general's own Vietnam experience.[70] "I could convince him to accept strategies based on the fact that they would save soldier's lives," Horner recalled. "That is why during *Desert Storm* we were able to conduct an extensive air campaign *prior* to initiation of ground combat."[71] In particular, Schwarzkopf ordered that airmen pound Saddam Hussein's Republican Guard so that, by the time the ground war began, it would be severely degraded.

Beyond his relationship with Schwarzkopf, Horner enjoyed generally good relations with his fellow component commanders. "The four of us—Walt Boomer, Stan Arthur, John Yeosock, and myself," he said, "were like brothers. We would never try to do anything to one another."[72] Indeed, relations between Schwarzkopf and all his component commanders were arguably better than Schwarzkopf's relations as land component commander with his corps command-ers, who occasionally disagreed with the decisions "Stormin' Norman" made and who were also dubious as to Horner's ability to furnish the support they believed necessary.[73]

Horner adamantly opposed Vietnam-style "route packs," as Vice Adm. Henry H. Mauz Jr. (a "black shoe" officer, or surface-warfare non-aviator, then serving as commander of naval forces in Central Command) discovered when they met in August 1990. "'I've got a great idea,'" Horner recalled Mauz saying as they studied a map. "'What we'll do is, we'll divide Iraq up into route packages, and the Navy will take these.' I said to him, 'Admiral, if you try and pull that bullshit, I will retire before I'll agree to it.'"[74] Mauz's successor, Vice Adm. Stanley Arthur, a highly decorated "brown shoe" light attack pilot, impressed Horner more favor-ably because, as an aviator, he "fully appreciated the need for a single commander for air, no matter what service uniform he wore."[75]

Horner jealously controlled air campaign planning and was stunned when Schwarzkopf announced he would ask the Joint Staff to develop a "strategic" target list. Alarmed, Horner warned him not to let Washington run targeting. Schwarzkopf, while reassuring Horner that he was in charge of the air campaign, nevertheless went ahead and contacted Powell and the USAF vice chief of staff, Gen. John "Mike" Loh, on August 8, requesting a strategic target list and air plan.[76] Loh in turn contacted Maj. Gen. Minter Alexander, the director of plans, who gave the tasking to his deputy director for war-fighting concepts, Col. John A. Warden III.

Warden ran Checkmate, an Air Staff planning and analysis cell tucked unobtrusively among the labyrinthine basement corridors of the Pentagon.[77] A forward air controller in Vietnam, an F-4 and F-15 fighter pilot, and a historically minded air power strategist, he had written a widely read treatise on air campaigns. Hearing that Iraq had invaded Kuwait, he had abandoned a vacation cruise, returned to Washington, and tasked his staff to look at possible military options. Checkmate put together a plan called "Instant Thunder" (in pointed contrast to Rolling Thunder), a concept where a whirlwind of effects-based strategic air attacks would destroy Iraq's war-fighting capabilities. The air force chief of staff (CSAF), Gen. Michael Dugan, and General Loh cleared it for presentation to Schwarzkopf. But TAC's Gen. Robert Russ thought Instant Thunder, despite its name, smacked of the worst aspects of Rolling Thunder. As he stated later, "What starts as a little bit of help from the Pentagon soon leads to more and more 'help' and pretty soon you get the President in on it. . . . Then you have people in the White House sitting on the floor trying to figure out what targets they are going to hit."[78]

Schwarzkopf received Instant Thunder on August 10 and exclaimed, "I love it!" A day later, Warden briefed Powell, who requested more emphasis on attriting the Iraqi Army. Over several days the plan underwent further refinement, still without involving Horner or TAC. Warden presented the revised plan to Schwarzkopf at MacDill AFB, Florida, on August 17, and again the general enthused, ordering Warden to brief Horner in Riyadh.[79] Accordingly, Warden and some of his team flew to Saudi Arabia and briefed Horner and his staff on August 20.[80] Horner considered the briefing as Warden's "job interview" for campaign planner. He thought that Instant Thunder had "some really good thoughts" but faulted it for not addressing how to stop Iraq's tanks.[81] When pressed, Warden replied dismissively (as Horner recalled), "Don't worry about the ground forces. They are going to be demoralized and quit."[82] Unsatisfied, Horner kept probing, with no result. When the briefing ended, so, too, had any chance of Warden's becoming the planner of the air campaign. Horner sent him home but retained some of his team.[83]

Waiting eagerly in the wings was Brig. Gen. Buster Glosson, then deputy commander of Joint Task Force Middle East.[84] Glosson had been one of Horner's squadron commanders, impressing him as a "go-getter" and "hard task-master."[85] In turn, Glosson considered Horner "bright, tough, with good instincts."[86] Glosson had met Horner on August 17 and volunteered his help, writing afterward that "Horner [is] upset about planning activities in Washington, no more Vietnams, war will be planned and fought in theater. I totally understand this issue."[87] When Horner called, he abruptly ordered him, "Get your ass up here now."[88]

BUILDING A PLAN AND THE FORCE TO EXECUTE IT

The contretemps over Instant Thunder has obscured many other challenges Horner faced. One was establishing—and quickly!—a streamlined, flattened, smoothly functioning combat force. Depending on their type, Horner assigned incoming units to one of four air divisions—fighters, electronic combat, strategic (bombers and tankers), and airlift—each commanded by a brigadier general. Wing commanders reported to their division commander, who reported to Horner.[89] Coalition partners could organize their forces as they saw fit, but their air operations had to be integrated into the master attack plan and the daily air tasking order (ATO).[90]

Horner readily delegated to trusted associates, finding and empowering energetic people who could help him immediately address the challenges he faced.[91] "This is your problem, go solve it. I don't have time to focus on this," Glosson recalls Horner telling him (referring to the air campaign plan).[92] Reflecting later, Glosson noted:

> Looking back, I've often thought that probably no other person in uniform would have given me the freedom that he did. I don't think there's a parallel for that anywhere in the history of the USAF. . . . He let me have unprecedented freedom to plan, and ultimately to command the fighters, and still keep the planning hat.[93] It was unique. He had total confidence that I would do the right thing and, more impressive, the confidence in himself to delegate.[94]

Not least among Horner's challenges was explaining what air attack could achieve. Despite being "extremely intelligent," Schwarzkopf (and his senior land force commanders) had little appreciation of air and space power. To Horner, it reflected their surface-centric backgrounds. "They don't have the basis for it," he said. "[Air Force] airmen do. Marine Corps airmen do, Navy airmen do. We can talk. But when you're dealing with a Joint Force Commander, nine times out of ten the Pentagon is going to make sure it's a *ground* guy, and you need to think about how you are going to communicate air matters with him ahead of time."[95]

The basic issue, he believed, was conveying air power's very different operational environment.[96] Horner noted,

Air operations are conducted at a speed and range that is difficult for our land forces brethren to capture mentally. The first time Buster Glosson brought me the Black Hole[97] briefing I threw him out of the office. His staff . . . had prepared a briefing that an airman would understand, but would be baffling to an Army audience, due to the massive scope, speed and range of air operations. Then I got to thinking, and concluded that all of us watch cartoons. So we built a cartoon. We had a map of Iraq, Saudi Arabia, and then plastic overlays, because the Army loves plastic overlays. "Here we are at 1:00 o'clock," and the little airplanes are flying over Saudi Arabia. "Here we are at 1:30," they're crossing the border. "Here they are at 2:00 o'clock," little orange explosions [appear] on the sector operations centers, stuff like that. That briefing, they could follow. They could understand it. It was a cartoon.[98]

Then they faced military traditionalism. For centuries, until after 1900, wars were fought on the surface, centered on major confrontations between massed armies, or force on force, and men waged bloody attrition battles until one side was too drained to continue fighting. The twentieth century introduced the submarine and the airplane. Yet armies and navies persisted in believing that what happened on the surface was more significant than what happened above and below it, even after combat experience indicated otherwise, and enforced that orthodoxy in joint planning and exercises. As a consequence, Horner recalled,

I never went to a joint force exercise "lessons-learned" meeting that wasn't absolute pure bullshit. In fact my staff would prepare my out-brief and tell me "you've got to say this and you've got to say that, because these are love-ins." The various components would stand up and say "this was the best exercise I've ever seen," and "the cooperation between the units was just perfect and we never had a problem." That just wasn't the case, often because the Army had never had to exercise realistically with air power. If they had, they would know how dominant air power can be on the modern battlefield. I would try to be diplomatic in pointing out that this was no longer World War II or Vietnam, but when your Army has not had to suffer modern air-power attacks, they tend to blow off the new imperatives of war. *Desert Storm* shocked our Army. For sure, the smart generals could recognize the impact of air power [but] the traditionalists chose to ignore it, as they saw it as a threat to their need to be the prime player.[99]

As CENTCOM Forward, Horner had to establish a trusting partnership with the Saudi military, some of whose leaders presumed that they would be commanding Coalition forces, including those of the United States. He worked assiduously to establish good relations with the Saudis, developing close friendships via delicate maneuvering and scrupulous concern for their culture and feelings. The Saudis naturally wished to know in great detail about the air plan, and Horner accommodated them.[100] Other issues included colocating headquarters—again decided via careful negotiation—and the role of female troops. Gen. Muhammad al-Hamad, Saudi Arabia's senior commander, asked if the United States would deploy women to the kingdom and, if so, whether they would expect to be able to drive. Horner declared military women were essential to America's effectiveness, adding, "General Hamad, these women are coming and in all likelihood will die defending your nation, and *you* are going to tell me they can't *drive*? I'm telling you that if it is their military duty, they *are* going to drive." It was not subject to negotiation.[101]

Various issues arose with some Coalition air forces, including disputes over rules of engagement (RoE), basing, and using aircraft. By mid-August, Britain's ambassador to Saudi Arabia, Alan Munro, and Air Chief Marshal Sir Andrew "Sandy" Wilson, the air commander of British Forces Middle East, had concluded that "the Americans were going to attack, no doubt about it," and passed this viewpoint to a visiting emissary from Whitehall.[102] But Horner and Wilson disagreed so strongly over RoE that Horner threatened to pull the RAF out of the campaign. "The RAF saw the Americans as adopting a cowboy approach," Munro recalled, "while General Horner and his staff regarded the RAF's attitude as wimpish."[103] In mid-November, Air Chief Marshal Sir William "Bill" Wratten succeeded Wilson and subsequently smoothed relations with Horner and his staff.[104]

FROM DESERT SHIELD TO DESERT STORM

Once he had F-15Cs, Horner had no doubt CENTAF would trounce the Iraqi Air Force, in large part because it had emulated Soviet-style air defense structure and practices.

> In 1988, I was in Pakistan having dinner with a group of Pakistani fighter pilots. One pilot had just returned from Iraq where he had served as an instructor pilot with the Iraqi air force. The overall program was under the control of the Russians, and he had been found guilty of trying to teach the Iraqi pilots how to use a variety of air combat tactics. This had enraged his Russian bosses, who insisted on teaching only very rigid close-controlled intercepts, to include orders from the ground controller when to fire their missiles. He went on at length how dependent the Iraqi pilots were on ground control, and how they were trained never to think independently.
>
> As a result, our planning to gain control of the air against the most effective air defense—the fighter aircraft—centered on severing the link between the Iraqi pilots and their ground controllers. [In Desert Storm] Our initial targets were the sector operations centers, and the communications links that tied the air defense system together. . . . When we showed up over Iraq, their radars found us and ordered their fighter pilots to scramble. The pilots would then attempt to contact their ground controllers, and were unable to find anyone to tell them what needed to be done. Shortly thereafter an Iraqi pilot would encounter a coalition fighter vectored by AWACS and would become a ball of fire. After a few nights of this, the Iraqi fighters quit flying, except for trying to escape to Iran.[105]

"All of us involved in planning the conflict," remembered Horner, "understood that the goal of Saddam Hussein was to maintain his position as undisputed ruler of Iraq." He added:[106]

> His attempt to steal the assets of Kuwait was a gamble he thought he could win, but that goal was secondary to his maintaining power in Iraq. He had

previously lost the gamble to steal the water-way into the Arabian Gulf from Iran, but he had maintained his grip over the Iraqi people.

Our air attacks on those Iraqi forces Saddam relied upon to maintain power—the Republican Guard and key armor elements—reduced those forces to very low states of effectiveness.[107] I discovered after the war during discussions with General Wafiq [al-Samarri],[108] the former Chief of Iraqi Military Intelligence, that Saddam offered to withdraw from Kuwait even before the coalition ground war was initiated.

Wafiq, who was at Saddam's side, described the Iraqi leader's growing despondency as he watched the Republican Guard and armor divisions experience significant losses to air attacks. He went on to tell me that when we suspended offensive operations as the Iraqis left Kuwait, Saddam suddenly proclaimed "We have won!"

He considered *Desert Storm* a victory *because he remained in power*, his ultimate goal. We in turn achieved our goal, *the withdrawal of Iraqi military from Kuwait*, by attaining an objective: removing Saddam's source needed to maintain political power [the Republican Guard], even though we failed to understand at the time what was occurring.[109]

In early October, JCS chairman Powell ordered Schwarzkopf to send a team to Washington to brief the state of air and ground planning to both the defense leadership and President Bush. It constituted a decisive inflexion point in campaign planning.

General Glosson first presented the air plan at a Pentagon pre-brief on October 10, with Powell finding it "bold, imaginative, and solid."[110] It capitalized upon the speed, range, flexibility, and precision of air forces, assisted by intelligence, deception, and imaginative strategy, to overwhelm Saddam Hussein's military machine. Horner's airmen would strike strategic targets, secure air supremacy, disrupt command and control, sever communications and transport links, and destroy Iraq's fielded forces.[111]

But air power unsettled Powell as well. More than a month earlier, Schwarzkopf had told Powell, "If you want to execute an air attack by itself, we're ready."[112] But Powell complained, "Air power was being portrayed as the 'answer to the problem.'"[113] Clearly uneasy, he told Glosson, "Be careful over at the White House tomorrow. I don't want the President to grab onto that air campaign as a solution to everything."[114] An air force general on the chairman's staff then reinforced the message, telling Glosson that Powell wanted him to "go through the plan much faster and not be so convincing"[115] The feisty one-star told Powell's multi-starred minion he "was not going to mislead the President about the capabilities of the offensive air campaign or make it sound more difficult to execute than I thought it really was." Glosson then received a *third* caution, this time from a CENTCOM colleague. Glosson called Schwarzkopf; who told him in "very direct" fashion to proceed as planned, and added, "Let me deal with Powell." The next day, Glosson briefed the president, noting Bush "paid close attention" and asked "many insightful questions."[116]

In contrast, the ground plan—a lightly armored airborne corps launching a Pickett's Charge–like assault into the heart of Iraqi defenses—elicited the greatest unease. Even its briefer lamely stated (as Cheney recalled), "No one in theater liked the straight-up-the-middle concept, but that it was all we could do with the numbers of forces deployed."[117] It projected two thousand Allied dead and eight thousand wounded.[118] "I mean you just cringed! They were trying to throw inadequate force against the enemy strength!" Horner exclaimed later.[119]

"I was appalled with the presentation and afterwards I called Cheney to say I thought we had to do better," said National Security Adviser Scowcroft. "It sounded unenthusiastic, delivered by people who didn't want to do the job. The option they presented us, an attack straight up through the center of the Iraqi army, seemed to me to be so counterintuitive that I could not stay silent. *I asked why not an envelopment to the west and north around and behind the forces in Kuwait to cut them off.*"[120]

Bush remembered that "the briefing made me realize we had a long way to go."[121] Cheney concurred, noting, "It didn't make any sense: Why would we send our forces—some of which were only lightly armored—up against the heavily armored core of Saddam's defenses?"[122] Subsequently, in reaction to Washington's displeasure, Schwarzkopf's planners developed the famed "Hail Mary" that bypassed Hussein's defensive belt.[123]

Bolstered by the deployment of the VII Corps from Europe, Schwarzkopf completed his plan with the left hook by mid-November, briefing it to CENTCOM at Dhahran on November 14. On November 29, the United Nations (UN) passed Resolution 678, authorizing forceful expulsion of Iraqi forces from Kuwait if they did not withdraw by January 15, 1991. In theater, Horner's staff developed plans for various contingencies, including rescuing American and British Embassy personnel trapped in Kuwait and countering Scuds and CBW. In early January, Congress held hearings on the UN resolution and approved the use of force by a vote of 250–183 in the House, 52–47 in the Senate. Secretary of State James Baker made one last effort to persuade Iraq to leave Kuwait, meeting with a stolid rebuff.

Horner now commanded more than 2,614 aircraft, three-quarters of which—1,990—were from U.S. forces, and fully 70 percent—1,838—were fighters and attack aircraft. Glosson visited the VII Corps to reassure its tankers that the Coalition's fighter and attack aircraft would hammer Iraq's Republican Guard divisions before the onset of the ground campaign. His planners had devised a grid of thirty-by-thirty-mile "kill boxes" in which F-16s and A-10s would prowl. (Subsequently, night-flying strike aircraft would use infrared sensors and laser-guided bombs to "tank plink," inflicting heavy losses). But, as Glosson recalled, "the Army commanders weren't buying. . . . Nothing in their grasp of history and air power supported that."[124] Glosson had a more favorable reception when he presented a briefing titled "Your Role in the Offensive Air Campaign" to his air division. It represented a change from Vietnam, where, he noted, "we never had a clue, at the unit level, what our overall effort was trying to accomplish."[125]

Afterward, one F-16 pilot wrote, "Got 'The Plan,' and my heart soared. The guys that wrote this plan have put together an incredible air campaign. I was worried that when push came to shove, the right people weren't going to be in the right places where they'd be needed. I am not nearly as apprehensive as before."[126]

On January 14, President Bush, Scowcroft, and Cheney had lunch with Gen. Merrill McPeak, the air force chief of staff, and reviewed plans. Bush recalled, "McPeak radiated confidence that the Air Force would carry out its mission with great precision and success."[127] On January 15, Bush signed a National Security Directive authorizing Operation Desert Storm; then Dick Cheney and Colin Powell cosigned its execution order. America and its partners were at war.

HORNER AND CENTAF GO TO WAR

At 6 a.m. on January 16, 1991, Horner issued an alert to his airmen, followed by the execute order shortly after noon: H-Hour was set at 3 a.m. on January 17. Twenty-two minutes after midnight, ten F-117 stealth fighters accelerated down a runway at Khamis Mushait and lifted into the night sky. At 1 a.m. Horner went to the Tactical Air Control Center (TACC), with the wait for the war constituting "the worst minutes of my life." Buster Glosson asked how many aircraft might be lost, and Horner scribbled "forty-two" in reply.[128] The coming bloodshed troubled him deeply: "It was a burden I'd been carrying around since I'd signed the orders that would start all of this carnage in motion," he said. "It was the understanding that someday I would probably have to explain my actions to God and there was no suitable explanation. When men are imperfect—and God knows we are—then there better be a forgiving God."[129]

"It seemed surreal to a certain extent," Glosson recalled.[130] B-52Gs with cruise missiles were inbound from the United States; the navy was readying cruise missiles and carrier aircraft for launch. Tankers, strike aircraft jammers, Weasels, and other support aircraft were airborne or nearly so.[131] At sea, the navy launched its cruise missiles and carrier aircraft, while, aloft, the B-52s launched their own cruise missiles and turned for home.

At 2:20 a.m., army gunships led by air force Pathfinders entered Iraq. So did the F-117s and the first cruise missiles. At 2:38, the helicopters destroyed a western radar site, dodging eighteen F-15E Strike Eagles streaking through the gap they opened. In Baghdad, at 3:02, the first F-117-delivered bomb obliterated a telecommunications center, taking Cable News Network (CNN) off the air. To Horner, "It was a wonderful moment" as he saw his hopes of shattering Iraq's air defense network being fulfilled.[132]

By morning 785 attackers (supported by 478 other aircraft) had struck approximately 144 targets (with 370 aim points), at the cost of just one airplane.[133] Iraq's air defenses and command and control were a shambles, and Coalition aircraft were already roaming across the Iraqi heartland. "Horner and his planners," Schwarzkopf noted, "clearly succeeded brilliantly at undoing Iraq's high-tech defense network. By jamming and bombing its radars, they'd blinded it; by striking at its command centers, they'd paralyzed it."[134] To Britain's Billière, the opening of the air war was "a masterpiece of human planning and computer-controlled aggression, directed with a degree of precision which far surpassed that of any air attack in the past." Moreover, he added, "many British service people, myself included, without direct experience of these [precision] weapons, had been faintly skeptical about the claims which the Americans made for them. Now we saw that everything they had said was justified."[135] Less than a week into the war, Lt. Gen. V. Gorbachev, faculty chief at the Voroshilov General Staff Academy in the then-tottering Soviet Union, wrote, "The outcome of the war has been determined by the fact that the coalition forces seized the initiative and won air superiority from the outset."[136]

Obedient to Schwarzkopf's directives, Horner's airmen battered the Republican Guard, with two of its divisions receiving 88 B-52 attacks and 579 F-16 strikes in a single week.[137] On February 24, Schwarzkopf launched the ground offensive. Abandoned vehicles littered Kuwait and Iraq, and 87,000 Iraqis surrendered.[138] Four days later, the war ended. "The paralysis and disorganization of the Iraqi Army came as a result of air power," analysts concluded. "Air power dominated the military outcome of Operation Desert Storm."[139] In forty-three days, airmen had flown 109,876 sorties of all kinds, with strike aircraft expending 88,500 tons of ordnance. Meanwhile, Saddam Hussein's army had gone from being the fourth largest army in the world to the fourth largest army in Iraq.[140]

Field Marshal Helmuth Graf von Moltke once famously remarked, "No campaign plan survives first contact with the enemy," but some plans withstand contact better than others. Desert Storm's air campaign plan was one example. That said, it was not free of Clausewitzian "fog and friction." These incidents included the RAF's high Tornado losses during low-altitude attacks (foreseen by Horner), the political dimension and strategic value of Iraqi Scuds, the terrible weather that seriously impacted the pace of air operations, the Iraqi attack on Khafji in late January, an intelligence debate over the state of Iraqi military effectiveness, the strike on Al Firdos bunker (an Iraqi command center that doubled as a shelter), and Washington's panicked reaction over the alleged "Highway of Death." All of these and other events have been well covered in the numerous accounts of the war published since its conclusion and are not addressed here.

Before the war, Coalition leaders demanded assurance that Hussein's CBW sites could be attacked "without collateral risk."[141] While most research, production, and storage sites could be struck with relative confidence, biological weapons constituted a more daunting challenge. Iraqi scientists had researched botulinum toxin and anthrax off and on since 1974, though no "smoking gun" existed to indicate whether either posed a weaponized threat.[142] Anthrax generated particular concern, with some experts predicting hundreds of thousands of deaths if live spores were released by Coalition bombing.[143] Horner thought such scenarios "a little bit Draconian," and a visiting scientist confirmed his suspicions and informed him that anthrax spores required a concentration and persistency not appreciated by popular fears. Attacking in calm air would minimize down-wind exposure, and sunlight would neutralize any surviving spores.[144] Thus reassured, Horner pressed ahead. He briefed Cheney, Powell, and Paul Wolfowitz (who concurred). Glosson's team used a "shake and bake" approach, bombing right before dawn, cracking the containment shells, incinerating their contents, and then trusting harsh desert sunlight to kill any spores that might survive. Subsequently, when Horner's airmen attacked the sites, no evidence of release was discovered.[145]

Horner believed strongly in the intrinsic relationship between trust and integrity, noting that "they feed off one another." From the onset of Desert Shield, he had placed a premium on air supremacy.[146] Once war came, the Iraqi Air Force had been swiftly shot out of the sky and bombed in its aircraft shelters. Then, in one of the war's strangest developments, Iraqi pilots began flying to Iran. On one occasion, two F-15s were so focused on chasing two Iraqi aircraft that they unknowingly followed them into Iranian airspace, where they shot both planes down. "In Vietnam our first casualty was integrity," Horner said afterward, "we didn't talk. We didn't ever tell the ugly things." But that was then. After a postflight review of their inertial navigation system coordinates, both pilots forthrightly reported the incursion. Horner immediately reported this incident to Schwarzkopf, who said, "No problem." Likewise, though, bound by his own integrity, the commander reported it to Washington.[147]

Horner feared it would trigger imposition of a buffer zone, one that, he opined later, had "worked wonderfully in Vietnam in terms of making us inefficient."[148] An Iranian buffer would constrain operations around Baghdad because of the extremely short distance (less than a hundred miles) from that city to the border. "My generals in Vietnam were unable to argue against the China buffer zone," he recalled,[149]

> and I was sure my thoughts would likewise be dismissed. As a result my only course of action would be to submit my resignation from the military. Here I was at the peak of any military career, leading troops in battle, and I was going to have to throw it all away because my vow of integrity would not let me do what my generals did not do for me. I hated it. I was despondent as I hand-wrote a letter of resignation that I concluded I needed to submit to battle a procedure that was of great importance to the crews flying combat, even though it was thought the right thing to do by the higher-ups. [But] the subject did not come up [and] I finally lost the letter. After the war I asked

Secretary of Defense Cheney if he heard about our crossing the Iranian border, and he had. I asked if he received any staff actions that provided means to preclude reoccurrence. He replied he had, but had not signed it, and wrote on the staff summary sheet "They will know what to do in theater."[150]

Intelligence and bomb damage assessment (BDA) posed particular challenges. Horner was a voracious consumer of intelligence and believed that "in war, it all starts and ends with intelligence. The operator only knows what he needs to *do* based on intelligence, and only knows what he has *done* based on intelligence."[151] Victory in the Gulf, he concluded, "depended greatly on how well we knew our enemy. We had a scalpel instead of club to use on our enemy; it provided a rare opportunity to limit the damage and loss of life on both sides of the battlefield. All that was required was to know where to best stick the scalpel and that depended on the quality of our intelligence."[152]

After the war, Horner reflected on intelligence from the command perspective:

Intelligence, surveillance and reconnaissance [ISR] data is only useful when it becomes *knowledge*. In the past we have taken ISR products and given the information to intelligence analysts, who turn it into finished products that the operator used in an attempt to know where, when, and how to take action. Unfortunately, in the past, walls were erected between the intelligence and operations communities that proved to be dysfunctional when their cooperation was most needed, in wartime. Intelligence persons were encouraged to hedge their prognostications. In peacetime, it was believed better to say what little they could prove with facts, rather than hazard a guess and then be wrong. Peacetime training exercises for operators pay too little emphasis on the role of intelligence, as employment is scripted to meet specific agendas, or training range limitations.[153]

CENTAF's intelligence staff (CENTAF/IN) and Glosson's planning staff worked in uneasy coexistence. While the planners needed swift, reliable targeting information, the intelligence staff insisted on thorough source vetting and analysis. At the outset, CENTAF/IN had incomplete and outdated information, and it was unable to satisfy Glosson's need for up-to-date imagery. Consequently, he directed planners to look elsewhere, stating, "I don't care where it comes from as long as it is timely and accurate."[154] They turned to Col. John Warden's Checkmate and the Joint Staff's J-2, Rear Adm. John M. "Mike" McConnell.[155] Horner did his best to mediate between Glosson and CENTAF's intelligence chief, Col. Christopher Christon, for he greatly respected both men. He noted later that "intelligence and operations have to converse, to argue, and make judgments in the face of uncertainty." Christon and Glosson, he said, "operated well in the chaos of war. Chris had the courage to state opinions not substantiated fully by our limited access to facts. Buster offered his own conclusions, as well as making a competitive search for truth that was seldom known prior to completion of an individual action."[156]

Since Horner was an avid user of intelligence, it may seem surprising that he was skeptical about the value of BDA, believing it less important for a commander to know what targets had been struck than to know what to strike next. BDA, he believed, focused too much attention on the past and not enough on what should be accomplished in the future. He wanted no part of ground-related BDA, feeling it was a subject best left to the army's component of Central Command (ARCENT). He recalled afterward that "I was not going to get involved in keeping track of the decimation of the Iraqi army in the field," adding, "One, it's something that the United States Army ought to be doing. Since they weren't fighting, they should have been doing something. Second, they were going to do it anyway, so why do I want to get crosswise?"[157]

Yet even ARCENT's analysts did not get their BDA straight. Schwarzkopf subsequently admitted that destruction criteria were so strict it seemed analysts would only count vehicles lying on their backs like "dead cockroaches." Worse, ARCENT's skepticism about air attack initially led its analysts to accept only A-10 claims while rejecting all those attributed to other aircraft. Since the most productive antitank aircraft in the Gulf were the F-111F and F-15E, which used sophisticated sensors and laser-guided bombs (that the A-10 lacked at the time) to attack tanks at night, ARCENT's low acceptance threshold led to serious overestimates of the Iraqi strength and risked the addition of numerous unnecessary sorties that would endanger airmen to no purpose. Fortunately, CENTAF discovered this bizarre practice before it got out of hand, restoring some credibility to the BDA process.[158]

Commenting two decades later, Horner remarked:

Think about the BDA scorekeeping that came out of the Vietnam War. The Pentagon wanted to keep track of how many of the enemy we killed each day.

Who cares? It did not provide knowledge of the *impact* we were having on the enemy, who just sent more people south. You don't ignore BDA, but it is only useful when it indicates the *effect* you are having on the enemy and how he will mutate as you move him toward your desired goal.[159]

[In *Desert Storm* one air intelligence officer] was responsible for the analysis of the Iraqi transportation system. Each night he would brief us on the results of our attacks from the previous twenty-four hour period. For about three days into the war, he kept giving me the recap of what he thought the BDA was. I told him, "*I don't care.*" He said, "What?" and I repeated "I don't care because *I need you to tell me what we have to do tomorrow.*"

After the verbal abuse, he got the idea and started briefing what needed to be done and the impact of the proposed action. For example, he would say "If we'll drop this bridge, we'll cut their through-put 13.5 percent." Now he had no clue if that was accurate, but I'll tell you, he was thinking in the right way and soon he became more accurate in his estimates. The lesson for me was that we need to train our intelligence people how to function in the chaos of war, not to fear that which they do not know for certain. We've got to make them think about *tomorrow*, not *yesterday*.[160]

The conflict between operators and intelligence came to a head over a tragic episode, one that illustrated Horner's view of leadership and command. In the midst of the war, F-111 crews came to believe a mysterious Iraqi fighter pilot, nicknamed "Baghdad Billy," was following them at night. CENTAF/IN reported these "encounters," spreading the rumor more widely. But the only Iraqi fighters airborne at that point in the war were trying to reach Iran. Glosson made a note to "stop [the rumor] before someone flies into the ground."[161] Unfortunately, one did: as two friendly F-15Es looked on, *Ratchet 75,* an EF-111A Raven jammer, was seen dispensing flares, making violent evasive maneuvers, and then impacting the ground in a fireball. No hostile aircraft was around. Glosson erupted, accusing Christon of "aiding and abetting this rumor and now two people [were] dead."[162]

Horner saw it differently. As he wrote later:

Both Buster and Chris were right. It was Chris's job to get the word out. And it was Buster's job as the fighter division commander to worry about the lives of his aircrew. But the real blame was mine. I should have been more forceful about dispelling the Baghdad Billy myth right from the start. I should have seen that a crew would get so engrossed with defeating the apparently real threat that they succumbed to the ever-present killer, the ground. My failure meant two needless deaths and bitter tears for the families of the crew of *Ratchet 75*.[163]

Crucial to the conduct of the war was effective decision making. Again, Horner's previous experiences with Creech and his own command background led him to emphasize a decentralized model of command and control that empowered subordinates to exert the widest range of latitude and authority in making decisions that involved, ultimately, the taking of human life. This arrangement did not mean there was not significant oversight—indeed, a CENTCOM lawyer reviewed every target Horner struck—but, from his perspective as the nation's first wartime Joint and Combined Force Air Component commander, he was comfortable delegating decision making to the lowest appropriate level consistent with his belief that "the nature of air wars requires that you decentralize decision making."[164]

Horner held to that credo even when sorely tempted to intervene. At the opening of the war, some of his wing commanders wanted to attack at low level. After assuming command of the Ninth Air Force, Horner had flown on a low-altitude F-15E familiarization sortie, stressing afterward the need to operate at medium or high altitudes with jamming and defense suppression. "There was absolute disbelief by the young aircrews," he noted later; for them, flying at low-level and high speed was an article of faith.[165] Horner disagreed, but he did not wish to overrule his commanders unilaterally. Instead, "I wanted them to make the decision." Thus, after they "pleaded to fly low-level missions," he let them do so. "The results turned out as I envisaged," he recalled drily, "and after a few days of combat all operations were at medium/high altitude."[166]

Another example involved the TACC at Royal Saudi Air Force headquarters in Riyadh. Staffed by Coalition officers, it maintained a sight picture on daily air operations. Horner recalled,

> I remember one time I'm sitting there, I'm watching the air picture, I've got a
> microphone on front of me on the desk, I can talk to any airplane over Iraq.
> I see two Iraqis take off out of Balad, and I see *Wolf Flight* orbiting nearby.
> Because I'm the world's greatest fighter pilot and know best what to do, I

want to reach for that microphone and issue the orders. Suddenly a lieutenant on the AWACS vectors *Tiger Flight* engaged, and they shoot both Iraqis
down. It was *exactly* the right decision. After that I used to sit on my hands.[167]

To Horner, the ATO was a critical aspect of decentralized decision making,
the "single sheet of music from which everybody played."[168] As Joint Force commander, Schwarzkopf determined "the weight of effort and where he wanted the
emphasis of air operations placed."[169] Next, Glosson's Black Hole formulated a
master attack plan. A planning team then prepared the ATO. Running to "hundreds of closely-detailed pages," it regulated the daily pace of the air campaign
virtually moment to moment, earning the admiration of those wondering how
such a campaign would be controlled.[170] Transmitted throughout the region and
flown out to carriers (which could not then receive it electronically), it detailed all
fixed-wing aircraft operations, cruise missile firings (though not battlefield rocket
artillery), and some helicopter operations (though not all). Finally, the Coalition's
flight leaders in individual units executed the order.[171] "By the time the unit received the ATO for a given day," Horner wrote after the war, "the next day's ATO
was well on the way to completion, and planning for the following day had begun."[172]

During the war and afterward, critics alleged that the ATO imposed too rigid
a system of control upon the air war, an accusation with which Horner vigorously
disagreed. He argued instead that, in contrast to the more rigid and hierarchical
tasking of "army → corps → division → brigade → battalion → company →
platoon → squad" characteristic of land-warfare forces, the relative "flatness" of
CENTAF's command chain, coupled with the decentralization of decision making, easily enabled "pop-up" changes to the ATO such as retargeting and adjusting
to new information, different circumstances, and enemy actions. "I hear Air Force
generals saying 'We've got to get rid of the ATO process, it's too long,'" Horner
recalled after the war.[173]

They don't understand. Speed and decision-making depend on two things,
decentralization and *command and control*. It has *nothing* to do with the ATO
process. The ATO process provides a foundation needed to initiate, coordinate, and, if needed, alter actions. You need a two-or-three-day ATO because

you've got guys that have got to knock lumber off bombs down in the bomb dump, maintenance folks who need to know how many and when jets are going to fly. They have to know what the people are thinking about three days from now.

If you go to a 12-hour ATO you're just going to screw the wrong people. You're going to jerk maintenance and supply around and they'll slow down because they will lose confidence in your leadership. When that happens they will lose confidence in *you*. Keep a three-day ATO cycle and build the best ATO you can, and if it is perfect, you'll never change a thing. I haven't seen anything perfect, so you need to then have a command and control structure that can execute decisions needed when things are not as planned.[174]

Much as Dwight Eisenhower did at the time of Normandy, Horner respected the media and their quest to report on military activities. "Some in the military blame our failure to maintain public support of our efforts in Vietnam on the media, but it was the same media who generated such public support for our operations in Desert Storm," Horner observed.

To be sure, you want to protect information that an enemy can use to his advantage. Also, you want to conduct operations in such a way that, if the enemy finds out what you are doing, you will succeed under any circumstances.

Most [journalists] are individuals who bring individual prejudices to a war, but [still] have a measure of integrity so that they will truthfully report what they see, even if it conflicts with what they want to say, or believe that they should report. I found you can work with many members of the media ahead of time, and they will keep promises of confidentiality prior to an operation. The advantage of doing this is they will better understand what is going on, and will be more accurate when they are free to report.

If the military is doing something that is so distasteful to the American public, then it is a good thing they get exposed, so the harm can be limited. If the military is doing something that the American public approves of, or even admires, then it is also a good thing to build public support for the efforts of the soldiers, sailors, Marines and airmen. In *Desert Storm* we did not contrive to skew or manage our information flow to the media, other than to protect classified information.[175]

AFTER THE STORM

At 8 a.m. on February 28, 1991, phase 4 of the Gulf campaign came to an end. It marked the conclusion of Desert Storm but not the end of the air forces' presence in the skies of Iraq. They would continue overflights for more than twenty more years—257 months in total—through Operations Provide Comfort, Northern Watch, Southern Watch, Vigilant Warrior, Desert Strike, Desert Fox, Iraqi Freedom, and New Dawn, with more than 500,000 sorties regulated by 7,635 ATOs.[176]

Richly honored, Horner stepped down as the Ninth Air Force and CENTAF commander in June 1992, pinning on his fourth star and assuming leadership of the North American Aerospace Defense Command and U.S. Space Command. During Desert Storm—America's first "space war"—the space community had furnished critical weather, communications, navigation, warning, and intelligence information, all essential to the conduct of combat operations.[177] But, as Horner noted, "if we had to launch a satellite during Desert Storm, we didn't have a real capability if the system wasn't already in the queue or already been programmed."[178] As CINCSPACE—the commander in chief, space command—Horner sought to change the command's culture from one where research and development predominated to one more responsive to the practical needs of the war fighter. "I had a small challenge when I took command of Air Force Space Command," Horner recalled:[179]

> Most of the space community thought of themselves as scientists, their orientation was on technology. They thought of themselves as builders and flyers of masterful spacecraft. They had trouble identifying themselves as part of the combat mission. One Officer's Call, I told them "You're all a bunch of nerds, a bunch of weenies, and a bunch of geeks. The only reason you exist is to fight wars." I wanted to see some warrior spirit. The older guys hated me. The younger guys took to it like water. The next morning, when I went out to my staff car, my license plate read "GEEK-1." I drove it that way for two-and-a-half years.[180]

Horner retired from the USAF at the beginning of October 1994, remaining active as an international businessman and defense consultant, a senior adviser to the air force leadership, and a strong air and space power advocate. He has frequently addressed what he has drawn from his own military experience and that of the United States in general, specifically the lessons and implications of Desert

Storm. While never minimizing the human aspect of war, he is a strong proponent of exploiting advanced technology. "Air and space operations leverage technology better than those on land and in the sea," he notes.

> While all services benefit from technological improvements in areas such as weapons, communications, sensors and defensive devices, air and space forces range over great distances at great speed, allowing for much greater opportunities to engage the enemy.
>
> In terms of contribution to the overall effort and total cost, air and space technology may be the best bargain available. Land forces require large numbers of people, both to engage directly with the enemy and an ever-increasing number of support personnel. In addition, as we maintain a volunteer armed force, each individual incurs longer-term costs such as retirement, recruiting, and medical expenses. Air and space technology is expensive up front; [but] systems may last from 15 to 70 years, and can be updated to maintain and/or increase utility and lethality.
>
> Technology has changed how we fight wars. Stealth; precision munitions; intelligence-surveillance-reconnaissance (ISR), all have changed the way people live or die in battle. In *Desert Storm* we had the technology, and our forces defeated an enemy force of similar size—half a million men—in six weeks with a loss of 148 killed in action, 35 of whom were killed by fires from their own side.[181] To be sure, factors such as leadership, training, and morale were major contributors, but you can trace much of our success in battle to having access to more advanced technologies.
>
> Technology also alters the culture of the warrior. Over the ages, technology has increased the distance between combatants. The sword and spear replaced the club and dagger; and gun powder permitted killing an adversary at even greater distances. But one of the drawbacks of distance was a loss of accuracy. Now, technologies such as the Global Positioning System (GPS) allow one to restore accuracy, yet maintain extended distance. Stealth technology affords the benefits of distance when engaging a radar-equipped defender.
>
> Robotics now allow one warrior to engage his adversary half a world away: Such is the case of a Remotely Piloted Aircraft [RPA] firing a missile in Afghanistan, with the human doing the attacking located at Creech Air Force

Base in Nevada. Historically, warriors are exposed to danger and hardships in battle. But the RPA operator does not share the same dangers and hardships as those whom he is attacking. Is he qualified to wear decorations awarded for bravery in battle? This is not to deny the value of robotic capabilities, but it does raise questions about the cultural aspects of modern warfare.

All war is ugly, but *Desert Storm* was less ugly due to the circumstances associated with factors such as the environment, strategy, precision, and efficiency of our operation. As such *Desert Storm*, like Vietnam, offers opportunity for subsequent generations to study. Lessons are difficult to learn from combat operations, for generals do not want to admit their mistakes, soldiers cannot fully describe what motivated their actions, and politicians will not recant easily their public announcements that led to war. Vietnam was so painful we vowed not to repeat its mistakes and I pray that our military of the future does not do so ever again.[182]

In retirement Horner and his wife (a gifted musician) lavish much love and attention on family and friends, have developed an eclectic art collection (and an impressive command of art history to go with it), generously support various philanthropic causes, and serve as pillars of both their church and community. Horner freely gives of his expertise to those seeking his views and insights and (as of this writing) chairs the Board of Trustees of the University of West Florida.

But Desert Storm will always be the measure by which he is evaluated. If, as the authors of the *Gulf War Air Power Survey* concluded, "The JFACC did not play by the book," preferring to work with a team of trusted associates rather than wrestle within the cumbersome architecture of an overly bureaucratic and ill-defined joint process, it was well that Horner did not.[183] On the eve of the war, Buster Glosson penned some thoughts in his diary. Of Horner he wrote, "Warrior mind . . . very savvy . . . super relationship with the CINC. . . . The results would speak for themselves. Thousands of lives will be saved as the result of his leadership!"[184] They did, and they were. No JFACC since Desert Storm has enjoyed the latitude and freedom of decision making that Horner did under Norman Schwarzkopf. And no air campaign since has been run as well, or better, or achieved as much or more.[185]

10

MICHAEL E. RYAN: ARCHITECT OF AIR POWER SUCCESS

Mark A. Bucknam

Informed airmen and military strategists knew that Bosnia and Herzegovina (BiH) was the wrong war in the wrong place against the wrong sort of adversary for air power to do much good. In the summer of 1995, the United Nations (UN) and the North Atlantic Treaty Organization (NATO) seemed poised on the brink of failure in BiH. After more than three years of brutal, internecine warfare in the Balkans and two years of disappointing attempts to employ NATO air power to curb the violence, the warring parties—Serb, Croat, and Bosniak (Muslim)—began descending deeper into ethnic cleansing, massacres, and indiscriminate shelling of civilians.

To schooled observers, it came as no surprise that NATO air power had been unable to live up to the high expectations of less knowledgeable politicians and pundits. At the start of the decade, Western air power had been so patently effective in the Gulf War against Iraq that it was easy to overestimate what it could accomplish. Unlike Iraq, however, BiH was small, mountainous, heavily wooded, and more complex in terms of the number and geographic disposition of warring parties. Yet the main factors inhibiting the effective use of air power were not physical; they were political.

By the start of 1995, senior UN officials, both military and civilian, had abandoned their responsibility to protect the six "safe areas" spread across BiH. NATO air power was supposed to help UN peacekeepers in BiH enforce the safe areas policy, but the top UN leaders were no longer interested in enlisting that help. In 1994, tentative attempts to use NATO air power led Bosnian Serb Army (BSA) forces to take UN peacekeepers hostage and threatened to collapse the UN mission in BiH. Forced to choose between peace support operations with lightly armed soldiers and the enforcement of UN Security Council resolutions through NATO air power, the UN ditched its enforcement mission and opted for peace support—even though there was little peace left to support. NATO air power was also supposed to enforce a no-fly zone over BiH. But doing so effectively meant NATO would first have to neutralize the BSA air defenses, and the UN withheld its consent for those operations to avoid BSA retaliation. The feckless UN and NATO performance seemed only to highlight the reputedly natural Balkan tendency toward violence.

That was why it appeared so extraordinary when a two-week NATO bombing campaign in the summer of 1995—Operation Deliberate Force—changed everything. The campaign contributed greatly to bringing the Bosnian Serb military to heel, establishing a basis for a negotiated end to the war, and paving the way for a political settlement in BiH that has lasted to this day. Air power alone did not work this dramatic turn of events, but it was a leading factor.[1] Lt. Gen. Michael E. Ryan, commander of that air campaign, deserves credit for conceiving of and skillfully executing Deliberate Force. His upbringing and air force career could hardly have been better designed to shape his personality, character, and expertise for successfully planning and commanding Operation Deliberate Force.

THE MAKING OF A COMMANDER

Mike Ryan was born in San Antonio, Texas, on December 24, 1941, three weeks after the Japanese attack at Pearl Harbor. He was the second child born to John "Jack" and Jo Carolyn Ryan. When Mike was born, his father was a young flight instructor. In February 1944, Jack Ryan was assigned to a base in southeastern Italy, from which he would lead B-17 missions against targets in northern Italy, Austria, and Germany.

Flying bomber missions in the European theater was far more dangerous than most people today realize. At twenty-eight years old, Jack Ryan commanded the Second Bomb Group and later served as operations officer for the Fifth Bombardment Wing before returning to Texas in April 1945, one month before the war in Europe ended. He survived fifty-eight combat missions, was promoted to colonel before his thirtieth birthday, and earned two Silver Stars, two Distinguished Flying Crosses, six Air Medals, and the Purple Heart. He nearly did not make it home. On his forty-second mission, he ran into heavy antiaircraft fire over northern Italy, and two members of his crew were killed and four others were wounded, as was Ryan himself. Despite significant damage to his B-17 and the injuries he had sustained, Jack Ryan successfully led his group to the target and brought his plane home safely.[2]

The men who succeeded in that environment rose rapidly through the ranks of the U.S. Army Air Forces, the forerunner of today's U.S. Air Force (USAF). Indeed, bomber generals would run the USAF for most of the first three decades of its existence. Jack Ryan would be one of those leading bomber generals. He rose through various assignments to command Strategic Air Command (SAC) and the Pacific Air Forces (PACAF) during the Vietnam War and ultimately became the seventh chief of staff of the USAF.

Mike Ryan was too young to remember his father's going off to fight in World War II, but he clearly recalled spending his elementary school years moving between bases in Texas and New Mexico. He received one of his strongest impressions from those early years when he was about twelve years old and his father took him up in a B-26 Marauder. That exhilarating experience convinced Mike that he wanted to be a pilot someday.[3] He knew military aviation had its serious side, for fatal aircraft mishaps were all too common. He also understood that military aircraft were weapons of war. Indeed, his father bore the visible scars of war, including a missing left index finger, which had been shot off during a mission in World War II. In the late 1940s, Mike's father took part in atomic weapons tests and later commanded the people who maintained, armed, and flew America's sole means for delivering nuclear weapons. From his earliest days, therefore, Mike was a child of the Cold War. He grew up attuned to the unforgiving and often hazardous nature of military flying and to the deadly serious realities of world affairs.

Mike was raised in a tight-knit family and was especially close to his sister, Patty Jo, and his brother, Jack, who had been born eighteen months before Mike. Dinners were a mandatory formation at the Ryan household, and although the dinner table conversations covered a wide variety of topics, Mike's father was guarded whenever talk turned to U.S. domestic politics. The older Jack Ryan subscribed to the tradition of not voting in political elections, adhering to the belief that a professional military officer had to be apolitical and that casting a ballot was a political act to be eschewed while on active duty. Mike would grow up following that same tradition. His father was the dominant figure in Mike's life, and he remembers him as a great dad and a highly disciplined man who lived by the watchwords "integrity" and "honesty." Discipline at home was reinforced in the Roman Catholic schools that Mike attended, where corporal punishment was commonly administered in the classroom.

The legendary Gen. Curtis LeMay had already commanded SAC for nearly eight years when in 1956 he brought Jack Ryan to SAC headquarters at Offutt Air Force Base near Omaha, Nebraska. There, Mike attended all four years of high school. He was not the bookish type. He liked sports and cars, interests he shared with his father. Mike attended a Catholic high school, and looking back from retirement, he recalled:

> I was not the most gifted student, but I was a big kid. I had to take the entrance exam several times to get into the school. But they were pretty intent on me getting in because I'd played football for three years down in Texas, and they prided themselves on their football team, even though it was a very small school of only about 700 boys—Jesuit run school. So I played football, basketball and track there.[4]

In 1960, Mike tried but failed to get into the Air Force Academy. Undeterred by this first rebuff, Mike went to the Millard preparatory school to improve his prospects for the following year. Located in the Oregon mountains, the school was, in Ryan's memory, "essentially a slave labor camp for a ranch that Colonel Millard had." Mornings were devoted to studying mathematics, afternoons were for English, and the remainder of the day was spent stringing fences or doing other work around the ranch. In early 1961, Ryan took the entrance exams for both the U.S. Military Academy at West Point and the Air Force Academy before taking the requisite physical exams. Although Mike had been an all-state high school football player a year earlier, the army declared him 4-F—physically unfit—because the arches of his feet were too high. So he applied again for admission to the Air Force Academy.

After finishing prep school, Ryan joined his family in Spain, where his father commanded SAC's Sixteenth Air Force, and waited to hear from the academy. At the time, his brother was living on his own and attending Creighton University in Omaha. Mike remembered Jack as a "brainiac," a national merit scholar who spent two years studying nuclear physics at the Rice Institute before returning to Omaha.[5] Mike recalled the day in 1961 when to everyone's puzzlement a telegram arrived congratulating his parents on Jack's acceptance to the Air Force Academy. The next day, another telegram arrived announcing Mike's acceptance to the academy. Jack had applied without telling anyone; thus the Ryan brothers ended up as classmates at the academy for the next four years.

Having his older brother as a classmate and tutor helped Mike, as did the structured and disciplined environment. Mike would later say, "I needed the discipline the Academy had with respect to academics."[6] It may have also helped him focus on his studies when a shoulder injury requiring surgical repair ended his days as a college football player. Close-up and in person, Ryan seems to stand taller than his six-foot, three-inch frame measures, but the punishment of playing college football caught up with him in the spring of his sophomore year. Advised that if another operation became necessary he would not go to pilot training, he decided football was not worth the risk.

While visiting Denver during his junior year, Mike met Jane Morgan, the woman he would marry soon after graduating from the academy. Mike's brother was his best man, and a year later Jack married Jane's best friend, Martha, whom he had met when she was the maid of honor at Mike and Jane's wedding.

Mike decided early on that he would rather fly fighters than bombers. During a break from the academy, he had an opportunity to fly aboard a B-52 on a "Chrome Dome" mission—a real-world airborne nuclear alert mission flown from Louisiana to the far northern latitudes. The plane carried thermonuclear weapons and mission matériels for striking targets in the Soviet Union. To Mike, the boring and uncomfortable twelve-hour ordeal did nothing to excite his interest in bombers. Near the end of his pilot training, he happily received an assignment to fly the F-4 Phantom II. His father, then commander in chief of SAC, came to Mike's graduation in 1966 and pinned wings on his chest. The next day, General Ryan flew to Texas and pinned wings on his elder son's chest. He too was going to fly F-4s.

By the end of the year, the Ryan brothers were flying F-4s at Eglin Air Force Base in Florida as members of the Sixteenth Tactical Fighter Squadron, but before long they went to war. In 1966, the air force had no formal F-4 training unit or any F-4 weapon system operators. Pilots flew in both the front and rear seats of F-4s. By October 1967, little more than a year after arriving at Eglin, Mike and Jack deployed with their squadron and its F-4Ds to Udorn Royal Thai Air Force Base in northern Thailand. Along the way, they stopped in Hawaii, where they met with their parents. General Ryan had become commander in chief of PACAF in February 1967, about the midpoint of the Johnson administration's Operation Rolling Thunder. This three-and-a-half-year-long campaign was intended to coerce the North Vietnamese leaders in Hanoi by carefully modulating America's bombing of targets in the north. Initially designed to send political signals, the campaign evolved into an attempt to constrain the north's ability to support the war in South Vietnam, and throughout it all, operations remained hamstrung by debilitating and ever-shifting political restrictions. This unorthodox use of military power failed miserably with the North Vietnamese and proved enormously frustrating and dangerous for the American airmen, including Mike and Jack Ryan, who were forced to implement it.

As an example of how political considerations affected operations in the field, on June 2, 1967, a few months before Mike and Jack arrived at Udorn, an F-105 from Takhli Air Base, Thailand, strafed an antiaircraft artillery (AAA) site near North Vietnam's main port of Hai Phong. The presence of a ship in close proximity to the AAA site greatly complicated matters and virtually ensured that the F-105 pilot would be subject to career-ending disciplinary action for making the attack. After the mission, the pilot lied to the intelligence officer conducting the debriefing to cover up the incident, and later he explained the situation to his vice wing commander, Col. Jack Broughton, a fighter pilot of World War II and Korean War fame who seemed to be on the path to bigger and better postings. To shield the younger pilot from the consequences of his actions, Broughton ordered that the F-105's gun camera film be brought to him, and he assisted in overexposing it to destroy any evidence of the strafing attack.[7]

The ship at the scene of the strafing attack turned out to be the Soviet *Turkistan*, and the Soviets' loud protests forced General Ryan to become directly involved in uncovering the origin of the unauthorized attack. The denouement of the drama came at the end of June at Takhli, where Broughton eventually admitted his part in covering up the affair to General Ryan.[8] General Ryan held Broughton personally accountable, ending his career. As Mike Ryan later explained, the lies and cover-up incensed his father more than the pilot's original action had. In Mike's view, honesty and integrity were black-and-white matters for his father, regardless of the shades of gray projected by the war's political complexities and its complicated rules of engagement (RoE). Later in the war, after General Ryan became chief of staff of the air force, he apparently came to believe that Gen. John

Lavelle had ordered his subordinates to lie and had himself misled the USAF inspector general during an investigation into unauthorized bombing of targets in North Vietnam, which led to Lavelle's dismissal, retirement, and loss of two stars. One upshot of General Ryan's absolute insistence on honesty was that all air force airmen at that time were required to sign statements reaffirming their commitment to integrity.[9]

As Mike and Jack accumulated sorties over North Vietnam, they came to share the intense frustration and exasperation that Colonel Broughton and others expressed at the way Washington was running the war. When Gen. Jack Ryan occasionally made swings through the bases in Southeast Asia, Mike and Jack avoided meeting him at his plane—just as all lieutenants and captains instinctively keep their distance from generals. But during his visits, they "would sneak over to his hooch at night and tell him what a [screwed up] war he was running."[10] This was mock criticism, for they understood that decisions about the bombing campaign were made in Washington and that their father was as frustrated as they were. Rolling Thunder continued until November 1, 1968, only days before the U.S. presidential election that brought Richard Nixon to the White House and a few weeks after General Ryan and his sons completed their tours in the Pacific.

Mike and Jack survived their tours at Udorn despite being shot at by the North Vietnamese, restrictive RoE, and a two-month banishment from the Officers' Club for some high jinks. In the process, Mike racked up 138 sorties, a Distinguished Flying Cross, and twelve Air Medals. In addition to his hundred missions over North Vietnam, he flew thirty-seven missions over Laos and one mission over South Vietnam.

By August 1968, many of Ryan's squadron mates at Udorn completed their tours and were sent to constitute a new F-4 unit at Holloman Air Force Base in New Mexico. Mike and Jack went as well, although this time the brothers were assigned to different squadrons. The air force equipped the new Forty-Ninth Tactical Fighter Wing with older F-4Ds brought home from bases in Europe. The jets had more than their share of maintenance problems and seemed to be the ones that Europe no longer wanted.[11]

Mike was the Seventh Tactical Fighter Squadron's assistant weapons officer, a position that was a stepping-stone to Fighter Weapons School, where the air force trained its best fighter instructors and tacticians. He did quite well at dropping bombs, but his squadron had trouble making qualifying scores in a technique called "dive toss bombing," which used the aircraft's radar to determine the range to a target for automatic bomb release. Accurate dive toss depended both on the skills of the crew flying the plane and on the F-4's avionics systems, and in Mike's squadron those systems seemed to be causing problems.

With an operational readiness inspection (ORI) approaching and the squadron's dive toss scores short of a passing grade, Mike was confronted with a challenge to his integrity. A senior officer told Mike to drop dive bombs on the bombing range but to log the deliveries as dive toss. Dive-bombing the target would surely put the bombs well within the hit criteria for dive toss, but doing so would be a blatant attempt to deceive the ORI inspectors. Undoubtedly Mike was not the only pilot whom that senior officer approached, but he may well have been the only one to turn him down flat. As Mike recalled, at the end of that encounter, "he just turned his back on me. I thought I was a dead man. . . . Even though it sounded like an order, I wasn't going to do it."[12] The squadron ultimately failed that ORI, and the inspector general from Tactical Air Command (TAC) would return within a year to reinspect Mike's squadron.

The maintenance unit's poor performance was one of the principal reasons for the failure, and Mike was about to become far more involved in maintenance than he had ever imagined. Air force fighter squadrons at that time included the maintenance function within the squadrons; thus, Mike's squadron comprised nearly five hundred people, most of them enlisted maintenance personnel. In the wake of the failed ORI, his squadron commander made him the new squadron maintenance officer. Because the position was usually filled by a nonflying officer whose entire career was spent working in maintenance, it was the last assignment the young fighter pilot wanted, but he did not have a choice in the matter. A bit stunned at the news, Mike had the presence of mind to make a request: if squadron maintenance earned a passing grade on the ORI retake, he wanted to go to Fighter Weapons School. He later recalled his squadron commander's blunt response: "If we pass the ORI, I will get you into Fighter Weapons School. If we don't pass the ORI, you are never going to Fighter Weapons School."[13] Not surprisingly, Mike was a highly motivated maintenance officer.

Captain Ryan set about improving maintenance operations using a simple formula: "Have a plan, put someone in charge, and follow up." At the start of his ten-month stint, he gathered the heads of each department within the maintenance section and directed them to come up with plans to bring their departments up to standard, while he put together an overall plan that integrated their efforts. Ryan met with these department heads semiweekly to review the progress in implementing the plans. He also took measures to instill a sense of ownership among the maintainers. In addition to their maintaining aircraft and painting the squadron's aerospace ground equipment (AGE), under Ryan's instruction, the maintainers responsible for the AGE painted their names on it. Squadron maintainers also stenciled the crew chiefs' names on the squadron's airplanes so that when a jet flew well the crew chief received praise; if it did not, the crew chief knew who would get the blame and could be expected to rectify the situation. It was basic management and leadership, and it worked. Ryan learned a great deal from his time as a maintenance officer; and it would not be his last disappointing assignment to turn out as a positive, formative experience for him.

As his squadron readied to retake its ORI, Mike and his brother continued to enjoy parallel careers at Holloman. About midway through his tenure as squadron maintenance officer, Mike was sent to Maxwell Air Force Base in Alabama to attend Squadron Officer School (SOS)—the first of three rungs up the air force officer's ladder of professional military education (PME). Jack attended the two-month course at the same time, and the two finished SOS in November 1969, a few months after their father became USAF chief of staff.

By 1970 Mike and Jack both had young children. Less than two weeks into the new year, Jack died in an F-4 mishap. Jack's loss hit Mike hard. Still, life went on, as it always must. When Mike returned from visiting the accident site in California, about four days after Jack's plane crash, he told his squadron commander he was ready to fly again. He believed it would be best if he got back to flying F-4s quickly.[14] Thus, even as the mishap board retrieved the wreckage of Jack's plane and endeavored to discover the cause of the fatal crash, Mike stoically went back to being the best F-4 pilot he could, including flying riskier functional check flights to verify the airworthiness and proper functioning of the planes that had recently undergone extensive maintenance. Not long afterward, his squadron passed the retake of its ORI. Maintenance earned good marks, and Mike went to Fighter Weapons School that summer.

Ryan did not spend much time at Holloman after he returned from Fighter Weapons School; instead, he began a series of flying assignments that would end with his first nonflying assignment, which was another fortuitous disappointment in his career. Starting in January 1971, Mike and his family spent two and a half years in Williamstown, Australia, where he flew French-built Mirage III fighters as an exchange officer. Although Ryan had wanted to return to Vietnam, the war wound down while he was in Australia, so in July 1973—the same month his father retired from the air force—he arrived at Luke Air Force Base, Arizona. After little more than a year at Luke, where he served as an instructor pilot and flight commander, he departed on a one-year, remote assignment (without family) to Kunsan Air Base, South Korea.

At Kunsan, Ryan was the wing weapons officer, overseeing the weapons and tactics training programs for the Eighth Tactical Fighter Wing. Just as at Holloman, the wing at Kunsan was a true multi-mission unit that trained for all manner of air-to-air and air-to-ground missions, including the delivery of nuclear weapons. Indeed, Kunsan kept two F-4s armed with nuclear weapons on alert at all times. For many fighter pilots, a tour at Kunsan was professionally rewarding because it provided a year of focused training in relatively unrestricted airspace and in close proximity to an adversary who routinely made the threat of conflict palpable. To Ryan's immense satisfaction, he knew that when his tour ended he would be rejoining his family at Luke, where he would be part of the initial cadre of instructors for the F-15 Eagle—indisputably the world's premier air-to-air fighter at that time.

Around Christmas, while still at Kunsan, Ryan learned he had been selected for promotion to major—a year below the zone—and that announcement changed all of his plans. Although his early promotion recognized his leadership and high potential, it also meant that he would not return to Arizona and the F-15. Hugely disappointed, Ryan thought it was the worst thing that could ever happen to him.[15] Instead of flying F-15s, he moved with his family to Maxwell Air Force Base, where he and Jack had attended SOS. This time, he was going to Air Command and Staff College (ACSC), the second rung of the PME ladder.

ACSC was, and still is, a ten-month course designed to teach a class of six hundred officers to think in a more sophisticated way about international affairs, national security, and the profession of arms. Ryan filled whatever spare time he might have had that year obtaining a master's degree in business administration from nearby Auburn University. He excelled at ACSC and was a distinguished graduate. Leaving ACSC in the summer of 1976, he received an assignment to return to flying as part of TAC's inspector general team, but once again he would be deeply disappointed when a last-minute diversion sent him to a nonflying job in TAC's plans directorate.

Though he did not realize it at the time, Ryan would later recognize the value of that staff assignment to his development as a future leader. TAC comprised all the fighter units based in the continental United States. Although the TAC staff was headquartered at Langley Air Force Base in southeastern Virginia, Ryan spent most of his first year working on a project that required him to spend significant amounts of time in Washington. As he described it:

> I was the action officer for the disestablishment of Air Defense Command and the absorption of . . . the radars and the fighters, etc., into TAC. We were locked in the anteroom of the Chief's office [in the Pentagon] for almost a year—going back and forth [to TAC headquarters]. And only five of us could work on it, and I was the only one at TAC. I would have to drive to TAC regularly to brief the commander and the 2-star XP [TAC's deputy chief of staff for plans].[16]

There were other programs for which Ryan also served as the primary briefer to senior leaders in TAC and the air force; therefore, in addition to receiving an education in the complexities of planning the future of a major command, he met some influential people. Most important, one year into Ryan's assignment Brig. Gen. Larry Welch arrived to head TAC/XP and became Ryan's new boss. A career fighter pilot, Welch would rise to become the USAF's twelfth chief of staff.

Near the end of his tour at TAC, Ryan was contacted by two men he respected deeply, each offering him the chance to command a squadron—one an A-10 squadron, the other an F-4 squadron. Not wanting to offend either wing commander, Ryan turned to General Welch for guidance. Welch soon informed Ryan that he would go to MacDill Air Force Base, Florida, to command the F-4 squadron and that within a year he would convert the unit to flying F-16s. Ryan found his return to F-4s was like riding a bike. Within a month of taking command of the Sixty-First Tactical Fighter Squadron, he won a squadron bombing competition. And, as General Welch had predicted, Ryan later led the squadron in its transition to flying the USAF's newest fighter, the F-16.

In August 1981, after two years at MacDill, the air force handed Ryan another career disappointment. Having been selected for promotion to colonel, he was looking forward to another flying job when the USAF's assistant deputy chief of staff for operations, Maj. Gen. Jack Chain, called and said that he wanted Ryan to come to the Pentagon and be the chief of Checkmate. When Ryan mentioned that he was not a volunteer, Chain let him know he was not being asked. Checkmate was an organization within air force headquarters that studied highly classified intelligence about the Soviet Union and other potential U.S. adversaries and developed air power solutions to the most difficult tactical and operational war-fighting challenges. Later during that Pentagon tour, Ryan became the deputy assistant director for joint and national security matters, working on operational, strategy, and policy issues related to the USAF chief's responsibilities as a member of the Joint Chiefs of Staff (JCS). Ryan later reflected on his Pentagon assignment and other unwelcome postings: "All of those things were not in my game plan, but all of them were terribly, terribly important I think to opening my eyes to a world I had not seen before."[17]

From the Pentagon, Ryan reached the top rung of the PME ladder and enjoyed a year at the National War College in Washington, D.C., the premier institution for studying strategy and national security. After graduation in 1984, Colonel Ryan was assigned to reestablish and command the 432nd Tactical Fighter Wing, flying F-16s, at Misawa Air Base, Japan. But he did not escape the Pentagon for long. In June 1986, he returned to the Pentagon in another good deal gone wrong. Ryan had received orders to serve as inspector general at PACAF headquarters in Honolulu, Hawaii. He would have continued flying and had the opportunity to travel throughout the Pacific region while inspecting USAF units. Everything was set, with the children enrolled in parochial schools in Hawaii. Instead, then–chief of staff of the air force General Welch phoned Ryan, telling him to be in Washington within ten days to be his executive officer (exec).

As with earlier "bad deals" during Ryan's career, this one turned out to be of enormous benefit. He hired a new junior executive officer, Lt. Col. Chuck Wald, an F-15 pilot who had, in addition to other talents, the raw energy necessary to function effectively in the chief's front office. Ryan would later draw on Wald's leadership during Operation Deliberate Force. In summarizing the value of that assignment, Ryan said the most important aspects were

watching General Welch work through decisions for the Air Force. He was kind enough to let me sit through almost every meeting he had. He was a wonderful mentor and a brainiac of the highest order . . . and just the issues we covered, everything from nuclear weapons and ICBMs [intercontinental ballistic missiles], which I'd never been involved with at all, and . . . watching the decision process, preparing for the Hill, going through all of the motions you have to go through to get ready for testimony, and working the budget. It was just a real education.[18]

On the one hand, Ryan was putting in grueling hours at the Pentagon, he was not living in Hawaii, and he was not flying. On the other hand, he was getting an invaluable education in the workings of the air force and, more important, in the workings of Washington.

In June 1988, the forty-six-year-old Ryan returned to Langley Air Force Base as a newly pinned-on brigadier general with twenty-three years of service. Ryan began this tour as head of the office where he had once worked, as TAC's deputy chief of staff for plans. He left Langley three years later—six months after pinning on his second star—having served as TAC's deputy chief of staff for operations during Operations Desert Shield and Desert Storm. In that capacity, Ryan had supported the Gulf War's joint force air component commander (JFACC), Lt. Gen. Chuck Horner, by creating "TAC Ops as reach-back for anything that Horner and his guys needed. We did all of the deployment planning, all of the logistical support of all of the tactical [fighter] forces over there—worked very hand-in-hand with all of my buddies at [Air Mobility Command] and SAC."[19]

Among the matériel that Horner needed were intelligence, maps, and reconnaissance imagery. Ryan and the TAC chief of intelligence, Brig. Gen.-select Ken Minihan, ensured that General Horner received what he needed and with classification markings that would allow the information to be shared with Coalition partners. Ryan believed that the close collaboration between intelligence and operations was vital to the latter's success. Speaking about the 1991 Gulf War, Ryan later stated:

The demand for intelligence and integration of intelligence into the planning over there was terribly necessary. And in my mind you can't separate operations from intelligence; they are co-dependent in a lot of ways. And so from that and from my time in Checkmate, which was very intelligence dependent, . . . I came to appreciate what they [intelligence] could draw on, because they could reach out to all the agencies in many ways and bring in stuff that you as an operator didn't have the reach for.[20]

That deep appreciation for intelligence also led General Ryan to partner with Minihan and TAC's vice commander, Lt. Gen. Joe Ashy, to expand the Fighter Weapons School to include intelligence officers.[21]

In July 1991, Ryan was again assigned to the Pentagon, where he served in two important joint jobs—the first in his career. His first duties were as vice director for strategic plans and policy on the Joint Staff, which supports the chairman of the JCS. The Directorate for Strategic Plans and Policy functions as the chairman's interface with policymakers in the Office of the Under Secretary of Defense for Policy, and its portfolio is worldwide, dealing with all manner of policy and strategy issues. When Ryan began his tenure on the Joint Staff, Gen. Colin Powell was chairman of the JCS. In May 1993, early in President Bill Clinton's first administration, Ryan received his third star and moved to the prestigious position of assistant to the chairman of the JCS (ACJCS).

The ACJCS functions as the de facto military adviser to the secretary of state and usually travels with the secretary. In his first month on the job, Ryan traveled to Europe with the recently confirmed secretary of state, Warren Christopher, to brief America's NATO allies on Washington's preferred policy toward the former Yugoslavia. That policy, known as "lift and strike," would lift the arms embargo on the Bosniaks—the primary victims of the war in BiH, in Washington's view—and strike the Bosnian Serbs, whom Washington saw as the primary aggressors. The U.S. proposal for lift and strike landed with a thud in Europe. European unification was on the ascent, and the Western European Union was striving to formulate and implement a common foreign and security policy. America's European partners wanted to handle the situation in BiH themselves, and many Americans thought that would be just fine. Despite the Europeans' rejection of lift and strike, back in the United States high-level administration officials periodically pressed Ryan about ways in which American air power might be brought to bear to end the war in BiH.

In October 1993, Gen. John Shalikashvili became Ryan's new boss as chairman of the JCS. "General Shali," as he was known, had returned recently from serving as the top U.S. and NATO commander in Europe, so he was well aware of the problems in BiH and of the disparate European attitudes toward the Balkans.

Having previously served as ACJCS himself, Shali relied on Ryan to represent the uniformed military in interagency deliberations, to prepare recommendations for the Deputies Committee of the National Security Council, and, in the vice chairman's absence, to represent the chairman on the Deputies Committee. Ryan also became a member of a high-level working group supporting the Contact Group, an informal body established to deal with the crisis in the Balkans, consisting of the American secretary of state and the foreign ministers of France, Germany, the United Kingdom, and Russia.

Throughout the summer of 1994, Ryan spent considerable time focusing on BiH, and he may have begun to formulate ideas for using air power there. On June 23, he testified before a U.S. Senate committee about how impractical and dangerous it would be for the United States to unilaterally lift the arms embargo against the Bosniaks.[22] Earlier that day, Maj. Gen. Rupert Smith of the British Army had testified before the same committee and delivered essentially the same message. As the British assistant chief of defence staff (operations and plans), Smith was quite familiar with the situation in BiH, where in addition to a large contingent of British soldiers, a British three-star, Sir Michael Rose, commanded all UN forces. Although the lift part of lift and strike seemed to be off the table that summer, the strike part still held potential. At the end of July, General Smith traveled to Geneva to brief Contact Group ministers on "options of extending NATO air action to bombing a number of Bosnian Serb targets simultaneously"—a briefing attended, if not informed, by Ryan.[23]

In mid-August 1994, near the end of Ryan's tour as ACJCS, Senator Charles Grassley spoke to his Senate colleagues in support of Ryan's pending nomination "to be 'dual-hatted' as commander, Allied Air Forces, Southern Europe, NATO, and commander, 16th Air Force, U.S. Air Force, Europe."[24] That position, which required Senate confirmation, would also put Ryan in charge of NATO air operations over BiH. Ryan's integrity and courage had impressed Grassley, and the senator lauded those traits in telling other senators of Ryan's central role in exposing another powerful three-star's improper interference with a board considering brigadier generals for promotion to major general. Ryan undoubtedly made the ethical choice, but doing so was also personally quite risky for him, since that other powerful three-star had especially strong ties to the Senate Armed Services Committee charged with screening all three- and four-star-officer assignments and promotions. By the end of the next month, however, Ryan was confirmed and in place in Italy to take command.

BACKGROUND TO OPERATION DELIBERATE FORCE

As the Cold War died out and in the power vacuum that followed the death of Josip Broz Tito in 1980, Slobodan Milošević rose to power in Belgrade, the capital of Serbia, stoking dormant ethnic tensions to further his political ambitions. In large measure, Milošević's own handiwork ensured Yugoslavia disintegrated in a grim and bloody manner, and he was a key powerbroker for anyone wishing to end the war in BiH. For the purposes of this chapter, three of the states that emerged from the breakup of Yugoslavia are of primary importance: Serbia, Croatia, and BiH. Sitting in the center of the three states, BiH is insulated from the Adriatic by a thin strip of Croatia except in the south, where a six-mile-wide opening gives BiH its only access to the sea. Thus, Croatia encircles BiH to the southwest, west, and north, and Serbia borders BiH to the east.[25]

Although political ambition and mutual fear among ethnic groups rather than religious ideology drove the dissolution of Yugoslavia, religious alignments helped to define the ethnic groups fighting in BiH. Croats tended to be Catholic, the Serbs mostly belonged to the Serbian Orthodox Church, and the group ruling BiH from Sarajevo was mainly Muslim and was referred to as Bosniaks.

Many Croats and Serbs lived within the territory of BiH, and they benefited significantly from the support of their kinsmen in neighboring Croatia and Serbia. Only the Bosniaks lacked outside support. Therefore, when the UN Security Council approved an arms embargo against the former Yugoslavia on September 25, 1991, the Bosniaks were most disadvantaged. Serbia inherited the bulk of the arms, army, and military production capacity from the former Yugoslavia, and Milošević made sure the Bosnian Serb Army received a significant share of the military spoils. Croatia enjoyed friendly relations with the European countries to its west and managed to build up its military forces in spite of the arms embargo. But BiH, very nearly landlocked, had great difficulty acquiring arms.

In October 1992, the UN Security Council declared the skies over BiH off-limits to unauthorized military aircraft. After numerous violations—including bombing attacks by Serb aircraft—the Security Council authorized NATO to impose a complete no-fly zone, which it did beginning on April 12, 1993. Though there were many violations of that no-fly zone as well, most unauthorized flights were by helicopters, and NATO enforcement generally curbed violations by fixed-wing aircraft.

In the early spring of 1993, the UN Security Council designated six towns in BiH as "safe areas." In addition to the BiH capital of Sarajevo, they included the towns of Goražde, Žepa, Tuzla, and Srebrenica in eastern BiH, and Bihac in the far northwest. In the spring of 1994, the UN and NATO strengthened the policy by establishing twenty-kilometer heavy weapons exclusion zones around all the safe areas. Tanks, artillery, mortars, and antiaircraft artillery had to be removed from these exclusion zones or secured within UN-guarded cantonment areas. This policy was backed up by the threat of NATO airstrikes.

In March 1994, the United States helped to fashion a workable, if somewhat unnatural, federation of BiH's Croats and Bosniaks. Thus, by late 1994, the complexity of the Balkan equation had been greatly reduced, with two main forces opposing one another—Croatia supporting the joint Croat-Bosniak Federation and Serbia supplying the Bosnian Serbs. President Radovan Karadžić and an army general who was the real center of Serb military power in BiH, Ratko Mladić, led the Bosnian Serbs. From their capital in Pale, immediately east of Sarajevo, Mladić and Karadžić had easy access to the border with Serbia, their main source of external support.

Despite UN Security Council resolutions to protect the safe areas, little was done to actually rein in the Bosnian Serbs. According to the rules governing the use of NATO air power, UN and NATO authorities needed to agree before airstrikes could be conducted to enforce the safe areas policy. The UN used this arrangement, called "dual-key" control, to block nearly all NATO action.

In September 1994, Lieutenant General Ryan moved to Naples, Italy, to take command of Allied Air Forces Southern Europe (AIRSOUTH) from Lieutenant General Ashy, who was instrumental in establishing the command structure and processes so essential to the air operations that followed. In the NATO chain of command, Ryan worked for an American admiral, Leighton W. "Snuffy" Smith Jr., who headed Allied Forces Southern Europe, the command tasked to conduct operations in and around BiH. Admiral Smith, in turn, worked for the supreme allied commander Europe, Gen. George Joulwan of the U.S. Army. His headquarters was in Mons, Belgium, not far from NATO's political headquarters in Brussels. NATO's military chain of command took its political orders from the North Atlantic Council (NAC), which was made up of ambassadors from the then-sixteen NATO member countries. Below Ryan in the NATO chain were two numbered Allied Tactical Air Forces, but only one—the Fifth Allied Tactical Air Force—was involved in BiH. Headquartered at Vicenza, Italy, its commander was an Italian Air Force three-star, Andrea Fornasiero, and his deputy was Brig. Gen.

Dave Sawyer (USAF). General Fornasiero, who later became chief of the Italian Air Force, worked closely with the Italian government on the many political, logistical, and operational matters associated with the military flying operations from, in, and around Italy. The nerve center of Fornasiero's operation in Vicenza was the Combined Air Operations Center (CAOC), which another USAF general officer, Maj. Gen. Hal Hornburg, commanded.[26]

Ryan also commanded the U.S. Sixteenth Air Force headquartered at Aviano Air Base in northeastern Italy. That responsibility meant he was part of a separate U.S. chain of command that ran from the president through the secretary of defense to General Joulwan, who in addition to his NATO position was also the commander of one of America's geographic combatant commands, U.S. European Command. Below General Joulwan, the U.S. chain of command ran to Ryan through the four-star commander of U.S. Air Forces in Europe, Gen. James Jamerson, rather than through Ryan's NATO boss, Admiral Smith.

Although Ryan received matériel resources and other support through the U.S. chain of command, his political direction and operational orders came through the NATO chain and, ostensibly, only through that chain. The UN chain of command was simpler—at least in theory. Political direction came from the UN Security Council. UN secretary-general Boutros Boutros-Ghali personally oversaw decisions on using force to back up Security Council resolutions, and he exercised his control in the Balkans through his special representative, Yasushi Akashi. Based in the Croatian capital of Zagreb, Akashi worked alongside the senior military commander of all UN forces in BiH and Croatia, Lt. Gen. Bertrand de Lapresle of the French Army. While the French provided the most troops and held the top military post within the UN Protection Force (UNPROFOR), Sir Michael Rose of the British Army commanded operations in BiH. Despite these formal command structures, both the UN and NATO chains of command suffered routine interference from the capitals of nations contributing forces to UNPROFOR and AIRSOUTH, respectively.

By the time Ryan arrived on the scene, the UN was well along the way to abandoning its responsibility for enforcing the policies related to the safe areas and usually refused NATO's requests to take any enforcement measures, including those related to the no-fly zone. The UN believed that any NATO enforcement action against the Bosnian Serbs would lead to Serb retaliation, which in turn would threaten to unhinge the UN's peace support missions. This division of labor—with the UN engaged in peace support and NATO engaged in enforcement—caused serious friction between the two organizations in late 1994.

In November, two Bosnian Serb military operations helped drive a further wedge between the UN and NATO. First, in response to a Bosniak ground offensive in western BiH, Serb pilots flying from Udbina airfield in a Serb-controlled region of Croatia violated the no-fly zone and attacked Bosniak targets inside BiH. On the second day of these attacks, when a Serb pilot on a bombing run crashed into an apartment building north of Bihac, the irrefutable evidence of the Serbs' misconduct goaded NATO into airstrikes against Udbina. This significant military operation involved six NATO nations. Even though UNPROFOR leaders intervened to limit the strikes, the scale of the operation was unprecedented in NATO's history. The Bosnian Serbs responded by rounding up hundreds of UN peacekeepers as hostages, used some as human shields against further NATO air attacks, and threatened to go to war against UNPROFOR.

With hostages in hand, the Bosnian Serbs further widened the rift between the UN and NATO by using the BSA's most lethal radar-guided surface-to-air missiles (SAMs) to threaten NATO aircraft enforcing the no-fly zone. General Ryan and Admiral Smith appealed to NATO political leaders for new authority to counter the heightened SAM threat, and the NAC responded by authorizing the suppression of enemy air defenses (SEAD). However, that authority was contingent upon UN concurrence, thus extending dual-key control to SEAD missions. Because the UN commanders refused to turn their key, NATO airmen were left in an untenable position. As Ryan later explained:

> I was the commander of the air campaign in Bosnia and had lived with almost-Vietnam rules the first year that I was there, and it was the most frustrating thing that I have ever dealt with. . . . I may have been frustrated as an aircrewman by some of the stupidity in Vietnam, but I was doubly frustrated [in Bosnia] because . . . I guess I took it on myself to be frustrated for all our aircrews, when [the Bosnian Serbs] could shoot at us with SAMs and we had to go back and ask the UN's permission to come back and take out the same site.[27]

Thereafter, Ryan only allowed NATO aircraft over BiH in the company of specialized SEAD escort. Ryan and Smith repeatedly asked for permission to eliminate Bosnian Serb air defenses, but the UN would not agree. In December, former U.S. president Jimmy Carter brokered a four-month cease-fire with the Bosnian Serbs and the situation quieted down for the winter. This lull in the fighting only masked NATO's difficulties, which remained unresolved and would reappear later.

Early 1995 saw some personnel changes in the UN command structure. In January, General Rose turned over his command in BiH to Lt. Gen. Rupert Smith. In March, another French Army officer, Lt. Gen. Bernard Janvier, replaced General de Lapresle. That command soon changed its name from the UN Protection Force to the UN Peace Force to be more consistent with its preferred mission and capabilities. The name UNPROFOR was transferred to the subordinate command in BiH, where General Smith would soon test the UN's readiness to live up to its responsibility to protect.

For all concerned, 1995 seemed to be a year of decision in BiH. The widespread expectation was that the cease-fire would vanish with the arrival of spring, and General Smith worked on the assumption or thesis that the Bosnian Serbs would attempt to settle the war in their favor. If the Bosnian Serbs did make a final push to achieve their objectives, then the UN mission would fail, for Rupert Smith's peacekeepers lacked the numbers, equipment, and authority to effectively oppose the Serbs. They would need significant NATO help simply to evacuate from BiH.

Since late 1994, NATO planners had been preparing plans for a variety of scenarios, and the air power components to those plans fed into planning for what would become Operation Deliberate Force. One NATO plan considered ways of aiding the withdrawal of UNPROFOR, and the United States—in a move that could well have scuttled President Clinton's chances for reelection in 1996—had committed to employing twenty-five thousand ground troops for the task. With the increased threat to NATO airmen from Serbian radar-guided SAMs, planners at the CAOC began working on a plan called "Deadeye" that would neutralize BSA air defenses. When Ryan saw the Deadeye plan, he ordered additional planning to attrit BSA military capabilities. In essence, this effort addressed the strike part of lift and strike. No one above Ryan had ordered the planning; he simply had seen it as part of his responsibility as a commander.

By the spring of 1995, the Deliberate Force plan was sufficiently developed to be briefed to Ryan's bosses, and his planners continually refined the details. As

Ryan later remarked: "If we did not do the planning, I think we would have been as remiss as the UN was in not upholding the mandates they were supposed to. . . . We planned it, and I briefed it to Smith and Joulwan—we started briefing it [in] March [or] April [1995]."[28] They also briefed the plan to the U.S. national security adviser Anthony Lake and to NATO secretary general Willy Claes.

The plan included three categories of targets, labeled Options 1, 2, and 3. Option 1 targets were those military targets closest to a safe area and posing a direct threat to it; for example, they included any heavy weapons removed from UN custody that could be used to attack a safe area. Option 2 targets were those farther from safe areas and posing a less dire threat, such as ammunition depots that supplied rounds for the heavy weapons threatening a safe area. Finally, Option 3 targets were those farthest from a threatened safe area and with the least immediate bearing on the tactical situation. Any targets outside BiH would fall into the Option 3 category. Inside BiH, judgment and circumstances came into play, but infrastructure targets and military-related items, such as arms production factories and vehicle maintenance facilities, were likely to be counted as Option 3 targets.

To refine the Deliberate Force plan, Ryan drew upon the services of Checkmate and other planning and intelligence agencies, including the Joint Warfare Analysis Center, the National Security Agency, and a USAF intelligence outfit from San Antonio, Texas, that specialized in command and control warfare. The planning for Deliberate Force, and later its execution, represented teamwork; it was not the sole product of Ryan's thinking or efforts. He insists on crediting Ashy; Fornasiero; Sawyer; Hornburg; the CAOC planners; his own staff from Naples, especially Col. Daniel "Doc" Zoerb; and many other permanent and temporarily assigned officers—American and allied—whose expertise, dedication, and hard work were essential in building, refining, and executing the plans.

When fighting did break out in the spring of 1995, it was in Croatia, not BiH. On May 1, Croatian forces launched Operation Flash, and within a few days they had captured a number of Serb forces and pushed the remainder south into BiH. The UN was helpless to stop the Croatian offensive, and more than a hundred UN peacekeepers in Croatia were taken hostage, some by Croatian forces, others by Serbian soldiers.[29] General Mladić kept his BSA forces out of the fight, fueling speculation that the BSA was stretched too thin in eastern BiH to support the Serbs fighting in Croatia.

Later in May 1995, General Mladić's artillery struck targets in Sarajevo, leading General Smith to issue an ultimatum. The UNPROFOR commander set a deadline for the BSA to return its heavy weapons to UN cantonment sites or suffer NATO airstrikes. When the BSA failed to meet Smith's deadline, NATO planes pounded ammunition storage bunkers at a BSA complex near Pale. The next day, the Bosnian Serbs failed to meet another of Smith's deadlines, and NATO airmen destroyed additional munitions sites at the Pale complex. This action was by far the most robust one that the UN had ordered in BiH, and it infuriated Mladić, who had become accustomed to receiving advanced warnings of NATO's pin-prick strikes. Mladić predictably seized UN soldiers as hostages and human shields. Most knowledgeable observers, including Ryan, believed that Smith had taken a calculated risk in authorizing the Pale airstrikes. According to this view, Smith wanted to force the UN hierarchy to confront the untenable nature of UNPRO-FOR's position in BiH and to give the UNPROFOR commander the leverage he needed to redeploy his forces to more defensible positions.[30]

To better protect their soldiers in BiH, the British, French, and Dutch governments quickly deployed a combat-capable rapid reaction force (RRF) to BiH but without first seeking the UN's consent for the deployment. The RRF's main fighting element was a multinational brigade equipped with British and French armored fighting vehicles and augmented with British and French artillery, a Dutch heavy mortar company, French antitank guided missiles, and other lethal hardware.[31] The speed with which the RRF deployed hinted at some level of premeditation and planning, and the UN's enhanced ground power was soon matched by improvements in NATO air power.

Before the first elements of the RRF arrived in BiH, and with hundreds of UN soldiers still held hostage, the Bosnian Serbs shot down a USAF F-16 piloted by Capt. Scott O'Grady. While patrolling the no-fly zone O'Grady and his flight lead were baited by Serb aircraft flying from Udbina in Croatia, slightly west of BiH, and only two or three minutes' flying time from Bihac. In retrospect, Ryan and Admiral Smith concluded that the Serbs had set a trap and that NATO airmen had fallen into it.[32] Ryan later said, "The O'Grady shoot down was my fault. . . . We became predictable, and that was my mistake." Suddenly the American public was paying attention to the war in BiH. Even after O'Grady's rescue six days after being shot down, Ryan received a deluge of equipment and personnel to support him and Major General Hornburg at the CAOC.

Within a month of the O'Grady shootdown, the U.S. fighter wing at Aviano Air Base in Italy became the 7490th Wing (Provisional). The temporary designation allowed the recently arrived wing commander, Colonel Wald, to exercise command authority over the disparate USAF units flying from Aviano. Wald also transformed the wing's small Operation Deny Flight coordination cell into a more capable operations center. By the time Deliberate Force began, the number of aircraft operating from Aviano stood at more than 100, and that number would climb to as high as 140 during the operation.[33]

The UN's persistent refusal to allow Admiral Smith and General Ryan to attack the Bosnian Serb air defenses caused the two NATO commanders to pull their air patrols back to the safety of the Adriatic, where they were largely ineffective. Only with heavy SEAD escort would NATO missions be allowed over BiH, and the limited number of SEAD assets meant that for long windows each day NATO was in no position to perform its enforcement missions. The Bosnian Serbs soon took advantage of their newfound freedom by flying missions from Banja Luka in northwestern BiH. Though pressed to do more to enforce the no-fly zone, Admiral Smith refused to hazard NATO aircrews unnecessarily. This stance forced NATO planners and political officials in Mons and Brussels to review the entire NATO mission in BiH and paved the way for a future NAC decision to back more forceful action.[34]

By July 1995, events in BiH were moving rapidly toward some sort of culmination, but who would prevail was not clear. In five days, starting on July 6, Bosnian Serb forces under General Mladić's command brushed aside the battalion of 450 Dutch peacekeepers in the UN safe area of Srebrenica and purged the town of its Muslim population. The Muslim men and older boys who did not escape into the surrounding hills were separated from their families and neighbors and massacred. The Serbs methodically killed several thousand, but no one knows the exact number. From Srebrenica, the BSA soldiers moved on to the nearby, smaller town of Žepa to continue their horrific work of ethnic cleansing.

Western governments expressed outrage at the BSA's actions, and those governments with peacekeepers in BiH feared their soldiers would soon face the same embarrassing fate that the Dutch at Srebrenica had suffered—or worse. With Goražde as the next likely target of Serb ethnic cleansing, the British were especially concerned, for their First Battalion, Royal Welch Fusiliers, was there. On July 21 and 22 in London, British prime minister John Major hosted a conference of leaders from the UN, Europe, and the Contact Group. Ryan's Deliberate Force plan was briefed to senior British officials on the eve of the conference, and in the days following the conference it was briefed to NATO ambassadors in Brussels.[35]

Two significant decisions emerged from this London conference. First, the attendees agreed to threaten the Bosnian Serbs with forceful and sustained NATO airstrikes if they committed any future transgressions. Second, they removed the UN authority to allow those NATO airstrikes from the secretary-general's special representative Akashi and passed it to the UN military commander, General Janvier.

In the two weeks following the conference, the NAC in Brussels affirmed its support for the decisions taken in London, authorizing in principle strikes against Option 1 and Option 2 targets. Strikes against Option 3 targets would require a separate political decision from NATO. Farther to the south, Admiral Smith worked with General Janvier to produce a memorandum of understanding formalizing the mechanisms by which they would coordinate targeting decisions and other details for using air power. Because no doctrine governed the coordination of NATO air action with UN ground operations, Generals Ryan and Smith hammered out an air-land coordination document. The two operational commanders agreed that for close air support (CAS), Smith would call the shots; for airstrikes or interdiction far from UN forces, Ryan would be in charge; and for targets falling between those categories the commanders would share decision-making authority.

During the collaboration between Ryan and Smith, the latter made a useful contribution to planning for Deliberate Force. Ryan did not believe air power could defend the safe areas; instead, he maintained it required a competent ground force. He thought that air power could best be used to end the war by eliminating BSA capabilities across BiH and not only in the vicinity of a threatened safe area. Therefore, if Ryan were given the opportunity to execute Deliberate Force he wanted as much latitude as NATO political authorities would give him. General Joulwan helpfully intervened with the NAC to win approval for Ryan to operate in undefined, broad zones of action (ZOAs). NATO air planners interpreted this authority liberally by noting that "zones" was plural, thus that meant they had to have at least two. They therefore divided the Deliberate Force targets into a northwest ZOA and a southeast ZOA along a straight line, running from southwest to northeast and bisecting BiH fairly evenly. When General Smith saw the proposed line, however, he suggested that the scheme be changed so that the safe area of Tuzla in northeastern BiH would be in both ZOAs. Now, the ZOAs would overlap in northeastern BiH, and an incident in Tuzla could trigger operations in either ZOA. Even more important, the narrow stretch of Serb-controlled land around Posavina, through which BSA forces would have to travel to move between eastern and western BiH, could be attacked regardless of which ZOA was approved for operations. Smith's recommendation was readily adopted.

Early on the morning of August 4, 1995, Croatian military forces launched Operation Storm to physically wrest control of Croatia's frontier from the Krajina Serbs. As writer and photojournalist Tim Ripley described it: "Operation Storm was a massive operation, involving more than 100,000 assault troops backed up by hundreds of artillery pieces and armoured vehicles. A similar number of troops were mobilized to support it. Dozens of helicopters and fighter-bombers participated in the attack."[36] Within two days, the Croatian army overran the Krajina Serb capital of Knin, sending nearly 100,000 Serb refugees fleeing north and east into Serb-controlled areas of western BiH.[37] Western outrage was muted. By August 8, the offensive had achieved its objectives, and again General Mladić and his BSA provided no help to their kinsmen in Croatia. With Zagreb now firmly in control of Croatian territory, except for Eastern Slavonia, all eyes were on BiH.

OPERATION DELIBERATE FORCE

The action that initiated Operation Deliberate Force turned out not to be a ground assault on Goražde or one of the other safe areas, as many observers had anticipated. Instead, the explosion of a 120mm mortar round at a busy marketplace in Sarajevo on the morning of Monday, August 28, triggered the campaign. Though the Bosnian Serbs denied responsibility for the blast, a UN investigation soon concluded the deadly shell was one of a salvo fired from Bosnian Serb positions.[38] The explosion left thirty-eight people dead and more than eighty wounded. As soon as Admiral Smith saw televised images of the carnage, he contacted his UN counterparts to inform them that his key was turned.

Because General Janvier was in France at his son's wedding, the UN key was in the hands of Lt. Gen. Rupert Smith. In the wake of the market attack, General Smith hastened the departure of the remaining Royal Welch Fusiliers from Goražde and ordered the withdrawal of UN military observers from vulnerable positions. Before midnight on Tuesday, August 29, General Smith had postured his forces to minimize their vulnerability, and General Janvier, who had returned to his headquarters in Zagreb, agreed to go ahead with the air campaign. Now the UN key was also turned. In the early hours of Wednesday, August 30, NATO airmen began what was by far the largest military operation of the alliance's forty-six-year history.

Ryan flew to the CAOC at Vicenza soon after the market bombing, and NATO airmen there and at bases in Italy and around the region readied for the first airstrikes. To mask NATO's preparations, Major General Hornburg ordered that a reduced schedule of sorties be flown on Tuesday. In contrast to some previous airstrikes, the Bosnian Serbs were to have no warning from the UN of the pending attacks—or at least that was the agreement among the senior commanders in NATO and the UN. But when the first wave of air attacks reached BiH airspace at around two o'clock in the morning of August 30, the BSA's air defenders remained suspiciously unresponsive to the air-launched decoys designed to expose their radar to lethal SEAD strikes.[39]

While Ryan might have preferred to eliminate all BSA air defenses before conducting Deliberate Force airstrikes, he opted instead for a minimalist approach to suppressing those defenses and concentrated the bulk of NATO air power against key combat elements of the BSA. After a single wave of strikes to suppress the enemy air defenses, NATO airmen began the first of five packages of airstrikes designed to attrit BSA capabilities.[40] Ryan wanted to destroy as many of the BSA's combat capabilities as possible before either the Bosnian Serbs stopped the campaign by yielding to UN demands or NATO political leaders called a halt to the strikes. Individual NATO countries had frequently intervened to stop earlier air operations, and Serb president Milošević contacted the UN's Yasushi Akashi on the afternoon of August 30, asking him to inform General Mladić of the UN's terms for halting the bombing.[41]

It would have been highly impolitic to say so at the time, but Ryan was consciously and quickly implementing the strike component of Washington's lift-and-strike policy. As he admitted after the campaign, he was trying to level the playing field that had previously been tilted in favor of the Bosnian Serbs, "That was the premise of the bombing operation. That was the heart of the bombing operation. You had heard about lift and strike. . . . Lift was not going to occur. So if you are going to level the playing field, you do it the other way around, by attriting."[42] Ryan had studied the BSA and understood its dependence on a relatively small number of highly effective forces and their ability to maneuver and draw on arms caches throughout BiH. He had reasons for not wanting to kill BSA soldiers, so he went after the weapons, logistical capabilities, munitions depots, command and control, and mobility targets that were key to the BSA's effectiveness.

After some initial friction between senior UN and NATO officials, the target approval process ran smoothly, and Ryan was left to run the air campaign.[43]

Initially, Admiral Smith and General Janvier approved only twenty-five targets: fifteen air defense targets from the Deadeye plan and ten targets from the Deliberate Force plan.[44] Generals Ryan and Smith nominated the targets, and, according to the memorandum of understanding that had been worked out after the London conference, Admiral Smith and General Janvier approved them. In most cases, these targets could be better described as large target sites containing multiple aim points or desired mean points of impact at which NATO airmen would aim their bombs. That distinction between targets and aim points, and the mismatch between the names given to certain large target sites (e.g., barracks) and the actual aim points within them (e.g., munitions bunkers), created confusion for General Janvier and initially caused him to balk at approving some targets, but that confusion was quickly cleared up. On day 2 of the campaign, Admiral Smith informed the press, "Once General Janvier and I decided it was time to execute air operations, we turned the air operations over to General Ryan and he is responsible for execution."[45]

Ryan controlled nearly every aspect of the air campaign, from target selection to bomb damage assessment and much in between, including the time of day, axis of attack, sequence for striking targets, and the type of weapons to be used. He could do this because the scope of the operation was small enough; there were only fifty-six target sites, and within those sites there was a combined total of just 338 aim points.[46] With scores of strike aircraft at his disposal, each capable of flying three to five sorties per day and of carrying two or more precision-guided munitions (PGMs), General Ryan could, theoretically, hit all of the targets within a single week in good weather conditions. Of course, the weather was not always good, and the fog and friction of war and politics ensured a sizable gap between the theoretical programming of sorties and the reality of achieving the campaign's desired effects. Still, after barely eleven days of bombing Ryan found he had very few targets left to strike.

Ryan exercised extremely tight control over targeting because he wanted to achieve the desired military effects quickly while avoiding collateral damage and the killing of Bosnian Serb soldiers. Significant collateral damage could easily have undermined NATO's political resolve and the UN's willingness to countenance the bombing; thus, as the air commander Ryan believed his responsibility was to ensure that no such damage occurred. On the one-year anniversary of Deliberate Force, Ryan told the audience at an air power conference in London, "If you're the commander of an air operation [collateral damage is] your business, nobody else's business. . . . Don't let it get down to the individual aircrew or unit. If they screw up, it's normally your screw-up, not theirs."[47]

Ryan sought to minimize collateral damage in a variety of ways, including through RoE and special instructions (SPINS). "Every section of ROE included a statement concerning the need to minimize collateral damage," noted the official U.S. Air University study of the campaign.[48] Though it frustrated some allied pilots and tacticians, Ryan issued SPINS mandating certain tactics that lowered the chances of success for a given attack and may have marginally increased risks to the aircrews, but they also decreased the likelihood that an errant bomb would cause civilian casualties. For example, when attacking a bridge with a laser-guided bomb, tactics manuals called for a pilot to fly and drop the bomb along an axis that nearly paralleled the bridge. General Ryan ordered such attacks be made on axes along rivers and perpendicular to bridges, so that bombs that missed their intended aim points would most likely land in the water, thereby reducing the chances of collateral damage. As an added precaution, Ryan ordered that they be struck at night, when civilian traffic on the bridges would be less likely.[49]

In addition, Ryan went to great lengths to avoid killing BSA soldiers. Ryan's planners at AIRSOUTH ranked Bosnian Serb fielded forces as the second-highest-priority targets, right behind BSA integrated air defenses,[50] yet Ryan still refused to target BSA forces intentionally. In explaining his targeting calculus, he later stated: "There was one that was unsaid . . . no one ever told me to do this, but, limit carnage—limit loss of life. So, we didn't hit buildings that had apparent administrative functions. . . . So we limited by time of day, by function, by location, loss of life on the Bosnian Serb Army side."[51] Minimizing BSA casualties helped to preserve the UN's backing for the air campaign and paved the way for a better state of peace. It also made it easier to negotiate with the Bosnian Serbs to end the fighting, and it avoided giving the Bosnian Serbs a motive for exacting retribution against the NATO ground forces that would eventually deploy to BiH to implement a peace settlement.

In addition to the twenty-five targets that NATO air power struck on day 1, the RRF used its guns and mortars on Mount Igman, which looms north of Sarajevo and commands most of the roads into the BiH capital, to hit fifteen targets in the vicinity of Sarajevo. Through a process of airspace management, the CAOC allotted time to various elements of the UN and NATO forces and allowed for

SEAD attacks, airstrikes, CAS, reconnaissance flights, and the firing of the RRF's guns. About two hours after the first airstrikes, nearly a hundred artillery and mortar tubes of the RRF began a seventy-five-minute sequence of attacks against the fifteen BSA targets. The RRF was reined in after the first day of Deliberate Force, when UN leaders in New York pointed out the RRF's lack of an offensive mission and called upon it to desist. Still, the RRF continued its efforts to break the siege of Sarajevo and to support the air campaign with missions against BSA air defenses, including some short-notice missions against man-portable weapons. By 6 a.m. on August 30, it was time to clear the air of artillery and mortar rounds and make way for NATO CAS missions.

French tactical air control parties talked NATO pilots onto BSA targets in the vicinity of Sarajevo. Though many CAS missions were programmed and flown, only ten aircraft actually attacked CAS targets on August 30.[52] After an hour of CAS on the morning of August 30, ownership of BiH airspace shifted back to the NATO planes conducting airstrikes. The Bosnian Serbs did not organize for offensive action until September 10, when they shelled Tuzla, eliciting the only other CAS missions of the campaign that expended their ordnance against actual CAS targets.[53]

At around 7 a.m., the second strike package pounded ammunition storage bunkers at several Bosnian Serb military sites to the west, north, and east of Sarajevo and at Pale. NATO strike packages contained aircraft formations from all of the NATO countries participating in Deliberate Force. The various national formations followed one another in a stream of jets, with each formation separated from the others by a few miles. Once in the vicinity of the target area, in this case Sarajevo, the formations split from the packages and attacked their separate targets. Aircraft capable of employing PGMs were tasked to hit most of the targets, and those incapable of dropping PGMs undertook missions where their lack of precision carried little risk of collateral damage.

On the evening of August 30, Bosnian Serb air defenders shot down a French Mirage 2000, call sign Ebro 33, with a shoulder-fired SAM. NATO aircrews operating nearby spotted two parachutes, indicating the plane's two crew members might have ejected safely. Ebro 33 may well have been operating below the 10,000-foot floor that General Ryan had set to keep his planes above many of the short-range air defense systems and small-arms fire, but excursions below the floor were permitted during certain phases of an attack, particularly when required to successfully hit a target.[54] A week after the shootdown, Ryan received inconclusive evidence of contact with the Ebro 33 crew, and on three consecutive days he launched missions to find and rescue them. In the process, the BSA almost shot down one of the rescue helicopters. The American airmen's willingness to take such risks earned great respect from the French contingent at the CAOC. For the Vietnam generation of airmen involved, such as Ryan, it was an article of faith that they would attempt a rescue if there were any chance to save a downed airman. Only after the campaign and the safe return of the Ebro 33 crew did General Ryan and others in NATO learn that the Bosnian Serbs had captured the two Frenchmen almost immediately after they parachuted to the ground.

On the second day of the campaign, NATO continued to launch sorties over BiH, but poor weather inhibited air operations. Although some of the fighters operating over BiH could use the Global Positioning System (GPS) for navigation, the USAF did not receive its first GPS-guided bombs until two years after Deliberate Force. Meanwhile, the overwhelming majority of PGMs used in Deliberate Force were laser-guided bombs, and the remainder relied on electro-optical guidance. Thus, to use their PGMs, NATO aircrews needed good weather over their targets. In addition to constraints that the contemporary PGMs imposed, restrictions against flying low meant that NATO aircrews needed uncommonly favorable weather conditions to hit their targets. Many of the missions scheduled for August 31 were scrubbed or failed to hit their targets because of adverse weather.[55]

PAUSE

After two days of bombing, Richard Holbrooke, President Clinton's chief negotiator for the Balkans, and Serb president Milošević interceded to suspend the campaign so that Generals Janvier and Mladić could meet and discuss terms for ending it. After the meeting, Janvier returned to his headquarters at Camp Pleso in Croatia convinced that Mladić would soon take the steps required to end the bombing permanently, and he persuaded Admiral Smith to extend the pause to ninety-six hours to give Mladić time to comply. Ryan's chief of staff, Maj. Gen. Mike Short—whom Ryan entrusted with many tough tasks—attended the meeting at Camp Pleso and relayed to Ryan that it appeared Deliberate Force was over. As Short later noted, Ryan "just postured the forces, getting ready to go again."[56]

The bombing pause not only allowed political authorities in the UN and NATO to set terms for permanently ending the bombing but also gave Ryan time for some badly needed rest. To maximize the damage NATO air power inflicted on the BSA's ability to fight, Ryan had remained awake and directed the campaign from the time he flew to Vicenza on the morning of August 29 until the pause went into effect early on September 1—nearly three days without sleep.[57] Experience strongly suggested that the UN's and NATO's willingness to use force in BiH would prove fragile, and the bombing pause seemed to confirm that notion. However, during the pause, NATO political authorities demonstrated their resolve to continue the campaign when the NAC issued an ultimatum on September 3 threatening further airstrikes if the Bosnian Serbs did not meet the following three conditions: "(1) remove all heavy weapons from the 20-kilometer exclusion zone around Sarajevo; (2) cease all attacks on the remaining four safe areas; and (3) lift the siege of Sarajevo by allowing unhindered access by road and air to the BiH capital."[58] By the evening of September 4, General Mladić clearly was not complying with UN and NATO demands. Bombing recommenced that night.

RESUMPTION

The bombing campaign resumed with airstrikes against the same types of targets struck during the first two days and then expanded to include new targets and new parts of BiH. Throughout September 5, NATO airmen eliminated Bosnian Serb ammunition bunkers; command, control, and communications targets; and military storage facilities in the southeastern zone of action.[59] The rapidly changing assessment of the situation in BiH eventually led planners at the CAOC to publish the air tasking message with all the information needed to fly the missions; however, it did not provide target information for missions flown later in the day until planners had assessed the progress of the campaign. As a consequence, some crews did not receive their target information until they were airborne.[60]

On September 6, weather forced many cancellations, led to ineffective sorties, and caused pilots to abort sorties after takeoff, including a combat search and rescue (CSAR) mission launched from the USS *Theodore Roosevelt* to locate the Ebro 33 crew.[61] Although the weather improved on September 7, another attempt to find the two French aviators ran into fog and was forced to turn back. On September 8, when BSA forces shot up a Special Operations helicopter, injuring two of its crew members, Ryan concluded that the Serbs were baiting NATO and that absent positive contact with the crew of Ebro 33 he would not launch any further CSAR missions to find them.

On September 7, NATO attacked targets in northeastern BiH and continued attacks in the southeast. Soon after bombing resumed, NATO began attacking bridges, eventually dropping seven of them and damaging five others.[62] Hitting bridges isolated Mladić from Bosnian Serb forces in central and western BiH and greatly hindered his ability to support them; so did destroying his command, control, and communication nodes, several of which were eliminated on the third day after the pause.[63]

Another expansion of bombing operations grew from Ryan's strong desire to destroy the BSA's integrated air defense system in northwestern BiH; he wanted to execute Deadeye Northwest. On September 5, Ryan requested permission to employ cruise missiles—namely, Tomahawk land-attack missiles (TLAMs)—against Serb air defenses, and on September 7 asked for U.S.-based F-117 stealth fighter-bombers.[64] He envisioned a three-step sequence of attacks against the Bosnian Serb air defenses: first he would attack known SAM sites, next he would take out the communications and early warning radar in northwestern and north-central BiH, and finally he would use airstrikes, including TLAMs and F-117s, to eliminate air defense and radio-relay targets.[65]

Although Ryan did not get everything he wanted, the Deadeye plan went forward and did more than secure the airspace over BiH. President Clinton reportedly approved the TLAM strikes on September 7, and Secretary of Defense William Perry okayed the deployment of F-117s on September 9.[66] However, the Italian government, unhappy at being left out of the Contact Group, refused to allow the F-117s into Italy. Ryan went ahead with the SEAD strikes against the SAMs on September 8, with disappointing results. The next night, USAF F-15Es using television-guided bombs (GBU-15s) and U.S. Navy F/A-18s launching TV-guided standoff land-attack missiles attacked integrated air defense system targets on Lisina Mountain and at Prnjavor but again with limited success.[67] A similar mix of assets went out the following night, September 10, with a heavy SEAD escort and thirteen TLAM missiles launched from the USS *Normandy*. Despite electronic interference between the air force and navy jets' TV-guided bombs, the USAF attacks that night were largely successful, and the TLAMs proved extremely effective.[68]

As hinted earlier, the Deadeye airstrikes in northwestern BiH significantly inhibited Mladić's ability—and that of the BSA generally—to respond to a Croat-Bosniak ground offensive. Mladić remained in Belgrade during the bombing pause and for a while afterward, though the reason for his absence from the battle-field remains unclear. Regardless of why or how long Mladić stayed in Belgrade, NATO air power was decimating his army's ability to function effectively. In the midst of the Deadeye attacks in northwestern BiH, Bosnian Croat and Croatian Army forces launched an offensive in central BiH.[69] Although the ground and air campaigns were not coordinated, they were mutually supportive and quickly overwhelmed the BSA. As Croatian and BiH Army forces remade the map defining the ethnic boundaries in central BiH, thousands of Bosnian Serbs fled north toward Banja Luka.

Ryan tightly controlled information about the details of the bombing operations. The Deliberate Force plan had been briefed to many NATO military and political leaders, but once the campaign commenced, only the military leaders in Naples and the CAOC knew the precise details of each day's operations. In Brussels discomfited NATO ambassadors wanted to know more about the campaign, and UN leaders in New York constantly pressed Special Representative Akashi and General Janvier for details. According to Air Commodore Mike Rudd, the British NATO liaison officer to Janvier's headquarters, "Janvier didn't tell them anything. . . . He only told the UN Secretary General Boutros Boutros-Ghali and Akashi big picture stuff, but did not give them militarily useful information."[70] In fact, Janvier did not have the operational details to give. While he and Admiral Smith approved targets for the campaign, the details of when and how to attack those targets were left to Ryan.

Ryan also held back information on the results of the air campaign, including bomb damage assessment (BDA). After the campaign he noted that "experience from other action [including Vietnam and Desert Storm] told me that somebody had to get control of BDA, so we put out a message that said the only [one] who will evaluate BDA will be the CAOC." Various national-level agencies, such as the Central Intelligence Agency and the Defense Intelligence Agency, were expected to feed data into the process but not to offer their own assessments.[71] By tightly controlling information about targeting and BDA, Ryan secured a large measure of autonomy and avoided outside interference. He later explained why he withheld details of the operation:

> So that we didn't have nations, or particular intelligence agencies briefing BDA that was not corroborated and coming up with conclusions from that.

None of the nations knew what targets were approved. . . . If you don't know what the target set is, you can't measure how you're doing, because you don't know what your objective is. And therefore, none of the other agencies were empowered in any way to say . . . whether we were accomplishing what we thought we needed to accomplish.[72]

Ryan did not want pundits, the press, or policymakers on the fringes of UN, NATO, or U.S. decision making second-guessing the progress of air operations. Fortunately for him, Admiral Smith supported him, ran interference, and screened questions from the press and from high-level political authorities.

On the days Deadeye Northwest was prosecuted, poor weather hampered NATO efforts in the southeast ZOA. On September 9, adverse weather in the target area prevented the first two strike packages from dropping their bombs. Though weather delayed the three strike packages later that day, they eventually flew and had some success in hitting their targets.[73]

By September 11, more than half of the original targets and aim points had been destroyed, and the majority of the remainder were destroyed that day. Of the original twenty Deadeye and thirty-six Deliberate Force targets, the day began with only twenty-two—seven Deadeye and fifteen Deliberate Force—still intact.[74] Favorable weather allowed Ryan to fly six strike packages instead of the usual five that were scheduled.[75] The targets NATO struck were monotonously similar to those described earlier.[76] By September 12, Ryan was down to a mere eleven targets with a scant sixty aim points.[77] Talk of going to Option 3 targets began to circulate in the press, but political approval for that route never seemed realistic.

News of the dwindling number of targets caused Richard Holbrooke, who was attending meetings in Washington, to return to the Balkans earlier than he had planned. Skeptical that NATO was running out of targets, Holbrooke wanted to stretch out the bombing campaign because of the leverage it gave him in negotiations with Serb president Slobodan Milošević. The one time Holbrooke tried telephoning Ryan to discuss the campaign, however, Ryan referred him to Admiral Smith. When Holbrooke did phone Admiral Smith, Smith refused to consider input from outside the formal chain of command. When General Joulwan subsequently pressed Smith, the admiral adamantly resisted any suggestion of sending NATO aircrews over BiH without valid targets to hit. Though Holbrooke did not like the situation, he could not change it; so he hurried on to Belgrade to meet with Milošević.

Perhaps fortunately for Holbrooke's negotiations, the weather over BiH prevented Ryan from making much progress against the remaining targets, thereby stretching out the campaign and preserving the threat of further airstrikes. On September 12, a NATO strike on a well-stocked ammunition site at Doboj, near Tuzla, caused such an explosion that, reportedly, "Serb radio went on the air to accuse NATO of using tactical nuclear weapons."[78] The next day, Ryan sent aircraft to revisit Lisina Mountain to hit an air defense target and a command, control, and communications target. Navy aircraft employing standoff land-attack missiles destroyed one target and heavily damaged the other.[79]

Entirely separate from the NATO bombing, on September 13 BiH Army and Croatian forces launched a new phase in their ground offensive in central BiH. This move was part of a mounting land campaign that would rumble on into October, weeks after Deliberate Force ended. For Holbrooke's purposes, that ground campaign almost certainly compensated for any adverse impact caused by weather or NATO's shrinking target list. Weather again severely hindered NATO air operations on September 14. By then only eight Option 2 targets and forty-three aim points had not been destroyed. That evening, Milošević surprised Holbrooke by bringing Bosnian Serb leaders Karadžić and Mladić to join the negotiations. After hammering out a few details, the Bosnian Serb leaders finally acceded to the terms of the NAC's ultimatum. Admiral Smith instituted a seventy-two-hour bombing pause that night to give the Serbs a chance to comply with the NAC's terms, effectively bringing the campaign to an end. The Croat and Bosniak ground offensive continued for several weeks, and the Bosnian Serbs never quite regained their footing, remaining on the defensive until the war ground to a halt. By the start of November, Slobodan Milošević was in Dayton, Ohio, with representatives from BiH and Croatia to negotiate a comprehensive settlement to the fighting that had raged in the Balkans for more than four years. The resulting Dayton Peace Accords were signed in Paris on December 14, 1995, and remain in effect seventeen years later.

Although air power by itself did not end the war in BiH, it made an essential contribution. General Ryan deserves much of the credit, even if he insists the credit belongs to the many members of his team involved in the planning and execution of Deliberate Force.

AFTER DELIBERATE FORCE

Ryan remained as commander of AIRSOUTH until April 1996, when he pinned on his fourth star and moved to Ramstein Air Base, Germany, to take command of U.S. Air Forces in Europe. In November 1997, he returned to Washington to become the sixteenth chief of staff of the U.S. Air Force and earned a reputation among the other air force four-stars for being collaborative and inclusive in leading the service.

Though Ryan arrived at the chief's office believing that fundamentally the air force was headed in the right direction, he counted several initiatives as the most important of his tenure. Even before becoming chief, Ryan had a hand in advancing the air force's operational doctrine. Having supported General Horner during Desert Shield and Desert Storm and then having commanded Operation Deliberate Force, Ryan helped codify the lessons underpinning successful air campaigns. Indeed, he was a primary contributor to the Air Force Doctrine Center's production of *Presentation of USAF Forces*, commonly referred to as "The Little Red Book," which helped inform Air Force Doctrine Document 2, *Operations and Organization*. As chief he continued to support the additional development of that doctrine and took it a step further by pushing the CAOC as a weapon system. He used his statutory responsibility to organize, train, and equip the air force to enable future air commanders by giving them the systems and trained personnel they needed to orchestrate air campaigns effectively. In doing so, he made sure to integrate intelligence and space capabilities into the CAOC. He also fostered an initiative to train and educate future JFACCs at a course conducted at Maxwell Air Force Base, bringing in retired generals with experience commanding air operations to mentor future JFACCs.

The major innovation that Ryan brought to the service was the Air Expeditionary Force (AEF) concept. By the time he became chief, the air force had been supporting flying operations over Iraq nonstop for more than six years. While other services deployed forces to the Gulf War and came home when the fighting stopped, the deployments never ended for the air force. Operations Northern Watch and Southern Watch created a constant demand on the USAF, in addition to other operations such as Deny Flight and Deliberate Force. Though the air force's pattern of operations had changed enormously since the Cold War, the way the service was organized to meet the new demands had not changed. The AEF concept rationalized what had been an ad hoc scheme of deciding which units and individuals to deploy, thereby making deployments more predictable and creating a greater sense of stability. The AEF also helped the air force justify the service's force structure and explain the impacts of adding to, or reducing, that force structure.

CHARACTERISTICS OF COMMAND

At least ten aspects of Gen. Mike Ryan's command of Deliberate Force warrant the attention of students of air power. The first is that Ryan was a tactical expert. He thoroughly understood the capabilities and limitation of the tools at his disposal and the adversary weapon systems that threatened NATO airmen. He understood the platforms, the weapons, the tactics, and the operational rhythm of the flight line and how they all fit together. This expertise came from a career focused on combat aviation, including flying F-4s over Vietnam, spending time as a maintenance officer, attending Fighter Weapons School, serving as wing weapons officer, and commanding a fighter squadron and later a fighter wing.

The second aspect of Ryan's command that stands out was his appreciation for the importance of intelligence and his knowledge of how to get it and how to use it. From his time at Checkmate and his later experience at TAC supporting General Horner, he knew that detailed intelligence in all its forms was a foundation for successful military operations. Indeed, as the command's deputy chief of staff for operations, Ryan had helped to create a section for training intelligence officers at Fighter Weapons School. In planning Deliberate Force, he tapped the expertise of intelligence organizations—at the USAF, joint, and national levels—to gain a detailed understanding of the BSA's operational center of gravity, and he later put it to good use in executing the campaign.

Vision, initiative, and planning combined to make up the third significant aspect of Ryan's command of Deliberate Force. Ryan had a plan to accomplish the job in BiH because he decided to create that plan; no one told him to do it. He had peered into BiH's future and envisioned possibilities that would solve not only the problems he faced as an air commander but also the complex tangle of political problems that confronted NATO and the United States. Ryan's ability to conceptualize and plan for complex challenges undoubtedly received a boost from his education at both the Air Command and Staff College and the business administration program at Auburn University. His assignments with TAC's planning staff and Checkmate further complemented that knowledge, and every step beyond that point enhanced his prowess and his confidence in taking the initiative to implement his plans and fulfill his vision.

The time Ryan spent on the Joint Staff as vice director for strategic plans and policy and then as assistant to the chairman of the JCS honed his sensitivity to the concerns of top civilian policy makers and political authorities. That understanding of the political environment is the fourth noteworthy aspect of Ryan's command. The air campaign over BiH was remarkable for its military efficacy, but even more impressive was its achievement of political objectives without significant unintended effects. Here Ryan displayed the genius—in the sense that Clausewitz used the term—needed to conceive of and to prosecute Deliberate Force despite the friction inherent in multinational military operations and the adverse weather during the campaign. That he led such a successful campaign when a single misstep could have ended it prematurely testifies to his political-military acumen.

In addition to meeting the military ends and political demands of the day, Ryan built and executed a campaign leading to a better state of peace. By minimizing casualties among BSA forces, Ryan helped to prevent the campaign from going in unanticipated and undesired directions, as commonly happens in war. Deliberate Force had an enormous impact on BSA fielded forces, but it did so without ruining negotiations to end the war in BiH and without poisoning the well for the international forces that deployed to BiH to implement the peace agreement. This fifth aspect of his command stemmed from Ryan's understanding of the nature of war and his appreciation for international affairs. He probably began developing these insights subconsciously at an early age as the son of an air force general; they truly started to mature through his assignments as a field-grade officer and never stopped evolving.

The sixth outstanding aspect of Ryan's command was his sense of responsibility for NATO airmen and his refusal to take unnecessary risks with their lives. In the run up to Deliberate Force, Ryan established requirements for SEAD escort whenever NATO aircraft operated over BiH, even though various political and military higher-ups complained about the detrimental impact that Ryan's SEAD requirements were having on the NATO mission. He knew from his experience in Vietnam how dangerous it was for airmen and their integrity if they were pushed to risk their lives without very good reasons for doing so. He would put airmen in harm's way, but only to accomplish meaningful objectives and only after giving them the tools they needed to defend themselves. When the Serbs shot down Ebro 33 on the first day of Deliberate Force, Ryan did all he reasonably could to rescue the crewmen and bring them back safely. He was not shy about pushing to obtain additional aircraft, the latest standoff weaponry, and the political permissions needed to minimize the risks to NATO airmen. Although some airmen complained at the time about Ryan's SPINs, which seemed to increase the risks they faced in dropping certain PGMS, the campaign's results support the contention that his instructions did not put those airmen at undue risk.

Another significant aspect of Ryan's command resulted from his collaborative nature and his ability to work across organizational boundaries and with Coalition partners. He forged strong and effective working relationships with people over whom he had no real authority, including his counterparts across NATO and General Smith. At the higher levels of command—especially in joint, interagency, and international settings—a commander often lacks authority to give orders to others whose cooperation and active collaboration he needs. As Ryan put it: "You can't command by commanding. You need people to buy in to where you want to go, and you need people to give you advice, because you're not [going to be] the smartest guy in the room."[80] Ryan noted that Generals Powell and Shalikashvili had different styles of leadership, but they were both skilled consensus builders. During Deliberate Force, Ryan helped forge and maintain consensus by giving all participants a stake in the mission; he ensured that every Coalition partner contributed to the campaign without compromising its key features. Furthermore, in the final design and execution of the campaign he worked very effectively with General Smith.

An eighth element of Ryan's command involves doctrine, particularly operational-level doctrine, and not merely the written documents. In large, complex operations that employ deadly force, it is imperative that all those involved understand their roles and that mechanisms exist for effective command and control of the forces. For Deliberate Force, Ryan worked out the air-land coordination document with General Smith because no doctrine existed for using NATO air power in conjunction with UN peacekeepers. Moreover, Ryan demonstrated strong respect for the two top principles of war—objective and unity of command. He kept the campaign focused on attriting BSA military capabilities and prevented people outside the chain of command from hijacking the operation. He streamlined chains of command wherever he could, as in the creation of the 7490th Wing (Provisional) at Aviano, and he ensured unity of effort where unity of command was not possible, as with the UNPROFOR. Finally, he helped secure equipment and people for the CAOC, creating tangible capabilities for an effective air campaign and setting the example that ultimately informed the USAF's operational doctrine.

Yet another key aspect of Ryan's command of Deliberate Force was his preference for using military force in a strong and decisive manner. If the Serbs violated the no-fly zone by flying from Udbina airfield in Croatia, Ryan believed Udbina should be hit hard to knock out Serb air power where it was concentrated rather than trying to intercept aircraft one at a time in BiH airspace. From his experiences in Vietnam, the 1991 Gulf War, and elsewhere during his career, he came to believe that using the blunt instrument of military force gradually and in small doses to try to send subtle signals was foolish and dangerous. In BiH, he worked through the target lists as rapidly as the weather allowed. When he attacked various target sets, such as the Deadeye Northwest targets, he relentlessly pounded their every element. Having been an assistant to General Powell, Ryan clearly inclined toward his former boss's preference for overwhelming force.

Finally, Ryan's integrity and strength of character stand out as key aspects of his personality and his command style. Indeed, it was his integrity that was cited by the first senator to speak on behalf of his pending confirmation to command AIRSOUTH. His integrity and strength of character shone through in his claim of responsibility for the loss of Scott O'Grady's aircraft. Those same characteristics underpinned Ryan's deep sense of responsibility for the effectiveness of Deliberate Force, driving him to remain at the helm from its start until the pause and compelling him to exercise tight control over every aspect of the bombing. They led him to believe that he was accountable for any collateral damage. The self-discipline, honesty, and integrity of his upbringing had been reinforced at the Air Force Academy and were tested and ultimately sustained throughout his long and successful career. Ryan's integrity was the foundation for his intellectually honest appraisal of the situation in BiH and his role as a commander. It not only helped him to develop a viable and appropriate solution but also enabled him to direct the operation through to its successful conclusion. It is difficult to imagine a life, education, and career that could better prepare the commander of an air campaign than those of Gen. Mike Ryan. In Deliberate Force, he was truly an architect of air power success.

11

MICHAEL C. SHORT:
AIRMAN UNDAUNTED

REBECCA L. GRANT

Unintended civilian casualties. An F-117 down. Higher-ups doubting his leadership. All these unfortunate circumstances happened to Lt. Gen. Michael C. Short as combined forces air component commander (CFACC) in the seventy-eight-day air campaign known as Operation Allied Force in the spring of 1999. And it had all happened to him before.

History logs Operation Allied Force as a success, yet few campaigns have involved greater tension between doctrinal views of air power. The internal debates over striking fixed, strategic targets or attacking fielded forces made for some of the most colorful episodes and enduring lessons of the war.

Long before Short was a "three-star general with a drilling blue stare and gruff manner," as Dana Priest of the *Washington Post* described him, he was a colonel dealing with crashes at Tonopah Test Range in Nevada. At 9:11 on the morning of October 20, 1987, an air force A-7 Corsair belonging to Col. Mike Short's group at Tonopah crashed into the lobby of the Airport Ramada Inn in Indianapolis, Indiana. Nine hotel employees died, as did one passerby who had stopped in the lobby to make a telephone call. The pilot, Maj. Bruce Teagarden, ejected and survived. "I heard the three booms, but I wasn't sure at first if it was somebody working on the roof. It was three loud booms because the plane hit the bank first and then hit the ground then went back up in the air and hit the hotel," said firefighter Paul Spurlin, who had been working across the street and was one of the first on the scene.[1]

Teagarden had been flying the A-7 on a cross-country route as part of a program to maintain currency for the real aircraft assigned to his squadron, the F-117. Six days prior to Teagarden's crash the wing had lost an F-117 when Maj. Michael C. Stewart crashed aircraft 83-815 into the ground on the Tonopah test range slightly before 8 p.m. Finding the crash site took almost twenty-four hours owing to the desert terrain. "The F-117 in a fast dive makes a tight little hole," Short recalled.[2]

"I'm not comfortable with things at Tonopah," Gen. Robert Russ, the commander of Tactical Air Command (TAC), told Short after the incidents. It was a clear warning. In those days, crashes at TAC units were widely deemed to be the fault of the commander, even if the accident board's investigations later revealed mundane and disparate reasons for crashes on his watch.[3] Wing commanders were expected to push their units hard, but they had to maintain a fine balance. Crash too many airplanes at a wing and common sense said it was good idea to fire the commander. Perhaps the commander was not up to the job, or maybe he was simply unsuccessful. Either was a reason to sweep him aside and thereby end his unlucky streak before he infected more of the air force. Firing wing commanders was considered a healthful tonic, an outgrowth of the blistering honesty and accountability demanded in daily flying operations. This service was the Cold War air force, manned at twice the level it would have twelve years later for Operation Allied Force, and many colonels could quickly step into Short's job.

In October 1987 the immediate future of the 4450th Tactical Group, and certainly the future career of Michael Short himself, were on the line. For Short, "the next five or six months were tough sledding." He survived and gained experience that proved useful a decade later. "Those six months of my career prepared me for the darkest days of Operation Allied Force," Short reflected years later.

His preparation, of course, had begun decades earlier, at a time when the Cold War and Vietnam dominated air force operations. Growing up as a self-described army brat, Short's dream was to attend West Point. He was born in Princeton, New Jersey, in 1944 while his father was in England waiting to make the D-Day jump with the Seventeenth Airborne Division. As he grew up, Short and his family later lived in Japan and France. Short graduated from the Orléans American High School in Orléans, France. West Point did not give him an appointment in the year he graduated from high school. He considered waiting a year and applying to West Point again but took an offer from the U.S. Air Force Academy instead.

Short graduated from the still-new U.S. Air Force Academy in 1965 and flew F-4s in Vietnam from 1967 to 1968. After Vietnam, his assignments flying fighters and commanding fighter units continued almost unbroken until he pinned on his first star in September 1991. During his air force career, while primarily in fighters, Short amassed more than forty-six hundred flying hours, easily a thousand hours greater than many of his peer general officers logged. For sheer experience in combat employment, few air war commanders could top him.

Short stayed in command at the 4450th and, in the ultimate sign of approval, went on to command other wings: the 355th Tactical Training Wing at Davis-Monthan Air Force Base (AFB), Arizona, and the 67th Tactical Reconnaissance Wing at Bergstrom AFB, Texas. Next he moved to the temple of TAC, its headquarters at Langley AFB in Virginia, as the assistant director of operations. During that time he also held command of the 4404th Provisional Wing at Dhahran, Saudi Arabia, from late 1992 to the spring of 1993.

Short went to Europe in July 1995 as chief of staff of the Allied Air Forces Southern Europe (AIRSOUTH), North Atlantic Treaty Organization (NATO), Naples, Italy. He arrived at a time of crisis in Bosnia and Herzegovina (BiH), marked by the July Srebrenica massacre and then the Operation Deliberate Force air campaign, which was waged for nearly three weeks from late August to mid-September 1995. Short saw all these events firsthand, spending nearly a year in the Naples job before moving up to Ramstein Air Base in Germany as director of operations under Gen. Michael E. Ryan.

In May 1998, Short pinned on a third star and assumed command of AIRSOUTH and Stabilization Forces Air Component in Naples, Italy, and served as commander of the Sixteenth Air Force and Sixteenth Air and Space Expeditionary Task Force, U.S. Air Forces in Europe (USAFE), at Aviano Air Base, Italy. This long title, laden with NATO responsibilities, would also make him the CFACC for Operation Allied Force.

One month after Short assumed his new role, Yugoslav forces pounded western Kosovo with mortar and artillery fire. British officials said that London wanted Western governments "to consider a direct threat of air strikes against Serbia to force a settlement in Kosovo rather than getting bogged down in lengthy border deployments."[4] As a result, planning for limited air strike options began in earnest. In July 1998, Short took a briefing on planning and targeting to Gen. John P. Jumper, who was then the USAFE commander, and to NATO's supreme allied commander, Europe (SACEUR), Gen. Wesley Clark (U.S. Army [USA]). These plans represented what airmen termed "U.S.-only" work, because they included aircraft such as the stealthy F-117 and the new B-2 stealth bomber, and the mission details were highly classified.

Clark raised few issues regarding the strategic targets, but he had another question. "Mike, what will you do when Milošević kills Muslims?" Clark asked him. "I'll go after the leadership in Belgrade," Short told Clark.

Here was the first indication of the fundamental controversy that would plague Operation Allied Force: what would make Serbia's president Slobodan Milošević give in? Short focused on strategic targets. "I thought Clark had grudgingly agreed with me that we must strike strategically, not tactically," Short later said. As it turned out, Clark wanted to emphasize attacks on Serb Army forces. Clark's question foreshadowed the dilemmas ahead.

Operation Allied Force ultimately proved a triumph for NATO and for air power. The air campaign was designed to drive the Serbs out of Kosovo, and it succeeded. Milošević withdrew his forces, leaving Kosovo to the care of an international peacekeeping force and subsequent negotiations. The alliance had waged and won its first collective fight on European territory.

Diplomacy involving Russia and other nations had been active prior to the conflict and played no small part in ending it. However, the military aspect of the campaign was unique among twentieth-century displays of air power because alliance airmen had the field of battle to themselves. Apart from Kosovar resistance irregulars, no friendly ground forces featured in the campaign. NATO announced from the start that it would not consider inserting ground forces to push Serbian forces out of Kosovo or to stop their ethnic cleansing spree. Thus, whatever military action NATO brought to bear would come exclusively from the air. Airmen then had the familiar double task of attacking an army in the field while also going after strategic target pressure points—provided NATO approved them first.

But in March 1999, the positive outcome was hazy indeed. Short did not think air power was being applied properly, Clark wanted Apache helicopters, and NATO wanted to bomb as delicately as possible. For CFACC Mike Short, accommodating these conflicting priorities was a tall order indeed. As a case study about how to command air power, Operation Allied Force offered many enduring lessons—all illuminated by the vibrant personality of Short himself.

COMPROMISING ON AIR POWER

Every air commander's story is set against the background of the campaign as a whole and against the politics that define it. That joint campaign is a panorama defined by the ground force commander, who in every case so far has also been the overall joint and Coalition force commander. Metrics drawn from land warfare doctrine measure the campaign's success. For U.S. Army officers at least, it is most natural to picture the campaign as a large and intricate maneuver whose borders are defined by the contours of the land. Decisive operations rest with the ground force when it closes with and destroys the enemy. Operations may contain preparation, offense, defense, and stabilization, but the metrics fit boots on the ground.

Air commanders work within this framework. For Col. William Mitchell at St. Mihiel in 1918 or for Lt. Gen. Chuck Horner in Saudi Arabia in 1991, the framework was the same. Gen. John J. Pershing saw the air campaign operating on a map of the St. Mihiel salient. Gen. H. Norman Schwarzkopf saw Operation Desert Storm as a long line of American and Coalition divisions arrayed against Iraqi infantry and Iraqi mechanized and Republican Guard divisions, with air power applied on top. No matter how dominant the air actions on any given day might be, though, the metrics of the battle itself were tied only to the ground map. What was the enemy force's position? What were friendly forces doing? Territory lost, held, regained, and occupied provided the full measure of the campaign. At St. Mihiel victory was the collapse of the salient. In 1991 it was the final surrender in a tent at Safwan ringed with tanks.

General Clark was from this same mold. He viewed air power mainly through the lens of army doctrine, which, in turn, categorized it essentially as a form of indirect fires to be coordinated with maneuver. Air power might be a powerful force within a given operation, but, according to this view, air power alone could scarcely define the battle, much less be said to win it.

"He did not trust airmen at all," Short said of Clark. Nor did he "trust or understand air power." Short had heard that Clark had subjected airmen at U.S. Southern Command, his previous duty station, to lectures on how air power was undependable.

Clark came from a generation of army generals who had only rare contact with detailed air planning and had deliberately chosen to remember Operation Desert Storm as a stunning four-day ground war. Large force exercises at the National Training Center in Fort Irwin, California, emphasized the integration of maneuver (tanks) and fires (artillery) with minor and highly scripted appearances by leashed A-10s. These army officers had last seen air power close up when they were young, company-grade officers in Vietnam. Their experiences of air power were very personal and specific, far from the campaign-level view for which they were responsible as four-star commanders. Furthermore, the rapid modifications that enabled the majority of U.S. fighters and bombers to carry precision weapons had taken place in the years immediately before Kosovo, and many army leaders had not yet understood the new capabilities that these munitions brought to the fight. Unfortunately, their careers had given them no opportunity to expand their war-fighting perspective or to understand the attributes—both good and bad—of air power as it existed circa 1999.

Pair an airman with deep understanding of a complex weapon with an army superior who had thought little about air power, and the results—as in previous decades—would hinge on the level of trust the airman could inspire in his army superior and how fast he could do it. Personality was a factor, of course. The CFACCs whose task was easiest were those whose army bosses fell into one of two categories. The men in the first category understood something about air power from recent planning experience. For example, Gen. Dwight Eisenhower had gained such knowledge from serving as Gen. George Marshall's de facto operations deputy from late December 1941, writing war plans in which he had to devise how to take down the Luftwaffe, and experiencing the campaign in North Africa. Others hungered for the extra edge that air power could give them in a campaign. Examples here included Pershing, who ultimately became willing to add Mitchell's air sweeps and interdiction to his 1918 St. Mihiel offensive, and Schwarzkopf, who embraced air power for Operation Desert Storm in 1991.

Clark fell into another, more common category. He summed up his views in the memoir he wrote after Operation Allied Force, noting that he had not believed in the efficacy of air power for BiH when first briefed on it in the summer of 1994. Discussing measured air strikes, Lt. Gen. Marvin Covault (USA) told him there were not enough targets in BiH to accomplish objectives and added that those targets did not "represent any kind of a center of gravity. With five days of good weather we could take them all out, and then we would find that the Serbs would just keep on doing whatever they were doing. Air strikes just won't be decisive." As Clark described his reaction, "I filed the information away. It certainly was consistent with my Vietnam experience and some of what we had learned about air power during the Gulf war."[5]

The success of air power in Operation Deliberate Force did not impress Clark either. Instead, he gave great credit to "a powerful Croat ground offensive."[6] This explanation may have better fit the ground framework with which Clark was familiar.

He would continue to talk of flawed ground force planning and marred Apache helicopter deployment as major elements of the Kosovo operation.

THE SLIDE TOWARD CRISIS

Clark's indifference might have been swept aside if NATO itself had agreed wholeheartedly on the wisdom and nature of an air campaign. Instead, NATO found running a bombing campaign in Europe an unappealing prospect. Throughout the alliance, the hope in the latter part of 1998 was that using the simple threat of air power might press Milošević toward a negotiated solution.

In the fall of that year, Clark gave Short an unusual assignment: he sent him to join a negotiating team led by Richard Holbrooke, the man who had brokered the BiH peace in Dayton three years earlier after Operation Deliberate Force. The team went to Belgrade, hoping to persuade Milošević to allow an air verification mission whereby U.S. and NATO surveillance aircraft would keep close track of the Serbian Army and its activities in order to discourage attacks on civilians in Kosovo. Holbrooke wanted to bring a "blue suit" (an air force officer) along to remind Milošević of what he could face and to work out the surveillance details.

"Short had experience in the region and was an extraordinarily well-qualified airman," Clark wrote later. "He brought along the kind of gruff humor, with an edge, that made him a strong leader and a forceful personality, and in no time, with Holbrooke's coaching, he seemed to bludgeon Milošević into accepting the air mission."[7]

However, the agreement ultimately hit snags. By September 1998, Clark was telling Gen. Henry H. Shelton, the chairman of the Joint Chiefs of Staff, about his "growing concern with NATO's visible failure to prevent the heavy handed Serb military and police operations which were destroying village after village in Kosovo."[8] Secret planning for limited air strike options accelerated. A fragile cease-fire commenced in October 1998, but it ended when Serbs killed forty-five ethnic Albanian Kosovars in a January 1999 incident at Racak. After Racak, the situation deteriorated further. Peace talks led by the United States, Russia, and the European Union in Rambouillet in February failed. Milošević would not agree to international peacekeepers on the ground. By the time Milošević backed away from Rambouillet in late February, his forces had already achieved battlefield dominance in Kosovo. The Yugoslav army reportedly numbered about 90,000 men, equipped with 630 tanks, 634 armored personnel carriers, and more than

800 howitzers. By mid-March, his army had displaced 250,000 ethnic Albanians, and a crisis was unavoidable.

NATO was still locked into a diplomatic mind-set. On the one hand, the collective hope was that three days of sharp air strikes would cause Milošević to change his mind and put him in a mood to accede to international demands. The general consensus was that a quick, efficient, diplomatic utilization of air power was acceptable, but ongoing bombing was not. On the other hand, failure to act would be unconscionable. To NATO secretary-general Javier Solana, the atrocities that the Serbs had committed were "things that my generation thought never again would we see." NATO saw Operation Allied Force as the lesser of two evils. When talks over Kosovo broke down, air power again seemed the obvious answer. Holbrooke recalled: "Milošević said to me at one point, 'Are you crazy enough to bomb us over these issues we're talking about in that lousy little Kosovo?' And I said, 'You bet. We're just crazy enough to do it.'"

The precedent, of course, was BiH. In a little over two weeks, the short NATO air campaign had pushed Milošević to the negotiating table in Dayton, Ohio, along with his Croatian and Bosnian counterparts. The show of NATO resolve, together with fortuitous maneuvers in the three-way civil war on the ground, had closed off Milošević's options. Holbrooke had led canny negotiations that quickly delivered the lasting peace plan known as the Dayton Accords.

But this time NATO faced a bigger problem. BiH had been wracked by civil war long before Operation Deliberate Force began. In the Kosovo crisis, however, NATO faced the prospect of attacking the capital city of Belgrade, which as Secretary-General Solana reminded everyone was "a city of Europe." NATO also had to reckon with the past. Serbia had played key roles in the wars of twentieth-century Europe and had been an ally of the Western powers in two world wars. From the outset, lingering myths and images from World War II dogged the very idea of waging a bombing campaign there. Clark was well aware of these emotional overtones. "In Europe, there's a terrible aftermath of World War II, and nations and individuals have memories of the terror of bombing and what it does to civilian populations," he explained. "And I think European leaders were acutely aware of the sensitivity of their publics, their electorate, their leaderships, to the dangers of unrestricted aerial warfare."[9]

Clark, as SACEUR, might have stepped into the role of explaining and facilitating the role of air power, especially since it was the only military weapon he wielded in the Kosovo crisis. Despite all the distaste for bombing, neither the United States nor its NATO partners ever seriously entertained the idea of using ground forces. President William J. Clinton had announced from the outset that he had no intention of putting troops in Kosovo to fight a war. Air power had succeeded in BiH; it was the only acceptable form of military force for NATO in the Kosovo crisis as well.

Short approached the problem differently than either Clark or NATO did. He viewed air power as a powerful means of coercion; air power was a weapon, not a diplomat's gambit. That interpretation meant he had to use speedy, direct, lethal force once NATO committed itself. "You want to crush the enemy," he explained. "To use a phrase I've used before, you go after the head of the snake. You put a dagger in the heart of the adversary, and you bring to bear all the force that you have at your command."[10] He felt that action would be the best way to accomplish NATO's goals and stop the Serb atrocities.

Short believed air power should be used as overwhelming force from night 1. As he put it:

I believe there is a right way to use air power, and that is to maximize the potential of our capabilities. That means to me that on the first day or the first night of the war, you attack the enemy with incredible speed and incredible violence. Violence that he could never have imagined. It should be his worst possible nightmare with an incredible level of destruction, relative again, to what he thought was possible. You should use every bit of technology that you have to shock him into inaction until he is paralyzed so that you can get ahead of him inside his decision-loop and force him to accept your terms. It is about modifying his behavior as rapidly as you can. That was how I thought air power should be used in Serbia.[11]

Neither NATO nor Clark was ready for such bold action. Clark had led as many as forty revisions to air strike plans by early 1999; however, wide gaps still existed between Short's concept of an efficient use of air power and what NATO was willing to approve. This discrepancy happened largely because all parties involved thought they were planning for a limited series of strikes. That short-term focus precluded opportunities for Short to straighten out his differences with Clark or to work through the sensitivities of the NATO allies. The disparate viewpoints would turn into a heavy burden when the first three days were up and there was sudden urgency to intensify a campaign.

Nor was there any guarantee that spending more time going over briefings would have improved matters. Short was working under handicaps that would become apparent to him only much later. First, the NATO command structure complicated matters. The structure had been established for a much more integrated and focused war between NATO and the Warsaw Pact. In such a conflict, the NATO supreme commander would have exercised operational command through his regional four-stars, and the trio of three-star airmen would have been fully occupied with their specific sub-theaters. In 1999, Short was outranked by Adm. James Ellis, a U.S. Navy carrier pilot who commanded NATO's southern region from a navy-run headquarters in Naples. Short also worked via the numbered air force chain for General Jumper, the USAFE commander. Clark in the Stuttgart headquarters of U.S. European Command was layers away. His work as AIRSOUTH commander was mediated through the chain above. "I thought I had top cover in either chain," said Short. "In my worst nightmare I wasn't working for Clark."

THE CAMPAIGN BEGINS

On March 18, 1999, the United Nations High Commissioner on Refugees estimated that there were 240,000 displaced persons—internal refugees—in Kosovo, accounting for more than 10 percent of the population. Roughly one-third of the Yugoslav army's forces now massed on the border of Kosovo. Estimates placed the numbers at around 40,000 Yugoslav army troops and about 300 tanks. Motivated by the need to stop atrocities, NATO agreed to three days of preplanned air strikes to demonstrate its resolve. Operation Allied Force began on the night of March 24, 1999.

Short's initial plan envisioned a few days of air operations against a carefully chosen set of about fifty targets, which had already been approved through the NATO process. Target categories included air defense sites, communications relays, and fixed military facilities, such as ammunition dumps. Air planners had targeting data on far more than fifty targets, but the consensus in NATO was only strong enough to support limited action. The list for the initial strikes included no targets in downtown Belgrade.

Obtaining air superiority was the first task. Conventional air-launched cruise missiles and Tomahawk land-attack missiles hit air defense sites and communications. Two B-2s flew more than thirty hours on a round-trip mission and launched the first joint direct attack munitions (JDAMs) ever used in combat against multiple targets. Many U.S. and NATO fighters in theater maintained combat air patrols, while others bombed targets.

To Short this situation was less than satisfying because the campaign was limited to three days—although forces were contending with a modern air defense system. "We began bombing the first night with our objective being to show NATO resolve," Short recounted later. "That is tough to tell the kids at Aviano—to go out and put it on the line to 'demonstrate resolve.'"[12]

No one knew exactly what it would take to make an impact on Milošević. Two statements made at the start of the campaign suggested how operations might unfold. "We have plans for a swift and severe air campaign," Pentagon spokesman Kenneth Bacon explained on March 23. "This will be painful for the Serbs. We hope that, relatively quickly . . . the Serbs will realize that they have made a mistake."[13] Clark took a firm stance on March 25: "We're going to systematically and progressively attack, disrupt, degrade, devastate, and ultimately—unless President Milošević complies with the demand of the international community—we're going to destroy these forces and their facilities and support."[14]

Milošević ignored the initial NATO air strikes. The Central Intelligence Agency predicted that Yugoslav forces could respond to NATO military action by accelerating the ethnic cleansing. Now Milošević gambled that his forces could push ethnic Albanians and the Kosovo Liberation Army out of Kosovo before NATO could react. The Yugoslav Third Army was assigned to Kosovo operations, along with reinforcements from the First and Second Armies. About 40,000 troops and 300 tanks crossed into Kosovo on March 28, spreading out in abandoned burned-out villages and buildings, whose former inhabitants were now refugees.[15] Paramilitary security forces from the Interior Ministry were engaged in multiple areas across Kosovo.

NATO had no doubts about continuing the campaign. U.S. secretary of state Madeleine Albright explained on March 28 that NATO intended to force Milošević to back off by "making sure that he pays a very heavy price."[16]

Determining how to do it was another matter. All the simmering disagreements about applying air power boiled over. From Clark's point of view, he had to stop the Serb Army. Short fundamentally disagreed with Clark's priorities. "I never felt that the [Serb] 3rd Army in Kosovo was a center of gravity," Short said in an interview published in September 1999. Short believed that "Milosevic had written the 3rd Army off. He went on, 'And body bags coming home from Kosovo didn't bother [Milošević], and it didn't bother the leadership elite [in Belgrade].'"[17]

NATO attacked integrated air defense targets and Serb air force facilities from the night of March 24 on; however, Short wanted to go further and hit a strategic target set that might hurt Milošević directly. He later said that, left to his own devices, he "would have arranged for the leaders in Belgrade to wake up 'after the first night . . . to a city that was smoking. No power to the refrigerator and . . . no way to get to work.'"[18]

Short's planners had not carried out much detailed study of how to go about striking the Serb ground forces now terrorizing ethnic Albanians in Kosovo. Without a land component going into action, they had not had any need to plan and brief battlefield coordination measures. The doubts over what NATO would do had postponed early discussions on the specifics of targeting land forces. Now, the scramble to sustain the campaign preempted much of the dialogue on air power that had preceded past wars.

Short contrasted Operation Allied Force with the deliberate planning for Operation Desert Storm. After Iraq invaded Kuwait on August 2, 1990, Horner was summoned to Camp David early in the crisis to brief President George H. W. Bush on air campaign effects. Brig. Gen. Buster Glosson and Chief of Staff Gen. Merrill "Tony" McPeak also had opportunities to brief details on evolving air campaign plans, expectations, casualty predictions, and the like. Short had none of these opportunities because of the prevailing belief that a three-day punch would do the job.

Clark and Short had to concoct the campaign as they went along and confront their differences at the same time. Short continued to push hard to make the air strikes as effective as possible in the abysmal early spring weather. In the process, he found the new B-2 bomber invaluable. "The F-117s drive nails when they're on and the weather is good," Short said later. But poor weather obscuring targets for the infrared guidance systems degraded their effectiveness.

With the B-2, Short had a new capability: the JDAM. The B-2 was the only aircraft to carry JDAMs during Operation Allied Force. The 2,000-pound bombs received their guidance from Global Positioning System navigation systems. For

Short, the JDAMs were a revelation. Finally, the B-2 was "confirming a manned capability to drop through the weather"—an ability airmen had sought for decades. It was "sixteen quality DMPIs [designated mean points of impact] every night regardless of how bad the weather was," said Short. He therefore used B-2s as much as possible. "I understand that JDAMs are a national asset," Short remembered thinking at the time, "but there's no other war going on and I think JDAMs are keeping F-16 and F-15 pilots alive and that's about the only pressure I can place on Milošević." It also suited Clark. Short appreciated that Clark was "letting the B-2 go at least around Belgrade and against targets in Serbia proper."[19]

Although the job of a combined forces air component commander is to make the air war function effectively, CFACCs themselves would probably say that their top task is maintaining a good working relationship with the joint force commander (JFC). Short, however, had a poor foundation for such a relationship with Clark. The lack of a personal relationship was not unusual; neither was Short's having to deal with Clark's inbred prejudice and lack of knowledge about air power. In this aspect, Short and Clark were a laboratory-grade sample of the problem.

Another common feature, as Short described it, was Clark's focus on the role of the AC-130 gunship. "Like all of the Army, he's in love with the AC-130 gunship. He bugged me for weeks" to bring them into the war. Short feared that because they presented such a big target, it would be too easy to lose one. Clark insisted on having the AC-130s fly on the border between Albania and Kosovo. Short finally did it to placate his boss.

The frustration between Short and Clark over the gunships typified the arguments between airman and soldier. The soldier wanted to direct tactical details. With solid tactical reasons for his opposition, the airman wished that the supreme commander would spell out effects rather than sorties. The airman's opposition made the soldier impatient, while the latter's seeming inability to comprehend the details aggravated the airman. Neither could be satisfied unless their mutual trust increased to the point where the soldier would not interfere with the airman's tactical decisions and the airman trusted the soldier's strategic insight. Short and Clark never truly built that trust.

RUNNING THE WAR

As Operation Allied Force rolled past the three-day war, Short prepared the Combined Air Operations Center (CAOC) for a steady effort. Operation Allied Force proved to be one of the longer air campaigns of the precision era. It lasted nearly a month longer than Operation Desert Storm had in 1991 and was also longer than the major combat operations phase of Operation Iraqi Freedom four years later.

Clark was all for intensifying the air war. NATO leaders meeting on April 7 came away with a clear commitment to stay the course. "Whatever General Clark feels he needs in order to carry out this campaign successfully, he will receive," vowed U.S. secretary of defense William Cohen after the NATO meeting.[20]

First, Short required more air power. NATO also needed enough aircraft to sustain twenty-four-hour operations over the dispersed Yugoslav forces in Kosovo. Plans were formulated for an augmented package of forces known as the "Papa Bear" option that would more than double the strike aircraft in theater.

In this situation, factors such as battle rhythm and the people surrounding the CFACC became especially important. "Figure out how many hours a day you can work and still be effective," cautioned Short. Day and night operations could have kept a CFACC on his feet around the clock. Short realized keeping that pace would not be wise. Thus, the membership of his team became crucial. He put Brig. Gen. Randy Gelwix in charge of the night shift and Maj. Gen. Garry Trexler in charge of daytime operations. General Jumper also sent Short additional staff from USAFE—Col. Al Peck, who headed the Thirty-Second Air Operations Group at Ramstein, and Col. Eddie Boyle, who became chief of the intelligence, surveillance, and reconnaissance cell that would pioneer work in predictive analysis and craft ways to find Serbian air defense sites. Short also had high praise for his deputy CFACC, Gen. Leonardo Tricarico of Italy. Beyond the technical expertise that these airmen provided, Short found value in having trusted individuals near him to provide feedback. "I needed guys I could trust to close the door and tell me if I was making a mistake," he said. "Every three- or four-star needs someone he can talk to."

NATO expanded and clarified the air campaign plan in early April. The goal was to conduct simultaneous attacks against two target sets—fixed targets of unique strategic value and fielded military forces and their sustainment elements. This effort was the heart of the air campaign as it would be carried out over the next two and a half months. Target set 1 included national command and control; military reserves; infrastructure, such as bridges, communications, and petroleum, oils, and lubricants (POL) production; and the military-industrial base of weapons and ammunition factories and distribution systems. Serbia's electric power grid was soon added to the list. Target set 2 included Yugoslav military forces, particularly their tactical assembly areas, command and control nodes, bridges in southern Serbia and Kosovo, supply areas, POL storage and pumping stations, choke points, and ammunition storage. Initial guidance focused on forces south of the forty-fourth parallel, but soon military targets north of the line also made the list.

As this guidance made clear, NATO had decided to pursue a multipronged strategy with its air campaign. It had enough targets to satisfy both Short's and Clark's views of air power priorities. The goal was not simply to demonstrate NATO resolve and hope to coerce Milošević; it was to directly reduce and eliminate the Yugoslav forces' ability to wage their campaign of destruction in Kosovo. Fortunately, NATO's air forces could make the transition. "NATO had one consensus, and that was for application of air power," said Secretary of Defense Cohen.

This new focus for Operation Allied Force finally combined the best capabilities of air power. Conflicts in the past had proven the value of attacking both target sets. Problems arose when limited sorties forced commanders to pick and choose among them. This situation was no different from the World War II debates about using air power on strategic targets in Germany or on bridges and railroads in France before D-Day. It was also normal for emotions to run high during these discussions.

Clark continued to downplay the role of air power even as he led an air campaign. In his mind, dropping bombs in Operation Allied Force was best described as "diplomacy backed by force." He stated, "Only when we invaded, using ground troops to wrest Kosovo away from Serb control, could we say we were really using 'force backed by diplomacy.'"[21]

Fortunately, Short was soon bringing Clark enough air power to put serious weight into attacking both target sets. "Most of the surge came from U.S. forces," Short recalled. Getting more out of the F-15E proved highly effective. Marines supplied EA-6B Prowlers on the ground to increase their sortie rate. Aircraft were stuffed into bases all over Europe. Tankers were in extraordinary demand. At one point, 40 percent of all USAF tankers and 80 percent of their crews were contributing to Operation Allied Force.

"I never felt we were going to be able to stop ethnic cleansing, and in fact we did not," Short said. "Most of the damage had been done before we ever started attacking targets on the ground." In his opinion, the way to force Milošević's hand was not by mounting attacks in kind. "I think it was the total weight of our effort that finally got to him," he said.

Short was willing to push when it made sense and to accept risk to achieve results. For example, he layered assets for suppressing enemy air defenses into virtually every strike package. The Prowlers served as the primary defensive jamming platform. A mid-1990s Pentagon decision had retired the Air Force's EF-111A Raven jammers, largely because more than a hundred Prowlers were still in the force. But the navy and Marine Corps never planned to mass them for an air campaign in Europe. Providing enough Prowlers was difficult, and as the war continued the navy began to fear the drain on the Prowlers would cut deep into the stateside training pipeline.

Short started to plan alternatives. "We were about to get to the point where I was going to risk forces coming into eastern Serbia without EA-6B escort because we thought the threat would allow us to do that," he said later.[22] The decision was vintage Short. His risk calculation was based on necessity and driven home by a sharp sense of the degree of risk his aviators could handle.

A more famous case of risk calculation concerned altitude restrictions. Serbia had a robust force of integrated air defenses and another category of threat—mobile, shorter-range surface-to-air missiles (SAMs) and antiaircraft guns that were particularly dangerous to operations at lower altitudes. Short was also concerned about antiaircraft fire and handheld SAMs. These threats were almost impossible to eradicate. For that matter, NATO had located only a few of the twenty-two larger SA-6 missile sites that they believed the Serbs possessed. Accordingly, to promote aircrew safety, Short imposed a 15,000-foot "floor" on missions, but mission requirements allowed aircrews to go lower if needed. Airborne forward air controllers were one example of pilots who had to fly at lower altitudes to complete their missions.

The altitude decision was almost immediately misinterpreted. Airmen were used to flying in altitude blocks for everything from routine training to major exercises such as Red Flag, where aircraft were assigned altitudes for mock dogfights. To airmen, this arrangement was routine, but the press could not leave the issue alone. As a result, Short and others spent much time explaining that laser-guided bombs, the principal precision weapons of the war, were best launched from higher altitudes. In fact, many NATO aircraft using laser targeting actually achieved better aiming at higher altitudes. Was it worth risking a short-range SAM shot or antiaircraft fire to ferret out a Serbian tank? To a point it was, but it was Short's job to keep the risk balance tilted in favor of having his fliers return safely to base after their combat missions. For Short and the aviators it was common sense. More to the point, the pilots rarely saw any advantage in going lower. The days of P-47s dipping low to strafe Nazi trains were long gone.

The 15,000-floot floor also led to another quarrel with Clark. "Mike, you've got to get down there with them!" Clark insisted at one point.

"We do JDAM from medium altitude," Short had to tell him That answer was not good enough, as Short recalled.

"Go down lower," Clark said to him, "or I'll get someone who will."

"If we have no [NATO] force on the ground we'll be up at 15,000 feet," Short insisted. That was one of the rough conversations. "My aide thought I'd been fired," Short said.

Short's visceral concern for the "kids," as he called them, was also a factor. It particularly galled him when political restrictions forced changes on aircrews inbound for combat missions. Short recounted how one or two nations could veto a target at the last minute, causing packages in the air to be recalled via airborne warning and control system aircraft and tankers. "There were numerous occasions where airplanes were airborne, and the senior national rep would run in to me and say, 'Our parliament won't allow us to strike that target,' or 'Our authorities will not allow your airplanes, which took off from our soil, to strike that target,'" said Short.[23] One B-2 strike had to turn back when a target was denied en route. According to Short, such last-minute changes "played havoc with a mission commander's plan, because now all of a sudden he's lost part of his train, and you don't want to send those kids in there if they're not going to drop [their bombs]."

CAREFUL LINE

Short was the first air component commander to deal regularly with extensive assessments of collateral damage associated with particular targets. This tasking resulted partly from NATO's concern over waging a careful campaign that minimized civilian casualties. It was also the product of the bounty of precision weapons platforms in theater. Simply put, NATO now had the luxury of running an effective campaign with extremely tight collateral damage calculations.

"These were the strictest rules of engagement I've seen in my twenty-seven years," commented then-Maj. Gen. Charles F. Wald of the Joint Staff's Strategic Plans and Policy Division, a key spokesman during the operation.[24] In fact, the restrictions increased throughout the campaign. "Toward the end of the air effort, we were restricted by enormous concern for collateral damage and unintended loss of civilian life," said Short. During the last days of the campaign, "that was the litmus that we used to pick a target."[25]

NATO was able to impose such stringent rules of engagement because aircrew training and the technical capacities of air power permitted rapid conferences about whether to strike a target. Often, getting clearance to attack a target required a pilot to make a radio call back to the CAOC and obtain approval from the one-star general on duty. Short told a revealing story about monitoring the activities of an A-10 pilot attempting to find the tanks that an unmanned Predator reconnaissance plane had spotted.

About 45 days into the war, Predator was providing great coverage for us. About 5 o'clock in the afternoon, we had live Predator video of three tanks moving down the road in Serbia and Kosovo. We had a FAC [Forward Air Controller] overhead and General Clark had the same live Predator video that I had. He said, "Mike, I want you to kill those tanks." I quickly responded, I had something else in mind, "Boss, I'll go after that for you." When shift time came, [Maj. Gen.] Garry Trexler was on the floor, finishing up in the daytime, and Gelwix arrived to take the night shift. I was there because the SACEUR wanted those three tanks killed. We had a weapon school graduate on the phone talking direction to the FAC on the radio.[26]

For better or for worse, this new level of control was possible in seeking pop-up targets. The tight focus would become standard operating procedure in future air wars.

To his great credit, Short delivered impressive results against a target set that was never his own choice. In the war's concluding phase the effort against Serbian military forces hit its stride, with the last three weeks being especially productive. From May 13, when strikes increased, to the end of the month an average of eighteen successful strikes across all categories occurred each day. From June 1 to the end of the air war on June 9, the average was about twenty-eight successful strikes per day. The day-by-day figures reinforced what the pilots said: it took time to find and hit the Yugoslav army forces.

Clark could hardly have asked for more. In fact, he was pleased with the results. After Operation Allied Force, Clark put together a summer assessment team to evaluate air strikes on Serbian-fielded forces. The Serbs disputed the reported findings, claiming minimal losses. Clark called them sore losers who were twisting the truth. "It's no wonder that the Serbs are trying so hard to conceal the damage that NATO did," Clark said at a September 1999 press conference. He estimated the Yugoslav army had 350 tanks, 450 armored personnel carriers, and 750 artillery pieces in Kosovo. Over seventy-eight days, NATO airmen scored validated hits on 26 percent of the tanks, 34 percent of the armored personnel carriers, and 47 percent of the artillery pieces. The raw numbers reported damages of 93 tanks and self-propelled guns, 153 armored personnel carriers, 389 artillery and mortar pieces, and 339 other military vehicles.[27] Operation Allied Force had accomplished its mission. NATO now had the complex task of providing the Kosovo stabilization force, but that effort, too, proved successful in time.

By any measure, Short's campaign was a stunning success. It marked the beginning of a new chapter for air power. Hunting targets with a sophisticated blend of intelligence, surveillance, and reconnaissance was pioneered on a large scale in Kosovo. Two years later it would become a primary means of conducting air operations. Precision and rapid retargeting made up a significant fraction of the NATO campaign. Within a few years they were de rigeur in the wars in Afghanistan and Iraq.

Operation Allied Force also brought NATO airmen together in a new way. This cooperation, too, would reach new heights in the fight against terrorism. The result was a battle-hardened NATO force whose airmen had deeper tactical experience and more time in command shifts at the CAOCs.

REFLECTIONS ON THE CAMPAIGN

Short was unsparingly honest during Operation Allied Force. He discussed the air war in detail less than a year after it ended. Years later, he extended his analyses to include a blunt review of what he saw as some of his own failings as CFACC. He thought a great deal about what had worked well in the Kosovo war and what had gone wrong. Many of his insights focused on relationships with allies. Over time, Short also concluded that he should have handled himself differently.

RELATIONSHIPS WITH ALLIES

Not surprising, the subject of the allies loomed large for Short after the campaign. From the beginning, the air war had been nearly as much about fighting for the legitimacy of NATO as about defeating the Serbs. General Short later wished he had included more Dutch and British airmen, specifically, in his command staff.

But he continued to believe the United States should be firm and unapologetic about its leadership role.

"Let me shoot very straight with you," Short told a *Frontline* interviewer a year after the campaign. "I believe before the first bomb was dropped that the door should have been closed with all those who wished to go to war." To Short, this essential policy position stemmed from the unique capacity of the United States in its air operations. As it was, the nineteen-member North Atlantic Council had a great deal of sway over target selection. "At least one nation consistently refused to let us attack targets that we wished to target, so that made it even more difficult," Short said later. The French also raised many objections over possible targets near Montenegro, even when they posed potential military threats. In his opinion,

The United States should have said very clearly, "It appears NATO wants to go to war in the air, and in the air only. If that is the case and that is the sentiment of the nations here, we will lead you to war. We, the United States, will provide the leadership, the enabling force, the majority of the striking power, the technology required. We will take the alliance to war, and we will win this thing for you. But the price to be paid is we call the tune. We are not just one of 19."[28]

CONDUCTING COALITION AIR OPERATIONS

Short also wished there had been a greater level of trust inside the CAOC. As noted previously, in Operation Allied Force, the United States built a separate U.S.-only air tasking order (ATO) that included stealth assets such as the F-117. This arrangement led to some awkward moments for Short. On a night early in the campaign, a top ally asked him why certain SA-6 sites were not being targeted. The sites were being targeted, of course, but the ATO was kept in U.S.-only channels to prevent its being leaked and falling into the hands of the Serb air defenders. Short understood the reasons, but they also made him uncomfortable. In a campaign where trust among allies was practically a center of gravity all on its own, the existence of double ATOs smarted. "A German full colonel walked off the floor" of the CAOC after learning he didn't know about the F-117s. The experience made Short a firm believer that "there should be one team, with no secrets." U.S.-only information had to be much more limited.

Furthermore, Short treated allied airmen like *airmen*—that is, with the bluntness born of the unforgiving fighter-pilot environment. He was tough when necessary. Nor did he hesitate to go to the top when needed. Several times he called the air chiefs of various allied nations directly to say that they needed to "assure me this mess is cleared up."

At the same time, Short warned the allies that they had to be willing to take the same risks as their American counterparts. In the 1999 campaign, Short quickly found that airmen from the Netherlands, the United Kingdom, and Spain would "do whatever we asked." Others were more limited in what they could do. Short realized the limits were a product of politics in their home capitals, but it frustrated him all the same. At one point, representatives from the French Air Force declined to fly missions in Serbia proper. Here was an air force with a long history and strong capabilities, including its own nuclear fighter-bombers, a strong French defense and aerospace industry, and highly skilled pilots. Short minced no words. "If you don't want to fly in Serbia, you won't fly at all," he told them.

Command Relationships

Not surprisingly, Short also drew important lessons from his uneasy relationship with Clark and decided to accept the responsibility as his own. He had not created the problem—it stemmed partly from Clark's personality and to a large extent from the U.S. Army's traditions and beliefs as manifested in the 1990s. The disagreements they had could well have happened to any airman and soldier paired together, and from this experience Short drew his lessons. He refined them in a series of talks given to senior airmen when he worked as an official mentor. "Your job is to make the Joint Force Commander successful," Short said.

He first cited his own limited view of the political objectives of the campaign—another casualty of the weak airman-soldier relationship. The airman, at least as Short viewed himself, did not have nearly the same level of insight as the JFC into the politics surrounding the air campaign. Most likely, neither did the maritime nor the land force commander. As Short described it: "I didn't understand the impact politics and NATO were having. I wasn't sophisticated enough to understand. I never understood the strategic endstate." In Short's view, he "had a vision of going after strategic centers of gravity to bring conflict to a close. NATO was not willing to do that. They were content to slowly escalate. I should have understood we'd be very conservative."

In the years after Operation Allied Force Short concluded that he should have taken the initiative to repair the relationship with Clark. "At the time, I thought I had good reasons," Short explained, but he later came to feel that he had pushed so hard that he had added to Clark's burdens. "A difficult subordinate did not have to be on his plate." He should have confronted the bad relationship directly. One step he might have taken was to seek help from Admiral Ellis. Taking another option, Short could have talked straight to Clark. "I should have had that one session with him," Short said.

Had Short ever had this heart-to-heart discussion with Clark, he might not have focused on changing the daily tasking or advocated that another set of targets be hit. Instead, Short believed he could have at least attempted to attain a better level of trust. He further concluded that making a deliberate effort to gain the trust of the JFC was part of the duty of the CFACC. Perhaps it was not a duty easy to recognize in advance or from the outside, but it was a duty nonetheless. Whether Short (or anyone else) would have succeeded in building trust with Clark under the conditions that pertained in the spring of 1999 can never be known. What is certain is that Short believed building that relationship was an essential step both to help ensure maximum success for the air campaign and to achieve the Coalition's larger objectives.

Short also wanted—as most commanders would—a greater level of trust in the connections with Washington and other capitals. This complaint was a common one, but his was still heartfelt. Short remembered receiving a call from Gen. Joseph Ralston, the vice chairman of the Joint Chiefs of Staff, during the thick of the search for the downed F-117. "Mike, I'm in the Oval Office," came Ralston's voice over the telephone. "The President wants to know why it's taking so long to recover the pilot."

Short did not spare in critiquing anyone, including himself and the U.S. Air Force. His major, lingering concern was that future CFACCs take more seriously the dilemmas of the Air Force Forces forward (AFFOR) job. The CFACC not only ran sorties for the air war but also had to fulfill the forces' forward role, including logistics, civil engineering, air base operations, munitions, and so on. All this activity generally had to be mastered in very little time. Short gave himself the grade of C+ or B– as CFACC, but he said he "almost failed" as AFFOR. In his view, the situation was worse in Afghanistan two years later.

LONG MEMORY

Few men have had the responsibility of command of air power in war. Short commanded a unique campaign, truly one of air power only, in a display of precision far more sophisticated than anything that had come before it.

Short retired from active duty on July 1, 2000. In retirement, he devoted considerable time to serving as an air force senior mentor. Several years later a spate of negative publicity about retired senior officer mentors made the job especially difficult, but Short did not retreat. He continued to devote time to coaching the next generation of air commanders.

Perhaps even more unusual was his willingness to share what he saw as his mistakes as well as his overall successes. To Short, his top success in Operation Allied Force was that no airmen died in combat. "To have flown that number of sorties and not to have lost anybody," he marveled later, "was remarkable." Rescue forces recovered both the F-117 and F-16 pilots who were shot down during the war.

Success number 2 was, of course, the victory itself. "NATO got it done," Short reflected. "Airmen were given the mission. There was no one else doing anything. In the application of military power, it was all air power and it was done well."

The alliance also proved strong enough to weather internal storms. For this accomplishment, much credit had to go to the increasing triumph of the campaign itself. Disarray after the first three days could have turned into a fatal paralysis, but Short did not allow it to happen. As CFACC, he fueled the air war, expanded forces, and kept the allied airmen in the fight together. His arguments with Clark may have singed both, but they were never incendiary enough to burn the alliance itself. Ultimately, Short's campaign accomplished what all campaigns should: it hit strategic targets to the maximum extent possible and carried out the gritty work of persistent attacks on enemy forces attempting maneuver in the field.

Keeping the air war going foiled Milošević's only chance to win. "Milošević's course of action was to splinter the alliance, and he couldn't do that," Short said with satisfaction. The seventy-eight days of strikes added up to the one pressure Milošević could not resist. Other factors almost certainly helped induce him to capitulate, and the end came through a mix of military and diplomatic power. However, it is significant that so many nations in 1998 and early 1999 tried every negotiating tactic and applied combinations of pressure to compel Milošević to back off on Kosovo. None of these measures worked for more than a few days or a few weeks before Milošević grew bold again. Only NATO's air campaign took that boldness away.

The experience of command and victory was indelible for Short. In 2012 he said: "My last conscious thought will be of my family and not losing anyone as CFACC."

12

T. MICHAEL MOSELEY: AIR POWER WARRIOR

JAMES D. KIRAS*

Air leaders, and especially air generals, are often the subjects of great scrutiny and criticism. The tenure of certain air leaders, and in particular the decisions they have made, generate considerable controversy. Some, like Gen. Curtis E. LeMay, were controversial throughout their careers. LeMay remains contentious as an air general for his polarizing leadership style, abrasive personality, and ethically questionable decisions, such as the firebombing of Tokyo. Other leaders become the subjects of inquiry in retirement on moral, ethical, or financial grounds; for instance, some were connected with the much-publicized "senior mentor" program, which has raised concerns about undue influence on acquisition programs and charges of conflict of interest.[1] Ironically, the most virulent criticism of an air general is usually generated within his service by peers and subordinates alike. Such criticism

* First I would like to express my deep gratitude and appreciation to General Moseley for taking the time to review an earlier draft of the chapter and provide comments on it. In addition, he generously sent a variety of material that was exceptionally useful in sketching a biography of his early career, lessons learned, and thoughts on generalship and leadership. I would also like to thank a number of students and colleagues at the School of Advanced Air and Space Studies for their insights and observations. In particular, Col. S. Clinton Hinote provided some of the keenest insights into "Buzz" Moseley's generalship through his research and his tolerance of my often pedantic questions. Lt. Col. Brook Leonard did not know it at the time, but he helped me understand the concept of operations and tactical innovation as I guided him on his research project. Col. Michael Kometer and Col. Melvin Deaile provided insights and observations from their experience or research on Operation Anaconda and Operation Iraqi Freedom. Col. Kometer also managed to educate a civilian academic on the intricacies of the Air Operations Center and the command and control of air. I owe Colonels Hinote, Kometer, and Deaile additional thanks for comments and feedback they provided on a draft version of this chapter. Last, and by no means least, I would like to thank Margaret S. MacDonald for her peerless editing of the text that made it a far better product.

often reflects personal opinion, tribal or individual rivalry or jealousy, or idle gossip and speculation about the quality of a general's leadership and decision making.

Few generals in the history of the U.S. Air Force (USAF) have generated as much controversy as Teed Michael Moseley. Better known by the nickname he acquired in the fighter community, "Buzz," Moseley has the dubious distinction of being one of the few generals forced to resign while serving as chief of staff of the air force. The proximate cause for Secretary of Defense Robert Gates's action was Moseley's handling of two incidents involving the mismanagement of nuclear weapons or their components. More informed sources suggest the secretary's actions were based on his continued displeasure with the actions of General Moseley and Secretary of the Air Force Michael Wynne's seemingly intractable stance on highly visible, expensive platform acquisition programs. In particular, Moseley was seen as too strident in his advocacy for the F-22 fighter program, even when Congress and the press questioned its cost and relevance in the contemporary security environment. Others characterized Moseley's defense of the F-22 program as a symptom of a much more insidious and troublesome problem: the seemingly unshakeable primacy of the "fighter generals" who had dominated the senior leadership positions in the USAF from 1982 onward and cemented their influence with the dissolution of the Strategic Air Command a decade later. In some communities, "fighter general" has become synonymous with "bias and narrowness of perspective" resulting in "insularity and narrow doctrinal focus" to the detriment of the overall health and welfare of the service.[2] In the eyes of his critics, the investigations into Moseley's alleged role in the so-called Thundervision scandal cement his place as the epitome of what is wrong with modern air generalship and, more specifically, with fighter air generalship.[3]

It is still too early to form a comprehensive portrait of T. Michael Moseley's career that would reflect all facets of his generalship, including his stewardship over the USAF during his time as chief of staff. That task will fall to a future biographer or historian. Only the passage of time, the distancing from events and personalities, and access to information that is currently classified or not in the public domain will allow a more complex portrait, reflecting a balanced perspective, to emerge.[4]

This chapter does not adopt the most expansive definition of generalship, which includes stewardship; instead, it assesses four qualities of air generalship: innovation, preparing for combat, building relationships, and leading forces in a major combat operation. In particular, the chapter focuses on how Gen. T. Michael Moseley exhibited these qualities in his own unique form of air generalship during his twenty-two-month tenure as commander of U.S. Central Command Air Forces (CENTAF) and combined forces air component commander (CFACC) for Operation Iraqi Freedom (OIF).

This review of Moseley's generalship starts with a brief biographical sketch of his background prior to his promotion to command the Ninth Air Force during Operation Enduring Freedom (OEF) in November 2001 and ends with the completion of major combat operations in OIF on May 1, 2003. This chapter breaks down this period into three phases: Operation Anaconda (March 2002); a period of adaptation, experimentation, and preparation for OIF (December 2002–February 2003); and the conduct of OIF itself (March 2003–May 2003). Although written chronologically, these sections attempt to illustrate Moseley's qualities as an air general through specific examples placed in context. The chapter ends with some broad conclusions on Moseley's air generalship.

A BRIEF BIOGRAPHY

Perhaps Teed Michael Moseley can be described best in one word, "Texan." He was born in Dallas on September 3, 1949, a member of the sixth generation of a Texas family. Several traits define those who come from the largest of the contiguous United States and Moseley is no exception: larger than life, traditional, virtuous, and plainspoken. Senator Phil Gramm once famously summarized the qualities of Texans when he said, "I love Texas because Texas is future-oriented, because Texans think anything is possible. Texans think big."[5] Educated in the Texas public school system, which reinforced Moseley's love of his country, his state, and their virtues and values, he sought to excel in every challenge he faced. For example, at the age of twelve he received two prestigious awards from the Boy Scouts of America. The first was his Eagle Scout award and the second—perhaps more remarkable given his young age—was the God and Country Award. Moseley went on to graduate from high school in Grand Prairie, Texas, and started his university education at Texas A&M during the height of the Vietnam War in 1967.[6]

Moseley's dream, from the earliest time he can remember, was to fly fighters. To say that he pursued this dream relentlessly is an understatement; he admits that he "never thought about being anything else." At age fourteen, when most other teenagers were thinking about learning how to drive a car, Moseley began flying lessons. As Moseley says, he "went to Texas A&M to be in the Corps of Cadets to become a fighter pilot." His dream of flying fighters also shaped his major subject of study: he took every available opportunity to feed his personal and professional interests in the context of military and air campaigns and other historical perspectives on war fighting. He excelled in the Corps of Cadets and graduated with a bachelor of arts degree in political science and history in 1971. That same year Moseley took his first major step toward his dream and received his commission as a second lieutenant in the USAF.

Shortly thereafter, three decisive events occurred in Moseley's life in quick succession. He continued his education by pursuing a master of arts degree in political science with a focus on Northeast Asia. More important in terms of achieving his goal, he started undergraduate pilot training with the USAF at Webb Air Force Base in Big Spring, Texas, graduating in 1973 with a recommendation for fighters and trainers. Most important of all, Moseley asked his high school sweetheart, Jennie Willman, to marry him, and she accepted. They were married in Houston, Texas, in May 1971. Within three years the Moseleys had two children—a daughter born in 1974 and a son born in the following year.

Moseley faced new challenges as he pursued his ambition of becoming a fighter pilot, and he met them with his characteristic commitment, enthusiasm, and energy. He followed up undergraduate pilot training with air force pilot instructor training at Randolph Air Force Base, Texas, and graduated with distinction. Almost immediately, Moseley put his instructor training to use in the USAF's only Security Assistance Program Squadron, where he trained South Vietnamese Air Force cadets and officers as well as airmen from various Middle Eastern and Latin American countries. From this assignment Moseley was promoted to first lieutenant and, in a demonstration of remarkable institutional confidence in his abilities, was selected to serve at this rank as a standardization/evaluation flight examiner. His superiors noted his personal commitment to excellence and his willingness to pursue what he believed to be the right course of action. As a result, in 1975 they awarded him one of the highest honors an instructor pilot can achieve, the Air Training Command's Instructor Pilot of the Year.

The following year Moseley received an even greater honor, which, in one way, represented the fulfillment of his lifelong dream. His talent and flying skill led to his selection as one of the initial cadre for the Forty-Ninth Tactical Fighter Wing, where he would fly the most advanced fighter in the world, the F-15A

Eagle, which was then entering operational service. In 1979 Moseley was chosen to join the first group of pilots to fly the more advanced version of the F-15, the *C* model, with the Eighteenth Tactical Fighter Wing at Kadena Air Base in Japan. Moseley not only flew the first operational F-15C to Kadena in the summer of 1979, but in the following spring he also led the first F-15C intercept of a Russian bomber—a Tupolev Tu-95 (NATO codename "Bear")—while operating out of Clark Air Base in the Philippines. Moseley's superior officers recognized his abilities and achievements by granting him further awards and selecting him for prestigious programs, including the U.S. Navy's Fighter Weapons ("Top Gun") School at Naval Air Station Miramar, California, as well as the air force's own Fighter Weapons School at Nellis Air Force Base (AFB), Nevada. He had become a consummate fighter pilot and master tactician at a relatively early stage in his air force career.

Moseley's star within the service was definitely on the rise during the 1980s, as his various promotions, distinctions, and assignments suggest. To some extent this reflected his skill as a pilot, but superior officers also recognized Moseley's other skills and qualities. One character trait he demonstrated time and again was his readiness to stand up for his beliefs, as long as those beliefs were founded on operational competence and personal honesty. Put simply, Moseley was willing to assume a degree of calculated risk without being reckless, leading superior officers to entrust him with responsibilities above his pay grade. For example, one of his earliest mentors, Col. Moody Suter (considered the father of the USAF's "Red Flag" series of exercises), asked Moseley to lead preparations for several operational readiness inspections, which involved particularly grueling reviews of equipment and operational compliance with demanding and detailed procedures to ensure the highest possible rating. Such inspections can make or break the chances for promotion of group and wing leaders. As Moseley related, "[Colonel Moody] absolutely trusted me to make things happen when the chips were down and there was risk involved."[7] Given his outstanding performance, Moseley was promoted to major and lieutenant colonel early, and between these promotions he attended Air Command and Staff College at Maxwell AFB, Alabama, graduating not merely with distinction but at the top of his class.

The years prior to Moseley's promotion to general officer rank were filled with numerous rewarding challenges and opportunities. Like most officers, Moseley had a tour of duty in the Pentagon after graduating from Staff College and served as an action officer on the Air Staff. It would be the first of several staff tours in the Pentagon that leveraged his expertise in fighters and their equipment and systems. For example, he was requested by name to work on so-called black world, or highly classified, applications of fighter radar; the development, testing, acquisition, and deployment of such weapon systems as the AIM-120 advanced medium-range air-to-air missile; and the early specifications and plans to acquire a replacement fighter for the F-15, or the advanced tactical fighter (which later became the F-22). Such was the confidence in his knowledge of fighter aircraft and their weapons systems that the secretary of defense personally picked him as one of four officers to provide a rationale both for protecting the AIM-120 missile program from termination and for reversing a production stop order for the F-15. Moseley accomplished it by "aggressively engag[ing] with historical fact and actual experience in flying the F-15 and in my experience of firing eight different air-to-air missiles. Eventually [the combination of] truthful and factual data and experience [helped save the program]."[8] In an example of contemporary challenges mirroring those of the past, Moseley later would stake his reputation, and some would say his legacy, in the bitter fight to guarantee the continuation of the F-22 program during his tenure as air force chief of staff.

The fourteen years from his first Pentagon tour until his promotion to lieutenant general in command of the Ninth Air Force brought Moseley greatly increased responsibility and several opportunities to exercise his leadership. Command of a squadron (F-15 Division, Fighter Weapons Instructor Course, Fighter Weapons School, Nellis AFB), an operations group (Thirty-Third Operations Group, Eglin AFB), and later a wing (Fifty-Seventh Weapons Wing, Nellis AFB) would teach him two valuable lessons in leadership. The first was that a commander's primary duty and obligation is "taking care of war fighting personnel, [both] enlisted and officer."[9] The second was that "not everyone has outstanding combat skills . . . others must be led and nurtured."[10] He incorporated these lessons into his own unique leadership style, one that combined Texan forthrightness; a love of fighters, service, and country; and an approach in which he was "[n]ever reluctant to engage superiors on challenges and issues" to obtain the best outcome.[11]

Moseley's staff tours represented a mix of USAF and Joint Staff assignments, the most important of which was his first direct experience with Iraq as the director of operations (J-3) for Joint Task Force–Southwest Asia. This experience included flying combat missions as part of Operation Southern Watch, an effort sanctioned by the United Nations (UN) to maintain a "no-fly" zone in Iraq following the Gulf War. Other staff assignments familiarized Moseley with the workings of the air force general officer corps, the Joint Staff regional planning process, and the air force's dealings with Congress and the executive branch of government. Moseley not only attended the prestigious National War College at Fort Lesley J. McNair in Washington, D.C., as his senior service school, but also served on the faculty for two years, holding the chief of staff of the air force's "chair." In this role he taught courses on air campaigns and the planning of joint-combined operations and had the opportunity to indulge his passion for air power history.

Reflecting on the events, Moseley typically and succinctly summarized his career in a way that revealed his directness, beliefs, passions, and interests:

> I would suggest my 38+ years in the Air Force were characterized by looking to obtain the right skill set, the right set of credentials, and the right set of experiences to better staff, lead and/or command Airmen and joint/combined operations. I also believe my career is most characterized by my willing[ness] to take risk in taking care of people, fighting bad guys, articulating American Air Power and defending what I believe to be right . . . with no compromise in defending the faith and the American people.[12]

OPERATION ANACONDA, NOVEMBER 2001–MARCH 2002

Shortly after being promoted to command of the Ninth Air Force and commander, U.S. Central Command Air Forces (COMUSCENTAF), Moseley would find himself in the midst of one of the earliest controversies of OEF. Operation Anaconda was the name given to an eighteen-day operation in one of the most contested regions of Afghanistan, the Shah-i-Kot Valley and the Arma Mountains in Paktia Province. Although officially a Coalition victory, Anaconda fell short of its objective of encircling and preventing the escape of remaining Taliban and Al Qaeda forces in Afghanistan.

Considerable friction, miscues, and lack of coordination between different assault and support elements beset the operation. Of the many mistakes made during the planning and initial execution of Anaconda, one would reignite perhaps the most persistent source of tension between air and ground units. Ground commanders alleged that despite an overabundance of resources, the USAF's dogmatic insistence on centralized control of air assets by an airman led to promises of intelligence and fire support being unfulfilled and that air power failed to respond to needs on the ground.

BACKGROUND

Exactly one month after OEF officially began, Moseley assumed command of the Ninth Air Force. Unlike most commanders before him, Moseley did not take command of the Ninth at its base in South Carolina. The nation was at war, and, as COMUSCENTAF, the Ninth Air Force commander served as the air component commander and force presenter to the geographic combatant commander of U.S. Central Command (CENTCOM), Gen. Tommy Franks. The change of command ceremony between Moseley and Lt. Gen. Charles "Chuck" Wald and Moseley's promotion to lieutenant general took place at the Combined Air Operations Center (CAOC) at Prince Sultan Air Base (PSAB) in the Kingdom of Saudi Arabia.[13] The timing appeared auspicious for Moseley's career. COMUSCENTAF was supporting missions in Afghanistan and using air power in ways previously undreamed of, pounding Taliban and Al Qaeda forces and scattering them from their bases, fortified positions, and cities. For the next twenty-two months PSAB would be Moseley's base of operations and his home.

OEF had formally started on October 7, 2001, when a mix of air force bombers, navy fighters, and cruise missiles hit thirty-one different targets throughout Afghanistan. Over the next few days and weeks air activity in support of OEF shifted from attacking largely static, infrastructure targets to providing close air support (CAS) of ground forces. This shift did not result only from "the bad guys moving" but also reflected a highly dynamic and fluid situation on the ground. Paramilitary forces, among others, had infiltrated the country weeks before the campaign began and had made contact with Afghan warlords and leaders who were hostile to the Taliban. Leaders of indigenous forces, such as Hamid Karzai and Abdul Rashid Dostum, subsequently linked up with U.S. Army Special Forces (SF) teams inserted into the country as part of Task Force Dagger.

One of the resources that SF teams had was access to American air power through enlisted or joint tactical air controllers, who were either part of or embedded with the SF Operational Detachments Alpha (ODAs).[14] Changes in the means of control of air power, the distances that platforms could reach thanks to aerial refueling, and the precision of munitions and their terminal guidance were rewriting how SF and other special operations forces (SOF) conducted their missions. In military parlance, air power was a "force multiplier" and a source of firepower that most indigenous forces could not have imagined.

FRICTION POINTS

Yet behind the early successes in Afghanistan friction was building up from different sources and came to a head for Moseley and CENTAF during Anaconda. One source of tension that preceded Moseley's arrival at PSAB was the relationship between the CENTCOM commander, General Franks, and the CENTAF staff, particularly staff in the CAOC that had the means to develop strategy and command and control the flow of resources into the theater and eventually into Afghanistan. The first night of air strikes, for example, involved coordinating the ingress, egress, and timing of strikes coming from ships in the Indian Ocean, from B-1 and B-52 bombers flying from Diego Garcia, and from B-2 bombers making forty-hour round-trip flights from Whiteman AFB in Missouri. The CAOC was more than sufficiently manned and equipped to interpret CENTCOM guidance and determine how best to utilize the resources at hand to achieve Franks's four-phase plan.[15] However, rather than provide broad guidance for the components to execute, Franks and his staff sent specific targeting information to the CAOC, and such CENTCOM-directed targets became much more limited as time went on.[16] In one instance, Franks upbraided Moseley's predecessor, General Wald, for placing air force priorities above those of the joint team.[17] As a result, many bombers and other strike aircraft proceeded to "burn holes in the sky" while waiting for calls to provide CAS.

Friction also resulted from the very means of U.S. and Coalition success in Afghanistan. To conduct operations as quickly as they did, the various component elements under CENTCOM—air, special operations, and maritime—stood up or utilized their own command and control mechanisms with little reference to one another. These standing or ad hoc commands functioned well in simple operations against distributed targets, such as fire support, but fissures in the command architecture appeared during more tactically complex operations that required synchronization and integration in limited space. For example, while U.S. Navy and U. S. Marine Corps (USMC) planners were preparing Task Force (TF) 58 to seize the airfield at Objective Rhino in November 2001, the size of the forces to be inserted grew beyond the ability of Marine Corps KC-130s to lift them. The TF-58 commander tried to arrange for air force lift transport, but the director of Mobility Forces in the CAOC, who was responsible for managing the flow of airlifters, found out about this requirement only three days prior to the start of the operation: Brig. Gen. Richard A. Mentemeyer recalled,

> I first got wind of the operation, on the 20th of November from [Lt. Gen. T. Michael Moseley], the Combined Forces Air Component commander at the time. I went down to the two MARLOs [Marine liaison officers in the CAOC] and asked about TF 58, and they just stared at me.[18]

During the preparations for Operation Anaconda the imposition of an additional command and control layer further confused an already complex and chaotic situation. For the planned operation, CENTCOM's combined forces land component commander (CFLCC), Lt. Gen. Paul Mikolashek, stood up Combined Joint Task Force (CJTF) Mountain, which was led by Brig. Gen. Franklin "Buster" Hagenbeck of the Tenth Mountain Division. The CJTF staff, located in Bagram, conducted their own planning and coordination through CFLCC headquarters in Camp Doha, Kuwait, for almost two months, largely without reference to other joint planning and control organizations. The staff's initial plan was a variation of the so-called hammer and anvil approach, where assault and maneuver elements drive the enemy to blocking positions and the former become force anvils that crush the enemy (see figure 1). Given that SOF would form part of the hammer element of the operation, planners from Joint Special Operations Task Force–North were involved in the planning process, although other SOF elements were not. The air elements integrated into the planning at the level of execution were organic and attached rotary-wing army aviation from the brigade executing the attack, or from the Third Brigade of the 101st Airborne Division under Task Force Rakkasan. While such aviation offers unprecedented mobility for ground forces, it is nevertheless vulnerable to small-arms and other antiaircraft artillery. A small air command element, the Twentieth Air Support Operations Squadron, was attached to SOF planning elements in Bagram, but it had neither the manpower nor the authority to generate air plans of its own.[19]

Separation in time and space added to the complications of planning and executing Operation Anaconda. The CENTCOM staff, located in Tampa, Florida, operated on eastern standard time. CFLCC army planners in Camp Doha, Kuwait, more than seven thousand miles away, conducted operations eight hours ahead of CENTCOM but based their planning on Greenwich mean time, or three hours behind local time. The air force CAOC operated using the same time zones as the CFLCC but was located in neighboring Saudi Arabia. To further complicate matters, CJTF and Air Support Operations Center (ASOC) staff in Afghanistan were two and a half hours ahead of the "Charlie" time of their parent CFLCC and CFACC headquarters and almost half a day ahead of CENTCOM planners. Coordination among these headquarters took place through video teleconferencing. Technological means could facilitate communication among the various components, but they did nothing to create and establish the relationships and, more important, the horizontal and vertical trust required at the service component and joint force levels to promote effective unity of effort and command.

The multiple, and to some degree independent, command and control architectures and the lack of coordination would lead to needless confusion throughout the battle's early phases. Although personal relationships between component commanders might have mitigated this source of friction, neither Mikolashek nor Hagenbeck appears to have made an effort to develop contacts with Moseley and his counterparts. Indeed, at least one source has characterized the relationship between Mikolashek and Moseley in polite terms as a "personality conflict."[20] Regardless of their personal differences, Moseley later stated that as component commanders supporting the operation, "General Mikolashek and I knew less of ANACONDA than I desired to know at that time."[21] Given that the plan for Anaconda relied almost exclusively on air assets for fire support, and that the Tenth Mountain and TF Rakkasan had left all but their mortars and other small tube artillery in garrison as they deployed forward, the reason why planners failed to seek greater cooperation with the air element remains a mystery.

While Operation Anaconda was based on an approved concept of operations (CONOPS), faulty assumptions threatened to unhinge the entire plan. For reasons that remain unclear, neither CJTF Mountain nor CFLCC planning staffs sought to use air component resources to refine estimates of the enemy's situation. Such assets could have included MQ-1 Predator drones to provide persistent surveillance as well as other manned intelligence, surveillance, and reconnaissance (ISR) platforms. One possible reason for this omission has to do with the strain and fatigue of CJTF Mountain staff, drawn from the Tenth Mountain Division headquarters, which one author has characterized as "the most undermanned,

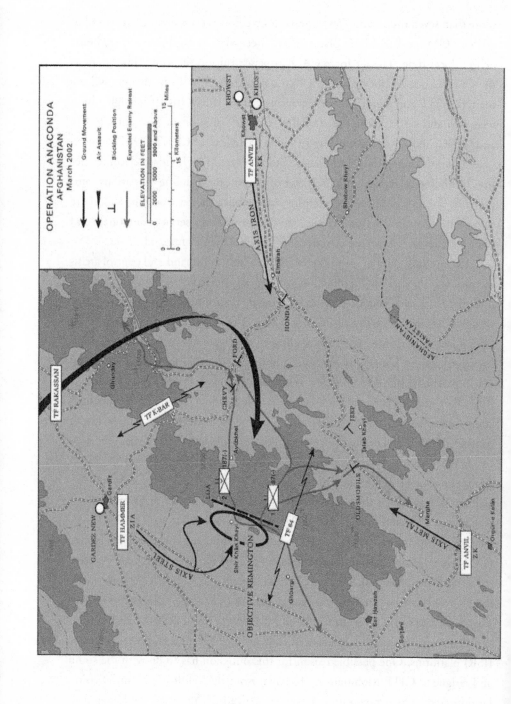

OPERATION ANACONDA
AFGHANISTAN
March 2002

Ground Movement
Air Assault
Blocking Position
Expected Enemy Retreat

ELEVATION IN FEET
2000 5000 9000 and Above

0   15 Kilometers
0   15 Miles

stretched, and stressed division headquarters in the Army."[22] The assumption that the Taliban and Al Qaeda forces were shattered, defeated, and incapable of coordinated resistance would prove fatal to some soldiers executing the plan at the tactical level.

Synchronizing fires and maneuver elements to generate specific effects in time is difficult enough to do well in a large battle space. The battle space of Operation Anaconda was a mere forty square miles in area but with differences of more than nine thousand feet in elevation between the surrounding valleys and the key mountain, nicknamed the "Whale." Furthermore, the border of another sovereign nation, Pakistan, was only a little more than fifteen miles away to the southeast, placing severe limitations on ingress and egress routes for aircraft and their holding areas. The problem, as seen from the air perspective, is best illustrated in figure 2, which depicts aircraft performing CAS in holding "stacks" and their routes. Finally, at least thirty-seven enlisted tactical air controllers were in this limited area of complex terrain, which required further deconfliction and synchronization.[23] Earlier notification and coordination with air planners, beyond the five to eight days alleged by some sources, could have prevented some of the unnecessary problems that faced Moseley and his staff when the combat portion of Operation Anaconda began on March 2.[24]

The notification of the impending operation surprised Moseley; he recalled only becoming aware of the operation five days prior to its start. When Franks asked for his assessment of the air support required, Moseley answered that he and his staff could run two simultaneous CAS operations if certain conditions were met.[25] Another surprising element of the operation, particularly for those engaged in fighting it, was the strength and quality of the Taliban and Al Qaeda resistance on the Whale and elsewhere. This resistance had two immediate effects. Almost immediately CJTF Mountain's CONOPS was rendered moot. Both American and Afghan maneuver elements were either pinned down by heavy machine gun fire and mortars, drastically slowing their advance, or they turned from tactical offensive to defensive rescue operations.[26] Attack helicopters also took unexpected damage and casualties, limiting their ability to provide expected air support. Operation Anaconda was turning from a plan designed to squeeze Taliban and Al Qaeda forces through coordinated maneuver and firepower into a disconnected and chaotic series of small unit, close combat actions that presented further challenges for air power to support. Over the course of the next two weeks, Moseley

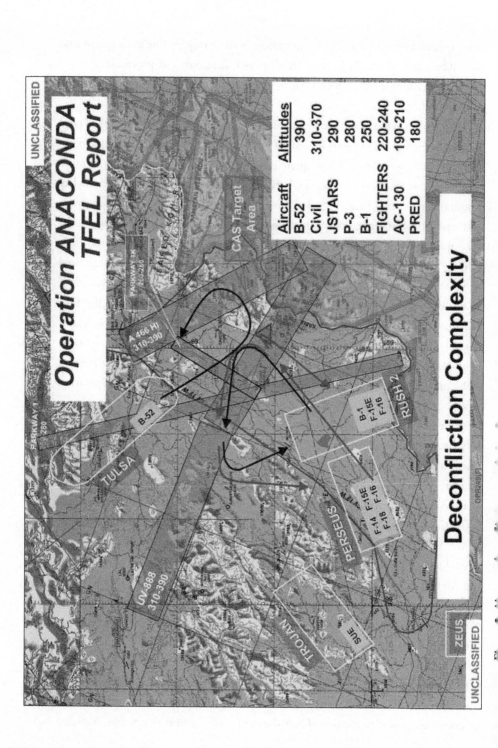

would exert his generalship and exhibit three qualities that made him an air leader as he responded to the challenges these surprises presented.

The first quality evident in Moseley's air generalship during Operation Anaconda was his sense of responsibility and accountability. This characteristic extended beyond himself; indeed, in his actions and decisions, Moseley held the air force as an armed service and all of its personnel, processes, and systems to his own high standards. It was obvious to Moseley that airmen had been included late in the planning process for Anaconda and that actions were not going particularly well in the first twenty-four hours of the actual operation. Moseley and his staff sought to identify both the proximate and underlying problems that were preventing the delivery of air power effects on the battlefield in a timely, relevant, and coordinated way. He imposed his own standards on the service and its personnel, and—as would any graduate of the Fighter Weapons School—Moseley expected the unvarnished truth and recommendations for improving near-term support to those relying upon air power in Anaconda. Other processes could be modified and improved with an eye toward providing a more comprehensive solution once Anaconda was over.

In this regard, one of the greatest challenges was imposing a level of discipline on how air strikes were apportioned and controlled. CJTF Mountain was dissatisfied with how long it took for the CAOC to authorize precision-guided munition strikes, but the CAOC had to observe weapons release procedures and calculations to help prevent fratricide.[28] Left unchecked, the existing system of command and control that flowed through the special operations liaison elements with the CAOC had a higher-than-average potential of causing friendly fire casualties, especially given the restricted operating area and the number of calls for air support that were coming in. All levels of air control—from the air support operations group commander, Col. Michael A. Longoria, who first stood up an ASOC, down to the assistant division air liaison officer in the ASOC itself—understood the need for a more rigorous system to avoid "a complete disaster."[29] Unfortunately, in an incident that strained relations between Coalition partners, two Air National Guard F-16 pilots misinterpreted ground fire near Tarnak Farms as hostile, disobeyed instructions to hold for confirmation from an airborne warning and control system, and rolled in, killing four Canadian soldiers and wounding eight others.[30] Following this tragedy, Moseley made certain that his air commanders and aircrews understood their responsibilities in responding to threats, warning them that there was "a well-defined mechanism to ensure you and I do not engage friendly forces. It is difficult to imagine a scenario, other than troops in contact, whereby we will not have time to egress the threat area, regroup, deconflict and then engage in a well thought-out and coordinated plan that ensures success. . . . We cannot afford another tragic incident."[31]

Enforcing the changes necessary to ensure command and control discipline was upheld was not easy, given that many soldiers and airmen thought the existing processes worked well enough in theater. Imposing discipline on theater air control, including bringing the recently established ASOC back in line with CAOC directives, required Moseley to impose his will to force change.[32] Yet he eventually succeeded through a number of actions during the battle. In addition, after the operation ended, Moseley took such corrective steps as establishing an air control coordination element (ACCE) within the CFLCC staff in Camp Doha.

Responsibility and accountability are also related to the calculation and acceptance of risk, or more specifically to recognizing unnecessary risk and seeking solutions to minimize it. Moseley later indicated just how risky it had been, for both ground and air forces, to provide air support under the system of control that existed in the opening days of Anaconda: "The air component contributed far more than the predicted two simultaneous CAS events at a time 'but we did it at extremely high risk to our folks,' General Moseley later said. 'We ended up dropping bombs through orbits. We simultaneously attacked sites from adjacent ground parties with not the right amount of comfort with ingressing and egressing fighters, all while taking weapons fire and surface-to-air missiles or MANPAD [man portable air defense] fire through all of this,' he added."[33]

Other risks made deconfliction and discipline necessary. Figure 2 depicts not only these potentially conflicting routes but also the different altitudes at which aircraft were operating. Moseley's CAOC director, Maj. Gen. John D. W. Corley, gave an idea of how congested the airspace above the mountains was, stating: "[There were] B-52s at higher altitudes dropping JDAMs [joint direct attack munitions]; B-1s at lower altitudes; unmanned vehicles such as Predator flying through there; P-3s, aircraft contributing to the ISR assets; helicopters down at the ground; fast-moving aircraft, F-14s, F/A-18s, F-16s, F-15Es; tanker aircraft that are flying through there. So you begin to see and sense the degree of difficulty of deconfliction."[34] In addition to military aircraft, the CFACC had to account for the risk to civil aviation operating on three established flight routes at altitudes between the B-52s and the joint surveillance target attack radar system (JSTARS).

In Moseley's mind, discipline and risk were inseparable, and the risks that ground forces assumed when calling in strikes could be resolved only through an improved system of control coupled with "better target ID and target coordinates, generating additional strike targets, prioritizing CAS, and [solving] the problems caused because not all GFACs [ground forward air controllers] had the equipment to determine precise target coordinates."[35] Such risk mitigation was required because, contrary to popular opinion, OEF was not fought exclusively with precision-guided weapons. Indeed, the tempo of air operations supporting Anaconda meant that more "dumb" bombs were dropped than smart ones were.[36] Both the preventable level of risk inherent in Operation Anaconda and the lack of proper control mechanisms and procedures led Moseley to conclude that on "day one or day two, I'm not happy now with what we're seeing." And he observed that even when staffs were augmented as immediate fixes "when we got [the ASOC at Bagram] up there, we didn't have it right."[37]

The strength of his convictions, which in turn informed his judgment, certainly shaped his generalship. In the most extreme cases, conviction can become dogma and overrule sound judgment. While Moseley remained true to his conviction that there was a correct way to use air and space power in support of Anaconda, he recognized the need to provide the effects that the soldiers in danger on the ground required. Because CENTAF only became involved late in the planning process for Anaconda he had little possibility of preparing the battle space by flowing intelligence assets into the theater and using them to collect information from the wide range of technical means at his disposal. The air force process for conducting intelligence preparation of the battle space involved everything from remotely piloted vehicles, such as Global Hawk, to manned E-8 JSTARS.

In Moseley's estimation an air general could provide not only an airman's unique, theater-wide perspective on the operation but also crucial information during the later planning stages and early execution. In retrospect he stated: "We didn't really survey this right, nor did we put the collection assets on this right, nor did we prioritize the collection deck right to find out where these people were, so we would know about where they were and how many there were before we put in our ground teams."[38] Moseley's conviction regarding a better use of air power was reinforced when he learned that B-52s were making 3,000-mile trips from Afghanistan back to Diego Garcia with full munitions loads. The problem was not merely one of unexpended ordnance; he knew that with adequate oversight and control these aircraft could be used much more effectively and perhaps even stopped from going on a sortie if not required.

Like many of his predecessors, Moseley was also convinced that an airman should control air power in order to generate the desired effects. Some have interpreted this insistence on control of all air assets as nothing more than a service-specific, borderline pathological obsession. Through his actions in two areas, Moseley made a convincing case for having an airman control air assets. First, given his particularly sound grasp of the technical aspects of modern air power to generate the desired effects, he authorized but did not micromanage ordnance loads. During the battle, Moseley authorized the use of both 1,000-pound cluster munition bombs (CBU-87) and 500-pound Mark-82s fused to detonate above ground.[39] In addition, he provided "top cover" that allowed his subordinates to experiment using novel techniques, such as "skip-bombing" ordnance into tunnel and cave openings, and to field new ordnance, such as thermobaric bombs.[40]

The second aspect of his approach to control in Anaconda—that is, his translation of the concept of centralized control and decentralized execution—demonstrates that Moseley was not dogmatic in his approach to air power. Those who interpret this doctrinal concept in its most literal and dogmatic sense are apt to demand control and oversight of all air assets all the time. When Moseley realized, however, that response times to calls for support had to be shortened, he took immediate action. During Anaconda responses could be inhibited by the requirement for strike approval from CENTCOM, delays in prestrike assessments of collateral damage, the long flight time needed for aircraft to reach the battle space, and the relatively short time on station of the preponderant types of aircraft (fighter-bombers) available. Long before the term was adopted in common usage, Moseley approved a "surge" of A-10 attack aircraft to serve two purposes—to provide CAS with a high degree of survivability against the Taliban's and Al Qaeda's weapons and to fill a gap in local airspace control and deconfliction by having A-10 pilots serve as airborne forward air controllers.[41] In another instance he fought for and received approval for the creation of de facto kill boxes, which gave pilots the freedom and discretion to use their unexpended ordnance and attack targets in certain areas before returning to base.

Air power played a crucial role during the battle, providing CAS in the form of 235 bombs dropped on average per day.[42] In addition, ISR platforms helped identify other targets on the mountains, improve the situational awareness of ground forces, and detect attempts by Al Qaeda to maneuver on the battlefield or to reinforce its men. On March 5, for example, a group of Taliban reinforcements numbering in the hundreds was detected and destroyed in the valley south of Takur Ghar.[43] The CJTF Mountain commander, "Buster" Hagenbeck, stated that air power inflicted the preponderance of casualties upon Taliban and Al Qaeda forces, although elsewhere he minimized air power's effectiveness.[44]

Despite the tensions, uncertainties, and tragedies, CENTCOM described Anaconda as a success when the battle concluded on March 18. Friendly losses were fourteen American and Afghan dead and fewer than 150 men wounded. Taliban and Al Qaeda forces not only gave up valuable ground but also suffered casualties estimated at between a hundred to more than a thousand dead.[45] Surviving Taliban and Al Qaeda escaped across the border into Pakistan.

Subsequent narratives about the battle have added to the controversy by depicting specific individuals as heroes or villains, including Moseley.[46] One true indicator of generalship is learning lessons and applying them to improve overall force performance. Moseley certainly did.

FROM ANACONDA TO OPERATION IRAQI FREEDOM

Even though Operation Anaconda was over, another battle regarding Anaconda was only now beginning. In print, including popular media and military publications, disputes ignited over individual and service reputations and responsibility for mistakes. Anaconda had been the first engagement of OEF that used conventional forces. It was also the first set-piece battle that U.S. ground forces had fought in an otherwise unconventional war against terrorism, making it more readily understood and therefore scrutinized by pundits and analysts outside the military.

Outside the public eye a struggle of a different sort was occurring. The army and air force senior leadership, including Moseley, engaged in some soul-searching of their own. Activities included such analytic efforts as Task Force Enduring Look as well as discussion by all four-star air force generals at their Corona summit.[47] The purpose of this critical, reflective examination was to determine how to improve interservice collaboration and cooperation for future operations. Continued lack of effective coordination between the services particularly concerned those leaders exploring options for a higher-stakes venture on the horizon, namely, the potential military invasion of Iraq. Almost immediately Moseley, as CFACC, focused on planning the air campaign in support of the invasion while simultaneously directing activities in support of Operation Southern Watch in Iraq.

Effective generalship and joint operations begin with unity of command and effort. Moseley was determined to forge improved working relationships across the joint force, including among component elements separated in both space and time.[48] Following Operation Anaconda, Moseley set about establishing strong collaborative relationships with both General Franks and the new CFLCC commander for CENTCOM, army Lt. Gen. David D. McKiernan.

Developing a trusting relationship with his boss was relatively easy for Moseley. The two had some common background, as both had grown up in Texas, although Franks was a transplant from Wynnewood, Oklahoma. They enjoyed a degree of healthy rivalry fostered by the fact that Moseley was a Texas A&M alumnus while General Franks had received his undergraduate degree from the University of Texas.[49] Their Texas heritage may have given them one crucial shared attribute: both officers had a no-nonsense, no-excuses, direct style in exercising leadership and command.

The two men also respected each other's obvious tactical and operational expertise. In reviewing the problems that occurred during Operation Anaconda, Moseley concluded that "if you exclude a component from the planning and you exclude a component that will provide the preponderance of support, logistic and kinetic, then you will have to live with the outcome of this not playing out very well."[50] In subsequent discussions with Franks, Moseley was direct to the point of being blunt: "We shouldn't go into [operations] thinking that the air component's going to come in like the cavalry and bail everybody out. We should have all of this happen at the beginning."[51] Franks responded equally directly: "Well, if we had [an operation like Anaconda] to do all over again, we would."[52] Candid assessments and exchanges such as these, punctuated by self-deprecating humor even in times of stress and crisis during the planning for OIF, demonstrate that Franks and Moseley had gained each other's trust and respect for their expertise and judgment.[53]

To improve information sharing and develop horizontal relationships and trust with his other service counterparts, Moseley advocated and received approval from the chief of staff of the air force, Gen. John Jumper, to establish ACCEs at the headquarters of each component command and at various task forces to act as Moseley's personal representatives and liaison officers. Although the ACCE concept had not yet been tested, validated, or accepted doctrinally, Moseley set up seven ACCEs that were composed of six to ten airmen.[54] To cement the relationships with his component counterparts and the task forces, Moseley handpicked the ACCE detachment commanders. He did not simply send "trusted agents" to command ACCEs; he chose his best officers, those who understood air power co-ordination at the highest levels and would represent the air force and the CFACC well. For example, Brig. Gen. F. C. "Pink" Williams was dispatched to lead the ACCE at the Coalition forces' special operations component commander's head-quarters that would meet SOF air requirements.[55] To guarantee the most effective coordination with General McKiernan and his staff, Moseley entrusted the ACCE of the combined forces land component command to Maj. Gen. Daniel P. Leaf.[56]

Sustaining a healthy working relationship between staffs is not simply a func-tion of sending highly qualified people to work with others. Although it might seem simple on the surface, it is equally important for the partners to demonstrate their commitment. A historical friction point between USAF officers and their aviation counterparts in other services was the desire of each group to maintain its own authority and control. Col. Michael Kometer explains how General Moseley resolved the issue:

In fall of 2002, he . . . conven[ed] a conference with top Marine generals to work out the C2 [command and control] of Marine airpower. *Without any formal written agreements, the generals worked out an arrangement* that allowed the Marine air commander to tell the air component how many sorties the 1st Marine Expeditionary Force (MEF) needed. The planners in the CAOC then allocated these sorties, arranged all the support for them, and sent that information back out in the [air tasking order]. To make this plan work, *Moseley insisted the Marines provide some of their best officers to serve as liaison officers, one of whom became the CAS planner for the entire theater.*[57]

Kometer illustrates three aspects of Moseley's generalship: a willingness to engage directly, yet informally, with his other service counterparts to resolve issues; an insistence that his counterparts send officers as good as the ones he dispatched, thereby ensuring a degree of shared commitment and costs; and a trust in these liaison officer's abilities, demonstrated by empowering them with extremely im-portant tasks on his staff, which reinforced their importance.

As a general officer with an exceptionally sound grasp of all aspects of air power, Moseley had well understood the two most troublesome aspects of providing air support to ground forces during Anaconda. The first was the significant "seam" between air strikes that had to undergo a lengthy review process, while the second related to flexible support, or immediate response, to emerging or fleeting requirements. In Moseley's words, "to strike a target, 'you had to either have a [joint special operations area] stood up, or a killbox [engagement zone] stood up, or targets outside of that had to be blessed through an elaborate process' reaching 'back to Tampa and in some cases back to Washington.'"[58]

During Anaconda, Moseley and his staff had developed a short-term fix for the first problem in the form of preplanned emergency CAS, which, according to air force doctrine, appeared to be a contradiction in terms. Even with such innovations, response times for some requests for air support were still too long. Moseley recognized that lengthy response times in providing effective air support were bad enough in a fixed battle space, such as that of Anaconda, and would only worsen when dealing with important targets that would be identified rapidly and just as quickly disappear. To address such fleeting targets he embraced and entirely changed a concept that was developed as a result of working with special operations forces and air cooperation in OEF, namely, time-sensitive targeting (TST).

The requirement to prosecute TST was not particularly new. The contemporary imperative to develop responsive TST in 2002–2003 reflected the same problem that Lt. Gen. Charles A. Horner and his CENTAF staff confronted in 1991. CENTCOM planners working from 2002 onward expected that Saddam Hussein would again use the western desert as a launching area for his mobile Scud ballistic missiles.[59] During Operation Desert Storm the CENTCOM commander and CENTAF planners had been caught off guard and reacted as best they could by sending in SOF teams and diverting significant aircraft to hunt Scuds. Despite the considerable resources thrown at the problem, without preparation and a coherent plan or process to tackle "flex targeting" the Coalition destroyed few mobile Scud launchers.[60]

The need for more responsive targeting and for using air power had become evident during OEF once the number of preplanned targets in Afghanistan had been exhausted. Dispersed SOF teams hunted Al Qaeda and Taliban leaders deemed high-value targets, a category that included Osama bin Laden and Mullah Muhammad Omar. Meanwhile, authorizations for air strikes involving TST continued to be refined, but collateral damage concerns made the process unwieldy:

The rules of engagement required that at least one SOF team member have eyes on the target before the target could be struck, with no slack allowed for presumptions or blind judgment calls. A second SOF team member also was required to double-check and confirm all target coordinates before they were passed to the assigned strike aircraft. Later in November [2001], General Franks received permission to delegate sensitive-target approval authority yet a further step downward to his director of operations at CENTCOM headquarters.[61]

Owing to the sensitive nature of some information and SOF activities against these high-value targets, however, a separate and, to large degree, isolated TST cell within CENTCOM operations center performed much of the planning for and execution of air strikes.

Moseley's expansion of the TST concept demonstrates an additional aspect of his air generalship, namely, vertical trust within his organization. Moseley knew that closer integration between air power and SOF was required to make the TST process more responsive against fleeting targets. As it happened, General Franks and his chief of operations, Maj. Gen. Victor "Gene" Renuart Jr., had come to the same realization in January 2003, and Franks became more responsive to Moseley's arguments.[62] As mentioned previously, Moseley had improved horizontal relationships between components, including SOF, by sending some of his most talented general officers to command ACCEs at the partners' headquarters. Their efforts increased coordination and synchronization between components through information sharing based on trust. Moseley now set to work on obtaining greater authority and freedom of action from Franks to deal with the TST problem. Drawing on their working relationship and mutual trust, he used two arguments to support transferring much of the authority for TST from CENTCOM's operations center to the CAOC. First, the CAOC possessed advanced and unique computer systems and management tools that were already "in theater"; and, second, the majority of the TSTs would be confirmed and attacked using integrated air and space resources.[63]

Moseley then turned to the problem of actually executing TST missions and streamlining the process by refining the necessary tactics, techniques, and procedures through service and joint war games and exercises. One of the first steps he took to deal specifically with the anticipated Scud threat in western Iraq was to sponsor, through the Air Combat Command (ACC), the Early Victor series of exercises conducted at Nellis AFB in Nevada. During these exercises, SOF teams and aircrews had the opportunity to test both the CONOPS and the practical details of air-ground coordination for hunting Scuds, including mock mission rehearsals to identify any potential tactical, technical, or procedural problems and find solutions to them.[64] Most important, Early Victor provided SOF operators and air force pilots the chance to view the operations from each other's very different tactical perspectives and develop a "keypad" system of sectors to identify the locations of friendly ground forces.[65]

One example, among many that occurred in the run up to OIF, illustrates the degree of confidence and depth of vertical trust that Moseley had in his airmen. As Colonel Leonard relates, CENTAF planners placed the responsibility for improving the technical means of acquiring and locking on to mobile Scud launchers on ACC, confident that its officers could perfect a solution. A working group from ACC's Weapons and Intelligence Directorate, consisting largely of majors and lieutenant colonels, was charged with developing a working CONOPS that included targeting pods, data links, and brevity codes to ease communications. At subsequent CENTAF and ACC planning conferences, the team gained a better sense of the planning assumptions for OIF and had the opportunity to discuss and refine its CONOPS and its digital architecture with other specialists.[66] Moseley demonstrated his forthright approach even to tactical CONOPS. As one of its authors relates, he received an uncomfortable series of "finger in the chest" questions from Moseley, who verified the soundness of the trusted team's work.[67]

Moseley also ensured that his CAOC staff took advantage of all available opportunities to work through targeting, intelligence sharing, and collaborative planning in the war games and exercises prior to OIF, including the CENTCOM-sponsored Internal Look 03. Previous exercises, including Joint Forces Command's Joint Force Exercise Millennium Challenge 2002, had presented the opportunity to further test and validate CAOC operating systems and processes and to identify and fix flaws.[68] To ensure the CAOC systems and cells were fully manned and functional Moseley requested and received more than triple the manpower the CAOC had when he first arrived.[69] The net result was, in his words, that "we had the chance to rehearse [OIF] several times . . . [through] a series of exercises and 'chair flys,' and all of that is relative to training the people, to streamline the process, to streamline the plan . . . [to] be able to stay ahead of [the enemy]."[70]

OPERATION IRAQI FREEDOM

THE OPENING SHOT: DORA FARMS

Before the Coalition launched the operation, Saddam Hussein had focused on maintaining his grip on power in Iraq while frustrating the efforts of weapons inspectors. With the United States tied down in Afghanistan, Hussein had taken every available opportunity to challenge U.S. relationships and interests in the region. By September 2002, U.S. and Coalition aircraft had dropped 54.6 tons of bombs on Iraqi targets as part of Operation Southern Focus.[71] For his part, Hussein continued to engage in high-profile, provocative behavior such as providing $25,000 payments to the families of Palestinian suicide bombers and making repeated, if veiled, threats that he not only had but also was willing to use weapons of mass destruction, presumably produced after the UN Special Commission's mandate expired and UN inspectors left Iraq in 1999. In addition, Hussein tasked his generals with restructuring plans and defensive schemes designed to thwart Coalition air and space power.[72]

Toppling Hussein and removing him from power was the focus of OIF, but in the months prior to the invasion planners appear to have given little thought to targeting him specifically. Hussein protected himself well, relying on a mixture of domestic security, intelligence, and military organizations, and this effort limited Coalition intelligence on his whereabouts and activities. He was even rumored to have used "doubles," or look-alikes, to mask his actual movements and minimize the chances of assassination. Furthermore, even if Hussein's location could be pinpointed and he could be killed, the Coalition still faced the problem of who would succeed him. The two most likely candidates were his sons Uday and Qusay. Uday, the elder of the two, was known for his unpredictable behavior, whereas Qusay was the quieter but much more ruthless one. The possibility that either son might succeed Hussein created the potential of replacing a known, if problematic, dictator with someone much worse.

Intelligence efforts in the lead-up to OIF were progressively getting closer to tracking Hussein's movements and hideouts. A huge break came on March 18, when a Central Intelligence Agency source placed Hussein at Dora Farms, a location of interest immediately south of Baghdad. References to Dora Farms had appeared repeatedly in communications, and vehicles associated with Hussein's security detachments had been observed there. Not one but two intelligence sources believed, with almost absolute certainty, that Hussein and his two sons would be at the complex on that day.[73] Here was an opportunity to topple the regime at a single stroke before Coalition forces set foot in Iraq. In evaluating possible strike options either the chairman of the Joint Chiefs of Staff, Gen. Richard E. Myers, or the CENTCOM commander and his staff thought that Tomahawk cruise missiles would be the most responsive option.[74] With additional information from other sources, analysts continued to refine the intelligence picture about the buildings at Dora Farms, and the word "bunker" was added to the planning considerations.[75] Targeteers (and their commanders) inferred that they were now dealing with a command and control center, as opposed to a hiding place. Given that Tomahawks lacked the ability to penetrate and destroy underground targets, the only other possible option was an air strike. President George W. Bush appeared willing to authorize the strike if the attack could be executed.

After Moseley took the phone call in the CAOC in the minutes before March 19 (local time), he had several significant questions to answer. First he had to determine whether the strike was even possible, given such considerations as aircraft and weapons availability and risk. The refining, scheduling, and tasking of all aspects of the air campaign of OIF, set to begin on March 21, were in full swing. Moseley sought advice from key individuals on his CAOC staff, including Maj. S. Clinton Hinote, who recalled:

> After we set the wheels in motion, Gen Moseley brought me up to his office and said, "The answer I owe the President is, is this doable, and what is the risk?" He then looked straight at me. I told him, "Sir, it is doable (then gave details of the operation, a couple of options and what support assets we needed) but the risk is high." I simply didn't know if the Iraqis would be expecting us—they still had a formidable air defense capability (their air defenses were more dense around Baghdad than during Desert Storm). I was in the room as General Moseley talked with CENTCOM and told them what I had said. I remember walking down the stairs praying that I was right in the advice I had given and also thinking, "I wasn't expecting to have to give advice to the President."[76]

This strike put to the test all of Moseley's investment in improving CAOC processes to better attack fleeting targets. Given the intelligence cue flashing on one of the CAOC screens, Moseley ordered one F-117 to be readied even before receiving a request from the CENTCOM commander. Questions immediately arose about the probability that one F-117 attack would succeed. Although the F-117 could carry two 2,000-pound precision-guided bombs in its bay, the on-board laser designator could only paint a single target. It could use GPS-guided JDAMs, but existing tactics, techniques, and procedures specified that only one could be dropped in a pass. Dropping both weapons together ran the risk that they would collide mid-air and perhaps detonate. Last but not least, responding to this fleeting target of opportunity would expose the F-117 to an additional level of risk by operating in daylight.[77] The window of approval for the mission was narrow and meant that the F-117 would strike right before dawn, exposing the plane to visual observation and risking that it might be shot down. Furthermore, any aircraft, even a stealthy one, always had the potential for mechanical, avionics, or munitions failure.

When asked his opinion about the probability of success when using one F-117, Moseley replied in his characteristically direct way: no more than 50 per-cent. Doubling the strike to two F-117s would increase the odds 100 percent. General Franks later recalled that Moseley did everything within his capacity to make the strike happen, including bringing the F-117s, their pilots, the munitions, and the plan together in one location.[78] Moseley weighed the risks and ultimately approved and accepted the responsibility for this untried and perilous method of delivery.

Despite the stress and all-night activity, Moseley appeared calm as the F-117s from the Eighth Expeditionary Fighter Squadron made their way toward their target. Hinote recalls feeling the tension and, even more bothersome, the weight of responsibility he bore because of the advice he had provided. As they watched the CAOC screens, Hinote remembered: "I don't know if Gen. Moseley sensed this [stress], but just minutes before the strike, he looked over to me and said, 'They're going to make it, you watch.' His confidence and control did make me feel better."[79]

Despite the sources' high level of confidence, the intelligence that prompted the Dora Farms strike was faulty. Hussein and his sons were not there. Fueling later criticism, at least one Coalition official quoted in a media report called into question the accuracy of the air strike itself without knowing what the specific aim point actually was.[80] Another opportunity to target Saddam Hussein occurred on April 7, and despite a rapid response from a B-1 bomber, it missed killing him by mere minutes.[81]

THE AIR CAMPAIGN

To label the use of air power in OIF as an "air campaign" is somewhat misleading, because it suggests actions independent of the land and sea campaigns. OIF truly was a joint fight that integrated elements from all of the components involved. Given that Franks had delegated much of the planning and coordinating responsibilities for OIF to his component commanders, the outcome says much about the ability of commanders such as Moseley to coordinate, integrate, and synchronize their efforts through liaison staffs and during commander's conferences.

Moseley's desire to synchronize air and space and to provide necessary and novel air power effects in supported and supporting efforts places his air generalship squarely in the same category as that of World War II's Lt. Gen. Elwood R. "Pete" Quesada and Lt. Gen. Millard "Miff" Harmon, among others.[82] What separates his generalship from such operational or "tactical" generals is that Moseley's air and space portion of OIF combined simultaneous elements of strategic attack, operational art, and tactical support.

OIF officially began on March 20, 2003, with little in the way of a preceding air campaign, but the operation used air and space power during the first week as forms of strategic attack. Activities conducted as part of Operation Southern Focus had probed Iraqi air defenses and softened them up, but from the standpoint of intelligence preparation of the battle space, they had been more useful for upcoming operations (including a proposed air and missile campaign code-named "Desert Badger") than as strategic attacks against Saddam Hussein's regime. In the months prior to OIF, air planners had developed a strategic attack campaign to target Iraqi command, control, and communications (beginning on "A-Day") that would pave the way for a ground invasion ("G-Day" for CFLCC planners and "D-Day" at CENTCOM and in Washington). Moseley agreed to align the start of the air campaign with the beginning of the SOF and ground campaigns to inflict "shock and awe" on Hussein's regime.[83] For at least the first seventy-two hours of OIF, Moseley's airmen focused on suppressing enemy air defenses, achieving air dominance, targeting state security and other symbolic regime offices and headquarters, and disrupting the regime's command and control through strikes against fiber optic links, cell phone towers, and other means of coordination. Almost all of these targets presented challenges for targeting and gave rise to concern over causing civilian casualties, or so-called collateral damage. As Moseley had discovered during Operation Southern Focus, targeting fiber optic links required exceptional precision to hit the "manhole-sized targets."[84] One minor source of friction between Franks and his CFACC during the course of OIF resulted from the ability of Hussein's regime to find innovative ways to continue communicating and broadcasting its messages despite the best attempts of Moseley's personnel to identify, target, and silence them.[85]

Air power played a crucial strategic and operational role in western and northern Iraq. The western desert of Iraq contained a number of airfields and had been the primary maneuver and launch area for Scud missiles during Operation Desert Storm. Franks demonstrated his confidence in Moseley's generalship and preparations by designating him as the supported commander in the area of operations (AO) in western Iraq. Although no Scud launchers were detected or destroyed there during OIF, the following statistics show the degree of integration between air power and the combined SOF team (Task Force Dagger).

The United States, Great Britain, and Australia committed almost 400 SOF personnel and approximately 2,300 fighter, attack, and bomber sorties plus an additional 500 C2ISR sorties over 27 days. . . . The CST [counter-Scud team] engaged more than 10,000 Iraqi troops, provided more than 25,000 hours of combined coverage on more than 20,000 areas (the 410th AEW [airborne early warning] alone surveyed more than 11,000 of these areas during NTISR [nontraditional ISR] missions), and reduced the ATO [air tasking order] planning cycle to as little as 12 hours when necessary. The CST executed 393 joint fires deconflictions, a successful CSAR [combat search and rescue] operation, and 100 troops in contact CAS missions with an average response time of less than 10 minutes and a maximum response time of less than 17 minutes.[86]

The success in the western AO had much to do with not only the preparations outlined earlier but also the degree of trust Moseley placed in his strategy division and TST cell chiefs in the CAOC to distinguish and coordinate time-sensitive and dynamic targets.[87] In the northern AO, air power backed Combined Joint Special Operations Task Force–North (Task Force Viking) and local Kurdish Peshmerga forces through a combination of CAS and mobility support. The mobility support included air dropping elements of the 173rd Airborne Brigade on March 26 and airlifting the remaining vehicles and troops the next day to augment Task Force Viking.[88]

The activities in both AOs generated at least one crucial operational and strategic effect. Senior Iraqi military leaders, including Saddam Hussein, had difficulty determining the Coalition forces' primary axis of advance. In addition, attacks on Iraqi communications prevented communication or coordination throughout the campaign, resulting in a degree of confusion and operational paralysis among the Iraqi forces.

After March 24 the preponderance of the air and space effort, by a margin of at least two to one, shifted to support the ground forces on the primary axis of advance from southern Iraq to Baghdad. Coordinating with CFLCC, and particularly army, planners was not without its challenges, especially over the issue of fire support coordination lines. Moseley insisted on providing General Franks, General McKiernan, Lt. Gen. William "Scott" Wallace (U.S. Army, V Corps commander), and Lt. Gen. James Conway (USMC, 1 Marine Expeditionary Force commander) with as much early warning and advanced and direct support as possible. The air elements delivered such support on March 24–27, at a crucial point in the campaign. Moseley's weather staff had picked up indications that a sizable *shamal* (a northerly wind that creates sandstorms) was developing. In past campaigns, enemy leaders had taken advantage of opportunities that such weather provided and moved their forces while American aircraft were grounded. Moseley recognized the problem, and his CAOC staff devised the novel solution of comparing pre-storm imagery with real-time radar mapping and then blind bombing any anomalies with precision weapons in so-called smack-down targeting.[89] To further support ground forces and to refine their intelligence estimates of the enemy, Moseley authorized high-value assets, such as E-8 JSTARS, to fly progressively deeper and riskier orbits into Iraq in order to extend the range of their sensor coverage.[90]

As a testimony to the effectiveness of air power during OIF, not once during the campaign were U.S. or Coalition ground forces tactically surprised and forced into a dangerous and chaotic meeting engagement battle with Iraqi conventional forces. The only meeting engagements that did occur involved suicidal attacks by irregular Fedayeen forces, which were quickly dispatched by ground and air forces.

Although problems with complete battle space awareness and battle damage assessment continued during OIF, there is little doubt as to the devastating effect of air targeting and interdiction on the Iraqi Army. The personnel of some divisions simply abandoned their tanks, armored personnel carriers, artillery, and defensive positions and went home. In other cases, the combined effects of air power denied the Iraqis the opportunity to defend themselves as they would have liked and as their doctrine specified.[91]

When the major combat portion of OIF concluded on May 1, 2003, Moseley could be justifiably proud. The airmen and platforms under his command had performed magnificently in one of the most successful air campaigns since the birth of manned flight. The campaign's statistics give some idea of its tremendous accomplishments, including a number of combat firsts. All told, more than 1,800 aircraft (and thirty different airframes) from four countries flew more than 41,000 sorties and dropped almost 300,000 bombs and missiles, 68 percent of which were precision guided.[92] At the height of the campaign the CAOC was controlling more than 2,000 flights a day.[93] Overall, the CAOC staff had prosecuted 156 TST and 686 dynamic targets.[94] Only one fixed-wing aircraft was lost due to enemy action, compared to three during Operation Allied Force in the former Yugoslavia.[95]

Moseley received a hero's welcome on his return to Shaw AFB in South Carolina on May 4, 2003.[96] As he always did in public, he assigned credit for the success of air power in Operation Iraqi Freedom to the airmen under his command. He particularly singled out their skill, dedication, and experience:

> We had the luxury of probably the most combat-experienced air component that an air commander has ever been blessed to go to war with. . . . [We had] the most lethal airmen ever to enlist. You would be hard pressed to find a young captain or major who hadn't flown combat sorties in the area of operations. And that's why it's so easy to execute these things because we have the most disciplined people in the world.[97]

CONCLUSION

All too often the term "generalship" is used loosely. Assessments of generalship can become a comparison between one general and another, based on their personalities, accomplishments, failures, or other relative performance. Sometimes the term is used as shorthand for effective leadership or command in combat. At other times, generalship is distilled to a presumably helpful, if intangible, characteristic or quality that should be emulated. For example, one best-selling work on generalship identifies "character" as the master quality that a successful general needs and further outlines the ten qualities that constitute it.[98]

Trying to grasp the concept of "air generalship" becomes more difficult. In land campaigns, generalship is most often equated with both the will and the persistence to carry out a plan or with the dash and cunning to outfox the opponent. The skill of generalship then becomes a function of either determination or drive, with progress measured by the movement of land forces toward their objectives on maps. Air generalship has no such concrete frame of reference, making its criteria difficult for others to comprehend. Discussions of historical air generalship often focus on either the degree to which a general advocated the independence of air assets or fought to achieve control over all air assets in theater, or the extent to which the general made air a "team player," and therefore merely a support function, within a joint or combined campaign. Even worse, explorations of air generalship can again degenerate into studies of personality and become either hate manifestos or hagiography.

Modern air generalship is further complicated by the systems required to provide a span of control over elements widely dispersed in space and time. The general cannot be everywhere he needs to be at once. This situation can lead to excessive delegation and reliance on subordinates or to a penchant for micromanaging details, both of which remove the general's will—the net sum of his personality, expertise, insight, and command style—from the equation. Maj. Gen. J. F. C. Fuller of the British Army identified one of the most significant problems that the modern (air) general faces: "More and more do strategical, administrative and tactical details occupy his mind and pinch out the moral side of his nature. Should he be a man of ability, he becomes a thinker rather than a doer, a planner rather than a leader, until morally he is as far removed from his men as a chess player is from the chessmen on his board."[99]

"Buzz" Moseley managed not to fall into this trap first and foremost because of his Texan and fighter-pilot directness, which bordered on brashness. This quality both inspired his subordinates and fostered a strong relationship with his OIF commander, General Franks, who increasingly delegated responsibility to him. And as Franks delegated responsibility to him, Moseley did the same for his subordinates, from his deputy and chief of strategy on down. Moseley set high personal standards of technical and leadership competence and expected his subordinates to do the same. He rewarded those subordinates, including field grade officers, with both trust and great responsibilities, particularly for devising solutions to battlefield problems. As one of his junior officers in the CAOC commented, what made Moseley an effective air general is that "[h]e empowered his subordinates while owning their decisions."[100] Moseley further inspired and fostered trust within CENTAF by accepting the risk and responsibility for certain decisions and defending risks taken on individual initiative, provided they were not reckless. Above all else, he held those people whom he trusted accountable for their actions, as his actions following the Tarnak Farm incident suggest. To those under his command, Moseley's blunt approach and faith in the performance of systems and solutions were a source of inspiring leadership. Other, more sensitive souls, and critics outside the air force, could interpret this quality according to their own injuries or prejudices.

During his time of generalship between Operation Anaconda and the end of OIF, Moseley acted as an advocate for both the value of air power and the need to integrate it within the joint force. He observed the problems in Anaconda and immediately sought to correct them. Moseley had fought hard to have the control of air and space assets placed under his command so that he could provide the joint force commander with the right air power solution for the job. He repaid Franks's trust by ensuring that air assets remained flexible and responsive to the most pressing unfolding requirements. Moseley did not elevate the presumed interests of the air force above those of the joint force or the nation. Instead, throughout OIF he would continue to balance the strategic effects that air power could generate, which were best understood by an airman, and the operational and tactical needs of the joint force team. Regardless of how future historians or biographers choose to interpret his life and leadership, undoubtedly future airmen will evaluate "Buzz" Moseley's twenty-two-month tenure as CENTAF commander, and his accomplishments during that time, as an exemplary case of modern air generalship in the early twenty-first century.

NOTES

Introduction

1. Jo Owen, *How to Lead*, 2nd ed. (Harlow, UK: Pearson Education Limited, 2009), xv–xvi.

2. Colin S. Gray, *Airpower for Strategic Effect* (Maxwell Air Force Base [AFB], AL: Air University Press, 2011), xvi.

3. To mention a few great and worthy studies of American airmen who held command of large air forces in World War II: David R. Mets, *Master of Airpower: General Carl A. Spaatz* (Novato, CA: Presidio Press, 1988); Richard G. Davis, *Carl A. Spaatz and the Air War in Europe, 1940–1945* (Washington, DC: Center for Air Force History, 1993); Thomas A. Hughes, *Over Lord: General Pete Quesada and the Triumph of Tactical Air Power in World War II* (New York: Free Press, 1995); Thomas E. Griffith Jr., *MacArthur's Airman: General George C. Kenney and the Air War in the Southeast Pacific* (Lawrence: University Press of Kansas, 1998); Charles R. Griffith, *The Quest: Haywood Hansell and American Strategic Bombing in World War II* (Maxwell AFB, AL: Air University Press, 1999); Robert S. Jordan, *Norstad, Cold War NATO Supreme Commander: Airman, Strategist, Diplomat* (New York: St. Martin's Press, 2000); Martha Byrd, *Chennault: Giving Wings to the Tiger* (Tuscaloosa: University of Alabama Press, 1987); Phillip S. Meilinger, *Hoyt S. Vandenberg: The Life of a General* (Bloomington: Indiana University Press, 1989); and Thomas M. Coffey, *Iron Eagle: The Turbulent Life of General Curtis LeMay* (New York: Crown Publishers, 1988). I would also like to acknowledge Vincent Orange's series of great biographies of British commanders of air power.

4. For example, Correlli Barnett, *The Swordbearers: Supreme Command in the First World War* (New York: William Morrow, 1964); Michael Carver, ed., *The War Lords: Military Commanders of the Twentieth Century* (Boston: Little, Brown, 1976); Byron Farwell, *Eminent Victorian Soldiers: Seekers of Glory* (New York: W. W. Norton, 1985); Correlli Barnett, ed., *Hitler's Generals* (New York: William Morrow, 1989); Stephen Howarth, *Men of War: Great Naval Leaders of World War II* (New York: St. Martin's Press, 1992); Eliot A. Cohen, *Supreme Command: Soldiers, Statesmen, and Leadership in Wartime* (New York: Free Press, 2002); and Michael Beschloss, *The Conquerors: Roosevelt, Truman, and the Destruction of Hitler's Germany, 1941–1945* (New York: Simon & Schuster, 2002). I am indebted to Richard P. Hallion for his input to this introduction and particularly these paragraphs, including the quotation from Montgomery.

5. Edward N. Luttwak, *Strategy: The Logic of War and Peace*, rev. and enlarged ed. (Cambridge, MA: The Belknap Press of Harvard University Press, 2002), 267.

6. Carl von Clausewitz, *On War*, ed. and trans. Michael Howard and Peter Paret (Princeton, NJ: Princeton University Press), 102.

7. Martin van Creveld, "Napoleon and the Dawn of Operational Warfare," in *The Evolution of Operational Art: From Napoleon to the Present*, ed. John Andreas Olsen and Martin van Creveld (Oxford, UK: Oxford University Press, 2011), 18.

8. Napoleon conversing with Montholon at St. Helena, quoted in J. F. C. Fuller, *The Generalship of Alexander the Great* (New Brunswick, NJ: Rutgers University Press, 1960), 281–82.

9. John Smyth, *Leadership in War, 1939–1945: The Generals in Victory and Defeat* (New York: St. Martin's Press, 1974), 10, 12.

10. Bernard L. Montgomery, *The Path to Leadership* (New York: G. P. Putnam's Sons, 1961), 49–50.

11. See David Jablonsky for Clausewitz, foreword to *Great Captains of Antiquity*, by Richard A. Gabriel (Westport, CT: Greenwood Press, 2001), xvi; and Mordechai Gichon, foreword, ibid., xiii.

12. Phillip S. Meilinger, *Airmen and Air Theory: A Review of the Sources* (Maxwell AFB, AL: Air University Press, 2001), 3. This is the best starting point for biographies, autobiographies, and the historiography of U.S. air power.

13. Ibid., 5, 7. Interesting biographies of these two, respectively, are Robert P. White, *Mason Patrick and the Fight for Air Service Independence* (Washington, DC: Smithsonian Institution Press, 2001); and Alfred F. Hurley, *Billy Mitchell: Crusader of Air Power* (Bloomington: Indiana University Press, 1975).

14. Henry H. "Hap" Arnold never saw combat service in World War I or in World War II when he commanded the U.S. Army Air Forces, but his command of the B-29s and his overall leadership are extraordinary. Among the several interesting studies of this five-star airman are: Richard G. Davis, *HAP: Henry H. Arnold, Military Aviator* (Washington, DC: Air Force History and Museums Program, 1997); Dick A. Daso, *Hap Arnold and the Evolution of American Airpower* (Washington, DC: Smithsonian Institution Press, 2000); and the more recent Herman S. Wolk, *Cataclysm: General Hap Arnold and the Defeat of Japan* (Denton: University of North Texas Press, 2010).

15. John L. Frisbee, ed., *Makers of the United States Air Force* (Washington, DC: Air Force History and Museums Program, 1996; first published 1987 by Office of Air Force History). The anthology includes chapters on Benjamin D. Foulois, Frank M. Andrews, Harold L. George, Hugh J. Knerr, George C. Kenney, William E. Kepner, Elwood R. Quesada, Hoyt S. Vandenberg, Benjamin O. Davis Jr., Nathan F. Twining, Bernard A. Schriever, and Robinson Risner.

16. Seventh Air Force commanders: Lt. Gen. Joseph H. Moore (April 1, 1966–June 30, 1966); Gen. William W. Momyer (July 1, 1966–July 31, 1968); Gen. George S. Brown (August 1, 1968–August 31, 1970); Gen. Lucius D. Clay Jr. (September 1, 1970–July 31, 1971); Gen. John D. Lavelle (August 1, 1971–April 6, 1972); and Gen. John W. Vogt Jr. (April 10, 1972–September 30, 1973).

17. General Lavelle assumed command of the Seventh Air Force on August 1, 1971, but was removed from command on April 7, 1972, as a result of allegations that he ordered unauthorized bombing missions into North Vietnam and that he authorized the falsification of reports to conceal the missions. Lavelle had to retire in the grade of major general, two grades lower than the last grade in which he had served on active duty. In 2007, newly released and declassified information resulted in evidence

that President Nixon had authorized Lavelle to conduct the bombing missions. Further, the Air Force Board for Correction of Military Records found no evidence that Lavelle caused, directly or indirectly, the falsification of records or that he was even aware of their existence. Once he learned of the reports, Lavelle took action to ensure the practice stopped. At the request from the Air Force Board of Correction of Military Records, the secretary of defense and secretary of the air force posthumously reinstated the grade of general, Lavelle's last grade while on active duty. *U.S. Department of Defense*, release no. 695-10, August 4, 2010.

18. Gen. George E. Stratemeyer left a diary, edited and annotated by William T. Y'Blood: *The Three Wars of Lt. Gen. George E. Stratemeyer: His Korean War Diary* (Washington, DC: Air Force History and Museums Program, 1999). Gen. William W. Momyer wrote *Air Power in Three Wars: WWII, Korea, Vietnam* (Maxwell AFB, AL: Air University Press: York, 2003).

19. Robert Dallek, *The Lost Peace: Leadership in a Time of Horror and Hope, 1945–1953* (New York: Harper, 2010), xii.

20. Cohen, *Supreme Command*, 173–207.

1. Carl A. Spaatz: Bomber Baron

1. "Army Specifications for Flyers, 1917," in Frank Freidel, *Over There: The Story of America's First Great Overseas Crusade* (New York: Bramhall House, 1964), 152.

2. Richard G. Davis, *Carl A. Spaatz and the Air War in Europe, 1940–1945* (Washington, DC: Center for Air Force History, 1993), appendix 8, November 1944. The number cited includes first line strength of B-17s, B-24s, P-38s, and P-51s only.

3. Ibid. Included B-26s, A-20s, A-26s, and P-47s.

4. Dwight D. Eisenhower, *The Papers of Dwight D. Eisenhower: The War Years*, ed. Alfred Chandler (Baltimore: John Hopkins University Press, 1970), item 2271, memo (for the record), February 1, 1945, 4:2466–69.

5. In 1937 Spaatz, at the urging of his wife and daughters, added an extra *a* to his name in hopes of encouraging its correct pronunciation—"spots," as in spots on a leopard, rather than "spats" as in the Edwardian footgear.

6. As with all military schools, the student body of West Point is organized into a military unit. The cadets are the ones who organize and command the unit while under faculty supervision. Thus many students/cadets have a "cadet rank," which they lose once they graduate and receive their formal officer commission. One who stays four years at West Point and earns no rank is considered not to be motivated and, hence, to have less-than-average prospects of a successful career. One without rank is considered not to have any interest in "leadership." As Spaatz demonstrated, this assessment was not always an accurate prediction of the individual cadet's future performance.

7. U.S. Military Academy, *The Howitzer, 1914* (West Point, NY: USMA, 1914), 84.

8. Minutes, conference with Gen. Carl Spaatz and the Gillem Board, October 18, 1945, Papers of Carl A. Spaatz, U.S. Library of Congress, Manuscript Division, Diary File (hereafter cited as Spaatz Papers Diary).

9. Ira C. Eaker, "Anatomy of Leadership: Images and Reflections—the Pattern of Air Leadership," address at the Industrial War College, Fort Lesley J. McNair, Washington, DC, April 14, 1977, 352.

10. Mattie E. Treadwell, *The Woman's Army Corps*, United States Army in World War II: Special Studies (Washington, DC: U.S. Army Center of Military History, U.S. Government Printing Office, 1954), 384.

11. Maurer Maurer, ed., *The U.S. Air Service in World War I*, vol. 1, *The Final Report and a Tactical History* (Washington, DC: Office of Air Force History, 1978), 1:97. This

citation is from the Official Final Report of the Air Service, 1919, also known as the "Gorrell's History," which is published in full in the Maurer volume.

12. Freidel, *Over There*, 153.

13. Maurer, *The U.S. Air Service*, 1:106, 112–13.

14. Ibid., 110.

15. Ibid.

16. Interview, Gen. Carl A. Spaatz by Donald Shaughnessey, Washington, DC, 1959–1960, Henry H. Arnold Oral History Project, Columbia University, New York, 2.

17. Edwin I. James, "Pershing's Airmen All-American Now," *New York Times*, September 30, 1918, 2. The story's dateline is September 29, 1918.

18. Message, J-205, Mitchell to Spaatz, September 26, 1918, Spaatz Papers Diary.

19. Spaatz interview, 24.

20. Ibid., 77.

21. Mets, *Master of Airpower*, 53–66. Mets provides a thorough description of Spaatz's intellectual and doctrinal activities regarding pursuit aviation in this period.

22. U.S. Congress, House, *Select Committee of Inquiry into the Operations of the United Air Services*, Hearings, 68th Cong., 2nd sess., 1925, part 3, 2246.

23. Richard K. Smith, *Seventy-Five Years of Inflight Refueling Highlights, 1923–1998* (Washington, DC: USAF History and Museum Program and the Government Printing Office, 1998), 3.

24. DeWitt S. Copp, *A Few Great Captains: The Men and Events that Shaped the Development of U.S. Air Power* (New York: Doubleday, 1980), 82–85; and Smith, *Seventy-Five Years of Inflight Refueling*, 3–6.

25. See the essay "The U. S. Military Intelligence Service: The ULTRA Mission," in *ULTRA and the Army Air Forces in World War II: An Interview with Associate Justice of the U.S. Supreme Court Lewis F. Powell, Jr.*, ed. Diane T. Putney (Washington, DC: The Office of Air Force History, 1987), 65–110, for a good introduction to the importance of Ultra to the AAF.

26. See Edward R. Zilbert, *Albert Speer and the Nazi Ministry of Arms: Economic Institutions and Industrial Production in the German War Economy* (Rutherford, NJ: Farleigh Dickinson University Press, 1981), especially chapter 6, "The Aircraft Industry," 185–258.

27. See Williamson Murray, *German Military Effectiveness* (Baltimore: The Nautical & Aviation Publishing Company of America, 1992), especially chapter 4, "The Air Defense of Germany: Doctrine and the Defeat of the Luftwaffe," 69–86.

28. See Davis, *Spaatz*, appendix 3, for growth of AAF strength in Europe and the Mediterranean.

29. Eighth Air Force Operations Analysis Section, "Report on Bombing Accuracy," Eighth Air Force, September 1 to December 31, 1944, Library of Congress, Manuscript Division, Washington, DC, the Papers of Carl A. Spaatz, Subject File, 1929–1945.

30. Charles W. McArthur, *Operations Analysis in the U.S. Army Eighth Air Force in World War II* (Providence, RI: The American Mathematical Society, 1990), 292.

31. Eighth Bomber Command, Mission of September 27, 1943, USAF Research Center, Microfilm Reel A5940, frame 746.

32. Davis, *Spaatz*, 298–302.

33. Wesley F. Craven and James L. Cate, eds., *The Army Air Forces in World War II*, vol. 2, *Europe: Torch to Pointblank, August 1942 to December 1943* (Chicago: University of Chicago Press, 1949), 755–56.

34. Letter, Spaatz to Arnold, March 16, 1944, Spaatz Papers Diary.

35. Message, Smith to Eisenhower, January 1, 1944, Spaatz Papers Diary.
36. Entry for January 1, 1944, Command Diary, Spaatz Papers Diary.
37. Sir Frederick Morgan, *Overture to Overlord* (Garden City, NY: Doubleday, 1950), 257.
38. F. H. Hinsley, *British Intelligence in the Second World War*, vol. 3, *Its Influence on Strategy and Operations* (London: Her Majesty's Stationery Office, 1988), part 2, 317.
39. Minutes, Eighth Air Force Commanders' Meeting, January 21, 1944, Air Force Historical Studies Office (AF/HSO) Microfilm Reel A5871, frame 1217.
40. Letter, Spaatz to Maj. Gen. Barney Giles, chief AAF Staff, April 18, 1944, Spaatz Papers Diary. This letter was received by Major General Giles, Chief of the Air Staff, who was standing in for Arnold while he recovered from a heart attack.
41. Memo, commanding general (CG), VIII Fighter Command, to CG, Eighth Air Force, Subject: Tactics and Techniques of Long-Range Fighter Escort, July 25, 1944, AF/HSO Microfilm Reel B5200, frames 142–61.
42. Richard G. Davis, *Bombing the European Axis Powers: A Historical Digest of the Combined Bomber Offensive, 1939–1945* (Maxwell AFB, AL: Air University Press, 2006). See worksheet for February–May 1944.
43. Davis, *Spaatz*, 321–22.
44. Richard G. Davis, "Pointblank versus Overlord: Strategic Bombing and the Normandy Invasion," *Air Power History* 41, no. 2 (Summer 1994): 12.
45. Teletype conference transcript, March 17, 1944, Spaatz Papers Diary.
46. Wesley F. Craven and James L. Cate, eds., *The Army Air Forces in World War II*, vol. 3, *Europe: Argument to V-E Day, January 1944 to May 1945* (Chicago: University of Chicago Press, 1951), 174.
47. Charles Webster and Noble Frankland, *The Strategic Air Offensive Against Germany, 1939–1945*, vol. 4, *Annexes and Appendices*, History of the Second World War (London: Her Majesty's Stationery Office, 1961), appendix 49, 516.
48. D/SAC/TS.100, letter, Tedder to Spaatz, April 19, 1944, Spaatz Papers Diary.
49. Davis, *Spaatz*, 392.
50. Ibid., 392–93.
51. Williamson Murray, *The Luftwaffe, 1933–1945: Strategy for Defeat* (Washington, DC: Brassey's, Inc., 1996), 273; and Adolf Galland, *The First and the Last: The Rise and Fall of the German Fighter Forces, 1938–1945*, trans. Mervyn Savill (New York: Bantam Books, 1978), 280.
52. AAF, *Ultra and the History of the United States Strategic Air Forces in Europe vs. the German Air Force* (Frederick, MD: University Publications of America, 1985), 98–99. This publication is a reprint of USSTAF's National Security Agency Special Research History No. 13 (SRH-13) from September 1945.
53. Walter W. Rostow, *Pre-Invasion Bombing Strategy: General Eisenhower's Decision of March 25, 1944* (Austin: University of Texas Press, 1981), 52.
54. Albert Speer, *Inside the Third Reich: Memoirs* (New York: Macmillan, 1970), 346.
55. Ibid., 346–47.
56. Webster and Frankland, *Strategic Air Offensive*, 4:321–25.
57. AAF, *Ultra and the History*, 104.
58. USAF oral history interview K239.0512-0793, Lt. Gen. James H. Doolittle, by Maj. Ronald R. Fogleman, Capt. James P. Tate, and Lt. Col. Robert M. Burch, September 26, 1970, 53, Air Force Historical Research Center, Maxwell AFB, AL.
59. Letter, Arnold to Spaatz, n.d. [February 1944], AF/HSO Microfilm Reel A1657, frames 1082–85. Spaatz received this letter on March 1, 1944, and returned his copy, one of only two made, with his reply. A copy of Spaatz's copy, with his handwritten notes faithfully transcribed, found its way into AAF files and thence to microfilm.

60. Dwight Eisenhower, *The Eisenhower Diaries*, ed. Robert H. Ferrell (New York: W. W. Norton, 1981), 94–95, entry for June, 11, 1943.

61. Letter, Maj. Gen. Laurence Kuter, AAF Staff, to Arnold, January 28, 1945, Library of Congress, Manuscript Division, Washington, DC, the Papers of Henry H. Arnold, Correspondence File.

62. Alfred Goldberg, "Spaatz," in *The War Lords: Military Commanders of the Twentieth Century*, ed. Michael Carver (Boston: Little, Brown, 1976), 580.

63. Craven and Cate, eds., *Army Air Forces in World War II*, 3:155.

64. Ibid.

65. Eighth Air Force, "Eighth Air Force Statistical Summary of Operations, August 17, 1942 to May 8, 1945," June 10, 1945. Found in USAFHRA Microfilm Reel A6482, beginning frame 800.

66. Ibid.

67. See Martin Blumenson, *Breakout and Pursuit*, United States Army in World War II: European Theater of Operations (Washington DC: Office of the Chief of Military History (OCMH), 1961), for a detailed study of COBRA.

68. Hugh M. Cole, *The Lorraine Campaign*, United States Army in World War II: European Theater of Operations (Washington, DC: OCMH, 1950), 424–25.

69. Roger A. Freeman, *Mighty Eighth War Diary* (London: Jane's, 1981), 399.

70. Davis, *Spaatz*, 487.

71. See Webster and Frankland, *Strategic Air Offensive*, 4:142–83, section 3, appendix 8, "Directives to the Air Officer Commanding-in-Chief, Bomber Command," directives 22–45 (a).

72. Davis, *Bombing the European Axis Powers*, 571–74. The AAF figure is the maximum and includes what is described as "area-like" missions, defined in the pages cited in this note. The U.S. Fifteenth Air Force conducted a negligible portion of such missions.

73. F. L. Anderson, USSTAF director of operations, to directors of operations, Eighth and Fifteenth Air Forces, July 21, 1944, Spaatz Papers, Subject File 1929–1945.

74. Letter, Spaatz to Arnold, August 27, 1944, Spaatz Papers Diary.

75. Wesley F. Craven and James L. Cate, eds., *The Army Air Forces in World War II*, vol. 5, *The Pacific: Matterhorn to Nagasaki, June 1944 to August 1945* (Chicago: University of Chicago Press, 1953), citing letter, Arnold to Spaatz, May 21, 1945.

76. Ibid., 676–90.

77. Ibid., 733.

78. During the first few years the U.S. government held all information about the A-bomb extremely tightly and closely (except from the spies whom Joseph Stalin's security services had inserted into the project from the beginning). The U.S. government even withheld information from the U.S. Air Force, which would have to fly and plan any atomic bomb drops. As more bombs were manufactured and the use of atomic weapons was driven to lower tactical levels in the 1950s and later, the granting of nuclear security clearances became more widespread and reached much lower ranks, such as aircrew and pilots.

79. Phillip S. Meilinger, *Hoyt S. Vandenberg: The Life of a General* (Bloomington: Indiana University Press 1989), 62–63.

80. This is a very rough paraphrase of the ACT text to be found in Wesley F. Craven and James L. Cate, eds., *The Army Air Forces in World War II*, vol. 1, *Plans and Early Operations, January 1939 to August 1942* (Chicago: University of Chicago Press, 1948), 52.

81. Meilinger, *Hoyt S. Vandenberg*, 62–63.

82. Ibid., 63.

83. Vincent Orange, *Tedder: Quietly in Command* (London: Frank Cass, 2003), 316.
84. Mets, *Master of Airpower*, 334–35. Mets provides a thorough description of Spaatz's life out of uniform.

2. George C. Kenney: "A Kind of Renaissance Airman"

1. Herman S. Wolk, "The Genius of George Kenney," *Air Force Magazine* 85, no. 2 (April 2002).
2. Samuel P. Huntington, *The Soldier and the State: The Theory and Politics of Civil-Military Relations* (Cambridge, MA: Harvard University Press, 1957).
3. Harold Lasswell, "The Garrison State and Specialists on Violence," *American Journal of Sociology* 66 (January 1941): 455–68.
4. John Keegan, *The Mask of Command* (London: Jonathan Cape, 1987), 1–11.
5. "Characteristics" and "behavior" are individual. Nevertheless, common patterns exist. Vincent Orange has identified ten elements in the characteristics and behavior of one of the greatest air commanders, Marshal of the Royal Air Force Lord Arthur Tedder, that he believes were central to Tedder's success: ambition, sacrifice, knowledge, welfare, listening, the ability to give orders, ruthlessness, patronage, calmness, and grasp of strategy. Most successful commanders could be expected to possess similar qualities. Vincent Orange, "The Hard Stone," *RAF Air Power Review* (Winter 1999): 76–87.
6. Carl von Clausewitz, *On War*, trans. J. J. Graham, ed. Anatol Rapoport (New York: Penguin, 1982), 138–58.
7. Martin van Creveld, *Command in War* (Cambridge, MA: Harvard University Press, 1985).
8. The best insight into Grant's character and leadership style comes from his autobiography, *The Personal Memoirs of U. S. Grant* (New York: Da Capo Press, 1982).
9. John Andreas Olsen, ed., *Global Air Power* (Washington, DC: Potomac Books, 2011), xv–xvi.
10. For a representative sample, see Valston Hancock, *Challenge* (Northbridge, MN: Access Press, 1990); Tom Clancy with Chuck Horner, *Every Man a Tiger: The Gulf War Air Campaign* (New York: Berkley Publishing Group, 2005); Carl H. Builder, *The Icarus Syndrome: The Role of Air Power Theory in the Evolution and Fate of the U.S. Air Force* (New Brunswick, NJ: Transaction Publishers, 1994); and Col. Mike Worden, *The Rise of the Fighter Generals: The Problem of Air Force Leadership, 1945–1982* (Maxwell AFB, AL: Air University Press, 1998).
11. There is some uncertainty about Kenney's citizenship, arising primarily from the "porous" border between the United States and Canada at the time. See Thomas E. Griffith Jr., *MacArthur's Airman: General George C. Kenney and the War in the Southwest Pacific* (Lawrence: University Press of Kansas, 1998), 2–3.
12. Ibid., 5.
13. Ibid., 9. Acosta also made a transatlantic flight in 1927, only thirty-three days after Charles Lindbergh did.
14. DeWitt S. Copp, *A Few Great Captains: The Men and Events that Shaped the Development of U.S. Air Power* (New York: Doubleday, 1980), 282.
15. The USAAC was renamed the USAAF in March 1942.
16. Roger Beaumont, quoted in D. Clayton James with Ann Sharp Wells, *A Time for Giants: Politics of the American High Command in World War II* (New York: Franklin Watts, 1987), 103–4.
17. Copp, *A Few Great Captains*, 274.
18. Ibid., 282.

19. Robert Frank Futrell, *Ideas, Concepts, Doctrine: Basic Thinking in the United States Air Force*, vol. 1, *1907–1960* (Maxwell AFB, AL: Air University Press, 1989), 69; and editors' introduction to Giulio Douhet, *The Command of the Air* (Washington, DC: Office of Air Force History, 1983), ix.
20. Copp, *A Few Great Captains*, 270.
21. Ibid., 342–43.
22. James, *A Time for Giants*, 196.
23. Ibid., 98.
24. Wesley F. Craven and James L. Cate, eds., *The Army Air Forces in World War II*, vol. 4, *The Pacific: Guadalcanal to Saipan, August 1942 to July 1944* (Chicago: University of Chicago Press, 1950), 26.
25. Douglas Gillison, *Royal Australian Air Force, 1939–1942* (Canberra: Australian War Memorial, 1962), 570.
26. Wolk, "The Genius of George Kenney."
27. George C. Kenney, *General Kenney Reports: A Personal History of the Pacific War* (Washington, DC: Office of Air Force History, 1987), 29–30.
28. Ibid., 99–100.
29. George Odgers, *Air War Against Japan, 1943–1945* (Canberra: Australian War Memorial, 1968), 92.
30. Samuel E. Morison, *History of United States Naval Operations in World War II*, vol. 6, *Breaking the Bismarcks Barrier, 22 July 1942–1 May 1944* (Boston: Little, Brown, 1950), 288.
31. H. H. Arnold Papers, Reel 87, Richardson to Arnold, 15-7-1942, Library of Congress; and Gen. George C. Kenney Papers, vol. 1, 13-7-1942, Office of Air Force History, Maxwell AFB, AL.
32. See Robert C. Owen, ed., *Deliberate Force: A Case Study in Effective Air Campaigning* (Maxwell AFB, AL: Air University Press, 2000); John E. Peters, Stuart E. Johnson, Nora Bensahel, Timothy Liston, and Traci Williams, *European Contributions to Operation Allied Force* (Santa Monica, CA: Rand Corporation, 2001); and Richard Norton-Taylor, "Operation Odyssey Dawn Echoes Previous US-Led Attacks," *Guardian*, March 20, 2011.
33. Gillison, *Royal Australian Air Force*, 656–57.
34. Kenney, *General Kenney Reports*, 137.
35. Gillison, *Royal Australian Air Force*, 598.
36. William F. Halsey and J. Bryan, *Admiral Halsey's Story* (Whitefish, MT: Kessinger Publishing, 2007), 231.
37. Air Marshal Sir Richard Williams Papers, "Memorandum on the Development of the Royal Australian Air Force in Australia and the Provision of Air Forces in the South-West Pacific Area," 10-4-1943, Royal Australian Air Force Museum, Point Cook, Victoria.
38. Kenney, *General Kenney Reports*, 341.
39. War Cabinet Agendum 90/145, 14-3-1945, Royal Australian Air Force Historical Records Section, Canberra.
40. Kenney, *General Kenney Reports*, xiv.
41. Gillison, *Royal Australian Air Force*, 636.
42. Craven and Cate, *Army Air Forces in World War II*, 4:118.
43. Ibid., 4:101.
44. Herman S. Wolk, "George C. Kenney: MacArthur's Premier Airman," in *We Shall Return! MacArthur's Commanders and the Defeat of Japan, 1942–1945*, ed. William M. Leary (Lexington: University Press of Kentucky, 1988), 108.
45. Gillison, *Royal Australian Air Force*, 676.

46. Quoted in Craven and Cate, *Army Air Forces in World War II*, 4:128.
47. Kenney, *General Kenney Reports*, passim.
48. Ibid., 41.
49. Craven and Cate, *Army Air Forces in World War II*, 4:151.
50. Gillison, *Royal Australian Air Force*, 623–24.
51. Gen. George C. Kenney Papers, vol. 2, 30-11-1942; and H. H. Arnold Papers, Reel 158, Memorandum 5-10-1942.
52. Gillison, *Royal Australian Air Force*, 654–55.
53. Ibid., 573–74.
54. Ibid., 654.
55. Craven and Cate, *Army Air Forces in World War II*, 4:587.
56. The A-20 was known as the Havoc by the USAAF and as the Boston by the British Commonwealth air forces.
57. Kenney, *General Kenney Reports*, 106–7.
58. Gillison, *Royal Australian Air Force*, 655.
59. For more background on skip bombing, see Steve Birdsall, *Flying Buccaneers: The Illustrated Story of Kenney's Fifth Air Force* (Newton Abbot, UK: David & Charles, 1978), 25–26.
60. Craven and Cate, *Army Air Forces in World War II*, 4:174.
61. Kenney, *General Kenney Reports*, 35–36.
62. Gillison, *Royal Australian Air Force*, 690–95.
63. Odgers, *Air War Against Japan*, 76–78.
64. Craven and Cate, *Army Air Forces in World War II*, 4:650.
65. Worden, *Rise of the Fighter Generals*, 30–32.
66. See, for example, Gen George C. Kenney, "Survival in the Atomic Age," *Air Affairs* 3, no. 3 (December 1950).
67. Worden, *Rise of the Fighter Generals*, 31. General Doolittle made similar assertions.
68. Ibid., 55–56; and Wolk, "The Genius of George Kenney."
69. Quoted in D. Clayton James, *The Years of MacArthur*, vol. 2, *1941–1945* (Boston: Houghton Mifflin, 1975), 197–202.

3. Otto P. Weyland: "Best Damn General in the Air Corps"

1. Henry H. Arnold, *Global Mission* (New York: Harper & Brothers, 1949), 519.
2. To date, Weyland has not been the subject of a full biography, though he certainly merits one. David Spires, in *Patton's Air Force: Forging a Legendary Air-Ground Team* (Washington, DC: Smithsonian, 2002), has produced a first-rate operational narrative and analysis of XIX Tactical Air Command's activities in 1944–1945. Spires also provides a concise treatment of the Weyland-Patton partnership in "Patton and Weyland," in *Airpower and Ground Armies: Essays on the Evolution of Anglo-American Air Doctrine, 1940–1943*, ed. Daniel Mortensen (Maxwell AFB, AL: Air University Press, 1998). John J. Sullivan, in *Air Support for Patton's Third Army* (Jefferson, NC: McFarland, 2003), also covers the story of XIX TAC from August through December 1944. Weyland's later years with TAC have been addressed in two important doctoral dissertations: Caroline F. Ziemke, "In the Shadow of the Giant: USAF Tactical Air Command in the Era of Strategic Bombing, 1945–1955" (PhD diss., Ohio State University, 1989); and Jerome V. Martin, "Reforging the Sword: United States Air Force Tactical Air Forces, Air Power Doctrine, and National Security Policy, 1945–1956" (PhD diss., Ohio State University, 1988).
3. Weyland maintained that his official air force biography, which states to this day that he was born in 1902, was in error. U.S. Air Force, "Biography: General Otto Paul

Weyland," www.af.mil/information/bios/bio.asp?bioID=7565 (accessed April 10, 2011).

4. Weyland's brother, four years his senior, remained in the engineering profession. Weyland noted, "He made more money than me, but I had more fun."

5. United States Air Force Oral History Program, "Interview of General O. P. Weyland," November 19, 1974, U.S. Air Force Historical Research Agency (USAFHRA), Maxwell AFB, AL K239.0512-813, 20.

6. Otto P. Weyland, oral history interview, September 17, 1967, USAFHRA K239.0512-1032, 1.

7. Peter R. Faber, "Interwar US Army Aviation and the Air Corps Tactical School: Incubators of America Airpower," in *The Paths of Heaven: The Evolution of Airpower Theory*, ed. Philip Meilinger (Maxwell AFB, AL: Air University Press, 1997), 219–20.

8. Student and faculty information are contained in Robert T. Finney, *History of the Air Corps Tactical School, 1920–1940* (Washington, DC: Center for Air Force History, 1992). Weyland's most distinguished classmate was probably Thomas Dresser White, future Chief of Staff of the USAF.

9. Otto P. Weyland, "Training Program for Observation Aviation: A Study Prepared by Otto P. Weyland, Captain, Air Corps, May 14, 1938," Air Corps Tactical School, Maxwell Field, Alabama, USAFHRA 248.262-29.

10. Ibid., 30.

11. USAF Oral History Program, "Weyland interview," 42.

12. Ibid., 46–47.

13. Ibid., 60ff.

14. Kent Roberts Greenfield, "Army Ground Forces and the Air-Ground Battle Team," Study No. 35 (Fort Monroe, VA: Historical Section, Army Ground Forces, 1948), 3–5; and Spires, *Patton's Air Force*, chapter 1.

15. War Department Field Manual FM 100-20, *Command and Employment of Air Power* (Washington, DC: GPO, July 1943), section 1, paragraph 3.

16. Army Air Forces Historical Office, AAF Historical Studies no. 36, "Ninth Air Force: April to November 1944" (Washington, DC: Headquarters, Army Air Forces, 1945), 1.

17. Ibid., 161.

18. XIX TAC, "Tactical Air Operations in Europe: A Report on Employment of Fighter-Bomber, Reconnaissance and Night Fighter Aircraft by XIX Tactical Air Command, Ninth Air Force, in Connection with the Third US Army Campaign from 1 August 1944 to VE Day, 9 May 1945," May 19, 1945, USAFHRA 537.04A, 41.

19. Spires, *Patton's Air Force*, 27.

20. Weyland, oral history interview, 1967, 140.

21. Spires, "Patton and Weyland," 148.

22. Spires, *Patton's Air Force*, 27.

23. USAF Oral History Program, "Weyland Interview," 1974, 68–74.

24. Ibid., 75–76.

25. Organizational chart of XIX TAC in XIX TAC, "A Report on the Combat Operations of the XIX Tactical Air Command," May 30, 1945, USAFHRA 537.04E, 2.

26. Weyland diary, September 19, 1944. Weyland's diary exists in two forms at the USAF Historical Research Agency at Maxwell AFB, AL. The original handwritten diary is at USAFHRA 168.7104-1. A typescript of highlights from the diary is at USAFHRA 537.13.1.

27. Spires, *Patton's Air Force*, 127.

28. XIX TAC, "Report on Combat Operations," 25.

29. The following narrative depends heavily on XIX TAC, "Twelve Thousand Fighter-Bomber Sorties: XIX TAC's First Month of Operations in Support of Third U.S. Army in France," September 30, 1944, USAFHRA 537.04B; XIX TAC, "Report on Combat Operations"; XIX TAC, "Tactical Air Operations in Europe"; Weyland diary; XIX TAC, "History 1 July 1944–28 Feb 1945, part II, Operations Narrative," USAFHRA 537.01, 10; USAAF Historical Office, "Ninth Air Force"; Spires, *Patton's Air Force*; and Sullivan, *Air Support for Patton's Third Army*.

30. XIX TAC, "Twelve Thousand Fighter-Bomber Sorties," 5–6.

31. XIC TAC, "Tactical Air Operations," 47.

32. XIX TAC, "Twelve Thousand Fighter-Bomber Sorties," 6.

33. XIX TAC, "History 1 July 1944–28 Feb 1945, part II, Operations Narrative," USAFHRA 537.01, 10.

34. XIC TAC, "Twelve Thousand Fighter-Bomber Sorties," 7.

35. XIX TAC, "History, August Operations," 21.

36. Bradford J. Shwedo, *XIX Tactical Air Command and ULTRA: Patton's Force Enhancers in the 1944 Campaign in France* (Maxwell AFB, AL: Air University Press, May 2001), chapter 5; and Sullivan, *Air Support*, 54–55.

37. XIX TAC, "Twelve Thousand Fighter-Bomber Sorties," 9.

38. Shwedo, *XIX Tactical Air Command*, 46ff; and Ralph Bennett, *ULTRA in the West: The Normandy Campaign of 1944–45* (New York: Scribner's, 1979), 111ff.

39. Shwedo, *XIX Tactical Air Command*, 50.

40. XIX TAC, "Twelve Thousand Fighter-Bomber Sorties," 17.

41. Ibid., 24.

42. Oberkommando der Luftwaffe, "Taktische Bemerkungen des Oberkommandos der Luftwaffe Nr. 5/44," July 15, 1944, BA/MA RH11 III/76, 7.

43. Shwedo, *XIX Tactical Air Command*, 85.

44. XIX TAC, "Twelve Thousand Fighter-Bomber Sorties," 29.

45. George S. Patton, *The Patton Papers*, vol. 2, *1940–1945*, ed. Martin Blumenson (Boston: Houghton Mifflin, 1974), 516.

46. USAAF Historical Office, "Ninth Air Force," 205.

47. XIX TAC, "Tactical Air Operations," 50.

48. Ibid., 1; and Shwedo, *XIX Tactical Air Command*, 107.

49. XIX TAC, "Tactical Air Operations," 48–49; and Spires, *Patton's Air Force*, 110–11.

50. Weyland diary, October 14, 1944. Young Stroh, West Point class of 1943, flew with the 362nd Fighter Group, 378th Fighter Squadron.

51. "Surrender on the Field of Battle: Gruppe Elster, Beaugency, France, 1944," *After the Battle* 48 (1985): 1–6.

52. Weyland diary, September 16, 1944.

53. Shwedo, *XIX Tactical Air Command*, 94–96.

54. USAF Oral History Program, "Weyland interview," 78.

55. XIX TAC, "Fly, Seek, Destroy: The Story of the XIX TAC," 1944, USAFHRA 537.04, 34.

56. Weyland diary, September 21, 1944.

57. Ibid., September 24, 1944.

58. Spires, *Patton's Air Force*, 121.

59. XIX TAC, "Tactical Air Operations," introduction.

60. Spires, *Patton's Air Force*, 89, 130.

61. Weyland diary, September 28, 1944.

62. XIX TAC, "Tactical Air Operations," 54.

63. Spires, *Patton's Air Force*, 177.

64. Air plan for Tink is at Annex 3, XIX TAC, "Report on Combat Operations."
65. Weyland diary, December 13, 1944.
66. Ibid., December 20, 1944.
67. XIX TAC, "Tactical Air Operations," 56.
68. Donald L. Caldwell and Richard R. Muller, *The Luftwaffe over Germany: Defense of the Reich* (London: Greenhill, 2007), 262.
69. John Manrho and Ron Pütz, *Bodenplatte: The Luftwaffe's Last Hope—the Attack on Allied Airfields, New Year's Day 1945* (Mardens Hill, UK: Hikoki, 2004), 221–46.
70. Ibid., 245.
71. Adolf Galland, *The First and the Last: The German Fighter Force in World War II* (Mesa, AZ: Champlin Museum Press, 1986), 319.
72. Weyland diary, January 22, 1945.
73. Spires, *Patton's Air Force*, 177.
74. XIX TAC, "Tactical Air Operations," 59.
75. Ibid., 59–60.
76. Ibid., 61.
77. Ibid., 62.
78. Ibid., 63.
79. Spires, *Patton's Air Force*, 281.
80. XIX TAC, "Tactical Air Operations," 67; and Spires, *Patton's Air Force*, 288.
81. XIC TAC, "Tactical Air Operations," 67.
82. HQ XIX TAC, General Orders No. 34, May 9, 1945.
83. Patton, *Patton Papers*, 810.
84. Weyland, oral history interview, 1967, 15.
85. Spires, *Patton's Air Force*, 296.
86. USAF Oral History Program, "Weyland Interview," 23.
87. Spires, *Patton's Air Force*, 117.
88. Weyland diary, November 11, 1944.
89. Philip S. Meilinger, *Hoyt S. Vandenberg: The Life of a General* (Bloomington: Indiana University Press, 1989), 51.
90. Thomas A. Hughes, *Over Lord: General Pete Quesada and the Triumph of Tactical Air Power in World War II* (New York: Free Press, 1995), 231. Quesada's biographer also notes, "Weyland plays a conspicuously small role in Quesada's memory of the war."
91. Weyland, oral history interview, 1967, 6.
92. USAF Oral History Program, "Weyland Interview," 24.
93. Weyland diary, December 31, 1944.
94. XIX TAC, "Tactical Air Operations," 35.
95. Weyland diary, April 12, 1945.
96. "Questions put to Generalfeldmarschall Gerd von Rundstedt by Major General O.P. Weyland, CG of Ninth Air Force, at Bad Kissingen on 2 July 1945," USAFHRA 168.7104-95.
97. USAF Oral History Program, "Weyland Interview," 148.
98. Weyland diary, November 16, 1944.
99. Hughes, *Overlord*, 241.
100. USAF Oral History Program, "Weyland Interview," 144–45.
101. XIX TAC, "Report on Combat Operations," introduction.
102. Spires, *Patton's Air Force*, 299.
103. XIX TAC, "Tactical Air Operations," 60–61.
104. Sullivan, *Air Support*, 60.
105. USAF Oral History Program, "Weyland Interview," 152.

106. XIX TAC, "Tactical Air Operations," 1–2; and XIX TAC, "Report on Combat Operations," 25.
107. Weyland, oral history interview, 1967, 9.
108. Spires, *Patton's Air Force*, 140.
109. Shwedo, *XIX Tactical Air Command*, 4.
110. Ibid., 15ff.
111. Ibid., 50, 85.
112. Weyland diary, November 9, 1944.
113. Jeffrey G. Barlow, *Revolt of the Admirals: The Fight for Naval Aviation, 1945–1950* (Washington, DC: Government Reprints Press, 2001), 45–46.
114. Weyland diary, December 16, 1944.
115. Patton, *Patton Papers*, 537 (entry for September 7, 1944).
116. Letter, Giles to Weyland, February 8, 1945, USAFHRA 168.7104-92.
117. Letter, Edey to Weyland, May 28, 1945, USAFHRA 168.7104-92.
118. Assistant Chief of Air Staff, Intelligence, "U.S. Tactical Air Power in Europe: A Special Issue," *IMPACT* 3, no. 5 (May 1945).
119. Mark Grimsley, *And Keep Moving On: The Virginia Campaign, May–June 1864* (Lincoln: University of Nebraska Press, 2002), xiii.
120. USAF Oral History Program, "Weyland interview," 107–10, 190.
121. Conrad C. Crane, *American Airpower Strategy in Korea, 1950–1953* (Lawrence: University Press of Kansas, 2000), 34.
122. Robert F. Futrell, *Ideas, Concepts, Doctrine: A History of Basic Thinking in the United States Air Force*, vol. 1, *1907–1960* (Maxwell AFB, AL: Air University Press, 1989), 450.
123. Gen. Otto P. Weyland, "The Air Campaign in Korea," *Air University Quarterly Review* 6 (Fall 1953): 28.

4. Curtis E. LeMay: Airman Extraordinary

1. For the development of doctrine in the U.S. Army Air Corps, see Robert F. Futrell, *Ideas, Concepts, Doctrine: A History of Basic Thinking in the United States Air Force*, vol. 1, *1907–1960* (Maxwell AFB, AL: Air University Press, 1971), among others.
2. For a discussion of the development of Luftwaffe doctrine during the interwar period, see Williamson Murray, *Luftwaffe* (Baltimore, MD: Nautical and Aviation Press, 1985), chapter 1.
3. Interview, Group Captain Tony Mason with Air Vice Marshal D. C. Bennett, archive, RAF Staff College, now located at the Joint Command and Staff College Archives, Shrivenham, United Kingdom.
4. Gen. Curtis E. LeMay with MacKinlay Kantor, *Mission with LeMay: My Story* (Garden City, NY: Doubleday, 1965), 227.
5. For the inaccuracy of German flak, see Friedhelm Golücke, *Schweinfurt und der strategische Luftkrieg, 1943* (Paderborn: Ferdinand Schöningh, 1980), 106–7.
6. The naval officer responsible for designing and then developing the proximity fuse also designed the firing mechanisms for the atomic bombs dropped over Japan.
7. LeMay, *Mission with LeMay*, 242.
8. For losses of bombers and crews by Eighth Air Force in 1943 and 1944, see the tables in Murray, *Luftwaffe*, 170 and 225.
9. Ibid., 224.
10. In this regard see Adam Tooze, *The Wages of Destruction: The Making and Breaking of the Nazi Economy* (New York: Viking Adult, 2007), 597–604.
11. Murray, *Luftwaffe*, 228.
12. In May the losses of B-17s and B-24s took a nosedive.

13. LeMay, *Mission with LeMay*, 323.
14. Ibid., 347.
15. See, in particular, Richard B. Frank, *Downfall: The End of the Imperial Japanese Empire* (New York: Random House, 1999). Frank's book, based on impeccable research, demolishes once and for all the persistent myth that the Japanese were on the brink of surrender when the atomic bombs were dropped.
16. LeMay, *Mission with LeMay*, 416.
17. For another viewpoint, see Alan Stephens, "George C. Kenney: 'A Kind of Renaissance Airman,'" in this volume.
18. Boeing produced the last B-52s in 1963, and those aircraft are still flying combat missions in 2011, forty-nine years after their construction.
19. Murray, *Luftwaffe*, 177.
20. The pilot of that aircraft, Col. Harry Deutschendorf, was the father of singer John Denver.
21. For a devastating account of Taylor's dishonest role in the making of American strategy, see H. R. McMaster, *Dereliction of Duty: Lyndon Johnson, Robert McNamara, the Joint Chiefs of Staff, and the Lies that Led to Vietnam* (New York: HarperCollins, 1998).
22. Thomas M. Coffey, *Iron Eagle: The Turbulent Life of General Curtis LeMay* (New York: Avon Books, 1988), 434.
23. LeMay, *Mission with LeMay*, 565. Note that LeMay's biographer Thomas M. Coffey states in his book that LeMay never said those words, although they appear in his autobiography, written with the significant help of novelist MacKinlay Kantor.

5. William H. Tunner: Master of Airlift

1. There are two major sources for William H. Tunner's biography—his autobiography, *Over the Hump* (Washington, DC: Office of Air Force History, 1985, first printing 1964), and the first full-length biography of Tunner in Robert A. Slayton's *Master of the Air: William Tunner and the Success of Military Airlift* (Tuscaloosa: University of Alabama Press, 2010).
2. Tunner, *Over the Hump*, 6.
3. Ibid., 3–6.
4. Ibid., 8.
5. Tunner was married twice. He had two children by his first wife, who died of cancer in 1947. Tunner remarried in 1951 to a former Ferrying Command auxiliary pilot and had a third child.
6. This expression is early aviation parlance, when pilots decided a course of action as they went along, using their own initiative, judgment, and perceptions rather than a predetermined plan or mechanical aids. The term emerged in the 1930s and was used in reports of Douglas Corrigan's flight from the United States to Ireland in 1938.
7. Robert F. Futrell, *Ideas, Concepts, Doctrine: Basic Thinking in the United States Air Force*, vol. 1, *1907–1960* (Maxwell AFB, AL: Air University Press, 1989), 101.
8. Assistant chief of the Air Staff, Intelligence, Historical Division, *Administrative History of the Ferrying Command, 29 May 1941–30 June 1942*, AAF Historical Studies No. 33 (U.S. Army Air Forces: Washington, DC, 1945). Document in USAF Historical Research Agency, Maxwell AFB, AL, (hereafter cited as USAFHRA).
9. Futrell, *Ideas, Concepts, Doctrine*, 63.
10. James Tate, *The Army and Its Air Corps: Army Policy toward Aviation, 1919–1941* (Maxwell AFB, AL: Air University Press, 1998), 131–34.
11. Futrell, *Ideas, Concepts, Doctrine*, 68–70.

12. On U.S. airlift doctrine before World War II, see Charles E. Miller, *Airlift Doctrine* (Maxwell AFB, AL: Air University Press, 1998), 1–26.

13. On the AAF's use of women pilots in World War II, see AAF Historical Office, *Women Pilots with the AAF, 1941–1944*, AAF Historical Study No. 55 (AAF Headquarters, Washington, DC, March 1946). Document in USAFHRA.

14. On training American transport pilots, see *Combat Crew and Unit Training in the AAF, 1939–1945*, AAF Historical Study No. 61 (Air Historical Office, Headquarters USAF, 1954), 89–101. Document in USAFHRA.

15. Tunner, *Over the Hump*, 26–27.

16. Miller, *Airlift Doctrine*, 34.

17. Tunner, *Over the Hump*, 41–42.

18. Ibid., 40.

19. Barbara W. Tuchman, *Stillwell and the American Experience in China, 1911–45* (New York: Grove, 2001), 312–13. The Hump operation took its name from flying over the 16,000-foot gap in the Himalayas through which all traffic had to be channeled.

20. Ibid., 372.

21. For a good overview of the air transport operations carried out for the Allies in Burma, see Joe Taylor, *Air Supply in the Burma Campaigns*, USAF Historical Study No. 75 (Maxwell AFB, AL: Air University, USAF Historical Division, Research Studies Institute, April 1957). Document in the USAFHRA. An excellent recent study is John Plating's *The Hump: America's Strategy for Keeping China in World War II* (College Station: Texas A&M Press, 2011).

22. Tuchman, *Stillwell and the American Experience*, 458–59.

23. Tunner, *Over the Hump*, 114–15.

24. Ibid.

25. Tuchman, *Stillwell and the American Experience*, 484.

26. Ibid.

27. Tunner, *Over the Hump*, 115–16.

28. An excellent description of Tunner's operations in the CBI theater and of his leadership style in general is found in David Hanson, *"When You Get a Job to Do, Do It": The Airpower Leadership of Lt. Gen. William H. Tunner* (Maxwell AFB, AL: Air University Press, 2008). On the CBI operations, see pages 27–36.

29. Miller, *Airlift Doctrine*, 57.

30. Tunner, *Over the Hump*, 158–60.

31. Ibid., 160.

32. Phillip S. Meilinger, *Hoyt S. Vandenberg: The Life of a General* (Bloomington: Indiana University Press, 1989), 99. Meilinger also notes that Vandenberg later promoted Smith to major general and made him the MATS commander, bypassing Tunner, who remained vice commander. See note 64, page 235.

33. Ibid.

34. Walton S. Moody, *Building a Strategic Air Force* (Washington, DC: Air Force History and Museums Program, 1995), 209.

35. Tunner, *Over the Hump*, 161.

36. For an overview of the airlift and the problems associated with it, see Tunner, *Over the Hump*, 161–75.

37. Ibid., 178.

38. Clayton Chun, *Aerospace Power in the Twenty-First Century: A Basic Primer* (Maxwell AFB, AL: Air University Press, 2001), 195.

39. Gen. T. Ross Milton, "Inside the Berlin Airlift," *Air Force Magazine*, October 1998.

40. Tunner, *Over the Hump*, 175–76.
41. Chun, *Aerospace Power*, 191–95.
42. There are several good books that provide the details of the Berlin Airlift. See Richard Collier, *Bridge Across the Sky: The Berlin Blockade and Airlift, 1948–1949* (New York: McGraw-Hill, 1978); Robert Jackson, *The Berlin Airlift* (Wellingborough, UK: Thorsons, 1988); Oliver La Farge, *The Eagle in the Egg* (Boston: Houghton Mifflin, 1949); Roger G. Miller, *To Save a City: The Berlin Airlift, 1948–1949* (College Station: Texas A&M Press, 2000); and Walter Boyne, *Beyond the Wild Blue: A History of the U.S. Air Force, 1947–1997* (New York: St. Martin's Press, 1997).
43. Tunner, *Over the Hump*, 161–62.
44. Daniel L. Haulman, *The United States Air Force and Humanitarian Airlift Operations, 1947–1994* (Washington, DC: Air Force History and Museums Program, 1998), 234–35.
45. Cited in Meilinger, *Hoyt S. Vandenberg*, 102; and quote from Frank Johnson, "Airlift to Berlin," *Air Classics*, September 1978, 30.
46. Gen. Curtis E. LeMay with MacKinlay Kantor, *Mission with LeMay: My Story* (Garden City, NY: Doubleday, 1965), 416.
47. Tunner, *Over the Hump*, 191.
48. Ibid., 222.
49. A. Timothy Warnock, ed., *The U.S. Air Force's First War: Korea, 1950–1953: Significant Events* (Maxwell AFB, AL: USAF Historical Research Agency, 2000).
50. USAF Historical Division, *United States Air Force Operations in the Korean Conflict*, USAF Historical Study No. 71 (Department of the Air Force, 1 July 1952), 101–2. Document in USAFHRA.
51. Ibid.
52. Ibid., 101–3.
53. Futrell, *Ideas, Concepts, Doctrine*, 311.
54. Ibid.
55. Haulman, *The United States Air Force*, 402.
56. See Warnock, *The U.S. Air Force's First War*.
57. Miller, *Airlift Doctrine*, 234–36.
58. Meilinger, *Hoyt S. Vandenberg*, 235.
59. For an overview of the whole process of rearming Germany and integrating Germany into NATO from 1949 to 1959, see James S. Corum, ed., *Rearming Germany* (Leiden: Brill Press, 2011).
60. On the process of developing the Luftwaffe and the USAF and on Luftwaffe strategic planning, see James S. Corum, "Building a New Luftwaffe: The US Air Force and Bundeswehr Planning for Rearmament, 1950–1960," *Journal of Strategic Studies*, March 2004, 88–113.
61. James S. Corum, "Starting from Scratch: Establishing the Bundesluftwaffe as a Modern Air Force, 1955–1960," *Air Power History*, Summer 2003, 16–29.
62. Corum, "Building a New Luftwaffe."
63. The airlift debates of this period are best described in Miller, *Airlift Doctrine*, 235–50.
64. Tunner, *Over the Hump*, 281–83.
65. Ibid., 289.
66. Ibid., 307–11. See also Miller, *Airlift Doctrine*, 265–66.
67. For a detailed review of the congressional debates about airlift, see Miller, *Airlift Doctrine*, 258–64.
68. Tunner, *Over the Hump*, 314.

6. George E. Stratemeyer: Organizer of Air Power

1. Biographical sketch of Stratemeyer in William T. Y'Blood, ed., *The Three Wars of Lt. Gen. George E. Stratemeyer: His Korean War Diary* (Washington, DC: Air Force History and Museums Program, 1999), 3–9; and Phillip S. Meilinger, *Hoyt S. Vandenberg: The Life of a General* (Washington, DC: Air Force History and Museums Program, 2000), 162.

2. Y'Blood, *Stratemeyer Korean War Diary*, entries of October 20, 1950 and April 6, 1951, 244, 468. While microfilm of the actual diary exists, the Y'Blood-edited version both remains accurate to the original and includes numerous footnotes providing explanations of terms, biographies of individuals referenced, and added context to explain situations that Stratemeyer noted but did not explain himself.

3. Ibid., 1.

4. Ibid., 2–3.

5. Ibid., 4–5.

6. Maurer Maurer, *Aviation in the U.S. Army, 1919–1939* (Washington, DC: Office of Air Force History, 1987), 394.

7. James Tate, *The Army and Its Air Corps: Army Policy toward Aviation, 1919–1941* (Maxwell AFB, AL: Air University Press, 1998), 192.

8. DeWitt S. Copp, *A Few Great Captains: The Men and Events that Shaped the Development of U.S. Air Power* (McLean, VA: The Air Force Historical Foundation, 1980), 152–53; and David R. Mets, *Master of Airpower: General Carl A. Spaatz* (Novato, CA: Presidio Press, 1988), 56, 98–99.

9. Spaatz's biographer Richard G. Davis cites numerous communications in which Stratemeyer provides recommendations of his own to Spaatz and not simply orders from Arnold. See Richard G. Davis, *Carl A. Spaatz and the Air War in Europe, 1940–1945* (Washington, DC: Center for Air Force History, 1993).

10. Arnold admitted as much to his daughter in a letter written after the war. Dik Alan Daso, *Hap Arnold and the Evolution of American Airpower* (Washington, DC: Smithsonian Institute Press, 2000), 201.

11. United States Air Force Academy, McDermott Library, Clark Special Collections Branch, the Thomas and Margaret Overlander Collection (hereafter cited as Clark Special Collections), MS 28, Box 1, Folder 2; and Y'Blood, *Stratemeyer Korean War Diary*, various entries.

12. Y'Blood, *Stratemeyer Korean War Diary*, various entries.

13. The command arrangements are laid out in detail in James L. Cate, "The Twentieth Air Force," in *The Army Air Forces in World War II*, vol. 5, *The Pacific: Matterhorn to Nagasaki, June 1944 to August 1945*, ed. Wesley F. Craven and James L. Cate (Washington, DC: Office of Air Force History, 1981), 44–49. This account also credits Stratemeyer with great success as a diplomat in these circumstances.

14. Chennault's perspective is provided in his *Way of a Fighter: The Memoirs of Claire Lee Chennault*, ed. Robert B. Hotz (New York: G. P. Putnam's Sons, 1949), 347–52.

15. Clark Special Collections, MS 28; and Y'Blood, *Stratemeyer Korean War Diary*, entry of May 22, 1944.

16. Lee Bowen, "The Liberation of Burma," in Craven and Cate, *Army Air Forces in World War II*, 5:238.

17. Clark Special Collections, MS 28; and Y'Blood, *Stratemeyer Korean War Diary*, entry of December 4, 1944.

18. Clark Special Collections, MS 53, Series 1, Box 6, notebook, entry of January 6, 1945.

19. James F. Schnabel and Robert J. Watson, *The Joint Chiefs of Staff and National Policy*,

vol. 3, *1950–1951, the Korean War: Part One* (Washington, DC: Office of Joint History, Office of the Chairman of the Joint Chiefs of Staff, 1998), 20–22.

20. Damage caused by having dust or objects ingested into the engines.

21. William H. Tunner, *Over the Hump* (Washington, DC: Office of Air Force History, 1985), 229–31.

22. Y'Blood, *Stratemeyer Korean War Diary*, entries for July 14–16 and 20, 1950, 72, 75–76, 79–80.

23. Oral History Transcript 215, Otto Weyland, June 1960, McDermott Library, Clark Special Collection.

24. Phillip S. Meilinger, *Airmen and Air Theory: A Review of the Sources* (Maxwell AFB, AL: Air University Press, 2001), 36–39.

25. Missing from this account of General Stratemeyer's command relationships is any mention of other members of the United Nations coalition. The omission is intentional. While units from other nations participated in the war, they did so while attached to lower-level USAF units and without representation at General Stratemeyer's command level, except for courtesy calls or brief visits. Thus General Stratemeyer's duties did not involve coalition operations to any appreciable extent.

26. Y'Blood, *Stratemeyer Korean War Diary*, entry for September 24, 1950, 204.

27. Ibid., entries for September 9 and 21, 1951, 179, 202. The letter to commanders asked that they destroy the letter after reading.

28. James F. Schnabel, *United States Army in the Korean War: Policy and Direction: The First Year* (Washington, DC: Office of the Chief of Military History, 1972), 108, 110; and William T. Y'Blood, *Down in the Weeds: Close Air Support in Korea* (Washington, DC: Air Force History and Museums Program, 2002), 7. For example, the targeting group used a map to select bridges, which in reality were only fords for river crossings.

29. Y'Blood, *Down in the Weeds*, 3–6.

30. See ibid.; Partridge comments in Richard H. Kohn and Joseph P. Harahan, eds., *Air Interdiction in World War II, Korea, and Vietnam: An Interview with Earle E. Partridge, Jacob E. Smart, and John W. Voght, Jr.* (Washington, DC: Office of Air Force History, 1986); Allan R. Millett, "Korea, 1950–1953," in *Case Studies in the Development of Close Air Support*, ed. Benjamin F. Cooling (Washington, DC: Office of Air Force History, 1990); and Gary R. Lester, *Mosquitoes to Wolves: The Evolution of the Airborne Forward Air Controller* (Maxwell AFB, AL: Air University Press, 1997), 45–52, for the experiences and development of the air-ground system in the early days of the war.

31. Robert Frank Futrell, *Ideas, Concepts, Doctrine: Basic Thinking in the United States Air Force*, vol. 1, 1907–1960 (Maxwell AFB, AL: Air University Press, 1989), 294–95; and Y'Blood, *Stratemeyer Korean War Diary*, entries of July 16 and 20, 1950 and September 17, 1950, 76–80.

32. Y'Blood, *Stratemeyer Korean War Diary*, entries for July 11 and September 2–4, 1950, 67, 161–68.

33. Letter to LeMay, ibid., entry for September 2, 1950, 160.

34. Robert Frank Futrell, *The United States Air Force in Korea, 1950–1953* (Washington, DC: Air Force History and Museums Program, 1996), 51–55.

35. Y'Blood, *Stratemeyer Korean War Diary*, entry of October 7, 1950, 223; and William T. Y'Blood, "Command and Control of Air Operations in the Korean War," in *Golden Legacy, Boundless Future: Essays on the United States Air Force and the Rise of Aerospace Power*, eds. Rebecca H. Cameron and Barbara Wittig (Washington, DC: Air Force History and Museums Program, 2000).

36. Wayne Thompson, "The Air War over Korea" in *Winged Shield, Winged Sword: A History of the United States Air Force*, ed. Bernard C. Nalty (Washington, DC: Air Force History and Museums Program, 1997), 18–20; and see Millett, "Korea 1950–1953," for a discussion of the army's and air force's positions.

37. Y'Blood, *Stratemeyer Korean War Diary*, entries of July 6 and September 4, 1950, 58, 165.

38. Ibid., entry of September 1, 1950, 158.

39. Ibid., Stratemeyer's eyes-only letter, September 9, 1950, and entry of September 6, 1950, 179.

40. Ibid., entry of October 21, 1950, 244.

41. Ibid., entry of October 2, 1950, 217–19.

42. Ibid., entry of October 14, 1950, 232.

43. Ibid., entries of October 19, 20, and 24, and November 6, 1950, 240–42, 245, 278. MacArthur did not get this award.

44. Ibid., entry of February 14, 1951, 418–21.

45. Schnabel and Watson, *The Joint Chiefs of Staff*, 93–107.

46. Y'Blood, *Stratemeyer Korean War Diary*, entries for August 30, September 27, and October 10–13, 1950, 150, 206–7, 226–32.

47. John Darrell Sherwood, *Officers in Flight Suits* (New York: New York University Press, 1996), 88–90.

48. Futrell, *Air Force in Korea*, 222, 248.

49. Y'Blood, *Stratemeyer Korean War Diary*, entries of November 5–8, 1950, 258–67. Of particular note is General MacArthur's extreme concern over the entry of Chinese troops into Korea weeks before the Chinese offensive in late November.

50. Ibid., entries of October 17–18, 1950, 236–37.

51. Ibid., entry of November 3, 1950, 253.

52. Futrell, *Air Force in Korea*, 320–22.

53. William Stueck, *The Korean War: An International History* (Princeton, NJ: Princeton University Press, 1995), 145–46.

54. Schnabel and Watson, *The Joint Chiefs of Staff*, 181.

55. Y'Blood, *Stratemeyer Korean War Diary*, entry of December 8, 1950, 342.

56. See particularly the minutes of several meetings and messages to General Vandenberg during the desperate days of December 1950. Ibid., entries for November 27–29 and December 2, 5, 11, and 21–23, 1950, 308, 313, 323–46, 356–72.

57. Ibid., entries for December 4–7, 1950, 325–39. The diary provides the text of General Stratemeyer's note.

58. Kenneth P. Werrell, *Archie to SAM: A Short Operational History of Ground-Based Air Defense*, 2nd ed. (Maxwell AFB, AL: Air University Press, 2005), 75–76.

59. A. Timothy Warnock, ed., *The USAF in Korea: A Chronology, 1950–1953* (Washington, DC: Air Force History and Museums Program, 2000), 40; Y'Blood, *Stratemeyer Korean War Diary*, entries for April 12–13, 1951, 477–79; and Sherwood, *Officers in Flight Suits*, 76.

60. George M. Watson Jr., *The Office of the Secretary of the Air Force, 1947–1965* (Washington, DC: Center for Air Force History, 1993), 118.

61. Y'Blood, *Stratemeyer Korean War Diary*, entry of May 8, 1951, 500. Little more was said of this incident, even though it was followed by an inspector general report.

62. Ibid., entry of May 11, 1951, 509–11.

63. Ibid., entry of April 16, 1951, 481–82.

64. Ibid., entry of April 6, 1951, 468.

65. Ibid., entry of April 11, 1951, 476.
66. Ibid., entry of May 2, 1951, 500.
67. Quotes and information in ibid., introductory section written by the book's editor, 28–32.
68. The only in-depth treatment of General Stratemeyer's service in Korea, and one used extensively here, comes from William T. Y'Blood's excellent work in editing General Stratemeyer's diary and in providing expanded explanations and biographical information. In addition, Nicholas M. Sambaluk wrote a master's thesis, "The Actions and Operational Thinking of Generals Stratemeyer and Partridge during the Korean War: Adjusting to Political Restrictions in Air Campaigns" (University of North Texas, 2008); and Gregory M. Corn completed a thesis, "Air Leadership in Joint/Combined Operations: Lt. General George E. Stratemeyer of Eastern Air Command, 1943–45" (USAF School of Advanced Air Power Studies, Maxwell AFB, AL, 1999).

7. William W. Momyer: An Air Power Mind

1. Wesley F. Craven and James L. Cate, eds., *The Army Air Forces in World War II*, vol. 2, *Europe: Torch to Pointblank, August 1942 to December* 1943 (Chicago: University of Chicago Press, 1949), 77; and James E. Reed, *The Fighting 33rd Nomads during World War II: A Diary of a Fighter Pilot with Photographs and Other Stories of 33rd Fighter Group Personnel* (Memphis, TN: Reed Publishers, 1988), 2:51.
2. John T. Correll, "The Vietnam War Almanac," *Air Force Magazine*, September 2004, 42–61.
3. Gen. William W. Momyer Oral History, by Lt. Col. John N. Dick, 31 January 1977, 2–4, K239.0512-1068, IRIS No. 1029788, U.S. Air Force Historical Research Agency (USAFHRA).
4. Momyer Oral History, 11–18; and Allan R. Scholin, "Momyer and TAC: A Perfect Fit," *Air Force Magazine*, July 1968, 31.
5. Frederick A. Johnsen, *P-40 Warhawk* (Osceola, WI: MBI Publishing, 1998), 74.
6. Momyer Oral History, 31.
7. Reed, *The Fighting 33rd Nomads during World War II*, 1:86.
8. U.S. Air Force Historical Research Agency, "Organizational History Branch, Squadrons and Flights," http://www.afhra.af.mil/organizationalrecords/squadronsandflights.asp (accessed September 15, 2011), 58th, 59th, and 60th Fighter Squadrons; and *History of the 58th Fighter Squadron, 10/42–6/44*, 19, SQ-FI-58-HI 15 Jan 1941–Dec 1943, IRIS No. 00056741, USAFHRA.
9. Headquarters (HQ) I Fighter Command, Special Order Number 145, IRIS No. 00056767, in the U.S. Air Force (USAF) Collection, USAFHRA; and USAFHRA, "Organizational History Branch, Wings and Groups," http://www.afhra.af.mil/organizationalrecords/squadronsandflights.asp (accessed September 15, 2011).
10. Craven and Tate, *Army Air Forces in World War II*, 2:53.
11. Paul Yarnell, "USS *Chenango* (ACV-28)," NavSource Online: Escort Carrier Photo Archive, http://www.navsource.org/archives/03/028.htm.
12. Reed, *Fighting 33rd Nomads*, 1:52–74.
13. Momyer Answers to Questionnaire, Attachment to Letter, Capt. Richard L. Dunn to Gen. William W. Momyer, Commander, TAC, October 18, 1972, 168.7041-58, IRIS No. 1001170.
14. Benjamin F. Cooling, ed., *Case Studies in the Achievement of Air Superiority* (Washington, DC: Center for Air Force History, 1994), 225–26; *History of the 58th Fighter*

Squadron, 7–13; and McNair as quoted in Richard G. Davis, *Carl A. Spaatz and the Air War in Europe, 1940–1945* (Washington, DC: Center for Air Force History, 1993), 135.

15. Jack Coggins, *The Campaign for North Africa* (New York: Doubleday, 1980), 74.

16. Charles R. Anderson, *Algeria-French Morocco: The United States Army Campaigns of World War II*, CMH Pub 72-11 (Washington, DC: Army Center of Military History, 1993), 10.

17. Reed, *Fighting 33rd Nomads*, 1:86–87; U.S. Air Force Historical Study No. 105 (AAFRH-5), *Air Phase of the North African Invasion*, Assistant Chief of Air Staff, Intelligence, November 1944, 75; *History of the 60th Fighter Squadron*, 10, SQ-FI-60-HI October 1942–December 1943, IRIS No. 00056791, AFHRA.

18. HQ, 47th Wing, General Orders No. 3 (March 11, 1943), Silver Star Citation for Col. William Wallace Momyer (Air Corps), for actions in November 1942.

19. *The Twelfth Air Force in the North African Winter Campaign: 11 November 1942 to the Reorganization of 18 February 1943*, U.S. Air Force Historical Study No. 114 (AAFRH-14) (Washington, DC: Army Air Forces Historical Office, January 1946), 8; and Craven and Cate, *Army Air Forces in World War II*, 2:77.

20. Craven and Cate, *Army Air Forces in World War II*, 2:88–89; and Daniel R. Mortensen, *A Pattern for Joint Operations: World War II Close Air Support in North Africa* (Washington, DC: Office of Air Force History and U.S. Army Center of Military History, 1987), 60–61.

21. Craven and Cate, *Army Air Forces in World War II*, 2:127–28; HQ XII Air Support Command (ASC), Report on Operations, Tunisia, January 13, 1943–April 9, 1943, 2, 651.3069-1, IRIS No. 00246452, USAFHRA; and David R. Mets, *Master of Airpower: General Carl A. Spaatz* (Novato, CA: Presidio Press, 1988), 149.

22. Citation of 33rd Fighter Group, February 7, 1945, GP-33-SW-AW, Oct 1942–10 July 1943, IRIS No. 00079425, USAFHRA; *59th Fighter Squadron History*, 19; and *History of the 58th Fighter Squadron*, 73.

23. HQ XII ASC, Report on Operations, Tunisia, 2, 10; George F. Howe, *Northwest Africa: Seizing the Initiative in the West* (Washington, DC: Office of the Chief of Military History, Department of the Army, 1957), 351; and Craven and Cate, *Army Air Forces in World War II*, 2:140.

24. *History of the 58th Fighter Squadron*, 80–81.

25. *59th Fighter Squadron History*, 23; HQ XII ASC, Report on Operations, Tunisia, 3; H. S. Warwick, "XII Air Support Command in the Tunisian Campaign," 5, 655.01-2, IRIS No. 00246459, USAFHRA; and *History of the 58th Fighter Squadron*, 99.

26. Vincent Orange, *Coningham: A Biography of Air Marshal Sir Arthur Coningham, KCB, KBE, DSO, MC, DFC, AFC* (London: Methuen, 1990), 143.

27. Air Marshal Coningham, Air Officer Commanding, Northwest Africa Tactical Air Force, "General Operational Directive, 20 February 1943," 1, 614.201-2, AFHRA.

28. *History of the 58th Fighter Squadron*, 103.

29. Howe, *Northwest Africa*, 564–72.

30. *History of the 58th Fighter Squadron*, 107.

31. Momyer Oral History, 34.

32. Headquarters, U.S. Army–North African Theater of Operations, General Orders No. 43 (June 26, 1943), Distinguished Service Cross Citation for Col. (Air Corps) William Wallace Momyer, for actions on March 31, 1943.

33. Warwick, "XII Air Support Command," 5.

34. Headquarters, Northwest African Tactical Air Force, "The Implications of the Present Situation," 17 April 1943, 1, 614.316, IRIS No. 00242503, USAFHRA.

35. Ibid., 2; and Warwick, "XII Air Support Command," 2.

36. Lt. Gen. Fred M. Dean Oral History, by Maj. Richard H. Emmons, 25–26 February 1975, 34, K239.0512-834, IRIS No. 01027517, USAFHRA.

37. Quoted in Robert Frank Futrell, *Ideas, Concepts, Doctrine: Basic Thinking in the United States Air Force*, vol. 1, *1907–1960* (Maxwell AFB, AL: Air University Press, 1989), 134.

38. Maj. Gen. Eugene L. Eubank Oral History, by Mr. Hugh N. Ahmann, 30 June–1 July 1982, 128, K239.0512-1345, IRIS No. 1052996, USAFHRA.

39. Army Air Forces (AAF) Board Minutes, October 21, 1943–January 31, 1944; and Historical Branch, AC/S-2, Air Proving Ground Command, *AAF Board: Its Divisions and Their Work, 1943–1946*, vol. 2, *1946*, 315–17, 240.04-6 v. 2, IRIS No. 00155453, USAFHRA.

40. Air Proving Ground Command, *AAF Board*, 1:69; and Report of the AAF Board, "Isolation of the Battlefield," Project No. 3763A373.1, October 17, 1944, 1–2, MICFILM 28222, IRIS No. 205-3567, USAFHRA.

41. AAF Board, "Isolation of the Battlefield," 5–13.

42. Gen. William W. Momyer, Commander, TAC, to Lt. Col. Ellis C. Vander Pyl, Letter, November 17, 1972, 168.7041-58, IRIS No. 1001170, USAFHRA.

43. Col. W. W. Momyer, Executive, AAF Board, to Col. Henry Viccellio, Headquarters, AAF, Letter, June 30, 1945, 245.6051, IRIS No. 00156485, USAFHRA; AAF Letter 201-10, June 3, 1946, in *Air Proving Ground Historical Data, 2 Sep 45–30 Jun 49*, vol. 2, 240.01v. 2, IRIS No. 00155430, USAFHRA.

44. Caroline F. Ziemke, "The Shadow of the Giant: USAF Tactical Air Command in the Era of Strategic Bombing, 1945–1955" (PhD diss., Ohio State University, 1989), 29–33; *History of the Tactical Air Command, March 1946–December 1946*, vol. 1, 417.01, IRIS No. 00198690, USAFHRA; and Mission statement from AAF Reg. No. 20-19, "Organization: The Tactical Air Command," October 10, 1946, quoted in *History of the Tactical Air Command for 1947*, vol. 1, 2, 417.01, IRIS No. 00198695, USAFHRA.

45. Lt. Gen. Elwood R. Quesada Oral History, by Lieutenant Colonel Stephenson and Lieutenant Colonel Long, U.S. Army Military History Institute, May 12–13, 1975, 34, K239.0512-838, IRIS No. 1037750, USAFHRA.

46. Col. William W. Momyer, "A Concept of Tactical Air Operations" (thesis, Air War College, Maxwell AFB, AL, 1949), 2–24.

47. Ibid., 25.

48. Futrell, *Ideas, Concepts, Doctrine*, 381.

49. "Air University History: 1 July 1950–31 December 1950," vol. 1, 167–69, K239.01 v. 1, IRIS No. 0479038, USAFHRA.

50. "Air University History: 1 January 1951–30 June 1951," vol. 2, Personnel Rosters, 2, K239.01 Jan–June 1951, v. 2, IRIS No. 0479043, USAFHRA; AWC Instruction Circular Number 51A-2, "Study No. 2: National Strategies in Action During World War II," in "Air University History: 1 January 1951–30 June 1951," vol. 3, K239.01 V.3, Jan–June 51, IRIS No. 0479044, USAFHRA; and "Air University History: 1 January 1951–30 June 1951," vol. 1, 137.

51. "Air University History: 1 July 1951–31 December 1951," vol. 1, 29–33, K239.01 Jul–Dec 1951, v. 1, IRIS No. 0479047, USAFHRA; "Classified Annex to AWC History, Jul–Dec 1951," 1-7, K239.01 Jul–Dec 1951, v. 1, Pt. 2, IRIS No. 00917436, USAFHRA; and "History of Air War College: 1 Jul 1952–30 Jun 1953," vol. 1, 39–44, K239.07B, Jul 1952–Jun 1953, IRIS No. 0480916, USAFHRA.

52. Col. Royal H. Roussel, "The Air Force Doctrinal Manuals," *The United States Air Force Air University Quarterly Review 7*, no. 1 (Spring 1954): 126–31.
53. Ibid., 130; and "History of Air War College: 1 Jul 1952–30 Jun 1953," 1:41.
54. "History of the 8th Fighter Bomber Wing: 1 Jul 1954–31 Dec 1954," K-WG-8-HI, IRIS No. 447584, USAFHRA; and "History of the 8th Fighter Bomber Wing: 1 Jan 1955–30 June 1955," K-WG-8-HI, IRIS No. 447585, USAFHRA.
55. "314th Air Division Historical Report: 15 March–30 June 1955," K-DIV-314-HI, Mar-Jun 1955, IRIS No. 0466096, USAFHRA; and "314th Air Division Historical Report: 1 July–31 December 1955," K-DIV-314-HI, Jul-Dec 1955, IRIS No. 0466098, USAFHRA.
56. Lt. Gen. Edward Timberlake, Ninth Air Force Commander, to Col. William Momyer, 312th Fighter-Bomber Wing Commander, September 1955, K-WG-312-HI, Jul–Dec 1955, vol. 2, IRIS No. 455298, USAFHRA.
57. "Biography of Brigadier General Momyer" in *History of the 832nd Air Division, 8 October–31 December 1957*, K-DIV-832-HI, IRIS No. 0467468, USAFHRA.
58. *History of the 832d Air Division.*
59. Gen. Frank F. Everest Oral History, by Lt. Col. John N. Dick Jr., August 23–25, 1977, 358–59, K239.0512-957, IRIS No. 1034248, USAFHRA.
60. History, DCS, Operations, 1 July–31 Dec 31 61, K143.01, vol. 7, IRIS No. 00470476, USAFHRA.
61. Col. William Hovde Oral History, January 19, 1977, 256, K239.0512-1062, IRIS No. 1031210, USAFHRA.
62. Major General Richard Catledge Oral History, September 30, 1987, 31, K239.0512-1768, IRIS No. 1095061, AFHRA.
63. Maj. Gen. Gordon H. Austin Oral History, by Hugh N. Ahmann, May 18–20, 1982, 233, K239.0512-1325, IRIS No. 1058219, USAFHRA.
64. Gen. Gabriel P. Disosway Oral History, by Dr. Edgar F. Puryear Jr., January 17, 1979, 8, K239.0512-1401, IRIS No. 01053206, USAFHRA.
65. Brig. Gen. Kenneth R. Johnson Oral History, by Hugh N. Ahmann, September 18, 1988, 29, K239.0512-1842, IRIS No. 1125014, USAFHRA.
66. Air Training Command History, vol. 1, K220.01: Jul-Dec 64, IRIS No. 0477280; Jan–Jun 65, IRIS No. 0477296; and Jan-Jun 66, IRIS No. 047737, USAFHRA.
67. Richard H. Kohn and Joseph P. Harahan, ed., *Air Superiority in World War II and Korea: An Interview with Gen. James Ferguson, Gen. Robert M. Lee, Gen. William Momyer, and Lt. Gen. Elwood R. Quesada* (Washington, DC: Office of Air Force History, 1983), 70.
68. General Momyer to General Ellis, Vice Chief of Staff, HQ/USAF, Memorandum, Subject: Corona Harvest (Command and Control of Southeast Asia Operations, 1 January 1965–31 March 1968).
69. John T. Correll, "Disunity of Command," *Air Force Magazine 88*, no. 1 (January 2005): 34.
70. Gen. William W. Momyer, *Airpower in Three Wars: WWII, Korea, Vietnam* (Maxwell AFB, AL: Air University Press, 2003), 106.
71. Ibid., 108.
72. Ibid., 104.
73. Gen. William W. Momyer, "Observations of the Vietnam War, July 1966–July 1968," November 1970, 2-3, K740.151, IRIS No. 00524451, USAFHRA.
74. Dennis M. Drew, *Rolling Thunder 1965: Anatomy of a Failure* (Maxwell AFB, AL: Air University Press, 1986), 1.

75. Momyer, *Airpower in Three Wars*, 18–21.
76. Ibid., 24–27.
77. General Wheeler, chairman JCS, testimony to US Senate, *Air War Against North Vietnam: Hearings Before the Preparedness Investigating Subcommittee of Committee on Armed Services*, 90th Cong., 1st sess., August 16, 1967, part 2, 139–40.
78. Momyer, "Observations," 2–3.
79. Maj. Gen. Gordon F. Blood Oral History, by Maj. S. E. Riddlebarger and Maj. R. B. Clement, April 6, 1970, 49-51, K239.0512-257, IRIS No. 904161, USAFHRA.
80. Momyer, *Airpower in Three Wars*, 309–13.
81. Blood Oral History, 49–51.
82. "Rolling the Thunder," *Time*, December 29, 1967, 23.
83. "Our Top Airman in Vietnam," *Airman*, May 1967, 4–5.
84. Ibid., 6–7.
85. Memo from W. W. Rostow to President Lyndon B. Johnson, General Momyer's Briefing Re: "Operations in Route Package VIA," July 18, 1967, Folder 27, Box 01, Veteran Members of the 109th Quartermaster Company (Air Delivery) Collection, the Vietnam Center and Archive, Texas Tech University.
86. When engaging with enemy aircraft, American aircraft often had to jettison their bombs so their aircraft would perform better in combat.
87. Memo, Rostow to Johnson.
88. Ibid.
89. Memo to President Lyndon B. Johnson from Tom Johnson, Meeting with Ken Crawford, July 20, 1967, Folder 09, Box 07, Larry Berman Collection (Presidential Archives Research), the Vietnam Center and Archive, Texas Tech University.
90. W. W. Rostow to President Lyndon B. Johnson; Meeting with General Eisenhower, 10 August 1967, Folder 30, Box 01, Veteran Members of the 109th Quartermaster Company (Air Delivery) Collection, the Vietnam Center and Archive, Texas Tech University.
91. Momyer testimony to U.S. Senate, 143.
92. Ibid., 143–44.
93. Ibid., 164.
94. "General Momyer Receives Fourth Star," HQ Seventh Air Force, news release, December 14, 1967, K740.951-2, IRIS No. 00527896, USAFHRA.
95. Gen. Gabriel P. Disosway, Commander, TAC, to Gen. William W. Momyer, Commander, Seventh Air Force, Letter, December 8, 1967, 168-7041-3, IRIS No. 01042242, from General Momyer Papers, USAFHRA.
96. Gen. John D. Ryan, Commander in Chief, USAF, to Lt. Gen. William W. Momyer, Commander, Seventh Air Force, Letter, June 26, 1967, 168.7041-3, IRIS No. 01042242, from General Momyer Papers, USAFHRA.
97. Momyer, *Airpower in Three Wars*, 337–40.
98. Ibid., 340–43.
99. Message from General Westmoreland to Admiral Sharp and General Wheeler, AIR CONTROL (SPECAT VOL 1), January 1, 1968, Folder 003, U.S. Marine Corps History Division, Vietnam War Documents Collection, the Vietnam Center and Archive, Texas Tech University.
100. HQ Pacific Air Forces (PACAF), Directorate, Tactical Evaluation, Contemporary Historical Examination of Current Operations (CHECO) Division, "Project CHECO Report: Khe Sanh (Operation Niagara), 22 January–31 March," 1.
101. Message from General Westmoreland to Admiral Sharp and General Wheeler Re: taking operational control of First Marine Air Wing, January 17, 1968, Folder 19,

Box 01, Veteran Members of the 109th Quartermaster Company (Air Delivery) Collection, the Vietnam Center and Archive, Texas Tech University.

102. Momyer, *Airpower in Three Wars*, 345–46.

103. General Westmoreland to Admiral Sharp Re: anticipated enemy attack on Khe Sanh, 21 January 1968, Folder 06, Box 01, Veteran Members of the 109th Quartermaster Company (Air Delivery) Collection, the Vietnam Center and Archive, Texas Tech University.

104. General Cushman to General Westmoreland, 19 February 1968, AIR CONTROL (SPECAT VOL 1), February 1, 1968, Folder 003, U.S. Marine Corps History Division Vietnam War Documents Collection, the Vietnam Center and Archive, Texas Tech University.

105. General Momyer to General Westmoreland, 22 February 1968, AIR CONTROL STUDY, 01 January 1968, Folder 003, U.S. Marine Corps History Division Vietnam War Documents Collection, the Vietnam Center and Archive, Texas Tech University.

106. General Krulak to General Cushman, 22 February 1968, AIR CONTROL (SPECAT VOL 1), February 1, 1968, Folder 003, U.S. Marine Corps History Division Vietnam War Documents Collection, the Vietnam Center and Archive, Texas Tech University.

107. HQ PACAF, Directorate, Tactical Evaluation, CHECO Division, "Project CHECO Report: Single Manager for Air in SVN," March 10, 1969, 6.

108. Khe Sanh Daily Reports to the White House, volume 6, #45-55, February 24 to March 7, 1968 (Part 2), no date, Folder 14, Box 01, Veteran Members of the 109th Quartermaster Company (Air Delivery) Collection, the Vietnam Center and Archive, Texas Tech University.

109. General Krulak to General Cushman, 28 February 1968, AIR CONTROL (SPECAT VOL 1), February 1, 1968, Folder 003, U.S. Marine Corps History Division Vietnam War Documents Collection, the Vietnam Center and Archive, Texas Tech University.

110. Bernard C. Nalty, *Air Power and the Fight for Khe Sanh* (Office of Air Force History, United States Air Force, Washington, D.C., 1986), 74–80.

111. Jack Schulimson et al., *U.S. Marines in Vietnam*, vol. 5, *The Defining Year, 1968* (Washington, DC: History and Museums Division, United States Marine Corps, 1997), 496.

112. HQ PACAF, "Project CHECO Report: Khe Sanh," 1.

113. Ray L. Bowers, *Tactical Airlift* (Office of Air Force History, United States Air Force, Washington, DC, 1983), 315.

114. Ibid.

115. BDM Corporation, *U.S. Defense Logistics Agency - A Study of Strategic Lessons Learned in Vietnam*, vol. 6, *Conduct of the War*, Book 1: *Operational Analysis* (McLean, VA: BDM for U.S. Army, May 9, 1980), part 2, chapter 3, 3–101, in Defense Technical Information Center (DTIC) Technical Reports.

116. Momyer, *Airpower in Three Wars*, 346–47.

117. Westmoreland as quoted in John Schlight, *The War in South Vietnam: The Years of the Offensive, 1965–1968* (Washington, DC: Air Force History and Museums Program, 1999), 285.

118. W. W. Rostow to President Lyndon B. Johnson; Meeting with General Momyer, March 28, 1968, Folder 15, Box 03, Veteran Members of the 109th Quartermaster Company (Air Delivery) Collection, the Vietnam Center and Archive, Texas Tech University.

119. Momyer, *Airpower in Three Wars*, 350–57.
120. As quoted in Scholin, "Momyer and TAC," 33.
121. "Rolling the Thunder," 23.
122. Memo to Secretary McNamara from Harold Brown: Air War In Southeast Asia, March 21, 1968, Folder 05, Box 11, Larry Berman Collection (Presidential Archives Research), the Vietnam Center and Archive, Texas Tech University.
123. Maj. Gen. John C. Giraudo Oral History, by Lt. Col. Charles M. Heltsley, January 8–12, 1985, 427, K239.0512-1630, IRIS No. 1105191, USAFHRA.
124. Gen. William W. Momyer to Gen. Horace M. Wade, letter, January 17, 1977, Momyer Miscellaneous File.
125. Gen. William W. Momyer to Maj. Gen. Woodard E. Davis, Letter, 16 March 1977, Momyer Miscellaneous File.
126. Lt. Gen. Jay T. Robbins Oral History, by Dr. James C. Hasdorff, 24–25 July 1984, 104–5, K239.0512-1593, IRIS No. 1064469, USAFHRA.
127. Col. Ben R. Blair, USAF (Ret.), to Gen. William W. Momyer, Commander, TAC, letter, July 19, 1973; Gen. William W. Momyer, Commander, TAC, to Col. Ben R. Blair, USAF (Ret.), letter, August 28, 1973, 168.7041-67, IRIS No. 100117, from General Momyer Papers, USAFHRA.
128. Gen. William W. Momyer, Commander, TAC, to Lt. Col. J. D. Moore, National War College, letter, October 17, 1970, 168.7041-33, IRIS No. 1001145, from General Momyer Papers, USAFHRA.

8. John W. Vogt: The Easter Offensive and Nixon's War in Vietnam

1. Executive Office Building conversation 700-3, April 3, 1972. All Nixon White House tapes conversations transcribed by the author from the Nixon Presidential Library and Museum in Yorba Linda, CA, unless otherwise noted.
2. Ibid.
3. Haldeman Diaries, April 6, 1972, CD edition, Sony Imagesoft, 1993.
4. Executive Office Building conversation 22-80, April 5, 1972.
5. Executive Office Building conversation 329-13, April 6, 1972.
6. Kissinger-Vogt teleconference (telcon), 1:55 p.m., April 5, 1972. NPMP/HAK Telcons /Box 14.
7. Kissinger-Vogt telcon, 8:37 a.m., April 8, 1972. NPMP/HAK Telcons/Box 14.
8. Gen. John W. Vogt, oral history interview with Edgar F. Puryear, September 9, 1981, U.S. Air Force Oral History Program, 61. Available through USAFHRA.
9. Richard H. Kohn and Joseph P. Harahan, ed., *Air Interdiction in World War II, Korea, and Vietnam: An Interview with Earle E. Partridge, Jacob E. Smart, and John W. Vogt, Jr.* (Washington, DC: Office of Air Force History, 1986), 36–38.
10. This chronology differs from that in Vogt's official biography, which does not include the periods of inactive status and misstates some dates. It is based on a summary compiled by Col. William Goodyear, USAF (Ret.), from Vogt's service records and supplemented by interviews with Vogt's family.
11. This character sketch, and some details of Vogt's World War II experience, is based on interviews with Col. Bill Goodyear, USAF (Ret.), on December 11–12, 2011 in Atlanta.
12. Politburo Cable No. 119, March 27, 1972, "On the Politburo Decision to launch a General Offensive on three fronts—military, political, and diplomatic—to defeat the enemy's 'Vietnamization' policy." Provided and translated by Merle Pribbenow.
13. Dale Andradé's *America's Last Vietnam Battle: Halting Hanoi's 1972 Easter Offensive* (Lawrence: University of Kansas Press, 2001) offers the most comprehensive and ac-

curate account of ground combat in the Easter Offensive and focuses on the role of American advisers in the campaign.

14. Stephen Randolph, in *Powerful and Brutal Weapons: Nixon, Kissinger, and the Easter Offensive* (Cambridge, MA: Harvard University Press, 2007), addresses strategic decision making in Washington and in Hanoi and describes the opening months of the Linebacker air campaign in detail. Wayne Thompson's *To Hanoi and Back: The United States Air Force and North Vietnam, 1966–1973* (Washington, DC: Smithsonian Institution Press, 2000) is the finest single-volume history of USAF operations over North Vietnam yet written.
15. Moorer Diary, NARA, RG 218, April 5, 1972.
16. The account of Vogt's arrival in Saigon and his first months in command is derived from interviews with Col. William Goodyear, USAF (Ret.), on October 14 and 21, 2011 in Washington, D.C.
17. Executive Office Building conversation 700-2, April 3, 1972.
18. See Randolph, *Powerful and Brutal Weapons*, 119–30, for a full account of these early B-52 raids and the confrontation between Nixon and Abrams.
19. Moorer Diary, December 27, 1972.
20. Seventh Air Force working paper, "Application of Air Power in SVN 1 April–31 May 1972." Forwarded from Maj. Gen. Alton Slay to Lt. Gen. George Eade, July 12, 1972, Vogt Papers, Air Force Historical Studies Office (AFHSO), Bolling AFB, Washington, DC.
21. End of tour report, Col. Stanley Umstead, 388 TFW/CC, April 1971–August 1972, 4, USAFHRA, Maxwell AFB, AL.
22. End of tour report, Lt. Col. Lachlan Macleay, 23 TASS/CC, 20, Vogt papers, AFHSO, Bolling AFB, Washington, DC.
23. Paul T. Ringenbach and Peter J. Melly, *The Battle for An Loc, 5 April–26 June 1972* (Hickam AFB, HI: Headquarters Pacific Air Forces (HQ PACAF), Contemporary Historical Examination of Current Operations (CHECO) Division, January 31, 1973), 12.
24. Ibid., 18.
25. Combat Operations Division, General Staff of the People's Army of Vietnam, *History of the Combat Operations Department 1945–2000* (Hanoi: People's Army Publishing House, 2005). Provided and translated by Merle Pribbenow; unpaginated translation.
26. Vogt Situation Report (SITREP), 011115Z May 72, Vogt Papers, AFHSO, Bolling AFB, Washington, DC.
27. Combat Operations Division, *History of the Combat Operations Department.*
28. Vogt SITREP, 091055Z May 72, 7, Vogt Papers, AFHSO, Bolling AFB, Washington, DC.
29. Ibid., 12–13.
30. Executive Office Building conversation 334-44, May 4, 1972.
31. Connally was a Democrat serving as Nixon's secretary of the treasury. Nixon considered him to be his only worthy successor as president.
32. Moorer Diary, May 8, 1972.
33. Ibid.
34. Vogt interview with Claude G. Moritz, January 24, 1973, "Implications of Modern Air Power in a Limited War," PACAF History Office, November 29, 1973, 7–8.
35. See Randolph, *Powerful and Brutal Weapons*, 198–213, for a more detailed description of air force and navy attack tactics. Jeffrey Ethell and Alfred Price's *One Day in a Long War: May 10, 1972, Air War, North Vietnam* (New York: Random House, 1989) provides a vivid and balanced account of the May 10 air battles.

36. Ho Si Huu et al., *History of the Air Defense Service,* vol. 3 (Hanoi: People's Army Publishing House, 1994), 117.
37. Vogt SITREP, 131110Z May 1972, 9, Vogt Papers, AFHSO, Bolling AFB, Washington, DC.
38. Vogt interview with Puryear, 70–75; and author's interview with Col. William Goodyear, USAF (Ret.), October 21, 2011, Washington, DC.
39. Vogt SITREP, 121140Z May 1972, 10, Vogt Papers, AFHSO, Bolling AFB, Washington, DC.
40. Oval Office conversation 726-1, May 19, 1972.
41. See William M. Hammond, *Reporting Vietnam: Media and Military at War* (Lawrence: University Press of Kansas, 1998), 158–290.
42. End of tour report, Col. Charles Gabriel, 432 TRW/CC, April 4, 1971–June 15, 1972, Vogt Papers, AFHSO, Bolling AFB, Washington, DC.
43. Clay began sending messages to Vogt noting deficiencies in the Linebacker missions on May 12, two days after the campaign began, and continued a steady stream of commentary throughout the first weeks of the operation. These messages can be found in Vogt's read file, Vogt Papers, AFHSO, Bolling AFB.
44. Vogt SITREP, 271215Z June 1972, 7, Vogt Papers, AFHSO, Bolling AFB, Washington D.C.
45. For more details, see Randolph, *Powerful and Brutal Weapons,* 309–19.
46. Vogt oral history, by Hugh N. Ahmann, June 10–11, 1985, 210, K239.0512-1652. Lt. Gen. Joseph Moore was Gen. William Momyer's predecessor as commander of the Second Air Division and then Seventh Air Force, serving in that position from 1964 to 1966.
47. Quoted in Pacific Air Forces, *Command History* 1 July 1971–30 June 1972 (Hickam AFB, HI: Office of History, Pacific Command), vol. 2, IV–147.
48. Marshall L. Michel III, *Clashes: Air Combat over North Vietnam, 1965–1972* (Annapolis: Naval Institute Press, 1997), 283–85.
49. Vogt interview, "Implications of Modern Air Power in a Limited War," 12–13.
50. Memorandum from Philip Odeen to Henry Kissinger, "CIA Assessment of the Mining and Bombing," August 12, 1972, NPMP/NSC Files/Vietnam Country Files/Box 161. Reprinted in John Carland, ed., *Foreign Relations of the United States (FRUS), 1969–1976,* vol. 8, *Vietnam, January–October 1972* (Washington, DC: U.S. Government Printing Office, 2010), 827.
51. Moorer to McCain, "Line Backer Targets," 2018Z 6 August 1972. Reprinted in ibid., 815.
52. Calvin R. Johnson, *Linebacker Operations, September–December 1972* (Hickam AFB, HI: HQ PACAF: Project CHECO, 1974), 41–43.
53. Nguyen Van Loi and Nguyen Anh Vu, *Le Duc Tho–Kissinger Negotiations in Paris* (Hanoi: The Goia Press, 1996), 239–40.
54. Message from Haig to Kennedy, Hakto 14, 0115Z December 6, 1972. Reprinted in John Carland, ed., *FRUS, 1969–1976,* vol. 9, *Vietnam, October 1972–January 1973* (Washington, DC: U.S. Government Printing Office, 2010), 528. Haig was in Paris with Kissinger in the negotiation sessions with Le Duc Tho and sent these instructions to his National Security Council staff aide Kennedy for guidance to Moorer.
55. James Reston, "Power Without Pity," *New York Times,* December 19, 1972.
56. Brig. Gen. James R. McCarthy and Lt. Col. George B. Allison, *Linebacker II: A View from the Rock* (Maxwell AFB, AL: Airpower Research Institute, 1979), 27.
57. Ho et al., *History of the Air Defense Service,* 3:184–88.
58. PACAF, *1972 Command History,* 2:IV-308.

59. Johnson, *Linebacker Operations*, 68.
60. PACAF, *1972 Command History*, 2:IV-304.
61. Paul W. Elder, *Air Operations in the Khmer Republic, 1 December 1971–15 August 1973.* (Hickham AFB, HI: HQ PACAF: Project CHECO, April 15, 1974). Accessed through the Vietnam Center, http://www.vietnam.ttu.edu/virtualarchive/items .php?item=0390101001.
62. Vogt interview with Puryear, 28–37.
63. Ibid., 41–44.
64. William Shawcross, *Sideshow: Kissinger, Nixon and the Destruction of Cambodia* (New York: Simon & Schuster, 1979). Vogt's response was printed as an appendix in the second volume of Kissinger's memoirs.
65. John W. Vogt Jr., "A Commander's View of the Vietnam War," in *The Vietnam Debate: A Fresh Look at the Arguments*, ed. John Norton Moore (Lanham, MD: University Press of America, 1990), 183–92.
66. PACAF, *1972 Command History*, 2:IV-146 to IV-158.

9. Charles A. Horner: Desert Storm Maestro

1. Remarks of President George H. W. Bush, Air Force Academy, Colorado Springs, CO, May 29, 1991, in *Weekly Compilation of Presidential Documents* (Washington, DC: Executive Office of the President, June 3, 1991), 683–86.
2. Gen. H. Norman Schwarzkopf, memorandum through chief of staff, U.S. Air Force [Gen. Merrill A. McPeak] for Secretary of the Air Force [Hon. Dr. Donald Rice], Subject: Commander Evaluation—Lt. Gen. Charles A. Horner (August 9, 1991), 1, copy in office files of the SecAF Staff Group, Headquarters Air Force, Pentagon. I thank General Horner for permission to quote from it. See also Lt. Gen. Michael A. Nelson, USAF, "Aerospace Forces and Power Projection," in *The Future of Air Power in the Aftermath of the Gulf War*, ed. Richard H. Shultz, Jr., and Robert L. Pfaltzgraff (Maxwell AFB, AL: Air University Press, 1992), 120, who called Horner "the quarterback for all the air players in the Gulf."
3. Gen. Sir Peter de la Billière, *Storm Command: A Personal Account of the Gulf War* (London: HarperCollins, 1992), 43, 205.
4. Conversation with Horner by the author in Horner's home, December 12, 2011. Tom Clancy has written a book about the war that includes an excellent biography in association with Horner, *Every Man a Tiger* (New York: G. P. Putnam's Sons, 1999). The author has also benefited from a lengthy missive, which is in the author's possession (hereafter cited as Horner to Hallion, June 1, 2011).
5. Horner to Hallion, June 1, 2011.
6. Clancy and Horner, *Every Man a Tiger*, 46.
7. Ibid., 52.
8. Ibid., 54. Horner continues to practice a quiet faith that infuses his daily life.
9. See Jack Broughton, *Thud Ridge* (Philadelphia: J. B. Lippincott, 1969); Ed Rasimus, *When Thunder Rolled: An F-105 Pilot over North Vietnam* (New York: Ballantine Books, 2003); and Kenneth Werrell, *Archie, Flak, AAA, and SAM: A Short Operational History of Ground-Based Air Defense* (Maxwell AFB, AL: Air University Press, 1988), 102.
10. "Oral History: Charles Horner," *Frontline: The Gulf War* PBS-WGBH (January 9, 1996), http://www.pbs.org/wgbh/pages/frontline/gulf/oral/horner/1.html (accessed August 10, 2011).
11. "We are considering air action against [North Vietnam] as the means to a limited

objective—the improvement of our bargaining position with the North Vietnamese." George W. Ball, "How Valid Are the Assumptions Underlying Our Viet-Nam Policies?" *Atlantic Monthly* 230 (October 5, l964): 38.

12. Lt. Col. Mark Clodfelter, USAF, *The Limits of Air Power: The American Bombing of North Vietnam* (New York: Free Press, 1989), 121; and John T. Correll, "Rolling Thunder," *Air Force Magazine* 88, no. 3 (March 2005): 61–63.

13. Correll, "Rolling Thunder," 63.

14. Edward J. Drea, *McNamara, Clifford, and the Burdens of Vietnam, 1965–1969* (Washington, DC: Office of the Secretary of Defense, 2011), 82; and Vietnam Task Force, *United States–Vietnam Relations, 1945–1967*, vol. 4, C.3, *Evolution of the War: The Rolling Thunder Program Begins, January–June 1965* (Washington, DC: Office of the Secretary of Defense, 1969), 100, 135, 139. See U.S. National Archives and Records Administration website, http://www.archives.gov/research/pentagon-papers (accessed December 27, 2011).

15. John T. Correll, "Disunity of Command," *Air Force Magazine* 88, no. 1 (January 2005): 34; Wayne Thompson, *To Hanoi and Back: The United States Air Force and North Vietnam, 1966–1973* (Washington, DC: Smithsonian Institution Press, 2000); and C. R. Anderegg, *Sierra Hotel: Flying Air Force Fighters in the Decade after Vietnam* (Washington, DC: Air Force History and Museums Program, 2001), 181.

16. Al Santoli, *Leading the Way—How Vietnam Veterans Rebuilt the U.S. Military: An Oral History* (New York: Ballantine Books, 1993), 20.

17. Ibid., 21.

18. Horner to Hallion, June 1, 2011.

19. For the Weasel program, see John T. Correll, "Take It Down! The Wild Weasels in Vietnam," *Air Force Magazine* 93, no. 7 (July 2010): 66–69; and Larry Davis, *Wild Weasel: The SAM Suppression Story* (Carrollton, TX: Squadron/Signal Publications, 1986), 3–13. Initially the F-100F was employed, but it proved only an interim solution.

20. Rolling Thunder cost 171 aircraft in 1965 and 318 in 1966. In the last week of April 1967 alone, the United States lost 16. See Vietnam Task Force, *United States–Vietnam Relations, 1945–1967*, vol. 4, C.7(a), *Evolution of the War: Air War in the North, 1965–1968* (Washington, DC: Office of the Secretary of Defense, 1969), 1:178, http://www.archives.gov/research/pentagon-papers (accessed December 27, 2011); John M. Granville, *Summary of USAF Aircraft Losses in SEA*, Report 7409 (Langley Air Force Base, VA: HQ Tactical Air Command, June 1974), tables 2, 4, 6, 15; Marcelle Size Knaack, *Encyclopedia of U.S. Air Force Aircraft and Missile Systems*, vol. 1, *Post-World War II Fighters, 1945–1973* (Washington, DC: Office of Air Force History, 1978), 204; and Stuart I. Rochester and Frederick T. Kiley, *Honor Bound: American Prisoners of War in Southeast Asia, 1961–1973* (Washington, DC: Office of the Secretary of Defense, 1998).

21. See U.S. Congress, Senate, Preparedness Investigation Subcommittee of the Committee on Armed Services, *Air War Against North Vietnam*, 90th Cong., 1st sess. (Washington, DC: U.S. Government Printing Office, 1967); Vietnam Task Force, *United States–Vietnam Relations, 1945–1967*, vol. 4, C.7(b) *Evolution of the War: Air War in the North, 1965–1968* (Washington, DC: Office of the Secretary of Defense, 1969), 2: 90–99 and 98–99, http://www.archives.gov/research/pentagon-papers/ (accessed December 27, 2011); and "The War: Into Exile," *Time* 90, no. 18 (November 3, 1967).

22. Horner to Hallion, June 1, 2011.

23. Other veterans of the Southeast Asia war share this view. See Colin L. Powell with

Joseph E. Persico, *My American Journey* (New York: Random House, 1995), 464; Douglas Kinnard, *The War Managers: American Generals Reflect on Vietnam* (New York: Da Capo Press, 1991), 25 and 75; and H. R. McMaster, *Dereliction of Duty: Lyndon Johnson, Robert McNamara, the Joint Chiefs of Staff, and the Lies that Led to Vietnam* (New York: HarperCollins, 1998).

24. See Donald J. Mrozek, *The U.S. Air Force after Vietnam: Postwar Challenges and Potential for Responses* (Maxwell AFB, AL: Air University Press, 1988); and Benjamin S. Lambeth, *The Transformation of American Air Power* (Ithaca, NY: Cornell University Press in association with the Rand Corporation, 2000).

25. U.S. Air Force, "Biography: General William Wallace Momyer," http://www.af.mil/information/bios/bio.asp?bioID=6504 (accessed August 8, 2011); and Horner to Hallion, June 1, 2011. He also wrote an influential memoir-history on air power; see William W. Momyer, *Air Power in Three Wars* (Maxwell AFB, AL: Air University Press, 1978), 337–39.

26. Creech assumed command in 1978, replacing Gen. Robert Dixon, who had replaced General Momyer in 1973. U.S. Air Force, "Biography: General Wilbur L. 'Bill' Creech," http://www.af.mil/information/bios/bio.asp?bioID=5110, (accessed August 8, 2011); and "Retired Gen. Creech, 'Father of the Thunderbirds,' Dies," *Las Vegas Sun*, August 28, 2003.

27. Lt. Col. James C. Slife, *Creech Blue: Gen. Bill Creech and the Reformation of the Tactical Air Force, 1978–1984* (Maxwell AFB, AL: Air University Press, 2004), 1.

28. Horner returned to the Fourth TFW at Seymour Johnson as deputy commander of operations. For his career, see U.S. Air Force, "Biography: General Charles A. Horner," http://www.af.mil/information/bios/bio.asp?bioID=5859, (accessed August 8, 2011).

29. Clancy and Horner, *Every Man a Tiger*, 148.

30. Horner to Hallion June 1, 2011; and Juliet V. Casey, "Wilbur Creech, Retired Air Force General, Dies," *Review Journal*, August 28, 2003, http://www.reviewjournal.com/lvrj_home/2003/Aug-28-Thu-2003/news/22036248.html.

31. Horner to Hallion, June 1, 2011.

32. Ibid. See also Slife, *Creech Blue*, 86–93.

33. Horner to Hallion, June 1, 2011.

34. He replaced Lt. Gen. Merrill A. "Tony" McPeak, who left to command the Twelfth Air Force (and who was air force chief of staff during Desert Storm).

35. Horner to Hallion, December 12, 2011.

36. Horner to Hallion, June 1, 2011.

37. Horner to Hallion, December 12, 2011. I also thank Ron "Buffalo" Hoerter, who flew with Horner, for his confirmatory insights.

38. For contemporary perspectives, see Osman A. Eisa, *Iran-Iraq War (Background, Development, and Regional Responses)*, AU-AWC-86-165 (Maxwell AFB, AL: Air University Press, 1986), 20–21; Maj. Gen. Davis C. Rohr, "Forging New Paths of Military Planning: Challenges of the Middle East/Persian Gulf," in *Military Planning in the Twentieth Century: Proceedings of the Eleventh Military History Symposium, 10–12 October 1984*, ed. Lt. Col. Harry R. Borowski (Washington, DC: Office of Air Force History, 1986), 416–22; Michael A. Palmer, *On Course to Desert Storm: The United States Navy and the Persian Gulf* (Washington, DC: U.S. Naval Historical Center, 1992), 103–46; and Caspar W. Weinberger, *Fighting for Peace: Seven Critical Years in the Pentagon* (New York: Warner Books, 1990), 410–20.

39. Diane T. Putney, *Airpower Advantage: Planning the Gulf War Air Campaign, 1989–1991* (Washington, DC: Air Force History and Museums Program, 2005), 1–3. Other components were ARCENT (army), NAVCENT (navy), MARCENT

(USMC), and SOCCENT (joint service).

40. The JFACC concept dated to March 1986 and the establishment of a JCS-directed joint doctrine for theater counterair operations. The JFACC was more than an "air boss"; he was charged to develop a "conops" to fulfill the objectives that the joint force commander established. See David E. Thaler and David A. Shlapak, *Perspectives on Theater Air Campaign Planning*, Report MR-515-AF (Santa Monica, CA: Rand Corporation, 1995), 16.

41. Horner to Hallion, June 1, 2011.

42. Ibid.

43. Gen. H. Norman Schwarzkopf with Peter Petrie, *It Doesn't Take a Hero* (New York: Bantam, 1992), 282–83.

44. Horner to Hallion, June 1, 2011; emphasis in original.

45. Conversation with Lornie Palmgren, Ft. Walton Beach, FL, January 7, 2012. At the time Palmgren was an air force major and SOCCENT liaison officer.

46. Transcript of interview of Lieutenant General Horner by Lt. Col. Suzanne Gehri and Lt. Col. Rich Reynolds (December 2, 1991), 5, Cat. No. K239.0472–493, Air Force Historical Research Agency, Maxwell AFB, AL (hereafter cited as Horner Interview 1).

47. Transcript of interview of Lieutenant General Horner by Barry Jamison, Richard Davis, and Barry Barlow (March 4, 1992), 13, Cat. No. K239.0472-94, Air Force Historical Research Agency, Maxwell AFB, AL (hereafter cited as Horner Interview 2).

48. Ibid., 11.

49. Ibid.

50. Horner Interview 1, 2–3. See also Horner Interview 2, 11–12, for additional detail.

51. Putney, *Airpower Advantage*, 18.

52. For TACWAR, see Francis P. Hoeber, *Military Applications of Modeling: Selected Case Studies* (New York: Gordon and Breach Science Publishers, 1982), 132–38; Lt. Col. Steve McNamara, USAF, "Assessing Airpower's Importance: Will the *QDR* Debate Falter for Lack of Proper Analytical Tools?," *Armed Forces Journal International*, March 1997, 36–37; and the following reports available from the Defense Technical Information Center (http://www.dtic.mil): John C. Ingram, "A Detailed Review of the TACWAR Model," Report HDL-TM-80-15 (Adelphi, MD: U.S. Army Harry Diamond Laboratories, December 1980), DTIC Accession ADA101134; Lowell Bruce Anderson, "A J-8 TACWAR Ground Combat Attrition Primer," Paper P-2549 (Alexandria, VA: Institute for Defense Analyses, July 1991), DTIC Accession ADA245435; and Maj. James E. Parker, USAF, "Experiments in Aggregating Air Ordinance [*sic*] Effectiveness Data for the TACWAR Model," Thesis AFIT/GOA/ENS/97M-12 (Wright-Patterson AFB, OH: Air Force Institute of Technology, 1997), DTIC Accession ADA324076. I thank Lt. Gen. David Deptula, USAF (Ret.), for further insights.

53. Horner to Hallion, June 1, 2011; emphasis in original.

54. "Jointness has been difficult to achieve because the reluctance of Services to cede prerogatives to another service," Horner wrote to the author. "This is because doctrine is written by non-combatants in service headquarters or the Joint Staff, while battle demands joint cooperation, or the consequences may range from a needless loss of life to defeat. The extent that warriors learn to exploit the capabilities of new technologies and integrate the efforts of land, sea, air and space forces depends on their training during peacetime" (Horner to Hallion, June 1, 2011). Horner was not opposed to doctrine, but he felt that it should be relevant and appropriate. "Doctrine made sense when I was a young fighter pilot," he once said to the author, "because it was just a few pages long and comprehensible."

55. "The JFACC concept works," Horner told an army audience. "Consistency and unity

in guidance reduce coordination conflicts. Operating under one coordinated plan improved efficiency and lessens the possibility of fratricide." See Lt. Gen. Charles A. Horner, USAF, "The Air Campaign," *Military Review* 71, no. 9 (September 1991): 26.

56. Dick Cheney with Liz Cheney, *In My Time: A Personal and Political Memoir* (New York: Threshold Editions, 2011), 425. For other accounts, see Powell and Persico, *My American Journey*, 132–33; Bob Woodward, *The Commanders* (New York: Simon & Schuster, 1992), 233–34; and Putney, *Airpower Advantage*, 24.

57. George H. W. Bush and Brent Scowcroft, *A World Transformed* (New York: Alfred A. Knopf, 1998), 334.

58. Clancy and Horner, *Every Man a Tiger*, 165.

59. Schwarzkopf and Petrie, *It Doesn't Take a Hero*, 300; and Bush and Scowcroft, *A World Transformed*, 327.

60. Bush and Scowcroft, *A World Transformed*, 321.

61. Ibid., 325; Cheney and Cheney, *In My Time*, 187; and Powell and Persico, *An American Life*, 465.

62. Schwarzkopf and Petrie, *It Doesn't Take a Hero*, 305.

63. Quoted in Clancy and Horner, *Every Man a Tiger*, 185. See also Cheney and Cheney, *In My Time*, 190–91.

64. Margaret Thatcher, *The Downing Street Years* (London: HarperCollins, 1995), 820–23. Many other British aircraft followed, including Buccaneer strike aircraft, Nimrod maritime patrol aircraft, and VC-10K tankers.

65. Schwarzkopf and Petrie, *It Doesn't Take a Hero*, 312.

66. Keith A. Hutcheson, *Air Mobility: The Evolution of Global Reach* (Vienna, VA: Point One and VII Publishing in association with USAF Air Mobility Command, September 1999), 71.

67. Horner, "The Air Campaign," 19.

68. Schwarzkopf and Petrie, *It Doesn't Take a Hero*, 351.

69. Capt. Rob A. Scofidio, USAF, "Transportation and Maintenance at King Fahd," in *From the Line in the Sand: Accounts of USAF Company Grade Officers in Support of Desert Shield/Desert Storm*, ed. Capt. Michael P. Vriesenga, USAF (Maxwell AFB, AL: Air University Press, 1994), 62.

70. Horner Interview 2, 22; emphasis in original.

71. Horner to Hallion, June 1, 2011.

72. Horner Interview 2, 26, 73. Horner worked closely with the ARCENT, Lt. Gen. John Yeosock, a War College classmate and friend. Other intimates were Adm. Grant Sharp (CENTCOM's director of plans); Maj. Gen. Don Kaufman (chief of the U.S. training mission to Saudi Arabia); Maj. Gen. John Corder (Horner's deputy commander for operations); Planning Chief Buster Glosson; Colonels Tom Olson, William Rider, Jim Crigger, Al Doman, Mike Grevey, and Charlie Hoss; and Lieutenant Colonels David Deptula, Sam Baptiste, Clyde "Joe Bob" Phillips, Dave Waters, and Jeffrey "Fang" Feinstein.

73. "Tensions between the Air Force and American ground commanders persisted," Keaney and Cohen conclude, "because the commanders did not understand that many decisions causing them problems were Schwarzkopf's and not Horner's." See Thomas A. Keaney and Eliot A. Cohen, *Gulf War Air Power Survey Summary Report* (Washington, DC: U.S. Government Printing Office, 1993), 152–53, 155. See also Eliot A. Cohen, *Gulf War Air Power Survey*, vol. 2, *Part I: Operations* (Washington, DC: U.S. Government Printing Office, 1993), 257; Rick Atkinson, *Crusade: The Untold Story of the Persian Gulf War* (Boston: Houghton Mifflin, 1993), 338–40; and Thaler and Shlapak, *Perspectives on Theater Air Campaign Planning*, 17. Late in

the war, the XVIII Airborne Corps shifted the fire support coordination line (FSCL) beyond the Euphrates to enable army gunships to operate without having to integrate with the JFACC and ATO. The action aided, rather than hindered, the escape of Iraqi forces, for the gunships did not show, and the fighters could not operate. Horner "hit the ceiling," and Schwarzkopf (not having known of the change) ordered the FSCL shifted back. See Perry D. Jamieson, *Lucrative Targets: The U.S. Air Force in the Kuwaiti Theater of Operations* (Washington, DC: Air Force History and Museums Program, 2001), 157–58.

74. Horner to Hallion, June 1, 2011.

75. Ibid. Arthur, an A-4 pilot, had completed more than five hundred combat missions over SEA, for which he received no less than eleven Distinguished Flying Crosses and fifty-one Air Medals.

76. Horner Interview 2, 13; Schwarzkopf and Petrie, *It Doesn't Take a Hero*, 313, 320; Clancy and Horner, *Every Man a Tiger*, 186–87; and Putney, *Airpower Advantage*, 32–43. The chief, Gen. Michael Dugan, was out of town. Secretary of Defense Dick Cheney subsequently dismissed Dugan after he discussed with reporters how air power could defeat Iraq and replaced him with Tony McPeak. See Cheney and Cheney, *In My Time*, 186–87; and Powell and Persico, *An American Life*, 476–78. The offending article was Rick Atkinson's "U.S. to Rely on Air Strikes if War Erupts," *Washington Post*, September 16, 1990, 1.

77. For Warden, see David R. Mets, *The Air Campaign: John Warden and the Classical Airpower Theorists* (Maxwell AFB, AL: Air University Press, 1999); and John Andreas Olsen, *John Warden and the Renaissance of American Air Power* (Washington, DC: Potomac Books, 2007).

78. Putney, *Airpower Advantage*, 55.

79. Instant Thunder is examined in Putney's *Airpower Advantage* and Olsen's *John Warden*, so it is not reviewed here.

80. Horner Interview 1 discusses this issue. See also Clancy and Horner, *Every Man a Tiger*; Olsen, *John Warden*; Putney, *Airpower Advantage*; Richard T. Reynolds, *Heart of the Storm: The Genesis of the Air Campaign against Iraq* (Maxwell AFB, AL: Air University Press, 1995); and Frederick W. Kagan, *Finding the Target: The Transformation of American Military Policy* (New York: Encounter Books, 2006), 132–35.

81. Horner Interview 1, 34.

82. Ibid.

83. Horner Interview 2, 14. Horner concluded Warden was "a genius" and "a superb targeteer" but also felt he was "out of touch with reality" and unable to translate a target strategy into an executable plan.

84. Buster Glosson, *War with Iraq: Critical Lessons* (Charlotte, NC: Glosson Family Foundation, 2003), 1–3.

85. Horner Interview 1, 35. For Glosson, see RAAF air commodore Gary Waters, "Master of Air Power—General Buster Glosson," in *Masters of Air Power: The Proceedings of the 2005 RAAF History Conference*, ed. Wing Commander Keith Brent (Canberra: RAAF Air Power Development Centre, 2005), 147.

86. Glosson, *War with Iraq*, 15.

87. Ibid., 10.

88. Ibid., 7, 13. Glosson was ably assisted by Brig. Gen. Larry Henry, an expert on defeating air defense networks. General Russ sent him to help Horner. Of the Warden team, Lt. Col. David A. Deptula most influenced the campaign, with Glosson finding him "invaluable, way up in the top 1% of officers . . . a thinker and a doer."

89. Horner, "The Air Campaign," 20.

90. As subsequently discussed.
91. Keaney and Cohen, *Summary Report*, 147, note that "Horner tailored the Tactical Air Control System for the task at hand in ways that made some of his staff uncomfortable." True, but any organization has its share of malcontents. Horner's intimates and, more important, his chief—Schwarzkopf—were quite content with his decision making.
92. Glosson, *War with Iraq*, 15. Horner's directive to Glosson was hardly unique. As Lt. Col. Joe Bob Phillips, a Fighter Weapons School expert sent at Glosson's request to the Gulf to help work battlefield air support issues, put it in his notes, "'Figure it out, shithead, that's your job' is a phrase I'm getting accustomed to from General Horner." See Clancy and Horner, *Every Man a Tiger*, 499; and Eliot A. Cohen, *Gulf War Air Power Survey*, vol. 1, *Part 1: Planning* (Washington, DC: U.S. Government Printing Office, 1993), particularly chapter 3, which examines Horner's decentralization and delegation leadership style in detail.
93. In December 1990, Horner designated Glosson (by then a major general) as commander of the Fourteenth Air Division, encompassing all of the USAF fighter forces in the Gulf.
94. Glosson, *War with Iraq*, 15–16.
95. Horner to Hallion, June 1, 2011.
96. After the war, trying to find a framework within which they could evaluate the air war, Watts and Keaney noted, "Upon reflection *it became less and less obvious that what had worked well for thinking about large-scale land warfare in the past could be just as readily applied to air warfare in the present or the future*" [emphasis added]. See Eliot A. Cohen, *Gulf War Air Power Survey*, vol. 2, *Part II: Effects and Effectiveness* (Washington, DC: U.S. Government Printing Office, 1993), 7.
97. The "Black Hole" was the planning cell Glosson had established.
98. Horner to Hallion, June 1, 2011. See also Glosson, *War with Iraq*, 29–30.
99. Horner to Hallion, June 1, 2011.
100. As Saudi Arabia's Gen. Khaled bin Sultan, commander of Saudi Joint Forces, put it, "I recognized that the air campaign was very nearly an all-American show, but I wanted to be sure that I knew 100 percent what was going on." He added, "It was inevitable that the command structure of the air campaign should reflect American supremacy." See Khaled bin Sultan, with Patrick Searle, *Desert Warrior: A Personal View of the Gulf War by the Joint Forces Commander* (New York: HarperCollins, 1995), 325, 338; and Schwarzkopf and Petrie, *It Doesn't Take a Hero*, 329–31.
101. Horner Interview 2, 68; and Horner and Clancy, *Every Man a Tiger*, 196–98. The Saudis preserved "face" by rationalizing that they were "soldiers," not "women."
102. Alan Clark, *Diaries: In Power, 1985–1992* (London: Phoenix, 1994), 331–32.
103. Alan Munro, *Arab Storm: Politics and Diplomacy Behind the Gulf War* (London: I. B. Tauris, 2006), 83.
104. Billière, *Storm Command*, 84–87, 114.
105. Horner to Hallion, June 1, 2011.
106. Ibid.
107. Discussed in depth in Jamieson's *Lucrative Targets*.
108. "General Plots Saddam's Downfall Step-by-Step," *Daily Telegraph*, December 13, 2002, http://www.telegraph.co.uk/news/worldnews/northamerica/usa/1416065/General-plots-Saddams-downfall-step-by-step.html (accessed October 12, 2011). Wafiq al-Samarri defected in 1994, making his way to London, where he met Horner.
109. Emphasis added. Schwarzkopf wanted to target the deployed Republican Guard be-

cause he saw it as the logical "center of gravity" that had to be weakened before he launched his ground offensive. Warden wanted to target sources of Hussein's political power rather than its fielded army, but the source of his political power *was* the Republican Guard. Therefore, by targeting the Republican Guard, the Coalition was targeting what Hussein held most dear—namely, his hold on power—fulfilling both men's goals. Thus, as Horner commented to the author, "Both Schwarzkopf and Warden did the right thing, but each for the wrong reasons."

110. Powell and Persico, *My American Journey*, 484.
111. As fully developed, it involved a four-phase campaign, with some overlap: Phase 1, Strategic Air Campaign; Phase 2, Air Superiority in the KTO; Phase 3, Preparation of the Battlefield; and Phase 4, Ground Attack.
112. Schwarzkopf and Petrie, *It Doesn't Take a Hero*, 354.
113. Glosson, *War with Iraq*, 45.
114. Putney, *Airpower Advantage*, 221. Coincidentally, also on October 10, a Rand study team headed by David Ochmanek briefed air force secretary Donald Rice, CSAF-select McPeak, acting CSAF Loh, and other officials on the projected Iraqi campaign. It stressed that Iraq's fielded military forces would have to be heavily attacked from the air, thus confirming Horner and Glosson's view (and that of Schwarzkopf as well) of what needed to be done.
115. Glosson, *War with Iraq*, 59. To Horner, "Powell was terrified of [the air campaign plan] because it made the air campaign *the campaign*. It promised success and put the role of the ground forces as a supporting element" [emphasis in original]. See Horner Interview 2, 16.
116. Glosson, *War with Iraq*, 58–59.
117. Cheney and Cheney, *In My Time*, 199.
118. Schwarzkopf and Petrie, *It Doesn't Take a Hero*, 356–61.
119. Horner Interview 2, 19.
120. Bush and Scowcroft, *A World Transformed*, 381; emphasis added.
121. Ibid.
122. Cheney and Cheney, *In My Time*, 198, 200. Afterward he asked Paul Wolfowitz to explore an end run known as the "Western Excursion."
123. Schwarzkopf and Petrie, *It Doesn't Take a Hero*, 362. Schwarzkopf gained the extra ground forces with deployment of the VII Corps in November.
124. Glosson, *War with Iraq*, 105–6. The "kill box" was devised by Lt. Col. (later Maj. Gen.) Rick Lewis. See also Cohen, *Gulf War Air Power Survey*, vol. 2, Part II, 266.
125. Ibid., 109.
126. William Andrews, "Gulf War Journal (I)," *Code One* 6, no. 4 (January 1992): 10.
127. Bush and Scowcroft, *A World Transformed*, 447–48.
128. Clancy and Horner, *Every Man a Tiger*, 339. Horner's forty-two anticipated only USAF losses (which actually totaled fourteen). Coalition losses totaled thirty-eight. See Eliot A. Cohen, *Gulf War Air Power Survey*, vol. 5, *A Statistical Compendium and Chronology* (Washington, DC: U.S. Government Printing Office, 1993), table 205, 651.
129. Clancy and Horner, *Every Man a Tiger*, 339–40.
130. Glosson, *War with Iraq*, 120–21.
131. For aircrew reflections, see Vriesenga, *From the Line in the Sand*, 177–247.
132. Clancy and Horner, *Every Man a Tiger*, 341.
133. Equating to a loss rate of 0.79 aircraft lost per 1,000 sorties. Compare this number to the March 1944 RAF night raid on Nuremberg, where a roughly equivalent-size force experienced a loss rate of 139 airplanes lost per 1,000 sorties while basically

attacking a single aim point.

134. Schwarzkopf and Petrie, *It Doesn't Take a Hero*, 415.

135. Billière, *Storm Command*, 205, 212.

136. "Tanks Will Not Save the Day," *Isvestiya*, January 21, 1991.

137. Cohen, *Gulf War Air Power Survey*, vol. 2, *Part II*, 271.

138. Group Captain Andrew P. N. Lambert, RAF, *The Psychology of Air Power* (London: Royal United Services Institute for Defence Studies, 1994), 59–69.

139. Cohen, *Gulf War Air Power Survey*, vol. 2, *Part II*, 264, 381. While some armor clashes did occur (such as 73 Easting), a USMC analysis found in a "typical ground engagement the Iraqi tanks were stationary, there was no sign of Iraqi soldiers, except those surrendering, and the Iraqi tanks were not firing." See Cohen, *Gulf War Air Power Survey*, vol. 2, *Part II*, 263, citing USMC Battlefield Assessment Team, *Armor/Anti-armor Operations in Southwest Asia*, Research Paper No. 92-0002 (Quantico, VA: USMC Research Center, July 1991), 18. For a contrary view, see Stephen Biddle, "Victory Misunderstood: What the Gulf War Tells Us about the Future of Conflict," *International Security* 21, no. 2 (Fall 1996).

140. Statistics from Gen. Merrill A. McPeak, "Desert Storm: The Air Campaign," DOD News Briefing, Pentagon, Washington, DC, March 15, 1991, reprinted in Merrill A. McPeak, *Selected Works: 1990–1994* (Maxwell AFB, AL: Air University Press, 1995), figure 14, 31.

141. Quote from John Major, *John Major: The Autobiography* (London: HarperCollins, 1999), 231. See also Cheney and Cheney, *In My Time*, 220; and Judith Miller, William Broad, and Stephen Engelberg, *Germs: Biological Weapons and America's Secret War* (New York: Simon & Schuster, 2001), 121.

142. Postwar investigation revealed Iraq produced 11,800 liters of concentrated botulinum and 8,575 liters of anthrax in 1990, up to the onset of the Gulf War. Iraq tested 122mm artillery rockets filled with BW in 1990 and, at the end of that year, began filling 150 bombs and 50 warheads with BW, developing as well a spray tank for aircraft that could dispense up to 2,000 liters of anthrax onto a target. See "Continuing Threat from Weapons of Mass Destruction," Statement for the Record by Dr. Gordon C. Oehler, director, Nonproliferation Center, to the Senate Armed Services Committee, March 27, 1996, https://www.cia.gov/news-information/speeches-testimony/1996/go_toc_032796.html#iraq-s-biological-warfare (accessed January 21, 2012).

143. Some analysts forecast bombing might release 10 percent of spores, but subsequent study indicated at most the release might be 0.1 percent, or a hundredth of the larger figure. See Miller et. al., *Germs*, 114–15, 121–22.

144. Statement by Horner on *Frontline*.

145. Horner to Hallion, December 12, 2011. See also Major, *John Major*, 231. Not all sites were attacked, and CBW troops hid much of their stock. The prospect of a massive U.S. retaliatory effort apparently also factored into Iraq's decision not to use battlefield CBW.

146. Afterward, he recalled, "interceptors could have caused havoc. If they had a MiG-21 inside one of the refueling tracks, can you imagine what that would have done to us?" Horner Interview 1, 59.

147. Gen. Charles A. Horner, "New Era Warfare," in *The War in the Air, 1914–1994*, ed. Alan Stephens (Maxwell AFB, AL: Air University Press, in cooperation with the RAAF Aerospace Centre, 2001), 371.

148. Ibid.

149. Horner to Hallion, June 1, 2011.

150. Cheney did not hesitate to intervene over the threat Scuds posed to Coalition unity. But usually he stayed clear, consistent with the comment in his memoirs: "The execution of this war would be in the hands of the generals." See Cheney and Cheney, *In My Time*, 206.
151. Horner to Hallion, June 1, 2011.
152. Ibid.
153. Ibid.
154. Glosson, *War with Iraq*, 26.
155. Ibid., 84. Of McConnell, Glosson wrote, "He will never know how important he has been and will be to our overall success." After the war, Keaney and Cohen rightly concluded, "The Washington bypass violated formal channels, but it worked. Operations planners got expert intelligence more rapidly than otherwise might have been the case." See Keaney and Cohen, *Summary Report*, 133, 130–31, 148; and Putney, *Airpower Advantage*, 283–86.
156. Horner to Hallion, June 1, 2011.
157. Putney, *Airpower Advantage*, 277.
158. Cohen, *Gulf War Air Power Survey*, vol. 2, Part II, 262–64; Jamieson, *Lucrative Targets*, 81–85; and Glosson, *War with Iraq*, 187–89.
159. As Watts and Murray note, "In the final analysis, much of the bean counting entirely missed the point. The number of tanks, vehicles, trucks, and artillery pieces destroyed did not determine whether the Iraqi Army would fight or even how well it would fight. . . . The impact of the air war depended, to a great extent, on psychological imponderables, and such uncertainties are not congenial to staff officers or to those statistical managers that have so bedeviled American military and intelligence agencies over the past twenty years." Cohen, *Gulf War Air Power Survey*, vol. 2, *Part II*, 264.
160. Horner to Hallion, June 1, 2011.
161. Glosson, *War with Iraq*, 219.
162. Ibid., 220.
163. Clancy and Horner, *Every Man a Tiger*, 364.
164. Horner to Hallion, June 1, 2011. About the CENTCOM lawyer, see Horner Interview 1, 55.
165. Horner to Hallion, June 1, 2011.
166. Ibid. Losses were two F-15Es and eight Tornados. A ninth Tornado was later lost but at medium altitude from an undetected SA-2 launch. See Cohen, *Gulf War Air Power Survey*, vol. 5, table 205, 651.
167. Horner to Hallion, June 1, 2011.
168. Quoted in Capt. Keith E. Kennedy, "Geeks Go to War: Programming Under Fire," in Vriesenga, *From the Line in the Sand*, 80.
169. Horner, "The Air Campaign," 22.
170. In Major's *John Major*, 235, he marveled how "each aircrew had to follow [it] to the second," their operations being "most successfully achieved."
171. The computer system was called the Computer-Assisted Force Management System. For a detailed discussion of its functioning by an associated programmer, see Kennedy, "Geeks Go to War," 74–80.
172. Horner, "The Air Campaign," 23.
173. Horner to Hallion, June 1, 2011.
174. Adding later, "Beware of generals making short notice decisions."
175. Horner to Hallion, June 1, 2011. It is worth noting that he held these views even

after General Dugan's press encounter had led to his dismissal as air force chief of staff.

176. Lt. Gen. David Goldfein, USAF, "An Iraqi End-of-Mission Message," *Air Force Print News*, January 5, 2012, http://www.afcent.af.mil/news/story_print.asp?id=123285128 (accessed January 19, 2012). I thank Lieutenant General Goldfein and his staff for their assistance to my research.

177. See Lt. Gen. Thomas S. Moorman Jr., "Space: A New Strategic Frontier," *Airpower History* 6, no. 1 (Spring 1992): 19–20; David N. Spires, *Beyond Horizons: A Half Century of Air Force Space Leadership* (Peterson AFB, CO: Air Force Space Command, 1997), 243–62; and Lt. Col. Michael W. Kometer, USAF, "Command in Air War: Centralized vs. Decentralized Control of Combat Airpower" (Ph.D. diss., Massachusetts Institute of Technology, May 2005), 90–91.

178. Charles A. Horner, "Rethinking National Security Strategy," Air Force Association Symposium, Colorado Springs, CO (May 24, 1996), http://www.afa.org/aef/pub/cs3.asp (accessed September 17, 2011).

179. Horner to Hallion, June 1, 2010.

180. "I long for the day," he wrote, "when a space geek walks into a fighter pilot bar and announces, 'You boys better get out of here. I've had a bad day flying my satellite, I intend to get drunk, and if that happens I may get mean and hurt one of you.'" Clancy and Horner, *Every Man a Tiger*, 520.

181. "Friendly fire" caused 18 percent of casualties and 24 percent of deaths. The ratio between land-caused casualties versus air-caused casualties was 2.14 to 1.0.

182. Horner to Hallion, June 1, 2011.

183. Keaney and Cohen, *Summary Report*, 161. They rightly note, "But it is by no means clear that playing by the book would have achieved more."

184. Glosson, *War with Iraq*, 117.

185. James A. Winnefeld and Dana J. Johnson, in *Joint Air Operations: Pursuit of Unity in Command and Control, 1942–1991* (Annapolis, MD: Naval Institute Press and the Rand Corporation, 1993), note: "*Desert Storm* was a vindication of the Air Force doctrine of unity of theater air control and (up to a point) its strategic concept of air operations separate from ground operations" (110). For subsequent experiences, see Col. Christopher M. Campbell, USAF, "The *Deliberate Force* Air Campaign Plan," in *Deliberate Force: A Case Study in Effective Air Campaigning*, ed. Robert C. Owen (Maxwell AFB, AL: Air University Press, 2000), 89–126; Gen. Michael C. Short, USAF (Ret.), "An Airman's Lessons from Kosovo," in *From Manoeuvre Warfare to Kosovo?*, ed. John Andreas Olsen (Trondheim: The Royal Norwegian Air Force Academy, 2000), 257–88; Col. Mark A. Bucknam, USAF, *Responsibility of Command: How UN and NATO Commanders Influenced Airpower over Bosnia* (Maxwell AFB, AL: Air University Press, 2003), 230–33, 316–22; Benjamin S. Lambeth, *Air Power Against Terror: America's Conduct of Operation Enduring Freedom*, Rand Report MG-166 (Santa Monica, CA: Rand National Defense Research Institute, 2005), 295–329; and Jeffrey Hukill and Daniel R. Mortensen, "Developing Flexible Command and Control of Airpower," *Air & Space Power Journal* 25, no. 1 (Spring 2011): 55.

10. Michael E. Ryan: Architect of Air Power Success

1. For a good account of the ground war in Bosnia and Herzegovina (BiH), see Tim Ripley, *Operation Deliberate Force: The UN and NATO Campaign in Bosnia, 1995* (Lancaster, UK: Centre for Defence and International Security Studies, 1999).

2. Citation to accompany the award of the Silver Star, second award, to Col. John D. Ryan (Air Corps), Headquarters, 15th Air Force, General Orders No. 2105 (April 5, 1945). See "John D. Ryan," Hall of Valor, *Military Times*, http://militarytimes.com/

citations-medals-awards/recipient.php?recipientid=49636.

3. Matt Kleve, "2005 Distinguished Graduates," *Checkpoints* (March 2006), 26–27; and Gen. Michael E. Ryan, USAF (Ret.), telephone interview with author, November 29, 2011 (hereafter cited as Ryan interview, November 29, 2011).

4. Ryan interview, November 29, 2011.

5. Ibid.

6. Kleve, "2005 Distinguished Graduates," 26–27.

7. Jack Broughton, *Going Downtown: The War Against Hanoi and Washington* (New York: Orion Books, 1988), 224.

8. Ibid., 242.

9. It was later revealed that President Nixon, probably with the knowledge of the Chairman of the Joint Chiefs of Staff, had authorized the bombing activities that Lavelle had supposedly tried to cover up—facts believed to have been unknown to Gen. Jack Ryan.

10. Ryan interview, November 29, 2011.

11. Ibid.

12. Gen. Michael E. Ryan, USAF (Ret.), interview with author, November 30, 2011 (hereafter cited as Ryan interview, November 30, 2011).

13. Ryan interview, November 29, 2011.

14. Ibid.

15. Ibid.

16. Ibid.

17. Ryan interview, November 30, 2011.

18. Ibid.

19. Ibid.

20. Ibid.

21. Ryan interview, November 29, 2011.

22. United States Senate, *Impact of the Unilateral United States Lifting of the Arms Embargo on the Government of Bosnia-Herzegovina: Hearings before the Committee on Armed Services*, 103d Cong., 2d sess., 1994, S. Hrg. No. 103-777, June 23, 1994, 20–21.

23. Robert Fox, "Gulf Commander Named to Take Over from Rose," *Daily Telegraph* (London), December 10, 1994, 17.

24. "Nomination of Lt. Gen. Michael Ryan," *Congressional Record* 140, no. 115 (August 16, 1994).

25. Technically, in 1993 it was the Federal Republic of Yugoslavia that bordered BiH to the east, with Serbia facing the northern half of BiH, and Montenegro opposite the southern half; but Serbia was far more powerful politically and militarily than Montenegro was.

26. Hornburg arrived in November 1994 and replaced Lt. Gen. James "Bear" Chambers, USAF, who had originally established flying operations to enforce the no-fly zone.

27. General Ryan cited in John A. Tirpak, "Chief Holds Course," *Air Force Magazine* 81, no. 1 (January 1998): 39 (bracketed comments appeared in original article).

28. Gen. Michael E. Ryan, USAF, interview with author, Ramstein Air Base, Germany, June 6, 1997, transcript of interview, author's personal collection (hereafter cited as Ryan interview, June 6, 1997).

29. Ripley, *Operation Deliberate Force*, 100.

30. Ryan interview, June 6, 1997; and Ryan interview, November 30, 2011.

31. Ripley, *Operation Deliberate Force*, 133.

32. Adm. Leighton W. Smith, USN, interview with author, February 10, 1998, Arlington, Virginia, transcript of interview, author's personal collection (hereafter cited as Smith

interview); and Ryan interview, November 30, 2011.

33. Lt. Col. Mark J. Conversino, "Executing Deliberate Force, 30 August–14 September 1995," in *Deliberate Force: A Case Study in Effective Air Campaign Planning*, ed. Col Robert C. Owen (Maxwell AFB, AL: Air University Press, 2000), 134.

34. Mark Bucknam, *Responsibility of Command: How UN and NATO Commanders Influenced Airpower over Bosnia* (Maxwell AFB, AL: Air University Press, 2003), 228–30.

35. Ripley, *Operation Deliberate Force*, 157, 164.

36. Ibid., 190.

37. Ibid., 192.

38. Ibid., 228.

39. Ibid., 245.

40. Allied Forces Southern Europe Fact Sheet, "Operation Deliberate Force," December 16, 2002, http://www.afsouth.nato.int/factsheets/DeliberateForceFactSheet.htm (accessed August 9, 2011).

41. Conversino, "Executing Deliberate Force," 138.

42. Ryan interview, June 6, 1997.

43. Smith interview.

44. Conversino, "Executing Deliberate Force," 133; and Air Commodore Mike Rudd, NATO liaison officer to commander, UN Peace Force, Zagreb, interview with author, September 15, 1997, Easton-on-the-Hill, England, transcript of interview, author's personal collection.

45. Adm. Leighton W. Smith, USN, "NATO Air Strike against Bosnia Serbs," transcript of news conference, August 31, 1995 (10 a.m.), http://marcosaba.tripod.com/bosnia 02.html.

46. Lt. Col. Richard L. Sargent, USAF, "Deliberate Force Targeting," in Owen, *Deliberate Force*, 290.

47. Gen. Michael E. Ryan, USAF, "NATO Air Operations in Bosnia-Herzegovina: Deliberate Force, 29 August–14 September 1995," transcript of briefing to Air Power Conference, London, September 13, 1996.

48. Lt. Col. Ronald M. Reed, "Chariots of Fire: Rules of Engagement in Operation Deliberate Force," in Owen, *Deliberate Force*, 412.

49. Sargent, "Deliberate Force Targeting," 287.

50. Ibid., 288–90.

51. Ryan interview, June 6, 1997.

52. Sargent, "Deliberate Force Tactics," in Owen, *Deliberate Force*, 318; and Ripley, *Operation Deliberate Force*, 248–50.

53. Sargent, "Deliberate Force Tactics," 318.

54. Ripley, *Operation Deliberate Force*, 255.

55. Conversino, "Executing Deliberate Force," 138.

56. Maj. Gen. Michael C. Short, USAF, chief of staff, Allied Air Forces Southern Europe, interview with author, May 2, 1997, Ramstein Air Base, Germany, tape recording, author's personal collection.

57. Ryan interview, November 30, 2011.

58. Bucknam, *Responsibility of Command*, 287.

59. Conversino, "Executing Deliberate Force," 147–48; and Ripley, *Operation Deliberate Force*, 269.

60. Conversino, "Executing Deliberate Force," 147–48.

61. Ibid., 148; and Ripley, *Operation Deliberate Force*, 271.

62. Conversino, "Executing Deliberate Force," 150; and Ripley, *Operation Deliberate*

Force, 272.
63. Ripley, *Operation Deliberate Force*, 268–70.
64. Conversino, "Executing Deliberate Force," 150–51.
65. Ibid., 152–53.
66. Ibid., 151; and Bucknam, *Responsibility of Command*, 294.
67. Conversino, "Executing Deliberate Force," 152.
68. Ibid., 153.
69. Ripley, *Operation Deliberate Force*, 276–78, 286–89.
70. Ibid., 239.
71. Ryan interview, June 6, 1997.
72. Ibid.
73. Conversino, "Executing Deliberate Force," 155.
74. Sargent, "Deliberate Force Combat Air Assessments," in Owen, *Deliberate Force*, 344.
75. Conversino, "Executing Deliberate Force," 156.
76. Sargent, "Deliberate Force Combat Assessments," 342.
77. Ibid., 344.
78. Ripley, *Operation Deliberate Force*, 290.
79. Conversino, "Executing Deliberate Force," 154; and Ripley, *Operation Deliberate Force*, 290. Note: Ripley places the attack on September 12, rather than September 13.
80. Ryan interview, November 30, 2011.

11. Michael C. Short: Airman Undaunted

1. John Stehr, "City Marks 20th Anniversary of Plane Crash Tragedy," WTHR Indianapolis, October 20, 2007, http://www.wthr.com/global/story.asp?s=7234226.
2. This and all other uncited quotations are from author's interview with Lieutenant General Short, October 6, 2011.
3. The investigation later determined that a defective gear in the accessory gearbox caused the Indianapolis crash.
4. Reuters News Service, June 9, 1998.
5. Wesley K. Clark, *Waging Modern War* (New York: PublicAffairs, 2001), 39.
6. Ibid., 431.
7. Ibid., 144.
8. Ibid., 133.
9. Holbrooke and Clark quoted in "War in Europe, Part 2: The Real War," *Frontline*, PBS-WGBH, original airdate February 29, 2000.
10. Ibid.
11. Michael C. Short, quoted in John Andreas Olsen, ed., *From Manoeuvre Warfare to Kosovo?* (Trondheim: The Royal Norwegian Air Force Academy, 2000), 260.
12. Michael C. Short, remarks to Air Warfare Symposium, Orlando, Florida, February 24, 2000 (hereafter cited as Short remarks).
13. Pentagon spokesman Kenneth Bacon, Pentagon briefing, March 23, 1999.
14. U.S. Army Gen. Wesley Clark, SACEUR, NATO briefing, March 25, 1999.
15. Cited in R. Jeffrey Smith, "Belgrade Rebuffs Final U.S. Warning," *Washington Post*, March 23, 1999.
16. U.S. Secretary of State Madeleine Albright on *Face the Nation*, CBS, March 28, 1999.
17. John A. Tirpak, "Washington Watch: Short's View of the Air Campaign," *Air Force Magazine* 82, no. 9 (September 1999), http://www.airforce-magazine.com/Magazine Archive/Pages/1999/September%201999/0999watch.aspx (accessed March 5, 2012).
18. Ibid.
19. Rebecca Grant, *The B-2 Goes to War* (Washington, DC: IRIS Press, 2001), 53.

20. U.S. Secretary of Defense William S. Cohen, remarks, Brussels, April 7, 1999.
21. Clark, *Waging Modern War*, 245.
22. Short remarks.
23. "War in Europe."
24. Air Force Association, "Operations in April: A Tough Job for Aerospace Power," *The Kosovo Campaign: Airpower Made It Work*, Special Report, http://www.afa.org/media/reports/april.asp (accessed March 5, 2012).
25. Tirpak, "Washington Watch."
26. Short remarks.
27. Rebecca Grant, "True Blue: The Kosovo Numbers Game," *Air Force Magazine* 83, no. 8 (August 2000).
28. "War in Europe."

12. T. Michael Moseley: Air Power Warrior

1. The authors of the article examine the senior mentor program that utilizes retired general officers from all of the U.S. armed services, not only the U.S. Air Force. Tom Vanden Brook, Ken Dilanian and Ray Locker, "How Some Retired Military Officers Became Well-Paid Consultants: Retired Military Officers Cash in as Well-Paid Consultants," *USA Today*, online edition, November 18, 2009, http://www.usatoday.com/news/military/2009-11-17-military-mentors_N.htm (accessed November 12, 2011).
2. Col. Mike Worden (USAF), *The Rise of the Fighter Generals: The Problem of Air Force Leadership, 1945–1982* (Maxwell AFB, AL: Air University Press, March 1998), 236–37.
3. The "Thundervision scandal" involved the letting of a sole-source, five-year $49.5 million contract to produce audiovisual presentations played during shows put on by the U.S. Air Force Thunderbirds flight demonstration team. Two official Department of Defense inspector general (DOD/IG) investigations were conducted. The first exonerated Moseley of any undue influence with members of the production company, Strategic Message Solutions. A redacted version of the 251-page report on the Thunderbirds Air Show Productions Services contract was cleared and released through a Freedom of Information Act request. See Inspector General, Department of Defense, "Report of Investigation," Nellis Air Force Base (AFB), Nevada, January 30, 2008, http://www.dodig.mil/fo/foia/ERR/ROI_20080130_0408.pdf. The second DOD/IG investigation was much more pointed, charging Moseley with a range of violations and recommending that "the Secretary of the Air Force consider appropriate corrective action with regard to Gen Moseley." Inspector General, Department of Defense, "Alleged Misconduct: General T. Michael Moseley, Former Chief of Staff, U.S. Air Force," Report H08L107249100, July 10, 2009, 46, http://www.airforce-magazine.com/SiteCollectionDocuments/Reports/2009/July%202009/Day13/IG_TAPS_071009.pdf. Previous and subsequent Department of the Air Force IG investigations and reports by other air force organizations have cleared Moseley of any wrongdoing or unprofessional or improper behavior.
4. Files to which future historians will have access, after eventual review and declassification, include numbered air force histories, interviews conducted as part of the Enduring Look project to capture significant events, and lessons from Operation Enduring Freedom, as well as General Moseley's e-mail correspondence while serving as commander of the Ninth Air Force. The electronic email files are greater than 600 megabytes alone. These records are held at the Air Force Historical Research Agency at Maxwell Air Force Base, Alabama.
5. Donna Ingham, ed., *1001 Greatest Things Ever Said About Texas* (Guilford, CT: Lyons

Press, 2006), 166.

6. Unless otherwise indicated, the information contained in this biographical sketch is derived from two sources. The first is U.S. Air Force, "Biography: General T. Michael Moseley," July 2008, http://www.af.mil/information/bios/bio.asp?bioid=6545 (accessed January 30, 2012). The second is personal correspondence from General Moseley to the author, January 19, 2012, in the author's possession.

7. Personal correspondence with General Moseley.

8. Ibid.

9. Ibid.

10. Ibid.

11. Ibid.

12. Ibid.

13. The development of the CAOC, and the role it played as a system of command in four air campaigns, is dealt with masterfully in Lt. Col. Michael W. Kometer (USAF), *Command in Air War: Centralized versus Decentralized Control of Combat Airpower* (Maxwell AFB, AL: Air University Press, 2007).

14. Operational Detachments Alpha (ODA) are more popularly known as A Teams. The primary task of an ODA is to train and advise foreign military counterparts to conduct foreign internal defense (counterinsurgency) or unconventional warfare (insurgency). An ODA is composed of twelve personnel: an officer, a senior enlisted man (a warrant officer), and ten sergeants (from E-6 to E-8, or staff to master sergeant in rank). In addition to language proficiency, the personnel within the ODA are cross-trained in medical, weapons, and cross-cultural communication skills. Although army SF personnel can be certified as joint terminal attack controllers, a more effective alternative is to attach an air force enlisted combat controller from a special tactics squadron to the team.

15. Tommy Franks with Malcolm McConnell, *American Soldier* (New York: Regan Books, 2004), 270–72.

16. Kometer, *Command in Air War*, 131–32.

17. Franks, *American Soldier*, 288.

18. Quoted in Maj. James G. Young (USAF), "Lessons from Rhino LZ: How the Afghanistan Invasion Changed Combat Airlift," *Armed Forces Journal*, November 2011, http://armedforcesjournal.com/2011/11/7948194/ (accessed November 12, 2011).

19. Lester W. Grau, "The Coils of the Anaconda: America's First Conventional Battle in Afghanistan" (Ph.D. diss., University of Kansas, April 27, 2009), 207.

20. Sean Naylor, *Not a Good Day to Die: The Untold Story of Operation Anaconda* (New York: Berkeley, 2005), 136.

21. Headquarters Air Force, AF-XOL, *Operation Anaconda: An Air Power Perspective* (Washington, DC: Headquarters Air Force, February 7, 2005), 34.

22. Naylor, *Not a Good Day to Die*, 86.

23. Col. Matt "El Cid" Neuenswander, "Operation Anaconda: Points to Ponder (U)," unpublished briefing slides, undated, slide 2, in the author's possession.

24. Grau contends that TF Summit issued its operations order, and sent a courtesy copy to the CFACC, on 20 February, and concludes that air planning is not as quick or adaptive as ground or army planning. "The Coils of the Anaconda," 207–8.

25. The conditions are outlined in more detail in Headquarters Air Force, AF-XOL, *Operation Anaconda*, 55.

26. The Department of Defense released basic details of the battle and rescue in 2002. See Department of Defense, *Executive Summary of the Battle of Takur Ghar* (Washington, DC: Department of Defense, May 2002), http://www.defense.gov/news/

May2002/d20020524takurghar.pdf#search=%22takur%20ghar%22 (accessed November 14, 2011). The personalities and events outlined in the report are brought to life in Malcolm MacPherson, *Roberts Ridge: A Story of Courage and Sacrifice on Takur Ghar Mountain, Afghanistan* (New York: Delacorte Press, 2005).

27. Derived from Neuenswander, "Operation Anaconda," slide 4. Colonel Neuenswander, an A-10 pilot, was the air force element director at the U.S. Army Command and General Staff College when he built this briefing.
28. Robert H. McElroy and Patrecia Slayden Hollis interviewed Maj. Gen. Franklin L. Hagenbeck for their article, "Afghanistan: Fire Support for Operation Anaconda," *Field Artillery* (September–/October 2002), 8.
29. HQAF/XOL, *Operation Anaconda*, 81.
30. For details, see Michael Friscolanti, *Friendly Fire: The Untold Story of the U.S. Bombing That Killed Four Canadian Soldiers in Afghanistan* (New York: Wiley & Sons, 2005).
31. Benjamin Lambeth, *Air Power Against Terror: America's Conduct of Operation Enduring Freedom*, Rand Report MG-166 (Santa Monica, CA: Rand National Defense Research Institute, 2005), 161.
32. HQAF-XOL, *Operation Anaconda*, 78.
33. Ibid., 80.
34. Ibid., 39.
35. Ibid., 78.
36. Ibid., 102. According to the staff of Task Force Enduring Look, non-precision munitions accounted for 53 percent of all weapons air dropped.
37. Ibid., 78.
38. Ibid., 30.
39. Ibid., 78.
40. I owe this observation to Colonel Deaile, who was in the CAOC during Operation Anaconda. Conversation with the author, SAASS, Maxwell AFB, December 8, 2011.
41. HQAF-XOL, *Operation Anaconda*, 79.
42. Ibid., 101.
43. Ibid., 8.
44. Hagenbeck's praise of air power's effectiveness is contained in Lambeth, *Air Power Against Terror*, 199. He provides a much different perspective in McElroy and Hollis, "Afghanistan," 7–8.
45. Grau, "The Coils of Anaconda," v.
46. Sean Naylor, a correspondent for the *Army Times*, goes out of his way to caricature Moseley as both a fighter pilot who does not understand close air support and a politician doing the White House's bidding and not focusing on the operation at hand. For example, see *Not A Good Day to Die*, 136, 271–72.
47. Corona meetings among air force four-stars now take place three times a year. Gen. Henry "Hap" Arnold held the first meeting on February 18, 1944, and the Corona meetings have continued ever since. The purpose of and historical tradition behind Corona is covered in Staff Sgt. Julie Weckerlein, "Top Generals Meet at Corona," *Air Force Times*, online edition (February 9, 2006), http://www.af.mil/news/story.asp?id=123016180 (accessed November 15, 2011).
48. In their historical study for Rand, James Winnefield and Dana Johnson conclude that joint air operations should be based on both unity of command and effort. They offer four criteria for evaluating unity of effort that all potential joint force and component commanders would do well to consider during their planning and coordination. Winnefield and Johnson, *Joint Air Operations: Pursuit of Unity in Command and Control, 1942–1991* (Annapolis, MD: Naval Institute Press and Rand Corporation,

1993), 2.
49. U.S. Air Force, "Biography: General T. Michael Moseley"; and Franks, *American Soldier*, 27–33, 117.
50. HQAF-XOL, *Operation Anaconda*, 114.
51. Ibid.
52. Ibid.
53. See, for example, Franks, *American Soldier*, xii–xiii.
54. Kometer, *Command in Air War*, 141.
55. U.S. Air Force, "Biography: Major General F. C. "Pink" Williams" April 2009, http://www.af.mil/information/bios/bio.asp?bioID=10793 (accessed December 1, 2011).
56. Kometer, *Command in Air War*, 141–42; and U.S. Air Force, "Biography: Lieutenant General Daniel P. Leaf," September 2006, http://www.af.mil/information/bios/bio.asp?bioID=6162 (accessed December 1, 2011).
57. Kometer, *Command in Air War*, 142. Emphasis added.
58. HQAF-XOL, *Operation Anaconda*, 46.
59. Bob Woodward, *Plan of Attack* (New York: Simon & Schuster, 2004), 52–55; and a graphic depiction in U.S. Central Command, "1003-V, Full Force—Force Disposition, Tab K," undated, slide 3, declassified through FOIA request by the National Security Archive, the George Washington University, posted online at http://www.gwu.edu/~nsarchiv/NSAEBB/NSAEBB214/Tab%20K.pdf (accessed December 7, 2011). The evolution of the plan for OIF—from its initial starting point as Operations Plan 1003-98 through various alternatives to the final plan, nicknamed "Cobra II"—is surveyed in Michael R. Gordon and Gen. Bernard E. Trainor, *Cobra II: The Inside Story of the Invasion and Occupation of Iraq* (New York: Pantheon, 2006).
60. For analysis of air operations in the counter-Scud campaign during Operation Desert Storm, see Thomas A. Keaney and Eliot A. Cohen, *Gulf War Air Power Survey Summary Report* (Washington, DC: Government Printing Office, 1993), 83–88. A much more optimistic evaluation of the campaign, in terms of the strategic effect generated by SOF activities, is given in William Rosenau, *Special Operations Forces and Elusive Enemy Ground Targets: Lessons from Vietnam and the Persian Gulf War*, MR-1408-AF (Santa Monica, CA: Rand Corporation, 2001), 29–44.
61. Lambeth, *Air Power Against Terror*, 312. Lambeth outlines the range of constraints placed on General Wald and General Moseley during OEF, including Coalition partner concerns, in considerable detail on pages 311–24.
62. Woodward, *Plan of Attack*, 77–78.
63. The rationale for moving TST authorities, as well as the systems available in the CAOC to facilitate information sharing, planning, and targeting, are outlined in Kometer, *Command in Air Warfare*, 168–71.
64. Robin Moore, *Hunting Down Saddam: The Inside Story of the Search and Capture* (New York: St. Martin's Press, 2004), 120.
65. Linda Robinson, *Masters of Chaos: The Secret History of the Special Forces* (New York: PublicAffairs, 2004), 197–98.
66. Maj. Brook Leonard (USAF), *How the West Was Won: The Essence of Network Centric Operations (NCO)* (Maxwell AFB, AL: School of Advanced Air and Space Studies, June 2006), 34–38.
67. Quoted in ibid., 40.
68. Kometer, *Command in Air War*, 169.
69. Ibid.
70. Quoted in Capt. Christine Kunz, "Teamwork on High: Success Over the Skies in

Iraq Was More Than a Solo Venture," *Airman*, October 2003, 20–21.

71. Michael Smith, "The War Before the War," *The New Statesman* online edition, May 30, 2005, http://www.newstatesman.com/200505300013 (accessed December 8, 2011).

72. Kevin Woods et al., *Iraqi Perspectives Project: A View of Operation Iraqi Freedom from Saddam's Senior Leadership* (Norfolk, VA: Joint Center for Operational Analysis, March 2006), 75–79.

73. Woodward, *Plan of Attack*, 373–74, 382–84.

74. Franks, *American Soldier*, 451; and Woodward, *Plan of Attack*, 385.

75. Woodward suggests that word "manzul" was responsible for the confusion. *Plan of Attack*, 385.

76. Maj. S. Clinton Hinote, "Appendix A: Author's Personal Notes Concerning the Opening Strike on Saddam Hussein," *More Than Bombing Saddam: Attacking the Leadership in Operation Iraqi Freedom* (Maxwell AFB, AL: School of Advanced Air and Space Studies, June 2006), 188.

77. Franks, *American Soldier*, 459–60.

78. Ibid., 455.

79. Hinote, *More Than Bombing Saddam*, 188.

80. Joel Roberts, "At Saddam's Bombed Palace," CBS News online, February 11, 2009, http://www.cbsnews.com/stories/2003/05/28/eveningnews/main555948.shtml (accessed December 8, 2011). The correspondent covering the story quotes Col. Tim Madere (USA), who assumed that because three of the bomb craters were outside the walls of the main farm compound that the bombs must have missed their intended target (the main farm compound).

81. Williamson Murray and Maj. Gen. Robert H. Scales Jr., *The Iraq War: A Military History* (Cambridge, MA: Belknap Press, 2003), 176; and Hinote, *More Than Bombing Saddam*, 2.

82. On Quesada's career and generalship, see Thomas A. Hughes, *Overlord: General Pete Quesada and the Triumph of Tactical Air Power in World War II* (New York: Free Press, 1995). The same author provides a model for scholarship and the evaluation of air generalship in his article on what made Harmon outstanding as a "joint" airman: "A General Airman: Millard Harmon and the South Pacific in World War II," *Joint Forces Quarterly* 52 (First Quarter 2009): 156–62.

83. Murray and Scales, *The Iraq War*, 166–67. The term "shock and awe" was the subject of a National Defense University study from 1996 to describe the effect that rapid dominance would have on an enemy system. The authors wrote, for example, that "the key objective of Rapid Dominance is to impose this overwhelming level of Shock and Awe against an adversary on an immediate or sufficiently timely basis to paralyze its will to carry on." Harlan Ullman and James P. Wade, *Shock and Awe: Achieving Rapid Dominance* (Washington, DC: National Defense University Press, October 1996), xxvi. The term first appeared in the media related to Iraq a little longer than a month prior to the start of OIF. See, for example, Suc Chan, "Iraq Faces Massive U.S. Missile Barrage," CBS News online edition, January 24, 2003, and most recently updated February 11, 2009, http://www.cbsnews.com/stories/2003/01/24/eveningnews/main537928.shtml (accessed December 16, 2011).

84. Hinote, *More Than Bombing Saddam*, 141.

85. Gordon and Trainor, *Cobra II*, 324.

86. Leonard, *How the West Was Won*, 89–90. The specific details of the campaign from the perspective of the SF teams are available in Robinson, *Masters of Chaos*, 191–223.

87. Kometer, *Command in Air War*, 171.

88. Charles Briscoe, et al, *All Roads Lead to Baghdad: Army Special Operations Forces in*

Iraq (Fort Bragg, NC: USASOC History Office, 2006), 190.

89. Trainor and Gordon, *Cobra II*, 324.

90. Murray and Scales, *The Iraq War*, 171.

91. Woods et al., *Iraqi Perspectives Project*, 82–83.

92. Lt. Gen. T. Michael Moseley, *Operation Iraqi Freedom: By the Numbers* (Prince Sultan Air Base, Saudi Arabia: CENTAF, April 30, 2003), 6, 11.

93. Susanne Schafer, "Air War Chief: Time to Get Crews Home 'so They Can Have a Life,'" *Argus Press* [Owosso, MI], April 19, 2003, 6.

94. Moseley, *Operation Iraqi Freedom*, 9.

95. Daniel L. Haulman, "USAF Manned Aircraft Losses 1990–2002," unpublished report (Maxwell AFB, AL: Air Force Historical Research Agency, December 9, 2002), 1.

96. Sharron Haley, "9th Air Force commander returns to Shaw," *The Item* [Sumter, SC], May 5, 2003, 201.

97. Kunz, "Teamwork on High," 22.

98. Edgar F. Puryear Jr., *American Generalship: Character Is Everything: The Art of Command* (Novato, CA: Presidio Press, 2000).

99. J. F. C. Fuller, *Generalship: Its Diseases and Their Cure: A Study of the Personal Factor in Command* (Harrisburg, PA: Military Service Publishing, 1936), 58.

100. Col. S. Clinton Hinote (USAF), personal correspondence with the author, November 17, 2011, in the author's possession.

SELECTED BIBLIOGRAPHY

Anderegg, C. R. *Sierra Hotel: Flying Air Force Fighters in the Decade after Vietnam.* Washington, DC: Air Force History and Museums Program, 2001.

Anderson, Charles R. *Algeria-French Morocco: The United States Army Campaigns of World War II.* CMH Pub 72-11. Washington, DC: Army Center of Military History, 1993.

Andradé, Dale. *America's Last Vietnam Battle: Halting Hanoi's 1972 Easter Offensive.* Lawrence: University of Kansas Press, 2001.

Arnold, Henry H. *Global Mission.* New York: Harper & Brothers, 1949.

Atkinson, Rick. *Crusade: The Untold Story of the Persian Gulf War.* Boston: Houghton Mifflin, 1993.

Barlow, Jeffrey G. *Revolt of the Admirals: The Fight for Naval Aviation, 1945–1950.* Washington, DC: Government Reprints Press, 2001.

Barnett, Correlli, ed. *Hitler's Generals.* New York: William Morrow, 1989.

———. *The Swordbearers: Supreme Command in the First World War.* New York: William Morrow, 1964.

Berntsen, Gary, and Ralph Pezzullo. *Jawbreaker: The Attack on Bin Laden and Al Qaeda: A Personal Account by the CIA's Key Field Commander.* New York: Crown, 2005.

Beschloss, Michael. *The Conquerors: Roosevelt, Truman, and the Destruction of Hitler's Germany, 1941–1945.* New York: Simon & Schuster, 2002.

Biddle, Stephen. *Afghanistan and the Future of Warfare: Implications for Army and Defense Policy.* Carlisle Barracks, PA: Strategic Studies Institute, 2002.

Billière, Peter de la. *Storm Command: A Personal Account of the Gulf War.* London: HarperCollins, 1992.

bin Sultan, Khaled. *Desert Warrior: A Personal View of the Gulf War by the Joint Forces Commander.* With Patrick Searle. New York: HarperCollins, 1995.

Birdsall, Steve. *Flying Buccaneers: The Illustrated Story of Kenney's Fifth Air Force.* Newton Abbot, UK: David & Charles, 1978.

Blumenson, Martin. *Breakout and Pursuit.* United States Army in World War II: European Theater of Operations. Washington, DC: Office of the Chief of Military History, 1961.

Boyne, Walter. *Beyond the Wild Blue: A History of the U.S. Air Force, 1947–1997.* New York: St. Martin's Press, 1997.

Broughton, Jack. *Going Downtown: The War Against Hanoi and Washington.* New York: Orion Books, 1988.

————. *Thud Ridge*. Philadelphia: J. B. Lippincott, 1969.

Bucknam, Mark A. *Responsibility of Command: How UN and NATO Commanders Influenced Airpower over Bosnia*. Maxwell Air Force Base, AL: Air University Press, 2003.

Builder, Carl H. *The Icarus Syndrome: The Role of Air Power Theory in the Evolution and Fate of the U.S. Air Force*. New Brunswick, NJ: Transaction Publishers, 1994.

Bush, George H. W., and Brent Scowcroft. *A World Transformed*. New York: Alfred A. Knopf, 1998.

Byrd, Martha. *Chennault: Giving Wings to the Tiger*. Tuscaloosa: University of Alabama Press, 1987.

Caldwell, Donald L., and Richard R. Muller. *The Luftwaffe over Germany: Defense of the Reich*. London: Greenhill, 2007.

Cameron, Rebecca H., and Barbara Wittig, eds. *Golden Legacy, Boundless Future: Essays on the United States Air Force and the Rise of Aerospace Power*. Washington, DC: Air Force History and Museums Program, 2000.

Carver, Michael, ed. *The War Lords: Military Commanders of the Twentieth Century*. Boston: Little, Brown, 1976.

Chandler, Alfred. *The Papers of Dwight D. Eisenhower: The War Years*. Vol. 4. Baltimore: John Hopkins University Press, 1970.

Cheney, Dick. *In My Time: A Personal and Political Memoir*. With Liz Cheney. New York: Threshold Editions, 2011.

Chennault, Claire. *Way of a Fighter: The Memoirs of Claire Lee Chennault*. Edited by Robert B. Hotz. New York: G. P. Putnam's Sons, 1949.

Chun, Clayton. *Aerospace Power in the Twenty-First Century: A Basic Primer*. Maxwell Air Force Base, AL: Air University Press, 2001.

Clancy, Tom. *Every Man a Tiger*. With Charles Horner. New York: G. P. Putnam's Sons, 1999.

Clodfelter, Mark. *The Limits of Air Power: The American Bombing of North Vietnam*. New York: Free Press, 1989.

Coffey, Thomas M. *Iron Eagle: The Turbulent Life of General Curtis LeMay*. New York: Avon Books, 1988.

Coggins, Jack. *The Campaign for North Africa*. New York: Doubleday, 1980.

Cohen, Eliot A. *Gulf War Air Power Survey*. Vol. 1, *Part I: Planning*. Washington, DC: U.S. Government Printing Office, 1993.

————. *Gulf War Air Power Survey*. Vol. 1, *Part II: Command and Control*. Washington, DC: U.S. Government Printing Office, 1993.

————. *Gulf War Air Power Survey*. Vol. 2, *Part I: Operations*. Washington, DC: U.S. Government Printing Office, 1993.

————. *Gulf War Air Power Survey*. Vol. 2, *Part II: Effects and Effectiveness*. Washington, DC: U.S. Government Printing Office, 1993.

————. *Gulf War Air Power Survey*. Vol. 5, *A Statistical Compendium and Chronology*. Washington, DC: U.S. Government Printing Office, 1993.

————. *Supreme Command: Soldiers, Statesmen, and Leadership in Wartime*. New York: Free Press, 2002.

Cole, Hugh M. *The Lorraine Campaign*. United States Army in World War II: European Theater of Operations. Washington, DC: Office of the Chief of Military History, 1950.

Collier, Richard. *Bridge Across the Sky: The Berlin Blockade and Airlift, 1948–1949*. New York: McGraw-Hill, 1978.

Cooling, Benjamin F., ed. *Case Studies in the Achievement of Air Superiority*. Washington, DC: Center for Air Force History, 1994.

Copp, DeWitt S. *A Few Great Captains: The Men and Events that Shaped the Development of U.S. Air Power.* New York: Doubleday, 1980.

Corum, James S., ed., *Rearming Germany.* Leiden: Brill Press, 2011.

Crane, Conrad C. *American Airpower Strategy in Korea, 1950–1953.* Lawrence: University Press of Kansas, 2000.

Craven, Wesley F., and James L. Cate, eds. *The Army Air Forces in World War II.* Vol. 1, *Plans and Early Operations, January 1939 to August 1942.* Chicago: University of Chicago Press, 1948.

———, eds. *The Army Air Forces in World War II.* Vol. 2, *Europe: Torch to Pointblank, August 1942 to December 1943.* Chicago: University of Chicago Press, 1949.

———, eds. *The Army Air Forces in World War II.* Vol. 3, *Europe: Argument to V-E Day, January 1944 to May 1945.* Chicago: University of Chicago Press 1951.

———, eds. *The Army Air Forces in World War II.* Vol.4, *The Pacific: Guadalcanal to Saipan, August 1942 to July 1944.* Chicago: University of Chicago Press, 1950.

———, eds. *The Army Air Forces in World War II.* Vol. 5, *The Pacific: Matterhorn to Nagasaki, June 1944 to August 1945.* Chicago: University of Chicago Press, 1953.

Dallek, Robert. *The Lost Peace: Leadership in a Time of Horror and Hope, 1945–1953.* New York: Harper, 2010.

Daso, Dik Alan. *Hap Arnold and the Evolution of American Airpower.* Washington, DC: Smithsonian Institute Press, 2000.

Davis, Larry. *Wild Weasel: The SAM Suppression Story.* Carrollton, TX: Squadron/Signal Publications, 1986.

Davis, Richard G. *Bombing the European Axis Powers: A Historical Digest of the Combined Bomber Offensive, 1939–1945.* Maxwell Air Force Base, AL: Air University Press, 2006.

———. *Carl A. Spaatz and the Air War in Europe, 1940–1945.* Washington, DC: Center for Air Force History, 1993.

———. *HAP: Henry H. Arnold, Military Aviator.* Washington, DC: Air Force History and Museums Program, 1997.

Douhet, Giulio. *The Command of the Air.* Washington, DC: Office of Air Force History, 1983.

Drea, Edward J. *McNamara, Clifford, and the Burdens of Vietnam, 1965–1969.* Washington, DC: Office of the Secretary of Defense, 2011.

Drew, Dennis M. *Rolling Thunder 1965: Anatomy of a Failure.* Maxwell Air Force Base, AL: Air University Press, 1986.

Eisenhower, Dwight. *The Eisenhower Diaries.* Edited by Robert H. Ferrell. New York: W. W. Norton, 1981.

Ethell, Jeffrey, and Alfred Price. *One Day in a Long War: May 10, 1972, Air War, North Vietnam.* New York: Random House, 1989.

Farwell, Byron. *Eminent Victorian Soldiers: Seekers of Glory.* New York: W. W. Norton, 1985.

Finney, Robert T. *History of the Air Corps Tactical School, 1920–1940.* Washington, DC: Center for Air Force History, 1992.

Frank, Richard B. *Downfall: The End of the Imperial Japanese Empire.* New York: Random House, 1999.

Franks, Tommy. *American Soldier.* With Malcolm McConnell. New York: Regan Books, 2004.

Freeman, Roger A. *Mighty Eighth War Diary.* London: Jane's, 1981.

Freidel, Frank. *Over There: The Story of America's First Great Overseas Crusade.* New York: Bramhall House, 1964.

Frisbee, John L., ed. *Makers of the United States Air Force.* Washington, DC: Air Force History and Museums Program, 1996. First published 1987 by Office of Air Force History.

Friscolanti, Michael. *Friendly Fire: The Untold Story of the U.S. Bombing that Killed Four Canadian Soldiers in Afghanistan.* New York: Wiley & Sons, 2005.

Fuller, J. F. C. *Generalship: Its Diseases and Their Cure: A Study of the Personal Factor in Command.* Harrisburg, PA: Military Service Publishing, 1936.

Fury, Dalton [pseud.]. *Kill Bin Laden: A Delta Force Commander's Account of the Hunt for the World's Most Wanted Man.* New York: St. Martin's Press, 2008.

Futrell, Robert F. *Ideas, Concepts, Doctrine: Basic Thinking in the United States Air Force.* Vol. 1, *1907–1960.* Maxwell Air Force Base, AL: Air University Press, 1989.

———. *The United States Air Force in Korea, 1950–1953.* Washington, DC: Air Force History and Museums Program, 1996.

Gabriel, Richard A. *Great Captains of Antiquity.* Westport, CT: Greenwood Press, 2001.

Galland, Adolf. *The First and the Last: The Rise and Fall of the German Fighter Forces, 1938–1945.* Translated by Mervyn Savill. New York: Bantam Books, 1978.

Gillison, Douglas. *Royal Australian Air Force, 1939–1942.* Canberra: Australian War Memorial, 1962.

Glosson, Buster. *War with Iraq: Critical Lessons.* Charlotte, NC: Glosson Family Foundation, 2003.

Gordon, Michael R., and Bernard E. Trainor. *Cobra II: The Inside Story of the Invasion and Occupation of Iraq.* New York: Pantheon, 2006.

Grant, U. S. *The Personal Memoirs of U.S. Grant.* New York: Da Capo Press, 1982.

Griffith, Charles R. *The Quest: Haywood Hansell and American Strategic Bombing in World War II.* Maxwell AFB, AL: Air University Press, 1999.

Griffith, Thomas E., Jr. *MacArthur's Airman: General George C. Kenney and the War in the Southwest Pacific.* Lawrence: University Press of Kansas, 1998.

Grimsley, Mark. *And Keep Moving On: The Virginia Campaign, May–June 1864.* Lincoln: University of Nebraska Press, 2002.

Halsey, William F., and J. Bryan. *Admiral Halsey's Story.* Whitefish, MT: Kessinger Publishing, 2007.

Hammond, William M. *Reporting Vietnam: Media and Military at War.* Lawrence: University Press of Kansas, 1998.

Hancock, Valston. *Challenge.* Northbridge, MN: Access Press, 1990.

Hanson, David. *"When You Get a Job to Do, Do It": The Airpower Leadership of Lt. Gen. William H. Tunner.* Maxwell Air Force Base, AL: Air University Press, 2008.

Haulman, Daniel L. *The United States Air Force and Humanitarian Airlift Operations, 1947–1994.* Washington, DC: Air Force History and Museums Program, 1998.

Hinote, S. Clinton. *More Than Bombing Saddam: Attacking the Leadership in Operation Iraqi Freedom.* Maxwell Air Force Base, AL: School of Advanced Air and Space Studies, 2006.

Hinsley, F. H. *British Intelligence in the Second World War.* Vol. 3, *Its Influence on Strategy and Operations.* London: Her Majesty's Stationery Office, 1988.

Hoeber, Francis P. *Military Applications of Modeling: Selected Case Studies.* New York: Gordon and Breach Science Publishers, 1982.

Howarth, Stephen. *Men of War: Great Naval Leaders of World War II.* New York: St. Martin's Press, 1992.

Howe, George F. *Northwest Africa: Seizing the Initiative in the West.* Washington, DC: Office of the Chief of Military History, Department of the Army, 1957.

Hughes, Thomas A. *Overlord: General Pete Quesada and the Triumph of Tactical Air Power in World War II.* New York: Free Press, 1995.

Huntington, Samuel P. *The Soldier and the State: The Theory and Politics of Civil-Military Relations.* Cambridge MA: Harvard University Press, 1957.

Hurley, Alfred F. *Billy Mitchell: Crusader of Air Power.* Bloomington: Indiana University Press, 1975.

Jackson, Robert. *The Berlin Airlift.* Wellingborough, UK: Thorsons, 1988.

James, D. Clayton. *A Time for Giants: Politics of the American High Command in World War II.* With Ann Sharp Wells. New York: Franklin Watts, 1987.

———. *The Years of MacArthur.* Vol. 2, *1941–1945.* Boston: Houghton Mifflin, 1975.

Jamieson, Perry D. *Lucrative Targets: The U.S. Air Force in the Kuwaiti Theater of Operations.* Washington, DC: Air Force History and Museums Program, 2001.

Johnsen, Frederick A. *P-40 Warhawk.* Osceola, WI: MBI Publishing, 1998.

Johnson, Calvin R. *Linebacker Operations, September–December 1972.* Hickam Air Force Base, HI: Pacific Air Forces Headquarters, Project Contemporary Historical Evaluation of Combat Operations, 1978.

Jordan, Robert S. *Norstad, Cold War NATO Supreme Commander: Airman, Strategist, Diplomat.* New York: St. Martin's Press, 2000.

Kagan, Frederick W. *Finding the Target: The Transformation of American Military Policy.* New York: Encounter Books, 2006.

Keaney, Thomas A., and Eliot A. Cohen. *Gulf War Air Power Survey Summary Report.* Washington, DC: U.S. Government Printing Office, 1993.

Keegan, John. *The Mask of Command.* London: Jonathan Cape, 1987.

Kenney, George C. *General Kenney Reports: A Personal History of the Pacific War.* Washington, DC: Office of Air Force History, 1987.

Kinnard, Douglas. *The War Managers: American Generals Reflect on Vietnam.* New York: Da Capo Press, 1991.

Kohn, Richard H., and Joseph P. Harahan, eds. *Air Interdiction in World War II, Korea, and Vietnam: An Interview with Earle E. Partridge, Jacob E. Smart, and John W. Vogt, Jr.* Washington, DC: Office of Air Force History, 1986.

———, eds. *Air Superiority in World War II and Korea: An Interview with Gen. James Ferguson, Gen. Robert M. Lee, Gen. William Momyer, and Lt. Gen. Elwood R. Quesada.* Washington, DC: Office of Air Force History, 1983.

Kometer, Michael W. *Command in Air War: Centralized versus Decentralized Control of Combat Airpower.* Maxwell Air Force Base, AL: Air University Press, 2007.

La Farge, Oliver. *The Eagle in the Egg.* Boston: Houghton Mifflin, 1949.

Lambert, Andrew P. N., *The Psychology of Air Power.* London: Royal United Services Institute for Defence Studies, 1994.

Lambeth, Benjamin S. *Air Power Against Terror: America's Conduct of Operation Enduring Freedom.* Rand Report MG-166. Santa Monica, CA: Rand National Defense Research Institute, 2005.

———. *The Transformation of American Air Power.* Ithaca, NY: Cornell University Press in association with the Rand Corporation, 2000.

LeMay, Curtis E. *Mission with LeMay: My Story.* With MacKinlay Kantor. Garden City, NY: Doubleday, 1965.

Lester, Gary R. *Mosquitoes to Wolves: The Evolution of the Airborne Forward Air Controller.* Maxwell Air Force Base, AL: Air University Press, 1997.

Major, John. *John Major: The Autobiography.* London: HarperCollins, 1999.

Manrho, John, and Ron Pütz. *Bodenplatte: The Luftwaffe's Last Hope—the Attack on Allied Airfields, New Year's Day 1945.* Mardens Hill, UK: Hikoki, 2004.

Maurer, Maurer. *Aviation in the U.S. Army, 1919–1939.* Washington, DC: Office of Air Force History, 1987.

————, ed. *The U.S. Air Service in World War I*. Vol. 1, *The Final Report and a Tactical History*. Washington, DC: Office of Air Force History, 1978.

McArthur, Charles W. *Operations Analysis in the U.S. Army Eighth Air Force in World War II*. Providence, RI: The American Mathematical Society, 1990.

McCarthy, James R., and George B. Allison. *Linebacker II: A View from the Rock*. Maxwell Air Force Base, AL: Airpower Research Institute, 1979.

McMaster, H. R. *Dereliction of Duty: Lyndon Johnson, Robert McNamara, the Joint Chiefs of Staff, and the Lies that Led to Vietnam*. New York: HarperCollins, 1998.

Meilinger, Phillip S. *Airmen and Air Theory: A Review of the Sources*. Maxwell Air Force Base, AL: Air University Press, 2001.

————. *Hoyt S. Vandenberg: The Life of a General*. Bloomington: Indiana University Press, 1989.

————, ed. *The Paths of Heaven: The Evolution of Airpower Theory*. Maxwell Air Force Base, AL: Air University Press, 1997.

Mets, David R. *The Air Campaign: John Warden and the Classical Airpower Theorists*. Maxwell Air Force Base, AL: Air University Press, 1999.

————. *Master of Airpower: General Carl A. Spaatz*. Novato, CA: Presidio Press, 1988.

Michel, Marshall L., III. *Clashes: Air Combat over North Vietnam, 1965–1972*. Annapolis: Naval Institute Press, 1997.

Miller, Charles E. *Airlift Doctrine*. Maxwell Air Force Base, AL: Air University Press, 1998.

Miller, Judith, William Broad, and Stephen Engelberg. *Germs: Biological Weapons and America's Secret War*. New York: Simon & Schuster, 2001.

Miller, Roger G. *To Save a City: The Berlin Airlift, 1948–1949*. College Station: Texas A&M Press, 2000.

Momyer, William W. *Air Power in Three Wars: WWII, Korea, Vietnam*. Maxwell Air Force Base, AL: Air University Press, 2003.

Montgomery, Bernard L. *The Path to Leadership*. New York: G. P. Putnam's Sons, 1961.

Moody, Walton S. *Building a Strategic Air Force*. Washington, DC: Air Force History and Museums Program, 1995.

Moore, John Norton, ed. *The Vietnam Debate: A Fresh Look at the Arguments*. Lanham, MD: University Press of America, 1990.

Moore, Robin. *Hunting Down Saddam: The Inside Story of the Search and Capture*. New York: St. Martin's Press, 2004.

Morison, Samuel E. *History of United States Naval Operations in World War II*. Vol. 6, *Breaking the Bismarcks Barrier, 22 July 1942–1 May 1944*. Boston: Little, Brown, 1950.

Mortensen, Daniel R., ed. *Airpower and Ground Armies: Essays on the Evolution of Anglo-American Air Doctrine, 1940–1943*. Maxwell Air Force Base, AL: Air University Press, 1998.

————. *A Pattern for Joint Operations: World War II Close Air Support in North Africa*. Washington, DC: Office of Air Force History and U.S. Army Center of Military History, 1987.

Mrozek, Donald J. *The U.S. Air Force after Vietnam: Postwar Challenges and Potential for Responses*. Maxwell Air Force Base, AL: Air University Press, 1988.

Munro, Alan. *Arab Storm: Politics and Diplomacy Behind the Gulf War*. London: I. B. Tauris, 2006.

Murray, Williamson. *German Military Effectiveness*. Baltimore: The Nautical & Aviation Publishing Company of America, 1992.

————. *The Luftwaffe, 1933–1945: Strategy for Defeat*. Washington, DC: Brassey's, Inc., 1996.

Murray, Williamson, and Robert H. Scales Jr. *The Iraq War: A Military History*. Cambridge, MA: Belknap Press, 2003.

Nalty, Bernard C., ed. *Winged Shield, Winged Sword: A History of the United States Air Force.* Washington, DC: Air Force History and Museums Program, 1997.

Naylor, Sean. *Not a Good Day to Die: The Untold Story of Operation Anaconda.* New York: Berkeley, 2005.

Odgers, George. *Air War Against Japan, 1943–1945.* Canberra: Australian War Memorial, 1968.

Olsen, John Andreas, ed. *From Manoeuvre Warfare to Kosovo?* Trondheim: The Royal Norwegian Air Force Academy, 2000.

———, ed. *Global Air Power.* Washington, DC: Potomac Books, 2011.

———, ed. *A History of Air Warfare.* Washington, DC: Potomac Books, 2010.

———. *John Warden and the Renaissance of American Air Power.* Washington, DC: Potomac Books, 2007.

Orange, Vincent. *Coningham: A Biography of Air Marshal Sir Arthur Coningham, KCB, KBE, DSO, MC, DFC, AFC.* London: Methuen, 1990.

———. *Tedder: Quietly in Command.* London: Frank Cass, 2003.

Owen, Robert C., ed. *Deliberate Force: A Case Study in Effective Air Campaigning.* Maxwell Air Force Base, AL: Air University Press, 2000.

Palmer, Michael A. *On Course to Desert Storm: The United States Navy and the Persian Gulf.* Washington, DC: U.S. Naval Historical Center, 1992.

Peters, John E., Stuart E. Johnson, Nora Bensahel, Timothy Liston, and Traci Williams. *European Contributions to Operation Allied Force.* Santa Monica, CA: Rand Corporation, 2001.

Plating, John. *The Hump: America's Strategy for Keeping China in World War II.* College Station: Texas A&M Press, 2011.

Powell, Colin L. *My American Journey.* With Joseph E. Persico. New York: Random House, 1995.

Puryear, Edgar F., Jr. *American Generalship: Character Is Everything: The Art of Command.* Novato, CA: Presidio Press, 2000.

Putney, Diane T. *Airpower Advantage: Planning the Gulf War Air Campaign, 1989–1991.* Washington, DC: Air Force History and Museums Program, 2005.

Randolph, Stephen. *Powerful and Brutal Weapons: Nixon, Kissinger, and the Easter Offensive.* Cambridge, MA: Harvard University Press, 2007.

Rasimus, Ed. *When Thunder Rolled: An F-105 Pilot over North Vietnam.* New York: Ballantine Books, 2003.

Reed, James E. *The Fighting 33rd Nomads during World War II: A Diary of a Fighter Pilot with Photographs and Other Stories of 33rd Fighter Group Personnel.* 2 vols. Memphis, TN: Reed Publishers, 1987–1988.

Reynolds, Richard T. *Heart of the Storm: The Genesis of the Air Campaign against Iraq.* Maxwell Air Force Base, AL: Air University Press, 1995.

Ripley, Tim. *Operation Deliberate Force: The UN and NATO Campaign in Bosnia, 1995.* Lancaster, UK: Centre for Defence and International Security Studies, 1999.

Robinson, Linda. *Masters of Chaos: The Secret History of the Special Forces.* New York: PublicAffairs, 2004.

Rochester, Stuart I., and Frederick T. Kiley. *Honor Bound: American Prisoners of War in Southeast Asia, 1961–1973.* Washington, DC: Office of the Secretary of Defense, 1998.

Rosenau, William. *Special Operations Forces and Elusive Enemy Ground Targets: Lessons from Vietnam and the Persian Gulf War.* MR-1408-AF. Santa Monica, CA: Rand Corporation, 2001.

Rostow, Walter W. *Pre-Invasion Bombing Strategy: General Eisenhower's Decision of March 25, 1944*. Austin: University of Texas Press, 1981.

Santoli, Al. *Leading the Way—how Vietnam Veterans Rebuilt the U.S. Military: An Oral History*. New York: Ballantine Books, 1993.

Schlight, John. *The War in South Vietnam: The Years of the Offensive, 1965–1968*. Washington, DC: Air Force History and Museums Program, 1999.

Schnabel, James F. *United States Army in the Korean War: Policy and Direction: The First Year*. Washington, DC: Office of the Chief of Military History, 1972.

Schnabel, James F., and Robert J. Watson. *The Joint Chiefs of Staff and National Policy*. Vol. 3, *1950–1951, the Korean War: Part One*. Washington, DC: Office of Joint History, Office of the Chairman of the Joint Chiefs of Staff, 1998.

Schulimson, Jack, Leonard Blasiol, Charles R. Smith, and David A. Dawson. *U.S. Marines in Vietnam*. Vol. 5, *The Defining Year, 1968*. Washington, DC: History and Museums Division, United States Marine Corps, 1997.

Schwarzkopf, H. Norman. *It Doesn't Take a Hero*. With Peter Petrie. New York: Bantam, 1992.

Shawcross, William. *Sideshow: Kissinger, Nixon and the Destruction of Cambodia*. New York: Simon & Schuster, 1979.

Shultz, Richard H., Jr., and Robert L. Pfaltzgraff Jr., eds. *The Future of Air Power in the Aftermath of the Gulf War*. Maxwell Air Force Base, AL: Air University Press, 1992.

Shwedo, Bradford J. *XIX Tactical Air Command and ULTRA: Patton's Force Enhancers in the 1944 Campaign in France*. Maxwell Air Force Base, AL: Air University Press, May 2001.

Slayton, Robert A. *Master of the Air: William Tunner and the Success of Military Airlift*. Tuscaloosa: University of Alabama Press, 2010.

Slife, James C. *Creech Blue: Gen. Bill Creech and the Reformation of the Tactical Air Force, 1978–1984*. Maxwell Air Force Base, AL: Air University Press, 2004.

Smyth, John. *Leadership in War, 1939–1945: The Generals in Victory and Defeat*. New York: St. Martin's Press, 1974.

Speer, Albert. *Inside the Third Reich: Memoirs*. New York: Macmillan, 1970.

Spires, David. *Patton's Air Force: Forging a Legendary Air-Ground Team*. Washington, DC: Smithsonian, 2002.

Stephens, Alan, ed. *The War in the Air, 1914–1994*. Maxwell Air Force Base, AL: Air University Press, in cooperation with the Royal Australian Air Force Aerospace Centre, 2001.

Stueck, William. *The Korean War: An International History*. Princeton, NJ: Princeton University Press, 1995.

Sullivan, John J. *Air Support for Patton's Third Army*. Jefferson, NC: McFarland, 2003.

Tate, James. *The Army and Its Air Corps: Army Policy toward Aviation, 1919–1941*. Maxwell Air Force Base, AL: Air University Press, 1998.

Thaler, David E., and David A. Shlapak. *Perspectives on Theater Air Campaign Planning*, Report MR-515-AF. Santa Monica, CA: Rand Corporation, 1995.

Thatcher, Margaret. *The Downing Street Years*. London: HarperCollins, 1995.

Thompson, Wayne. *To Hanoi and Back: The United States Air Force and North Vietnam, 1966–1973*. Washington, DC: Smithsonian Institution Press, 2000.

Tooze, Adam. *The Wages of Destruction: The Making and Breaking of the Nazi Economy*. New York: Viking Adult, 2007.

Treadwell, Mattie E. *The Woman's Army Corps*. United States Army in World War II: Special Studies. Washington, DC: U.S. Army Center of Military History, U.S. Government Printing Office, 1954.

Tuchman, Barbara W. *Stillwell and the American Experience in China, 1911–45*. New York: Grove, 2001.

Tunner, William H. *Over the Hump*. Washington, DC: Office of Air Force History, 1985.

Van Creveld, Martin. *Command in War*. Cambridge, MA: Harvard University Press, 1985.

Vriesenga, Michael P., ed. *From the Line in the Sand: Accounts of USAF Company Grade Officers in Support of Desert Shield/Desert Storm*. Maxwell Air Force Base, AL: Air University Press, 1994.

Warnock, A. Timothy, ed. *The USAF in Korea: A Chronology, 1950–1953*. Washington, DC: Air Force History and Museums Program, 2000.

———, ed. *The U.S. Air Force's First War: Korea, 1950–1953: Significant Events*. Maxwell Air Force Base, AL: USAF Historical Research Agency, 2000.

Watson, George M., Jr. *The Office of the Secretary of the Air Force, 1947–1965*. Washington, DC: Center for Air Force History, 1993.

Webster, Charles, and Noble Frankland. *The Strategic Air Offensive against Germany, 1939–1945*. History of the Second World War. London: Her Majesty's Stationery Office, 1961.

Weinberger, Caspar W. *Fighting for Peace: Seven Critical Years in the Pentagon*. New York: Warner Books, 1990.

Werrell, Kenneth. *Archie, Flak, AAA, and SAM: A Short Operational History of Ground-Based Air Defense*. Maxwell Air Force Base, AL: Air University Press, 1988.

White, Robert P. *Mason Patrick and the Flight for Air Service Independence*. Washington, DC: Smithsonian Institution Press, 2001.

Winnefeld, James A., and Dana J. Johnson. *Joint Air Operations: Pursuit of Unity in Command and Control, 1942–1991*. Annapolis, MD: Naval Institute Press and the Rand Corporation, 1993.

Wolk, Herman S. *Cataclysm: General Hap Arnold and the Defeat of Japan*. Denton: University of North Texas Press, 2010.

Woods, Kevin, Michael R. Pease, Mark E. Stout, Williamson Murray, and James G. Lacey. *Iraqi Perspectives Project: A View of Operation Iraqi Freedom from Saddam's Senior Leadership*. Norfolk, VA: Joint Center for Operational Analysis, March 2006.

Woodward, Bob. *Bush at War*. New York: Simon & Schuster, 2002.

———. *The Commanders*. New York: Simon & Schuster, 1992.

———. *Plan of Attack*. New York: Simon & Schuster, 2004.

Worden, Mike. *The Rise of the Fighter Generals: The Problem of Air Force Leadership, 1945–1982*. Maxwell Air Force Base, AL: Air University Press, 1998.

Y'Blood, William T. *Down in the Weeds: Close Air Support in Korea*. Washington, DC: Air Force History and Museums Program, 2002.

———, ed. *The Three Wars of Lt. Gen. George E. Stratemeyer: His Korean War Diary*. Washington, DC: Air Force History and Museums Program, 1999.

Zilbert, Edward R. *Albert Speer and the Nazi Ministry of Arms: Economic Institutions and Industrial Production in the German War Economy*. Rutherford, NJ: Farleigh Dickenson University Press, 1981.

INDEX

Biographical Notes

Mark A. Bucknam is a colonel in the U.S. Air Force, currently serving on the faculty of the National War College (NWC). He is a career fighter pilot who has flown more than 2,400 hours in the A-10, AT-38, and F-16 and has had commands at squadron and group levels. Bucknam has served in three staff tours, all in the Pentagon, including tours on the Air Staff, Joint Staff, and most recently as director for campaign and contingency plans on the staff of the undersecretary of defense for policy. He has published several articles and one book—*Responsibility of Command: How UN and NATO Commanders Influenced Airpower over Bosnia* (2003). Bucknam earned a bachelor's degree in physics and a master's degree in materials science and engineering from Virginia Tech; a master's degree from the U.S. Air Force School of Advanced Airpower Studies at Maxwell Air Force Base, Alabama; and a master's at the NWC. In 1999, he was awarded a PhD in war studies from Kings College, University of London. He has been assigned overseas for nearly ten years of his career, mostly in Europe and the Republic of Korea. He is a member of the Council on Foreign Relations and the International Institute for Strategic Studies.

James S. Corum is the dean of the Baltic Defence College. From 1991 to 2004, he was a professor at the U.S. Air Force School of Advanced Air and Space Studies, Maxwell Air Force Base, Alabama. In 2005 he was a visiting fellow at All Souls College, Oxford, where he held a Leverhulme Fellowship, and then an associate professor at the U.S. Army Command and General Staff College, Fort Leavenworth, Kansas. Corum is the author of several books on military history, including *The*

Roots of Blitzkrieg: Hans von Seeckt and German Military Reform (1992); *The Luft-waffe: Creating the Operational Air War, 1918–1940* (1997); *The Luftwaffe's Way of War: German Air Force Doctrine, 1911–1945*, with Richard Muller (1998); *Air-power in Small Wars: Fighting Insurgents and Terrorists*, with Wray Johnson (2003); *Fighting the War on Terror: A Counterinsurgency Strategy* (2007); and *Rearming Germany* (2011). He has also authored more than fifty book chapters and journal articles on a variety of subjects related to air power and military history, and was one of the primary authors of *Field Manual 3-24*, which sets forth the U.S. Army and Marine Corps's doctrine on counterinsurgency. Corum served in Iraq in 2004 as a lieutenant colonel in the U.S. Army Reserve. He holds a master's degree from Brown University, a master of letters from Oxford University, and a PhD from Queen's University, Canada.

Case Cunningham is an active duty lieutenant colonel in the U.S. Air Force. A career fighter pilot, his assignments have included tours as the commander and leader of the U.S. Air Force Thunderbirds, director of operations of an F-22 squadron, and an F-15 instructor pilot at the U.S. Air Force Weapons School. He has logged nearly 2,800 hours in the F-15, F-16, and F-22, with more than 160 hours of combat experience. He graduated from the U.S. Air Force Academy, Colorado Springs; has a master's degree in strategic leadership from the Air Force Institute of Technology; a master's degree in national security studies from American Military University; and a master's degree in air power art and science from the School of Advanced Air and Space Power Studies, Maxwell Air Force Base, Alabama. He is currently a doctoral candidate at the Air Education and Training Command.

Richard G. Davis is currently serving as senior historian at the National Museum of the U.S. Army. His previous positions include U.S. European Command historian (2010–2012), division chief at the U.S. Army Center of Military History (2004–2010), and U.S. Air Force historian (1990–2001). He has published several biographies, including *Carl A. Spaatz and the Air War in Europe* (1993), and *HAP: Henry H. Arnold, Military Aviator* (1997); an official operational history of the U.S. Air Force in the first Gulf War, *On Target: The Planning and Execution of the Strategic Air Campaign against Iraq* (2003); and *Bombing the European Axis Powers: A Historical Digest of the Combined Bomber Offensive, 1939–1945* (2006). He is also the author of "The 31 Initiatives: A Study in Air Force–Army Cooperation" (1987) and "Anatomy of a Reform: The Aerospace Expeditionary Force" (2000). He has published seven monographs, thirteen journal articles, and several chapters in anthologies, such as the "The Bombing of Auschwitz: Comments on a Historical Speculation" (2000). Davis also served as the U.S. Air Force historical adviser for the movie *Pearl Harbor*, first screened in 2001.

Rebecca L. Grant is the director of the General Billy Mitchell Institute for Airpower Studies at the Air Force Association, Washington, D.C. She has more than twenty years of experience as an air, space, and cyber power analyst. In the early 1990s, she worked in the operations group of the chief of staff of the U.S. Air Force, for the secretary of the air force, and for the Rand Corporation. In 1995, she founded IRIS Independent Research and served as its president; in that capacity she authored *The First 600 Days of Combat* (2004), *The B-2 Goes to War* (2001), and *The Radar Game: Understanding Stealth and Aircraft Survivability* (1998), among other titles. Grant has written extensively for the *Air Force Magazine* and in 2002 was named a contributing editor. She is the author of numerous Mitchell Institute products, including *Airpower in Afghanistan: How a Faraway War is Remaking the Air Force* (2009). Grant is a graduate of Wellesley College and earned her PhD in international relations at the London School of Economics.

Richard P. Hallion, a Smithsonian research associate, retired in 2006 as a senior adviser for air and space issues in the Directorate for Security, Counterintelligence, and Special Programs Oversight, Office of the Secretary of the Air Force, while remaining as a senior adviser for aerospace technology (hypersonics and global strike) in the Office of the Air Force Chief Scientist. Hallion began his government career at the National Air and Space Museum (NASM) in 1974, serving as curator of science and technology. In 1982 he moved to the U.S. Air Force, where, among other positions, he was a senior issues and policy analyst for Secretary Donald B. Rice and, for eleven years, was the U.S. Air Force historian. He has been a Daniel and Florence Guggenheim Fellow, held the H. K. Johnson Chair at the U.S. Army Military History Institute and the Charles A. Lindbergh Chair at the NASM, was the Alfred Verville Fellow at the NASM, and is a Fellow of the Earthshine Institute, the American Institute of Aeronautics and Astronautics, the Royal Aeronautical Society, and the Royal Historical Society. He has mission observer flying experience in a variety of aircraft, from biplanes to the F-15E, and teaches, lectures, and consults widely. Among his other works, Hallion is the author of *Rise of the Fighter Aircraft, 1914–1918* (1984); *The Naval Air War in Korea* (1986); *Strike from the Sky: The History of Battlefield Air Attack, 1911–1945* (1989); *Storm over Iraq: Air Power and the Gulf War* (1992); *Taking Flight: Inventing the Aerial Age, from Antiquity through the First World War* (2003); and he also edited *Air Power Confronts an Unstable World* (1997). He holds a PhD in history from the University of Maryland and is a graduate of the Federal Executive Institute and the National Security Studies Program, John F. Kennedy School of Government, Harvard University.

Thomas A. Keaney is the associate director of strategic studies at Johns Hopkins University School of Advanced International Studies (SAIS), executive director of the Philip Merrill Center, and a senior adjunct professor of strategic studies at SAIS. Before coming to SAIS in 1998, he spent ten years as a professor of military strategy at the National War College, Washington, D.C., and director of NWC's core courses on military thought and strategy. A retired colonel, during his U.S. Air Force career Keaney served in various positions, including associate professor of history at the U.S. Air Force Academy, planner on the Air Staff, chairman of the department of military strategy at NWC, forward air controller in Vietnam, and B-52 squadron commander. During 1991 and 1992 he was a researcher and author with the Gulf War Air Power Survey, and then coauthored two reports of that survey—*Summary Report* (1993) and *The Effects and Effectiveness of Air Power* (1993)—and a subsequent book with Eliot A. Cohen, *Revolution in Warfare? Air Power in the Persian Gulf* (1995). Among his publications are *U.S. Allies in a Changing World* (2001) and *Armed Forces in the Middle East: Politics and Strategy* (2002), both edited with Barry Rubin; *War in Iraq: Planning and Operations* (2007), edited with Thomas Mahnken; and *Understanding Counterinsurgency: Doctrine, Operations, and Challenges* (2010), edited with Thomas Rid. Keaney received a bachelor's degree from the U.S. Air Force Academy and a master's degree and PhD in history from the University of Michigan.

James D. Kiras is an associate professor at the School of Advanced Air and Space Studies (SAASS), Maxwell Air Force Base, Alabama. He holds a bachelor's degree in history from the University of Massachusetts at Boston, a master's degree in history and international relations from the University of Toronto, and a PhD from the University of Reading. At SAASS, Kiras directs the school's course on irregular warfare and lectures, publishes, and consults extensively on counterinsurgency, counterterrorism, special operations, and suicide bombing. He is also an associate fellow of the Joint Special Operations University, Hurlburt Field, Florida. Before teaching at SAASS, Kiras was a defense consultant with Booz Allen Hamilton and an analyst at the National Institute for Public Policy. In these jobs he provided analytic and strategic planning support to the Office of the Secretary of Defense, the combatant commands, the unified commands, and the Joint Staff. In 2002 he joined the strategy, concepts, and initiatives team in the Office of the Assistant Secretary of Defense for Special Operations and Low-Intensity Conflict. Kiras is the author of *Special Operations and Strategy: From World War II to the War on Terrorism* (2006), and coauthor of *Understanding Modern Warfare* (2008).

Richard R. Muller is a professor of military history at the School of Advanced Air and Space Studies (SAASS), Maxwell Air Force Base, Alabama. As a military historian specializing in the history of World War II and the development of air power, he teaches core courses in air power history, strategy, and decision making. Prior to joining the SAASS faculty in June 2005, Muller spent fourteen years on the faculty at the U.S. Air Force Air Command and Staff College, where he served as course director, department chairman, and dean of education and curriculum. He is the author of *The German Air War in Russia* (1992); *The Luftwaffe's Way of War: German Air Force Doctrine, 1911–1945*, with James S. Corum (1998); *The Luftwaffe over Germany: Defense of the Reich*, with Donald L. Caldwell (2007); and many articles, book chapters, and reviews. Muller received his bachelor's degree in history from Franklin and Marshall College and his master's degree and PhD in military history from Ohio State University. He has held fellowship posts at Yale University and the National Air and Space Museum.

Williamson Murray has taught at a number of academic and military institutions, including the Air War College, the U.S. Military Academy at West Point, and the Naval War College, where he most recently served as a Minerva Fellow over the academic year 2011–2012. He has been a consultant at the Institute of Defense Analyses, where he worked on the Iraqi Perspectives Project, and recently completed two years as the distinguished visiting professor of naval heritage and history at the U.S. Naval Academy. He graduated from Yale University in 1963 and then served five years as an officer in the U.S. Air Force, including a tour in Southeast Asia with the 314th Tactical Airlift Wing. He returned to Yale, where he received his PhD in military-diplomatic history, working under Hans Gatzke and Donald Kagan. After teaching for two years he moved to Ohio State University in 1977 and retired in 1995 as professor emeritus of history. He is the author of *The Change in the European Balance of Power, 1938–1939: The Push to Ruin* (1984), *Luftwaffe* (1985), *German Military Effectiveness* (1992), *The Air War in the Persian Gulf* (1995), and *The War in the Air, 1914–45* (1999). Murray coauthored *The Iraq War: A Military History* (2003) and has edited a number of books and articles on military matters while also holding numerous fellowships and chairs and giving lectures throughout the world. His latest works, all published by Cambridge University Press in 2011, include *The Shaping of Grand Strategy: Policy, Diplomacy, and War*; *Military Adaptation in War: With Fear of Change*; and *War, Strategy, and Military Effectiveness*.

John Andreas Olsen is an active duty colonel in the Royal Norwegian Air Force, currently serving in the Ministry of Defence, and a visiting professor of operational art and tactics at the Swedish National Defence College. He was the deputy commander and chief of the North Atlantic Treaty Organization (NATO) advisory team at NATO Headquarters in Sarajevo in the period of 2009 to 2012; prior to that he was the dean of the Norwegian Defence University College and head of its division for strategic studies. Other assignments include tours as the Norwegian liaison officer to the German Operational Command in Potsdam and the military assistant to the attaché in Berlin. Olsen is a graduate of the German Command and Staff College, has a doctorate in history and international relations from De Montfort University, a master's degree in contemporary British literature and politics from the University of Warwick, and a master's degree in English from the University of Trondheim. Professor Olsen is the author of *Strategic Air Power in Desert Storm* (2003) and *John Warden and the Renaissance of American Air Power* (2007). He is the editor of several books, including *A History of Air Warfare* (2010); *Global Air Power* (2011); *The Evolution of Operational Art*, with Martin van Creveld (2011); and *The Practice of Strategy*, with Colin Gray (2012).

Stephen P. Randolph, a former fighter pilot and retired U.S. Air Force colonel, is the general editor of the State Department's documentary history series *Foreign Relations of the United States*, which records U.S. foreign policy activities. He graduated from the Air Force Academy in 1974, beginning a twenty-seven-year-long career in the service. Through most of his active duty career he flew F-4s and F-15s, including a deployment to Desert Storm from Bitburg Air Base, Germany. He also served on the Joint Staff and the Air Staff before moving to the National Defense University in 1997, where he was a military faculty member, a department chairman, and an associate dean until moving to the State Department in 2011. He earned his doctorate from The George Washington University in 2005 and later published a study of the Easter Offensive and the end of America's war in Vietnam, *Powerful and Brutal Weapons: Nixon, Kissinger, and the Easter Offensive* (2007). He is now working on a book focusing on Nixon as commander in chief.

Alan Stephens is a visiting fellow at the University of New South Wales (UNSW) and a member of the Sir Richard Williams Foundation. Previously he has been a lecturer at UNSW, the Royal Australian Air Force historian, an adviser to the Australian federal parliament on foreign affairs and defense, a visiting fellow at the Strategic and Defence Studies Centre at the Australian National University, and a pilot in the Royal Australian Air Force, where his experience included the command of an operational squadron and a tour in Vietnam. Stephens has published and lectured extensively. His books include *Going Solo—the Royal Australian Air Force, 1946–1971* (1995); *High Fliers: Leaders of the RAAF* (1996); *The Australian Centenary History of Defence*, volume 2, *The Royal Australian Air Force* (2002); and *Making Sense of War: Strategy for the 21st Century* (2006). In 2008 he was made a member of the Order of Australia for his contribution to air force history and to Australian air power strategy.

CPSIA information can be obtained
at www.ICGtesting.com
Printed in the USA
LVOW03s0131101017

551751LV00004B/711/P